1938

TH

'RN

9

3

For con

ANTICIPATORY SYSTEMS

Philosophical
Mathematical
and
Methodological Foundations

IFSR International Series on Systems Science and Engineering — Volume 1

International Federation for Systems Research

International Series on Systems Science and Engineering

VOLUME 1

Editor-in-Chief: G. KLIR, State University of New York at Binghamton, USA

Other Titles of Interest

Pergamon Related Journals (free specimen copies gladly sent on request)

ANTICIPATORY SYSTEMS

Philosophical
Mathematical
and
Methodological Foundations

ROBERT ROSEN
Dalhousie University, Nova Scotia, Canada

PERGAMON PRESS

OXFORD · NEW YORK · TORONTO · SYDNEY · PARIS · FRANKFURT

U.K.	Pergamon Press Ltd., Headington Hill Hall, Oxford OX3 0BW, England
U.S.A.	Pergamon Press Inc., Maxwell House, Fairview Park, Elmsford, New York 10523, U.S.A.
CANADA	Pergamon Press Canada Ltd., Suite 104, 150 Consumers Road, Willowdale, Ontario M2J 1P9, Canada
AUSTRALIA	Pergamon Press (Aust.) Pty. Ltd., P.O. Box 544, Potts Point, N.S.W. 2011, Australia
FRANCE	Pergamon Press SARL, 24 rue des Ecoles, 75240 Paris, Cedex 05, France
FEDERAL REPUBLIC OF GERMANY	Pergamon Press GmbH, Hammerweg 6, D-6242 Kronberg-Taunus, Federal Republic of Germany

First edition 1985

Library of Congress Cataloging in Publication Data

Rosen, Robert, 1934–
Anticipatory systems.
(IFSR international series on systems science and engineering; v.1)
1. System theory. I. Title. II. Series.
Q295.R667 1985 003 84-26626

British Library Cataloguing in Publication Data

Rosen, Robert
Anticipatory systems: philosophical, mathematical & methodological foundations.—
(IFSR international series on systems science and engineering; v. 1)
1. System theory
I. Title II. Series
003 Q295
ISBN 0-08-031158-X

Printed in Great Britain by A. Wheaton & Co. Ltd., Exeter

Foreword

This manuscript was written during the months between January and
June in 1979. The writing was done under difficult circumstances.
At that time, I had some reason to fear that I would no longer be
able to personally pursue a program of active scientific research.
Yet at the time, I felt (and still do) that I had arrived upon the
threshold of some entirely new perspectives in the theory of natural
systems, and of biological systems in particular. The issues involved were of sufficient interest and importance for me to wish
them to be pursued by others, if they so desired. On the other hand,
my own outlook and development are different from other people's,
and have with justification been called idiosyncratic. Thus I
resolved to try, while I knew I was still able, to set down a coherent narrative development, beginning with the most elementary matters,
which I hoped would permit others to understand why I was doing the
things I was doing.

This volume is the result. I have organized it around the concept
of anticipation, which is fundamental in its own right, and which
connects naturally to a cluster of other concepts lying at the heart
of natural science and of mathematics. Strictly speaking, an anticipatory system is one in which present change of state depends upon
future circumstances, rather than merely on the present or past. As
such, anticipation has routinely been excluded from any kind of
systematic study, on the grounds that it violates the causal foundation on which all of theoretical science must rest, and on the
grounds that it introduces a telic element which is scientifically
unacceptable. Nevertheless, biology is replete with situations in
which organisms can generate and maintain internal predictive models
of themselves and their environments, and utilize the predictions of
these models about the future for purpose of control in the present.
Many of the unique properties of organisms can really be understood
only if these internal models are taken into account. Thus, the
concept of a system with an internal predictive model seemed to
offer a way to study anticipatory systems in a scientifically
rigorous way.

This book is about what else one is forced to believe if one grants
that certain kinds of systems can behave in an anticipatory fashion.
I begin with an autobiographical account of how I came to believe

that anticipatory systems were important, and why. I then proceed
to an extensive discussion of the central concept of anticipation,
namely, the modelling relation between a system and a model, or a
system and an analog. In the process of exploring this relation,
and by exhibiting manifold and diverse examples of this relation,
I try to establish the basic threads between the concepts of science
and mathematics. I hope that this discussion will be of interest in
its own right, and will also serve to illustrate that the approaches
I take are not really as idiosyncratic as might at first appear.
Only when this background is laid do I turn to the concept of anticipation itself, and explore some of the elementary properties of
systems which can anticipate. Here I well realize, the surface is
barely scratched. But this was as far as I had been able to progress
at the time, and the point of the book is to guide the reader to the
surface.

For a variety of external reasons, the manuscript was not published
immediately. However, none of the fundamental material has changed
in the intervening five years, and I have not altered the original
text. I have, however, added an Appendix. It has turned out that
the initial anxieties which generated the book were unfounded, and
since that time, I have been able to push some of the fundamental
implications of the relation between system and model much further.
In the Appendix, some of these more recent developments are sketched,
and some of their rather startling implications are pointed out. I
hope to enlarge this Appendix into a separate monograph in the near
future, giving full details to justify what is merely asserted
therein.

I would like to take this occasion to thank the many colleagues and
friends who have lent precious moral support as a beacon through
dark times. Among them I may mention J. F. Danielli, George Klir,
I. W. Richardson, Otto Rössler, Ei Teramoto, and Howard Pattee. I
hope that this volume will justify at least some small part of their
exertions on my behalf over the years.

Preface

The present volume is intended as a contribution to the theory of those systems which contain internal predictive models of themselves and/or of their environment, and which utilize the predictions of their models to control their present bahavior.

Systems of this type have a variety of properties which are unique to them, just as "closed-loop" systems have properties which make them different from "open-loop" systems. It is most important to understand these properties, for many reasons. We shall argue that much, if not most, biological behavior is model-based in this sense. This is true at every level, from the molecular to the cellular to the physiological to the behavioral. Moreover, model-based behavior is the essence of social and political activity. An understanding of the characteristics of model-based behavior is thus central to any technology we wish to develop to control such systems, or to modify their model-based behavior in new ways.

The essential novelty in our approach is that we consider such systems as single entities, and relate their overall properties to the character of the models they contain. There have, of course, been many approaches to planning, forecasting, and decision-making, but these tend to concentrate on tactical aspects of model synthesis and model deployment in specific circumstances; they do not deal with the behavioral correlates arising throughout a system simply from the fact that present behavior is generated in terms of a predicted future situation. For this reason, we shall not at all be concerned with tactical aspects of this type; we do not consider, for instance, the various procedures of extrapolation and correlation which dominate much of the literature concerned with decision-making in an uncertain or incompletely defined environment. We are concerned rather with global properties of model-based behavior, irrespective of how the model is generated, or indeed of whether it is a "good" model or not.

From the very outset, we shall find that the study of such global aspects of model-based behavior raises new questions of a basic epistemological character. Indeed, we shall see that the utilization of predictive models for purposes of present control confront us with problems relating to causality. It has long been axiomatic that system behavior in the present must never depend upon future states or future inputs; systems which violate this basic axiom are collectively called *anticipatory*, and are routinely excluded from science. On the other hand, the presence of a predictive model serves precisely to pull the future into the present; a system with a "good" model thus behaves in many ways like a true anticipatory system. We must thus reconsider what is meant by an anticipatory system; the suggestion arising from the present work is that model-based behavior requires an entirely new paradigm, which we call an "anticipatory paradigm", to accomodate it. This paradigm extends (but does not replace) the "reactive paradigm" which has hitherto dominated the study of natural systems, and allows us a glimpse of new and important aspects of system behavior.

The main theoretical questions with which we deal in the present work are the following: (a) What is a model? (b) What is a *predictive* model? (c) How does a system which contains a predictive model differ in its behavior from one which does not? In the process of exploring these questions, starting from first principles, we are lead to a re-examination of many basic concepts: time, measurement, language, complexity. Since the modelling relation plays a central role in the discussion, we provide numerous illustrations of it, starting from models arising entirely within symbolic systems (mathematics) through physics, chemistry and biology. Only when the modelling relation is thoroughly clarified can we begin to formulate the basic problems of model-based behavior, and develop some of the properties of systems of the kind with which we are concerned.

It is a pleasure to acknowledge the assistance of many friends and colleagues who have aided me in developing the circle of ideas to be expounded below. A primary debt is owed to my teacher, Nicolas Rashevsky, who above all set an example of fearlessness in entering territory which others thought forbidden. An equally important debt is owed to Robert Hutchins, and to the Center which he created; it was there that I was first forced to confront the nature of anticipatory behavior. A third debt is to my colleagues at the Center for Theoretical Biology: James F. Danielli, Howard Pattee, Narendra Goel, and Martynas Ycas, for their intellectual stimulation and support over the years. Gratitude must also be expressed to Dalhousie University, where thought and the leisure to think are still valued, and especially to my colleague I. W. Richardson.

Contents

Chapter 6. Anticipatory Systems

CHAPTER 1

Preliminaries

1.1 General Introduction

The original germinal ideas of which this volume is an outgrowth were developed in 1972, when the author was in residence as a Visiting Fellow at the Center for the Study of Democratic Institutions in Santa Barbara, California. Before entering on the more formal exposition, it might be helpful to describe the curious circumstances in which these ideas were generated.

The Center was a unique institution in many ways, as was its founder and dominating spirit, Robert M. Hutchins. Like Mr. Hutchins, it resisted pigeonholding and easy classification. Indeed, as with the Tao, anything one might say about either was certain to be wrong. Despite this, it may be helpful to try to characterize some of the ambience of the place, and of the remarkable man who created it.

The Center's spirit and *modus operandi* revolved around the concept of the Dialog. The Dialog was indispensable in Hutchins' thought, because he believed it to be the instrument through which an intellectual community is created. He felt that "the reason why an intellectual community is necessary is that it offers the only hope of grasping the whole". "The whole", for him, was nothing less than discovering the means and ends of human society: "The real questions to which we seek answers are, what should I do, what should we do, why should we do these things? What are the purposes of human life and of organized society?" The operative word here is "ought"; without a conception of "ought" there could be no guide to politics, which, as he often said, quoting Aristotle, "is architectonic". That is to say, he felt that politics, in the broadest sense, is ultimately the most important thing in the world. Thus for Hutchins the Dialog and politics were inseparable from one another.

For Hutchins, the intellectual community was both means and end. He said,

> The common good of every community belongs to every member of it. The community makes him better because he belongs to it. In political terms the common good is usually defined as peace, order, freedom and justice. These are indispensable to any person, and no person could obtain any one of them in the absence of the community. An intellectual community is one

1

in which everybody does better intellectual work because he belongs to a
community of intellectual workers. As I have already intimated, an intellectual community cannot be formed of people who cannot or will not think,
who will not think about anything in which the other members of the community are interested. Work that does not require intellectual effort and
workers that will not engage in a common intellectual effort have no place
in [the intellectual community].

He viewed the Dialog as a continuation of what he called "the great
conversation". In his view,

> The great conversation began with the Greeks, the Hebrews, the Hindus and
> the Chinese, and has continued to the present day. It is a conversation
> that deals - perhaps more extensively than it deals with anything else -
> with morals and religion. The questions of the nature and existence of
> God, the nature and destiny of man, and the organization and purpose of
> human society are the recurring themes of the great conversation...

More specifically, regarding the Dialog at the Center, he said,

> Its members talk about what ought to be done. They come to the conference
> table as citizens, and their talk is about the common good...It does not
> take positions about what ought to be done. It asserts only that the issues
> it is discussing deserve the attention of citizens. The Center tries to
> think about the things it believes its fellow citizens ought to be thinking
> about.

The Dialog was institutionalized at the Center. Almost every working
day, at 11.00 am, the resident staff would assemble around the large
green table to discuss a pre-circulated paper prepared by one of us,
or by an invited visitor. At least once a month, and usually more
often, a large-scale conference on a specific topic, organized by
one or another of the resident Senior Fellows, and attended by the
best in that field, would be held. Every word of these sessions was
recorded, and often found its way into the Center's extensive publication program, through which the Dialog was disseminated to a wider
public.

It might be wondered why a natural scientist such as myself was
invited to spend a year at an institution of this kind, and even
more, why the invitation was accepted. On the face of it, the
Center's preoccupations were far removed from natural science.
There were no natural scientists among the Center's staff of Senior
Fellows, although several were numbered among the Center's Associates
and Consultants; the resident population, as well as most of the
invited visitors, consisted primarily of political scientists,
journalists, philosophers, economists, historians, and a full spectrum of other intellectuals. Indeed, Mr. Hutchins himself, originally trained in the Law and preoccupied primarily with the role of
education in society, was widely regarded as contemptuous of science
and of scientists. Immediately on assuming the presidency of the
University of Chicago, for instance, he became embroiled in a
fulminating controversy on curricular reform, in which many of the
faculty regarded his position as anti-scientific, mystical and
authoritarian. At an important conference on Science and Ethics,
he said, "Long experience as a university president has taught me
that professors are generally a little worse than other people, and
scientists are a little worse than other professors".

However, this kind of sentiment was merely an expression of the well-
known Hutchins irony. His basic position had been clearly stated
as early as 1931:

Science is not the collection of facts or the accumulation of data. A
discipline does not become scientific merely because its professors have
acquired a great deal of information. Facts do not arrange themselves.
Facts do not solve problems. I do not wish to be misunderstood. We must
get the facts. We must get them all....But at the same time we must raise
the question whether facts alone will settle our difficulties for us. And
we must raise the question whether...the accumulation and distribution of
facts is likely to lead us through the mazes of a world whose complications
have been produced by the facts we have discovered.

Elsewhere, he said,

The gadgeteers and data collectors, masquerading as scientists, have
threatened to become the supreme chieftains of the scholarly world.

As the Renaissance could accuse the Middle Ages of being rich in principles and poor in facts, we are now entitled to enquire whether we are
not rich in facts and poor in principles.

Rational thought is the only basis of eduation and research. Whether
we know it or not, it has been responsible for our scientific success; its
absence has been responsible for our bewilderment...Facts are the core of
an anti-intellectual curriculum.

The scholars in a university which is trying to grapple with fundamentals will, I suggest, devote themselves first of all to a rational analysis
of the principles of each subject matter. They will seek to establish
general propositions under which the facts they gather may be subsumed.
I repeat, they would not cease to gather facts, but they would know what
facts to look for, what they wanted them for, and what to do with them
after they got them.

To such sentiments, one could only say Amen. In my view, Hutchins
was here articulating the essence of science, as I understand it.

However, I had more specific intellectual reasons for accepting an
invitation to spend a year at the Center, as, I think, the Center
had for inviting me to do so. It maybe helpful to describe them
here. My professional activities have been concerned with the theory
of biological systems, roughly motivated by trying to discover what
it is about certain natural systems that makes us recognize them as
organisms, and characterize them as being alive. It is precisely
on this recognition that biology as an autonomous science depends,
and it is a significant fact that it has never been formalized. As
will be abundantly seen in the ensuing pages, I am persuaded that
our recognition of the living state rests on the perception of
homologies between the behaviors exhibited by organisms, homologies
which are absent in non-living systems. The physical structures of
organisms play only a minor and secondary role in this; the only
requirement which physical structure must fulfill is that it allows
the characteristic behaviors themselves to be manifested. Indeed,
if this were not so, it would be impossible to understand how a
class of systems as utterly diverse in physical structure as that
which comprises biological organisms could be recognized as a unity
at all. The study of biclogical organization from this point of
view was pioneered by my Major Professor in my days as a graduate
student at the University of Chicago, Nicolas Rashevsky (who, through
no coincidence, idolized Robert Hutchins). Rashevsky called this
study "relational biology", and we will have much more to say about
it below.

The relational approach to organisms is in many ways antithetical

to the more familiar analytic experimental approach which has culminated in biochemistry and molecular biology. Particularly in these
latter areas, the very first step in any analytic investigation is
to destroy the characteristic biological organization possessed by the
system under study, leaving a purely physical system to be investigated by standard physical means of fractionation, purification, etc.
The essential premise underlying this procedure is that a sufficiently
elaborate characterization of structural detail will automatically
lead to a functional understanding of behaviors in the intact organism. That this has not yet come to pass is, according to this view,
only an indication that more of the same is still needed, and does
not indicate a fault in principle. The relational approach, on the
other hand, treats as primary that which is discarded first by
physico-chemical analysis; i.e. the organization and function of
the original system, In relational biology, it is the structural,
physical detail of specific systems which is discarded, to be recaptured later in terms of *realizations* of the relational properties
held in common by large classes of organisms, if not universally
throughout the biosphere. Thus it is perhaps not surprising that
the relational approach seems grotesque to analytic biologists, all
of whose tools are geared precisely to the recognition of structural
details.

In any case, one of the novel consequences of the relational picture
is the following: that many (if not all) of the relational properties
of organisms can be realized in contexts which are not normally
regarded as biological. For instance, they might be realized in
chemical contexts which, from a biological standpoint, would be
regarded as exotic; this is why relational biology has a bearing on
the possibility of extraterrestrial life which is inaccessible to
purely empirical approaches. Or they might be realized in technological contexts, which are the province of a presently ill-defined
area between engineering and biology often called Bionics. Or, what
is more germane to the present discussion, they may be realized in
the context of human activities, in the form of social, political
and economic systems which determine the character of our social
life.

The exploration of this last possibility was, I think, the motivation
behind the extending of an invitation to me to visit the Center, as
it was my primary motivation for accepting that invitation. The
invitation itself was extended through John Wilkinson, one of the
Center's Senior Fellows, whose interest in the then novel ideas
embodied in the structuralism of Levi-Strauss clearly paralleled my
own concern with relational approaches in biology.

It is plain, on the face of it, that many tantalizing parallels exist
between the processes characteristic of biological organisms and
those manifested by social structures or societies. These parallels
remain, despite a number of ill-fated attempts to directly extrapolate
particular biological principles into the human realm, as embodied,
for example, in Social Darwinism. Probably their most direct expression is found in the old concept of society as a "super-organism";
that the individuals comprising a society are related to one another
as are the constituent cells of a multicellular organism. This idea
was explored in greatest detail by the zoologists Alfred Emerson and
Thomas Park, who studied insect societies, and who carefully established the striking degree of homology or convergence between social
and biological organizations. (Coincidentally, both Emerson and
Park were professors of zoology at the University of Chicago).

What would it mean if common modes of organization could be demonstrated between social and biological structures? It seemed to me

that, in addition to the obvious conceptual advantages in being able
to effectively relate apparently distinct disciplines, there were a
number of most important practical consequences. For instance, our
investigation of biological organisms places us almost always in the
position of an external observer, attempting to characterize the
infinitely rich properties of life entirely from watching their
effects without any direct perception of underlying casual structures.
For instance, we may watch a cell in a developing organism differentiate, migrate, and ultimately die. We can perceive the roles played
by these activities in the generation and maintenance of the total
organism. But we cannot directly perceive the casual chains responsible for these various activities, and for the cell's transition or
switching from one to another. Without such a knowledge of casual
chains, we likewise cannot understand the mechanisms by which the
individual behaviors of billions of such cells are integrated into
the coherent, adaptive behavior of the single organism which these
cells comprise.

On the other hand, we are ourselves all *members* of social structures
and organizations. We are thus direct participants in the generation
and maintenance of these structures, and not external observers;
indeed it is hard for us to conceive what an external observer of
our society as a whole would be like. As participants, we know the
forces responsible for such improbable aggregations as football
games, parades on the Fourth of July, and rush hours in large cities.
But how would an external observer account for them?

It is plain that a participant or constituent of such an organization
must perceive and respond to signals of which an external observer
cannot possibly be aware. Conversely, the external observer can
perceive global patterns of behavior which a participant cannot even
imagine. Certainly, if we wish to understand the infinitely subtle
and intricate processes by which biological organisms maintain and
adapt themselves, we need information of both types. Within the
purely biological realm, we seem eternally locked into the position
of an external observer. But if there were some way to effectively
relate biological processes to social ones; if, more specifically,
both biological and social behaviors constituted alternate realizations of a common relational scheme, it might become possible to
utilize our social experience as a participant to obtain otherwise
inaccessible biological insights. Indeed, this capacity for trans-
ferring data and information from a system in which it is easy to
obtain to a similar system in which it is hard to obtain is a unique
characteristic of the relational approach. This was my basic hope;
that I as a theoretical biologist could learn something new about
the nature of organisms by judiciously exploiting the cognate properties of social systems.

The other side of that coin was equally obvious; that by exploiting
biological experience, obtained from the standpoint of an external
observer, we could likewise develop entirely new insights into the
properties of our social systems. At that time, however, my detailed
knowledge of the human sciences was essentially nil; to explore
the possibilities raised above would require what appeared to me to
be a major educational effort, and one which at first sight seemed
far removed from my own major interests and capabilities.

It was at this point that I perceived the benefits of the community
of scholars which Robert Hutchins had created. At the Center I
could explore such ideas, while at the same time it was possible for
me to learn in the most painless possible fashion how the political
scientist, the anthropologist, the historian, and the economist each

viewed his own field and its relation to others. In short, the
Center seemed to provide me with both the opportunity and the means
to explore this virgin territory between biology and society, and to
determine whether it was barren or fertile. I thus almost in spite
of myself found that I was fulfilling an exhortation of Rashevsky,
who had told me years earlier that I would not be a true mathematical
biologist until I had concerned myself (as he had) with problems of
social organization. At the time, I had dismissed these remarks of
Rashevsky with a shrug; but I later discovered (as did many others
who tried to shrug Rashevsky off) that he had been right all along.

Thus, I expected to reap a great deal of benefit from my association
with the Center. But, as stressed above, the Center was an intellectual community, and to participate in it, I was expected to contribute to the problems with which the other members of that community
were concerned. Initially, it appeared that I would have no tangible
contribution to make to such problems as the constitutionalization
of the oceans, the role of the presidency, or the press as an institution. Gradually, however, I perceived the common thread running
through these issues and the others under intense discussion at the
Center, and it was a thread which I might have guessed earlier. As
I have noted, Hutchins' great question was: what should we do now?
To one degree or another, that was also what the economists, the
political scientists, the urban planners, and all the others wanted
to know. However different the contexts in which these questions
were posed, *they were all alike in their fundamental concern with
the making of policy, the associated notions of forecasting the future
and planning for it.* What was sought, in each of these diverse areas,
was in effect a technology of decision-making. But underlying any
technology there must be a substratum of basic principles;
a science, a theory. What was the theory underlying a technology
of policy generation?

This was the basic questions I posed for myself. It was a question
with which I could feel comfortable, and through which I felt I could
make an effective, if indirect, contribution to the basic concerns
of the Center. Moreover, it was a question with which I myself had
had extensive experience, though not in these contexts. For the
forecasting of the future is perhaps the basic business of theoretical
science; in science it is called *prediction*. The vehicle for prediction must, to one degree or another, comprise a *model* for the
system under consideration. And the making of models of complex
phenomena, as well as the assessment of their meaning and significance,
had been my major professional activity for the preceding fifteen
years. In some very real sense, then, the Center was entirely
concerned with the construction and deployment of predictive models,
and with the use of these predictive models to regulate and control
the behaviors of the systems being modelled. Therefore, the basic
theory which must underlie the technologies of policy making in all
these diverse disciplines is the theory of modelling; the theory
of the relation between a system and a model of that system.

This in itself was a pleasing insight. And it led to some immediate
consequences which were also pleasing. For instance: why did one
need to make policies in the first place? It was clear that the
major purpose of policy-making, of planning, was to eliminate or
control *conflict*. Indeed, in one form or another, much attention
at the Center was devoted to instances of conflict, whether it be
between individuals or institutions; that was what the Law, for
example, was all about. In each specific case, it appeared that the
roots of conflict lay not so much in any particular objective situation, but rather in the fact that differing *models* of that situation

had been adopted by the different parties to the conflict; consequently, different predictions about that situation were made by these parties, and incompatible courses of action adopted thereby. Therefore, a general theory of policy making (or, as I would argue, a general theory of modelling) would have as a corollary a theory of conflict, and hopefully of conflict resolution.

I proceeded by attempting to integrate these thoughts with my overall program, which as I noted above was to establish homologies between modes of social and biological organization. Accordingly, I cast about for possible biological instances of control of behavior through the utilization of predictive models. To my astonishment, I found them everywhere, at all levels of biological organization. Before going further, it may be helpful to consider a few of these examples.

At the highest level, it is of course clear that a prominent if not overwhelming part of our own everyday behavior is based on the tacit employment of predictive models. To take a transparent example: if I am walking in the woods, and I see a bear appear on the path ahead of me, I will immediately tend to vacate the premises. Why? I would argue: because I can *foresee* a variety of unpleasant consequences arising from failing to do so. The stimulus for my action is not *just* the sight of the bear, but rather the output of the model through which I predict the consequences of direct interaction with the bear. I thus change my *present* course of action, in accordance with my model's prediction. Or, to put it another way, my present behavior is not simply *reactive*, but rather is *anticipatory*.

Similar examples of anticipatory behavior at the human level can be multiplied without end, and may seem fairly trivial. Perhaps more surprising is the manifestation of similar anticipatory behavior at lower levels, where there is no question of learning or of consciousness. For instance, many primitive organisms are negatively phototropic; they move towards darkness. Now darkness in itself has no physiological significance; in itself it is biologically neutral. However, darkness can be *correlated* with characteristics which are not physiologically neutral; e.g. with moisture, or with the absence of sighted predators. The relation between darkness and such positive features comprises a *model* through which the organism predicts that by moving towards darkness, it *will* gain an advantage. Of course this is not a conscious decision on the organism's part; the organism has no real option, because the model is, in effect, "wired-in". But the fact remains that a negatively phototropic organism changes state in the present in accord with a prediction about the future, made on the basis of a model which associates darkness (a neutral characteristic in itself) with some quality which favors survival.

Another example of such a "wired-in" model may be found in the wintering behavior of deciduous trees. The shedding of leaves and other physiological changes which occur in the autumn are clearly an adaptation to winter conditions. What is the cue for such behavior? It so happens that the cue is not the ambient temperature, but rather is day length. In other words, the tree possesses a model, which *anticipates* low temperature on the basis of a shortening day, regardless of what the present ambient temperature may be. Once again, the adaptive behavior arises because of a wired-in predictive model which associates a shortening day (which in itself is physiologically neutral) with a *future* drop in temperature (which is not physiologically neutral). In retrospect, given the vagaries of weather, we can see that the employment of such a model, rather than a direct temperature response, is the clever thing to do.

A final example, this one at the molecular level, illustrates the
same theme. Let us consider a biosynthetic pathway, which we may
represent abstractly in the form

$$A_0 \xrightarrow{\;E_1\;} A_1 \xrightarrow{\;E_2\;} A_2 \xrightarrow{\;E_3\;} \ldots \xrightarrow{\;E_n\;} A_n$$

in which each metabolite A_i is the substrate for the enzyme E_{i+1}.
A common characteristic of such pathways is a *forward activation*
step, as for example where the initial substrate A_0 activates the
enzyme E_n (i.e. increases its reaction rate). Thus, a sudden increase in the amount of A_0 in the environment will result in a
corresponding increase in the activity of E_n. It is clear that the
ambient concentration of A_0 serves as a *predictor*, which in effect
"tells" the enzyme E_n that there *will be* a subsequent increase in
the concentration A_{n-1} of its substrate, and thereby pre-adapts the
pathway so that it will be competent to deal with it. The forward
activation step thus embodies a model, which relates the present
concentration of A_0 to a subsequent concentration of A_{n-1}, and
thereby generates an obviously adaptive response of the entire
pathway.

I remarked above that I was astonished to find this profusion of
anticipatory behavior at all levels of biological organization. It
is important here to understand why I found the situation astonishing,
for it bears on the developments to be reported subsequently, and
raises some crucial epistemological issues.

We have already seen, in the few examples presented above, that an
anticipatory behavior is one in which a change of state in the
present occurs as a function of some predicted future state, and
that the agency through which the prediction is made must be, in the
broadest sense, a model. I have also indicated that obvious examples
of anticipatory behavior abound in the biosphere at all levels of
organization, and that much (if not most) conscious human behavior
is also of this character. It is further true that organic behaviors
at all of these levels have been the subject of incessant scrutiny
and theoretical attention for a long time. It might then be expected
that such behavior would be well understood, and that there would
indeed be an extensive body of theory and of practical experience
which could be immediately applied to the problems of forecasting
and policy-making which dominated the Center's interests. But in
fact, nothing could be further from the truth. The surprise was
not primarily that there was no such body of theory and experience,
but rather that almost no systematic efforts had been made in these
directions; and moreover, almost no one recognized that such an
effort was urgently required. In retrospect, the most surprising
thing to me was that I myself had not previously recognized such a
need, despite my overt concerns with modelling as a fundamental scientific activity, and despite my explicit involvement with biological
behavior extending over many years. Indeed, I might never have
recognized this need, had it not been for the fortuitous chain of
circumstances I have described above, which led me to think seriously
about apparently alien problems of policy-making in a democratic
society. Such are the powers of compartmentalization in the human
mind.

In fact, the actual situation is somewhat worse than this. At its deepest level, the failure to recognize and understand the nature of anticipatory behavior has not simply been an oversight, but is the necessary consequence of the entire thrust of theoretical science since earliest times. For the basic cornerstone on which our entire scientific enterprise rests is the belief that events are not arbitrary, but obey definite laws which can be discovered. The search for such laws is an expression of our faith in causality. Above all, the development of theoretical physics, from Newton and Maxwell through the present, represents simultaneously the deepest expression and the most persuasive vindication of this faith. Even in quantum mechanics, where the discovery of the Uncertainty Principle of Heisenberg precipitated a deep re-appraisal of causality, there is no abandonment of the notion that microphysical events obey definite laws; the only real novelty is that the quantum laws describe the statistics of classes of events rather than individual elements of such classes.

The temporal laws of physics all take the form of differential equations, in which the rate of change of a physical quantity at any instant is expressed as a definite function of the values of other physical quantities at that instant. Thus, from a knowledge of the values of all the relevant quantities as some initial instant t_0, the values of these quantities at the succeeding instant $t_0 + dt$ are determined. By iterating this process through an integration opertion, the values of these quantities, and hence the entire behavior of the system under consideration, may be determined for all time. Carrying this picture to its logical conclusion, Laplace could say,

> An intelligence knowing, at a given instant of time, all forces acting in nature, as well as the momentary position of all things of which the universe consists, would be able to comprehend the motions of the largest bodies of the world as well as the lightest atoms in one single formula...To him nothing would be uncertain; both past and future would be present in his eyes.

This picture of causality and law, arising initially in physics, has been repeatedly generalized, modified and extended over the years, but the basic pattern remains identifiable throughout. And one fundamental feature of this picture has remained entirely intact; indeed itself elevated to the status of a natural law. That feature is the following: *in any law governing a natural system, it is forbidden to allow present change of state to depend upon future states*. Past states perhaps, in systems with "memory"; present state certainly; but *never* future states. It is perfectly clear from the above discussion why such a commandment is natural, and why its violation would appear tantamount to a denial of causality in the natural world.

A denial of causality thus appears as an attack on the ultimate basis on which science itself rests. This is also the reason why arguments from final causes have been excluded from science. In the Aristotelian parlance, a final cause is one which involves a purpose or goal; the explanation of system behavior in terms of final causes is the province of *teleology*. As we shall see abundantly, the concept of an anticipatory system has nothing much to do with teleology. Nevertheless, the imperative to avoid even the remotest appearance of telic explanation in science is so strong that all modes of system analysis conventionally exclude the possibility of anticipatory behavior from the very outset.[2]

And yet, let us consider the behavior of a system which contains a predictive model, and which can utilize the predictions of its model

to modify its present behavior. Let us suppose further that the
model is a "good" model; that its predictions approximate future
events with a sufficiently high degree of accuracy. It is clear
that such a system will behave *as if it were* a true anticipatory
system; i.e. a system in which present change of state does depend
on future states. In the deepest sense, it is evident that this
kind of system will not in fact violate our notions of causality in
any way, nor need it involve any kind of teleology. But since we
explicitly forbid present change of state to depend on future states,
we will be driven to understand the behavior of such a system in a
purely *reactive* mode; i.e. one in which present change of state
depends only on present and past states.

This is indeed what has happened in attempting to come to grips
theoretically and practically with biological behavior. Without
exception (in my experience), all models and theories of biological
systems are reactive in the above sense. As such, we have seen that
they *necessarily* exclude all possibility of dealing directly with
the properties of anticipatory behavior of the type we have been
discussing.

How is it, then, that the ubiquity of anticipatory behaviors in
biology could have been overlooked for so long? Should it not have
been evident that the "reactive paradigm", as we may call it, was
grossly deficient in dealing with systems of this kind? To this
question there are two answers. The first is that many scientists
and philosophers have indeed repeatedly suggested that something
fundamental may be missing if we adopt a purely reactive paradigm
for consideration of biological phenomena. Unfortunately, these
authors have generally been able only imperfectly to articulate
their perception, couching it in terms as "will", "Geist" "élan",
"entelechy", and others. This has made it easy to dismiss them as
mystical, vitalistic, anthropomorphic, idealistic, or with similar
unsavory epithets, and to confound them with teleology.

The other answer lies in the fact that the reactive paradigm is
universal, in the following important sense. Given any mode of
system behavior which can be described sufficiently accurately,
regardless of the manner in which it is generated, there is a purely
reactive system which exhibits precisely this behavior. In other
words, any system behavior can be *simulated* by a purely reactive
system. It thus might appear that this universality makes the
reactive paradigm completely adequate for all scientific explanations,
but this does not follow, and in fact is not the case. For instance,
the Ptolemaic epicycles are also universal, in the sense that any
planetary trajectory can be represented in terms of a sufficiently
extensive family of them. The reason that the Copernican scheme
was considered superior to the Ptolemaic lies not in the existence
of trajectories which cannot be represented by the epicycles, but
arises entirely from considerations of *parsimony*, as embodied for
instance in Occam's Razor. The universality of the epicycles is
regarded as an extraneous mathematical artifact irrelevant to the
underlying physical situation, and it is for this reason that a
representation of trajectories in terms of them can only be regarded
as a simulation, and not as an explanation.

In fact, the universality of the reactive paradigm is not very
different in character from the universality of the epicycles.
Both modes of universality ultimately arise from the mathematical
fact that any function can be approximated arbitrarily closely by
functions canonically constructed out of a suitably chosen "basis
set" whose members have a special form. Such a basis set may for

instance comprise trigonometric functions, as in the familiar Fourier expansion; the polynomials 1, x, x², ... form another familiar basis set. From this it follows that if any kind of system behavior can be described in functional terms, it can also be *generated* by a suitably constructed combination of systems which generate the elements of a basis set, and this entirely within a reactive mode. But it is clear that there is nothing unique about a system so constructed; we can do the same with *any* basis set. All these systems are different from one another, and may be likewise different from the initial system whose behavior we wanted to describe. It is in this sense that we can only speak of simulation, and not of explanation, of our system's behavior in these terms.

Nevertheless, I believe that it is precisely the universality of the reactive paradigm which has played the crucial role in concealing the inadequacy of the paradigm for dealing with anticipatory systems.

Indeed, it is clear that if we are confronted with a system which contains a predictive model, and which uses the predictions of that model to generate its behavior, we cannot claim to understand the behavior unless the model itself is taken into account. Moreover, if we wish to construct such a system, we cannot do so entirely within the framework appropriate to the synthesis of purely reactive systems.

On these grounds, I was thus led to the conclusion that an entirely new approach was needed, in which the capability for anticipatory behavior was present from the outset. Such an approach would necessarily include, as its most important component, a comprehensive theory of models and of modelling. The purpose of the present volume in fact, is to develop the principles of such an approach, and to describe its relation to other realms of mathematical and scientific investigation.

With these and similar considerations in mind, I proceeded to prepare a number of working papers on anticipatory behavior, and the relation of this kind of behavior to the formulation and implementation of policy. Some of these papers were later published in the *International Journal of General Systems*.[3] The first one I prepared was entitled, "Planning, management, policies and strategies: Four fuzzy concepts", and it already contained the seeds of the entire approach I developed to deal with these matters. For this reason, and to indicate the context in which I was working at the Center, it may be helpful to cite some of the original material directly. The introductory section began as follows

It is fair to say that the mood of those concerned with the problems of contemporary society is apocalyptic. It is widely felt that our social structure is in the midst of crises, certainly serious, and perhaps ultimate. It is further widely felt that the social crises we perceive have arisen primarily because of the anarchic, laissez-faire attitude taken in the past towards science, technology, economics and politics. The viewpoint of most of those who have written on these subjects revolves around the theme that if we allow these anarchies to continue we are lost; indeed, one way to make a name nowadays is to prove, preferably with computer models, that an extrapolation of present practices will lead to imminent cataclysm. The alternative to anarchy is management; and management implies in turn the systematic implementation of specific plans, programs, policies and strategies. Thus it is no wonder that the circle of ideas centering around the concept of *planning* plays a dominant role in current thought.

However, it seems that the net effect of the current emphasis on planning

has been simply to shift the anarchy we perceive in our social processes
into our ideas about the management of these processes. If we consider,
for example, the area of "economic development" of the underdeveloped
countries (a topic which has been extensively considered by many august
bodies), we find (a) that there is no clear idea of what constitutes "development";   (b) that the various definitions employed by those concerned with
development are incompatible and contradictory;   (c) that even among those
who happen to share the same views as to the ends of development, there are
similarly incompatible and contradictory views as to the means whereby the
end can be attained. Yet in the name of developmental planning, an enormous
amount of time, ink, money and even blood is in the process of being spilled.
Surely no remedy can be expected if the cure and the disease are indistiguishable.

If it is the case that planning is as anarchic as the social developments
it is intended to control, then we must ask whether there is, in some sense,
a "plan for planning" or whether we face an infinite and futile anarchic
regress. It may seem at first sight that by putting a question in this form
we gain nothing. However, what we shall attempt to argue in the present
paper is that, in fact, this kind of question is "well-posed" in a scientific
sense: that it can be investigated in a rigorous fashion and its consequences
explored. Moreover, we would like to argue that, in the process of investigating this question, some useful and potentially applicable insights into
planning itself are obtainable.

After a brief review of the main technical concepts to be invoked
(which was essential for the audience at the Center) I then proposed
a specific context in which anticipatory behavior could be concretely
discussed:

We are now ready to construct our model world, which will consist of a class
of systems of definite structure, involving anticipation in an essential
way, and in which the fuzzy terms associated with "planning" can be given a
concrete meaning.

Let us suppose that we are given a system S, which shall be the system
of interest, and which we shall call the *object system*. S may be an individual organism, or an ecosystem, or a social or economic system. For
simplicity we shall suppose that S is an ordinary (i.e. non-anticipatory)
dynamical system.

With S we shall associate another dynamical system M, which is in some
sense a *model* of S. We require, however, that if the trajectories of S are
parameterized by real time, then the corresponding trajectories of M are
parameterized by a time variable which goes faster than real time. That is,
if S and M are started out at time $t = 0$ in equivalent states, and if (real)
time is allowed to run for a fixed interval T, then M will have proceeded
further along its trajectory than S. In this way, the behavior of M *predicts*
the behavior of S; by looking at the state of M at time T, we get information about the state that S will be in at some time later than T.

We shall now allow M and S to be coupled; i.e. allow them to interact
in specific ways. For the present, we shall restrict ourselves to ways in
which M may affect S; later we shall introduce another mode of coupling
which will allow S to affect M (and which will amount to updating or improving
the model system M on the basis of the activity of S). We shall for the
present suppose simply that the system M is equipped with a set E of
effectors, which allow it to operate either on S itself, or on the environmental inputs to S, in such a way as to change the dynamical properties of
S. We thus have a situation of the type diagrammed in Figure 1.

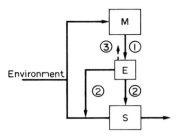

Fig. 1.1.1.

If we put this entire system into a single box, that box will appear to us to be adaptive system in which prospective future behaviors determine present changes of state. It would be an anticipatory system in the strict sense if M were a *perfect* model of S (and if the environment were constant or periodic). Since in general M is not a perfect model, for reasons to be discussed in Chapter 5 below, we shall call the behavior of such systems *quasi-anticipatory*.

We have said that "M sees" into the future of S, because the trajectories of M are parameterized faster than those of S. How is this information to be used to modify the properties of S through the effector system E? There are many ways in which this can be formalized, but the simplest seems to be the following. Let us imagine the state space of S (and hence of M) to be partitioned into regions corresponding to "desirable" and "undesirable" states. As long as the trajectory in M remains in a "desirable" region, no action is taken by M through the effectors E. As soon as the M-trajectory moves into an "undesirable" region (and hence, by inference, we may expect the S-trajectory to move into the corresponding region at some later time, calculable from a knowledge of how the M- and S-trajectories are parameterized) the effector system is activated to change the dynamics of S in such a way as to keep the S-trajectory out of the "undesirable" region.

From this simple picture, a variety of insights into the nature of "planning", "management", "policies", etc., can already be extracted.

The structure depicted in Fig. 1.1.1 possesses properties which relate directly to the generation and implementation of plans; I then proceeded to sketch these properties:

A. Choice of M.

The first essential ingredient in the planning process in these systems involves the choice of the model system M. There are many technical matters involved in choosing M, which will be discussed in more detail in Chapter 5 below. We wish to point out here that the choice of M involves paradigmatic aspects as well, which color all future aspects of the "planning" process. One simple example of this may suffice. Let us suppose that S is a simple early capitalist economic system. If we adopt a model system which postulates a large set of small independent entrepeneurs, approximately equivalent in productive capability and governed by "market forces", we find that the system S is essentially stable; coalitions are unfavored and any technical innovations will rapidly spread to all competitors. On the other hand, if we adopt a model system M in which there are positive feedback loops, then

we will see the same situation as *unstable*, much as an emulsion of oil and
water is unstable. That is, initially small local accretions of capital
will tend to be amplified, and the initially homogeneous population of many
small entrepeneurs will ultimately be replaced by a few enormous cartels.
This, in a highly oversimplified way, seems to represent the difference
between laissez-faire capitalism and Marxian socialism, proceeding from
two different model systems of the same initial economic system S, and hence
predicting two entirely different futures for S.

B. Selection of the Effector System E.

Once the model M has been chosen, the next step of the planning or management
process for S is to determine how we are to modify the dynamics of S according
to the information we obtain from M. The problem involves several stages.
The first stage involves a selection of "steering" variables in S or in the
environment of S, through which the dynamical properties of S can be modified.
In general, several different kinds of choices can be made, on a variety of
different grounds. In empirical terms, this choice will most often be made
in terms of the properties of the model system M; we will consider how M
can be most effectively steered, and use the corresponding state variables
of S (if possible) for the control of S. Thus again the initial choice of
the model system M will again tend to play a major role in determining the
specifics of the planning process.

C. Design of the Effector System E.

Once having chosen the control variables of S, we must now *design* a corresponding effector system. This is a technological kind of problem, governed
by the nature of the control variables of S and their response characteristics. We may wish, for example, to employ only controls which are easily
reversible.

D. Programming of the Effector System E.

The final aspect of the planning process involves the actual programming of
the effector system; i.e. the specification of a dynamics on E which will
convert the input information from M (i.e. information about the future
state of S) into a specific modification of the dynamics of S. This transduction can be accomplished in many ways, and involves a mixture of "stra-
tegic" and "tactical" considerations.

E. Identification of "Desirable" and "Undesirable" Regions.

Ultimately the programming of the effectors E will depend heavily on the
character of the regions we consider "desirable" and those we consider
"undesirable". This choice too is arbitrary, and is in fact independent of
the model system M which we have chosen. It represents a kind of constraint
added from the outside, and it enters into the planning process in an equally
weighty fashion as does the model M and the effector system E.

F. Updating the States of M.

In Fig. 1.1.1 we have included a dotted arrow (labelled (3)) from the effector
system back to the model. This is for the purpose of resetting the states
of the model, according to the controls which have been exerted on the system
S by the effector system. Unless we do this, the model system M becomes
useless for predictions about S subsequent to the implementation of controls
through E. Thus, the effector system E must be wired into M in a fashion
equivalent to its wiring into S.

The enumeration (A)-(F) above seems to be a useful atomization of the
planning process for the class of systems we have constructed. Within this

class, then, we can proceed further and examine some of the consequences of planning, and in particular the ways in which planning can go wrong. We shall sketch these analyses in the subsequent sections.

The notion of "how planning could go wrong" was of course of primary interest to the Center; indeed, for months I had heard a succession of discouraging papers dealing with little else. It seemed to me that by elaborating on this theme I could establish a direct contact between my ruminations and the Center's preoccupations. My preliminary discussion of these matters ended as follows:

> We would like to conjecture further that, for any specific planning situation (involving an object system S, a model M, and suitably programmed effectors E), each of the ways in which planning can go wrong will lead to a particular kind of syndrome in the total system (just as the defect of any part of a sensory mechanism in an organism leads to a particular array of symptoms). It should therefore be possible, in principle, to develop a definite diagnostic procedure to "trouble-shoot" a system of this kind, by mimicking the procedures used in neurology and psychology. Indeed, it is amusing to think that such planning systems are capable of exhibiting syndromes (e.g. of "neurosis") very much like (and indeed analogous to) those manifested by individual organisms.

Such considerations as these led naturally to the general problems connected with system error, malfunction or breakdown, which have always been hard to formulate, and are still poorly understood. Closest to the surface in this direction, especially in the human realm, were breakdowns arising from the incorporation of incorrect elements into the diagram shown in Fig. 1.1.1 above; faulty models, inappropriate choice of effectors, etc. I soon realized, however, that there was a more profound aspect of system breakdown, arising from the basic nature of the modelling process itself, and from the character of the system interactions required in the very act of imposing controls. These were initially considered under the heading of *side-effects*, borrowing a medical terminology describing unavoidable and usually unfortunate consequences of employing therapeutic agents (an area which of course represents yet another branch of control therapy). As I used the term, I meant it to connote unplanned and unforeseeable consequences on system behavior arising from the implementation of controls designed to accomplish other purposes; or, in a related context, the appearance of unpredicted behavior in a system built in accordance with a particular plan or blueprint. Thus the question was posed: are such side-effects a *necessary* consequence of control? Or is there room for hope that, with sufficient cleverness, the ideal of the *magic bullet*, the miraculous cure which specifically restores health with no other effect, can actually be attained?

Since this notion of side-effects is so important, let us consider some examples. Of the medical realm we need not speak extensively, except to note that almost every therapeutic agent, as well as most diagnostic agents, create them; sometimes spectacularly so, as in the thalidomide scandal of some years past. We are also familiar with ecological examples, in which man has unwittingly upset "the balance of nature" through injudicious introduction or elimination of species in a particular habitat; well-known instances of this are the introduction of rabbits to Australia, to give the gentlemen farmers something to hunt on the weekend; or the importation of the mongoose into Santo Domingo, in the belief that because the mongoose kills cobras it would also eliminate local poisonous snakes such as the fer-de-lance. Examples from technology also abound; for instance, we may cite the presence of unsuspected oscillatory modes in the

Tacoma Bay Bridge, which ultimately caused it to collapse in a high
wind; or the Ohio Turnpike, which was built without curves on the
theory that curves are where accidents occur; this led to the discovery of road hypnosis. Norbert Wiener warned darkly of the possibility of similar disastrous side-effects in connection with the
perils of relying on computers to implement policy. He analogized
this situation to an invocation of magical aids as related in in-
numerable legends and folk-tales; specifically, such stories as The
Sorcerer's Apprentice, The Mill Which Ground Nothing but Salt, The
Monkey's Paw, and The Midas Touch. And of course, many of the social
and economic panaceas introduced in the past decades have not only
generated such unfortunate side-effects, but have in the long run
served to exacerbate the very problems they were intended to control.

The ubiquity of these examples, and the dearth of counter-examples,
suggests that there is indeed something universal about such behavior,
and that it might be important to discover what it is.

My first clumsy attempts to come to grips with this underlying principle, at this early stage, were as follows (the several references
to an "earlier paper" in these excerpts refer to a paper written
later than, but published before, the one being cited):

> There is, however, a class of planning difficulties which do not arise from
> such obvious considerations, and which merit a fuller discussion. This class
> of difficulties has to do with the problem of *side effects*; as we shall see,
> these will generally arise, even if the model system is perfect and the
> effectors perfectly designed and programmed, because of inherent system-
> theoretic properties. Let us see how this comes about.

> In a previous paper we enunciated a conjecture which I believe to have
> general validity: namely; that in carrying out any particular functional
> activity, a system S typically only uses a few of its degrees of freedom.
> This proposition has several crucial corollaries, of which we noted two in
> the preceding paper:

> (1) The same structure can be involved simultaneously in many different
> functional activities, and conversely.

> (2) The same functional activity can be carried out (or "realized") by
> many different kinds of structures.

> We stressed in that paper how the fact that *all* of the state variables
> defining any particular system S are more or less strongly *linked* to one
> another via the equations of motion of the system, taken together with the
> fact that the many state variables not involved in a particular functional
> activity were free to interact with other systems in a non-functional or
> dysfunctional way, implied that any particular functional activity tends to
> be modified or lost over time. This, we feel, is a most important result,
> which bears directly on the "planning" process under discussion. The easiest
> way to see this is to draw another corollary from the fundamental proposition
> that only a few degrees of freedom of a system S are involved in any particu-
> lar functional activity of S.

> (3) Any functional activity of a system S can be *modelled* by a system whose
> structure is simple compared to that of S (simply by neglecting the non-
> functional degrees of freedom of S). Indeed, it is largely because of this
> property that science is possible at all. Conversely,

> (4) No one model is capable of capturing the full potentialities of a system
> S for interactions with arbitrary systems.

The corollary (4) is true even of the best models, and it is this corollary which bears most directly on the problem of *side-effects*. Let us recall that S is by hypothesis a real system, whereas M is only a model of a particular functional activity of S. There are thus many degrees of freedom of S which are not modelled in M. Even if M is a good model, then, the capability for dealing with the non-functional degrees of freedom in S have necessarily been abstracted away. And these degrees of freedom, which continue to exist in S, are generally *linked* to the degrees of freedom of S which are modelled in M, through the overall equations of motion which govern S.

Now the planning process requires us to construct a real system E, which is to interact with S through a particular subset of the degrees of freedom of S (indeed, through a subset of those degrees of freedom of S which are modelled in M). But from our general proposition, only a few of the degrees of freedom of E can be involved in this interaction. Thus both E and S have in general many "non-functional" degrees of freedom, through which other, non-modelled interactions can take place. Because of the linkage of all observables, the actual interaction between E and S specified in the planning process will in general be affected. Therefore, we find that the two following propositions are generally true: (a) An effector system E will in general have other effects on an object system S than those which are planned; (b) The planned modes of interaction between E and S will be modified by these effects. Both of these propositions describe the kind of thing we usually refer to as *side-effects*. As we see, such side-effects are unavoidable consequences of the general properties of systems and their interaction. They are by nature unpredictable, and are inherent in the planning process no matter how well that process is technically carried out. As we pointed out in our previous paper, there are a number of ways around this kind of difficulty, which we have partially characterized, but they are only applicable in special circumstances.

The basic principle struggling to emerge here is the following: the ultimate seat of the side-effects arising in anticipatory control, and indeed of the entire concept of error or malfunction in system theory as a whole, rests on the discrepancy between the behavior actually exhibited by a natural system, and the corresponding behavior predicted on the basis of a model of that system. For a model is necessarily an *abstraction*, in that degrees of freedom which are present in the system are absent in the model. In physical terms, the system is *open* to interactions through these degrees of freedom, while the model is necessarily *closed* to such interactions; the discrepancy between system behavior and model behavior is thus a manifestation of the difference between a closed system and an open one. This is one of the basic themes which we shall develop in detail in the subsequent chapters.

My initial paper on anticipatory systems concluded with several observations, which I hoped would be suggestive to my audience. The first was the following: that it was unlikely that side-effects could be removed by simply augmenting the underlying model, or by attempting to control each side-effect separately as it appeared. The reason for this is that both of these strategies face an incipient infinite regress, similar to that pointed out by Gödel in his demonstration of the existence of unprovable propositions within any consistent and sufficiently rich system of axioms. Oddly enough, the possibility of avoiding this infinite regress was not entirely foreclosed; this followed in a surprising way from some of my earliest work in relational biology, which was mentioned earlier:

There are many ramifications of the class of systems developed above, for the purpose of studying the planning process, which deserve somewhat fuller consideration than we have allowed. In this section we shall consider two of them: (a) how can we update and improve the model system M, and the effector system E, on the basis of information about the behavior of S itself and (b) how can we avoid a number of apparent infinite regresses which seem to be inherent in the planning process?

These two apparently separate questions are actually forms of the same question. We can see this as follows. If we are going to improve, say, the model system M, then we must do so by means of a set of effectors E'. These effectors E' must be controlled by information pertaining to the effect of M on S; i.e. by a model system M' of the system (S+M+E). In other words, we must construct for the purpose of updating and improving M a system which looks exactly like Fig. 1.1.1 except that we replace M by M', E by E', and S by S+M+E. But then we may ask how we can update M'; in this way we see an incipient infinite regress.

There is another infinite regress inherent in the discussion given of side-effects in the preceding section. We have seen that the interaction of the effectors E with the object system S typically give rise to effects in S unpredictable in principle from the model system M. However, these effects too, by the basic principle that only a few degrees of freedom of S and E are utilized in such interactions, are capable of being modelled. That is, we can in principle construct a new model system M_1 of the interaction between S and E, which describes interactions not describable in M. If these interactions are unfavorable, we can construct a new set of effectors, say E_1, which will steer the system S away from these side-effects. But just as with E, the system S will typically interact with E_1 in ways which are in principle not comprehensible within the models M or M_1; these will require another model M_2 and corresponding new effectors E_2. In this way we see another incipient infinite regress forming. Indeed, this last infinite regress is highly reminiscent of the "technological imperative" which we were warned against by Ellul[1] and many others. Thus the question arises: can such infinite regresses be avoided?

These kinds of questions are well-posed, and can be investigated in system-theoretic terms. We have considered[2] questions like these in a very different connection; namely, under what circumstances is it possible to add a new functional activity to a biological organization like a cell? It turns out that one cannot simply add an arbitrary function and still preserve the organization; we must typically keep adding functions without limit. But under certain circumstances, the process does indeed terminate; the new function is included (though not *just* the new function in general) and the overall organization is manifested in the enlarged system. On the basis of these considerations, I would conjecture that (a) it is possible in principle to avoid the infinite regresses just alluded to in the planning process, and in particular to find ways of updating the model M and the effectors E; (b) *not every way of initiating and implementing a planning process allows us to avoid the infinite regress.* The first conjecture is optimistic; there are ways of avoiding this form of the "technological imperative". The second can be quite pessimistic in reference to our actual society. For if we have in fact embarked on a path for which the infinite regresses cannot be avoided, then we are in serious trouble. Avoiding the infinite regresses means that developmental processes will stop, and that a stable steady-state condition can be reached. Once embarked on a path for which the infinite regresses cannot be avoided, no stable steady-state condition is possible. I do not know which is the case in our own present circumstances, but it should at least be possible to find out.

I hope that the above few remarks on the planning process will provide food for thought for those more competent to investigate such problems than I am.

The theoretical principle underlying this analysis of failure in
anticipatory control systems is not wholly negative. In fact, we
shall argue later that it also underlies the phenomena of *emergence*
which characterize evolutionary and developmental processes in
biology. It may be helpful to cite one more excerpt of a paper
originally prepared for the Center Dialog, which dealt with this
aspect:

> It may perhaps be worth noting at this point that the above phenomenon is
> responsible for many of the evolutionary properties exhibited by organisms,
> and many of the developmental characteristics of social organizations. Con-
> sider, for example, the problems involved in understanding, e.g. the evolution
> of a sensory mechanism such as an eye. The eye is a complicated physiological
> mechanism which conveys no advantage until it actually sees, and it cannot
> see until it is complicated. It is hard to imagine how one could even get
> started towards evolving such a structure, however valuable the end-result
> may be, and this was one of the major kinds of objections raised by Darwinian
> evolution. The response to this objection is essentially as follows: the
> proto-eye in its early stages was in fact not involved in the function of
> seeing, but rather was primarily involved in carrying out some other functional
> activity, and it was on this other activity that selection could act. It we
> now suppose that this other activity involved photosensitivity in an initially
> accidental way (simply because the physical structure of the proto-eye happened
> to also be photosensitive), it is easy to imagine how selection pressure
> could successively improve the proto-eye, with its accidental sensory capacity,
> until actual seeing could begin, and so that selection could begin to act on
> the eye directly as an eye. When that happened, the original function of the
> eye was lost or absorbed into other structures, leaving the eye free to
> evolve exclusively as a sensory organ.
>
> This "Principle of Function Change" is manifested even more clearly by
> the evolution of the lung as an organ of respiration. Many fish possess
> swim bladders, a bag of tissue filled with air, as an organ of equilibration.
> Being a bag of tissue, the swim bladder is vascularized (possesses blood
> vessels). When air and small blood vessels are in contact, there will necess-
> arily be gas exchange between the blood and the air, and so a respiratory
> function is incipient in this structure, designed initially for equilibration.
> It is easy to imagine how successive increases in vascularization of this
> organ, especially in arid times, could be an advantage, and thus how selection
> could come to act on this structure as a lung. This Principle of Function
> Change is thus one of the cornerstones of evolution (and indeed of any kind
> of adaptive behavior), and it depends essentially on the fact that the same
> structure is capable of simultaneously manifesting a variety of functions.

Thus the basic problem of avoiding infinite regresses in anticipatory
control systems could be reformulated as follows: can we design
systems which are proof against a Principle of Function Change?

This was the circle of ideas which I was led to place on the table
at the Center. The response elicited thereby could perhaps best be
described as restrained, but encouraging. I received some comments
to the effect that my approach was logical and mathematical, and
hence fundamentally inapplicable to politics. In particular, there
seemed to be no room for perversity, a major factor in human behavior.
Indeed, I had often noted that almost the only way for man to prove
that he is truly free is to deliberately do himself an injury; to
deliberately act against his obvious best interests. But I did not
feel that this sort of objection was insuperable. Mr. Hutchins
himself made few direct comments, except at one point to remark that
one of my conclusions was the most outrageous thing he had ever
heard. I took this as a high compliment.

A number of the Senior Fellows did feel that these ideas bore directly on the major concerns of the Center. Rex Tugwell, on the basis of a long life of practical experience in government policy-making, and a commitment to constitutionalization, provided numerous specific instances of many of the points I tried to make in a general context, and always seemed to ask the right questions. Harvey Wheeler, a political scientist, was a most effective and sympathetic devil's advocate. The most enthusiastic response, however, was made by John Wilkinson, whose long advocacy of modelling and simulation for the understanding and exploitation of the lessons on history involved the questions I raised in an essential way.

For my own part, I continue to believe that the properties of anticipatory systems raise new questions for the scientific enterprise of the most basic and fundamental kind. These questions have led me to reformulate and refocus all of my previous work in the foundations of theoretical biology, and in the relation of biology to the physical and human sciences. Indeed, there is no aspect of science which can be untouched by so fundamental an activity as a reconsideration of the reactive paradigm itself. The results of this reconsideration, and its implications, are the basic subject-matter of the developments which follow.

Now that we have reviewed the genesis of the theoretical problems with which the present volume is concerned, we may turn to a consideration of the problems themselves. The first and most basic of them is simply this: what is a model? What is the nature of the relation between two systems which allows us to assert that one of them is a model for the other? The basic property of the modelling relation is that we can learn something about a system in which we are interested by studying a model of that system. The crucial point to be developed here is that *causality* in the system must be represented by *implication* in the model. Chapter 2 is devoted entirely to abstract considerations of how this is done, and how a given system may be *encoded* into another so as to establish a modelling relation. These ideas comprise the heart of the book.

Chapter 3 provides a concrete survey of modelling relations between systems of many diverse kinds, drawn from all corners of natural science and mathematics. These examples not only exemplify the abstract development, but throw new light on the inter-relationships generated among systems through the existence of relations between system models. This part culminates with a thorough discussion of relational models and metaphors, to which we have alluded several times above.

Chapter 4 is concerned with laying the basis for a theory of dynamical models, which are the essential features of anticipatory systems. The main point of this chapter is a comprehensive discussion of *time*. Chapter 5, which is in fact closely related, is devoted to a discussion of system reliability and system error, in terms of the deviation between the actual behavior of a system and the behavior predicted by some model of the system. The basic point of view we take here is the one proposed earlier; namely, that this deviation can be regarded as the difference in behavior between a system closed to certain environmental interactions, and the same system open to those interactions. We illustrate these ideas with a discussion of emergent novelty in biology, and its relation to the general notion of a *bifurcation*.

Finally, in Chapter 6 we pull these various threads together to obtain a general theory for feedforwards and anticipatory systems.

Of particular importance here is an extensive discussion of anticipation and causality. In the concluding part, we consider the unique possibilities for global failures in feedforward systems, which do not arise from local failure in any subsystem. We suggest how this possibility leads to a new theoretical approach to the spanning of biological properties, and to organism senescence.

As noted previously, the subsequent exposition will draw heavily on our previous work concerned with modelling and system epistemology. In particular, the material in a previous monograph entitled *Fundamentals of Measurement and the Representation of Natural Systems* will be extensively used. However, we have made every effort to keep the present treatment as self-contained as possible. Where this was not feasible, extensive references to the literature have been supplied.

In conclusion, I would like to refer the reader once again to Mr. Hutchins' epic view of the Great Conversation, resounding through all ages that have been and are to come. I hope that this volume can be regarded as a small contribution to it.

REFERENCES AND NOTES

1. Robert Hutchins died in 1978. A biography of this extraordinary man, who was Dean of the Yale Law School at 24, and President of the University of Chicago before he was 30, still awaits writing. At present, one can best learn about Hutchins from his own voluminous writings, or from the tapes of the dialogs in which he participated at the Center; these last reveal his unique and charismatic personality most directly.

   The Center for the Study of Democratic Institutions also deserves a biographer. The Center has undergone a radical transformation over the past few years; it still survives, in a vastly mutated form, as part of the University of California in Santa Barbara. Its former character, under Hutchins, can best be appreciated by looking at its lively little magazine, the *Center Reports*, which unfortunately is now extinct. Its sister publication, the *Center Magazine*, still appears (as of this writing) but was always far more traditionally academic in tone.

   The quotations of Hutchins cited in the text were taken from articles he prepared for Center publication, and from various talks and addresses he presented over the years.

2. The role of teleology in biological theory has had a long and confused history. In some forms of teleology (e.g. Lamarck) the individual organism is regarded as the telic agent; in others (e.g. Bergson) the organism is an instrumentality of an agent which lies outside itself. Further, the status of telic explanation has become inextricably confounded with the endless and futile mechanist-vitalist controversy. A bibliography of references on causality and teleology, and the philosophical issues they raise, would run to hundreds of pages; we content ourselves with a few representative discussions, from several different points of view, which the interested reader may pursue further:

   Bunge, M., *Causality*. Harvard University Press, Cambridge, Massachusetts (1959).

Driesch, H., *History and Theory of Vitalism*. MacMillan, London
  (1914).
Grene, M., *Approaches to Philosophical Biology*. Basic Books, New
  York (1968).
Grene, M. and Mendelsohn, E., *Topics in Philosophy of Biology*.
  Reidel, Boston (1976).
Mackie, J. L., *The Cement of the Universe: A Study of Causation*.
  Clarendon Press, Oxford (1947).
Nagel, E., *Teleology Revisited and Other Essays*. Columbia University
  Press, New York (1979).
Woodfield, A., *Teleology*. Cambridge University Press, Cambridge
  (1976).
Woodger, J. H., *Biological Principles*. Routledge & Kegan Paul,
  London (1967).
Wright, L., *Teleological Explanations*. University of California
  Press, Berkeley (1976).

Among more recent works involving purposiveness in biological systems,
we may especially mention Agar, W. E., *A Contribution to the Theory
of the Living Organism*. Melbourne (1943). A perhaps surprising
emphasis on purposiveness also appears in the book of the eminent
molecular biologist Jacques Monod (*Chance and Necessity*, Knopf, 1971),
for which he coins a new word ("teleonomy"). We may also cite some
of the papers of J. M. Burgers (e.g. "Causality and Anticipation".
Science, **189**, 194-98) which are based on the philosophical writings
of A. N. Whitehead.

There is of course an enormous literature on causality in physics,
much of it provoked by quantum mechanics and especially by the
uncertainty principle. A brief but clear discussion, which is still
valuable, may be found in Weyl, H., *Philosophy of Mathematics and
the Natural Sciences*. Princeton University Press (1949). More to
our present point: the idea that causality forbids the future from
influencing the present is all-pervasive in physics; as for instance
in the automatic exclusion of certain solutions of Maxwell's Equations
("advanced potentials") which refer to future time, while retaining
other solutions ("retarded potentials") which refer to past time;
see e.g. Sommerfeld, A., *Electrodynamics*. Academic Press (1954) or
Landau, L. D. and Lifshitz, E. M., *The Classical Theory of Fields*.
Pergamon Press (1975). The alacrity with which this is done has
worried a number of theoretical physicists over the years; perhaps
the most interesting attempt to rehabilitate advanced potentials
may be found in a little-known paper of Wheeler and Feynman (*Rev.
Mod. Phys.*, **21**, 425-43 (1949).

For a typical system-theoretic argument that causal systems cannot
be anticipatory, see e.g. Windeknecht, T. G., *Math. Syst. Theory.*,
1, 279 (1967).

3. Rosen, R., 1974a. *Int. J. Gen. Syst.* **1**, 6-66.
    Rosen, R., 1974b. *ibid.* **1**, 245-252.
    Rosen, R., 1975.   *ibid.* **2**, 93-103.

1.2 The Reactive Paradigm: Its Basic Features

Before we begin our systematic development, it will be well to briefly
review the basic features cf the reactive paradigm itself. This will
be important to us for several reasons. The first of these is, of
course, the overwhelming historical importance of reactive concepts
in the development of science up to this point. Indeed, as we have
noted, systems which appear to violate the hypotheses on which the
reactive paradigm is based are routinely excluded from the scientific
realm. This leads us to the second reason for being familiar with
the reactive paradigm: at the present time, this paradigm dominates
the very concept of modelling; since the concept of a model is the
central feature of anticipatory behavior, we need to understand
fully how the modelling relation and reactive behavior are related.
Third, our extensive familiarity with reactive systems will serve
us as a source of examples and motivation, and as an effective
contrast to the behavior of anticipatory systems as we proceed with
our development.

The treatment which follows will be necessarily sketchy, and will
be concerned entirely with formal aspects. We will leave it to
subsequent chapters to develop the relations which exist between
such formalisms and the natural systems these formalisms are intended
to represent. The reader will probably be familiar with much or all
of this material, and in any case we will provide extensive references to the literature in lieu of detailed discussions. Our inten-
tion is to exhibit the conceptual inter-relationships between the
underlying ideas, and not to go deeply into the technical details.

We begin by noting that the reactive paradigm has been embodied in
two distinct but related fcrmalisms. The first, which is most closely
related to the physics of material systems (from which it originally
arose) may be called the *state variable* approach. It is expressed
most directly in the mathematical theory of dynamical systems, and
various generalizations and modifications of that theory. The second
approach, which arose primarily from concerns of engineering, and
especially from control engineering, may be called the *input-output*
approach. Thus, the first approach arose from problems of system
analysis, while the second was concerned more directly with system
synthesis or system design. It is not surprising to find numerous
close relationships between these approaches, and we shall be concerned with developing some of them in the present chapter.

Let us begin by considering the state variable approach. As we mentioned previously, the temporal laws of particle mechanics provided the initial impetus for this approach, and provided the guide for all of its subsequent elaborations.[1] These temporal laws take the form of differential equations. These in turn were originally expressions of Newton's Second Law, which *defined* the force acting on a mass point to be the rate of change of momentum:

$$F = dp/dt$$

where momentum p is defined as the initial mass m of the point multiplied by the velocity v. In its turn, velocity is defined as rate of change of position or displacement from some origin of coordinates; hence we have

$$F = m \frac{d^2 x}{dt^2}$$

In order to apply this formulation to any specific systems, we must have an independent characterization of the force, expressed in terms of the varying quantities; in the present simple case, the force must be expressed in terms of the displacement x from some reference, and the velocity v. For instance, to obtain a representation of simple harmonic motion, we can posit

$$F(x, v) = -kx$$

where k is a *constitutive parameter*, whose magnitude is independent of the displacement and the velocity. We thus obtain the equation of motion

$$m \frac{d^2 x}{dt^2} = -kx$$

which is to be solved for the displacement x as an explicit function of time. As a second-order differential equation, its general solution will contain two arbitrary constants, which are evaluated in terms of the *initial values* of the displacement and the velocity.

The single second-order equation can be written as a pair of first-order equations:

$$\frac{dx}{dt} = \frac{p}{m}$$

$$\frac{dp}{dt} = -kx$$

(1.2.1)

The first of these equations simply defines velocity (or momentum), while the second specifies the force. It is in this form that the dynamics of mass points is most susceptible of useful generalizations to other situations.

We may also note that, according to Newton's Laws, the displacements and momenta of the particles constituting a given system are sufficient to characterize that system completely. That is, every other quantity pertaining to the system is assumed to be an explicit function of the displacements and momenta. Knowing these displacements and momenta at an instant of time thus suffices to specify the *state* of the system completely at that instant, and hence the positions and their associated momenta are said to constitute a set of *state variables* for the system. As we have seen earlier, a knowledge of the forces acting on the system (which allows us to write down explicitly the appropriate equation of motion) together with a set of initial values of the state variables completely determines the values of the state variables, and hence of every other system quantity, for all time. It should be noted explicitly that there is nothing unique about a set of state variables; indeed much of theoretical mechanics is concerned with transformations to new sets of state variables, in which the equations of motion take on particularly simple forms.

The system of first-order equations (1.2.1) can be considerably generalized. Let us suppose that x_1, ..., x_n represent a family of physical magnitudes which characterize the states of *any* given system, in the same way that position and momentum characterize the states of a system of particles. For instance, the x_i may represent the concentrations of reactants in a chemical system, or the population sizes in an ecosystem. Let us further suppose that the rates at which these quantities are changing, at any instant of time, is a specific function of the instantaneous values of the quantities themselves. Then we may write a set of first-order differential equations of the form

$$\frac{dx_i}{dt} = f_i(x_1, \ldots, x_n), \qquad i = 1, \ldots, n \qquad (1.2.2)$$

which are obvious generalizations of the equations of motion (1.2.1) for a simple particulate system. The system (1.2.2) is a mathematical object, which constitutes a *dynamical system*.[2] Let us note explicitly how the hypothesis of causality is embodied here; rate of change depends *only* on present state.

The basic paradigm of the dynamical system as embodied in (1.2.2) comprises the basic nucleus of all form of mathematical analysis of natural systems. It has of course been extended and modified in many ways; these modifications alter the technical character of the resulting theory, without affecting the conceptual features which are the main objects of present attention. For instance, if we wish to consider spatially extended or distributed systems, we must introduce appropriate spatial magnitudes as independent variables, in addition to the single independent variable (time) appearing in (1.2.2); the resulting equations of motion then become partial differential equations (field equations) instead of ordinary differential equations. Likewise, in many situations it is reasonable to pass from the continuous time parameter in (1.2.2) to a discrete-valued time parameter; the resulting equations of motion are difference equations, leading to a theory of discrete dynamical systems. If the set of states which such a system can occupy is likewise discrete, we obtain in effect a theory of automata. If we wish to consider systems with "memory", this can be done by introducing time lags into the equations of motion. In each of these situations we may construct analogs of the arguments to be developed below.

Dynamical systems of the form (1.2.2) play a predominant role in the modelling of real-world phenomena. The construction of a dynamical model of a real system involves the identification of a suitable set of state variables x_i, and the characterization of the forces imposed on the system in terms of them (and of the constitutive parameters, such as the quantities m and k in (1.2.1), which identify the system). The further investigation of the behavior of the system then becomes entirely a question of determining the *mathematical* properties of the equations of motion (1.2.2). The basic mathematical concept involved here is that of *stability*, which we will now proceed to describe.

In mathematical terms, a *solution* of the system (1.2.2) is an explicit expression of each of the state variables x_i as a function of time, $x_i(t)$, in such a way that these functions identically satisfy the equations of motion. Geometrically, each solution corresponds to a *curve*, or *trajectory*, lying in the manifold of all possible states of the system (this manifold comprises the *state space* of the system.) The fundamental existence and uniqueness theorems for dynamical systems of the form (1.2.2) assure us that, under very mild mathematical conditions on the functions f_i, through each state in the state space there passes *exactly one* trajectory of the system; this is the *unique trajectory property*. It embodies a very strong notion of causality for dynamical systems, for it asserts that only one history can give rise to a particular state, and only one future can follow from it. As such, it is a corollary of the basic hypothesis that present change of state depends only on present state.

We may note parenthetically that the unique trajectory property allows the entire theory to be reformulated in a manner which is often more convenient for specific applications. Let x denote an element of the state space, and let us suppose that our system is in this state at some initial instant $t = 0$. At some later time t, the system will be in a state $x(t)$, which by the unique trajectory property is uniquely determined by $x = x(0)$. Hence we may define a transformation T_t br writing $x(0) \rightarrow x(t)$ for every state in the state space; the unique trajectory property guarantees that this transformation is one-to-one and onto. We can do this for every instant t. The resultant family $\{T_t\}$ of mappings (often called a *flow*) possesses a group property; i.e. it satisfies the following conitions: (a) T_0 = identity; (b) $T_{t_1+t_2} = T_{t_2} T_{t_1}$; (c) $T_{-t} = T_t^{-1}$.

Such a family of transformations is called a *one-parameter group*. It is clear that the study of such one-parameter groups of transformations allows an alternate formulation (of somewhat different generality) of the theory of dynamical systems which we have been developing. For further details, the reader is invited to consult the references.

Very often, we are not interested in, or we cannot analytically determine, the specific solutions of (1.2.2). But we do wish to know the *asymptotic* behavior of the system (i.e. what happens as time becomes infinite). And we usually also wish to know how the system will respond to perturbations; i.e. how a particular trajectory is related to nearby trajectories. These are the province of stability theory.

Let us consider initially the simplest possible trajectories, those consisting of single states. Analytically, these correspond to solutions of (1.2.2) of the form $x_i(t)$ = constant. Such solutions represent the *steady states* of (1.2.2); intuitively, a system placed initially in such a state will never leave it, since the rates of change dx_i/dt of the state variables all vanish in that state. In principle, the steady states of (1.2.2) are found by solving the simultaneous system of algebraic equations

$$f_i(x_1, \ldots, x_n) = 0, \quad i = 1, \ldots, n.$$

The *stability* of such a steady state is basically determined by whether the nearby trajectories approach that steady state or not as time increases. This is a question which can usually be answered analytically; since it is of importance for the sequel, we shall briefly describe how this is done.

Let us suppose that $(x_1{}^*, \ldots, x_n{}^*)$ is a steady state of (1.2.2). Under very mild mathematical conditions, universally satisfied in applications, the functions $f_i(x_1, \ldots, x_n)$ occurring in (1.2.2) can be expanded in Taylor's series in a neighborhood of the steady state; such an expansion typically has the form

$$f_i(x_1{}^* + q_1, \ldots, x_n{}^* + q_n) = \sum_{j=1}^{n} q_i \frac{\partial f_i}{\partial x_j} + \sum_{j,k} q_j q_k \frac{\partial^2 f_i}{\partial x_j \, \partial x_k} + \cdots$$

The partial derivatives which appear here are evaluated at the steady state itself; hence they are simply numbers. Moreover, if the neighborhood we are considering is sufficiently small, the higher powers of the displacement from the steady state can be neglected. Thus, in the neighborhood, the original equations of motion (1.2.2) are closely approximated by another set of equations of the form

$$\frac{\partial u_i}{\partial t} = \sum_{j=1}^{n} a_{ij} u_j \qquad\qquad (1.2.3)$$

where we have written $a_{ij} = \dfrac{\partial f_i}{\partial x_j}$, evaluated at the steady state of (1.2.2). The new dynamical system (1.2.3) is *linear*; the state variables appear here only to the first power. Linear dynamical systems are completely tractable analytically; in general their solutions are sums of exponentials

$$u_i(t) = \sum_{j=1}^{n} A_{ij} \, e^{\lambda_j t} \qquad\qquad (1.2.4)$$

where A_{ij} are constants determined by initial conditions, and the λ_j are the *eigenvalues* of the system matrix (a_{ij}). Typically these eigenvalues are complex numbers

$$\lambda_j = p_j + i q_j$$

and so the exponentials in (1.2.4) can be written

$$e^{\lambda_j t} = e^{p_j t} \, e^{i q_j t}$$

Now the imaginary factor $e^{i q_j t}$ is bounded in absolute value between ±1. Therefore the time behavior of each of the exponentials is determined entirely by the real factor $e^{p_j t}$, and more specifically by the sign of p_j; if this sign is positive, the corresponding exponential will grow without limit; if negative, the exponential will decay to zero as time increases. Stated another way: if the

p_j are all negative, any trajectory of (1.2.3) sufficiently near the
origin will approach the origin as time increases; if all of the
p_j are positive, any such trajectory will move away from the origin;
if some are positive and others negative, the behavior of a specific
trajectory will depend entirely on the initial conditions; i.e. on
the constants A_{ij} in (1.2.4). In the first case, the steady state
is said to be *asymptotically stable*; in the second case is *unstable*;
in the third case the steady state is *conditionally stable*. Let us
also note here, for further reference, that the *magnitudes* of the p_j
determine the *rate* at which the trajectories of (1.2.3) are traversed.
Thus, systems for which all the p_j are large and negative are "more
stable" than those for which the p_j are small and negative, and
conversely.

It can be shown that, of all the p_j are not zero, then the behavior
of the trajectories of (1.2.3) near the origin are the same as the
trajectories of (1.2.2) near the steady state $(x_1{}^*, \ldots, x_n{}^*)$. If
all the p_j are zero, then we obtain no information about the stability
of the steady state from the approximating linear system (1.2.3). The
theorem expressing this fact is an assertion about the *structural
stability* of the linear system (1.2.3); i.e. the invariance of its
stability properties to perturbations of the *form* of the equations
of motion. This idea of structural stability will be one of our
main preoccupations in the ensuing chapters.

The above analysis refers to the stability of steady states. But we
can investigate the stability of arbitrary trajectories in the same
way; indeed, it can be shown that the stability of any trajectory
of (1.2.2) can be reduced to the stability of a steady state of an
associated dynamical system. For details on these matters, which
we repeat belong entirely to pure mathematics, we invite the reader
to consult the references.

Since the stability of trajectories embodies the manner in which a
system responds to perturbations, it is clear that the stability of
a trajectory represents the *homeostatis* of a particular mode of
system behavior. Conversely, the instability of a trajectory can
often be interpreted as representing a capacity for *self-organization*,
in that the initially small perturbations away from an unstable
trajectory are amplified by the system. This is true *independent* of
the specific form of the system dynamics; for this reason, stability
arguments have come to play a crucial role as metaphors for
developmental processes in general. We shall return to these matters
in a more comprehensive way below.

Let us now return to the other manifestations of the reactive paradigm, which we termed the input-output approach.[3]

Let us begin with a consideration of the proverbial "black box"; a

device whose inner mechanism is unknown, but on which we can impose
certain "signals", interchangeably called *inputs*, *forcings* or
stimuli. These signals can generally be regarded as function of
time. In its turn, the black box is able to generate corresponding
signals, variously called *outputs* or *responses*, which are also
functions of time, and which one can directly observe. We desire
to know how each particular output of the box is determined by the
corresponding input which elicits it, and from this to determine,
to the extent possible, what is actually inside the box. We note
explicitly that a knowledge of the relation of inputs to outputs
also allows us to *control* the behavior of the box; i.e. to elicit
any desired output, by supplying it to the corresponding input.

Clearly the box itself acts as a *transducer*, which converts inputs
to outputs. In mathematical terms, since both inputs and outputs
are represented as functions of time, the activity of the box is
correspondingly represented by some kind of operator, which maps
input functions into output functions. It is this operator which
we wish to characterize, and our only means for doing so are our
observations of how the box responds to inputs supplied to it.

Once again, this kind of question can only be answered completely
for a special class of systems, whose input-output relation is generated by a *linear* operator T. More specifically, if $\{y_i(t)\}$ represents a family of possible input functions to our box, and $u_i(t)$
represents the family of corresponding outputs, then we require that

$$T(\sum_i r_i\, y_i(t)) = \sum_i r_i\, u_i(t) \qquad\qquad (1.2.5)$$

where the r_i are arbitrary numbers. Simply stated, a linear box
maps arbitrary sums of inputs into sums of corresponding outputs.
A box represented by such a linear operator is called a *linear box*,
or linear input-output system. The reader will note that this
definition of linearity appears quite different from that employed
in connection with the dynamical system (1.2.3) above.

More generally, we shall suppose that linearity holds for even the
situation in which the index i, instead of running over a finite or
countable set, runs over a continuum. In this case, the summations
appearing in (1.2.5) are replaced by integrations over this continuum.

We can see intuitively that we can completely characterize the input-
output relation of a linear system, by invoking the kind of universality we mentioned above. Specifically, we have already noted
that any function $y(t)$ can be uniquely represented in terms of an
appropriate basis set $\{\phi_i(t)\}$, as a series of the form

$$y(t) = \sum_i a_i\, \phi_i(t). \qquad\qquad (1.2.6)$$

Thus, if we know the outputs of the box for just the functions in
the basis set, linearity allows us to determine the output of the
box for any input $y(t)$. More generally, the index i can be taken
as running over a continuum; in this case, the representation
(1.2.6) becomes an integral of the form

$$y(t) = \int_{\tau_0}^{\tau_1} a(\tau)\, \phi(t, \tau)\, d\tau \qquad\qquad (1.2.7)$$

Once again, if we know the response of the box to the particular
functions $\phi(t, \tau)$, we can determine the response of the box to *any*
input $y(t)$.

Let us speak now informally for a moment. If we are willing to
stray outside the domain of continuous functions, we can pick the
functions $\phi(t, \tau)$ in (1.2.7) very cleverly; in fact, in such a way
that they are all determined by a single one. That one is the familiar δ-function, introduced by Heaviside (although it was already
known to Cauchy, Poisson and Hermite) and most notably exploited by
Dirac. This function is defined by the properties

$$\int_{-\infty}^{\infty} \delta(t)\ dt = 1$$

$$\delta(t) = 0 \text{ for } t \neq 0.$$
(1.2.8)

Clearly $\delta(t)$ is a most peculiar function, viewed from any classical
standpoint. In fact it is not a function at all, but rather a
generalized function or *distribution* in the sense of Laurent Sch-
wartz. Briefly, it can be represented as a limit of a Cauchy
sequence of continuous functions as for example

$$\delta(t) = \lim_{n \to \infty} \frac{n}{\pi(n^2 t^2 + 1)}$$

or

$$\delta(t) = \lim_{n \to \infty} \frac{n}{\sqrt{\pi}}\ e^{-n^2 t^2}$$

in much the same way that a real number can be represented as the
limit of a Cauchy sequence of rational numbers. Its basic property
is that it defines a linear functional on spaces of functions of
the type we are considering, through what is usually called the
sifting property:

$$\int_{-\infty}^{\infty} y(t)\ \delta(t)\ dt = y(0)$$
(1.2.9)

for any function y defined in a neighborhood of the origin.

From $\delta(t)$, we can obtain a continuum of functions of the form
$\delta(t - \tau)$, one for each real number τ. These functions, the translates of $\delta(t)$, also satisfy a sifting property:

$$\int_{-\infty}^{\infty} y(t)\ \delta(t - \tau)\ dt = y(\tau)$$
(1.2.10)

Comparing (1.2.10) and (1.2.7), we see that we can represent any
input $y(t)$ to a linear system in an integral form, using the translates $\delta(t - \tau)$ of the δ-function as a basis set.

Thus, let us suppose that we can supply $\delta(t)$ as an input to our
linear black box, and let us suppose that the resultant output or
response is $K(t)$. Clearly, the response of the box to any translate $\delta(t - \tau)$ will be $K(t - \tau)$. But now any arbitrary input $y(t)$
to the box can be written in the form (1.2.10); hence the linearity
of the box implies that the corresponding output is

$$u(t) = \int_{-\infty}^{t} K(t - \tau)y(\tau)\ d\tau.$$
(1.2.11)

The relation (1.2.11) is the fundamental one which characterizes our linear black box, in the sense that it specifies the output $u(t)$ of the box when the input $y(t)$ is given. The function $K(t - \tau)$ is essentially what is called the *transfer function* of the system, although for technical reasons, the transfer function of the engineer is the Laplace Transform of K. The basic reason for this is that the Laplace transform converts the integral (1.2.11), which is a *convolution integral*, into an ordinary product of functions; thus, if L formally denotes the Laplace transform operation, (1.2.11) becomes

$$Lu(t) = G(s) \ L \ y(t) \tag{1.2.11A}$$

where $G(s)$, the Laplace transform of $K(t)$, is given by

$$G(s) = \int_0^\infty K(t) \ e^{-st} \ dt$$

For fuller details, see the Bibliography.[4]

We can cast the relation (1.2.11), expressing the input-output relations of our linear box, into a more familiar form under certain general circumstances. Namely, if the required derivatives exist, it is

$$\frac{du}{dt} = \int_{-\infty}^t \frac{\partial}{\partial t} K(t - \tau) y(\tau) \ d\tau$$

or more generally, that

$$\sum_{i=0}^n a_i(t) \frac{\partial^i u}{\partial t^i} = \int_{-\infty}^\infty \sum_{i=0}^n a_i(t) \frac{\partial^i}{\partial t^i} K(t - \tau) y(\tau) \ d\tau \tag{1.2.12}$$

where the $a_i(t)$ are the arbitrary functions of t. Let us suppose that we can find functions $a_0(t)$, $a_1(t)$, $\ldots$, $a_n(t)$ such that

$$\sum_{i=0}^n a_i(t) \frac{\partial^i}{\partial t^i} K(t - \tau) = \delta(t - \tau).$$

Then by the sifting property, (1.2.12) becomes

$$\sum_{i=0}^n a_i(t) \frac{\partial^i u}{\partial t^i} = y(t) \tag{1.2.13}$$

That is, *the relation between input $y(t)$ and corresponding output $u(t)$ is such that these functions satisfy the linear n^{th}-order differential equation (1.2.13)*. Stated another way, the differential operator

$$\sum_{i=0}^n a_i(t) \frac{\partial^i}{\partial t^i}$$

and the integral operator

$$\int_{-\infty}^t K(t - \tau) \ d\tau$$

are inverse of one another.

The relationship between (1.2.11) and (1.2.13) allows us to draw an important connection between the linear black box, characterized by the function $K(t - \tau)$, and the theory of linear dynamical systems we touched on earlier. For the single n^{th}-order linear differential equation (1.2.13) can be expressed as a set of n linear first-order equations: i.e. as a dynamical system. Specifically, if we introduce new variables x_1, x_2, ..., x_n by writing

$$x_i = d^{i-1} x / dt^{i-1}$$

we obtain the linear dynamical system

$$\frac{dx_1}{dt} = x_2$$

$$\frac{dx_2}{dt} = x_3$$

$$\vdots$$

$$\frac{dx_{n-1}}{dt} = x_n$$

$$\frac{dx_n}{dt} = - \frac{1}{a_n(t)} \sum_{i=1}^{n-1} a_i(t) \, x_i - y(t)$$

(1.2.14)

This dynamical system is, apart from technical details, of the form (1.2.3) which we have seen before. The details in which (1.2.14) differs from (1.2.3) are: (a) in (1.2.14) the coefficients $a_i(t)$ are in general functions of time, and not constant as they were in (1.2.3); (b) the system (1.2.14) is not homogeneous; the last equation involves an additive time-dependent function $y(t)$, the system input. But it is easy to generalize the theory of linear systems like (1.2.3) to the situation of non-homogeneous systems (i.e. non-zero input) and time-varying coefficients; the details can be found in almost any text on linear differential equations. It is also shown from this analysis the close relation which exists between the response function $K(t - \tau)$ of the linear box and the matrix $A(t)$ of the associated linear dynamical system (1.2.14); namely

$$K(t - \tau) = e^{(t-\tau)A}$$

(1.2.15)

There is a further consequence of the representation (1.2.14) which should be noted. Initially, we regarded our black box as opaque; by hypothesis we had no knowledge of the internal structure of the box, but we assumed that we could observe the output $u(t)$ generated by a given input $y(t)$. On the other hand, the variables x_i introduced in (1.2.14) can be regarded as constituting a set of variables for the *box itself*. Moreover, the transfer function allows us to determine, through the representation (1.2.13) and (1.2.14), the equations of motion governing these state variables. Thus to this extent a characterization of the input-output relation allows us to *open the box*, at least to the extent we have indicated.

It should also be noted that the integral (1.2.11), which character-izes the input-output relation of our box, expresses the reactive paradigm in the following form: the *value* of the output $u(t)$ at any instant is obtained as an integral over all present and past values

of the input $y(t)$, each appropriately weighted by the response function $K(t-\tau)$. In all linear theories of this form, the possibility
of future input values entering into the present value of the output
is expressly forbidden. When we represent the same system in
differential form, as in (1.2.13) or (1.2.14), we find this translates into the usual condition that rate of change of *state* depends
only on present state.

It should also be emphasized that the transfer-function approach to
input-output systems is restricted to *linear* systems. There is in
general no analog of the transfer function to describe the relations
between inputs and outputs in systems which are not linear.

Now let us, in effect, turn the entire argument of the past few
pages around. We shall *begin* with a linear dynamical system of the
form

$$\frac{dx_i}{dt} = \sum_{j=1}^{n} a_{ij} x_j, \qquad i = 1, \ldots, n. \qquad (1.2.15)$$

in which we can allow the coefficients a_{ij} to be definite functions
of time. Let us now suppose, by analogy with (1.2.14), that we
allow the rates of change dx_i/dt of the state variables x_i to depend
in a linear fashion on a family $y_i(t), \ldots, y_r(t)$ of functions of
time, which may be chosen from a class of admissible functions;
i.e. we write the equations of motion as

$$\frac{dx_i}{dt} = \sum_{i=1}^{n} a_{ij} x_j + \sum_{R=1}^{r} b_{ik} y_k \qquad (1.2.16)$$

Here the coefficients (b_{ik}) are assumed fixed. The functions $y_i(t)$
are generally called *controls* for the system (1.2.16). We shall
further assume that the object of imposing such controls is to
manipulate the values of some quantity H associated with the system.
Since by hypothesis $x_1, \ldots, x_n$ are state variables, the quantity H
must be a specific function $H(x_1, \ldots, x_n)$ of these variables, and
we assume it is a linear function:

$$H(x_1, \ldots, x_n) = \sum_{i=1}^{n} \beta_i x_i. \qquad (1.2.17)$$

This is the basic format for the theory of the control of linear
systems, resolved here into two distinct problems: (a) to determine,
from (1.2.16), the manner in which a set of control functions $y_i(t)$
modify an appropriate set of state variables; (b) to compute from
this the behavior of the output function H in which we are interested.

With appropriate modifications, we can in effect run backwards the
argument which led from (1.2.11) to (1.2.14) above. More specifically, we can write the family (1.2.16) of n first-order differential
equations as a single n-th order equation; this equation will in
general involve the control functions $y_i(t)$ and their time derivatives. From this nth-order equation, we can work backwards to write
down a generalized form of the input-output relation (1.2.11),

thereby obtaining the most general form of linear theory of input-output systems; it allows us to explicitly express the relation between multiple controls and the resultant outputs.

It must not be thought that there is a complete equivalence between the dynamical approach (1.2.16) and the transfer function approach based on (1.2.11). In fact, the set of state variables x_i which we obtain in passing from (1.2.11) to (1.2.14) need not completely characterize our black box; in effect, we can only detect through the transfer function such state variables of which the outputs we observe are functions, and which are themselves functions of the imposed inputs. All other state quantities characterizing the interior of the box are *invisible* to this approach. They can be made visible only by augmenting either the class of admissible inputs to the box, or by gaining access to a larger class of outputs of the box (or both). The extent to which we can characterize the interior of a linear box in terms of a definite set of inputs we can impose, and a definite set of outputs we can observe, is the subject of an elegant development by R. E. Kalman, under the heading of a general theory of *controllability and observability*.[5] As we shall see, the Kalman theory illuminates many important epistemological questions concerning systems in general. For further details regarding this theory, we refer the reader to the material cited in the Bibliography.

We now wish to develop another important relationship between the theory of input-output systems and that of stability of dynamical systems. We can motivate this development in the following way. We have already mentioned that the stability of a steady state of a dynamical system, or indeed of an arbitrary trajectory, can be thought of as a manifestation of homeostasis. On the other hand, the theory of control was largely developed precisely to generate and maintain homeostasis within a technological context. We have already formulated the basic notions of control, as far as linear systems are concerned, in the relations (1.2.16) and (1.2.17) above. What we wish to do now is to explicitly develop the relationship between dynamical stability and control theory. It is important to do this, because stability is a property of *autonomous* systems (i.e. whose equations of motion do not involve time explicitly) while control theory seems to involve time-varying quantities in an essential way; we can see at a glance that the control equations (1.2.16) do not fit under the rubric of stability as we defined it. We shall ultimately find that the relation between stability and control to be developed embodies all of the essential conceptual features of the reactive paradigm, in a particularly transparent and suggestive way. Before we take up this relationship, there is one more important point to be made about the input-output approach, which we now proceed to sketch.

We have seen that the basic unit of the input-output approach is the "black box", which receives inputs from its environment, and produces outputs to the environment. This situation can be represented pictorially as in Fig. 1.2.1. Here the y_i represent particular modalities of inputs presented to the box, and the u_j are correspondingly output modalities. In the case of a linear box, we have seen that the box itself can be assigned a family of state variables $x_1, \ldots, x_n$, whose temporal behavior depends on the inputs $y_i(t)$, and which in turn determine the properties of the outputs $u_j(t)$.

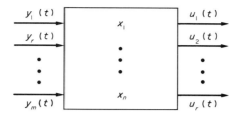

Fig. 1.2.1.

The reason that the representation of Figure 1.2.1 is so suggestive
is the following: *we can imagine that the inputs $y_i(t)$ to the box
are themselves outputs of other boxes; likewise, that the outputs
$u_j(t)$ of the box are themselves inputs to other boxes.* In other
words, we can construct *networks* of such boxes; the response
characteristics of such networks, considered as input-output systems
in their own right, may then be expressed in a canonical way in
terms of the properties of the constituent elements in the network,
and the manner in which these are inter-related. Conversely, a
given linear input-output system may be *analyzed* or resolved into
a network of simpler systems. This crucial capacity for analysis
and synthesis is not visible in a pure state-variable approach;
although as we shall soon see, it is present.

As an illustration, let us consider the simplest possible networks.
In Fig. 1.2.2, we see a system consisting of two linear boxes
arranged in series; the output of the first is the input of the
second.

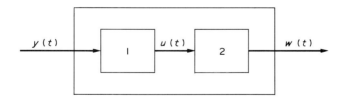

Fig. 1.2.2.

As we have seen, each of the component boxes is represented by a
response function, which we may denote by K_1, K_2 respectively. It
turns out for our present purposes to be more convenient to work
with the corresponding transfer functions G_1, G_2, where, as noted
above, $G_1 = LK_1$, $G_2 = LK_2$, and L is the Laplace transform operation.

For it is then immediate to verify that

$$Lw(t) = G_2 G_1 \, Ly(t).$$

In other words, *the transfer function of a pair of linear boxes connected in series is the product of the transfer functions of the boxes.*

Likewise, we may consider the simple parallel network shown in Fig. 1.2.3:

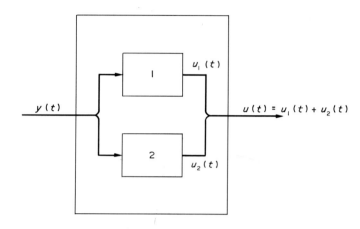

Fig. 1.2.3.

Using the same notation as before, it is easy to see that

$$L(u_1(t) + u_2(t)) = (G_1 + G_2)L_y(t);$$

or in other words, that *the transfer function of a pair of linear boxes connected in parallel is the sum of the transfer functions of the individual boxes.* From these two simple results, we can readily see how the transfer function of any array of linear boxes connected in series and parallel can be computed, from a knowledge of the transfer functions of the component boxes and of the pattern of interconnections. Conversely, if the transfer function of a given system can be expressed in terms of sums and products of simpler functions, then the system itself can be effectively decomposed into a series-parallel network of simpler subsystems.

The most important kind of application of these ideas, for our purposes, arises when *the input signal to a box in a network is partially derived from its own output, either directly, or through the intermediary of other boxes.* Such a situation is called *feedback,* and is exemplified by the network shown in Figure 1.2.4.

In control engineering, each aspect of this kind of network is given a special name, descriptive of the function of the network as a whole. These are as follows: The box labelled "1" is called the *controlled system;* The box labelled "2" is called the *controller;*

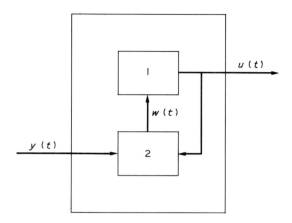

Fig. 1.2.4.

The input $y(t)$ is called the *command signal*; $w(t)$ is called the
control signal;   The closed loop passing from the first box through
the second and back to the first is the *feedback loop*.

Finally, if the entire system is to remain linear, it is clear that
the total input to the second box, or controller, must be of the
form $y(t) + u(t)$ or $y(t) - u(t)$. In the first case, we speak of
positive feedback; in the latter case, of *negative feedback*. If
the feedback is negative, then the total input $y(t) - u(t)$ to the
controller is called the *error signal*. In general, a negative
feedback tends to *oppose* the motion of the output $u(t)$, while a
positive feedback tends to amplify it.

Let us for the moment restrict ourselves to the case of negative
feedback. In this case, the diagram of Fig. 1.2.4 is the simplest
instance of a *pure servomechanism*. Intuitively, the function of
the controller here is to force the output signal $u(t)$ of the
controlled system to follow or track the command signal $y(t)$. The
controller's input, or error signal, is determined by the discrepancy
between $y(t)$ and $u(t)$; its output, the *command signal*, is designed
to minimize this discrepancy. Finally, if G_1, G_2 denote the transfer
functions of the controlled system and controller respectively, it
is not hard to show that the transfer function of the total system
shown in Fig. 1.2.4 is

$$G = G_1 G_2 / (1 + G_1 G_2).$$

A variant of the network shown in Figure 1.2.4 is given in Figure
1.2.5.

Here we assume that the command signal is constant (such a constant
command signal is often called a *set-point*). We now admit a new
signal $y_p(t)$ directly into the controlled system; $y_p(t)$ represents
ambient fluctuation or perturbation. If $y_p(t) = 0$, the output $u(t)$

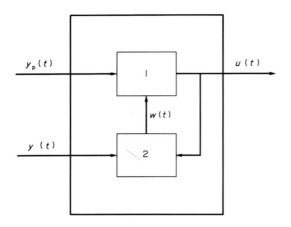

Fig. 1.2.5.

of Figure 1.2.5 will come to, and remain at, a constant value. A
non-zero perturbing signal will tend to move the controlled system
away from this value. The function of the feedback loop is to
offset the effect of the perturbation, again by comparing the actual
present value of the output with the set-point, and imposing a
control signal whose magnitude is determined by the degree of
discrepancy between the two. For this reason, the network of Figure
1.2.5 is often called a *pure regulator*, or *homeostat*.

We can now express the relationship between stability and control,
which is most transparent in the context of feedback control. To
fix ideas, let us consider the homeostat shown in Figure 1.2.5 above.
The purpose of imposing such a control is, of course, to maintain
some output $u(t)$ of the controlled box at a constant level, in the
face of externally imposed perturbations $y_p(t)$. It is precisely to
accomplish this that we attach the controller in the fashion indicated.

Let us suppose that $x_1, \ldots, x_n$ represent a set of state variables
for the controlled system, so chosen that the autonomous equations
of motion of that system, in the absence of external perturbation,
or any signal from the controller, are in the form corresponding to
(1.2.14) above; namely

$$\frac{dx_i}{dt} = x_{i+1}, \quad i = 1, \ldots, n-1$$

$$\frac{dx_n}{dt} = -a_1 x_1 - a_2 x_2 - \ldots - a_n x_n$$

(1.2.18)

We also arrange matters so that the state variable x_1 is also the
system output in which we are interested; i.e. $x_1 = u$. It can
readily be shown that these hypotheses involve no loss of generality.

Let us further suppose that the controller, considered in isolation, can be represented by a set of state variables $\xi_1, \ldots, \xi_m$, where once again we can express the automonous dynamics in the form

$$\frac{d\xi_i}{dt} = \xi_{i+1}, \qquad i = 1, \ldots, m-1$$

$$\frac{d\xi_n}{dt} = b_1\xi_1 - b_2\xi_2 - \ldots - b_m\xi_m \qquad\qquad (1.2.19)$$

and such that $\xi_1 = w(t)$; i.e. the command signal, or controller output, is the first of our state variables.

We now combine (1.2.18) and (1.2.19) in the fashion indicated in Figure 1.2.5, remembering the relation (1.2.13). First, let us agree to represent the command signal, or set point, by a new formal state variable ξ_{m+1} of the controller. The equations (1.2.19) then become

$$\frac{d\xi_i}{dt} = \xi_{i+1}, \qquad i = 1, \ldots, m-1$$

$$\frac{d\xi_m}{dt} = -b_1\xi_1 - b_2\xi_2 - \ldots - b_m\xi_m + \xi_{m+1}$$

$$\frac{d\xi_{m+1}}{dt} = 0 \qquad\qquad (1.2.20)$$

Furthermore, the output $x_1(t)$ of the controlled signal is to be *fed back* into the controller. Thus, (1.2.20) finally becomes

$$\frac{d\xi_i}{dt} = \xi_{i+1}, \qquad i = 1, \ldots, m-1$$

$$\frac{d\xi_m}{dt} = -b_1\xi_1 - b_2\xi_2 - \ldots - b_m\xi_m + (\xi_{m+1} - x_1)$$

$$\frac{d\xi_{m+1}}{dt} = 0 \qquad\qquad (1.2.21)$$

Now we must represent the command signal ξ_1 as input to the controlled system. When this is done, (1.2.18) becomes

$$\frac{dx_i}{dt} = x_{i+1}, \qquad i = 1, \ldots, n-1$$

$$\frac{dx_n}{dt} = -a_1x_1 - a_2x_2 - \ldots - a_nx_n + \xi_1 \qquad\qquad (1.2.22)$$

The equations (1.2.21) and (1.2.22) together form a single linear dynamical system, which represents the automonous behavior of the entire homeostat shown in Figure 1.2.5. We can see immediately that this system will have a unique steady state at which

$$x_1 = \xi_{m+1}$$

and all the other state variables are zero. This steady state will be stable if all the eigenvalues of the system matrix have negative real parts, and the degree of stability (i.e. the rate at which any particular trajectory approaches the steady state) will depend on the magnitudes of these real parts. In their turn, the eigenvalues themselves are determined entirely by the coefficients a_i and b_j, which are the constitutive parameters of the controlled system and the controller respectively. In particular, we can choose the b_j in such a way that, for a given system to be controlled, i.e. a given set of parameters a_1, all the eigenvalues of the total system have large negative real parts.

If we now impose an arbitrary perturbing signal $y_p(t)$ on the controlled system, subject only to the condition that $y_p(t)$ changes *slowly* compared to the rate at which the trajectories of the homeostat are approaching their steady state, it is intuitively clear that the homeostat will always remain close to its steady state. Thus, *the homeostatic property of the feedback control is directly identified with the stability property of the total system consisting of the controlled system and the controller*.

From this argument, we see that the *function* of a controller in a homeostat is to embed the controlled system in a larger system, in such a way that (a) the larger system possesses an asymptotically stable steady state, and (b) that steady state, when projected onto the states of the controlled system alone, possesses the desired property (here, the property that $x_1 = \xi_{m+1}$).

The above argument exemplifies the relation we sought between control theory and stability. Although we couched it in the language of linear feedback, the argument itself is perfectly general. Specifically, if we are given *any* dynamical system of the form (1.2.2), then in some neighborhood of any stable steady state, we have seen that the behavior of the system may be approximated by that of a linear system (1.2.3). In an approximate co-ordinate system (i.e. by a suitable choice of state variables) that approximating linear system may itself be decomposed into a part interpretable as a controlled system, and a part interpretable as a feedback controller. Of course this decomposition is not unique, but it does exhibit the essential equivalence between the concept of feedback control and the stability of steady states.

The same argument may be used to demonstrate the equivalence between positive feedback and instability; we leave the details to the reader.

It should be carefully noted that the linear formulation we have provided above is not adequate for the homeostats and servomechanisms which are found in biology. Basically, this is because biological feedback controls violate basic assumptions we have made: (a) that the autonomous dynamics of an input-output system are of the linear form (1.2.3), and (b) that the interaction between boxes is describable in the form (1.2.16), in which controls enter linearly into the autonomous dynamics. In connection with this latter point, it is found that interactions between biological systems, even if they could be regarded as linear, takes place through the modification of constitutive parameters; this is called *feedback through parameters*. Such control is analogous to a modification of the transfer functions through interaction; if we attempt to embody this type of control through arguments leading to the equations (1.2.21) and (1.2.22),

the resulting system will necessarily be nonlinear. This comment,
however, is primarily of a technical nature; it does not affect
the essential relation between feedback and stability which we have
developed above.

We may now conclude this brief overview of the basic aspects of the
reactive paradigm with a few general remarks.

The first remark is concerned with the frankly reactive nature of
feedback control. Indeed, the distinguishing feature of feedback
control is the presence of an "error signal", which is the difference between what the system output *should be* at a given instant (as
embodied in the command signal) and what the output actually *is* at
that instant. It is this error signal which is transduced by the
controller into a control signal, whose purpose is to minimize the
discrepancy between command signal and output. Clearly, the utilization of such an error signal means that the behavior of the controlled system *has already departed* from that which is desired
before any control can be imposed on it. The exercise of feedback
control is thus always corrective; always imposed as a reaction to
a deviation which has already occurred. Nothing could be more
indicative of the essential character of the reactive paradigm than
this.

We can now graphically illustrate the fundamental distinction between a reactive and an anticipatory mode of control. We have just
seen that all reactive behavior necessarily involves a response to
circumstances which have already occurred. It might be argued that
by making a reactive system more stable, in the sense of increasing
the magnitudes of the (negative) real parts of the system eigenvalues, or in other words by making the time constants of the system
sufficiently short, this difficulty can for practical purposes be
eliminated. Apart from the practical problems arising from attempting to do this, we can see that this is not so in principle by
comparing two apparently similar homeostats; one arising in biology,
and the other of a technological nature.

One of the best-studied biological homeostats is one involved in
maintaining an optimal constancy of light falling on the retina of
the vertebrate eye, the so-called *pupillary servomechanism*.[6] Roughly
speaking, in conditions in which there is a great deal of ambient
light, the pupil contracts, and admits a smaller amount of light to
the eye. Conversely, when the ambient light is dim, the pupil opens
to admit more light. It has been established that the control system involved here is a true feedback system, whose output is represented by the actual amount of light falling on the retina. Thus,
the sensor for the controller is at the retina, and the system
reacts to how much light has already been admitted to the eye. The
time constant for this servomechanism is not outstandingly small,
but the system clearly functions well for almost all conditions the
organism encounters.

Now let us consider the analogous problem of controlling the amount
of light entering a camera to ensure optimal film exposure. Here
again, the control element is a diaphragm, which must be opened
when the ambient light is dim, and closed when the ambient light is
bright. However, in this case, *we cannot in principle use a reactive
mechanism at all*, no matter how small its time constant. For
clearly, if the input to the controller is the light falling on the
film, in analogy to the situation in the eye, then the film is
already under- or over-exposed before any control can be instituted.
In this case, the *only* effective way to control the diaphragm is

through an anticipatory mode, and that is what in fact is done.
Specifically, a light-meter is used to measure the *ambient* light.
The reading of the light meter is then referred to a predictive
model, which relates ambient light to the diaphragm opening necessary
to admit the optimal amount of light to the camera. The diaphragm
is then *pre-set* according to the prediction of the model. In this
simple example we see all the contrasting features of feedforward
and feedback; of anticipatory as against reactive modes of control.

The crucial distinction between anticipation and reaction manifests
itself very strongly in what we may call the "style" of approach
that each imposes on the study of system behavior. For instance,
we have already discussed the anticipatory nature of simple organism
behaviors, such as phototropisms. We argued that these tropisms
embody predictive models, insofar as they correlate neutral ambient
characteristics such as darkness with circumstances which are physiologically favorable. On the other hand, we may cite a passage from
Norbert Wiener's seminal book *Cybernetics*,[7] dealing with negative
phototropism in the flatworm:

> ...negative phototropism...seems to be controlled by the balance of the
> impulses from the two eyespots. This balance is fed back to the muscles of
> the trunk, turning the body away from the light, and, in combination with
> the general impulse to move forward, carries the animal into the darkest
> region accessible. It is interesting to note that a combination of a pair
> of photo-cells, with appropriate amplifiers, a Wheatstone bridge for balancing
> their outputs, and further amplifiers controlling the input into the two
> motors of a twinscrew mechanism would give us a very adequate negatively
> phototropic control for a little boat.

There is in this discussion a total preoccupation with *mechanism*,
and more tacitly, with the idea that reactive simulation provides a
full understanding of the tropistic behavior. It can be seen from
this example that the reactive paradigm necessarily restricts us
from the outset to the *effector* aspects of behavior, and in itself
leaves the adaptive aspects of that behavior, which arise precisely
from its anticipatory features, untouched. In our little example
of the pre-setting of a camera aperture as a function of ambient
light, the analogous discussion to that cited above could only be
concerned with the specific mechanism by which the diaphragm is
actually moved, as a function of the predictions of the model.

Our final remark arises naturally from the preceding discussion, and
involves the relation between homeostasis and adaptation in general.
In the broadest terms, adaptation in biology refers to a modification
of system structure or behavior, in such a way that the overall
survival of the adapting system is enhanced. As such, adaptation
connotes a dynamical process, in which changed circumstances are
reflected in corresponding changes in the adapting organism. In
these terms, adaptation itself can occur through either a reactive
mode or an anticipatory mode; the former connotes responses to
changes which have already occurred, and the latter connotes
responses to changes which some model predicts will occur. Let us
restrict attention for the moment to reactive adaptation.

In particular, let us consider the homeostat shown in Figure 1.2.5;
or better, a specific realization of such a homeostat, as for
example the thermostatically controlled temperature of a room.
Although of course "survival" is not an appropriate concept in this
context, it is not too great an abuse of language to regard the
thermostat as adapting to ambient fluctuations of the temperature of
the room. We obtain two quite different pictures of the thermostat,

depending upon which part of it we focus our attention upon. For
instance, if we concentrate on the system output, we know that this
remains approximately constant in the face of ambient fluctuations,
and this reflects the homeostatic aspects of the system. On the
other hand, we could concentrate upon, say, the dampers which control the amount of air entering the furnace. This part of the
system is in more or less continual movement, and this movement
reflects the adaptive aspect of the system. We must say, in general, that adaptation and homeostasis in this sense are always
correlated; there is always some property of an adaptive system
which is homeostatic in character, and conversely there is always
some aspect of a homeostatic system which is adaptive in character.
Whether we consider such a system as adaptive or homeostatic is
determined entirely by whether we focus on the parts of the system
which are changing, or on the parts which are staying fixed. The
dualism between adaptation and homeostasis is in fact an essential
feature of biological systems, to which we shall return many times
as we proceed.

REFERENCES AND NOTES

1.   There are many excellent books dealing with classical mechanics,
     which is the wellspring of the reactive paradigm. Among more
     modern treatments, the following may be recommended:
          Abraham, A. and Marsden, J. E., *Foundations of Mechanics*.
          Benjamin, Reading, Pennsylvania (1978).
          Arnold, V. I., *Mathematical Methods of Classical Mechanics*.
          Springer-Verlag, New York (1978).
          Santilli, R. M., Foundations of Theoretical *Mechanics*.
          Springer-Verlag, New York (1978).
          Sudarshan, E. C. G. and Mukunda, N., *Classical Dynamics: A
          Modern Perspective*. Wiley, New York (1974).

2.   The theory of dynamical systems have developed along a number
     of fronts, which overlap considerably but are not quite equiv-
     alent mathematically. The form closest to its origin in Newton-
     ian mechanics is the theory of systems of first-order differenial
     equations; an early and still excellent reference is
          Birkhoff, G. D., *Dynamical Systems*. AMS, Providence (1927).
     A later but still classically oriented work is
          Nemitskii, V. V. and Stepanov, A., *Qualitative Theory of
          Ordinary Differential Equations*. Princeton University
          Press (1960).
     A more recent approach is to define a dynamical system as a
     vector field on a manifold. A good introduction, which never-
     theless stays close to the classical roots, is
          Hirsch, M. W. and Smale, S., *Differential Equations, Dynamical
          Systems and Linear Algebra*. Academic Press (1974).
     Still another approach is to regard a dynamical system as a
     flow; a parameterized family of automorphisms on a topological
     space or a measure space. As an example of the former, we may
     mention
          Gottschalk, W. H. and Hedlund, G. A., *Topological Dynamics*.
          AMS, Providence (1955).
     for the latter, the reader may consult, e.g.
          Ornstein, D., *Ergodic Theory, Randomness and Dynamical Systems*.
          Yale University Press (1971).

3.   The input-output approach is characteristic of engineering
     rather than physics. The theory of such systems is almost
     entirely restricted to the situation in which the system in

question is linear. On the mathematical side, this theory
connects linear differential equations with integral equations
(which is perhaps not surprising, if we recall that differentiation and integration are inverse operations). The application of this theory is broadly called *control theory*. The
classic text on linear system theory is still
> Zadeh, L. and Desoer, C. A., *Linear System Theory*. McGraw-
> Hill, New York (1963).

4. The mathematical theory underlying our discussion here is generally called harmonic analysis. A fairly typical exposition
(which nowadays can be found in most treatments of real variable
theory) is
> Loomis, L. H., *Abstract Harmonic Analysis*. van Nostrand, New
> York (1955).

Harmonic analysis is one of the most interesting and seminal
areas in all of mathematics; for an incredibly rich historical
survey of how these ideas ramify throughout mathematics, see
Mackey, G. W., *Bull. Am. Math. Soc.* (New Series) 3, 543-698
(1980). A far more restricted development of those portions
most familiar to engineers may still be found in
> van der Pol, B. and Bremer, H., *Operational Calculus*.
> Cambridge University Press (1955).

5. See for instance
> Kalman, R. E., Arbib, M. and Falb, P. L., *Topics in Mathemat-
> ical System Theory*. McGraw-Hill, New York (1969).

6. A detailed discussion of the pupillary servomechanism, as well
as many other examples of biological control, will be found in
> Stark, L., *Neurological Control Systems*. Plenum, New York
> (1968).

7. Cybernetic contol is in many ways the apotheosis of the reactive
paradigm. The best reference is
> Wiener, N., *Cybernetics*. MIT Press, Cambridge (1961).

CHAPTER 2

Natural and Formal Systems

2.1 The Concept of a Natural System

In the present chapter, we shall be concerned with specifying what we mean by a *natural system*. Roughly speaking, a natural system comprises some aspect of the external world which we wish to study. A stone, a star, the solar system, an organism, a beehive, an eco-system, are typical examples of natural systems; but so to are automobiles, factories, cities and the like. Thus, natural systems are what the sciences are about, and what technologies seek to fabricate and control. We use the adjective "natural" to dis-tinguish these systems from the *formal systems* which we create to represent and model them; formal systems are the vehicles for drawing inferences from premises, and belong to mathematics rather than science. There are of course close relations between the two classes of systems, natural and formal, which we hope to develop in due course.

In coming to grips with the idea of a natural system, we must necess-arily touch on some basic philosophical questions, on both an onto-logical and an epistemological character. This is unavoidable in any case, and must be confronted squarely at the outset of a work like the present one, because one's tacit presuppositions in these areas determine the character of one's science. It is true that many scientists find an explicit consideration of such matters irksome, just as many working mathematicians dislike discussions of foundations of mathematics. Nevertheless, it is well to recall a remark made by David Hawkins: "Philosophy may be ignored but not escaped; and those who most ignore least escape". The discussion presented in this chapter is not intended to be exhaustive or comprehensive; it will, however, provide much of the basic concep-tual underpinning for the detailed technical discussions of the subsequent chapters.[1]

It is perhaps best to begin our discussion of natural systems with our fundamental awareness of sensory impressions, which we shall collectively call *percepts*. These percepts are the basic stuff of science. It is at least plausible for us to believe that we do not entirely create these percepts, but rather discover them, through our experience of them. If we do not create them, then their source must lie, at least in part, outside of us, and thus we are led to the idea of an *external world*. We are further led to associate the sources of our percepts with definite *qualities* belonging to that external world; thence to identify such qualities with the percepts which they generate, and which we experience.

The first obvious step in our characterization of a natural system can then be stated: *a natural system is a member or element of the external world.* As such, then, it generates (or can generate, under suitable conditions) percepts in us, which we identify in turn with specific qualities, or properties, of the system itself.

The ability to generate percepts is not sufficient for us to say we have identified a natural system, although it is certainly a necessary part of such an identification. Intuitively, we would expect the concept of a system to involve some kind of inter-relation between the percepts it generates, and which then become identified with corresponding relationships between the external qualities which generated them.

The question of relations between percepts would be relatively simple if it were the case that such relations were themselves percepts. In that case, we could immediately extend our identification of percepts with qualities, so as to likewise identify perceptual relations with relations between qualities. However, we would not be justified in immediately taking such a step, because it is not clear that relations between percepts are themselves percepts or that they are discovered rather than created. This is a subtle and important point, which must be discussed in more detail.

Briefly, we believe that one of the primary functions of the mind is precisely to *organize* percepts. That is, the mind is not merely a passive receiver of perceptual images, but rather takes an active role in processing them and ultimately in responding to them through effector mechanisms. The *organization* of percepts means precisely the establishment of relations between them. But we then must admit that such relations reflect the properties of the active mind as much as they do the percepts which the mind organizes.

What does seem to be true, however, is the following: that the mind behaves *as if* a relation it establishes between percepts were itself a percept. Consequently, it behaves *as if* such a relation between percepts arises from a corresponding relation between qualities in the external world. Therefore it behaves as if such a relation between qualities in the external world were itself a quality, and as if the perception of this new quality consisted precisely of the relation it established between percepts. The basic point is simply that relations between percepts are, at least to some extent, creations of the mind which are then *inputed* to the external world. As such, they may be regarded as "working hypotheses", or, to use a more direct word, *models* of how the external world is organized.

Now we have already argued that the function of the mind, in biological terms, is to act as a transducer between percepts and specific actions, mediated by the organism's effector mechanisms. It is clear that these actions, and thus the models of the external world which give rise to them, are directly subject to natural selection. An organism which acts inappropriately, or in a maladaptive manner, will clearly not survive long. The very fact of our survival as organisms subject to natural selection thus leads us to suspect that the mechanisms of the mind for organizing percepts (i.e. for establishing relations between percepts) must have some degree of correspondence with objective relations existing between qualities in the external world which is, after all, the agency through which selection

mechanisms themselves operate). This type of argument from selection, while obviously not a proof (and equally obviously, hardly
an argument from first principles), makes it at least plausible that
(a) relations between perceived qualities exist in the external
world, and (b) that such relations, too, can be discovered by the
mind. The process by which such relations are discovered, however,
is not of the same character as the discovery of the qualities themselves; rather, it arises through the *imputation* of mentally created
relations between particular percepts to the qualities which generate
these percepts.

This discussion provides the second necessary ingredient in our characterization of a natural system. Specifically, we shall say that
*a natural system is a set of qualities, to which definite relations
can be imputed*. As such, then, a natural system from the outset
embodies a mental construct (i.e. a relation established by the mind
between percepts) which comprises a hypothesis or model pertaining
to the organization of the external world.

In what follows, we shall refer to a perceptible quality of a natural
system as an *observable*. We shall call a relation obtaining between
two or more observables belonging to a natural system a *linkage* between them. We take the viewpoint that the study of natural systems
is precisely the specification of the observables belonging to such
a system, and a characterization of the manner in which they are
linked. Indeed, for us *observables are the fundamental units of
natural systems, just as percepts are the fundamental units of
experience*.

To proceed further, we need first to discuss in more detail how
qualities, or observables, are defined in general. We have already
stated that a quality is a property of the external world which is,
or which can be made to be, directly perceptible to us. Let us
elaborate a bit on this theme.

The first thing to recognize is that our sensory apparatus, through
which qualities in the external world are transduced to percepts in
us, must themselves be part of the external world. That is, they
themselves are natural systems of a particular kind, or at least
involve such natural systems in an essential way. It is more precise to say that it is a specific interaction between a natural system
and our sensory apparatus which in fact generates a percept. In
fact, it must ultimately be a *change* or *modification* in the sensory
apparatus, arising from such an interaction, which actually does
generate the percept.

Furthermore, we know that we can also interact with the external
world through our own effector mechanisms; thus these effectors
themselves must project into the external world. Such interactions
cause changes in the external world itself, which can then be
directly perceived.

From these assertions, it is a small but significant act of extrapolation to posit that, in general, natural systems are capable of
interactions, and that these interactions are accompanied by changes
or modifications in the interacting systems. We have seen that, in
case one of the interacting systems is a part of our own sensory
apparatus, the vehicle responsible for its modification is *by definition* a quality, or observable, of the system with which that
apparatus interacts. It is a corollary of these propositions that
if an interaction between any two natural systems S_1, S_2 causes some

*change in S_2, say, then the vehicle responsible for this change is
an observable of S_1, and conversely.* That is, we wish to define
observables *in general* as the vehicles through which interactions
between natural systems occur, and which are responsible for the
ultimately perceptible changes in the interacting systems arising
from the interactions.

The above ideas are in fact crucial for science, because they
indicate how we can discover new qualities of observables of natural
systems, besides the ones which are immediately perceptible to us.
More specifically, since our own effectors are themselves natural
systems, they can be employed to bring systems into interactions
which were not so before. In this way we can actively perform
experiments, rather than being restricted to passive observation.
Suppose for example that we are interested in some specific natural
system S_1, some of whose qualities we can directly perceive. Suppose
further that we bring S_1 into interaction with some other system S_2.
Suppose that as a result of this interaction there occurs a directly
perceptible change in S_2. We may then associate the change in S_2
with some specific quality or observable of S_1, which may (or may
not) be *different* from those observables of S_1 which were directly
perceptible to us. In this situation, we are in effect employing
the system S_2 as a transducer, which renders the corresponding
observable of S_1 directly perceptible to us. As we shall see shortly,
this situation is the prototype for the idea of a *meter*, which not
only defines the observable through which S_1 interacts with it, but
actually enables us to *measure* this observable. And it is also
clear that such considerations directly generalize the manner in
which our own sensory apparatus generates percepts.

Let us return again to the situation above, in which we have placed
a system S_1 into interaction with another system S_2. Let us suppose
now, however, that the interaction results in a perceptible change
in S_1. We may then say that, as a result of the specific interaction with S_2, a new *behavior* of S_1 has been generated. It is
correct to say that this behavior is *forced* by the interaction with
S_2, or that it is an *output* to the input consisting of the observable
of S_2 through which the interaction occurs.

Both of these situations are fundamental to experimental science,
and are the prototypes of the two ways in which we acquire *data*
regarding natural systems. We shall have much to say about both of
them as we proceed.

The above ideas have one further crucial ramification, which we now
proceed to describe. This ramification is concerned with associating
quantity with qualities or observables, and is implicit in the
preceding discussion. Let us recall what we have *defined* an observable of a natural system S_1 as a capability for specific interactions

of S_1 with other systems, such as S_2, and that such an interaction
is recognized through a corresponding change in S_2. Let us imagine
now that the system S_2 has the following properties: (a) any change
in S_2 arising from interaction with another system S_1 can be associated with the *same* quality or observable of S_1; and (b) prior to
the establishment of interaction between S_2 and some other system
S_1, S_2 has been restored to an unchanged, fixed initial situation.
The property (a) means that, though S_2 can in principle interact
with many different systems S_1, the *agency* of S_1 responsible for a
change in S_2 is a fixed observable; (b) means that the system S_2
is always the same before interaction is instituted.

Under these conditions, it may still happen that the particular
perceptible change in S_2 arising from interaction with S_1 is different from that arising from interaction with another system S_1'.
Since by hypothesis the *quality* responsible for the change in S_2 is
in both cases the same, we can conclude that this quality may take
on different *values*. In fact, we can *measure* the values of this
quality by the differences between the changes arising in S_2. By
this means, we introduce a new *quantitative* aspect into the characterization of natural systems; we may say that *if a quality of such
a system corresponds to an observable, a quantity corresponds to a
specific value of an observable.*

The essence of quantitative measurement, or the determination of the
magnitude or value of an observable, is thus referred to the change
caused through interaction with a specific system like S_2 in the
above discussion. The role played by S_2 is then, as noted before,
that of a *meter* for the observable in question; under the conditions we have stated, the possible changes which can be induced
in S_2 can be identified with the set of possible values of the
observable which induces them. Such an identification introduces a
crucial notion: that the change in a meter for an observable can
represent, or replace, the specific value of the observable which
generated it. In other words, the change in a meter serves to *label*
the values of the associated observable. This will turn out to be
the crucial concept underlying the development of the subsequent
chapters, when we turn to the concept of formal systems, and the
representation of natural systems in terms of formal ones.

There now remains one more basic notion to be introduced before we
can proceed with a more comprehensive discussion of the linkage
relations which can obtain between observables of a system. This
is the notion of *time*, which is of course central to any discussion
of change, and hence is a fundamental ingredient in any discussion
of interaction of natural systems of the kind sketched above.[2] For

the present, we shall restrict ourselves to the notion of time as
quality; we shall return to the matter in more depth in Section 3
below, which is devoted to dynamics.

The notion of time is a difficult and complex one. We may recall
the plaintive words of Saint Augustine, who in his *Confessions* remarks: "What then is time? if no one asks me, I know: if I wish to
explain it to one that asketh, I know not."

In accord with the spirit of the discussion we have presented so far,
we must begin with our direct perception of time, or what is commonly
called the "sense" of time. This is a percept, in the sense in which
we have employed the term above. But it is apparently not a simple
percept; we can discern at least two quite distinct and apparently
independent aspects of our time perception. These distinct aspects
must be interpreted differently when, as with all percepts, we attempt to associate them with specific qualities pertaining to the
external world. These aspects are: (a) the perception of co-
temporality or *simultaneity*; and (b) the perception of *precedence*,
involving the distinction between past and future. It should be
noted at the outset that both of these aspects of time perception
involve *relations* between percepts. It clearly makes no sense to
apply either of them to a single percept. For this reason, it does
not seem appropriate to treat time directly as a *quality* or observable belonging directly to the external world. Indeed, we have
interpreted all such qualities as potential capacities for interaction, as manifested especially in the moving of meters. It does
not seem that either aspect of time perception is of this character.

On the other hand, we have the conviction that time can be "measured".
Thus, if time is not to be regarded as a quality or observable, we
must understand the sense in which it can be measured, or resolved
into specific time values (instants). We shall begin with a consideration of this question.

The crucial concept here will be that of a *label*; the employment
of qualities of one system to represent qualities of another. We
have seen, for instance, that the values of an observable can be
represented, or labelled, by the specific changes induced in other
systems, or meters. Now we have argued that one essential aspect
of our time perception expresses the *simultaneity* of other percepts.
If this aspect truly reflects a relation between percepts, it follows
from our earlier discussion that this relation involves a creative
mental act, or model, about the external world which generated the
percepts. It is at least plausible to infer that *the specific creative act of the mind involved here is the segregation of percepts
into mutually exclusive classes, in such a way that percepts assigned
to the same class are regarded as simultaneous, and percepts assigned
to different classes are not simultaneous*. In other words, the mind
imposes an equivalence relation, not on any specific set of percepts,
but on the set of *all possible percepts*; it is this act of extrapolation which characterizes the creative aspect of the sense of
simultaneity. Now in general, whenever we are given an equivalence
relation on a set of elements, we may select a single representative
from each equivalence class, and regard it as a specific *label* for
that entire class. As we shall see later, the search for a clever
choice of such a label or representative dominates all theories of
classification; in mathematics, for instance, we search for *canonical forms* to represent classes of equivalent objects. If this is
the case, we can conclude that a "time meter", or clock, is simply
a natural system chosen in such a way that the particular percepts

it generates serve as *labels* for the equivalence classes of simultaneous percepts to which they belong. Thus, a clock is not to be regarded as a meter at all, but rather as a generator of labels or representatives for these equivalence classes. In other words, a clock does not "measure" anything; it simply exemplifies the mentally constructed relation of simultaneity between percepts in a particularly convenient form. Its only relation to a true meter resides in its association of percepts with labels.

We may point out explicitly that there is no absolute or objective character to the classes of simultaneous percepts, or the corresponding classes of simultaneous qualities, which we have just described. Clearly, each of us creates these classes in his own way. We shall see later how we may use our basic time intuitions to construct an objective "common time", which all observers can use, in place of the subjective and idiosyncratic "time sense" which we have been describing.

We turn now to the other aspect of our time perception; that embodied in the distinction between past and future. This aspect imposes a different kind of relation on the set of possible percepts than that embodied in the sense of simultaneity; it is compatible with it, but apparently not directly inferable from it.

To describe this relation, which essentially expresses the idea of predecessor and successor, it is simplest to use a mathematical notation. Let t denote a particular instant; as we have seen, t is itself a percept belonging to the class $C(t)$ of all possible simultaneous percepts, and which serves to *label* the class. Let t' be another instant, $C(t')$ that class of simultaneous instants labelled by it. If we perceive that t' is later than t, then for each percept $p(t)$ in $C(t)$ there is a uniquely determined percept $p(t')$ in $C(t')$ such that $p(t)$ and $p(t')$ are related in the same way that t and t' are related. We alternatively say that $p(t)$ is a *predecessor* of $p(t')$, or $p(t')$ is a *successor* of $p(t)$. Thus, the relations of precedence in time serve to relate percepts belonging to *different simultaneity classes*. We must apparently posit separately that these precedence relations are such that the set of instants (i.e. the set of labels for the simultaneity classes) thereby acquires the mathematical structure of a totally ordered set; in fact, we shall see later that the natural mathematical candidates to represent such a set of instants are the integers or all real numbers.

If we take the now familiar step of inputing relations between percepts to corresponding relations in the external world, the above considerations suffice to characterize time in that world. However, simultaneity in the external world relates qualities or observables (or more precisely, the values of observables) and the set of instants serves to label classes of simultaneously manifested qualities; likewise, the relation of precedence serves to relate the qualities belonging to different simultaneity classes, again in such a way that the set of instants becomes totally ordered. We once again emphasize that these two relations reflect apparently different aspects of our sense of time, and it is important not to confuse them.

Let us now return to our discussion of natural systems, following this extensive detour into the character of observables and the nature of time. We recall that we had defined a natural system to be a collection of observables satisfying certain relations. We can now be somewhat more specific about the nature of the relations, or linkages, which may obtain between the observables of a natural system.

To do this, we are going to utilize in an essential way the structures we have discussed in connection with time. Namely, we have
described the sets $C(t)$ of simultaneous percepts, and the way these
sets are related through the successor-predecessor relation. If we
are given a natural system consisting of a set of related observables
or qualities, we can then naturally consider:

    a.   How these particular observables (or better, their specific
        values) are related as elements of a simultaneity class;

    b.   How these observables are related through the successor-
        predecessor relation.

The first of these will specify how the values assumed by particular
observables in the system at an instant of time are related to the
values assumed by other observables. The second will specify how
the values assumed by particular observables at a given instant are
related to the values assumed by these or other observables at other
instants.

In an intuitive sense, we would not say that a set of observables
actually constitutes a system unless both these kinds of linkages
can be specified, at least in principle. A direct expression of
these linkages would be equivalent to specifying the *system laws*.
For it is the function of system laws in science to tell us precisely
how the values of the system observables at an instant of time are
related, and how the values of these observables at a given time are
related to their values at other times. As we shall see, the formal
vehicles for expressing these laws are what we shall call *equations
of state*. However, we shall argue that the precise formulation of
such relations belongs not directly to the theory of natural systems,
but depends in an essential way on the manner in which observables
and their values are *represented* or *encoded* into corresponding formal
systems. We will turn to such questions in the subsequent chapters
of this section. For the present, it suffices to note that the
existence of definite linkage relations of the kind we have described
represent one embodiment of the notion of *causality*. Indeed, our
initial insistence that definite linkage relations exist between the
observables constituting a natural system restricts us from the outset
to situations in which such a notion of causality is expressed. We
shall later on see how this requirement can be loosened.

We wish to point out two other kinds of linkage relations which are
implicit in the discussion of observables and measurement which was
sketched above. However, whereas thus-far we have considered only
linkages between the observables comprising a single system, the
linkages we describe now relate observables belonging to *different*
systems.

The first of these is implicit in the very concept of a meter. As
we noted above, the essential function of a meter is to provide
labels for the specific values of some observable, through the
different changes arising in the meter when placed in interaction
with a system containing the observable. This means precisely that
the interaction between such a system and the meter establishes a
relation, or linkage, between the observable being measured and some
quality of the meter. Indeed, we shall see later that dynamical
interactions provide the vehicles whereby linkages are established
and lost in general; the case of the meter is a fundamental prototype for the modification of linkage relations. Thus in particular
we can see how *the linkage relations themselves may be functions of
time*. We note, for later reference, that the temporal variation of

linkage relations arising from interactions will provide us with the vehicle for discussing phenomena of *emergence* and emergent novelty.

A final kind of linkage between observables belonging to different systems arises when, speaking roughly, two different natural systems comprising two different sets of observables, satisfy the same linkage relations. This shall provide us with the conceptual basis for the discussion of *system analogy*, and it is exemplified for example in the relation between a scale model and a prototype. We shall take up this kind of linkage further in our discussion of similarity.

Now let us pause for a moment and see where our discussion has led us so far. We have described the way percepts in us are associated with qualities in an external world. We have argued that such qualities, or observables, provide the vehicles for interaction between natural systems in that world. Such interactions can be exploited, through experiment, to make new qualities, initially imperceptible to us, visible. Moreover, such interactions provide us with a way of labelling the qualities of a system with changes in other systems; this is the essence of the concept of a meter. The importance of this concept lies not only in the fact that it allows us to *define* observables, but actually allows us to *measure* them, in the manner we have described. The exploitation of these interactive capabilities provide us with *data* about the external world; the acquisition of such data is the basic task of experimental science.

We also described certain kinds of relations between observables, which we called *linkages*. We saw how the establishment of such relations involved a constructive or creative aspect of the mind, expressed in the organization of percepts. The concept of time plays a crucial role in this organization of percepts; first in establishing a relation of simultaneity, and then in establishing a relation of succession or precedence. These relations are then imputed to the external world, just as qualities or observables are imputed to percepts.

Much beyond this we cannot go without introducing a fundamental new idea. The basic reason lies in the fact that experiment (i.e. the acquisition of data) can only tell us about observables and their values; it cannot in principle tell us anything about the manner in which these observables are linked or related. This is because relations do not directly generate percepts; they do not directly move meters. As we have seen, such relations are posited or *imputed* to the external world, and this imputation involves an essentially creative act of the mind; one which belongs to *theoretical* science. But how do we know whether such imputations are correct? Observation and experiment cannot directly answer such a question; all that can be observed, in principle, are observables and their specific values.

This is why a new element is needed before we can proceed further. Put succinctly, this new element must enable us to make *predictions* about observables on the basis of *posited* linkages between them. There is absolutely no way to do this within the confines of natural systems alone. What we require, then, is a new universe, in which we can *create* systems . But in this universe, the systems we create will have only the properties we decide to endow them with; they will comprise only those observables, and satisfy only those linkages, which we assign to them. But the crucial ingredient of this universe must be a mechanism for making inferences, or predictions. This capacity will play the same role in our new universe that

causality plays in the external world. But whereas in the external
world we are confronted with the exigencies of time, and are forced
to wait upon its effects, in our new universe we are free of time;
the relation of inference to premise takes the place of the temporal
relation between predecessor and successor.

We have, of course, created such a universe. In its broadest terms,
that universe is mathematics. The objects in that universe are
formal systems. Hence, before we can go further in the universe of
natural systems, we must explore the one of formal systems. We
shall begin this exploration in the next chapter.

Looking ahead a bit further still, the next obvious task is to relate the worlds of natural systems with that of the formal ones;
to exploit the capability of drawing inferences in the latter to
make predictions about the former. This will be the subject of the
final section in this chapter.

REFERENCES AND NOTES

1. The epistemological considerations developed herein are idiosyn-
    cratic, but I think not arbitrary. I am sure that none of the
    individual elements of this epistemology is new, but I think
    that their juxtaposition is new and (judging by what it implies)
    significant. I see no purpose in contrasting my approach to
    others; this would at best be tangential to my primary purpose.
    For a fuller treatment of how the epistemological ideas developed
    herein arose out of definite scientific investigations, the
    reader is referred to
        Rosen, R., *Fundamentals of Measurement and the Theory of
        Natural Systems*. Elsevier, New York (1978).

2. For the purpose of the present discussion, it is sufficient to
    refer the reader to a general philosophical treatment of the
    problem of time, such as:
        Whitrow, G., *The Natural Philosophy of Time*. Nelson, London
        (1980).
    A more detailed discussion of how time in represented in different
    kinds of encodings will be found in the various Chapter 3 below,
    and the references thereto.

2.2 The Concept of a Formal System

The present chapter is devoted to developing the concept of a formal system. This development forces us to leave the external world of natural systems, with its observables which generate percepts and move meters. We must enter another world, populated entirely by mental constructs of particular kinds; this is the world of mathematics in the broadest sense.

This is not to say that the external world and the world of mathematics are entirely unrelated, or that our perception of natural systems plays no role in the construction of formal ones. As we shall see, there are many deep relations between the two worlds. Indeed, the main theme of the present book is the modelling relation, which rests precisely on linking the properties of natural systems with formal ones in a particular way. We wish merely to note here that mathematical objects, however they may initially be created or generated, possess an existence of their own, and that this existence is different in character from that of a natural one.

Furthermore, as we shall see, the world of mathematics really consists of two quite separate worlds, which are related to each other in very much the same way as the world of percepts is related to the external world. One of these mathematical worlds is populated by the familiar objects of mathematics: sets, groups, topological spaces, dynamical systems and the like; together with the mappings between them and the relations which they satisfy. The other world is populated with symbols and arrays of symbols. The fundamental relation between these two worlds is established by utilizing the symbols of the latter as *names* or *labels* for the entities in the former, and for regarding arrays of symbols in the latter as expressing *propositions* about the former. In this sense, the world of symbols becomes analogous to our previous world of percepts; while the world of mathematical objects becomes analogous to an external world which elicits percepts. The primary difference between the two situations (and it is an essential one) is that the mathematical worlds are entirely constructed by the creative faculty of the mind.

Perhaps the best way to illustrate the ideas just enunciated is to begin to construct the two mathematical worlds in parallel. We will do this by establishing a few of the rudiments of what is commonly called the *theory of sets*. This has been universally adopted as the essential foundation, in terms of which all the rest of mathematics can be built. As our purpose here is illustrative rather than expository, we shall suppose that the reader already has some familiarity with the concepts involved.[1]

Let us begin to populate our first world, which we shall denote by U. We will initially admit two kinds of entity into U, which we will call *elements* and *sets* respectively. We initially assume no relation of any kind between the entities called elements and those called sets.

Whenever we wish to speak of a particular *element*, we must characterize it by giving it a name; i.e. by labelling it with some symbol, say α, which serves to identify it, and distinguish it from others. This kind of labelling is very much like an act of perception; perceiving the particular element so labelled and its distinctness from others, which we labelled differently. Likewise, when we wish to speak of a particular *set* in U, we must provide it too with a name, or labelling symbol, say A.

Of course we must carefully distinguish the entities in and the symbols which we use to name these entities. The symbols themselves do not belong to U; only the entities themselves have this property. Their names thus must belong to another world, established in parallel with U; this world of names we shall call P.

As it stands, the world U is completely static and uninteresting. In order to proceed further, we must introduce some *relations* into it. We shall do this by admitting into our world a new kind of entity, neither a set nor an element. These new entities must also be labelled or named; let us agree to call such an entity (α, A), where α is the name of an element of U and A is the name of a set. Intuitively, we are going to interpret the presence of such a pair (α, A) in U by saying that α *is an element of* A.

At this stage, we can note that the *character* of U now depends entirely on which pairs are admitted into it. Thus already at this early stage we confront the necessity of *choice*; and indeed the choice we make here will determine everything which follows. Retrospectively, we can see that populating our universe U with different pairs will in effect create different (indeed, radically different) set theories, and hence different mathematics. We will return to this point several times as we proceed.

In accord with long tradition, we will agree to denote the presence of (α, A) in U by the introduction of a new symbol into P. This symbol serves to connect the names of the element and set constituting the pair; specifically, we will write

$$\alpha \ \varepsilon \ A \qquad\qquad\qquad (2.2.1)$$

The symbol ε thus names a *relation* obtaining between sets and elements in U, and the entire expression (2.2.1) is interpreted as naming the manifestation of the relation between a particular pair in U.

The expression (2.2.1) is our first example of a *proposition*. Such a proposition does not belong to U, but rather is the name of an *assertion* about U. Since this is a crucial point, we will spend a moment discussing it.

Once we have introduced the symbol ε into $\mathfrak{p}$, there is nothing to prevent us from taking the name of an arbitrary element of $\mathfrak{u}$, say β, and the name of an arbitrary set, say C, and producing the expression or proposition

$$\beta \ \varepsilon \ C \qquad\qquad (2.2.2)$$

This too is a *proposition*, and in effect it *asserts* something about $\mathfrak{u}$; namely, that (β, C) is a pair in $\mathfrak{u}$. But merely because the proposition (2.2.2) can be *expressed* in $\mathfrak{p}$, it does not follow that the relation it names actually *obtains* between β and C. Thus there are in general going to be *many more propositions in $\mathfrak{p}$ than there are entities in* $\mathfrak{u}$.

If the particular proposition (2.2.2) happens to name a relation that actually obtains in $\mathfrak{u}$; (i.e. is such that (β, C) actually is in $\mathfrak{u}$) then we shall say that the proposition (2.2.2) is *true*. Otherwise, we shall say that (2.2.2) is *false*. Thus, the truth or falsity of such a proposition depends entirely on the nature of $\mathfrak{u}$; it cannot be determined from within the world $\mathfrak{p}$ at all. In a sense, the characterization of (2.2.2) as a true proposition is an *empirical* question; we must look at $\mathfrak{u}$ to determine if the particular pair (β, C) is in it. If not, then (2.2.2) is the name of a situation which does not exist in $\mathfrak{u}$; a label which labels nothing. But such a label cannot be excluded from $\mathfrak{p}$ on any syntactical grounds; once the symbol ε is allowed, so are *all* propositions of the form (2.2.2). This is why, even at this most elementary stage, the world $\mathfrak{p}$ of propositions has already grown larger than the world $\mathfrak{u}$ which originally generated it. If we restrict ourselves only to the *true* propositions, then the two worlds remain in parallel. But as we emphasize, there is no way to do this within $\mathfrak{p}$. Indeed, the propositions (2.2.2) which now populate $\mathfrak{p}$ express all the choices which *could have been* made in constructing $\mathfrak{u}$; they cannot tell us which ones actually *were* made.

It should also be stressed before proceeding that truth and falsity are attributes of *propositions*. It is therefore meaningless to speak of these attributes in connection with $\mathfrak{u}$; they pertain entirely to $\mathfrak{p}$ alone. Basically, a false proposition is one which looks like a name, but which is in fact not a name (of anything in $\mathfrak{u}$).

Let us now proceed a bit further. The next step is, in effect, to change the rules of the game in $\mathfrak{u}$. What we shall do is to *identify* a set A in $\mathfrak{u}$ with the totality of elements which belong to it. In other words, the entity originally named A completely disappears from view, and the name itself is reassigned to a particular totality of elements. This procedure can be represented in $\mathfrak{p}$ with the aid of some new symbols introduced for the purpose:

$$A \equiv \{\alpha : \alpha \ \varepsilon \ A\}. \qquad\qquad (2.2.3)$$

In words, A now names a particular family of elements of $\mathfrak{u}$; namely those for which the proposition α ε A (in the original sense) is true. The symbol "≡" thus expresses a *synonymy* in $\mathfrak{p}$, and will be exclusively used for this purpose. The notation in (2.2.3) also serves to assign names to sets of elements α, characterized through the expression of a particular relation or property which they satisfy in $\mathfrak{u}$.

This identification makes it clear why the initial population of $\mathfrak{u}$ which pairs (α, A) is so important. For at this stage, with the identification of A with the totality of its elements, the character of all subsequent developments in mathematics is determined. Indeed, the "best" way to do this is far from a trivial matter, and in fact is not really known. We do possess a certain amount of retrospective experience bearing on this question, but it is mainly of a negative character. For instance, if we populate $\mathfrak{U}$ too liberally with such pairs, then some of our later set-theoretic constructions will turn out to have paradoxical properties; i.e. certain objects will need to be simultaneously included in and excluded from our universe. The well-known paradoxes of early set theory can all be regarded as arising in this manner.

Modulo the identification (2.2.3), we can now introduce all of the familiar relations and operations of elementary set theory. At each stage, we need to introduce corresponding *names* of these relations and operations into $\mathfrak{P}$. As we do so, we find exactly the same situation as we encountered with the introduction of ε; i.e. we are able thereby to form propositions in $\mathfrak{P}$ which name no counterpart in $\mathfrak{U}$, and hence are to be considered *false*. In other words, as we build structure into $\mathfrak{U}$, we introduce a corresponding *syntax* into $\mathfrak{P}$, which generates a *calculus of propositions*.

To illustrate these last remarks, and incidentally to introduce some important terminology, let us consider the relation in $\mathfrak{U}$ which expresses that a set A is a *subset* of a set B. By virtue of the identification (2.2.3) which specifies the sets of $\mathfrak{U}$ in terms of their constituent elements, such a relation will devolve upon corresponding relations pertaining to the *elements* of A and B. The subset relation is said to obtain if $\mathfrak{U}$ is such that, whenever a pair (α, A) is in $\mathfrak{U}$, the pair (α, B) is also; i.e. every element of A is also an element of B. Now to express this in $\mathfrak{P}$ we need to relate the *propositions* $\alpha \varepsilon A$ and $\alpha \varepsilon B$. There is no way to do this with the machinery we have introduced into $\mathfrak{P}$ so far; we need another *symbol* to express such a relation between propositions, just as we needed the new symbol ε to express a relation between names. This new symbol will be denoted by $\Rightarrow$, and will relate propositions in $\mathfrak{P}$, as in the expression

$$(\alpha \ \varepsilon \ A) \ \Rightarrow \ (\alpha \ \varepsilon \ B). \tag{2.2.4}$$

This expression is now a *new proposition*, which means: if $\alpha \varepsilon A$ is true, then $\alpha \varepsilon B$ is true. The subset relation can now be expressed in $\mathfrak{P}$, because if it obtains in $\mathfrak{U}$ between a pair of sets A, B, the proposition (2.2.4) is true; conversely, if the proposition (2.2.4) is true for some A and B, we say that A is a subset of B. We still need a name for the subset relation itself; we thus write

$$A \subseteq B \equiv (\alpha \ \varepsilon \ A) \ \Rightarrow \ (\alpha \ \varepsilon \ B). \tag{2.2.5}$$

This name $A \subseteq B$ expresses now a relation between sets, instead of the oblique form (2.2.4) which relates propositions about elements. The relation named by (2.2.5) is called *inclusion*.

The implication relation $\Rightarrow$ introduced above is going to be the cetnral feature of our discussion of formal systems. As we shall see, it will be our primary vehicle for expressing in $\mathfrak{P}$ all of the properties pertaining in $\mathfrak{U}$. Its basic characteristic is that *it never takes us out of the set of true propositions*; i.e. if p is any true proposition, and p $\Rightarrow$ q holds for some other proposition q, then q is also a true proposition. Stated another way, this implication relation between propositions enables us to express *linkages* between properties in $\mathfrak{U}$; it will play the same role in the universe of formal systems that causality plays in the universe of natural ones.

Let us note in passing that the inclusion relation just introduced
allows us to look at *synonymy* in a new light. For instance, if it
should be the case that *both* of the inclusion relations

A ⊆ B,   B ⊆ A

hold in $\mathbf{U}$, then both of the sets in question consist of exactly the
same elements. By virtue of (2.2.3), then, these sets are not
different in $\mathbf{U}$, even though they bear two different *names*. Hence
these names are synonyms for the *same* set in $\mathbf{U}$. We shall soon see
that much of mathematics consists of establishing that different
names, or more generally, different propositions in $\mathbf{P}$, are actually
synonyms; in the sense that they name the same object or relation
in $\mathbf{U}$. The vehicle for establishing such synonymy will consist of
chains of *implications* relating propositions in $\mathbf{P}$; this is the
essence of proof. We will take these matters up in more detail
subsequently.

So far, we have considered how a set-theoretic relation (inclusion)
is defined, and the manner in which it is acommodated in the world
$\mathbf{P}$ of propositions, through the introduction of a corresponding relation between propositions. Let us now turn to the question of
set-theoretic *operations*, using the specific example of the *union* of
two sets.

In a sense, we can encompass a concept like the union of two sets
under the rubric of set-theoretic relations, which we have already
introduced. Intuitively, an operation like union defines a new set
in a canonical fashion out of a pair of given sets. If C denotes
this new set, we can equivalently define it in terms of the unique
relation it bears to the sets from which it is built. That is, we
can proceed by adding to our universe $\mathbf{U}$ a family of triples (A, B, C)
satisfying the appropriate properties. For instance, we would informally require the set C in such a triple to be a subset of any
set D of which A and B are both subsets.

However, it is more convenient (and more traditional) to proceed by
specifying the new set C in terms of the specific elements of which
it is composed, via (2.2.3). Intuitively, we wish an element α to
belong to C in case α belongs to A, or α belongs to B, or belongs
to both. To define C in this way requires us to articulate this
idea as a *proposition* in $\mathbf{P}$. We have no proposition at our disposal
for this purpose in $\mathbf{P}$ so far, but we can *build* one if we allow ourselves a new operation on *propositions*. Of course, this is the
conjunction operation, which from any two propositions p, q in $\mathbf{P}$
allows us to produce a new proposition denoted p v q. In terms of
this operation on propositions, we can now specify the set we seek:

C ∃ {α: (α ε A) V (α ε B)}.   (2.2.6)

As before, we must give a specific name to the operation in $\mathbf{U}$ which
constructs C for us out of A and B; we do this by *defining*

C ≡ A ∪ B.

In words, the proposition (α ε A) V (α ε B) is true precisely when
at least one of its constituent propositions (α ε A) or (α ε B) is
true. The expression A ∪ B is now to be regarded as the *name* of the
set in $\mathbf{U}$ defined by (2.2.6).

Let us pause now to note a fundamental distinction between the world
$\mathbf{U}$ of mathematical objects and the world $\mathbf{P}$ of names and propositions

pertaining to these objects. In a certain important sense, a set
like A ∪ B already exists in 𝔘 from the outset; we need only find
a way of giving it an appropriate name, which exhibits explicitly
its relation to other sets in 𝔘. But the corresponding propositions
in 𝔭 need to be *created*, or *generated*; a proposition like p V q
does not exist in 𝔭 before we introduce the specific operation "V",
and directly apply it to particular propositions in 𝔭. This is a
crucial point, and marks the difference between those mathematicians
who believe that the mathematical universe pre-exists, possessing
properties which must be *discovered*, and those who believe that the
mathematical universe must be *constructed* or *created*, and that this
construction is an entirely arbitrary process. Ultimately, this
difference resides in whether one conceives of the natural habitat
for mathematics as 𝔘 or 𝔭. We need not regard these alternatives
as being mutually exclusive, though perhaps most mathematicians
have regarded them as such; this fundamental distinction, resting
as it does primarily on aesthetic grounds, is responsible for much
of the acrimony and bitterness surrounding the foundations of mathematics. But in any case we can discern once again the similarity
of the relation between 𝔘 and 𝔭 to the relation between qualities
and percepts which we discussed in the preceding chapter. We shall
return to this matter when we consider the question of axiomatics
below.

Let us return now to a consideration of the set-theoretic operation
of forming the union. Once it has been defined or named, we can
discover that it possesses certain properties. for instance that it
is associative. Associativity consists in the fact that certain
names of sets are in fact synonyms; specifically, that the two
names

$$(A \cup B) \cup C \quad \text{and} \quad A \cup (B \cup C)$$

both label the same set in 𝔘. The *proof* of synonymy consists of
establishing certain *implications* in 𝔭; namely, that

$$\alpha \; \varepsilon \; (A \cup B) \cup C \Rightarrow \alpha \; \varepsilon \; A \cup (B \cup C)$$

and

$$\alpha \; \varepsilon \; A \cup (B \cup C) \Rightarrow \alpha \; \varepsilon \; (A \cup B) \cup C$$

Thus, the sets named by (A ∪ B) ∪ C and A ∪ (B ∪ C) are each contained in the other; hence are identical. This identity is a
theorem; an assertion which is true in 𝔘 if the initial propositions

$$\alpha \; \varepsilon \; (A \cup B) \cup C$$

and

$$\alpha \; \varepsilon \; A \cup (B \cup C)$$

are true in 𝔘. We leave it to the reader to fill in the details.
The reader should also convince himself that the associativity of
the set-theoretic operation 𝔘 *forces* the associativity of the operation V on propositions in 𝔭. The nature of this forcing is most
illuminating in considering the relation between 𝔘 and 𝔭.

We can proceed in an analogous manner to define the other basic set-
theoretic operations of intersection (denoted by ∩) and complemen-
tation (denoted by ‾); these in their turn force us to introduce
new operations on propositions in 𝔭 (namely disjunction, denoted by
∧, and negation, denoted variously by - or ~). We will omit the
details, which the reader can readily supply. These simple ideas

already admit a rich calculus (or better, an algebra, which is usually associated with the name of the English mathematician Boole), in which one can prove many theorems of the character we have already described. For instance, we can establish the familiar de Morgan Laws

$$\overline{A \cup B} = \overline{A} \cap \overline{B}$$

$$\overline{A \cap B} = \overline{A} \cup \overline{B}$$

in $\mathfrak{U}$, and their corresponding analogs in $\mathfrak{p}$. The reader should establish the appropriate chains of implication in detail, and interpret their meaning in the light of the preceding discussion.

Before proceeding further, let us add a word about the intersection operation. Explicitly, in analogy with (2.2.6), the intersection of two sets A, B is defined as the set $A \cap B$ of elements which belong both to A and to B; i.e. for which the propositions ($\alpha \varepsilon$ A) and ($\alpha \varepsilon$ B) are true. But clearly there need be no elements α in $\mathfrak{U}$ for which ($\alpha \varepsilon$ A) and ($\alpha \varepsilon$ B) are both true. In this case we say that A and B are disjoint. By convention, and so that the intersection operation shall be universally defined for all pairs of sets A, B, we introduce a new concept; that of the *empty set*. The empty set intuitively possesses no elements, and is usually denoted by ϕ. Thus, if A and B are disjoint, we write

$$A \cap B = \phi.$$

The empty set is considered to be a perfectly respectable member of $\mathfrak{U}$ (indeed, it can be regarded as generating all of $\mathfrak{U}$, in a certain ironic sense)[2], and is likewise considered to be a subset of every set; i.e. $\phi \subseteq A$ for every set A.

We now possess all the machinery for defining in $\mathfrak{U}$ all of the familiar structures of methematics. These can all be regarded as arising from particular kinds of set-theoretic operations. The most important of these set-theoretic operations is the *cartesian product* operation; given any pair A, B of sets we can define a new set AxB in the following way:

$$AxB = \{(\alpha, \beta) : \alpha \varepsilon A, \alpha \varepsilon B\}.$$

An arbitrary subset $R \subseteq AxB$ defines a *binary relation* between the elements of A and the elements of B. If R is such a relation, it is traditional to abbreviate the proposition $(\alpha, \beta) \varepsilon$ R by writing α R β.

Binary relations formally lead us to some of the basic structures of mathematics, with which we shall be much concerned throughout the sequel. For instance, suppose that $R \subseteq AxB$ is a binary relation. Suppose further that R possesses the following property

$$\alpha \ R \ \beta \quad \text{and} \quad \alpha \ R \ \gamma \quad \Rightarrow \quad \beta = \gamma.$$

A relation of this kind can thus be regarded as establishing a *mapping*, or *correspondence*, between the elements of A and the elements of B. Indeed, given a relation of this kind, we can express the proposition α R β by writing $\beta = f(\alpha)$, where f is the symbol expressing the mapping or correspondence. As we shall see, these mappings (also denoted by the symbol f : A → B) introduce a dynamic element into $\mathfrak{U}$; they are the vehicles through which different structures in $\mathfrak{U}$ may be compared.

One of the basic properties of binary relations, which we shall exploit heavily in subsequent chapters, resides in the fact that they can be *composed*. Suppose that $R_1 \subseteq A \times B$, and that $R_2 \subseteq B \times C$, are two binary relations. We are going to define a new relation $R \subseteq A \times C$. To define it, we need to specify what elements of $A \times C$ are in R. We shall say that a pair (α, γ) is in R if and only if there is a β in B such that

$$(\alpha, \beta) \; \varepsilon \; R_1 \qquad \text{and} \qquad (\beta, \gamma) \; \varepsilon \; R_2.$$

We shall define this relation R to be the *composite* of R_1 and R_2, and write $R = R_2 R_1$.

In case R_1 and R_2 are *mappings*, it is easy to see that this definition produces a relation which is itself a mapping. This generates the familiar idea of *composition of mappings*. Specifically, if $f : A \to B$, and $g : B \to C$ are mappings, then there is a uniquely determined mapping $h : A \to C$ defined in accordance with the above construction, and we *define* h = gf.

These considerations lead directly to another set-theoretic construction, which is as important as the cartesian product. Namely, given two sets A, B in U, we can consider the set of *all* mappings from A to B. This is a new set, which we can denote by H(A, B). This set H(A, B) thus turns out to be intimately related to the cartesian product operation appropriately generalized, but we shall not develop that relation here.

If A = B, a binary relation $R \subseteq A \times A$ establishes a relation among the elements of A. By far the most important of these for our purposes are the *equivalence relations* on A. An equivalence relation $R \subseteq A \times A$ possesses the following properties:

(a) $\alpha \; R \; \alpha$ for every α in A   (reflexivity)

(b) $(\alpha \; R \; \beta) \; \Rightarrow \; (\beta \; R \; \alpha)$ (symmetry)

(c) $(\alpha \; R \; \beta)$ and $(\beta \; R \; \gamma) \; \Rightarrow \; (\alpha \; R \; \gamma)$ (transitivity).

Such equivalence relations will be of vital importance to us throughout our subsequent development. Intuitively, an equivalence relation is a generalization of equality (which is itself obviously an equivalence relation) which arises when we discard some distinguishing property which enabled us to recognize that particular elements were unequal; when the property is discarded, such elements now appear indistiguishable.

This central aspect of equivalence relations is manifested in their fundamental property, which we can formulate as follows: if R is an equivalence relation on a set A, and if $\alpha \; \varepsilon \; A$ is any element of A, then we can form the subset of A defined as follows:

$$[\alpha] = \{\alpha' : \alpha \; R \; \alpha'\}.$$

If β is another element of A, we can likewise form the subset

$$[\beta] = \{\beta' : \beta \; R \; \beta'\}.$$

It is then a *theorem* that either

$$[\alpha] = [\beta]$$

or

$$[\alpha] \cap [\beta] = \phi$$

The subset $[\alpha]$ defined above is called the *equivalence class* of α (under the relation R); the theorem just enunciated asserts that two such classes are either disjoint or identical. Hence the relation R can be regarded as partitioning the set A into a family of disjoint subsets, whose union is clearly all of A. The *set* of equivalence classes of A under an equivalence relation R is itself a set in $\mathcal{U}$, denoted A/R, and often called the *quotient set* of A modulo R. It is easy to see that the equivalence relation R on A becomes simple equality on A/R.

There is a simple but profound relation between mappings and equivalence relations. Let $f : A \rightarrow B$ be a mapping. For each $\alpha \in A$, let us define

$$[\alpha] = \{\alpha' : f(\alpha') = f(\alpha)\}.$$

These sets $[\alpha]$ are all subsets of A, and it is easy to see that they are either disjoint or identical. They can thus be regarded as the equivalence classes of a corresponding equivalence relation R_f on A. Intuitively, this relation R_f specifies the extent to which the elements of A can be distinguished, or resolved, by f. Thus, if we regard the mapping f as associating with an element $\alpha \in A$ a name or label $f(\alpha)$ in B, the equivalence relation R_f specifies those distinct elements of A which are assigned the same name by f. Moreover, it is a fact that *any* equivalence relation may be regarded as arising in this fashion. In this sense, equivalence is a kind of inverse of synonymy; equivalence involves two *things* assigned the same *name*; synonymy involves two *names* assigned to the same *thing*.

After all this extensive preamble, we are now in a position to discuss some familiar formal system as mathematical objects. In the world $\mathcal{U}$, such a formal system can be regarded as a set together with some other structure; a set and a mapping; a set and a relation; a set and a family of subsets. As a simple example, we may consider a typical algebraic structure, such as a *group*.

A group may be regarded as a pair (G, τ), where G is a set in $\mathcal{U}$, and $\tau : G \times G \rightarrow G$ is a definite mapping in $H(G \times G, G)$. This mapping τ is not arbitrary, but is supposed to satisfy the following conditions:

(a) $\tau(g_1, \tau(g_2, g_3)) = \tau(\tau(g_1, g_2), g_3)$ (associativity)

(b) $\tau(g, e) = \tau(e, g) = g$ for some distinguished element
      $e \in G$; the *unit element*

(c)   for every $g \in G$ there is a unique element $g^{-1} \in G$
      such that $\tau(g, g^{-1}) = \tau(g^{-1}, g) = e$.

It is more traditional to write $\tau(g_1, g_2)$ as $g_1 \cdot g_2$, and consider τ as defining a *binary operation* on G. The properties (a) to (c) above are ususally called the "group axioms".

We can establish the framework for studying groups in $\mathfrak{P}$ by mimicking
the machinery which was established for sets, appropriately modified
or constrained so as to respect the additional structure which distinguishes a group from a set. This machinery can be succinctly
characterized under the headings (a) substructures, (b) quotient
structures, (c) structure-preserving mappings. These are the *leit-
motifs* which establish the framework in terms of which all kinds of
mathematical structures are studied. For the particular case we are
now considering, this *leitmotif* becomes: (a) sub-groups; (b)
quotient groups; (c) group homomorphisms. Let us briefly discuss
each of these in turn.

(a)   Subgroups

As we have seen, a mathematical structure like a group is a set
together with something else; in this case, a binary operation
satisfying the group axioms. Thus a *subgroup* of a group G will
intuitively first have to be a *subset* $H \subseteq G$ of the set of elements
belonging to G. Further, this subset must bear a special relation
to the binary operation, which is the other element of structure.
It is clear what this relation should be: H should itself be a
group under the same operation which makes G a group; and further
should have the same unit element. A subset H with these properties
is said to define a *subgroup* of G.

(b) Quotient Groups

To define quotient groups, we must first consider equivalence relations on G, considered as a set. But by virtue of the additional
structure (the binary operation) we will only want to consider
certain special equivalence relations, which in some sense are
compatible with the additional structure. It is relatively clear
how this compatibility is to be defined. Suppose that R is some
equivalence relation on G. Let g_1, g_2 be elements of G. Suppose
that $g_1 \, R \, g_1'$, and that $g_2 \, R \, g_2'$. In G we can form the *products*
$g_1 \cdot g_2$ and $g_1' \cdot g_2'$. It is natural to require that *these two products
are also equivalent under* R; i.e. $(g_1 \cdot g_2) \, R \, (g_1' \cdot g_2')$. If we do
this, then the quotient *set* G/R can itself be turned into a group,
by *defining* the product of two equivalence classes $[g_1]$, $[g_2]$ in G/R
as

$$[g_1] \cdot [g_2] = [g_1 \cdot g_2].$$

That is: the product of equivalence classes in G/R is the equivalence **class** of the product in G. It is trivial to verify that
this operation in G/R turns it into a new group; this new group is
then called a *quotient group* of G.

(c)   Structure-Preserving Mappings

Suppose that G and H are groups. Just as we did not wish to consider all equivalence relations on a group, but only those which
were compatible with the additional structure, so we do not wish to
consider all mappings $f : G \to H$, but only those which are also compatible with the structures on G and H. Just as before, this

compatibility will consist in preserving the properties of the binary operations. Written succinctly, such compatibility means at least that

$$f(g_1 \cdot g_2) = f(g_1) \cdot f(g_2)$$

for any two elements g_1, g_2 in G. It should be noted that the binary operation appearing on the left side of this condition is the operation in G; the operation on the right side is the operation in H. We will also require explicitly that f *preserve units*; i.e. if e_G, e_H are the unit elements of G and H respectively, then $f(e_G) = e_H$. From this it immediately follows that such a mapping f also *preserves inverses*: $f(g^{-1}) = (f(g))^{-1}$.

A mapping $f : G \to H$ which satisfies these compatibility conditions is called a *group homomorphism*. Such a homomorphism is an instrument through which the group structures on G and H can be *compared*.

On the basis of these simple ideas, we can construct a world $\mathfrak{U}_G$ patterned after our original world $\mathfrak{U}$, except that instead of consisting of sets it consists of *groups*; instead of allowing arbitrary mappings, we allow only group homomorphisms; instead of allowing arbitrary equivalence relations, we allow only compatible equivalence relations. Such a world is now commonly called a *category*; what we have done in specifying $\mathfrak{U}_G$ is to construct the *category of groups*.

The above line of argument is generic in mathematics; it can be applied to any kind of mathematical structure, and leads to the construction of a corresponding *category* of such structures. Thus, we can consider categories of rings, fields, algebras, topological spaces, etc. Our original world $\mathfrak{U}$ can itself be considered as a category; the *category of sets*. One of our basic tasks, which we shall consider in the next chapter, is to see how different categories may themselves be compared; i.e. how different classes of mathematical structures may be related to one another. In abstract terms, this kind of study comprises the *theory of categories*[3] and it will play a central conceptual role in all of our subsequent discussion.

In our discussion of formal systems so far, we have been concentrating on the world $\mathfrak{U}$. Let us now return to the world $\mathfrak{P}$ of names and propositions, and see how such formal systems look in that world. As we shall see, the situation in that world is quite different. This is roughly because, as we pointed out before, we could essentially *discover* groups in $\mathfrak{U}$; but they must be *created* in $\mathfrak{P}$.

Let us then begin to create a group; the procedure we use will be typical of the constructive or generative procedures which characterize doing mathematics in $\mathfrak{P}$. We are going to initiate our construction by taking an array of symbols g, h, ... from $\mathfrak{P}$, now considered in the abstract; i.e. without regard for anything external to $\mathfrak{P}$ which these symbols might name; we establish by fiat that these symbols shall be in our group. Now we must introduce a special rule which allows us to combine our symbols to obtain new ones analogous to the operations ∨, ∧ etc., which allow us to combine propositions. We will call such a rule a *production rule*. The rule we use is a very simple one, called concatenation; if g, h are two of our symbols,

then their concatenation gh will also be a symbol in our group-to-be.
More generally, if we are given any finite number g_1, ..., g_n of such
symbols, then the concatenation $g_1...g_n$ is a symbol. In this way we
build up finite *strings* of the symbols with which we started; such
strings are conveniently called *words*. Most generally, if w_1, w_2
are words, then the concatenation w_1w_2 is also decreed to be a word.

Now concatenation is obviously associative: $(w_1w_2)w_3$ is the same
string as $w_1(w_2w_3)$. Moreover, if we admit the *empty word* e into our
system (where e is a string containing no symbols) then e plays the
role of a unit element for concatenation; we = ew = w for any word
w. In this way, we have constructed in effect an algebraic system
which has many grouplike properties; a binary operation (concatenation) which is associative and possesses a unit element. However,
it is clear that there are no inverses in this kind of system, which
is called the *free semigroup* generated by the symbols orignally chosen
(the significance of the word "free" will become clear in a moment).

To force the existence of inverses, we need to add them explicitly.
Let us do this by taking another family of symbols g', h', ..., one
for each of the generating symbols initially chosen, but such that
the two families of symbols are disjoint. Intuitively, we are going
to force g' to behave like g^{-1}, h' like h^{-1}, and so on. We do this
by adding the new primed generating symbols to the original ones,
and once again constructing all finite strings by concatenation.
But now on this larger set of strings, we are going to *force* a concept
of synonymy. In particular, we are going to decree that the string
gg' and the string g'g be synonymous with the empty word e; and
likewise for all of the generating symbols. From this it is easy to
see that, if $w = g_1...g_n$ is an arbitrary string, and if we define

$$w' = g_n'...g_1',$$

then ww' and w'w must also be synonymous with the empty word.

Intuitively, what this procedure does is to impose an equivalence
relation R on our second set of strings; two such strings being
called equivalent if one can be obtained from the other by the
insertion or removal of substrings of the form ww' or w'w. It
requires a bit of an argument to establish that the relation so
introduced is indeed an equivalence relation, and that it is compatible with concatenation, but the details are not difficult and
are left to the reader. Granting that this relation is a compatible
equivalence, we can pass then to the quotient set modulo R. This
quotient set, whose elements are *equivalence classes* of strings,
has now all the properties of a group; it is called the *free group*
generated by our original set of symbols.

The significance of the term "free" in these constructions is as
follows: there is a sense in which the group we have constructed
is the largest group which can be built from the generators we have
employed. Stated another way: no *relation* is satisfied by the
elements of this group, other than the one we have imposed to
guarantee that they do indeed form a group.

If G is such a free group, then we can impose further (compatible) equivalence relations on G, and obtain new groups by forming the corresponding quotient groups G/R. It is not difficult to show that there is a sense in which *every* group can be regarded as a quotient group of a suitable free group, and in that sense, we have succeeded in constructing all groups in $\mathfrak{P}$. However, it is clear that the kind of constructive procedure we had to use to generate groups in $\mathfrak{P}$ makes a group look much different from the simple definitions which could be employed to discover the same groups in $\mathfrak{U}$. The treatment adopted in the above constructive argument is often called *the definition of a group through generators and relations*. To construct any specific group, we must first construct a free group, and then impose on it precisely the relation R which ensures that the quotient modulo R is in fact the desired group. It may be imagined that this is not always easy to do.[4]

We may note in passing that the free groups are in fact in $\mathfrak{U}$, but they are there characterized by the satisfaction of what appears to be a quite different property. For the reader's interest, we might sketch this property. Suppose that G is a group in $\mathfrak{U}$, and that A is simply a set. Let $f : A \to G$ be a mapping of A into G. Let H be any other group, and let $g : A \to H$ be any mapping. If in this case we can always find a group homomorphism $\phi : G \to H$ such that the composite mapping $\phi f : A \to H$ is the same as the chosen mapping $h : A \to H$, then G is called the free group generated by A.

In fact, the two definitions are equivalent, in the following sense. If we start with a set A in $\mathfrak{U}$, we can use the names of its elements as the symbols in $\mathfrak{P}$ from which to begin our construction. When we do this, there is a direct *interpretation* of our construction in $\mathfrak{U}$ at every stage, and in particular, the free group we generate names an object in $\mathfrak{U}$. This object can be shown to satisfy the condition just enunciated. In fact, this kind of argument is used to establish the *existence* of free groups. Indeed, by allowing our symbols to possess a definite interpretation in $\mathfrak{U}$ from the outset, we may pass freely back and forth between $\mathfrak{P}$ and $\mathfrak{U}$, exploiting both the constructive aspects of the former and the existential qualities of the latter. Mathematicians do this routinely. But it raises some deep questions, which we must now pause to examine.

These questions devolve once again on the relative roles played by $\mathfrak{U}$ and $\mathfrak{P}$ in the development of the mathematical universe. We have already touched on this above, and indeed, we have seen how differently the same mathematical object (a group) could look in the two realms. In general, we may say that those concerned with mathematics can be divided into two camps, or parties, which we may call the $\mathfrak{U}$-ists and the $\mathfrak{P}$-ists. The $\mathfrak{U}$-ists minimize the role played by $\mathfrak{P}$ in mathematics; their basic position is roughly as follows: $\mathfrak{P}$ if we wish to establish some property of a mathematical system, we need merely look at that object in $\mathfrak{U}$ in an appropriate way, and *verify* the property. According to this view, mathematics is akin to an experimental science and, as noted before, $\mathfrak{U}$ is treated in the same way an experimental scientist treats the external world.

The $\mathfrak{P}$-ists have, however, cogent arguments on their side. For one thing, all of the machinery of proof; i.e. for the establishment of chains of interference, is in $\mathfrak{P}$. Moreover, we can build into $\mathfrak{P}$ an abstract image of any imaginable mathematical object, as a family of propositions generated from an appropriate set of symbols and production rules, whether $\mathfrak{U}$ is available for inspection or not. Hence, they argue, $\mathfrak{U}$ can be entirely dispensed with, for it can be invented entirely within $\mathfrak{P}$.

The 𝕌-ists can counter with a very powerful argument. Namely, as
long as at least some of the symbols and propositions in 𝕡 are interpretable as names of objects in 𝕌, the concept of truth or falsity
of the propositions in 𝕡 is not only meaningful, it is determined.
Within 𝕡 alone, there is no vehicle for assigning truth and falsity.
Thus, since as we have seen 𝕡 is inevitably much bigger than 𝕌, we
will never effectively be able to find an abstract image of 𝕌 in 𝕡.
Moreover, the fundamental weapon of *implication*, which as we have
seen never takes us out of a set of true propositions, is of no value
without a *prior* notion of truth and falsity.

The 𝕡-ists can counter such an argument to some extent, as follows.
We do not care, they may say, about any notion of truth or falsity
which is imported into 𝕡 from outside. From within 𝕡 itself, we may
by fiat declare a certain set of propositions to be *true*, together
with all the propositions which may be built from these according
to the syntactical rules in 𝕡. All we need care about is that this
choice be made in such a way that the set of propositions arising
in this fashion is *consistent*; in other words, that for no proposition p is it the case that both p and -p (the negation of p) belong to the set. And indeed, it may be argued that any such set of
consistent propositions is an abstract image of *some* mathematical
world 𝕌, and therefore *is* that world.

The 𝕡-ists have one more powerful argument, which is intended to
rebut the idea that mathematical properties can be determined by
inspection or verification in 𝕌. They point out that all mathematicians seek generality; i.e. to seek to establish the relation
between mathematical properties in the widest possible context.
Mathematicians seek to establish relations such as, "if G is *any*
group, then some property P is true of G". Or, stated another way,
for *all* groups G, P(G) holds. In 𝕡, a proposition like this is
represented through the introduction of the universal quantifier
∀, and would be expressed as

   ∀G P(G)

Now the universal quantifier is closely related to the operation ∧
of disjunction on propositions. For, if we had some way of enumer-
ating groups, as say G_1, G_2, G_3, ..., G_n, ..., the above universal
assertion could be written as

   $P(G_1) \wedge P(G_2) \wedge \ldots \wedge P(G_n) \wedge \ldots$

To *verify* a proposition of this type requires an infinite number of
verifications, which is impossible *in principle*. Thus, to the
extent that a universal quantifier is meaningful in mathematics at
all, it can only be meaningful within a limited constructive sense
in a universe of totally abstract propositions.

The same argument may be given in connection with another kind of
basic mathematical proposition, which asserts that for some particular property P, there *exists* an object A which satisfies the property.
To enunciate such a proposition requires another quantifier, the
existential quantifier ∃; in terms of it, the above assertion would
be expressed as

   ∃A P(A).

This existential quantifier is closely related to the conjunction

operation;   again, if all objects A could be enumerated in some
fashion as A_1, A_2, ..., A_n, ..., the existential assertion would
amount to the proposition

$$P(A_1) \lor P(A_2) \lor ... \lor P(A_n) \lor ...$$

Here again, to establish existence by verification requires an infinite number of separate acts of verification, which is impossible
in principle. Hence existence also can only be given a very circum-
scribed formal meaning, which involves the actual *construction* of the
object whose existence is asserted.

Once again the U-ists can rebut in a very powerful way. Quite apart
from the utter aridity of the manipulation of symbols devoid of
interpretation, which is the nature of the universe contemplated by
the P-ists, they can point out that the validity of the entire P-ists
program would depend on *effectively* being able to determine the
consistency of families of propositions arbitrarily decreed in
advance to be true. It is here that the name of Gödel[5] first appears.
To appreciate the full force of the argument we are now developing
we must digress for a moment to consider the concept of *axiomatization*.

Axiomatization is an old idea, dating back to the codification of
geometry by Euclid. The essence of the Euclidean development was
to organize a vast amount of geometric knowledge by showing that
each item could be established on the basis of a small number of
specific geometric postulates, and a similarly small number of rules
of inference or axioms. On this basis, it was believed for a long
time that every true proposition in geometry could be established
as a theorem;   i.e. as a chain of implications ultimately going back
to the postulates. Moreover, if some geometric assertion was not
true, then its negation was a theorem.

Mathematicians came to believe that every branch of mathematics was
of this character. Namely, they believed that the totality of true
propositions about every branch of mathematics (say number theory)
could all be established as theorems, on the basis of a small number
of assumed postulates and the familiar rules of inference. It was
this belief that in fact underlies the expectation that all of
mathematics can be transferred from U to P;   for the axiomatic
method is entirely formal and abstract, and in principle utterly
independent of interpretation. In this way, an axiomatic *theory* in
P proceeds by identifying some small (invariably finite) number of
propositions or symbols as axioms, and entirely by the application
of a similarly small number of syntactical production rules (rules
of inference) proceeds to generate the implications or theorems of
the system. As noted above, the only limitation imposed here is
that the resulting set of theorems be *consistent*;   i.e. that for no
proposition p are both p and -p theorems. The generation of theorems
in such a system is entirely a *mechanical* process, in the sense that
it can be done by a robot or machine;   and indeed one approach to
such systems proceeds entirely through such machines (Turing machines);[6]   this is the basis for the close relation between axiomatics and automata theory. But that is another story.

What Gödel showed in this connection was that this kind of procedure
is essentially hopeless. If we have some body of propositions that
we desire to declare true, and if this body of propositions is rich
enough to be at all interesting in mathematical terms, then there

will be no mechanical process for establishing all these propositions
on the basis of any finite subset of them chosen as axioms; i.e.
there will be true propositions which are unprovable from the axioms,
however the axioms may be chosen. There is only one exception; the
fatal one in which the body of propositions initially declared true
is inconsistent. Moreover, it is generally impossible, given a
system of axioms and a set of production rules, to determine whether
or not an arbitrary proposition is in fact a theorem; i.e. can be
reached from the axioms by chains of implications utilizing the given
rules.

Thus the U-ists can say to the P-ists: you claim that the impossi-
bility of carrying out infinitely many acts of verification means
that mathematics must become a game of manipulating meaningless symbols according to arbitrary rules. You say that truth or falsity of
propositions is likewise something which may be arbitrarily assigned.
But you cannot effectively answer any of the crucial questions; not
even whether a proposition is a theorem, nor whether a particular
set of propositions is consistent. Surely, that is no basis for
doing mathematics.

And in fact, this is where the matter still stands at present. The
dispute is over what mathematics *ought* to be; a question which would
gladden Mr. Hutchins' heart, but one which cannot apparently be
answered from within mathematics itself; it can only be answered
from within the mathematician.

We are going to make the best of this situation by ignoring it to
the extent possible. In what follows, we shall freely move back and
forth between the world U of formal mathematical systems and the
world P of propositions relating properties of these systems as if
it were legitimate to do so; unless the reader is a specialist in
foundation problems, this is in fact what the reader has always done.
We will freely make use of *interpretations* of our propositions; in
fact, the generation of such interpretations will be the heart of
the modelling relation. The above discussion is important in its
own right, partly because it teaches us the essential difference
between things and the names of things. But also it provides some
essential background for the discussion of modelling itself; many
of the purely mathematical struggles to provide meaning through
interpretation of sets of propositions are in themselves important
instances of the modelling relation, and will be discussed in some
detail in Chapter 3 below.

We now turn to the next essential item of business; the establishment of relationships between the worlds of natural systems and of
formal ones.

REFERENCES AND NOTES

1. Georg Cantor, the creator of set theory, envisioned it as pro-
    viding an unshakable foundation for all of mathematics, something
    on which all mathematicians could agree as a common basis for
    their discipline. He would have been astounded by what has
    actually happened; hardly two books about "set theory" are alike,
    and some are so different that it is hard to believe they purport
    to be about the same subject. We have tried to make this liveli-
    ness visible in the treatment we provide. Of the multitude of
    books about set theory, the one whose spirit seems closest to
    ours is:

van Dalen, D., Doets, H. C. and de Swart, H., *Sets: Naive,*
Axiomatic and Applied. North-Holland (1978).

2. The empty set is perhaps the only mathematical object which
    survives Cartesian doubt; it must *necessarily* exist, even if
    nothing else does. Since it exists, we can form the class which
    contains the empty set as its single element; thus a one-element
    set also exists, and hence the number 1 can be defined. By
    iterating this procedure, we can construct a set with two el-
    ements, a set with three elements, etc., and mathematics can
    begin.

3. We shall discuss the Theory of Categories at greater length in
    3.3 below; references are provided in the notes for that chap-
    ter.

4. In fact, it is generally impossible (in a definite, well-defined
    sense). At least, it is impossible in any sense that would be
    acceptable to a $\mathfrak{p}$-ist. The problem of determining effectively
    whether two words of even a finitely generated free group fall
    into the same equivalence class with respect to some relation is
    essentially the *word problem* for groups, and it can be shown to
    be unsolvable. See
        Boone, W. W., Cammonito, F. B. and Lyndon, R. C., *Word Problems.*
        North-Holland (1973).

5. In a celebrated paper, Gödel showed that any axiom system strong
    enough to do arithmetic must contain undecidable propositions,
    unless the system is inconsistent to begin with. Gödel's dis-
    covery devastated the so-called Hilbert Program, which sought
    to establish mathematical consistency entirely along $\mathfrak{p}$-ist lines.
    For a clear and simple exposition of Gödel's argument and its
    significance, we may recommend
        Nagel, E. and Newman, J. R., *Gödel's Proof.* Routledge & Kegan
        Paul, London (1962).

6. The term "machine" is used in mathematics for anything that
    executes an algorithm; it does not refer to a physical device.
    Such "Mathematical machines" provide an effective way to navi-
    gate in the universe $\mathfrak{p}$. The theory of such machines is known
    variously as recursive function theory and the theory of auto-
    mata. It also turns out to be intimately connected to the
    theory of the brain (cf. 3.5, Example 3B below) and cognate
    subjects. One way of showing that a class of problems (such as
    the word problems for finitely generated groups which was
    mentioned above) is unsolvable is to show that no machine can
    be programmed to solve the problem in a finite number of steps.
    General references bearing on these matters are:
        Davis, M., *Computability and Unsolvability.* McGraw-Hill, New
        York (1958).
        Minsky, M., Computation: *Finite and Infinite Machines.*
        Prentice-Hall, New York (1967).

2.3 Encodings between Natural and Formal Systems

In the preceding two chapters, we have discussed the concepts of
natural systems, which belong primarily to science, and *formal systems*, which belong to mathematics. We now turn to the fundamental
question of establishing relations between the two classes of systems.
The establishment of such relations is fundamental to the concept of
a model, and indeed, to all of theoretical science. In the present
chapter we shall discuss such relations in a general way, and consider a wealth of specific illustrative examples in Section 3 below.

In a sense, the difficulty and challenge in establishing such relations arises from the fact that the entities to be related are
fundamentally different in kind. A natural system is essentially
a bundle of linked qualities, or observables, coded or named by the
specific percepts which they generate, and by the relations which
the mind creates to organize them. As such, a natural system is
always incompletely known; we continually learn about such a system,
for instance by watching its effect on other systems with which it
interacts, and attempting to include the observables rendered perceptible thereby into the scheme of linkages established previously.
A formal system, on the other hand, is entirely a creation of the
mind, possessing no properties beyond those which enter into its
definition and their implications. We thus do not "learn" about a
formal system, beyond establishing the consequences of our definitions through the application of conventional rules of inference,
and sometimes by modifying or enlarging the initial definitions in
particular ways. We have seen that even the study of formal systems
is not free of strife and controversy; how much more strife can be
expected when we attempt to relate this world to another of a fundamentally different character? And yet that is the task we now
undertake; it is the basic task of relating *experiment* to *theory*.
We shall proceed to develop a general framework in which formal and
natural systems can be related, and then we shall discuss that framework in an informal way.

The essential step in establishing the relations we seek, and indeed
the key to all that follows, lies in an exploitation of *synonymy*.
We are going to force the name of a percept to be also the name of
a formal entity; we are going to force the name of a linkage between percepts to also be the name of a relation between mathematical

entities; and most particularly, we are going to force the various
temporal relations characteristic of causality in the natural world
to be synonymous with the inferential structure which allows us to
draw conclusions from premises in the mathematical world. We are
going to try to do this in a way which is *consistent* between the two
worlds;   i.e. in such a way that the synonymies we establish do not
lead us into contradictions between the properties of the formal system and those of the natural system we have forced the formal system
to name. In short, we want our relations between formal and natural
systems to be like the one Goethe postulated as between the genius
and Nature: what the one promises, the other surely redeems.

Another way to characterize what we are trying to do here is the
following: we seek to *encode* natural systems into formal ones in a
way which is consistent, in the above sense. Via such an encoding,
if we are successful, the inferences or theorems we can elicit
within these formal systems become *predictions* about the natural
systems we have encoded into them;   consistency then means that
these predictions will be *verified* in the natural world when appropriately *decoded* into linkage relations in that world. And as we
shall see, once such a relation between natural and formal systems
has been established, a host of other important relations will
follow of themselves;   relations which will allow us to speak precisely about analogy, similarity, metaphor, complexity, and a spectrum of similar concepts.

If we successfully accomplish the establishment of a relation of
this kind between a particular natural system and some formal system,
then we will obtain thereby a composite structure whose character is
crudely indicated in Fig. 2.3.1 below:

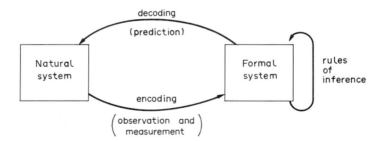

Fig. 2.3.1.

In this Figure, the arrows labelled "encoding" and "decoding" represent correspondences between the observables and linkages comprising the natural system and symbols or propositions belonging to
the formal system. Linkages between these observables are also
encoded into relations between the corresponding propositions in
the formal system. As we noted earlier, the rules of inference of
the formal system, by means of which we can establish new propositions of that system as implications, must be re-interpreted
(or decoded) in the form of specific assertions pertaining to the
observables and linkages of the natural system;   these are the
predictions. If the assertions *decoded* in this fashion are *verified*
by observation;   or what is the same thing, if the observed behavior

of the natural system *encodes* into the same propositions as those obtained from the inferential rules of the formal system, we shall say that (to that extent) the relation between the two systems which we have established, and which is diagrammed in Fig. 2.3.1, is a *modelling relation*. Under these circumstances, we shall also say that the formal system of Fig. 2.3.1, modulo the encoding and decoding rules in question, is a model of the natural system to which it is related by those rules.

Let us consider the situation we have described in somewhat more detail. We saw in the preceding chapter that rules of inference relating propositions in a formal system cannot be applied arbitrarily, but only to propositions of a definite form or character. If we are going to apply our rules of inference in accordance with the diagram of Fig. 2.3.1, then specific aspects of the natural system must code propositions to which they can be applied. In the broadest terms, the aspects so encoded can be called *states* of the natural system. A state of a natural system, then, is an aspect of it which encodes into a *hypothesis* in the associated formal system; i.e. into a proposition of that formal system which can be the basis for an inference. Speaking very informally, then, *a state embodies that information about a natural system which must be encoded in order for some kind of prediction about the system to be made.* It should be explicitly noted that, according to this definition, *the concept of state of a natural system is not meaningful apart from a specific encoding of it into some formal system.* For, as we are employing the term, a state comprises what needs to be known about a natural system in order for other features of that system to be determined. This in itself is somewhat a departure from ordinary usage, in which a state of a natural system is regarded as possessing an objective existence in the external world. It should be compared with our employment of the term "state" in Chapter 1.2 above; we will see subsequently, of course, that the two usages in fact coincide.

Let us now suppose that we have encoded a state of our natural system into a hypothesis of the associated formal system. What kind of inferences can we expect to draw from that hypothesis, and how will they look when they are decoded into explicit predictions?

We shall begin our discussion of this question by recalling our discussion of *time* and its relation to percepts. We pointed out that there were two different aspects of our time-sense, which we called simultaneity and precedence, which we impose upon percepts. We then *impute* similar properties to the qualities in the external world which generate these percepts. Accordingly, it is reasonable to organize assertions about natural systems (and in particular, the predictions generated from a model) in terms of temporal features.

We can then recognize three temporally different kinds of predictions: (a) predictions which are time-independent; (b) predictions which relate different qualities of our system at the same instant of time; and (c) predictions which relate qualities of our system at different instants of time. Predictions of the first type are those which are unrelated to the manner in which time itself is encoded into our formal system. Typically, they express relations or linkages between qualities which play an essential role in the recognition of the identity of the natural system with which we are dealing, and hence which *cannot* change, without our perception that our original system has been replaced by a new or different system. To anticipate subsequent discussion somewhat, qualities of this type are exemplified by constitutive parameters; hence a time-independent prediction would typically take the form of a linkage between such constitutive parameters.

Almost by definition, all time-dependent qualities pertaining to our natural system can change without our perceiving that our system has been replaced by another. Hence, the two kinds of time-dependent predictions we might expect to make on the basis of a model will necessarily pertain to such qualities.

Predictions of the second type itemized above will generally be of the following form: if a state of our natural system at a given instant of time is specified, then some other quality pertaining to the system *at the same instant* may be inferred. That is, predictions of this type will *express linkages between system qualities which pertain to a specific instant of time*, and which are simultaneously expressed at that instant.

Predictions of the third type will generally be of the form: if the state of our natural system at a particular instant is specified, then some other quality pertaining to the system *at some other instant* may be inferred. Thus, predictions of this type *express linkages between qualities which pertain to different instants of time*. In particular, we may be interested in inferences which link *states* at a given instant to states at other instants. As we shall see, linkages of this type essentially constitute the dynamical laws of the system.

It will be noted that all three types of inferences, and the predictions about a natural system which may be decoded from them, express *linkage* relations between system qualities. The corresponding inferential rules in the formal system which decode into these linkage relations are what are ususally called *system laws* of the natural system. It is crucial to note that, as was the case with the concept of state, the concept of system laws is meaningless apart from a specific encoding and decoding of our natural system into a formal one; the system laws belong to the formal system, and are in effect *imputed* to the associated natural system exactly by virtue of the encoding itself.

We shall see many specific examples of all of these ideas, in a broad spectrum of contexts, in Chapter 3 below; therefore we shall not pause to give examples here. However, the reader should at this point look back at the treatment of the reactive paradigm provided in Chapter 1.2 above, to gain an idea of just how much had to be tacitly assumed in writing down even the first line of that development.

We are now going to elaborate a number of important variations on the basic theme of the modelling relations embodied in Fig. 2.3.1 above. As we shall see, these variations represent the essential features of some of the most important (and hence perhaps, the most abused) concepts in theoretical science. They will all be of central importance to us in the developments of the subsequent chapters.

The first of these variations is represented in diagrammatic form in Fig. 2.3.2 below. In this situation, we have two natural systems, which we shall denote by N_1, N_2, encoded into the same formal system F, via particular encodings E_1, E_2, respectively.

The specific properties of the situation we have diagrammed depends

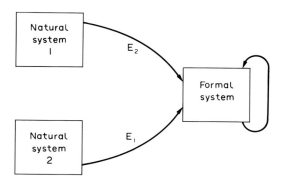

Fig. 2.3.2.

intuitively on the degree of "overlap" in F between the set $E_1(N_1)$
of propositions which encode qualities of N_1, and the set $E_2(N_2)$ of
propositions which encode qualities of N_2. Clearly, if the *same*
proposition of F simultaneously encodes a quality of N_1 and a quality
of N_2, *we may thereby establish a relation between* N_1 *and* N_2. It is
convenient for us to recognize three cases:

Case A1: $E_1(N_1) = E_2(N_2)$

In this case, every proposition of F which encodes a quality of N_1
also encodes a quality of N_2, and conversely. Utilizing this fact,
we may in effect construct a "dictionary", which allows us to *name*
every quality of N_1 by that quality of N_2 which encodes into the
same proposition in F; and conversely, every quality of N_2 can be
named by a corresponding quality in N_1. Since by definition of the
modelling relation itself, the system laws imputed to N_1 and N_2 are
also the same, this dictionary also allows us to decode the inferences
in F into corresponding propositions about N_1 and N_2 respectively.
In this case, we can say that *the natural systems* N_1 *and* N_2 *share a*
common model. Alternatively, we shall say that N_1 and N_2 are *anal-*
ogous systems, or analogs.[1] As usual, we point out explicitly that
this concept of analogy is only meaningful with respect to a particular choice of the encodings E_1, E_2 into a common formal system
F. A moment's reflection will reveal that our use of the term
"analog" is a straightforward generalization of its employment in
the term "analog computer". It must also be emphasized that the
relation of analogy is a relation between *natural systems*; it is a

relation established precisely when these natural systems share a common encoding into the same formal system. In this sense, it is different in character from the modelling relation, which (as we have defined it) is a relation between a natural system and a formal system. Despite this, we shall often abuse language, and say that N_1 and N_2 are *models of each other*; this is a usage which is ubiquitous in the literature, and can really cause no confusion. It should be noted that our "dictionary" relating corresponding qualities of analogous systems behaves like a *linkage* between them; but the origin of such a linkage has its roots in the formal system F and in the properties of the encodings E_1, E_2; it does *not* reside in the natural systems N_1, N_2 themselves.

Case A2: $E_1(N_1) \subset E_2(N_2)$

This case differs from the previous one in that, while every proposition of F which encodes a quality of N_1 also encodes a corresponding property of N_2, the converse is not true. Thus if we establish a "dictionary" between the qualities of N_1 and N_2 put into correspondence by the respective encodings, we find that every quality of N_1 corresponds to some quality of N_2, but not conversely. That is, there will be qualities of N_2 which do not correspond in this fashion to any qualities in N_1.

Let N_2' denote those qualities of N_2 which can be put in correspondence with qualities of N_1 under these circumstances. If we restrict attention to just N_2', then we see that N_1 and N_2' are analogs, in the sense defined above. If we say that N_2' defines a *subsystem* of N_2, then the case we are discussing characterizes the situation in which N_1 and N_2 are not directly analogs, but in which N_2 *contains a subsystem analogous to* N_1. By abuse of language, we can say further that N_2 *contains a subsystem* N_2' *which is a model of* N_1.

Of course, if it should be the case that $E_2(N_2) \subset E_1(N_1)$, we may repeat the above argument, and say that N_1 possesses a subsystem N_1' which is analogous to, or a model of, N_2.

Case A3: $E_1(N_1) \cap E_2(N_2) \neq \emptyset$

We assume here that neither of the sets $E_1(N_1)$, $E_2(N_2)$ of encoded propositions is contained in the other, but that their intersection is non-empty. In this case, an application of the above argument leads us to define subsystems N_1' of N_1, and N_2' of N_2, which can be put into correspondence by virtue of their coding into the same proposition of F. In this case, then, we may say that the natural systems N_1, N_2 possess *subsystems* which are analogous, or which are models of each other.

There is of course a fourth possibility arising from the diagram in Fig. 2.2.3; namely $E_1(N_1) \cap E_2(N_2) = \emptyset$. But this possibility is uninteresting, in that the encodings E_1, E_2 allow us to establish no relation between N_1 and N_2.

Now let us consider a further variation on our basic theme, which generalizes the above discussion in a significant way. Let us consider the situation diagrammed in Fig. 2.3.3 below:

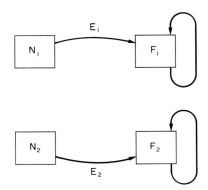

Fig. 2.3.3.

Here the natural systems N_1, N_2 encode into *different* formal systems F_1, F_2 respectively. We shall now attempt to establish relations between N_1 and N_2 on the basis of *mathematical* relations which may exist between the corresponding *formal* systems F_1, F_2, respectively.

Here again, it will be convenient to recognize a number of distinct cases, which are parallel to those just considered.

Case B1: $E_1(N_1)$ and $E_2(N_2)$ are *isomorphic*

In this case, there is a structure-preserving mapping between the sets of encoded propositions, which is one-to-one and onto. Since we are dealing here with formal systems, this mapping is a definite mathematical object, and can be discussed as such. By "structure-preserving", we mean here that this mapping can be extended in a unique way to all inferences in F_1, F_2 which can be obtained from $E_1(N_1)$, $E_2(N_2)$ respectively.

Under these circumstances, we can once again construct a dictionary between the qualities of N_1 and those of N_2, by putting qualities into correspondence whose encodings are images of one another under the isomorphism established between $E_1(N_1)$ and $E_2(N_2)$. This dictionary, and the fact that the system laws in both cases are also isomorphic, allows us to establish a relation between N_1 and N_2 which has all the properties of analogy defined previously. We shall call this relation an *extended analogy*, or, when no confusion is possible, simply an analogy, between the natural systems involved. It should be noted explicitly that the dictionary through which an extended analogy is established depends on the *choice* of isomorphism between $E_1(N_1)$ and $E_2(N_2)$.

Case B2: $E_1(N_1)$ is isomorphic to a subset of $E_2(N_2)$

This case is, of course, analogous to Case A2 above. As in that case, we can establish our dictionary between N_1 and a subsystem N_2' of N_2, and thereby establish a relation of extended analogy between N_1 and N_2'. It is clear that all aspects of our discussion of Case A2 also apply here. Likewise, we have

Case B3: A subset of $E_1(N_1)$ is isomorphic to a subset of $E_2(N_2)$

This case is the analog of Case A3 above, we can establish an extended analogy between subsystems N_1' of N_1 and N_2' of N_2 in the obvious fashion.

There is a final case to be considered before leaving the situation diagrammed in Fig. 2.3.3, which should be mentioned at this time, but about which we will not be able to be very precise until somewhat later. This is the circumstance in which the formal systems F_1, F_2 of that diagram satisfy some more general mathematical relation than that embodied in the existence of a structure-preserving mapping between them. As we shall see subsequently, such a relation will typically involve the satisfaction of some general criterion according to which formal systems may be classified; as for instance that F_1, F_2 are both "finite-dimensional" or "finitely generated" in some sense, but without any more detailed relationship which might be embodied in the existence of a structure-preserving mapping between them. In such a circumstance, we cannot establish a detailed dictionary relating qualities of the associated natural systems N_1, N_2. However, we can utilize the fact that F_1 and F_2 are related in some more general sense, and hence are to be counted as alike in that sense, to *impute* a corresponding relation to N_1, N_2 themselves. The situation we are describing will provide the basis for saying that N_1 is a *metaphor* for N_2, in the sense that *their models share*

some common general property. Subsequently we shall see many
examples of such metaphors, as for instance in the assertion that
open systems are metaphors for biological developmental processes.
This concept of metaphor will be important to us, but we will leave
the more detailed discussion for subsequent chapters.

So far, we have considered situations in which different natural
systems can be encoded into the same formal system, or into systems
between which some mathematical relation can be established. We
will now turn to the dual situation, in which the same natural system can be encoded into two (or more) formal systems; this situation
is diagrammed in Fig. 2.3.4 below:

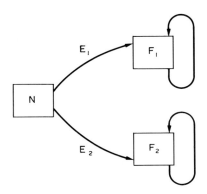

Fig. 2.3.4.

We will now take up the important question of the extent to which a
mathematical relation can be established between the *formal* systems
F_1 and F_2, simply by virtue of the fact that the same natural system
N can be encoded into both of them. Such a relation would essentially embody a *correspondence principle* between the encodings.

In a sense, the diagram of Fig. 2.3.4 can be regarded as a variant
of that shown in Fig. 2.3.3, in which we put both N_1 and N_2 equal
to N. Indeed, if we consider the simplest situation, in which
exactly the same variates of N are encoded into F_1 and F_2 (via the
encodings E_1 and E_2 respectively), then it is easy to see that we
are indeed in the situation previously discussed, and in fact essentially in the Case B1. However, we shall ignore this relatively
trivial situation, and instead consider what happens when *different
qualities* of N are encoded into F_1 and F_2. We are now in a quite
different situation from that diagrammed in Fig. 2.3.3, for the
following reason: we supposed that N_1 and N_2 represent *different*
natural systems; this means that their respective qualities are
generally unlinked. In Fig. 2.3.4, on the other hand, even though
we may generally encode different qualities of N into different
formal systems F_1, F_2, these qualities are linked in N through the
hypothesis that they pertain to the *same* system. However, the

linkages between these differently encoded qualities are themselves encoded neither in F_1 nor in F_2. Thus the question we are now posing is the following: *to what extent can these uncoded linkages manifest themselves in the form of purely mathematical relations between F_1 and F_2?* It will be seen that this is the inverse of the former cases, in which we *posited* a mathematical relation between F_1 and F_2, and *imputed* it to the natural systems encoded into them. Stated otherwise: whereas we formerly sought a relation between natural systems through a mathematical relation between their encodings, we presently seek a mathematical relation between encodings, arising from uncoded linkages between families of differently encoded qualities.

There are again a number of cases which must be considered separately.

Case C1

Let us suppose that we can establish a mapping of F_1, say, into F_2. That is, every proposition of F_1 can be associated with a unique proposition of F_2, but we do not suppose that the reverse is the case. Then every quality of N encoded into F_1 can thereby be associated with another quality of N, encoded into F_2, but not conversely. There is thus an important sense in which the encoding F_1 is *redundant*; every quality encoded into F_1 can be recaptured from the encoding of apparently different qualities into F_2. In this case, we would say intuitively that F_2 provides the more comprehensive formal description of N, and in fact that the encoding into F_1 can be *reduced* to the encoding into F_2.

The fundamental importance of this situation lies in its relation to *reductionism* as a basic scientific principle.[2] Reductionism asserts essentially that there is a universal way of encoding an arbitrary natural system, such that *every other encoding* is reducible to it in the above sense. It must be stressed, and it is clear from the above discussion, that reductionism involves a *mathematical* relation between certain formal systems, into which natural systems are encoded. In order for reductionism in this sense to be established as a *valid* scientific principle, the following data must be given: (a) a recipe, or algorithm, for producing the universal encoding for any given natural system N; (b) a *mathematical* proof that every other coding can be effectively mapped into the universal one. Needless to say, no arguments bearing on these matters have ever been forthcoming, and as we shall see abundantly, there are good reasons to suppose that the reductionistic principle is in fact false. Furthermore, in a purely practical sense, an attempt to obtain specific inferences about qualities of a given natural system N by detouring through a universal description would not be of much value in any case. Nevertheless, it is important to determine in what circumstances a given encoding $E_1(N)$ can be reduced to another one $E_2(N)$. For such a reduction implies important linkages between the qualities encoded thereby; linkages which as we noted above are themselves not explicitly encoded by either E_1 or E_2.

Case C2

Here we shall suppose that a mapping can be established from a *subset* of F_1 to a *subset* of F_2, in such a way that certain qualities of N encoded into $E_1(N_1)$ can be related to corresponding qualities encoded into $E_2(N_2)$. The mapping itself, of course, establishes a logical relation between the encodings, but one which does not hold universally. Thus in this case we may say that a *partial* reduction is possible, but one of limited applicability. As we shall see, when we leave the domain in which such a partial reduction is valid, the two encodings become logically independent; or what is the same thing, the linkage between the qualities in N which are encoded thereby is broken. Depending on the viewpoint which is taken, such a departure from the domain in which reduction is valid will appear as a *bifurcation*, or as an *emergence phenomenon*; i.e. the generation of an emergent novelty. We will develop explicit examples of these situations subsequently.

Case C3

In this case, no mathematical relation can be established between F_1 and F_2. Thus, these encodings are inadequate in principle to represent any linkages in N between the families or qualities encoded into them. Into this class, we would argue, fall the various *complementarities* postulated by Bohr in connection with microphysical phenomena. Here again, it must be stressed that it is the mathematical character of the encodings which determines whether or not relations between them can be effectively established; in this sense, complementarity is entirely a property of formal systems, and not of natural ones.

One further aspect of the basic diagram of Fig. 2.3.4 may be mentioned briefly here. We are subsequently going to relate our capacity to produce independent encodings of a given natural system N with the *complexity*[3] of N. Roughly speaking, the more such encodings we can produce, the more complex we will regard the system N. Thus, contrary to traditional views regarding system complexity, we do not treat complexity as a property of some particular encoding, and hence identifiable with a mathematical property of a formal system (such as dimensionality, number of generators, or the like). Nor is complexity entirely an objective property of N, in the sense of being itself a directly perceptible quality, which can be measured by a meter. Rather, complexity pertains at least as much to *us as observers* as it does to N; it reflects *our ability to interact with* N in such a way as to make its qualities visible to us. Intuitively speaking, if N is such that we can interact with it in only a few ways, there will be correspondingly few distinct encodings we can make of the qualities which we perceive thereby, and N will appear to us as a *simple* system; if N is such that we can interact with it in many ways, we will be able to produce correspondingly many distinct encodings, and we will correspondingly regard N as complex. It must be recognized that we are speaking here entirely of complexity as an attribute of *natural* systems; the same word (complexity) may, and often is, used to describe some attribute of a *formal* system. But this involves quite a different concept, with which we are not presently concerned. We shall also return to these ideas in more detail in subsequent chapters.

Let us turn now to an important re-interpretation of the various
situations we have discussed above. We have so far taken the viewpoint that the modelling relation exemplified in Fig. 2.3.1 involves
the encoding of a given natural system N into an appropriate formal
system F, through an identification of the names of qualities of N
with symbols and propositions in F. That is, we have supposed that
we *start* from a given natural system whose qualities have been directly perceived in some way, and that the encoding is established
from N *to* F. There are many important situations, however, in which
the same diagram is established from precisely the opposite point of
view. Namely, suppose we want to *build*, or create, a natural system
N, in such a way that N possesses qualities linked to one another in
the same way as certain propositions in some formal system F. In
other words, we want the system laws characterizing such a system N
to represent, or *realize*, rules of inference in F. This is, of
course, the problem faced by an engineer or an architect who must
design a physical system to meet given specifications. He invariably
proceeds by creating first a *formal system*, a blueprint, or plan,
according to which his system N will actually be built. The relation
between the system N so constructed, and the plan from which it is
constructed, is precisely the modelling relation of Fig. 2.3.1, but
now the relation is generated *in the opposite direction* from that
considered above.[4] From this we see that the analytic activities
of a scientist seeking to understand a particular unknown system,
and the synthetic activities of an engineer seeking to fabricate a
system possessing particular qualities, are in an important sense
inverses of one another. When we speak of the activities of the
scientist, we shall regard the modelling relations so established
in terms of the *encoding* of a natural system into a formal one;
when we speak of the synthetic activities of the engineer, we shall
say that the natural system N in question is a *realization* of the
formal system F, which constitutes the plan. Using this latter
terminology, then, we can re-interpret the various diagrams presented
above; for instance, we can say that two natural systems N_1, N_2 are
analogs precisely to the extent that they are *alternate realizations*
of the same formal system F. Likewise, in the situation diagrammed
in Fig. 2.3.4, we can say that the same natural system N can simultaneously realize two distinct formal systems; the complexity of N
thus can be regarded as the number of distinct formal systems which
we perceive that N can simultaneously realize. We shall consider
these ideas also in more detail in the course of our subsequent
exposition.

To conclude these introductory heuristic remarks regarding the
modelling relation, let us return again to the situations diagrammed
in Figs 2.3.2 and 2.3.3 above. We saw in our discussion of those
diagrams that the modelling relation is one established between a
natural system N and a formal system F through a suitable encoding
of qualities of N into symbols and propositions in F. We also saw
that when two distinct natural systems N_1, N_2 can be appropriately
encoded into the same formal system, it was meaningful to speak of
a relation of *analogy* as being established between the natural systems N_1 and N_2 themselves. We wish to pursue a few corollaries of
these ideas.

The main property of a modelling relation, which we shall exploit
relentlessly in what follows, is this: once such a relation has
been established (or posited) between a natural system N and a
formal system F, *we can learn about* N *by studying* F; a patently
different system. Likewise, once an analogy relation has been

established between two natural systems N_1 and N_2, *we can learn about one of them by studying the other*. In this form, both model-ling and analogy have played perhaps the fundamental role in both theoretical and experimental science, as well as a dominant role in every human being's daily life. However, many experimental scien-tists find it counter-intuitive, and therefore somehow outrageous, to claim to be learning about a particular natural system N_1 by studying a different system N_2, or by studying some formal system F, which is of a fundamentally different character from N_1. To them, it is self-evident that the only way to learn about N_1 is to study N_1; any other approach is at best misguided and at worst fraudulent. It is perhaps worthwhile, therefore, to discuss this attitude somewhat fully.

It is not without irony that the empiricist's aversion to models finds its nourishment in the same soil from which our concept of the modelling relation itself sprang. For they are both products of the development which culminated in Newton's *Principia*. In that epic work, whose grandeur and sweep created reverberations which still permeate so much of today's thought, it was argued that a few simple formal laws could account for the behavior of all systems of material particles, from galaxies to atoms. We have sketched a little of this development in Chaper 1.2 above. Newton also provided the technical tools required for these purposes, with his creation of the differen-tial and integral calculus; i.e. he also provided the formal basis for encoding the qualities of particulate systems, and drawing con-clusions or inferences pertaining to those systems from the system laws. Not only was the entire Newtonian edifice one grand model in itself, but it provided a recipe for establishing a model of *any* particulate system. To set this machinery in motion for any specific system, all that was needed was (a) a specification of the forces acting on the system (i.e. an encoding of the system laws), and (b) a knowledge of initial conditions.

The universality of the Newtonian scheme rests on the extent to which we can regard *any* natural system as being composed of material particles. If we believe that any system can in fact be resolved into such particles, then the Newtonian paradigm can always be in-voked, and the corresponding machinery of encoding and prediction set in motion. The belief that this is always possible (and more than this, is always necessary and sufficient) is the motivating force behind the concept of reductionism, which was mentioned earlier.

Now the determination of system laws, and even more, the specification of initial conditions, which are the prerequisites for the application of the Newtonian paradigm, are not themselves conceptual or theoreti-cal questions; they are empirical problems, to be settled by obser-vation and measurement, carried out on the specific system of interest. Thus, hand in hand with the grandest of conceptual schemes we necess-arily find the concomitant growth of empiricism and reductionism; two thankless offspring which incessantly threaten to devour that which gave them birth. For, once separated from the conceptual framework which originally endowed them with meaning and significance, they become in fact antithetical to that framework. Pursued in isolation, empiricism must come to claim (a) that measurement and observation are ends in themselves; (b) that measurement and obser-vation pertain only to extremely limited and narrow families of interactions which we can generate in the here-and-now; (c) and that, finally, whatever is not the result of measurement and observation in this narrow sense *does not exist*, and ergo cannot be part of science.

We can now begin to understand why the theoretical concept of a model, which has as its essential ingredient a freely posited formal system, is so profoundly alienating to those reared in an exlusively empirical tradition. This alienation can sometimes take bizarre and even sinister forms. Let us ponder, for example, the growth of what was called *Deutsche Physik*, which accompanied the rise of National Socialism in Germany not so very long ago.[5] At root, this was simply a rebellion on the part of some experimental physicists against a threatening new theoretical framework for physics (especially as embodied in general relativity); the ugly racial overtones of this movement were simply an indication of how desperate its leaders had become in the face of such a challenge. They were reduced to arguing that "those who studied equations instead of nature" were traitors to their abstract ideal of science; that the true scientist could only be an experimenter who developed a kind of mystic rapport with nature through direct interaction with it. Similarly, the phenomenon now called Lysenkoism in the Soviet Union was associated with a phobia against theoretical developments in biology, especially in genetics.[6] These are admittedly extreme situations, but they are in fact the logical consequences of equating science with empiricism (which in itself, it should be noted, involves a model).

Although perhaps most empirical scientists would dissociate themselves from such aberrations, they tend to share the disquiet which gave rise to them. They regard the basic features of the modelling relation, and the idea that we can learn about one system by studying another, as a reversion to magic; to the idea that one can divine properties of the world through symbols and talismans. Perhaps it must inevitably seem so to those who think that science is done when qualities are simply named (as meter readings) and tabulated. But in fact, that is the point at which science only begins.

From this kind of acrimony and strife, one might suppose that the modelling relation is something arcane and rare. We have already seen that this is not so; that indeed the modelling relation is a ubiquitous characteristic of everyday life as well as of science. But we have not yet indicated just how widespread it is. To do so, and at the same time to give specific instances of the situations sketched abstractly in our discussion so far, we will now turn to developing such instances, as they appear in many fields. We may in fact regard such instances as *existence proofs*, showing that the various situations we have diagrammed above are not vacuous. This will be the primary task of the chapters in Section 3 to follow.

REFERENCES AND NOTES

1. Aside from the special case of "dynamical similarity", which we shall consider at some length in 3.3 (especially Example 5), there has still been no systematic study of the circumstances under which two different systems are analogous. Our treatment here is based on ideas first expounded in a paper of the author's: Rosen, R., *Bull. Math. Biophys.* 30, 481-492 (1968).

2. See also 3.6 below.

3. See 5.7 below.

4. The relation between model and realization is discussed more fully in 3.1.

5. For a good discussion of the philosophical issues involved here,
    see
    Beyerchen, A. D., *Scientists Under Hitler*.   Yale University
        Press (1977).

6. The two definitive treatments of Lysenkoism are
    Medvedev, Zh. A., *The Rise and Fall of T. D. Lysenko*.   Columbia
        University Press (1969).
    Joravsky, D., *The Lysenko Affair*.   Harvard University Press
        (1970).
    These three books make fascinating reading, especially when
    read concurrently.

CHAPTER 3

The Modelling Relation

3.1 The Modelling Relation within Mathematics

We developed the modelling relation in the preceding chapter as a
relation between a natural system and a formal system. This relation
was established through an appropriate encoding of the qualities of
the natural system into the propositions of the formal system, in
such a way that the inferential structure of the latter correspond
to the system laws of the former.

As it happens, an analogous relation to the modelling relation can
be carried out entirely within the universe of formal systems. This
situation is, for example, tacitly embodied on the diagram of Fig.
2.3.4 above, in which we sought to relate two formal systems F_1, F_2
by virtue of the fact that they both encoded qualities pertaining to
the same natural system N. The various cases discussed under that
heading involved encodings between formal systems, and when accomplished, result in a diagram very similar in character to that
displayed in Fig. 2.3.1. The primary difference between these two
situations is, of course, that we must now consider encodings between
two *formal* systems which preserve the *inferential* structures in the
two systems, so that a theorem of the first corresponds to a theorem
of the second.

More precisely, an encoding of one formal system into another can
now itself be represented by a precise mathematical object, namely,
a specific mapping $\Phi : F_1 \to F_2$. In the analogous situation establishing a modelling relation, the encoding of N into F could not be
regarded as a mapping, because a natural system is not itself a
formal object. But in the present case, we can now formulate the
basic structure-preserving feature of the encodings we seek by saying
precisely that, if p is a theorem in F_1, then $\Phi(p)$ is a theorem in
F_2.

It is thus appropriate to begin our consideration of modelling relations by examining this analogous situation arising within mathematics itself. This will have the advantage that the relation of
"system" to "model" becomes far more transparent; the objects in a
formal system possess only the properties endowed to them through
their definitions, and are not an incompletely specified family of
qualities or observables. Moreover, very often in science we proceed

by in effect making a model of a model, through formal manipulations
of a formal system F in which some natural system has already been
encoded. Such formal manipulations lead precisely to a situation of
the type we will be considering.

Our first examples will be drawn from geometry. Until the beginning
of the last century, "geometry" meant the geometry of Euclid. As
was mentioned previously, Euclid provided the earliest and most
influential example of a mathematical theory as a system of axioms,
to which we have alluded briefly in 2.2 above. All the examples to
be considered now arose historically out of deeper investigations
into the Euclidean system. In our first example, we shall consider
the familiar arithmetization (or perhaps more accurately, algebraization) of geometry by Descartes, which was first published in 1637.

EXAMPLE 1: ANALYTIC GEOMETRY

The axiom system provided by Euclid involved both general rules of
inference, by which theorems could be proved, and specifically geometric postulates which, in effect, defined the properties of such
geometric objects as points, lines, planes and the like. Since
these axioms determines the entire geometry, it is necessary to
formulate them explicitly, and then see how they can be encoded into
another mathematical context.

The Euclidean axioms have been the subject of exhaustive study,
perhaps most especially during the last half of the nineteenth
century. Probably the most satisfactory reformulation of these
axioms was that of David Hilbert, who in his monumental *Grundlagen
der Geometrie* (first published in 1899) sought to place all geometric
investigations into a common perspective. His reformulation involved
eleven axioms, divided into five classes, which for plane geometry
(to which we restrict ourselves here) may be set down as follows:

(a) *Axioms of Incidence*

1. Any pair of points lie on exactly one straight line.
2. At least two points lie on every line.
3. Given any straight line, there is a point not lying on that line.

(b) *Axioms of Order*

1. If three points lie on a line, one of them is between the other
two.
2. Given any two points on a line, there is another point of the
line lying between them.
3. A straight line divides the plane into two disjoint half-planes.

(c) *Axioms of Congruence*

1. An admissible motion of the plane carries lines onto lines.
2. Motions can be composed; i.e. two motions carried out successively produce the same result as a uniquely determined single motion,
their composite.
3. Any motion is a composition of a translation, a rotation and a
reflection about a line.

(d) *Axiom of Continuity*

Let L be a line. Let P_1, P_2, ..., P_n, ... be any sequence of points such that P_{i+1} is between P_i and P_{i+2} for every i. If there is a point A of L such that for no i A between P_i and P_{i+1}, then there is a uniquely determined point B which also possesses this property, but if B' is any point for which B is between B' and A, then there is a P_i such that B' is between P_i and P_{i+1}.

(e) *Euclidean Axiom of Parallels*

Given a point P not lying on a line L, there is exactly one straight line through P which does not intersect L.

On the basis of these axioms, Hilbert showed that all of Euclidean geometry could be built up. Let us note that the various specific geometric terms, such as point, line, plane, between, etc., are considered as *undefined* (or more precisely, they possess only the properties endowed to them by the axioms).

We are now going to encode this system in another. This second system relies basically on the properties of the real number system, which can also themselves be developed axiomatically, but which we shall assume known (since our main purpose here is to establish the encoding, and not to do either geometry or arithmetic). To establish the encoding, we shall give the undefined terms in the above axioms new names, and then show briefly that the axioms, which define the properties of the undefined terms, are satisfied.

The new terminology we introduce is as follows:

    point = ordered pair (a, b) of real numbers

    plane = set of all ordered pairs of real numbers

    line = set of all pairs (x, y) satisfying the condition
            $ax + by + c = 0$, where a, b, c are any three real numbers

From just this, it is a matter of straightforward verification that the Axioms of Incidence are satisfied.

Further, let (a_1, b_1), (a_2, b_2), (a_3, b_3) be three points on a line. We define the second to be *between* the other two if and only if the inequalities

$$a_1 < a_2 < a_3,$$

$$b_1 < b_2 < b_3$$

are satisfied. Then the Axioms of Order can be verified.

To verify the Axioms of congruence, we must define the admissible motions in terms of ordered pairs. We will do this by expressing a motion as a mapping of the set of all ordered pairs onto itself; it is thus sufficient to specify what the motion does to each particular pair (x, y). If we define the motions as follows:

    (a) *Translation:* $(x, y) \rightarrow (x+h, y+k)$ for some fixed numbers h, k.

(b) *Rotation:* $(x, y) \to (ax+by, -bx+ay)$, where a, b are fixed
numbers such that $a^2+b^2 = 1$.

(c) *Reflection:* $(x, y) \to (-x + 2a, -y + 2b)$ where (a, b) is a
fixed point.

then it can be verified that the Axioms of Congruence are satisfied.
The Axiom of Continuity is also verified directly from properties of
real numbers.

Finally, if we are given a line, say in the form $y = mx + b$, and a
point (ξ, η) not on this line, consider the line

$$y = mx + (\eta - m\xi).$$

It is immediately verified that this is a unique line which contains
the point (ξ, η) and which has no point in common with the given
line. Thus the Euclidean Axiom of Parallels is verified.

The Cartesian algebraization of Euclidean geometry which we have
just described was one of the great syntheses of mathematics. It
showed that every geometric proposition had an algebraic counterpart. It also showed how geometry itself needed to be extended, if
the converse was to be true. We have become so accustomed to this
synthesis that its properties have become commonplace, and its
initial impact hard for us to imagine. But in fact, it was one of
the supreme intellectual achievements; one which was indispensable
for everything that followed. For instance, it is hard to imagine
how Newton could have developed the calculus had not Descartes first
established his encoding of geometry into algebra and arithmetic.

EXAMPLE 2: NON-EUCLIDEAN GEOMETRY[1]

Let us preface our discussion with a few historical remarks. The
encodings we are going to develop arose from consideration of the
Euclidean Axiom of Parallels cited above. Already in ancient times,
it was recognized that this axiom was of a different character than
the others. Although no one doubted it was in some sense true, it
seemed to lack the character of "self-evidence" which Euclid claimed
for his axioms and postulates. In particular, its verification in
any particular case involved a potentially infinite process; two
given lines might have the property that, after being prolonged an
arbitrarily long distance, they still had not met. But that fact
could not establish whether or not those lines were in fact parallel.
Thus it was felt in antiquity that the Axiom of Parallels should in
fact be a theorem inferable from the other axioms. Thus were born
the succession of attempts to "prove the Parallel Postulate".

By the early part of the nineteenth century, it finally had to be
admitted that these attempts had all failed. Most of these attempts
were direct; they attempted to establish a chain of inferences
from other Euclidean axioms to the Axiom of Parallels. But on close
examination, all these direct attempts made tacit use of propositions
equivalent to the Parallel Axiom itself, and hence were circular.
A number of attempts were of a different character; they proceeded
indirectly by assuming that the Parallel Axiom was false, and
endeavored to derive a logical contradiction. The best known of
these are associated with the names of Saccheri and Lambert. Finally,
after a great deal of effort had been expended, the possibility
gradually dawned that no logical contradiction could be derived in

this way; that the negation of the Parallel Axiom led to a body of
theorems which was logically consistent. The first publication of
this assertion was that of Lobatchevsky in 1826, although Gauss and
others had conceived of this possibility earlier. This was a sen-
sational claim, for it had long been believed that the geometry of
Euclid was the only "true" geometry. Moreover, the Cartesian
identification of Euclidean geometry with algebra which we have
just discussed was regarded as irrefutable evidence of at least the
logical consistency of Euclidean geometry.

The body of theorems obtained by postulating the negation of the
Parallel Axiom indeed seemed very peculiar. For instance, it was a
theorem that no two triangles could be similar; or that there were
no triangles of arbitrarily large area. However, there was no
logical inconsistency visible in these theorems; i.e. no case of a
theorem and its negation both being provable from these axioms. If
this is so, then (a) more than one geometry is *logically* possible,
and (b) it becomes an *empirical* question to decide which of the
logically possible geometries actually pertains to *physical* space.
This last assertion led, in a circuitous way, to the General Theory
of Relativity. But nearly one hundred years earlier, Lobatchevsky
was already suggesting astronomical observations as a test of this
question.

Now we have already seen in Chapter 2.2 above that the *consistency*
of a body of propositions, such as the one which constitutes the
geometry of Lobatchevsky, cannot be established from the perusal of
any finite sample, just as the parallelism or non-parallelism of a
pair of lines cannot be established by any limited prolongation of
them. Thus it could always be claimed that logical contradictions
were inherent in the "non-Euclidean" geometries; they simply had
not yet been discovered.

These hopes were laid to rest by the encodings we are now going to
describe. Namely, it was shown that, via such encodings, it was
possible to build a *model*[2] of the geometry of Lobatchevsky completely
within the confines of Euclidean geometry. These *models of non-
Euclidean geometry* in fact had the following profound consequences:
(a) they related the consistency of the non-Euclidean geometries to
the consistency of Euclidean geometry, in such a way that the former
could not be inconsistent without the latter at the same time being
inconsistent; this was the first important example of a *relative*
consistency proof; (b) they gave a concrete *meaning* to the "points",
"lines" and "planes" of non-Euclidean geometry; this was important
because it was clear that these terms could not be synonymous with
the traditional Euclidean usages; (c) at the same time, they
suggested that mathematics could, and perhaps should, be done
entirely in the abstract, devoid of *any* notion of meaning or interpretation; this paved the way for the position we described as
P-ist in Chapter 2.2 above, and which we shall take up again shortly.

The first model we shall describe is that of Beltrami, who showed
in 1868 that at least a portion of Lobatchevsky's non-Euclidean
geometry could be encoded into the intrinsic geometry of a surface
of constant negative curvature. The particular surface he used was
the *pseudosphere*, which is a surface of revolution obtained by
revolving a certain curve (called a tractrix) about its asymptote.
In turn, the tractrix is that curve defined by the following property: its tangent at any point P intersects the asymptote at a
point Q such that the segment PQ has constant length. Let us establish then the following encoding:

point   = point on the pseudosphere

line   = geodesic on the pseudosphere

motion = geodesic-preserving map of pseudosphere onto itself

All of the other undefined terms of Lobatchevskian geometry are
given their traditional Euclidean meanings, restricted to the
surface of the pseudosphere.

Then to every theorem of Lobatchevskian geometry there corresponds
a *fact* about the intrinsic geometry of the pseudosphere (or more
accurately, to every such theorem which pertains to a finite part
of the Lobatchevskian "plane"). What this encoding shows, then, is
that the non-Euclidean geometry of Lobatchevsky can be regarded as
an abstract version of the intrinsic geometry of the pseudosphere;
a geometry which itself exists in an entirely Euclidean setting.
More than this: as the curvature of the pseudosphere goes to zero,
the propositions of the Lobatchevsky geometry approach there Euclidean
counterpart in a certain well-defined sense; i.e. Euclidean geometry
can itself be regarded as a limiting case of the Lobatchevskian.

A more comprehensive *model* of this kind was developed by Felix Klein
in 1870;   Klein showed how to encompass the infinite Lobatchevskian
"plane" within the confines of Euclidean geometry. To develop
Klein's model, let us consider a circle in the ordinary Euclidean
plane. Let us agree to establish the following dictionary:

point   = interior point of this circle

line   = chord of this circle

motion = mapping of the circle onto itself, in such a way that
         chords are carried onto chords.

As examples of such motions, we may consider the ordinary rotations
of the circle;   these are the Lobatchevskian rotations also. The
translations are somewhat more complicated, and can best be described through reference to the Cartesian arithmetization of the
Euclidean plane. If we take our circle to be the unit circle in
the Euclidean plane, and establish a co-ordinate system in that
plane with the center of the circle as origin, then the set of
points interior to the circle are defined as those satisfying the
inequality $x^2 + y^2 < 1$. Now we define the transformation

$$x \rightarrow \frac{x + a}{1 + ax}$$

$$y \rightarrow \frac{y\sqrt{1 - a^2}}{1 + ax}$$

where a is any real number such that $-1 < a < 1$. It is an easy
exercise to verify that this transformation maps the interior of
the unit circle onto itself, and leaves the circumference of that
circle fixed. It is also readily verified that it maps chords onto
chords.

Finally, reflections of this circle are just ordinary reflections
in the Euclidean plane.

Once again, it can be readily shown that all the axioms of the
Lobatchevskian geometry are satisfied in this model. We may mention

that this model captures the infinite Lobatchevskian plane because
the definition of *distance* in the model is such that a segment of
unit length (in the Lobatchevskian sense) is such that its Euclidean
length shrinks to zero as the segment is translated towards the
boundary of the circle. We shall omit the details, but they can be
found in the references.

The Klein model shows explicitly that every theorem of Lobatchevskian
geometry expresses, via the above encoding, a fact of Euclidean
geometry within the chosen circle. In this case, the converse also
happens to be true; namely, every fact of Euclidean geometry within
the circle also corresponds to a theorem of Lobatchevskian geometry.
In this way, we can use Euclidean theorems to "predict" Lobatchevskian
theorems, thereby illustrating one of the fundamental properties of
the modelling relation, here entirely within a mathematical context.

The fascinating story of Euclidean models of non-Euclidean geometry
does not end here; we may describe one further ramification of it.
In 1904, Poincaré modified Klein's model, in the following way:
instead of interpreting the Lobatchevskian lines as chords of a
Euclidean circle, he interpreted them as arcs of circles intersecting
the given one perpendicularly. Further, instead of interpreting a
motion as a chord-preserving transformation of the circle onto itself,
he required instead that a motion be an arbitrary *conformal* mapping
(these are mappings which preserve Euclidean angles). Once again,
he could verify that all the Lobatchevskian axioms are satisfied in
this model. But it is well known that conformal mappings are also
intimately connected with properties of analytic functions of a
complex variable. Thus Poincaré could also encode important features
of the theory of functions of a complex variable into the same mathematical object for which Lobatchevskian geometry was also encoded.
In effect, then, he thus produced a diagram of the form

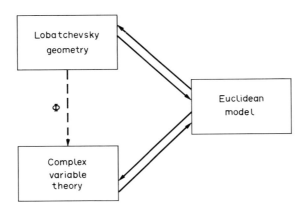

Fig. 3.1.1.

which should be compared to 2.3.4 above. In this case, Poincaré
was able to establish a partial correspondence, denoted by the
dotted arrow in the above figure, by means of which he was able to
re-interpret certain theorems of Lobatchevskian geometry as theorems

about analytic functions. He was thereby able to establish important
results in complex variable theory; results which apparently could
not be easily obtained *in any other way*. We obviously cannot enter
into the details here; nevertheless, the above story exhibits in a
remarkably graphic way the power of modelling relations, here developed entirely within mathematics itself. We invite the reader to
pursue the details independently.

EXAMPLE 3: FORMAL THEORIES AND THEIR MODELS[2,3]

The experience with non-Euclidean geometries, some of which was
described in the previous section, was but one of several profound
shocks experienced by mathematics in the last part of the nineteenth
century and the first part of the twentieth. Perhaps the worst of
these shocks was the discovery of the paradoxes generated by apparently legitimate employment of set-theoretic constructions; these
paradoxes precipitated the "foundation crisis" which is, in effect,
still going on. As we saw earlier, many mathematicians felt that
the only way to avoid such difficulties was to give up the idea that
mathematics was "about" anything; i.e. to give up all idea of interpretation of mathematical ideas, and to consider mathematics
itself as an entirely abstract game played with meaningless symbols
manipulated according to definite syntactical rules. This, together
with the Euclidean experience, led to an intense interest in formal
theories, and thence to the concept of *models* for such theories.
Since many of these ideas are direct generalizations of the preceding
examples, and since they are for many purposes important in their
own right, we will review them in more detail here.

Let us consider first what is meant by the term "formal". Initially,
any body of propositions in mathematics (and perhaps in all of science) is associated with a meaning or interpretation, which in general can be ultimately related back to corresponding percepts and
relations between percepts. These meanings or interpretations enter
tacitly into all arguments involving the propositions. The point is
to get these tacit meanings, which affect the manner in which propositions are manipulated, themselves explicitly expressed as propositions. Once this is done, the meanings are no longer necessary,
and can be forgotten. This process was perhaps best described by
Kleene (1952):

> This step (axiomatization) will not be finished until all the properties
> of the undefined or technical terms of the theory which matter for the
> deduction of theorems have been expressed by axioms. Then it should be
> possible to perform the deductions treating the technical terms as words
> in themselves without meaning. For to say that they have meanings
> necessary to the deductions of the theorems, other than what they derive
> from the axioms which govern them, amounts to saying that not all of
> their properties which matter for the deductions have been expressed by
> axioms. When the meanings of the technical terms are thus left out of
> account, we have arrived at the standpoint of formal axiomatics .....
> Since we have abstracted entirely from the content matter, leaving only
> the form, we say that the original theory has been *formalized*. In this
> structure, the theory is no longer a system of meaningful propositions,
> but one of sentences as sequences of words, which are in turn sequences
> of letters. We say by reference to the form alone which combinations
> of words are sentences, which sentences are axioms, and which sentences
> follow as immediate consequences from others.

This, of course, is the past $\mathfrak{p}$-ist position which we have considered
previously.

Now a formal theory of the type contemplated here turns out to possess a well-defined anatomy, very much like the anatomy of an organism, which we now proceed to describe in a systematic way.

Specifically, any formal theory $\mathfrak{I}$ must contain the following:

1. A class of elementary symbols called *variables*. This class is usually taken to be denumerably infinite, or at least indefinitely large.
2. Another class of elementary symbols called *constants*. Among this class, we discern two subclasses: (a) *Logical Constants*: These comprise the so-called sentential connectives ($V, \land, \tilde{}, \to$), the quantifiers ($\lor, \exists$), and the identity symbol ($=$). (b) *Non-Logical Constants*: These comprise the names of predicates and operations available in the theory. Each predicate and operation is associated with a number, its *rank*; thus a unary operation is of rank one; a binary operation is of rank two, and so on; likewise, a one-place predicate is of rank one, a two-place predicate is of rank two, etc. There are also symbols for "individual constants" as required.

Initially, we allow any string of constants to be an *expression*. Certain expressions are called *terms*; the simplest of these are the symbols for the individual constants; a compound term is obtained by combining simpler terms by means of an operation symbol of the appropriate rank. Likewise, the simplest *formulas* are obtained by combining terms through a predicate of appropriate rank; compound formulas are built from simpler ones through the sentential connectives and the quantifiers.

If a formula contains a variable (x, say) then the variable is called *bound* if it is quantified over; otherwise it is called *free*. A formula with no free variables is usually called a *sentence*.

3. A set L of sentences called *logical axioms*.
4. A distinguished set U of operations called *operations of inference* or *production rules*. This set U is invariably taken as finite. When these rules are applied to sentences, they yield new sentences. A sentence is called *logically provable* or *logically valid* if it can be obtained from the sentences of L by arbitrary application of the rules in U.

Within this framework, further structure is usually required:

5. A set A of sentences, which are regarded as *non-logical axioms*. A sentence is called *derivable* if it can be obtained from the sentences in A $\cup$ L by applications of the rules of U. If A is empty, so that the sentence is derivable from L alone, we are back in the previous situation. Sometimes a sentence derivable from A is called *valid*, or *provable*, from A.

As we see, a theory $\mathfrak{I}$ has a substantial amount of anatomy. Let us illustrate some of the anatomical units in the specific case of Euclidean geometry. A variable might be a symbol for "triangle"; a constant would be a symbol for a specific triangle. To say that two triangles are similar would express a two-place predicate. A logical axiom might be: "If equals are added to equals, the results are equal". A non-logical axiom would be one of the specific geometric postulates; e.g. "Any pair of points lie on exactly one straight line", or the Parallel Axiom itself. Thus, if we replace the Parallel Axiom by its negation, we obtain a different theory, with a different set of valid or provable sentences.

In the last analysis, a formal theory is determined by its set of valid sentences. It must be stressed here, as before, that this concept of validity depends on arbitrary choices of L, A and U; there is no way from inside the theory of making these choices in a unique way.

Let us now turn to the concept of a *model* of a theory J. Intuitively, the concept of a model is an attempt to re-introduce some notion of meaning or interpretation into the theory. Indeed, the choice of non-logical axioms in a theory J is generally made because we have some particular model in mind; the notion of validity in J, which as we saw was arbitrary from within J, can only be effectively made in this way.

In mathematics, we traditionally desire our models to themselves be mathematical objects, belonging to the universe $\mathbb{U}$ which was described in Chapter 2.2 above. We will proceed in two stages; the initial stage will be to construct a mathematical *realization* of a theory J, and then we shall say which of these realizations are in fact *models*.

Accordingly, let U be a set in $\mathbb{U}$; we shall call U the *universe* of the realization. Let us now enumerate all the non-logical constants of our theory J in some fashion; say as a sequence

$$c_1, \ c_2, \ \ldots, \ c_n, \ \ldots \ .$$

With each of these c_i, we are going to associate a structure involving U. Specifically, if c_i is an r-place predicate, we shall associate c_i with an r-ary relation on U; i.e. with a subset $R_i \subseteq U \times U \ldots \times U$, where there are r terms in this cartesian product. If c_i is an r-ary operation, we shall associate c_i with an r-ary operation on U; i.e. with a mapping

$$\Phi_i: \quad \underbrace{U \times U \ldots \times U}_{r \text{ times}} \to U.$$

On this basis, we can in the obvious way translate sentences from the theory J into propositions about this system Σ of relations and operations on U. A sentence of J is said to be satisfied in Σ if it translates into a true proposition.

The system Σ of relations and operations on a set U is thus what we shall call a realization of J. A realization becomes a *model* of J when the set of all valid sentences in J are satisfied in Σ. We remark once more that in practice, we generally choose a particular notion of validity in J because we want a certain mathematical system to be a model; formally, however, the above definition of model is always meaningful, however validity may be defined in J.

In any case, it is clear that once a modelling relation between J and Σ has been established, it has all of the properties of the modelling relation displayed in Figure 2.3.1 above. Specifically, any true proposition in Σ *decodes* into a valid proposition in J, and hence we may make *predictions* about from the properties of its model Σ. It should be noted that we may arrange matters so that a model of a formal theory J is another formal theory J'; in such a case we impart "meaning" to $\mathbb{J}$ through its encoding into the propositions of another formal theory. In this fashion, we come to some of the principal applications of the concept of a model in formal mathematics: the problem of consistency, which we have already mentioned several times in previous discussions.

In a formal theory, consistency means simply that no sentence and its negation can both be valid. It is a difficult, and indeed in some sense impossible, problem to establish the consistency of a formal theory which is at all mathematically interesting (e.g. such that the real number system can be a model). However, what the theory of models enables us to do is to establish *relative* consistency arguments: if Σ is a model of $\mathbb{J}$, then $\mathbb{J}$ can be consistent only if Σ is consistent. We have already seen specific examples of this kind of argument in our discussion of the models of Lobatchevskian geometry above. There is a very rich literature dealing with relative consistency arguments, which we urge the reader to consult for further examples.

Another principal application of the theory of models has been to a vexatious problem, already touched on above, which is generally called *decidability*. What is at issue here is the following problem: given an arbitrary sentence of a theory $\mathbb{J}$, is there some procedure for effectively deciding whether it is valid or not? In principle, all the valid expressions in such a theory can be effectively generated, one after another; but there are an infinity of them; hence the ability to *generate* them does not provide a means of *recognizing* one. For obviously, no matter how many valid sentences we have already generated, we have no way of knowing whether an arbitrary sentence not already generated ever will be generated. The fundamental distinction between the recognition problem and the generation problem is one of the vexing features of foundation studies and its offshoots; this includes such areas as automatic pattern recognition and cognate areas connected with the theory of the brain.

Let us give one example of a recognition problem which cannot be solved. We saw in 2.2 above that groups could be defined within the confines of a formal theory, by imposing compatible equivalence relations on a free group. The effect of such equivalence relations is to force certain words of the free group to be synonymous with each other. Let us ask the following deceptively simple question: given an arbitrary relation R, and an arbitrary pair of words w_1, w_2 in the free group, can we effectively decide whether these words are synonymous under R or not? This is the *word problem for groups*, and it can be shown that this problem is *unsolvable*; there is no recognition procedure which can answer this question for us in all cases in a finite number of steps.[4]

It will of course be noticed that the recognition problem is a generalization of the consistency problem; if we had a decision procedure for recognizing valid sentences, we could thereby establish consistency. Thus it is plausible that, just as we can establish relative consistency through the use of models, we can establish solutions to recognition problems in a theory $\mathbb{J}$ if we can solve them in a model Σ of $\mathbb{J}$. In fact, this idea leads to a very interesting theory in itself, concerned with *degrees* of unsolvability;[5] once again, a detailed discussion of such matters is not possible here, but we would encourage the reader to consult the literature.

EXAMPLE 4: EQUIVALENCE RELATIONS AND CANONICAL FORMS

We are now going to develop some examples which are going to be of
the utmost importance to us in our subsequent work. We will begin
with a consideration of a familiar problem of elementary linear
algebra, which is based on the Cartesian arithmetization of Euclidean
geometry described above.

Just as we identified the Cartesian plane as the set E_2 of all
ordered pairs (a, b) of real numbers, so we can identify Euclidean
n-dimensional space as the set E_n of all ordered n-tuples $(a_1, \ldots,
a_n)$ of real numbers. This is not just a set, but in fact inherits
definite algebraic and geometric properties from the real numbers;
indeed, Euclidean n-space is nothing but the cartesian product of
the real numbers with itself n times.

For instance, if $\alpha = (a_1, \ldots, a_n)$ and $\beta = (b_1, \ldots, b_n)$ are two
such n-tuples, we can form the sum $\alpha + \beta$, which is defined to be the
n-tuple

$$(a_1 + b_1, \ a_2 + b_2, \ \ldots, \ a_n + b_n).$$

This addition is associative, commutative, and in fact turns our
space into a commutative group, with the n-tuple $(0, 0, \ldots, 0)$ as
unit. Moreover, if α is any n-tuple, and r is any real number, we
can define the product $r\alpha$ as the n-tuple

$$(ra_1, \ ra_2, \ldots, \ ra_n);$$

this *multiplication by scalars* distributes over addition; $r(\alpha + \beta) =$
$r\alpha + r\beta$, and has all the other familiar properties.

Let us consider the n-tuple $e_1 = (1, 0, \ldots, 0)$. The set of all
scalar multiples of the form re_1 is a *line* in our space. Likewise,
if e_i is the n-tuple with zeros in all but the ith position, and 1
in that position, then the set of all multiples of the form re_i is
another line in the space.

These lines play a distinguished role, because we can express every
n-tuple α uniquely in the form

$$\alpha = a_1 e_1 + a_2 e_2 + \ldots + a_n e_n. \tag{3.1.1}$$

In fact, under this interpretation, the numbers a_i become the co-
ordinates of α. referred to the lines defined by the e_i; these
lines are then the *co-ordinate axes*; the n-tuples $e_i, \ldots, e_n$ form
a *basis* for E_n. Thus, labelling a point in Euclidean n-space by an
ordered n-tuple of numbers presupposes a specific choice of co-
ordinate axes, or basis, in that space.

If we choose another set of co-ordinate axes, the points in Euclidean
n-space would be labelled by different n-tuples. Thus we can ask
the following sort of question: if we label the points of E_n in two

different ways by choosing two different sets of co-ordinate axes,
how are these labellings related to each other?

We can express this question in diagrammatic form, as indicated in
Fig. 3.1.2 below:

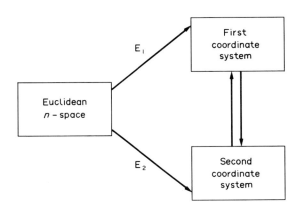

Fig. 3.1.2.

In this diagram, each point P of Euclidean n-space is given two
distinct encodings $E_1(P)$, $E_2(P)$ into the set of ordered n-tuples,
by virtue of two different choices of co-ordinate axes. In this
case, we would expect complete correspondences between these two
encodings; these correspondences would amount to one-one transformation of the set E_n of ordered n-tuples onto itself. Of course
we know that this is the case; all such encodings are thus *equivalent*
to each other.

Let us look at this matter in more detail; in particular, let us
see how these correspondences themselves can be expressed, with the
aid of a Cartesian encoding. Let $e_1, \ldots, e_n$ be as above, and let
$e_1', \ldots, e_n'$ define the new co-ordinate axes. Now each of the e_i'
can be referred back to the original axes; i.e. we can write

$$e_i' = p_{i1}e_1 + p_{i2}e_2 + \cdots + p_{in}e_n. \tag{3.1.2}$$

Thus, expressing the new axes in terms of the old involves the n^2

numbers p_{ij}; these numbers can be arranged in the familar way into
a *matrix* which we shall call P. The numbers in this matrix, which
are the co-ordinates of the new basis elements e_i' in the original
co-ordinate system, clearly also depend on that co-ordinate system.

This matrix P represents, in a sense, all we need to know about transforming co-ordinates, because once we know how the e_i transform to $e_i{}'$, we can express any n-tuple $\alpha = a_1 e_1 + \ldots + a_n e_n$ in the new co-ordinates.

Specifically, let us suppose we can write

$$\alpha = a_1 e_1 + a_2 e_2 + \ldots + a_n e_n \qquad (3.1.3)$$

in the original co-ordinate system. In the new co-ordinate system, we will have

$$\alpha = a_1{}' e_1{}' + a_2{}' e_2{}' + \ldots + a_n{}' e_n{}'. \qquad (3.1.4)$$

To find the $a_i{}'$, we need to express the e_i in terms of the $e_i{}'$; this is done analogous to (3.1.2) by finding the numbers q_{ij} such that

$$e_i = q_{i1} e_1{}' + q_{i2} e_2{}' + \ldots + q_{in} e_n{}' \qquad (3.1.5)$$

The numbers q_{ij} are related to the p_{ij} as follows: the two matrices $P = (p_{ij})$ and $Q = (q_{ij})$ are *inverses* of each other with respect to matrix multiplication; i.e.

$$Q = P^{-1}.$$

In any case, if we now substitute (3.1.5) in (3.1.3), then collecting terms and comparing the resulting coefficients of the $e_i{}'$ with (3.1.4), we find

$$a_i{}' = \sum_{j=1}^{n} q_{ij} a_j \qquad (3.1.6)$$

So far, we have regarded such matrices as representing different encodings of the *same* point of E_n, referred to different choices of co-ordinate systems. However, we can equally well interpret them as *moving* the points of E_n, with the co-ordinate system held fixed. In that case a relation like (3.1.6) expresses the co-ordinates of the point to which a particular point with co-ordinates $(a_1, \ldots, a_n)$ is moved. Under this interpretation, the matrices we have introduced represent *motions* of E_n. Thus, using the familiar matrix notation, we can write (3.1.6) as

$$\alpha' = Q\alpha = P^{-1}\alpha, \qquad (3.1.7)$$

where P is the matrix which describes how the basis vectors e_i move under the transformation according to (3.1.2) above.

Thus, under this last interpretation, we see that the *motions* of E_n

encode as matrices. But the entries of such matrices themselves depend upon the choice of co-ordinate system we have made in E_n; if we choose a different co-ordinate system, we will obtain a different matrix, i.e. a different encoding, for the same motion of E_n. Thus, just as before, we may ask the following question: *under what circumstances do two different matrices represent encodings of the same motion?*

This question can be easily answered from (3.1.7). Suppose that A is a matrix, and that we can write

$$\alpha = A\beta \qquad\qquad (3.1.8)$$

in some initial co-ordinate system $e_1, \ldots, e_n$. If we then change co-ordinates to $e_1', \ldots, e_n'$, then from (3.1.7) and (3.1.8) we can write

$$\alpha' = P^{-1}AP\beta' \qquad\qquad (3.1.9)$$

where P is the appropriate matrix defining the co-ordinate transformation according to (3.1.2). This relation means that the matrix

$$P^{-1}AP$$

represents the same transformation in the new co-ordinates that the matrix A represented in the original co-ordinates.

Thus, if A and B are two matrices such that

$$B = P^{-1}AP \qquad\qquad (3.1.10)$$

for some co-ordinate transformation P, they can be regarded as representing different encodings of the same motion, or transformation, of E_n. Under these circumstances, we say that A and B are *similar matrices*.

If we now look at the set of all square matrices of n^2 entries as itself a mathematical object, it is easy to see that (3.1.10) represents a binary relation between pairs of matrices A, B. In fact, this relation is an equivalence relation, as we might expect; reflexivity and symmetry are immediate, and transitivity follows from the ordinary properties of matrix multiplication (and the elementary theorem that the composition of the two co-ordinate transformations is again a co-ordinate transformation). Hence, the set of motions, or linear transformations, on E_n, is simply the set of all such square matrices, reduced modulo this equivalence relation.

Much of linear algebra is concerned intimately with this equivalence relation of similarity between matrices, and with the associated *decision problem* of deciding when two given matrices A, B are in fact similar. Since this circle of ideas will be vital to us in subsequent chapters, we will discuss it in some detail in this relatively familiar context.

Let us denote the set of all nxn square matrices by U_n, and let us denote the similarity relation by R. We wish to construct an effective *decision procedure* to decide when a pair of given matrices A, B in U_n are similar; i.e. fall into the same equivalence class under R.

One way to approach this problem involves seeking *invariants* of R. Let us suppose that f : $U_n \to \mathbb{R}$ is a mapping of matrices into real numbers. If this mapping f happens to be *constant on the equivalence classes of* R, then f is called an invariant of R. Specifically, if f is such an invariant, and if A, B are two matrices such that $f(A) \neq f(B)$, then A and B *cannot be similar*; i.e. the condition $f(A) = f(B)$ is a necessary condition for similarity. It is not in general a sufficient condition, unless f happens to take different values on *each* equivalence class. In that case, we find that our relation R on U_n is precisely the same relation as what we called R_f in Chapter 2.2 above; but in general, f is an invariant if every equivalence class of R_f is the *union* of classes of R (or, stated another way, if R *refines* R_f). We can thus solve the decision problem for equivalence of matrices if we can find enough invariants f_1, f_2, ..., f_m to satisfy the condition that $f_i(A) = f_i(B)$ *if and only if* A and B are similar. More explicitly, given any two matrices, we have only to compute the invariants $f_i(A)$, $f_i(B)$. If these numbers are different for any i = 1, ..., m, the matrices cannot be similar; if they are the same for each i, the matrices must be similar. In this case, f_1, ..., f_m is called a *complete set of invariants*.

We remark here, for later exploitation, that such invariants play a role analogous to the qualities or observables of natural systems; the machinery for their computation or observation are analogous to physical meters; a complete set of invariants is analogous to a set of state variables.

In the case of similarity of matrices, the finding of an appropriate set of invariants is intimately associated with the reduction of matrices to *canonical forms*. The question of finding canonical forms has two distinct aspects. Quite generally, if we are given any equivalence relation on a set, it is often helpful to be able to pick a specific representative from each equivalence class in a canonical way. A set of such representatives is then obviously in one-one correspondence with the quotient set modulo the given equivalence relation. In the present case, a set of such canonical representatives would itself be a set of matrices, and not a set of equivalence classes of matrices; this is a great convenience for many purposes. The second aspect is that if such a representative is chosen in a natural way, we can also solve the decision problem for two matrices A, B by reducing each of them to their canonical form; the matrices can be similar if and only if the canonical forms turn out to be identical.

The basic idea behind expressing a given matrix in a canonical form is, in effect, to find that co-ordinate system or basis of E_n in

which that matrix is encoded in an especially simple fashion. To do
this, of course, requires us to sepcify what we mean by "simple".
There are a variety of criteria which can be employed for this purpose; the best-known of these leads to the familiar *Jordan Canonical
Form*. It so happens that, in the process of establishing this form,
we simultaneously obtain a desired complete set of invariants. These
invariants turn out to be the *eigenvalues* of a given matrix, together
with their *multiplicities*. Once again, we shall omit the details,
which can be found in any text on linear algebra.

The reader may now with some justice inquire what this discussion
has to do with the modelling relation. The answer is this: we are
going to take the point of view that *two similar matrices are models
of each other*, in a sense now to be made precise.

Let A, B be matrices of the type under consideration. Then we have
seen that each of them may be regarded as a motion; i.e. a transformation of E_n into itself. If α is an element of E_n, which we may
think of as a possible *input* to the transformation, then $A\alpha$ is the
corresponding *output*. (The reader should compare this usage with
that employed in discussing linear input-output systems in 1.2
above.) [6]

Let us express this observation in a convenient diagrammatic form.
If A and B are similar matrices, then we can find a co-ordinate
transformation P such that (3.1.10) holds. If we regard A and B as
transformations of E_n, then (3.1.10) may be re-expressed as a *diagram
of transformations* of the form

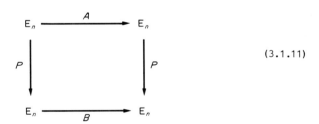

$$(3.1.11)$$

This diagram has the fundamental property that the composite mappings
PA and BP are in fact the same mapping. A diagram with this property
is called *commutative*. Thus, the relation of similarity between
matrices can be expressed through the existence of a commutative
diagram of the form (3.1.11).

Let us further look upon P as an *encoding* of the inputs to A into
the inputs to B, and the inverse mapping P^{-1} as a *decoding* of the
outputs of B into the outputs of A. *The commutativity of the diagram
then becomes precisely the statement that B is a model of A.* Likewise, we can regard P^{-1} as an encoding of the inputs to B onto the
inputs to A, and its inverse P as a decoding of the outputs of A
onto the outputs of A. By the same argument, A is also a model of
B; hence in this case, the two matrices A, B are, as claimed, models
of each other. Moreover, if we have a canonical form A* for the

equivalence class of similar matrices to which A belongs, then A*
is simultaneously a model for every matrix in that class.

Let us introduce some terminology which will be important to us
subsequently. If α is regarded as an input to A, then we shall call
P(α), which is its encoding into an input to B, as that input which
corresponds to α. If A(α) = α', then we shall say that P(α') likewise *corresponds* to α'. The commutativity of the diagram (3.1.11)
then says precisely that A, B *map corresponding elements onto
corresponding elements.* As we shall see, this kind of situation
arises ubiquitously in the modelling of natural systems, under such
guises as Laws of Dynamical Similarity or Laws of Corresponding
States.

EXAMPLE 5: A GENERALIZATION: STRUCTURAL STABILITY[7]

The situation described in the preceding example can be vastly
generalized. Some of the generalizations are among the deepest
and most interesting areas of the contemporary mathematics. For
instance: instead of looking at E_n, we may look at more general
metric spaces (i.e. sets on which a distance function, and hence a
metric topology, are defined). Thus, let X, Y be metric spaces.
Let H(X, Y) denote the set of continuous mappings or functions from
X into Y. Let us say that two mappings f, g in H(X, Y) are *equivalent*
if we can find a pair of one-one mappings ϕ : X → Y, ψ : Y → Y
such that the diagram

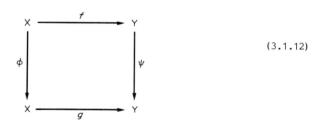

(3.1.12)

is commutative. It will be observed that this diagram (3.1.12) is
an immediate generalization of (3.1.11), and the verification that
the relation of equivalence between mappings in H(X, Y) is indeed an
equivalence relation on H(X, Y) proceeds in exactly the same way.

Thus, H(X, Y) is partitioned into equivalence classes. A major
question that becomes the analog of the decision problem for matrices:
given any particular mapping f in H(X, Y), to which equivalence class
does it belong? When are two mappings equivalent?

This question is rendered still more interesting by the following
fact. The set H(X, Y) of continuous mappings of X into Y is not
just a set; there is a sense in which it inherits a further structure from the fact that X and Y are metric spaces. In particular,
there are a variety of distinct and important ways in which H(X, Y)
can itself be made into a metric space; i.e. in which a distance
function can be defined in H(X, Y) itself.

Thus if $f \in H(X, Y)$, we can talk about the mappings f' which are *close* to f, in the sense that the distance between f' and f is small. Indeed, we can regard f' as a "perturbation" of, or an approximation to, a nearby mapping f. The main feature of an approximation is this: we would expect that important mathematical properties of f are also manifested by sufficiently good approximations to f; i.e. differing from f by a sufficiently small amount. In particular, we might expect that if f' is close to f in $H(X, Y)$, then f and f' are equivalent.

The fact is that this expectation turns out not to be in general true, no matter how the distance function on $H(X, Y)$ is defined. If it is true that, under a particular distance function, all nearby mappings f' are indeed equivalent to f, then f is called *stable*, or *structurally stable*. Some of the deepest questions of mathematics are associated with this notion of stability, which in turn reflects the interplay of the relation of equivalence on $H(X, Y)$ with a notion of closeness or approximation on $H(X, Y)$.

Speaking very roughly, for a moment, the question of stability of mappings we have just raised boils down to this. We have already seen that the relation of equivalence involves a precise sense in which one mapping can be regarded as a model of another. Likewise, the notion of closeness or approximation also refers to a modelling situation; namely, to the idea that mappings which are sufficiently close to one another in a topological sense are also models of each other. The fact that there are mappings which are not stable thus means that *these two notions of model are essentially different from one another*. We can thus see emerging here a specific example of the situation diagrammed in Fig. 2.3.4 above, in which *we cannot establish a correspondence between two models of the same object simply from the fact that they are both models*. This is the situation we called Case C2 in the previous discussion, and we see that it arises here in a completely mathematical context. As we noted previously, such a situation is intimately connected with ideas of reductionism; in this case, we see that we cannot reduce the topology on $H(X, Y)$ to equivalence, nor vice versa; the two notions are in general logically independent of one another.

We also pointed out that this situation is intimately related to the notion of *bifurcation*. Indeed, let f be a mapping in $H(X, Y)$ which is not stable. Then however close we come to f, in the topology of $H(X, Y)$, there will be mappings of f' which are closer still to f and which belong to a different equivalence class. This is the same as saying that certain arbitrarily small perturbations of f will manifest essentially different properties than f does; this is precisely what bifurcation means. We also see clearly how a bifurcation represents a situation in which two different representations of the same object (here the mapping f) become logically independent of one another under these circumstances.

Let us describe here one specific context in which these ideas manifest themselves. Consider a simple linear dynamical system, of the form

$$\frac{dx}{dt} = ax + by$$

$$\frac{dy}{dt} = cx + dy$$

(3.1.13)

We shall consider two situations: (a) the eigenvalues of the system matrix

$$\begin{pmatrix} a & b \\ c & d \end{pmatrix}$$

are real and negative;   (b) the eigenvalues of the system matrix are pure imaginary.

In each case, there is a unique steady state, at the origin of the state space. Near the origin, in case (a), the trajectories are essentially as shown in Fig. 3.1.3:

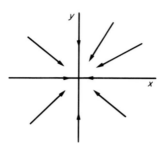

Fig. 3.1.3.

i.e. the origin is a stable node. The condition that the eigenvalues of A be real and negative may be expressed, in terms of the matrix coefficients, as a pair of inequalities:

$$(a + d)^2 > 4(ad - bc)$$

$$(a + d) < 0$$

Suppose we now perturb the system, by replacing the coefficients in the matrix A by new values a', b', c', d', which are close to the original values. It is evident that, if this perturbation is sufficiently small, it will not affect the above inequalities;   the perturbed system will have essentially the same dynamical behavior as the original one.

Now let us turn to case (b). In this case, which is essentially that of the undamped harmonic oscillator in one dimension, the trajectories will appear as shown in Fig. 3.1.4 below:

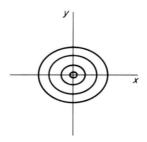

Fig. 3.1.4.

The trajectories here are closed orbits; concentric ellipses; the origin is a *center*, and is neutrally stable. The condition that the eigenvalues of the system be pure imaginary are now

$$(a + d) = 0$$

$$(ad - bc) > 0.$$

The first of these conditions is an *equality*. Thus, if we now perturb this system as we did the preceding one, by replacing the coefficients a, b, c, d by new values close to the original ones, we see that in general, no matter how small a perturbation we impose, the equality

$$a' + d' = 0$$

will in general *not hold*. The eigenvalues of the new system will then not be pure imaginary, but will have some non-zero real part. This is sufficient to turn the trajectories of the system from the original closed, neutrally stable orbits into open spirals, which approach or diverge from the origin according to whether the sign of the real part of the eigenvalues is positive or negative; this behavior is shown in Fig. 3.1.5:

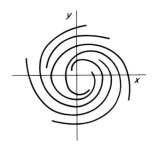

Fig. 3.1.5.

Thus in this case, an arbitrarily small perturbation can turn the origin from a neutrally stable center to a (stable or unstable) *focus*.

The first case we have discussed is an example of a structurally stable system. Let us recast its properties into the form exhibited in (3.1.12) above. As we saw earlier, we could regard a dynamics like (3.1.13) as generating a flow on the state space (in this case, on E_n); in turn, this flow could be represented by a one-parameter family of mappings $f_t : E_2 \to E_2$. Likewise, a perturbation of the system will generate a corresponding one-parameter family of mappings $f_t' : E_2 \to E_2$. The structural stability of the first system means that the character of the trajectories, although modified in a quantitative sense when we replace f_t by f_t', remains qualitatively the same. In mathematical terms, this means that we can establish continuous one-one mappings of E_2 onto itself which *preserve the*

trajectories. In general, then, if f_t is structurally stable, we
can find continuous, one-one mappings ϕ, ψ such that the diagram

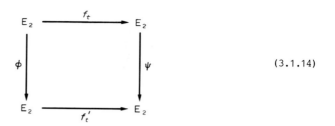

$$(3.1.14)$$

commutes for every t. That is, the original and the perturbed systems are in this sense *models of each other.*

The second case is an example of a structurally unstable system.
Indeed, it is clear from comparing Figs 3.1.4 and 3.1.5 that we
cannot hope to find continuous maps on E_2 which preserve trajectories.
Thus, an arbitrarily small perturbation of a structurally unstable
system can cause it to assume essentially new properties. In this
case, there is a bifurcation of the following character: some perturbations of the neutrally stable system will result in a stable
system; others will result in an unstable system. These two situations are not models of each other; nor is either of them a model
for the original unperturbed situation.

Before concluding this section, we shall make one further comment
about diagrams like (3.1.12) and (3.1.14). If in diagram (3.1.14)
we regard f_t' as a perturbation of f_t, the commutativity of the
diagram asserts precisely that *such a perturbation can be "annihilated" through suitable co-ordinate transformations* ϕ, ψ. That is,
if such a perturbation is imposed, in the sense that the map f_t is
replaced by a new map f_t', then we can recapture the original situation simply by replacing all elements in the domain and range of f_t
by their *corresponding* elements via the encodings ϕ, ψ. This too
will prove to be an essential characteristic of modelling relations
in general, with which we will meet constantly in subsequent chapters.

EXAMPLE 6: ALGEBRAIC TOPOLOGY AND THE THEORY OF CATEGORIES

In the preceding example, we briefly discussed the concept of the
stability of mappings $f : X \to Y$ of a metric (topological) space X
into a similar space Y. We saw that stability reflected the extent
to which two mappings which are close to one another in a suitable
topology of H(X, Y) are also members of the same conjugacy class.
We are now going to briefly describe a closely related circle of
ideas, applied to another kind of classification problem.

One of the basic problems of topology is again a decision problem:

given two spaces X, Y, to decide whether they are *homeomorphic*. A
homeomorphism $f : X \to Y$ is a mapping which is one-one and onto, and
such that both f and its inverse mapping f^{-1} are continuous; Two
homeomorphic spaces can be considered as abstractly the same; any
topological property of one can be transformed into a corresponding
property of the other. Thus, two homeomorphic spaces are *models of
each other*; any topological property of one of them can be encoded
(via a homeomorphism) into a corresponding property of the other, and
conversely.

We can try to approach this decision problem for topological spaces
in exactly the same way we approached the decision problem for similar matrices; we may attempt to construct suitable *topological
invariants*. These invariants need not be numbers; they may be
other mathematical objects G(X) associated with a topological space
X in such a way that if G(X) and G(Y) are different, then X any Y
cannot be homeomorphic. In what follows, we shall consider a few
of the simpler topological invariants of this type. We shall see
(a) that such a topological invariant G(X) is *itself a model of* X,
in that it represents an encoding of properties of X into G(X), and
(b) that the general procedure by which a space X is associated with
the invariant G(X) leads us directly to the *theory of categories*
which was mentioned earlier. In this sense, we shall see that the
theory of categories can itself be regarded as a *general theory of
modelling*, built up entirely within mathematics itself.

As we stated above, the topological invariants we shall describe
are not themselves numbers, but rather are certain algebraic systems;
in fact, they are groups. The basic idea behind the construction of
these invariants goes back to Poincaré. We shall describe them in
an informal fashion; full details can be found in any text on
algebraic topology.[8]

Let us first describe the *fundamental group*. Suppose that X is a
suitable topological space; e.g. a region of the plane, or the
surface of a sphere, or the surface of a torus. Let us fix a point
x_0 in X, and let us consider curves C of the type shown in Fig.
3.1.6 below:

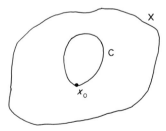

Fig. 3.1.6.

The curve C is just a closed curve which both initiates and termin-
ates at our chosen point x_0. We shall also provide such a curve C
with an *orientation*, as follows: we can, starting at x_0, traverse

the curve either in a clockwise or in a counter-clockwise direction and return to x_0; if we choose the former, we shall say that the curve is given a positive orientation; if we choose the latter, we shall say that the curve is given a negative orientation.

Given two such curves, say C_1 and C_2, we can obtain another such curve by traversing one of them from x_0 back to x_0 in a given orientation, and then traversing the other from x_0 back to x_0. In this way, we can introduce a binary operation into the set of such curves. It is easy to see that under this binary operation, the set of curves becomes a group; the inverse of a curve C is the same curve traversed in the opposite orientation, and the unit element for the group is just the point x_0 itself.

Now we shall introduce a compatible equivalence relation on this group, in the following intuitive way. First, let us suppose that such a curve C can be continuously *deformed* down to the point x_0; i.e. that we can make C smaller and smaller in a continuous fashion, without ever leaving the space X. Intuitively, this means that the "interior" of the curve C is simply connected; or that C does not enclose a "hole". We shall say that such a curve is "homotopic to zero". For instance, if X is the interior of a circle, or is the surface of the sphere, then any such path C is homotopic to zero. On the other hand, if X is the surface of a torus, then the curve C_1 shown in Fig. 3.1.7 is homotopic to zero, but the curve C_2 is not:

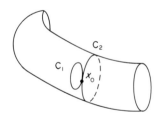

Fig. 3.1.7.

if the composite curve C_1-C_2 is homotopic to zero. It is easy to show that homotopy is an equivalence relation among such curves, and that it is compatible with the binary operation we have introduced. If $K(x_0)$ is the set of curves, and R is the homotopy relation, then $G(x_0)$ = $K(x_0)/R$ is a group; the *fundamental group*, or *first homotopy group*, of the space X (it should be noted that a simple argument is required to show that this group does not in fact depend on the choice of x_0).

We might mention that the homotopy relation just introduced is really intimately connected with conjugacy of mappings. For we may regard any curve in X as a mapping f of the unit interval

$$I = \{r \mid 0 \le r \le 1\}.$$

into X. The curves originating and terminating at x_0 are precisely
the ones for which $f(0) = f(1) = x_0$. Thus, homotopy of curves becomes an equivalence relation between certain mappings in the set of
mappings $H(I, X)$. Moreover, we can represent the "deformation" of
curves in X by means of curves in $H(I, X)$; two mappings f, g are
joined by a continuous curve in $H(I, X)$ if there is a continuous
mapping $\phi : I \to H(I, X)$ such that $\phi(0) = f$, $\phi(1) = g$; the existence
of such a ϕ establishes the homotopy relation between f and g. It
is not hard to show that this can be translated into a conjugacy
diagram of the form

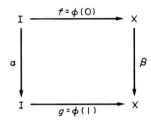

relating f and g. Thus, homotopy of curves can be regarded as a
special case of conjugacy of mappings.

In any case, once we have shown that the fundamental group is independent of our choice of x_0, it becomes in effect a function of the
space X alone, which we may denote by $G(X)$. It can readily be shown
that *homeomorphic spaces are associated with isomorphic fundamental
groups*; thus if two spaces X, Y are such that $G(X)$ and $G(Y)$ are not
isomorphic, it follows that X and Y cannot be homeomorphic. Thus
$G(X)$ is a topological invariant; the isomorphism of fundamental
groups is a necessary (but not sufficient) condition for X and Y to
be homeomorphic.

As an obvious application, we can see immediately that the surface
of a torus and the surface of a sphere cannot be homeomorphic. This
is because on the surface of a sphere, every curve is homotopic to
zero, while the torus admits curves which are not homotopic to zero,
as we have seen.

One further crucial property of this construction must now be described. Suppose X and Y are topological spaces, and that $G(X)$,
$G(Y)$ are their associated fundamental groups. If we are given a
continuous mapping $f : X \to Y$, then clearly f maps every curve in X
into some corresponding curve in Y. It is again not hard to show
that a continuous mapping preserves the homotopy relation between
curves; if two curves C_1, C_2 are homotopic in X, then their images
$f(C_1)$, $f(C_2)$ are homotopic in Y. From this it follows that, associated with the continuous mapping f, there is a corresponding group
homomorphism $f^* : G(X) \to G(Y)$. This fact may be represented by a
diagram

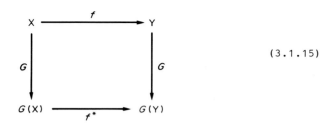

$$(3.1.15)$$

Here G is regarded as a correspondence (a *functor*) which associates
with any space X its corresponding fundamental group. As we shall
see in a moment, it is appropriate to write $f^* = G(f)$ as well. It
must be carefully noted that the arrows labelled G in (3.1.15) are
not mappings in the sense that f and f^* are mappings; G does not
associate *elements* x in X with corresponding elements $G(x)$ in $G(X)$.
Rather, G is a rule which shows how the *group* $G(X)$ is associated
with the *space* X. Thus this diagram (3.1.15) has a different significance from, say, the conjugacy diagrams (3.1.11) and (3.1.12)
above.

It should be noted that the construction we have just sketched can
be vastly generalized, to yield a sequence of *higher homotopy groups*.
The operations which associate a space X to these higher homotopy
groups have the same properties which we have just observed for G;
in particular, they all yield diagrams like (3.1.15). We refer the
reader to the literature for further details about these other topological invariants.

The study of what was traditionally called combinatorial topology
yields other kinds of groups which are topological invariants; the
homology groups, and their duals, the *cohomology groups*. We can
only here give the flavor of the ideas leading to their construction.
To take a very simple example, consider the tetrahedron ABCD shown
in Fig. 3.1.8 below:

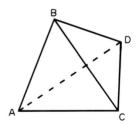

Fig. 3.1.8.

This tetrahedron is bounded by four *triangles*; these in turn determine six distinct *edges*, and four *vertices*. These will be called
the *elements* of the tetrahedron; the triangles are two-dimensional
elements, and the vertices are zero-dimensional.

Let us consider one of the triangles, say ABC. We can give the triangle an *orientation* by agreeing to traverse its boundary in a given direction; say clockwise or counter-clockwise. Two triangles are said to be *coherently oriented* if they are traversed in the same direction. It should be noticed that if two triangles with a common edge are coherently oriented, then the common edge is traversed in *opposite* directions in the two triangles. The reader should verify that the four triangles comprising the faces of our tetrahedron can be coherently oriented; it turns out that this property is itself a topological invariant.

We can also orient *edges*, in such a way that if, say, the edge AB is traversed from A to B in an orientation of ABC, then this orientation is inherited by the edge.

If we call one orientation positive (+) and the other negative (-), then we can designate the bounding faces of the tetrahedron as a *sum* of coherently oriented triangles:

$$ABCD = ABC + BDC + DBA + ACD. \qquad (3.1.16)$$

Indeed, we can in this way talk about *any* linear combination of these triangles, where the coefficients are any positive and negative integers, or zero. Such a linear combination of two-dimensional elements is an example of a 2-*chain*.

The particular 2-chain exhibited as (3.1.16) above is a special one; it represents the boundary of the tetrahedron. Now we can look at its boundary as a particular 1-chain; i.e. as a sum of one-dimensional elements, each with the proper orientation. If we write down this 1-chain explicitly, we see that it is *zero*. This illustrates the crucial fact that the *boundary of a boundary is always zero*.

Now a chain which is a boundary of another (and hence such that its own boundary is zero) is called a *cycle*.

The set of all r-chains of our tetrahedron (here r = 0, 1, 2, 3) is clearly an additive group under the binary operation + exemplified in (3.1.16) above. It can readily be verified that the set of all cycles is a *subgroup*. Let us call two r-chains *homologous* if they differ by a cycle; a cycle itself is thus *homologous to zero*. This relation of homology is easily seen to be an equivalence relation compatible with the group operation; hence we can form the quotient group. This quotient group is the r-dimensional homology group. These homology groups are the prototypes of the topological invariants we seek.

In general, we can construct such homology groups for any topological space which we can dissect into triangles, tetrahedra and their higher-dimensional analogs, by generalizing the above discussion in the appropriate way. This approach to such spaces is the essence of combinatorial topology, and hence of algebraic topology.

If $K^r(X)$ is the r-dimensional homology group of a space X, then it is not hard to verify that a diagram of mappings essentially similar to (3.1.15) can be built (see (3.1.17). As before, any continuous mapping $f : X \rightarrow Y$ induces a corresponding group homomorphism f^* : $K^r(X) \rightarrow K^r(Y)$. The homology groups are also topological invariants; if X and Y are homeomorphic, then their homology groups $K^r(X)$, $K^r(Y)$ are isomorphic as groups.

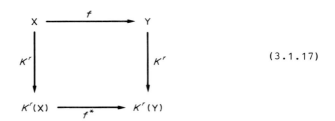

$$(3.1.17)$$

As noted above, we are going to take the point of view that algebraic objects like $G(X)$ and $K^n(X)$ are *models* of the space X; i.e. that *they encode in their algebraic properties particular features of the topological space* X. We are now going to describe how the relation between a space X and its algebraic models can be described in formal terms. This will lead us essentially into the theory of categories; in this theory, diagrams like (3.1.15) and (3.1.17) will play the fundamental role.

Let us recall that in Chapter 2.2 above, we briefly touched on the concept of a category[9]. At that time, we regarded a category as the totality of mathematical structures belonging to a certain type which belong to a particular mathematical universe $\mathfrak{U}$, together with the structure-preserving mappings through which different structures in the category could be compared.

One category we might consider, then, would be the category of all topological spaces in $\mathfrak{U}$. This category would comprise two distinct elements of structure: (a) its *objects*; in this case, all the topological spaces in $\mathfrak{U}$; (b) its *mappings*; in that, for every pair X, Y of topological spaces, we would associate the set $H_c(X, Y)$ of all *continuous* mappings from X to Y. Thus, the category itself becomes a mathematical object, bearing definite mathematical properties. Most of these revolve around the composition of mappings belonging to the category; for instance, if $f : X \to Y$ and $g : Y \to Z$ are continuous mappings, we know that there is a definite mapping $gf : X \to Z$ which is also in the category. These properties can be formulated in a completely abstract way (cf. the discussion of example 3 above) to define an axiomatic approach to categories as mathematical objects in their own right.

Likewise, we could consider the category of all groups in $\mathfrak{U}$. The objects of this category would be individual groups; to each pair G_1, G_2 of groups we associate the set $H_g(G_1, G_2)$ of all group homomorphisms of G_1 into G_2.

If such categories are themselves to be regarded as mathematical objects, bearing definite internal structures, we can study them in the same way we study any other mathematical objects; namely, by defining structure-preserving mappings between them. If $\mathfrak{A}, \mathfrak{B}$ are categories, then, we need to define what we mean by such a structure-preserving mapping F : $\mathfrak{A} \to \mathfrak{B}$. Such a structure-preserving map between categories will be called a *functor*.

A category contains two items of structure: its objects, and the mappings which relate these objects. A functor F must be specified according to its behavior on both. Accordingly, let us define a functor F in two steps: (a) a functor F is a rule which associated, with each object A in $\mathfrak{A}$, an object F(A) in $\mathfrak{B}$. (b) let f : A → B be a mapping in $\mathfrak{A}$. Then a functor F is also a rule which associated with f a mapping F(f) in $\mathfrak{B}$, such that

$$F(f) : F(A) \to F(B).$$

This rule F must respect composition of mappings, in the following sense: if gf : A → C is a composite mapping in $\mathfrak{A}$, then F(gf) is the same mapping as F(g)F(f) in $\mathfrak{B}$. Furthermore, if F : A → A is the *identity mapping* of A onto itself, then F(f) is the identity mapping for F(A).

We have essentially defined a particular kind of functor; a *co-variant* functor of a single argument. We often need to consider other kinds of functors; e.g. *contravariant* functors. These are defined in the same way as are convariant functors, except that F(f) is required to be a mapping of F(B) into F(A); i.e. contravariant functors reverse the arrows associated with mappings in $\mathfrak{A}$.

Since this concept of a functor is so basic, we will give a few simple examples.

1. Let $\mathfrak{A}$ = $\mathfrak{B}$ = category of sets. If X is a set, let F(X) be the set of all subsets of X. If f : X → Y is a mapping, let F(f) : F(X) → F(Y) be defined as follows: if S is a subset of X, let F(f)(S) = f(S). It is immediate to verify that F is indeed a covariant functor of the category of sets into itself.

2. Let $\mathfrak{A}$, $\mathfrak{B}$ be as in the preceding example, and let us again take F(X) = set of all subsets of X. However, let us now define F on mappings in a different way. If f : X → Y is a mapping, we will define F(f) as a mapping *from* F(Y) *to* F(X) according to the following requirement. If S is a subset of Y, then

$$F(f)(S) = f^{-1}(S).$$

Again, it is immediate to verify that F is a functor, but this time a *contravariant* functor.

3. Let us consider some examples of functors of more than one variable. Once again, let $\mathfrak{A}$ = $\mathfrak{B}$ = category of sets. If X, Y are sets, define

$$P(X, Y) = X \times Y.$$

That is, P associates with a pair of sets X, Y a new set, their cartesian product. To turn P into a functor, we must now describe what it does to mappings. Accordingly, let

$$f : X \to X', \qquad g : Y \to Y'$$

be mappings. Then we must have

$$P(f, g) : P(X, Y) \to P(X', Y');$$

we do this by simply defining

$$P(f, g)(x, y) = (f(x), g(y))$$

for all elements x ε X, y ε Y. Again, it is immediate to verify
that P is a functor under these conditions, covariant in both of
its arguments.

4.   A somewhat more involved, but equally important functor of two
     variables is one which enters into the very definition of a
     category. Specifically, if X, Y are sets, we can consider the
     new set H(X, Y) of all (set-theoretic) mappings from X to Y as
     being part of a functor. We will now see how it can be extended
     to mappings. Namely, we shall define a new mapping H(f, g),
     where f : X' → X and g: Y → Y' are given mappings. By definition,
     H(f, g) must map H(X, Y) into H(X', Y'); i.e. given any mapping
     θ : X → Y, we must specify a new mapping H(f, g)(θ) : X' → Y'.
     A moment's reflection reveals that if we define

   $$H(f, g)(\theta) = g\theta f$$

     then H becomes a functor, contravariant in its first argument,
     and covariant in its second argument.

From these few examples, it becomes clear that all of the important
mathematical constructions are functorial in this sense. Indeed, it
turns out that the functorial character of these constructions is
the reason for their significance.

In terms of the concepts we have just introduced, the next step
should be evident. Namely, the constructions which associate to a
topological space X its fundamental group $G(X)$, or its r-dimensional

homology group $K^r(X)$, are *functors of the category of topological
spaces into the category of groups*. They associate topological
spaces with groups, and continuous mappings with group homomorphisms,
in such a way that they become covariant functors from spaces to
groups. Indeed, it was primarily from a study of this relation that
the concept of a category was extracted initially. The detailed
study of these functors, from the standpoint of category theory, has
grown into an exceedingly rich mathematical theory in its own right:
homological algebra. We refer the reader to the references for
further details.

Before we proceed to investigate the sense in which functors establish
modelling relations, there is one more basic concept to be introduced.
We have seen that a functor is a vehicle for comparing categories;
we now wish to introduce a corresponding vehicle for comparing
functors. In doing so, we will introduce the idea of a *natural
transformation*. We shall preface our discussion with a few words of
motivation.

We saw above that the cartesian product could be regarded as a functor
of two variables; with each pair of sets X, Y, we could associate
another set P(X, Y) = XxY. If we interchange the roles of X and Y,
we thereby define another functor, which we can call P'(X, Y) = YxX.
Strictly speaking, these two functors P and P' are different. Nevertheless, there is an important sense in which we do not wish to
distinguish between P(X, Y) and P'(X, Y), nor between P(f, g) and
P'(f, g). This sense clearly has to do with the fact that P(X, Y)
and P(Y, X) are always *isomorphic* as sets; there is in fact a
distinguished isomorphism

   $$\phi : X \times Y \rightarrow Y \times X \qquad\qquad (3.1.18)$$

defined by writing φ(x, y) = (y, x). This isomorphism is always

present, for any pair of sets X, Y; therefore it must have something
to do with the *category*. In other words, it must be definable in
categorical terms, rather than as an *ad hoc* mapping pertaining to
individual sets X, Y. When we specify how P(X, Y) and P'(X, Y) are
related in general, we will thereby have an example of a natural
transformation (in fact, of a natural equivalence) which relates the
two functors.

We have just pointed out that, given any pair of sets X, Y, there is
a distinguished mapping ϕ(X, Y) defined by (3.1.18). The properties
of this mapping can be expressed in diagrammatic form as follows:

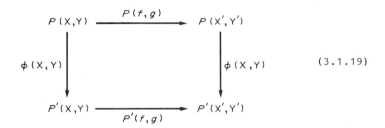

$$(3.1.19)$$

The totality of these mappings $\{\phi(X, Y)\}$ comprises a general way of
relating the two functors P, P'; i.e. of translating or encoding
the properties of P into the properties of P' in a systematic way.
We shall call such a family of mappings a *natural transformation*
between P and P', and write ϕ : P → P'. In the present case, of
course, the encoding can also be reversed, since each ϕ(X, Y) is
itself an isomorphism, and thus can be inverted. In such a case,
the natural transformation becomes a *natural equivalence*. Let us
notice explicitly that for any definite pair of sets X, Y, the
diagram (3.1.18) expresses a *conjugacy relation*.

In general, if F, G : $\mathfrak{a}$ → $\mathfrak{B}$ are (covariant) functors, we say that
these functors are *naturally equivalent* if for every pair of objects
A in $\mathfrak{a}$, B in $\mathfrak{B}$, we can find isomorphisms ϕ(A, B), ψ(A, B) in $\mathfrak{B}$ such
that the analog of (3.1.19), namely

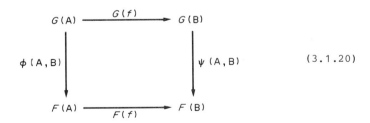

$$(3.1.20)$$

always commutes. The totality of these pairs of mappings constitutes
the natural equivalence. If these mappings are not isomorphisms,
the totality of these pairs constitutes a natural transformation of
F to *G*.

Let us note one final feature of this concept of natural transformations. If 𝕒 and 𝕓 are categories, then we can consider the class
of all functors from 𝕒 to 𝕓. To each pair (F, G) of such functors,
we can associate the set of all natural transformations from F to G.
It is then easy to verify that the totality of these functors and
natural transformations themselves form a category, the *functor
category* 𝕓(𝕒, 𝕓). Such functor categories will play an important
role in subsequent discussions, for the following reason: if we
consider F(X) to be a model of X, and G(X) to be another model of X,
then a natural transformation between F and G represents a sense in
which G(X) is a model of F(X); i.e. the extent to which we can
extract a relation between F(X) and G(X) simply from the fact that
they are both models of X. As a result, natural transformations
have a profound bearing on such problems as reductionism, and conversely, on the possibility of bifurcation between the two encodings
F, G of a system X. As we shall see later, such questions all devolve on the specific properties of a functor category. Thus, the
above discussion should be considered in the light of the diagram
shown in Fig. 2.3.4 in the preceding section, and the various cases
pertaining to that diagram.

Having now described at some length a number of specific examples
of encodings and modelling relations occurring entirely within
mathematics, let us see what general concepts pertaining to modelling
may be distilled from them. To do this, it may be helpful to review
our examples and see in each case what role the modelling relation
has played in understanding the system being modelled.

Our first example was that of the cartesian synthesis of Euclidean
geometry and algebra. The encoding of geometry into algebra and
arithmetic was not only a grand intellectual synthesis; it was of the
utmost practical importance. For the availability of algebraic
manipulative techniques made possible entirely new advances, which
would have been difficult or impossible to contemplate in purely
geometrical terms. In a certain sense, the inferential rules in the
model system (algebra) are infinitely more transparent than the
corresponding ones in the system being modelled (geometry). This fact
indicates one of the basic features of a modelling relation: via an
artful encoding, we can convert features difficult or impossible to
extract from the original system into a new form which renders them
visible, and amenable to study. Indeed, we may say that perhaps the
bulk of modern geometry would have been literally *unthinkable* in the
absence of algebraic encoding.

We also, however, see one important *caveat* to be borne in mind, which
became especially significant in our discussion of similar matrices.
Namely, the particular encoding we choose can introduce *artifacts*.
Namely, any cartesian encoding carries with it a reference to a
particular co-ordinate system, which of itself has no intrinsic
geometric significance. When attempting to do geometry via a
cartesian encoding, we must be careful to restrict ourselves to
algebraic features which are, in some sense, *independent* of the system of co-ordinates which the encoding imposes on us. Indeed, this
is why we must search for invariants and for canonical forms in the
first place. The lesson here is the following: when encoding a
system S_1 into another system S_2, we must remember that not every
property of S_2 is an encoding of some property of S_1. In general,
S_2 has properties of its own, unrelated to the encoding; we must
recognize this fact, and draw our conclusions accordingly.

We see similar lessons emerging in the Euclidean models of non-Euclidean geometry. Here again, the encodings we discussed were of incalculable significance for geometry; not only did they provide concrete interpretations of what had heretofore been purely formal structures, but they actually served to establish the logical consistency of these geometries relative to the Euclidean. And once again, we can see that such encodings made possible the discovery of many new theroems of non-Euclidean geometry, owing to the relatively much greater transparency of the properties of the model than those of their prototype. We repeat once again: a fundamental feature of the modelling relation is that it can convert relations obscure in the prototypic system into a tangible and graspable form. We will see this transductive feature of modelling relations again and again as we proceed.

Our discussion of similarity, conjugacy and stability brought to the fore another feature of the modelling relation; namely, its role in classification, discrimination and recognition among a set of related objects (matrices and mappings). Here the models were treated as *invariants*; we counted systems alike to the extent that they gave rise to identical models. Moreover, the models themselves could be constructed in a *canonical* fashion. Of particular interest here is the relation of our arguments to the notion of *metaphor*, which we mentioned earlier. In a certain sense, once we know how to construct a canonical form of *any* matrix, for instance, we know how to construct a canonical form for *every* matirx. All we need to know is that some mathematical structure is a matrix, or that it behaves "sufficiently like" a matrix, and we can instantly apply the battery of machinery which yields a canonical model. Indeed, it is precisely in this sense that we can regard any matrix as a metaphor for every other, regardless of its dimensionality or the character of its entries. Precisely this fact is exploited relentlessly in mathematics, as for example in the enormous theory of *representations*[10] of arbitrary groups by matrices; a subject we might well have included among our examples of modelling relations in mathematics.

All of these features manifested themselves most clearly in our discussion of categories. In a sense, all the objects in a given category are metaphors for one another, in the sense that once we know how to encode any one of them into a model, we know how to encode every one of them. For instance, given *any* triangulable space, we can construct the corresponding homology groups. This indeed is the essence of a functor; the construction of a functor on a category simultaneously establishes (a) a sense in which all objects in the category are related to one another, and (b) thereby produces an explicit model of each of them. It must also be emphasized that the functorial relation between, say, a topological space and an algebraic model like a homology group is not a pointwise correspondence between them, but rather embodies the capturing of a certain *global* feature of the space in corresponding global algebraic properties of the group; it is not in principle a reductionistic kind of relation.

In a certain sense, whenever we have established a modelling relation between mathematical systems of differing characters, we have built at least a piece of a functor. Thus we emphasize once more the intimate relation between category theory as a mathematical discipline, and the general theory of modelling. We shall exploit this relation in various important ways as we proceed. Before we do this, however, we shall return once again to a consideration of natural systems, and see how they may be explicitly encoded into formal systems in fruitful ways.

REFERENCES AND NOTES

1. A good historical treatment of the basic trends in Euclidean and
    non-Euclidean geometries may be found in
        Greenberg, M. J., *Euclidean and Non-Euclidean Geometries*.
        Freeman (1974).
    The various Euclidean models are succinctly described in
        Coxeter, H. S. M., *Non-Euclidean Geometry*. University of
        Toronto Press.
    A monumental and relatively recent study of axiomatic approaches
    to geometry is
        Borsuk, K. and Smidiew, W., *Foundations of Geometry*. North-
        Holland (1960).

2. The reader may observe that it is perhaps a matter of taste
    whether we regard the constructions of Beltrami, Klein and
    Poincaré (and even the arithmetization of Descartes) as models
    or realizations. Indeed, the mathematical utilization of the
    term "model", as we shall see it used throughout the present
    chapter, is often more closely akin to realization than it is to
    model. However, the terminology is so deeply entrenched that it
    is hopeless to change it now. The abstract distinction between
    the operation M of making a model, and the operation R of con-
    structing a realization, may crudely be put as follows: MRM = M,
    but RMR ≠ R in general.

3. The "theory of models" has grown rapidly in the past several
    decades, and has had an important influence on logic, foundations,
    set theory and algebra. There are a number of good introductory
    texts, among which we may mention the following:
        Smullyan, R. M., *Theory of Formal Systems*. Princeton University
        Press (1961).
        Robinson, A., *Introduction to Model Theory*. North-Holland
        (1963).
        Kopperman, R., *Model Theory and its Applications*. Allyn &
        Bacon (1972).
        Chang, C. C., *Model Theory*. Elsevier (1973).
    A general background text, still of great value for all of the
    foundational matters we have discussed, is
        Kleene, S. C., *Introduction to Metamathematics*. van Nostrand
        (1952).

4. See note 4 in 2.2 above.

5. Roughly, two unsolvable problems are said to be of the same
    degree if either implies the other. Thus, unsolvable problems
    come in many degrees. For a treatment of these matters, see
        Schoenfield, J. R., *Degrees of Unsolvability*. North-Holland
        (1971).

6. The usage is in fact identical. This can be seen by writing the
    elements a_{ij} of a matrix A as $a(i, j)$, thus revealing the true
    status of the indices as independent variables of which the
    matrix elements are functions. Likewise, we will write the
    components x_i of a vector $\vec{x}$ as $x(i)$. Then the action of a
    matrix A on a vector $\vec{x}$ (the "input") produces a new vector $\vec{y}$,
    (the "output"), whose ith component can be written as
    $$y(i) = \sum_{i=1}^{u} a(i, j) x(j).$$

If we now think of the variables i, j as ranging over continua instead of a discrete index set, the above sum goes over into an integral of precisely the form (1.2.11).

7. Stability of mappings is a subject of much current interest. In one sense, it is a straightforward generalization of the study of the following question: given a matrix A, under what conditions is every other matrix sufficiently close to A also similar to A? If a matrix A satisfies these conditions, then it is *stable* to all sufficiently small perturbations. Sability of mappings underlies bifurcation theory, structural stability of dynamical systems, and catastrophe theory. A good reference is
   Guillemin, V. and Golubitsky, M., *Stable Mappings and their Singularities*. Springer-Verlag (1973).
There are no texts devoted to the structural stability of dynamical systems *per se* (a subject which used to be known to engineers as sensitivity analysis, and to biologists as robustness). A good review of the basic approach may be found in Smale, S., *Bull. Am. Math. Soc.* **73**, 747-817 (1967).

8. Good general references for these important matters are
   Wallace, A. H., *Algebraic Topology*. Benjamin (1970).
   Switzer, R. M., *Algebraic Topology, Homotopy and Homology*. Springer-Verlag (1975).
   Bourgin, D. G., *Modern Algebraic Topology*. MacMillan (1963).
For deeper discussions of homotopy, see for example
   Hilton, P. J., *An Introduction to Homotopy Theory*. Cambridge University Press (1953).
   Hu, S., *Homotopy Theory*. Academic Press (1959).
   Gray, B., *Homotopy Theory*. Academic Press (1975).
For homology and cohomology, see
   Hilton, P. J., *Homology Theory*. Cambridge University Press (1960).
   MacLane, S., *Homology*. Springer-Verlag (1963).
Clearly, the techniques of algebraic topology grew out of geometry. However, it is interesting to note that the machinery characeristic of algebraic topology may be created and applied in purely algebraic situations. This creation of a kind of "fictitious geometry" in a purely algebraic setting is of the greatest interest, and is another application of the making of models of mathematical systems with mathematics itslef. A typical reference in this area is
   Weiss, E., *Cohomology of Groups*. Academic Press (1960).
It is also interesting to observe that classical homology theory was axiomatized by Eilenberg & Steenrod (*Foundations of Algebraic Topology*, Princeton 1952), and that the homology theory of algebraic systems, differential forms and the like can be regarded as *models* (or realizations) of these axioms.

9. As we have noted, category theory grew out of the construction of algebraic invariants of topological spaces. The paper which founded the subject was Eilenberg, S. and MacLane, S., *Trans. Am. Math. Soc.* **58**, 231-294 (1945). Initially it was very much skewed in these directions, under the guise of *homological algebra* (cf. Cartan, H. & Eilenberg, S., *Homological Algebra*, Princeton 1956), but it soon developed as an independent mathematical discipline, cutting obliquely across all others. As we have noted, we regard it as a general framework for the construction of models of mathematical objects. Some current references are:
   Mitchell, B., *Theory of Categories*. Academic Press (1965).

MacLane, S., *Categories for the Working Mathematician*.
Springer-Verlag (1971).
Arbib, M. and Manes, E. G., *Arrows, Structures and Functors*.
Academic Press (1975).

10. A representation of an arbitrary group is a homomorphism of the
group into the group of linear transformations acting on some
linear space. Representation theory has an enormous literature,
spurred in large part by its applications to physics. Good
general references are
Dornhoff, L., *Group Representation Theory*. Marcel Dekker
(1971).
Kirillov, A. A., *Elements of the Theory of Representations*.
Springer-Verlag (1972).
The reader should also consult the review of Mackey referred
to in Note 4 to Chapter 1.2 above.

3.2 Specific Encodings between Natural and Formal Systems

In the preceding chapter, we reviewed a number of examples illustrating the manner in which formal systems of a given type could be encoded into formal systems of a different type. We could then utilize these encodings to bring the inferential apparatus characteristic of the latter system to bear, yielding entirely new theorems about the encoded systems; these are the analogs of *predictions* in natural science. Before we turn to explicit consideration of encodings of *natural* systems, we must review some general principles which underlie these encodings. This is the purpose of the present chapter.

We obviously cannot proceed to develop encodings of natural systems in the same terms as were employed when dealing with purely formal systems. We have seen in the preceding chapter that such encodings typically take the form of mappings or functors relating mathematical objects. But as we have stressed, natural systems are not formal objects; indeed, the main purpose of establishing a modelling relation is precisely to bring an inferential structure to bear on them; a structure which will mirror whatever laws govern the behavior of the natural system itself. Thus, we cannot hope to talk of mappings and encodings without some basic preliminary discussion.

As we have seen in 2.2 above, the fundamental unit of a natural system is what we called a quality, or an observable. We recall that the defining characteristic of an observable is that it represents an interactive capability, through which a given system may interact with another. In particular, an observable embodies either the capability of a natural system to move a meter, or through which the effect of a particular mode of interaction on the system itself may be assessed. For the moment, we shall concentrate on observables defined through their effects on the specific meters which measure them; we shall return to their own capacity to change as a result of interactions imposed on them shortly.

In any case, since an observable is the basic unit of a natural system, all problems pertaining to the encoding of natural systems in formal ones ultimately devolve upon the problem of how observables are to be encoded.

Before attacking this fundamental question, let us make two simple observations. The first is the following: *the same observable can be manifested by many distinct natural systems*. Indeed, insofar as an observable is operationally defined through the specific meters which it moves, we may say that any system capable of moving those meters manifests the *same* observable quality. The second observation is: *different systems manifesting the same observable, or even the same system considered at different instants of time, may exhibit the capacity of moving a meter to a different degree*. The totality of different ways in which such a meter may be moved, as a result of an interaction with a natural system manifesting the quality in question, can be considered as the set of possible *values* which that quality can assume. Following customary usage, we shall refer to this set of values as the *spectrum* of the observable.

Intuitively, the simplest kinds of meters, and those customarily employed in natural science, are those for which the values of the corresponding observable are expressed as *numbers*. Indeed, it is a basic postulate of physics that it is *sufficient* for all scientific purposes to restrict ourselves entirely to observables whose values can be represented in this way. For the moment, we shall limit ourselves to observables of this type. We leave open for the moment the question of whether numerical-valued observables are in fact adequate for all of science; we shall return to this question subsequently, when we consider the sense in which, for example, feature extraction can be regarded as measurement. For now, we simply note that (a) most of the well-known examples of encoding of natural systems into formal ones tacitly restrict themselves to numerical-valued observables, and (b) the employment of such observables allows us to make the most immediate contact between formal systems and natural ones, through the use of mathematical objects (numbers) as names for observable values.

Thus, for our present purposes, we suppose that an observable is an entity capable of assuming numerical values. To that extent, then, an observable possesses some of the features of a purely mathematical object; namely, a mapping into real numbers. However, it thusfar lacks one of the basic properties of such a mapping; namely, we have as yet no idea about what the *domain* of such a mapping may be. An observable associates *something* with particular numbers; but until we specify in a formal sense what that something may be, an observable is not yet a real-valued mapping. We shall now endeavor to do this, by enlarging on the notion of *state* of a natural system which was developed earlier.

As we developed the concept of state in Chapter 2.3 above, we saw that it in principle only had meaning with respect to a particular encoding; we shall in fact enlarge on this as we proceed. Basically, we regard a state as comprising those qualities which needed to be encoded into a specific formal system so as to provide a hypothesis to which the inferential machinery of that system could be brought to bear. We will now make a small but essential epistemological step: we shall *impute* this concept of state back to the natural system under consideration, *as a conceptual entity which exists apart from any specific encoding; indeed, as that part of the natural system which is encoded*. To distinguish this kind of state from the encoding-dependent usage which we employed previously, we shall endow it with a name of its own: an *abstract state*.

Speaking very roughly, an abstract state of a system is that on which the observables of the system assume their values. In this sense,

the value of any observable on an abstract state is a way of naming
that state; i.e. is already an encoding of the abstract state. In
particular, if we restrict ourselves to observables which take their
values in real numbers, the evaluation of an observable on an abstract
state is an encoding of that state into a mathematical system; such
an observable names a state through a corresponding number. As we
shall see abundantly, these simple considerations in fact will lead
to the most profound consequences.

Through the employment of this idea of abstract state, our concept
of what constitutes a natural system becomes much enlarged. We
began with the simple idea that a natural system comprises a set of
qualities or observables. These could be defined through the effects
produced in other systems (e.g., in meters) as a result of specific
interactions; this in turn led to the idea that an observable could
be regarded as manifesting a set of values, which comprise its spectrum. Now we have introduced the idea of an abstract state, which
is the agency on which each particular observable assumes a definite
value in its spectrum. Finally, we have seen that the specific
value assumed by an observable on such an abstract state may be
regarded as a name of that state.

We suggested above that observables possessed features of real-
valued mappings, except that there was no way of specifying the
domain of the observable. The concept of abstract state precisely
fills this gap. For a natural system is now to be regarded not *only*
as a family of observables, but also as a set of abstract states on
which these observables are evaluated. Thus, to every natural system we shall associate a set of abstract states; we learn about
these abstract states through specific acts of measurement; each
such act results in the evaluation of some observable on a state,
and at the same time names or encodes that state into real numbers
in a particular way. We can express these considerations succinctly
into a diagram:

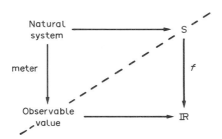

Fig. 3.2.1.

The dotted line bisecting this diagram separates those parts which
pertain to the external world from those which pertain to the world
of formal systems. The set S of abstract states sits partly in both
worlds; in its definition it is imputed to the natural system
itself, but as a set, it belongs to our mathematical universe $\mathfrak{U}$.
The meter readings pertain also to the external world, but by definition they can be directly encoded into real numbers $\mathbb{R}$. The meter,

which by definition serves to evaluate a specific observable on a particular state, is then itself encoded as a specific mathematical object; namely, as a real-valued function f defined on the set of abstract states of the natural system. Finally, since the meter *defines* the observable with which it is associated, we may regard the mapping f as *representing* that observable. Everything which follows will be seen to rest on these deceptively simple ideas.

Before proceeding further, let us note one crucial feature of the situation we have described. In a sense, an act of observation (i.e. an act of evaluating a specific observable on an abstract state) represents a description, or encoding, of that state. But any such act of observation clearly gives us only a *partial* description of the state. Thus any specific act of observation is at the same time an act of *abstraction*; an act of neglecting or forgetting all of the other ways in which that same state could be named; or what is the same thing, all of the other ways in which that same state could move other meters. It is usually considered a truism that abstraction is entirely a theoretical activity; but in fact, abstractions are imposed on us every time we make a measurement. Insofar as theoretical investigations must begin from the encodings provided by measurement, they are imposed on theory by the observer himself. Indeed, since one of the fundamental tasks of theory is to determine the relations between different descriptions or encodings, theory itself is one of the few ways that the shackles of abstraction imposed by measurement can be removed, or at least loosened. We shall return to this point several times as we proceed, for it is crucial to a proper understanding of the controversies revolving around the relative significance of "theory" and "experiment" in science.

Let us now examine some of the consequences of the picture we have drawn of an observable of a natural system encoded as a mapping $f : S \to \mathbb{R}$ from a set S of abstract states into the real numbers $\mathbb{R}$. Let us recall first that, given any mapping between sets, we can define an equivalence relation R_f on its domain, by saying that s_1 R_f s_2 if and only if $f(s_1) = f(s_2)$. In the present case, to say that two abstract states s_1, s_2 in S are so related means that both states produce the same effect on our meter, and are hence *indistinguishable* to it. They are thus both assigned the same name in $\mathbb{R}$; or, stated another way, the value assigned by f to such states is *degenerate*.

If we form the quotient set S/R_f, it is obvious that this set is in one-one correspondence with the spectrum $f(S)$ of S; namely, if r is a number in $f(S)$, we associate with r the entire equivalence class $f^{-1}(r)$ assigned the label r by the observable f. But $f(S)$ is a set of *numbers* into which the abstract states have been encoded; by hypothesis, since we are at present considering only the single observable f, this encoding represents *all* the information available about the states in S. Thus it is reasonable to *identify* the spectrum $f(S)$ with S itself; indeed, $f(S)$ is the prototype of what is generally called a "state space" of our natural system. It must be carefully observed that the encoding of abstract states in S into real numbers returns us to our previous definition of "state" as defined in terms of a specific encoding.

Let us now generalise these ideas slightly. Suppose that we have at our disposal two observables of our system, encoded into respective mappings $f, g : S \to \mathbb{R}$. Each of them has a definite spectrum (namely

$f(S)$ and $g(S)$ respectively) and these spectra are in one-one correspondence with the quotient sets S/R_f, S/R_g.

Let us suppose s_1, s_2 are two abstract states such that $f(s_1) = f(s_2)$.
Then as we have seen, the observable f cannot distinguish or resolve
these states, and assigns the same label to both of them. However,
it may very well be the case that the observable g can resolve these
states; $g(s_1) \neq g(s_2)$. Thus, as we would expect, we can obtain
more "information" about S by employing a second observable g than
we could with our original observable f alone.

Indeed, it is suggested that instead of naming a state s either with
$f(s)$ or $g(s)$ alone, we name s by encoding it into the *pair* $(f(s)$,
$g(s))$. Let us pursue this idea, and consider some of its consequences.

First, in a certain sense, we are treating the pair of observables
(f, g) as if they comprised a single observable. It is clear that
we may regard the pair (f, g) as imposing a single equivalence relation R_{fg} on S, defined by writing $s_1 R_{fg} s_2$ if and only if $f(s_1) =$
$f(s_2)$ and $g(s_1) = g(s_2)$; i.e. two abstract states are equivalent
under R_{fg} if and only if neither f nor g can distinguish between them.
It may be noted that the equivalence classes of this new relation R_{fg}
are the totality of intersections of the equivalence classes of R_f with
those of R_g; symbolically, $R_{fg} = R_f \cap R_g$. Thus, once again, we may
form the quotient set S/R_{fg}; given an equivalence class in S/R_{fg},
we may uniquely associate it with the pair of numbers $(f(s), g(s))$,
where s is any abstract state in that class.

It is clear that this procedure of labelling abstract states with
pairs of numbers produces a mapping

$$\phi : S/R_{fg} \rightarrow f(S) \times g(S). \tag{3.2.1}$$

However, we must note carefully that this mapping ϕ is not, in general
onto the cartesian product $f(S) \times g(S)$. In other words, given an
arbitrary number $r_1 \; \varepsilon \; f(S)$, and an arbitrary number $r_2 \; \varepsilon \; g(S)$, *there
need not exist an abstract state s such that* $\phi(s) = (r_1, r_2)$. Even
though $f(S)$ is the spectrum of f, and $g(S)$ is the spectrum of g,
the cartesian product $f(S) \times g(S)$ is not generally the spectrum of
ϕ; all we can say is that it *contains* that spectrum.

It is easy to verify that $f(S) \times g(S)$ will coincide with the spectrum
of ϕ if and only if every equivalence class in S/R_f intersects every
equivalence class in S/R_g, and conversely. Intuitively, when this
happens, we may say that a knowledge of $f(s)$ places *no restriction*
on the possible values of $g(s)$. In all other cases, a knowledge of
$f(s)$ generally does limit the possible values of (s); in the
extreme situation, where every class in S/R_f is a union of classes
in S/R_g, and hence can intersect only one such class, a knowledge
of $f(s)$ *completely determines* the value of $g(s)$. We have seen this

situation before; it is the case for which g is an *invariant* for
the equivalence relation R_f.

Thus, if the mapping ϕ of (3.2.1) above is not onto $f(S) \times g(S)$, we
may say that there is some *relation* obtaining between the values of
the observables f and g on the set S. This kind of relation is our
first indication of what we have previously called *linkage* between
qualities or observables; we see it emerging here directly out of
the formalism into which we encode the basic concept of an observable.
In precise terms, a linkage relation involves the *degree of logical
independence* between the labelling of abstract states by f and
labelling them by g. We shall explore this in more detail shortly.

Before taking up this point, however, let us look once again at the
cartesian product $f(S) \times g(S)$. We have seen so far that this set of
pairs of numbers contains the spectrum of the mapping ϕ, but is not
in general coincident with this spectrum. However, it is customary
to treat $f(S) \times g(S)$ as if it were the spectrum of ϕ, and thus, just
as before, to call it a "state space" of our natural system. Since
we now utilize two observables f, g in our encoding, this "state
space" is *two-dimensional*; we typically call a pair of numbers
(r_1, r_2) in this product a "state" of our system. Once again, we
point out explicitly that this use of the term "state" is dependent
on a particular encoding, and must not be confused with the abstract
states in S on which our observables are evaluated. Indeed, as we
have seen, if there is a linkage between the observables f and g,
not every pair (r_1, r_2) can be the name of an abstract state. When
such a situation arises in applications, it is customary to say that
the system is *constrained*, or that there is some *selection rule*
operating to eliminate those pairs which do not label abstract states.

Let us formalize the construction of this "state space" in more
detail. Given any set S, we can produce a mapping

$$\delta : S \to S \times S \qquad\qquad (3.2.2)$$

by defining $\delta(s) = (s, s)$; this mapping δ is often called the
diagonal map. Moreover, we have seen previously that the cartesian
product operation is a *functor*; thus in particular, given any pair
of mappings f, $g : S \to \mathbb{R}$, we can write

$$f \times g : S \times S \to \mathbb{R} \times \mathbb{R}. \qquad\qquad (3.2.3)$$

Thus, the process by which we label abstract states through pairs of
numbers can be represented, putting (3.2.2) and (3.2.3) together, by
a diagram of mappings of the form

$$S \xrightarrow{\delta} S \times S \xrightarrow{f \times g} f(S) \times g(S) \qquad\qquad (3.2.4)$$

and indeed, we see that the mapping ϕ in (3.2.1) is nothing but the
composite $(f \times g)\delta$.

The diagram (3.2.4) can be considerably generalized. In particular,
if we are given n observables $(f_1, \ldots, f_n)$, each of which is represented by a mapping of S into $\mathbb{R}$, we can construct an n-dimensional
"state space" by means of the diagram

$$S \xrightarrow{\delta} S^n \xrightarrow{f_1 \times \ldots \times f_n} \prod_{i=1}^{n} f_i(S) \qquad (3.2.5)$$

where we have written S^n as the n-fold cartesian product of S with itself, and δ is here the appropriate map of S into the n-fold product.

It is these spaces $\prod_{i=1}^{n} f_i$ (S) *of n-tuples of numbers which constitute the "state spaces" that are the point of departure for scientific investigations of natural systems.* It is perhaps not generally appreciated just how much conceptual work is involved before we can talk meaningfully about these spaces.

As with any encoding, we attempt to utilize the mathematical structure present in the formal system to learn about the properties of the natural system encoded into it. In the situation diagrammed in (3.2.5) above, these mathematical properties arise because we are dealing with cartesian products of sets of real numbers. The real numbers possess many rich mathematical structures of an algebraic, topological and measure-theoretic kind. Let us consider for a moment the topological properties, which arise from the ordinary Euclidean metric, or distance function. In particular, it is meaningful to inquire whether two n-tuples in such a cartesian product are close; i.e. whether the distance between them is small. If these n-tuples both name abstract states in S, *it is reasonable to impute the distance between the names of the states to the states themselves.* Thus, we would like to say that two abstract states s_1, s_2 are close in S if their images $(f_1 \times \ldots \times f_n)$ δ (s_1), $(f_1 \times \ldots \times f_n)$ δ (s_2) are close in the ordinary Euclidean metric. But it cannot be too strongly emphasized that this kind of imputation is dependent on the encoding, and has no intrinsic significance in S; if we choose other observables $(g_1, \ldots g_m)$: $S \to \mathbb{R}$, thereby creating another "state space" for S through the diagram

$$S \xrightarrow{\delta} S^m \xrightarrow{g_1 \times \ldots \times g_m} \prod_{i=1}^{m} g_i(S) \qquad (3.2.6)$$

we could be led to impute an entirely different metrical structure on S. Indeed, we could then ask the following kind of question: to what extent do the metrical structures arising from (3.2.5) and (3.2.6) coincide with S; i.e. to what extent does a knowledge that two abstract states s_1, s_2 appear close in (3.2.5) imply that these same states appear close in (3.2.6)? This is a question intimately related to notions of *stability* which we encountered in the previous chapter, and provides the general context in which *bifurcations* can be discussed. However, as we shall now see, questions of this type devolve once again to notions of linkage, and thence back to the essence of the modelling relation itself. Let us then take up the question of linkage of observables in more detail.

Let us begin with the simplest case, in which we are given two observables f, g : $S \to \mathbb{R}$. Let us represent this situation by means of the diagram shown in Figure 3.2.2 below. This diagram should remind the reader of that shown in Fig. 2.3.4 above, in which a single natural system (here represented by its set of abstract states) is encoded into two distinct formal systems; here the

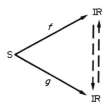

Fig. 3.2.2.

encodings are given by the observables f and g themselves, through
their evaluations on abstract states. The linkage between these two
observables is, as we have indicated, manifested by how much we
learn about $g(s)$ when $f(s)$ is known, and conversely; thus the linkage
between f and g involves the specification of relations between the
encodings themselves, considered as formal systems, arising from the
fact that the same abstract set of states is being encoded. Such
relations are expressed in the diagram by the dotted arrows. Thus,
if such relations exist, they measure the extent to which the two
encodings are models of each other, in the sense of the preceding
chapter.

Let us consider a few special cases, to fix ideas. The simplest
possible situation is that for which $R_f = R_g$; i.e. every equivalence
class in S/R_f is also an equivalence class for S/R_g. In this case,
the value $f(s)$ of f on any abstract state s completely determines
the g-value, and conversely. This means that there is actually an
isomorphism Φ between $f(S)$ and $g(S)$, and we can write

$$\Phi(f(s)) = g(s) \qquad\qquad (3.2.7)$$

for every abstract state s ε S.

Restated in slightly different language, if $R_f = R_g$, the $R_{fg} = R_f =
R_g$. The image of S/R_{fg} in $f(S)$ x $g(S)$ is then simply a *curve* in the
two-dimensional "state space", whose equation is given by (3.2.7).

The next most elementary case is that in which f is an invariant for
R_g; i.e. each class in S/R_f is a union of classes in S/R_g. In this
case, knowing the value $g(s)$ completely determines $f(s)$; but knowing
$f(s)$ does not in general determine $g(s)$. It is easy to see that, in
this case, $R_{fg} = R_g$. We can thus establish a mapping $\Phi : g(S) \to f(S)$,
but this mapping is not an isomorphism; it cannot be inverted. In
this case, the encoding arising from f is "coarser" than that arising
from g; the f-encoding may be *reduced* to the g-encoding, but not
conversely.

In this case, we shall say that f is *linked* to g. The linkage relation can again be represented geometrically in the two-dimensional
"state space" $f(S) \times g(S)$ as a curve;   i.e. as a relation

$$\Phi(f(s), g(s)) = 0 \tag{3.2.8}$$

in which $g(s)$ plays the role of independent variable;   i.e. (3.2.8)
can be solved as a single-valued function of $f(s)$, but not conversely.

In a still more general situation, where a given value $f(s)$ of f
partially constrains the possible values of $g(s)$, a repetition of
these arguments shows that the image of S/R_{fg} in $f(S) \times g(S)$ is no
longer a curve, but some more complicated subset of $f(S) \times g(S)$.
Nevertheless, we can still find a relation of the form (3.2.8);
it can however not be solved in general for $f(s)$ as a single-valued
function of $g(s)$, or conversely. Thus, there is in this case no
mapping between the encodings in either direction;   so that neither
of them can be regarded as a model of the other.

Finally, in the case that the value of $f(s)$ places no restriction on
the value of $g(s)$ and conversely (i.e. the case in which every class
in S/R_f intersects every class in S/R_g and conversely) there is no
relation of the form (3.2.8) at all; S/R_{fg} maps *onto* all of $f(S) \times$
$g(S)$, and we say that the two observables f, g are *unlinked*.

In general, we can say that a linkage between two observables f, g
can be expressed as a relation of the form (3.2.8), which characterizes some locus in $f(S) \times g(S)$. Such a relation (3.2.8) will be
called an *equation of state* for the system. An equation of state
is thus seen to be a relation between encodings of a natural system,
expressing the degree to which the codings are linked. *An equation
of state is not an observable*, but expresses a relation between
observables;   as we shall see, such equations of state represent the
encoding of system laws, imposed by a choice of encoding of individual
observables in the fashion we have described.

In the light of the above discussion, let us consider the more general
situation, in which we are given two *families* $(f_1, \ldots, f_n)$, $(g_1,
\ldots, g_m)$ of observables of our system S. With each of these families
we can associate corresponding "state spaces", which we can denote
by $\prod_{i=1}^{n} f_i(S)$, $\prod_{i=1}^{m} g_i(S)$ respectively. Using the notation of (3.2.5)
and (3.2.6) we can construct the following analog of the diagram of

Fig. 3.2.3, as shown overleaf. The arguments above can be repeated r
word for word in the new situation. Any linkages between the f_i
and the g_i considered individually or in sets will be expressed
by a more general equation of state, of the form

$$\Phi(f_1(s), \ldots, f_n(s), g_1(s), \ldots, g_m(s)) = 0 \tag{3.2.9}$$

which is the analog of (3.2.8). The character of Φ will express the manner in which the observables in these families are linked.

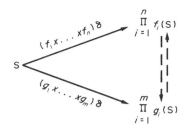

Fig. 3.2.3.

Of special importance is the case in which $m = 1$ (i.e. our second family of observables consists of only a single member) and in which the relation (3.2.9) can be solved for this member; i.e. put into the form

$$g(s) = \Psi(f_1(s), \ldots, f_n(s)). \tag{3.2.10}$$

In this case, the value of $g(s)$ is completely determined by knowing the values of the f_i on s, for any abstract state s. Stated another way the relation R_g is precisely the intersection of the relations R_{f_i}, $i = 1, \ldots, n$. In this case, the linkage is expressed by saying that the observable g is a *function* of the observables f_i, and the equation of state (3.2.10) can be used to determine its value if the values of the f_i are known. This is perhaps the simplest instance of how we may utilize the encodings we have discussed, and the equations of state to which they give rise, to make specific *predictions*. We shall see many examples of this as we proceed.

So far, we have not made any mention of dynamics; i.e. of the manner in which the states of a system may change in time; nor of the manner in which time itself must be encoded into a formal system. We will take up these important matters in due course. For the moment, we will content ourselves with pointing out how more general equations of state may be written within the scope of the discussion we have presented above, and of which dynamical laws can be regarded as a special case. Let us return to the diagram (3.2.5) above, which specifies how we may encode abstract states in terms of a family $(f_1, \ldots, f_n)$ of observables. A particular role is played in that diagram by the formal mapping δ, the diagonal mapping. Intuitively, we may think of δ as specifying an "instant of time" at which our natural system is in some abstract sense s, and it is at that instant that the observables f_i are evaluated. With this intuitive picture,

it is clear that if we replace δ by some more general mapping of S into its n-fold cartesian product, and then carry out the same analysis as before, we obtain thereby *equations of state which relate the values of the observables f_i evaluated on different states of* S.

Thus, in particular, if we think of these different abstract states of S as pertaining to different instants of time, *such an equation of state represents a linkage relation between observables evaluated*

at different instants. For instance, we might interpret an equation
of state like (10) under these circumstances as a relation linking
the value of an observable g at some instant to the values of the
observables f_i evaluated at some other instant. In this fashion,
such equations of state become the essential vehicles for dynamical
prediction. For the present, we content ourselves with these general
remarks; we shall take up dynamical questions in more detail in a
subsequent chapter.

Let us conclude this chapter with a few considerations bearing on
the encoding of observables we have described. Let us first suppose
that we have at our disposal a family $\}= (f_1, f_2, \ldots, f_n)$ of observables. One question we may ask is whether we may find a subset
$\}' \subset \}$ of these observables, such that every observable in $\} - \}'$
can be related to those in $\}'$ by an equation of state of the form
(3.2.10). In that case, we can speak of $\}'$ as constituting a family
of *state variables* for $\}$. In practice, we also try to pick such a
set $\}'$ which is of minimal size, and for which the observables of
$\}'$ are pairwise unlinked. The existence of such a subset $\}'$ is a
purely *formal* question, and receives its precise formulation in terms
of the corresponding equivalence relations involved. It is universally supposed in applications (a) that we can always find such a
set of state variables;   (b) that the number of observables in such
a set is always the same; i.e. in an invariant of $\}$; and (c) if $\}'$
is a set of state variables for $\}$, it is also a set of state variables
of a smaller set. It turns out, however, that none of these assumptions is generally valid; i.e. that there is nothing intrinsic about
a set of state variables. We shall not dwell on these matters here;
fuller details concerning problems of state variables, and indeed of
all of the encodings we have discussed in the present chapter, may
be found in our earlier monograph on measurement and system description.

We will conclude this chapter with a word about bifurcations. To
fix ideas, let us consider again the simple diagram shown in Figure
3.2.2 above, and let us suppose that some equation of state of the
form (3.2.8) relates the two encodings via f, g respectively. We
are going to inquire how the equation of state behaves with respect
to the topologies of $f(S)$ and $g(S)$, and the manner in which they
separately impute metric considerations to S. Basically, the question
we ask is this: if we know that $f(s)$ and $f(s')$ are close in $f(S)$,
can we conclude that $g(s)$ and $g(s')$ are likewise close in $g(S)$?
Stated in slightly different language: if $f(s')$ is an *approximation*
to $f(s)$, will $g(s')$ be an approximation to $g(s)$?

This question obviously devolves on the *continuity* of any relation
between $f(s)$ and $g(s)$ established by the equation of state Φ. More
specifically, suppose r ε $f(S)$. Let U be a small neighborhood of
r. Now consider $f^{-1}(U)$; the totality of abstract states in S
assigned a value in U by the observable f. Let us form $g(f^{-1}(U))$;
this is a set of values in $g(S)$. The relation between U and $g(f^{-1}(U))$
is obviously another way of expressing the equation of state (3.2.8).
Clearly, if $g(f^{-1}(U))$ is a small neighborhood in $g(S)$, and if $f(s) = $
r ε U, then replacing s by another abstract state s' for which $f(s')$
ε U will keep $g(s')$ within a small neighborhood of $g(s)$. Under such
circumstances, the equation of state (3.2.8) is a continuous relation
within U, and we can say that any r ε U is a *stable point* of f with
respect to g. The totality of such stable points comprises an open
subset of $f(U)$. The complement of the set of stable points will be
called the *bifurcation set* of f with respect to g; clearly, if a

number r belongs to the bifurcation set, then the relation between
any neighborhood U of it and the corresponding set $g(f^{-1}(U))$ established by the equation of state will not be a continuous one. In
other words, no matter how close $f(s')$ is to $f(s) = r$ in this case,
we cannot conclude that $g(s')$ and $g(s)$ are close; i.e. no matter
how closely we approximate to r in the f-encoding, we do not approximate correspondingly in the g-encoding. It will be seen that this
notion of bifurcation is exactly the same as that described in the
preceding chapter. We reiterate that in present circumstances, when
we are dealing with encodings of observables of natural systems,
bifurcation depends on the continuity of the linkage relations
between observables on a set of abstract states. Thus, as we pointed
out before, a bifurcation arises when the properties of distinct
encodings become logically independent; the properties in question
here are topological relations between respective sets of observable
values.

We point out explicitly that so far, we have considered stability
and bifurcation of the observable f with respect to the observable
g; in particular, the bifurcation set we defined was a subset of
$f(S)$. We can clearly interchange the roles of f and g in the above
discussion; we thereby obtain a dual notion of stability and bifurcation of g with respect to f. Thus, bifurcation sets come in pairs;
in the present case, as a pair of subsets of $f(S)$ and $g(S)$ respectively.

The discussion of stability and bifurcation can clearly be generalized to equations of state of the form (3.2.9). We leave the details
as an exercise for the reader.

We shall now turn to some specific examples of the encodings we have
described above, beginning with those which characterize the study
of physical systems. As we shall see, all of the deep problems in
the study of such systems arise from the attempts to inter-relate
distinct encodings; i.e. from attempts to establish equations of
state of the form (3.2.10). It should now be evident that all of
these problems involve at root the essence of the modelling relation
itself.

REFERENCES AND NOTES

The material presented in this chapter is an elaboration of some of
the ideas originally developed in the author's earlier monograph,
Fundamentals of Measurement and the Representation of Natural Systems
(Elsevier, 1978). Further background and details may be found there.

3.3 Encodings of Physical Systems

We are now in a position to discuss the modelling of natural systems
in detail. The present chapter will be concerned with the encoding
of physical systems. As in 3.1 above, we will subdivide our development into a number of examples, each of which will be concerned with
a different kind of encoding of a physical system into a formal or
mathematical one. We shall emphasize in our discussion how these
encodings are related formally to each other, or not, as appropriate.
We will thus construct an armory of specific examples of the modelling
relation between natural and formal systems, which we shall draw upon
heavily as we proceed.

EXAMPLE 1: PARTICLE MECHANICS[1]

Our first example will be concerned with the Newtonian approach to
systems of material particles, which we already touched on briefly,
in a superficial way, in 1.2 above. We will now bring to bear the
basic discussion of the previous chapter, to see what is actually
involved in the encoding of particulate systems.

The first order of business is to specify the fundamental observables
to be encoded, and to define the corresponding "state space". The
first great contribution of Newtonian mechanics was to propose such
a set of observables, or state variables, which provides the foundation for everything to follow.

In brief, Newton proposed that these fundamental observables could
be taken as: (a) the (instantaneous) displacements of the particles
in the system from some convenient reference, or origin of co-
ordinates, and (b) the corresponding (instantaneous) values of the
velocities of these particles. Thus, given a system composed of N
particles, each abstract state of the system is represented by a set
of 6N numbers; three co-ordinates of displacement for each particle,
and three corresponding co-ordinates of velocity. This gives us an
encoding of abstract states into the points of a 6N-dimensional
Euclidean space, corresponding to 3.2.5 of the preceding chapter.
This Euclidean space is the *phase space* of mechanics; the 3N-dimen-
sional space comprising the displacement co-ordinates alone is generally called the *configuration space* of the system; the 3N-dimensional

137

space of velocity co-ordinates is called the *velocity space*.

The next step in the Newtonian encoding is to postulate that *every other observable of a particulate system can be represented by a real-valued function on this phase space*. This innocent-sounding step is really of great profundity and significance, for it asserts that every other observable is totally linked to these state variables on the set of abstract states S. That is, if *g* is any observable of our system, then there is a linkage of the form (3.2.10) above, which expresses its value on any abstract state as a function of the values of the state variables on that state. We shall put aside for the moment the extent to which such a postulate can be expected to be universally satisfied; we shall simply treat it here as a definition of the scope of the Newtonian encoding; that is, the observables with which Newtonian mechanics deals are precisely those which are representable in this manner. The force of this postulate is that it removes the necessity of ever referring back to the set S of abstract states; we can confine ourselves from now on entirely to the phase space into which S is encoded by the state variables, and to the real-valued functions defined on this phase space.

We must now say a word about the manner in which *time* is encoded in the Newtonian scheme. Indeed, the very notion of velocity or rate, which enters into the choice of the basic state variables, presupposes some kind of temporal encoding. We have also tacitly utilized such an encoding when we used the term "instantaneous" in discussing these state variables. Basically, the Newtonian view of time involves two aspects: one of simultaneity, and one of temporal succession, as described in 2.1 above. For Newton, an *instant* of time is that at which the state variables must be evaluated in order to provide a coding of abstract states into points in the phase space. It follows that a particulate system must be in exactly one such state at any instant of time; the determination of which state our system is in at some instant is equivalent to the *simultaneous* evaluation of all of the state variables at that instant. It should be noted that it is precisely here that the modern treatments of quantum theory depart from the Newtonian scheme; in quantum theory it is in fact *impossible* (according to the Heisenberg uncertainty principle) to simultaneously evaluate these variables; hence in quantum theory there is (a) no such thing as an instantaneous state, and (b) the encoding of time itself in the quantum-theoretic formalism is shrouded in the deepest obscurity.

Thus, for Newtonian mechanics, a point in the phase space represents an *instantaneous* state; it tells us what our system is like at an instant of time, and thereby tacitly specifies what is meant by an instant.[2]

The next step, basic to dynamics, is to specify what is meant by temporal succession. It is here that we find the famous identification of the set of instants with the real number continuum, and of absolute time flowing along this continuum of itself. In terms of the phase space of a mechanical system, this must mean the following: if at some instant t of time our system is represented by a point $\sigma(t)$ in the phase space, then as time flows of itself along the time continuum, the state $\sigma(t)$ itself will in general move in the phase space, tracing out thereby a curve, or *trajectory*, which is a continuous image of the time continuum. Each system trajectory, then, will be represented by a continuous mapping of the set $\mathbb{R}$ of instants into the phase space.

We have already pointed out that in Newtonian mechanics, we assume
that *every* observable pertaining to a particulate system is repre-
resented by a function of the state variables.   In particular, the
rates at which the state variables themselves are changing in any
particular state must be a function of the state alone (it will be
noted that this basic hypothesis of the reactive paradigm, which was
described at length in Chapter 1.2 above, is seen here simply as a
consequence of the way observables are encoded in the Newtonian
scheme).   *Thus, if these rates are themselves observables, there
must be equations of state of the form (3.2.10), which express the
manner in which the rates of change of the state variables depend
on the values of the state variables themselves.*   It is this fact
which leads directly to the entire dynamical apparatus of Newtonian
physics.

Let us suppose that x_1, ..., x_n, v_1, ..., v_n are respectively the
instantaneous co-ordinates of displacement and velocity of a state
of a particulate system.   Let us denote their respective rates of
change of that state in the traditional way by dx_1/dt, ..., dx_n/dt,
dv_1/dt, ..., dv_n/dt.   Then by (3.2.10) we must have $2n$ equations of
state, of the form

$$\frac{dx_i}{dt} = \phi_i(x_1, \ldots, x_n, v_1, \ldots, v_n) \qquad i = 1, \ldots, n$$

$$\frac{dv_i}{dt} = \psi_i(x_1, \ldots, x_n, v_1, \ldots, v_n) \qquad i = 1, \ldots, n$$

(3.3.1)

These equations of state play the predominant role in the theory;
they are essentially the *equations of motion* of the system.

Before proceeding further, let us pause for a moment to look at the
equations (3.3.1).   Each of the functions ϕ_i, ψ_i appearing in these
equations will typically involve, in addition to the state variables
themselves, a number of numerical quantities *which are not themselves
functions of the state variables.*   For instance, if these functions
are represented mathematically in terms of some basis set, we will
find a corresponding family of coefficients.   Such numerical quantities pertain to the specific character of the system with which we
are dealing, for they determine the precise form of the linkage between the state variables and the rates at which these variables are
changing.   We cannot change them without in a precise sense changing
the *identity* of the system with which we are dealing (i.e. we would
thereby force a change in the way the observables of our system are
linked to each other).   These numerical quantities thus play the
role of *structural* or *constitutive parameters* of our system, which
were mentioned briefly in Chapter 2.3 above.   We see here that such
specific numerical parameters appear here automatically, by virtue
of the basic hypothesis that rates of change of state variables in
a state are linked in a specific way, via (3.3.1), to the values of
the state variables themselves.

Of course, such constitutive parameters may be measured independently
on our system;   we shall see in a moment that they correspond to such
quantities as inertial masses, elastic constants, coefficients of
viscosity, and the like.   Two points should be observed regarding
them: (a) they appear as necessary consequences of the encoding of

state variables and observables, and thus their appearance as a
logical consequence of the encoding itself represents a specific
prediction about the system; (b) since they are observable quantities, and not functions of the state variables, we see that our
initial identification of observables as functions of the state
variables is already proving to be too narrow. We shall see in a
moment how to broaden our encoding of observables so as to accomodate them.

Let us now return to the incipient equations of motion of our system,
embodied in (3.3.1) above. It was the second great step of Newton
to give a specific interpretation to the functions ϕ_i, ψ_i in these
equations of state. The specification of the first n of these functions is simple; we merely put

$$\phi_i(x_1, \ldots, x_n, v_1, \ldots, v_n) = v_i \qquad (3.3.2)$$

In fact, these n equations are nothing but the *definition* of velocity
as rate of change of displacement. The real innovation was Newton's
identification of the functions ψ_i with the mechanical concept of
force, and the essential identification of force with rate of change
of velocity. Since the forces imposed on a system can generally be
posited directly as functions of displacements alone (conservative
forces) or as functions of displacement and velocity, the second n
equations in (3.3.1) become not only non-circular, but in fact enable
us to specifically encode *any* particulate system in the fashion we
have indicated.

We thus can write our $2n$ equations of motion in the form

$$\frac{dx_i}{dt} = v_i$$

$$\frac{dv_i}{dt} = F(x_1, \ldots, x_n, v_1, \ldots, v_n) \qquad (3.3.3)$$

where F_i is the force acting on the particle for which dv_i/dt is a
velocity co-ordinate. It is in this form that we can bring the full
inferential power of mathematical analysis specifically to bear on
the encoding of our system, and obtain the most far-reaching predictions. But before dealing with this question, let us look again at
the constitutive parameters entering into the equations (3.3.3) by
virtue of the general discussion given above.

Let us first observe that these parameters appear in the equations
of motion precisely in the definition of the forces imposed on the
system; i.e. in the functions F_i. If we suppose that there are r
such parameters $q_1, \ldots, q_r$, then these equations of motion can be
written as

$$\frac{dx_i}{dt} = v_i$$

$$\frac{dv_i}{dt} = F_i(x_1, \ldots, v_n, q_1, \ldots, q_r) \qquad (3.3.4)$$

Since these parameters by definition cannot change without changing
the very identity of the system, and since they are *unaffected* by

the forces being imposed on the system, we can treat them as if they
were additional state variables for our system, governed by dynamical
equations of the form

$$\frac{dq_i}{dt} = 0 \qquad i = 1, \ldots, r \qquad\qquad (3.3.5)$$

Indeed, we can even treat time as if it were a state variable τ, by
writing

$$\frac{d\tau}{dt} = 1 \qquad\qquad (3.3.6)$$

Thus, with these assumptions, the constitutive parameters can be
included directly into the essential Newtonian formalism. Indeed,
utilizing (3.3.6), we can allow the forces F_i in (3.3.4) to contain
time t explicitly.

The next point to make is that we can imagine *changing* the values of
these constitutive parameters to new values q_i', leaving every other
aspect of our encoding unaffected. We would thereby in effect
create an encoding of *another system*, *quantitively* different from
the original one, but with the same phase space, and with the same
qualitative properties. Indeed, we can identify each such system
obtained in this fashion with the corresponding r-tuple $(q_1, \ldots, q_r)$
of structural parameters. The set of all possible r-tuples of constitutive parameters for these systems fills out a set Q, which is a
subset of r-dimensional Euclidean space; this set Q may be called
the *parameter space* for the systems so defined; each specific system
is obtained by identifying a single element of this parameter space.
Looked at in this light, the equations of motion (3.3.4) represent
not a single system, but an entire class of systems, differing from
one another only in the values assigned to their constitutive parameters.

If we denote the phase space shared by the systems in such a class
by X, then the class itself is represented by the cartesian product
QxX. We may note here, and we will enlarge upon this subsequently,
that the class of systems so obtained has many of the properties of
a mathematical object called a *fiber bundle*, with base space Q and
fiber X. In diagrammatic form, the class can be represented as
shown in Figure 3.3.1 below:

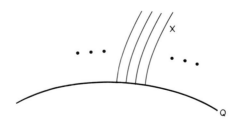

Fig. 3.3.1.

where each point q ε Q is associated with a copy of the phase space

X, and the equations of state obtaining in the pair (q, X) are given
by (3.3.4) and (3.3.5) with the appropriate numerical values of the
q_i inserted into them. We shall have extensive recourse to this
picture in some of the examples to be considered subsequently.

This, then, is the general picture of the Newtonian encoding of particulate systems. We do not encode a specific system as a general
rule, but an entire class of qualitatively similar but quantitatively
distinct systems, as we have just described. These classes are encoded into objects of the type shown in Fig. 3.3.1 above; objects
with an exceedingly rich mathematical structure, which themselves
form a category. This fact too will be exploited in the examples
to be considered subsequently.

Let us return briefly to a specific system in such a class, specified
by a definite pair (q, X), and with the equations of motion (3.3.5).
This is now a formal, mathematical object, and as we noted above, we
can impose the full power of mathematical analysis on such objects.
Let us briefly review some of its basic properties, and how these
may be decoded into predictions pertaining to the corresponding
natural system from which it was obtained.

Specifically, if we fix a q_0 in Q, then the equations of motion
(3.3.6) become, in mathematical terms, a family of $2n$ simultaneous
first-order differential equations. We have already discussed the
properties of such a system of equations in Chapter 1.2 above;
specifically, how we may obtain solutions of such a system in analytic form. In general, a solution comprises a family of $2n$ functions
of the independent variable t:

$$\{x_1(t), \ldots, x_n(t), v_1(t), \ldots, v_n(t)\}$$

which satisfy the equations of motion identically. We have seen
also (in Chapter 1.2) that, under very weak mathematical conditions
on the forces F_i, a solution is uniquely determined by any point in
the phase space through which it passes; this is the unique trajectory property in analytic form, when we note that a solution precisely defines a continuous mapping of the space of instants into
the phase space. Thus, in principle, knowing a point in the phase
space (i.e. knowing the values of the state variables x_i, v_i at a
single instant of time), the equations of motion determine the
entire trajectory on which the point lies.

In particular, the knowledge of such a set of initial conditions
$\{x_1(t_0), \ldots, x_n(t_0), v_1(t_0), \ldots, v_n(t_0)\}$ allows us to draw
inferences of the form

$$\{x_i(t_0), v_i(t_0)\} \rightarrow x_j(t) \tag{3.3.7}$$

and

$$\{x_i(t_0), v_i(t_0)\} \rightarrow v_j(t) \tag{3.3.8}$$

That is, knowing the values of the state variables at any instant t_0
allows us to *predict* the values of any state variable at any other
instant. These predictions are simply expressions of linkage between

the initial values of the state variables and their values at other
instants, of the type which were mentioned in the preceding chapter;
that is, they represent a linkage between observables evaluated on
different abstract states of our physical system. Further, using
the hypothesis that every relevant observable is directly linked to
the state variables, we can use the inferences (3.3.7) and (3.3.8)
to predict the value of *any* observable on the state of our system at
any instant t, knowing the values assumed by the state variables on
the state at some fixed instant t_0.

Thus, we can make an enormous number of inferences regarding the
temporal behavior of our physical system when we know: (a) the
forces acting on our system; i.e. the way in which rates of change
of the state variables are linked to the state variables themselves;
(b) the values assumed by the state variables on any initial state.
These inferences are then specific predictions about our physical
system, which decode into the results of specific measurements or
observations carried out on our physical system at particular instants. If such predictions are verified, then the mathematical
system we have described must, by definition, be related to the
physical system encoded into it by a modelling relation. That is,
the linkages embodied into the equations of motion, together with
the purely mathematical inferential structure which can be brought
to bear on these equations, faithfully represent the laws governing
the change of abstract states of that system in the external world.
If the predictions we have made on this basis are found *not* to be
realized when the appropriate observations are performed, and if the
discrepancy between prediction and observation is not due to faulty
observation, then we are faced with a number of obvious alternatives:
(a) we have not selected an adequate set of state variables, so that
the assumed linkage between rates of change of state variables and
the variables themselves fails to encode essential qualities, or (b)
our hypothesis about the form of the linkage, embodied in the specification of the forces on the system, do not faithfully mirror the
circumstances obtaining in the physical system, or (c) the entire
encoding procedure we are using is fundamentally inapplicable to the
given physical system, for one reason or another. We shall see
examples of all of these circumstances as we proceed.

We can carry out this procedure for each system in our family of
systems (q, X), by inserting the appropriate values of the constitutive parameters q in Q into the equations of motion. In terms of
the diagram of Fig. 3.3.1 above, we obtain thereby a fibering of
each of the state spaces X into trajectories, determined by solutions
of the equations of motion associated with the corresponding point
of q. It then becomes an interesting question to relate the fiberings
corresponding to different values q, q' of Q; it will be seen that
this question is a special case of structural stability, which was
discussed in Example 5 of Chapter 3.1 above. To see this, let us
recast the dynamical equations (3.3.4) above into the form of a one-
parameter family of transformations of X, which was described in
Chapter 1.2. Thus, to each q in Q, we will have a one-parameter
family

$$T_t^q : X \to X. \tag{3.3.9}$$

If q' is another point in Q, it will be associated with a corresponding one-parameter family

$$T_t^{q'} : X \to X. \tag{3.3.10}$$

Roughly speaking, if the effect of replacing q by q' in (3.3.9) can
be annihilated by co-ordinate transformations of X; i.e. if we can
find mappings $\alpha = \alpha(q, q')$, $\beta = \beta(q, q')$ such that the diagram

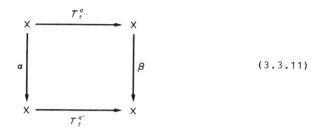

$$(3.3.11)$$

is commutative for every t, then by definition the dynamics imposed
by (3.3.4) is structurally stable to the perturbation $q \to q'$. In
this case, we may say that the particular system (q, X) is itself a
model of the different system (q', X). This kind of diagram, which
we have already seen in abstract terms in Figure 2.3.3 above, will
be the basis for our discussion of similarity in Example 5 below.
The reader should also note for future reference the relation between the situation diagrammed in (3.3.11) and the notion of a natural
transformation of functors. Briefly, what we have shown is the following: to the extent that a modification of constitutive parameters
in Q can be annihilated by co-ordinate transformations s on X, to
that extent are the two physical systems themselves related to one
another by a modelling relation; and to that extent is a model for
one of them also a model for any other. The ramifications of this
situation are most profound, and reach into every corner of both
theoretical and practical science.

Since the situation we have just described is so important, let us
recast (3.3.11) into a diagram analogous to that of Figure 3.3.1:

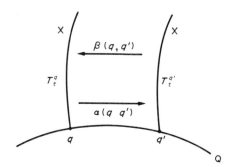

Fig. 3.3.2.

This diagram allows us to enlarge somewhat on our previous remark that QxX itself possesses the structure of a fiber bundle. On each "fiber" X there is imposed a group of transformations; namely the corresponding dynamics T_t^q; the notion of structural stability allows us to consider mappings of the entire space QxS which (a) leaves Q fixed, and (b) preserves dynamics on the fibers. Later, we shall consider a broader class of mappings on spaces QxX which do not leave Q fixed; these are intimately connected with what the physicist calls *renormalization*. We shall take up these matters once again in the appropriate sections below.

EXAMPLE 2: CONTINUUM MECHANICS[3]

We have seen in the preceding example how to encode a natural system consisting of a discrete set of mass points (particles) into a mathematical formalism, and how that formalism leads in turn to specific predictions about the system so encoded. This kind of encoding represents one of the two possible logical alternatives we may entertain about the ultimate nature of an extended physical system; namely, that it is comprised of such particles. The assertion that every material system is composed of particles forms the basis for the atomic theory; thus, to the extent that the atomic theory holds universally, the concepts of Newtonian mechanics (or some appropriate generalization, such as quantum theory) can be regarded as providing an encoding of every physical system.

The other logical alternative we may entertain regarding the structure of extended material systems is that, in some sense, they are continua. That is, they may be indefinitely subdivided, in such a way that any portion of the system, however small it may be, retains all of the qualities of the entire system. The pursuit of this logical alternative leads to a quite different mechanical theory, which is generally called continuum mechanics. As we shall see, the character of the encoding required for a continuum is in many ways radically different from the one we have just described. Furthermore, the point of departure for this encoding is logically incompatible with particle mechanics, as we have just seen. In the present section, we shall briefly explore the nature of the encodings appropriate to continua, and then we shall describe the manner in which these two incompatible encodings may be forced to co-exist as alternate descriptions of the same extended material system. We will thus be exploring a special case of the situation diagrammed in Figure 2.3.4 above; and as we shall see, much of classical physics is concerned precisely with the confrontation of these incompatible pictures, neither of which, by its very nature, can be reduced to the other.

The first item of business is to decide on the encoding of an *observable* of a continuous extended system. As this is far from a trivial matter, we shall discuss it in some detail.

It is reasonable to suppose initially that a quality or observable pertaining to a continuously extended system involves two distinct aspects: (a) an aspect involving the actual manner in which the system is extended in space, and (b) an aspect independent of the extension. For by the hypothesis of infinite divisibility, any portion of such a system, however small it may be, retains the characters of the system as a whole; this would be impossible if all characters were dependent on the way each particular system is extended. In the limit, then, each *point* of the system must manifest these characters, independent of all the others.

Moreover, we must relate the encoding of observables to the encoding
of time. We retain the idea that instants of time are encoded as
real numbers, and thus that the set of instants is the real number
system $\mathbb{R}$. We encode instants in a manner similar to that employed
for particulate systems; we assume that *both* aspects of observables
of continua (i.e. the aspect dependent on extension and the aspect
independent of it) are what are evaluated at specific instants.

We shall suppose that, at any instant t_0 of time, our system occupies
a region $U(t_0)$ of Euclidean three-dimensional space, E_3. Thus, we
assume that any point of $U(t_0)$ can be identified by a triple $(u_1, u_2,
u_3)$ of real numbers, where the point is referred to some convenient
system of co-ordinates in E_3. Thus, any quality pertaining entirely
to the spatial extension of the system can simply be regarded as a
real-valued function of $U(t_0)$; as examples, we may cite the observables used to describe the motions of rigid bodies in space.

We now turn to the representation of observables which are independent
of spatial extension. We will proceed analogously to the example of
particle mechanics, by assigning to any *point* of an extended system
a set S of abstract states. An observable will then, as usual, be
encoded into a real-valued function $f : S \to \mathbb{R}$ on this set of abstract
states. If we assume as before that any point of the system is in
exactly one abstract state $s(t_0) \varepsilon S$ at any instant of time t_0, then
the value of f at the instant t_0 is just $f(s(t_0))$.

Let us now put these two aspects together. If at an instant t_0 our
extended system occupies a definite region $U(t_0)$, then each point of
this region is assigned a copy of the set S of abstract states.
Moreover, we suppose that in each such copy of S, there is exactly
one distinguished state, on which observables independent of extension
may be evaluated at that instant. Thus, the extended system as a
whole is represented by a set of 4-tuples of the form

$$(s(t_0), u_1, u_2, u_3);$$

i.e. is a definite element of $S \times U(t_0)$. Thus, if $f : S \to \mathbb{R}$ is an
observable independent of extension, we may encode this observable
into a 4-tuple of real numbers.

$$(f(s(t_0)), u_1, u_2, u_3);$$

i.e. into the cartesian product $f(S) \times U(t_0)$. Thus, an observable of
S defines, at any instant of time, a *scalar field* of $U(t_0)$. Observables of this character are the ones predominant in studies of elastic
solids, and of fluids of various types. We shall call the number
$f(s(t_0))$ appearing at the first co-ordinate of such a 4-tuple the
value of f at the point (u_1, u_2, u_3) of our extended system at time
t_0. In this way, we can ultimately encode such observables as real-
valued functions of the four real variables $t, u_1, u_2, u_3;$ this is

analogous to, but quite different from, our encoding of observables of particulate systems.

The effect of this kind of encoding is to convert observables f which are independent of spatial extension into new observables of a particular extended system; these new observables can be regarded as *densities*. We invariably suppose that these densities, considered as functions of four real variables, are continuous and smooth in time and space. Thus, they have rates of change in time (velocities) and rates of change in space (gradients). If we assume that these rates of change are *themselves observables* of the same character, we have as before the possibility of establishing linkages between them; such linkages will be the analogs of the equations of motion for a particulate system, and will represent the encoding of system laws into mathematical objects, which are now *partial* differential equations.

In general, the encoding of such linkages does not proceed, as it did in particle mechanics, by attempting to find a set of "state variables" in terms of which any observable can be expressed, and then establishing equations of motion for the state variables. Rather, if we are interested in any particular observable f on an extended system, we attempt to find a family of observables g_1, $\ldots$, g_r such that f is linked to the g_i, and the equations of motion for each g_i depend only on the other g's. Thus the g_i play the role of state variables for the observable f in which we are interested, but they need not play the same role for another observable f'.

The actual expression of such linkages depends heavily on the local geometry of Euclidean space. For instance, if f is an observable of an extended system, we can talk about the rate at which f is changing in any direction $\vec{r} = (r_1, r_2, r_3)$ at some instant t_0 and some point (u_1, u_2, u_3); this is identified with the scalar product

$$r_1 \frac{\partial f}{\partial u_1} + r_2 \frac{\partial f}{\partial u_2} + r_3 \frac{\partial f}{\partial u_3} = \vec{r} \cdot \nabla f.$$

We can seek to establish a linkage between these rates, or *flows* of the quality f, with its velocity $\frac{\partial f}{\partial t}$; such a linkage may for instance take the familiar form

$$\frac{\partial f}{\partial t} = - \nabla^2 f + Q(f, g_1, \ldots, g_r) \qquad (3.3.12)$$

Such a linkage may be interpreted as follows: the rate at which a quality f is changing at an instant t, at a point (u_1, u_2, u_3) of our extended system, is given by the rate at which it flows from the point together with the rate at which it is produced or consumed at the point. Typically these rates themselves depend on other such observables g_i and their flows; to encode the system laws into a mathematical form from which inferences may be drawn, it is necessary to specify these observables as well, in the manner we have indicated. We then obtain a system of simultaneous partial differential equations, in terms of which we may make predictions about the observable in which we are interested.

Just as in the case of particle mechanics, linkage relations like
(3.3.12) typically involve numerical parameters which characterize
the *identity* of the system; these then play the role of constitutive
parameters. Likewise, the form of the linkages arising in the description of any particular system may be determined by subsidiary
relations among the observables involved, which are generally called
constituuve relations; these play the role of constraints in particle mechanics, and again refer to the specific nature of the system
with which we are actually dealing.

We cannot in the present limited space go too deeply into the detailed
features of continuum mechanics; for these the reader may consult
any of the excellent texts on e.g. elasticity or on hydrodynamics.
We have said enough, however, to point out the fundamental differences
between it and particle mechanics, not only in terms of the basic
hypothesis of the infinite divisibility of extended matter, but in
terms of the mathematical form of the symbolism into which observables and linkages of extended systems are encoded.

We now turn to the question of how the irreconcilable encodings of
extended material systems we have described can be related to each
other.[4] As we have already noted above, the atomic theory of matter
postulates precisely that matter is not infinitely divisible, but in
fact consists of discrete particulate units, However, it also follows
that these discrete units are exceedingly small compared to the units
of extension typically used in describing bulk matter; hence in any
bulk volume there will be an exceedingly large number of them. The
basic idea, then, is to use this fact to "approximate" to a continuum
by the exploitation of *average values* of observables pertaining to
such a family of particles; at the same time, we must "discretize"
the continuum by breaking it into regions which are (a) large enough
so that the average process is meaningful (i.e. large enough to
contain many particles) but (b) small enough so that they can be
treated as infinitesimals. In this way, we obtain a distortion of
both theories; it is these distortions which may then be related.
The basic question is whether, in the process of formal distortion,
we may lose the encodings themselves.

Let us look at the matter in more detail. Let us suppose that U is
a region of an extended system, containing a number N of particles
at some instant t_0. Then this particulate system can be encoded as
described previously, and in particular, the displacements and velocities of the particles form a set of state variables. We can then
think of representing the entire system of particles by a single
"mean particle", encoded into a single 6-tuple $(\bar{u}_1, \bar{u}_2, \bar{u}_3, \bar{v}_1, \bar{v}_2, \bar{v}_3)$, where each $\bar{u}_i$, $\bar{v}_i$, is the *average* of the corresponding co-ordinates for the individual particles. We can then further evaluate
any observable f of the particulate system on this "mean particle"
to obtain an average value $\bar{f}$ of f in the region, by writing

$$\bar{f} = f(\bar{u}_1, \bar{u}_2, \bar{u}_3, \bar{v}_1, \bar{v}_2, \bar{v}_3). \tag{3.3.13}$$

We see that, if we could suppose our region shrunk to a point in such
a way that the number of particles within the region was always
large enough to make these averages meaningful, they would converge
to what we earlier called *densities*. However, we clearly cannot do
this; therefore, the mean observables we have described can only be
regarded as formal *approximations* to such densities.

Conversely, let us suppose that we are given a continuum. Let (u_1, u_2, u_3) be a point of this cintinuum, and let V be a small neigborhood of this point. If now f represents a density (i.e. an observable of the continuum) then we can eliminate the pointwise variation of f in V by a process of integration; i.e. we can form the qualtity

$$\bar{\bar{f}} = \frac{1}{\|V\|} \int_V f \, du_1 du_2 du_3. \tag{3.3.14}$$

where $\|V\|$ is the volume of the neighborhood V. This is a kind of averaging in the *continuum*, which approximates to f at the given point (u_1, u_2, u_3) in the sense that $\bar{\bar{f}}$ converges to f as V shrinks to (u_1, u_2, u_3).

What we need to do is to identify these two kinds of averages. But we must note that the approximations involved themselves require incompatible hypotheses. The first approximation requires a large number of particles, and hence a large region over which the averages are formed. The second requires, on the other hand, a small region. If we suppose that these incompatible requirements can be satisfied, so that we can identify the two kinds of averages; i.e.write

$$\bar{f} = \bar{\bar{f}}, \tag{3.3.15}$$

then the two approaches become *equivalent*. In particular, we can treat the densities of continuum mechanics as if they were averages of appropriate observables of an underlying particulate system. The linkages of the continuum thus become expressions of how these *average* values are related. Further, the predictions made on the basis of equations of state on the continuum become exact predictions about the *average* behavior of this particulate system.

However, it is clear that no such formal compromise between the particulate and continuous pictures can be valid. In particular, if we insist on large volumes, so that the averages of the particulate system are meaningful, we lose the properties on which the encoding of the continuum are based. Conversely, if we insist on small volumes, we lose the meaningfulness of the averages. In either case, there will necessarily be a discrepancy between the predictions obtainable through such a compromise and the behavior to be expected in obser-vation of the system itself. Stated another way: if the particulate or continuum encoding of a natural system is a model of that system, then the compromise we have described above cannot be; conversely, if the compromise is a model, then neither the particulate or con-tinuum encodings of that system can be a model.

We can attempt formally to correct for this discrepancy by adding an *ad hoc* term to the equations of motion, which represents the *fluctu-ations* about the average value arising from the necessity for aver-aging over small regions. In a sense, then, these fluctuations encode *nothing* about the natural system; they are entirely mathemat-ical artifacts arising from an attempt to reconcile two fundamentally incompatible encodings of the same system. Indeed, the entire theory of *heat*, which is precisely the study of how the fluctuations must behave in order for the compromise to work at all, is in this sense an artifact. It arises entirely from the desire to use equations of motion appropriate to continua in dealing with systems assumed in fact to be particulate. To this extent, theories of heat, fluctuation and randomness which play such a predominant role in thermodynamics are simply the necessary formal consequences of utilizing incompatible encodings simultaneously. We shall see a further example of this kind of artifact when we take up the relation of particle mechanics to thermodynamics in our next example, and will meet with this circle of ideas in a more general context when we take up the concept of *error*.

There is one further important point to be noticed in regard to equations of motion like (3.3.12) above, which express linkages within an encoding of a continuously extended system. In the light of (3.3.13), (3.3.14) and (3.3.15), such an equation must represent the behavior of an *average* quantity, which may be interpreted *either* as an average of a particulate quality, *or* as the average of a continuous quantity. If in (3.3.14) we consider a quantity f which is independent of position, then there is a sense in which the average f becomes identical with the value of f. In such a case, the term in (3.3.12) representing flow drops out; the partial derivative $\partial f/\partial t$ becomes the total derivative df/dt, and (3.3.12) itself becomes an *ordinary* differential equation of first order. If the observables g_i in (3.3.12) are also of this character, then the equations of motion for the entire family become a set of simultaneous first-order differential equations in f and the g_i; i.e. a dynamical system.

This is indeed the origin of the dynamical systems described in Chapter 1.2 above, which are used as models for all kinds of rate processes in chemistry and biology. In Chapter 1.2, we considered them as analogs of the equations of motion of particle mechanics, but we see here that they are actually of quite a different character. The dependent variables in such a dynamical system must be interpreted as *averages* which are independent of position; the equations themselves describe the time course of these average quantities, and the linkages they embody have a physical meaning entirely different from those of particle mechanics (where they embody Newton's Second Law). Moreover, these average quantities *must* be supplemented by *ad hoc* fluctuations; in certain cases, as in the diffusion-reaction systems to be considered in the next chapter, the fluctuations become in fact the dominant factor in interpreting the system's behavior. Thus, despite the formal similarity between dynamical systems arising as encodings of particulate systems and other kinds of dynamical models, the nature of the encodings through which they respectively represent temporal phenomena is essentially different, and it is important to bear this in mind.

EXAMPLE 3:   THERMODYNAMICS, PARTICLE MECHANICS AND STATISTICAL
             MECHANICS[5]

We shall begin our considerations by briefly describing the nature of thermodynamics as a branch of physical science. It is distinguished from other branches of physics by its central concern with the concept of *heat*, and with the interconversion of heat into mechanical work.

The simplest kind of system with which thermodynamics deals is a homogeneous fluid, such as a gas. A system of this kind is considered as a continuum, and thus falls within the province of the encoding of continua described in the previous example. There is thus a certain overlap between thermodynamics and the dynamics of continua. However, the former is distingushed both by its preoccupation with heat and temperature, and by its *essential restriction to conditions of thermal and mechanical equilibrium*.

A thermodynamic system is, as are all the physical systems we have
considered thusfar, encoded in mathematical terms through the identification of the observables with which it deals into real-valued
functions. Like particle mechanics, certain of these observables
are distinguished as state variables, and all others are considered
to be functions of the state variables in the manner we have already
described. For a homogeneous gas, only three state variables are
necessary: the volume V occupied by the system, the pressure P, and
the temperature T. In this fashion, the abstract states of a thermodynamic system are encoded into a Euclidean three-dimensional space
in the familiar manner. However, the essential restriction to equilibrium conditions means that in general, these three state variables
are not independent, but are connected by an *equation of state* of
the form

$$F(P, V, T) = 0. \qquad (3.3.16)$$

Indeed, this is the origin of the terminology for "equations of
state" as expressions of linkage which we have used above. A thermodynamic system is completely characterized by its equation of state,
which can be interpreted geometrically as specifying a locus, or
surface, in the thermodynamic space of states.

For instance, (3.3.16) may be taken of the form

$$PV = rT \qquad (3.3.17)$$

which is generally called the *Ideal Gas Law*. The significance of the
parameter r appearing in (3.3.17) depends on our choice of units for
temperature and volume. If the choice of units is made arbitrarily,
then r is a *constitutive parameter* of the kind we have seen before;
its specific value is determined by the intrinsic character of the
gas we are describing. However, if we measure temperature on the
absolute scale, and we measure volume in *mols* (which means that we
must use a different unit of volume for each gas) then r becomes a
universal constant, *independent* of the nature of the gas; this is
because we have in effect incorporated the constitutive parameter
into the unit of volume.

The study of ideal gases in thermodynamic terms involves inferences
about the effect of infinitesimal changes in the state variables on
the equilibrium surface (3.3.17), and the effects of such changes
on other specific thermodynamic state variables, such as energy,
work, enthalpy, entropy, and the like. It turns out that all of
thermodynamics can be built up on the basis of a small number of
formal laws, limiting the form of the equations of state which link
the basic thermodynamic observables to the state variables. The
First Law of Thermodynamics expresses in effect the conservation of
energy, by relating the energy to heat absorbed by the system, and
work done by the system. The Second Law of Thermodynamics involves
the concept of entropy, and basically asserts that in any transition
to equilibrium in an isolated system, the entropy always increases.
We assume that the details are well known; they can be found in any
of the standard texts on thermodynamics.

The phenomenological development of thermodynamics which we have
briefly sketched was essentially completed before the end of the
last century; the ideal gas laws had been postulated a century
before that. However, during all this time, the atomic theory had
been extensively developed and applied to all parts of physics. As
we have seen, according to this theory, any physical system was to

be encoded according to the Newtonian scheme described in Example 1
above. In particular, a thermodynamic system such as a homogeneous
gas was accordingly to be regarded not as a structureless, infinitely
divisible continuum, but as a family of a large number of particles.
Moreover, the universality of the Newtonian encoding required that
every physical quantity be representable as a real-valued function
on an appropriately encoded space of states. The question thus arose:
what was the relation between the thermodynamic state variables and
the underlying atomic picture? In short: how could thermodynamics
be *reduced* to mechanics? The task here is thus a special case of
the situation diagrammed in Figure 2.3.4 above; to relate two
encodings of the same physical system (e.g. a homogeneous gas) in
such a way that the thermodynamic state variables become expressible
in terms of the purely mechanical ones.

From the consideration of the preceding example, the startegy to be
employed should be fairly clear: namely, to relate the thermodynamic
state variables to certain averages of the underlying mechanical
encoding, in such a way that not only the averages but also the
associated fluctuations can be expressed directly in mechanical
terms. The machinery for accomplishing this, being a relation between two *mathematical* systems, is itself of a purely mathematical
character, and has come to be called *statistical mechanics*. In fact,
the statistical appraoch to thermodynamics grew historically along-
side the more phenomenological approach, although from the formal
and logical point of view, the two are quite distinct; in principle
either of them can be developed in total ignorance of the other, or
indeed of any physical interpretation whatever.

The basic idea of statistical mechanics involves the transfer of
attention from the temporal behavior of individual states (i.e. from
trajectories) to the temporal behavior of *sets* of states. The
original motivation for doing this was the following: it was known
from the time of Avogadro that that macroscopic volumes of gases
contain enormous numbers of particles; according to Avogadro's Law,
one mol of a gas must contain of the order of 10^{24} particles. Thus,
the appropriate phase space for such a system would be a Euclidean
space of approximately 6×10^{24} dimensions; a complete knowledge of
a state of the gas in Newtonian terms would require the specification
of the same number of initial conditions. This was recognized as at
least a technical difficulty by even the most fervent disciples of
the atomic theory. Thus, the question became: what can we say about
a gas from this Newtonian picture when our knowledge about it is more
modest; e.g. if we know simply that our gas is initially in a state
for which the energy lies within a certain range?

In general, constraints of this form specify regions of the phase
space, in which initial states compatible with them may lie. Any
state in such a region is a candidate for the initial state of our
gas. Each such state will trace out a unique trajectory in time,
and accordingly, the initial *region* will correspondingly appear to
flow in the state space. If U_0 is our initial region in the phase
space X, then any point u(0) in U_0 will move to a point u(t) in X
after a time t has elapsed, and thus the region U_0 will move to a
new region U_t. What can we say about U_t from an initial specification
of U_0, knowing only the equations of motion of the system?

Briefly, the answer to this question is given by *Liouville's Theorem*:
if the total energy of the system is conserved on trajectories, then

the flow we have just described in the phase space is like that of
an incompressible fluid. Thus, if our initial region U_0 has a certain volume $\mu(U_0)$, and if after a time t this initial region has
moved to the region U_t, then $\mu(U_t) = \mu(U_0)$; or more succinctly,

$$\frac{d}{dt}\, \mu(U_t) = 0$$

This theorem, together with the conservation of energy (of which it
is a corollary) forms one of the great cornerstones of statistical
mechanics.

The other great cornerstone is a concept called *ergodicity*. This
may be explained as follows. If energy is conserved, then an exact
knowledge of the energy H_0 of our system constrains all possible
trajectories to lie on the hypersurface $H = H_0$ in the phase space X.
The "ergodic hypothesis" of Gibbs essentially states that a *typical*
trajectory (in a precise measure-theoretic sense) wanders through
this hypersurface in such a way that it spends roughly the same
amount of time in any neighborhood of any point in that hypersurface.
Thus, in a rough sense, watching a single typical trajectory for a
sufficiently long time gives the same result as a single random
sampling of the entire hypersurface. In other words, if we average
any mechanical quantity along a single trajectory in time, we obtain
the same answer as if we averaged the same quantity over the entire
energy hypersurface in which the trajectory lies; or in more technical language, time averages (on single trajectories) may be replaced by phase averages (over such hypersurfaces).

The totality of points in X consistent with some partial knowledge
about where an initial state lies is an example of what is called an
ensemble. An ensemble is just a set of points in the phase space X.
However, it may equally well be regarded as an encoding of a *set* of
samples of our gas, each initially in some different state. In other
words: our uncertainty as to exactly where the initial state of our
sample of gas lies in X is equivalent to an ensemble of different
samples, each of which may be perfectly known.

Let then $E \subset X$ denote such an ensemble. Let us *suppose* that there
is some observable $\rho : X \to \mathbb{R}$ which can be interpreted as the *density*
with which the points in E are distributed in X; it will be observed
that this notion of density in X is analogous to the one considered
in the previous example, except now we are dealing with density in
a phase space. If $U \subseteq X$ is now any subset, we can define a new
volume for U, which we will denote by $m_\rho(U)$, by writing

$$m_\rho(U) = \int_U \rho dt$$

It is then a corollary of Liouville's Theorem that

$$\frac{dm_\rho(U_t)}{dt} = 0 \quad \text{iff} \quad [\rho, H] = 0$$

where H is the energy observable (the Hamiltonian) and $[\rho, H]$ is the
Poisson Bracket, defined by

$$\sum_{i=1}^{n} \left[\frac{\partial \rho}{\partial x_i} \cdot \frac{\partial H}{\partial v_i} - \frac{\partial \rho}{\partial v_i} \cdot \frac{\partial H}{\partial x_i} \right]$$

The ensemble E is called *stationary* if $[\rho, H] = 0$; i.e. the density with which the points of E are distributed in X is independent of time.

It follows immediately from this argument and from the hypothesis of ergodicity that an ensemble is stationary only if its density ρ is constant on surfaces of constant energy; i.e. is a function of energy alone.

To bring this machinery to bear on thermodynamic questions, we need to find some way of talking about *temperature*. Intuitively, temperature is a measure of energy flow between systems brought into interaction or contact with each other; when two systems have the same temperature, then there is no net energy flow between them. Thus, to talk about temperature, we need to find a way of talking about stationary ensembles for interacting systems of this type.

We can make contact with our previous discussion in the following way. Suppose that X is the phase space considered before, but let us now suppose that it can be written as a cartesian product

$$X = \prod_{\alpha=1}^{k} X_{\alpha}$$

where each X_{α} is itself the phase space of some *subsystem*, which we shall also refer to as X_{α}. We shall suppose that the decomposition is made in such a way that, if $(x_1^{\alpha}, \ldots, v_m^{\alpha})$ are the state variables for X_{α}, the equations of motion of X can be written in the form

$$\frac{dx_i^{\alpha}}{dt} = v_i^{\alpha}$$

$$\frac{dv_i^{\alpha}}{dt} = F_i^{\alpha}(x_1^{\alpha}, \ldots, v_m^{\alpha}) + \phi_i$$

where each function ϕ_i is assumed (a) to be a function of the state variables of X not in X_{α}, and (b) ϕ_i is small compared to F_i; i.e. the interaction between the subsystems X_{α} is small.

By hypothesis, energy is conserved in the entire system X, but in general it is not conserved in the subsystems X_{α}. That is, we can regard the X_{α} as exchanging energy with one another. If we assume that our knowledge of X is represented by a *stationary* distribution ρ, we can ask such questions as: what fraction of the time would we expect X_{α} to be in a state with energy less than some given value E_0?

The answer to this question can be obtained from the equations of motion, Liouville's Theorem, and the ergodic hypothesis, with the aid of much mathematical manipulation and approximation. It involves an important function, called the *partition function*, defined as

$$Z \equiv \int_{-\infty}^{\infty} e^{-\beta E} \mu'(E) dE$$

where E is a given energy value, and $\mu(E)$ is the volume of the set
of all states in X_α with energy less than E. The parameter β depends
on the way in which X_α is coupled to the other subsystems, and on
their dynamics, and is thus intimately related to what we would call
the *temperature* of X_α; in fact, it turns out that

$$\beta = 1/kT$$

where k is a universal constant (the Boltzmann Constant) and T is
temperature in degrees Kelvin. We then proceed to *identify* the two
statements:

a. X_α has temperature T;

b.   The fraction of time during which X_α is in a state with
     energy less than E_0 is given by

$$\frac{1}{Z} \int_{-\infty}^{E_0} e^{-E_0 kT} \mu'(E)\,dE.$$

When this is done, we have a way of building a concept of temperature,
the fundamental thermodynamic variable, into the Newtonian picture,
in terms of an energy *distribution* in X_α. We have thus carried out
the essential step in relating the thermodynamic variables of state
to an underlying particulate picture; i.e. we have built a mapping
from the Newtonian encoding to the thermodynamic encoding of the
same system. This is what the physicist means by asserting that
thermodynamics can be *reduced* to mechanics.

It must be stressed that the character of this reduction is *entirely
mathematical*, and rests on the assumption of a number of important
mathematical properties which must be possessed by the equations of
motion of the particulate system. If a particulate system does not
admit an encoding with these mathematical properties, the reduction
we have described will not work. It is this fact which, more than
any other, has limited the scope of statistical mechanics. We shall
see this in more detail in the next chapter.

EXAMPLE 4:   THE MECHANO-OPTICAL ANALOGY[6]

In the previous example, we have described an instance of *reduction*
in physics; i.e. a specific example of the situation diagrammed in
Figure 2.3.4 above. We now wish to consider an example of the dual
situation, diagrammed as Figure 2.3.2. In this case, two distinct
kinds of physical systems are related through the fact that they
admit a common encoding; i.e. they stand in a modelling relation to
the *same* formal system. To use the terminology we developed before,
these two distinct kinds of physical systems are then analogs of one
another, and we can learn about one of them by studying the analogous
properties of the other. It will be noted that this relation of
analogy is a relation between natural systems, and not between
encodings or formal systems; thus it is necessarily of a completely
different character from reduction (which is a relation between
encodings).

Let us begin with a number of mathematically equivalent reformulations of the Newtonian encoding of a particulate system. We will exhibit these reformulations in a special simple example, but in fact these ideas are perfectly general. To that end, let us consider once more the one-dimensional undamped harmonic oscillator, whose equations of motion were given in (1.2.1) above. We note that in these equations we have replaced the velocity v by the momentum mv = p, where m is the mass (a constitutive parameter). The trajectories of this system were shown in Figure (3.1.4) above; they are a family of concentric ellipses, whose equations in the phase plane are

$$p^2/2m + kx^2/2 = \text{constant.}$$

The observable H(x, p) defined by

$$H(x, p) = p^2/2m + kx^2/2 \qquad\qquad (3.3.18)$$

plays a predomiant role in all of our subsequent considerations. It is called the *Hamiltonian* of our system, and its value on a state (x, p) is simply the *total energy* of the state. We see that it is a sum of two terms:

$$H(x, p) = T(p) + U(x), \qquad\qquad (3.3.19)$$

the first of which depends only on velocity or momentum, and the second of which depends only on displacement. Accordingly, T(p) is called *kinetic energy*, and U(x) is called *potential energy*. We note that the potential energy U(x) is related to the force imposed on the system by

$$F = -kx = -\frac{\partial U}{\partial x}$$

A force related to a potential in this way is called *conservative*.

It will also be observed that the equations of motion of our system are completely determined by the Hamiltonian, for we can verify that

$$\begin{cases} \dfrac{dx}{dt} = \dfrac{\partial H}{\partial p} \\[2mm] \dfrac{dp}{dt} = -\dfrac{\partial H}{\partial x} \end{cases} \qquad\qquad (3.3.20)$$

That is, the time derivatives of the state variables are precisely the partial derivatives of H as functions of phase. The equations (3.3.20) are the *Hamiltonian form* of the equations of motion.

If we differentiate the first of these equations with respect to time and substitute into the second, remembering that p = mdx/dt, we find

$$\frac{d}{dt}\left(\frac{\partial H}{\partial p}\right) + \frac{\partial H}{\partial x} = 0$$

If we now introduce a new observable

$$L(x, p) = T(p) - U(x)$$

we can rewrite this last expression in terms of L as

$$\frac{\partial L}{\partial x} - \frac{d}{dt}\left(\frac{\partial L}{\partial p}\right) = 0. \qquad\qquad (3.3.21)$$

This observable L is called the *Lagrangian* of the system, and (3.3.21)

is called the Lagrangian form of the equations of motion. It can be
regarded as a single second-order equation in the displacement x;
in fact, expanding the total derivative in (3.3.21), we have explicitly

$$\left(\frac{\partial L}{\partial x} - \frac{\partial^2 L}{\partial t \partial p}\right) - \left(\frac{\partial^2 L}{\partial x \partial p}\right) \cdot \frac{dx}{dt} - \left(\frac{1}{m}\frac{\partial^2 L}{\partial p^2}\right) \cdot \frac{d^2 x}{dt^2} = 0$$

It will be noted that all of our arguments can be run backward; the
original equations of motion are completely equivalent to both the
Hamiltonian and Lagrangian forms.

All of our arguments apply to general conservative systems. If we
know the total energy $H(x_1, \ldots, x_n, p_1, \ldots, p_n)$ then the equations
of motion of the system can be put into the Hamiltonian form

$$\begin{cases} \dfrac{dx_i}{dt} = \dfrac{\partial H}{\partial p_i} \\[2mm] \dfrac{dp_i}{dt} = -\dfrac{\partial H}{\partial x_i} \end{cases} \qquad i = 1, \ldots, n$$

or into the Lagrangian form

$$\frac{\partial L}{\partial x_i} - \frac{d}{dt}\left(\frac{\partial L}{\partial p_i}\right) = 0 \qquad i = 1, \ldots, n$$

and all of these are completely equivalent.

Now the Lagrangian form (21) of the equations of motion arise in
another class of problems in mathematics; namely, in that part of
mathematics called the *calculus of variations*. The basic problem
here is the following: to find that curve x = x(t) which minimizes
(or maximizes) some function of the form

$$J(x) = \int_{t_0}^{t_1} F(t, x(t), x'(t)) dt \tag{22}$$

For instance, we might wish to find that curve x(t) passing between
two points $(t_0, x(t_0))$, $(t_1, x(t_1))$ in the plane such that the arc
length

$$\int_{t_0}^{t_1} \sqrt{1 + \left(\frac{dx}{dt}\right)^2}\ dt$$

is minimal.

It is shown in the calculus of variations that a necessary condition
for a curve x = x(t) to extremize a function of the form (22) is
precisely that x(t) satisfy the differential equation

$$\frac{\partial F}{\partial x} - \frac{d}{dt}\left(\frac{\partial F}{\partial x'}\right) = 0$$

This equation is called the Euler equation associated with the
variational problem (3.3.22). On comparing (3.3.23) and (3.3.21),
we see that *the Lagrangian form of the equations of motion is the
Euler equation of the variational problem*

$$A(x, p) = \int_{t_0}^{t_1} L(x, p)\,dt = 0 \qquad\qquad (3.3.23)$$

We can interpret this situation as follows. In mechanics, x is a
co-ordinate of configuration; the totality of displacement co-ordinates define the configuration space of our system. If we ask the
question: of all paths in the configuration space between an initial
configuration $x(t_0)$ and a later configuration $x(t_1)$, which one will
actually be traced out by the system? We find that this path must
extremize the quantity $A(x, p)$ defined by (3.3.23). This quantity
is called the mechanical *action*, and the property we have just mentioned (i.e. that of all possible paths joining two configurations
in configuration space, the one actually followed by the system
extremizes action) constitutes essentially the *Principle of Least
Action*.

The discovery that all of Newtonian mechanics could be developed on
the basis of a global minimum principle of this type was a very
exciting one in its time, for it was in accord with the idea that
nature behaved in a way which was, in some sense, *optimal*. It was
thus very much in accord with the eighteenth century idea that the
actual world of nature was the "best of all possible worlds". It
also showed that under some circumstances, the differential equations
of motion, which strictly speaking express linkages between a given
state and infinitesimally nearby states, could be equivalent to global
principles pertaining to arbitrarily extended time intervals.

It was **W. R. Hamilton** who first formulated the Principle of Least
Action in definitive form, in the course of the most far-reaching
studies on the foundations of mechanics. He also noticed that this
principle was formally identical with an independent principle postulated by Fermat, from which all of geometric optics could be derived.
This was Fermat's Principle of Least Time, which we now proceed to
describe.

If we suppose that a ray of light is passing through a point x of
some optical medium, in a direction $\vec{r}$, then the velocity with which
it moves in general depends on both x and x'; i.e. $v = v(x, x')$.
If the light ray moves between two points of the medium along some
curve $x = x(s)$ (where s is some parameter), then the time of transit
for the ray between the two points along that curve is just

$$\tau = \int_{t_0}^{t_1} \frac{x'}{v(x, x')}\,ds = \int_{s_0}^{s_1} G(x, x')\,ds \qquad\qquad (3.3.24)$$

Fermat's Principle of Least Time states that, of all curves connecting
two points in an optical medium, light will *actually* move along that
curve which minimizes (3.3.24); i.e. for which the *time of transit*
is least.

On the basis of (3.3.24), all the facts of geometric optics can be
expressed; just as, on the basis of (3.3.23), all the facts of
particle mechanics can be expressed. Hamilton now noticed that a
dictionary could be established between mechanics and optics, by
analogizing action with time of transit, and the Lagrangian L with
refractive index G. In this way, by exploiting constructions in
optics such as Huyghens' Principle, and translating them via his
dictionary into mechanical terms, he was led to many deep insights
into mechanics itself. For instance, he was able to derive a partial

differential equation (the Hamilton-Jacobi equation) for the spreading
of "wave fronts" of constant action in configuration space, which
ultimately led directly to the Schrödinger equation of quantum mechanics. In fact, this synthesis of optics and mechanics was of such
power and beauty that one of the finest textbooks on the subject
(Lanczos) prefaces the discussion of the Hamilton-Jacobi equation
with the following words from Exodus: "Put off thy shoes from off
thy feet, for the place whereon thou standest is holy ground".

We stress again that there is in this discussion no question of a
reduction of optics to mechanics, or vice versa. Rather, by exploiting a purely mathematical relation between the manner in which
optical and mechanical systems are independently encoded, a dictionary
can be established between the *systems themselves*, in such a way that
the behavior of each system is a model for the behavior of the other.
Such analogies have had a most fruitful exploitation in theoretical
physics, through their suggestion of how to formulate equations of
motion (or their equivalent action principles) in particular physical
domains, assuming an analogy between such a domain and another for
which action principles are known. As far as we are aware, the
extent and significance of the employment of such analogies as a
basic methodological tool in theoretical physics has never been
systematically studied. But by any standard, its significance has
been at least as great as that of any reductionistic scheme.

EXAMPLE 5: SIMILARITY[7]

We are now going to consider an extension of the relation of analogy
discussed in the preceding example, so as to provide important illustrations of the situation diagrammed in Figure 2.2.3 above. In so
doing, we will throw new light on the discussion focused around the
diagram (3.3.2) above, which was originally proposed in the context
of encoding of particulate systems.

We shall begin with an example drawn from classical thermodynamics.
It had long been known that the behavior of real gases was only
approximately given by the ideal gas law (3.3.17), with the approximations between the predictions of this law and experimental observation becoming poorer as the temperature was lowered and the pressure
raised. Indeed, it was experimentally known that, past certain
critical values of pressure and temperature, a *phase transition* would
occur; the original gaseous phase would be replaced by a liquid
phase, possessing quite different physical properties. Of even the
possibility of such a phase transition, there is no hint in the ideal
gas law. Thus, the ideal gas law cannot be a universally valid
encoding of the equilibrium behavior of real gases.

By utilizing considerations based on atomic theory, a more general
equation of state was proposed by van der Waals in 1873. This
equation of state is of the form

$$(P + a/V^2)(V - b) = rT. \qquad\qquad (3.3.25)$$

It will be noticed that this new equation of state involves two new
constitutive parameters a, b, and that it reduces to the ideal gas
law (3.3.17) when a = b = 0. The parameters a, b are associated
with the particulate constitution of real gases. Thus, the parameter
a embodies the fact that the particles in such a gas will attract
each other; hence the pressure P actually experienced by a gas will
be larger than the value P' obtained from a manometer or other
measuring instrument. Likewise, the parameter b embodies the fact

that the particles of a gas themselves occupy a volume, which must
be subtracted from the measured volume V'. Indeed, we may think of
(3.3.25) as an admission that the instruments which we use to evaluate
the state variables P, V are in fact measuring *different* quantities
P', V', related to the ones we want by

$$P' = P - a/V'^2,$$

$$V' = V + b;$$

and when we take this into account, the ideal gas law in fact still
holds. This is an inportant point which should be kept in mind for
our later discussion of renormalization.

The van der Waals equation (3.3.25) describes the equilibrium behavior
of a family of "non-ideal" gases. Indeed, to every triplet of values
(a, b, r), there corresponds in principle such a gas. Let us describe
all these gases in a common framework, utilizing ideas which we have
seen before. Namely, let us denote by Q the totality of all triples
(a, b, r). To each point of Q, we associate a copy of the state
space E_3; i.e. the space of all triples (P, V, T). In each such
space there is a distinguished surface; the surface of steady states
of the gas given by the van der Waals equation (3.3.25), in which the
appropriate values (a, b, r) are inserted. Thus, our family of gases
is put into the form diagrammed in Figure 3.3.1 above, with $Q = E_3$.

We are now going to argue that a transition q → q' in Q can be annihilated by co-ordinate transformations of the associated (P, V, T)
spaces. In other words, we are going to show that all the different
gases obeying the equation of state (3.3.25) are *similar* to each
other. To see this, we shall digress for a moment to discuss some
general properties of (3.3.25).

We said earlier that the ideal gas law (3.3.17) did not admit phase
transitions. This can be seen as follows: if we fix any temperature
$T = T_0$, then (3.3.17) becomes the equation of a hyperbola in the
(P, V)-plane; this curve is called an *isotherm* for obvious reasons.
Clearly all these isotherms are hyperbolic, and each one behaves like
any of the others. If we do the same thing with the van der Waals
equation, however, we find a situation as diagrammed in Figure 3.3.3
below:

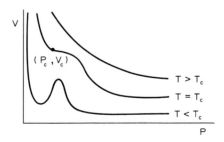

Fig. 3.3.3.

Heuristically, because of the fact that the volume V enters (3.3.25)
in a cubic fashion, there will be three qualitatively different kinds

of isotherms, depending on the number of real roots possessed by
(3.3.25) as a function of V. For large T, the isotherms are of the
same hyperbolic character as we found for the ideal gas law. For
very small T, the isotherms will no longer be monotonic functions,
but will possess a unique maximum and a unique minimum. Separating
these two classes of isotherms there will be a *critical* one; for
some definite temperature T = T_c the corresponding isotherm will
have a point of inflection. We have labelled this unique point of
inflection by (P_c, V_c) in Figure 3.3.3.

This very special point, whose co-ordinates in the state space are
(P_c, V_c, T_c), is called the *critical point* of the system. We can
easily evaluate its co-ordinates, using the facts that (a) the critical point is an equilibrium state of the gas, and hence satisfies
the van der Waals equation (3.3.25); (b) the critical point causes
the derivative dV/dP to vanish; (c) the critical point is a point
of inflection, thus causing the second derivative d^2V/dP^2 to vanish.
We can solve the resulting three equations for the three co-ordinates
of the critical point; we find

$$P_c = \frac{a}{27b^2}$$

$$V_c = 3b \qquad\qquad (3.3.26)$$

$$T_c = \frac{8a}{27rb}$$

Let us note that the co-ordinates of the critical point in the state
space depend *only* on the constitutive parameters (a, b, r). No other
point satisfying (3.3.25) has this property.

Thus, if we make a transition q → q' in Q (i.e. if we replace the
constitutive parameters (a, b, r) by new values (a', b', r')) we
clearly move the critical point from its original location to a new
one. If we want to annihilate such a transition, we need to find a
co-ordinate transformation of the state space which preserves critical points, and also maintains the manner in which arbitrary states
are related to the critical point. Let us consider the transformation
$\gamma(q, q') : E_3 \rightarrow E_3$ defined by

$$\gamma(P, V, T) = (P', V', T')$$

where

$$
\begin{cases}
P' = \dfrac{P_c'}{P_c} P \\[2ex]
V' = \dfrac{V_c'}{V_c} V \qquad\qquad (3.3.27) \\[2ex]
T' = \dfrac{T_c'}{T_c} T
\end{cases}
$$

and (P_c, V_c, T_c), (P_c', V_c', T_c') are the critical points corresponding to the values q = (a, b, r), q' = (a', b', r') in Q respectively. Then it is immediately verified that this transformation
indeed annihilates the transition q → q' made initially. Indeed,

the transformation (3.3.27) embodies what is usually called the *Law of Corresponding States* for gases satisfying (3.3.25); it is a precise assertion of the sense in which two such gases are similar to each other.

Let us reformulate these considerations in a slightly different fashion. If we fix a set of constitutive parameters (a, b, r), the van der Waals equation may be regarded as a rule for associating to each pair (P, T) a corresponding value of V. Let us denote the space of pairs (P, T) by X, and the space of values of V by Y. Then the van der Waals equation (3.3.25) can be represented as a mapping

$$\Phi_{abr} : X \to Y. \tag{3.3.28}$$

Here we have used the notation Φ_{abr} to indicate that the mapping (3.3.28) depends on the specific values of the constitutive parameters.

If we take a different set of constitutive parameters (a', b', r'), we obtain a different mapping

$$\Phi_{a'b'r'} : X \to Y \tag{3.3.29}$$

The Law of Corresponding States then says precisely that there exist co-ordinate transformations $\alpha : X \to X$, $\beta : Y \to Y$, which make the diagram

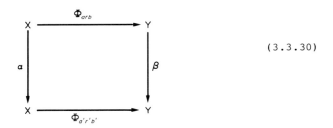

$$\tag{3.3.30}$$

commutative; i.e. which annihilate the transition from unprimed to primed constitutive parameters. These transformations α, β depend only on the initial and terminal values of these parameters, and are given in the obvious way from (3.3.27). Stated another way, the above construction shows that all the mappings Φ_{abr} are *conjugate*.

We will now point out a fundamental property of such conjugacy classes of equations of state, which generalizes a remark made earlier about ideal gases. We noticed, in connection with (3.3.17) above, that the parameter r appearing therein could be interpreted either as a constitutive parameter characteristic of the gas, or as a universal constant independent of the gas. In this last case, we saw that it was necessary to choose a unit of volume specifically related to the gas being measured (the mol), so that in effect the constitutive parameter disappears from the equation into the units in which its terms are measured.

Exactly the same thing is true for the van der Waals equation. This can be seen in two related ways. First, let us suppose that we wish

to choose our units so that *any* gas satisfying this equation has its
critical point located at (1, 1, 1) in the state space. Clearly,
the choice of unit will then depend on the gas. From (3.3.26), it
is easy to see that the specific values of a, b, r which assign unit
values to the critical volume, temperature and pressure are given by

$$a = 3; \qquad b = 1/3; \qquad r = 8/3;$$

and substituting these values into the van der Waals equation itself,
we find

$$(P + 3/V^2)(3V - 1) = 8T. \tag{3.3.31}$$

With this choice of units, *any* gas satisfying the van der Waals
equation will also satisfy the equation (3.3.31), in which *no constitutive parameters appear*. As before, these parameters are now hidden
in the units in which the constitutive parameters, and hence also
state variables, are measured.

Let us look at what we have just done in a slightly different way.
Given any gas satisfying the van der Waals equation, let us introduce
new state variables (π, ν, τ) by writing

$$\pi = \frac{P}{P_c}; \qquad \nu = \frac{V}{V_c}; \qquad \tau = \frac{T}{T_c} \tag{3.3.32}$$

These new variables have the property that they are *dimensionless;*
i.e. they are pure numbers, independent of the units in which pressure,
volume and temperature are measured. Once again, we see that these
dimensionless variables depend on the gas we are dealing with; the
constitutive parameters (a, b, r) appear explicitly in them through
their determination of the critical point of the gas. It is evident
that if we substitute these variables into the van der Waals equation,
we obtain precisely

$$(\pi + \frac{3}{\nu^2})(3\nu - 1) = 8\tau \tag{3.3.33}$$

which is identical with (3.3.31) in form. For this reason, (3.3.33)
is often called the *dimensionless form* of the van der Waals equation.

It will now be apparent that the conjugacy expressed in the diagram
(3.3.30) above is equivalent to the existence of a single "dimensionless form" into which all the equations of state of the conjugacy
class can be transformed; and that the co-ordinate transformations
α, β in that diagram are precisely the ones which express this fact.
In effect, what we have done is to pick a particular *canonical* gas
out of the conjugacy class (namely, the one for which the critical
point has co-ordinates (1, 1, 1)) and refer every other element of
the class to it. These remarks should be compared with our discussion
of similar matrices and canonical forms, in Example 4 of Chapter 3.1.

Using the notation that the dimensionless form (3.3.31) or (3.3.33)
is a canonical form of equation of state for an entire conjugacy
class, we can reformulate the Law of Corresponding States in the
following way. If (P, V, T) and (P', V', T') are respectively states
of gases (a, b, r) and (a', b', r'), then the states are corresponding
if and only if they are both mapped onto the *same* state of the
canonical gas by the appropriate transformations (3.3.27). Or,
stated somewhat differently: if (π, ν, τ) is a state of the canonical
system, and if (a, b, r) specify any gas, there is a unique state
(P, V, T) of that gas which maps onto (π, ν, τ) under (3.3.27). Any

two such states, for any two gases, are corresponding states, and conversely. Under this formulation, we see that we annihilate any change of constitutive parameters by in effect transforming the initial gas and the perturbed one to canonical form.

Let us agree in general to say that *two natural systems are similar if they admit encodings into equations of state which are conjugate*. This is a perfectly general definition of similarity among natural systems, and plays the same role in a class of natural systems as the modelling relation does between natural and formal systems. It should also be compared with the notion of natural equivalence between functors (taking a natural system as an object in a category, and their equations of state as their images under distinct functors).

These ideas find many important applications in engineering, because they underlie the notion of a "scale model". In general, let us suppose that we can encode some natural system into an equation of state analogous to (3.3.28) above;   i.e. as a mapping

$$\Phi_{a_1 \ldots a_r} : X \to Y$$

where $a_1, \ldots, a_r$ are constitutive parameters. As before, let us denote by Q the space of r-tuples $(a_1, \ldots, a_r)$;   then to each q in Q, we have a mapping Φ_q between copies of X and Y. In all the mappings Φ_q are conjugate, we can essentially repeat the discussion given above for the van der Waals equation word for word;   we can identify a canonical form of the equation of state which is *dimensionless* in the above sense. There is a Law of Corresponding States arising just as before;   if q, q' are distinct elements of Q, then a pair (x, y) of the first system corresponds to a pair (x', y') of the second if and only if they map onto the *same* state (ξ, n) of the canonical system.

To see how these ideas are applied, let us suppose for example that we are interested in the hydrodynamic properties of some airplane. We can in principle write down an equation of state, expressing the physics of the   situation, and attempt to draw inferences from it directly, in the fashion we have described in previous examples in this chapter. But we can also note that, by varying the constitutive parameters, we may be able to construct a different system, obeying the same equation of state, and which is thus *similar* to the case we are interested in. This second system is called a *scale model*. By *observing* the hydrodynamic behavior of the scale model, and by utilizing the transformations which establish similarity, we can thereby directly determine the hydrodynamic properties of the *corresponding states* of the actual airplane. Such ideas serve to bring many otherwise intractable problems within reach;   although we shall describe a number of other important examples of this character as we proceed, we cannot enter into full details here. We must once again urge the reader to consult the relevant literature.

EXAMPLE 6:   SYMMETRY AND INVARIANCE

In our discussion of similarity of matrices, we pointed out that the entire question arises from the cartesian encoding of geometry into arithmetic, through the fact that such an encoding distinguishes a particular system of co-ordinates. In this system, the n-tuples of cartesian n-space become the co-ordinates of specific points in the

geometric space. If we choose co-ordinates differently, the labelling
of points by n-tuples changes.

We may argue that exactly the same situation obtains in the encoding
of any natural system into a formal system; particularly into one
arising from numerical evaluations of observables through specific
meters. Such encodings are basic to our construction of phase spaces,
which in turn provide the foundation for the inferential structure
from which predictions are made, and which are supposed to mirror
the laws (linkages) obtaining in the natural system itself. Such
encodings are open to precisely the same problem that we found in
the cartesian encoding of geometry; if we change the encoding
through a change in meters, or more generally through any shift in
reference frame, we will thereby change all the linkages.

In physics, as in geometry, we feel that such different encodings
must in some precise sense be *equivalent*. In particular, it must
be the case that predictions about a *given* natural system, made on
the basis of two encodings differing by only a "change of co-ordinates", must be the same, in some precise sense. This is expressed
in physics through the proposition that system laws, or better, the
"laws of nature", must be *independent of the observer*, and hence of
any special way of encoding or co-ordinatizing a physical system.
Stated another way, the linkages obtained from any particular encoding must be *invariant* to transformations of co-ordinates. Thus,
if we have two distinct encodings related by such a transformation,
we must be able to (a) express the co-ordinates of either encoding
in terms of the other, and (b) show that any linkage in either encoding purporting to express system laws is invariant to the transformation relating the co-ordinates.

This kind of situation has in fact permeated all of our previous
discussions of conjugacy and similarity. For let us suppose that,
by virtue of some specific encoding of a natural system, we obtain
an equation of state of the form

$$\Phi(q, x, y) = 0 \qquad\qquad (3.3.34)$$

where q denotes an r-tuple of constitutive parameters, and x, y
denote vectors of state variables and observables respectively.
As we have seen, this kind of encoding presupposes a distinguished
co-ordinate system in each of the three spaces Q, X, Y whose elements
enter into the equation of state (3.3.34).

Let us suppose we perform a general co-ordinate transformation on
the space QxXxY into which our system is encoded; i.e. we introduce
a new co-ordinate of the form

$$\begin{cases} q' = q'(q, x, y) \\ x' = x'(q, x, y) \\ y' = y'(q, x, y) \end{cases} \qquad\qquad (3.3.35)$$

If this transformation can arise from a change of observer, or a
change of meter, then the invariance of natural laws to choice of
co-ordinate system means that the linkage (3.3.34) must be preserved;
i.e. that

$$\Phi(q', x', y') = 0 \qquad\qquad (3.3.36)$$

and hence that the linkage (expressed by the relation Φ) must be invariant to the transformation (3.3.35).

If we now suppose that (3.3.34) can be expressed as a family of mappings

$$\Phi_q : X \twoheadrightarrow Y \qquad\qquad (3.3.37)$$

and that all the mappings Φ_q are conjugate for each choice of $q \in Q$, then we have seen that (3.3.37) is indeed invariant to transformations of the form

$$\begin{cases} q \to q' \\ \alpha(q, q') : X \to X \\ \beta(q, q') : Y \to Y \end{cases} \qquad\qquad (3.3.38)$$

For the van der Waals equation, the invariance of the equation of state to the transformation (3.3.38) is simply the conjugacy diagram (30) above. Therefore, if we reinterpret the case of the van der Waals equation to refer to a *single* gas, encoded relative to different observers who measure (a, b, r) and (P, V, T) in different scales related to one another by (3.3.38), our previous discussion of similarity becomes precisely a discussion of invariance under co-ordinate transformations of particular types.

It is not hard to verify that the totality of transformations of the type (3.3.38) form a *group* of transformations acting on QxXxY, and that the conjugacy of all the mappings Φ_q means precisely that the equation of state (3.3.37) is invariant to every transformation of this group. We can now proceed just as well in the opposite *direction*: *given* a group G of transformations on the space QxXxY; under what circumstances will an equation of state of the form (3.3.36) or (3.3.37) be invariant to every transformation in the group? If we have independent reasons for believing that the transformations of such a group G are in fact simple changes of co-ordinatization or observer in the encoding of a natural system, then only those equations of state invariant to G can be candidates for expression of linkage relations of that system.

This was in fact the procedure underlying the development of the special theory of relativity[8] In the study of mechanical systems, it had long been known that Newtonian equations of motion were invariant to the transformations of the Galilean group; these transformations related observers moving relative to one another at constant velocities. However, Einstein observed that the equations of electro-dynamics (the field equations of Maxwell) were not invariant under these transformations, but rather under those of a different group (the Lorentz group). Invoking the invariance of *mechanical* laws under change of observer, and utilizing the Lorentz group instead of the Galilean, Einstein was led to a profound reformulation of all of mechanics, which by now is well known.

Similar ideas of invariance have come to be of decisive importance in quantum mechanics[9]

We wish to draw the reader's attention to several features of this kind of situation.

First, that symmetry and invariance are all variations on the basic ideas of conjugacy and similarity. They refer initially to mathematical relations between *encodings*, and are then imputed back to the natural systems which give rise to the encodings.

Second, we must point out that the often rather mysterious ideas collectively called *renormalization*[10] can be looked upon as arising from considerations of invariance under transformation. To see this, let us compare the general transformation (3.3.35) with the special transformations (3.3.38), under which the equation of state (3.3.37) is invariant. As we saw, this invariance is simply an expression of conjugacy of the mappings Φ_q. But suppose that (3.3.38) is invariant to a larger class of transformations of QxXxY than those given by (3.3.38). Under such a larger class, the new constitutive parameters q' will, according to (3.3.35), now depend on the original state variables in X and Y; likewise, the new state variables x', y' will depend on the original constitutive parameters in Q. In other words, the new constitutive parameters cannot be defined in terms of the original ones; nor can the new state variables be defined entirely in terms of the original ones. We thus retain the *form* of the original equation of state, now referred to a set Q'xX'xY', but we can no longer identify this product directly with QxXxY in a simple fashion. As we noted above, in connection with the van der Waals equation, this is tantamount to passing to a completely *new encoding* of our natural system, and the introduction of a completely new set of observable quantities. We cannot go deeply into the details of specific renormalization procedures in physics, but the reader can observe from what has already been said its essential theoretical significance.

Third, the idea that system laws are invariant to the observer refers only to the case in which *the observers are basically measuring the same set of observables*. Specifically, the observables measured by any particular observer must be totally linked to those measured by any other observer. *Indeed, this fact is what makes transformations between the encodings generated by these different observers possible at all*. But we have seen that different encodings of the *same* system may involve unlinked observables; this was the case in our discussion of discrete versus continuous encodings, which constituted the first two examples of this chapter. In that case, we cannot expect these encodings to be related by any kind of transformation; they are fundamentally irreducible one to the other. We have already alluded to this possibility in Chapter 3.2 above, and we suggested that it plays the essential role in our perception of *complexity* of natural systems; this is a point we will develop in detail subsequently. Indeed, as we shall see, there is a sense in which biology is possible only *because* there exist intrinsically inequivalent observers, whose encodings cannot be transformed into one another. Nevertheless, within their sphere of applicability, symmetry and invariance arguments are of fundamental importance; they may roughly be regarded as expressing a sense in which different *observers* are models of each other.

REFERENCES AND NOTES

1. The references cited in Note 1 to 1.2 above are appropriate here also.

2. See especially the discussion in 4.2 below.

3. Continuum mechanics comprises, among other things, the traditional

approaches to hydrodynamics, aerodynamics, elasticity, plasticity
and the like. It its mathematical form, it can be regarded as
transmuting into the theory of fields (e.g. electrodynamics and
electromagnetism). Some good general references on the mechanics
of continuous media are:
  Truesdell, C. A., *Elements of Continuum Mechanics*. Springer-
  Verlag (1966).
  Eringen, A. C., *Mechanics of Continua*. Wiley (1966).
  Scipio, L. A., *Principles of Continua with Applications*. Wiley
  (1966).
For a treatment of fluid mechanics from the same general point of
view, see
  Aris, R., *Vectors, Tensors and the Basic Equations of Fluid
  Mechanics*. Academic Press (1962).
For a cognate treatment of elastic solids, see
  Brillouin, L., *Tensors in Mechanics and Elasticity*. Academic
  Press (1964).
The volumes of Elasticity and Fluid Mechanics in the Landau-
Lifschits series are worth consulting. A treatment of fields
may be found in
  Artley, J., *Fields and Configurations*. Holt, Reinhart & Winston
  (1964).

4. In the main, the relationship between particle and continuum
mechanics has tacitly been treated as a complementarity (in the
sense of Bohr), like the wave-particle duality of quantum mechanics. From the purely mechanical point of view, the problem is
not urgent; the atomic theory tells us that matter is ultimately
particulate, but we may use continuum methods when dealing with
bulk phenomena, whose scale of length is large compared to the
interatomic distances. The problem becomes unavoidable when we
deal with the effects of fields on matter. At this point, the
usual approach is to quantize the fields, which in effect buries
the epistemological issues in an opaque formalism . Our main
point here is not with the applicability of continuum of particulate encodings of specific situations, but rather to point out
that the encodings are distinct and mutually irreducible.

5. Each of these subjects has an enormous literature. Thermodynamics
is a subject which can be, and has been, treated as a logically
closed entity, independent of the rest of physics (indeed, for
an axiomatic treatment, see Giles, R., *Mathematical Foundations
of Thermodynamics*, Pergamon Press (1964). The classical texts,
such as those of Planck (*Treatise on Thermodynamics*, 1867, reprinted Dover 1965) and Sommerfeld (*Thermodynamics and Statistical
Mechanics*, Academic Press 1956) are perhaps still the best. Of
the many standard references on statistical mechanics, one of
which the author is particularly fond is
  Khinchine, A. I., *Statistical Mechanics*. Dover (1949).
We shall discuss the formalism of statistical mechanics more
deeply in 4.3 below.

6. The two best current references for the relation between geometric
optics and the action principles of mechanics are:
  Lanczos, C., *The Variational Principles of Mechanics*. University
  of Toronto Press (1966).
  Yourgrau, W. and Mandelstam, S., *Variational Principles in
  Dynamics and Quantum Theory*. Saunders (1968).
It is interesting to note further that the very same formalism
is exploited nowadays in yet another context; that of the theory
of optimal control. The two basic approaches to optimal control

theory, namely the Maximum Principles of Pontryagin, and the
Dynamic Programming of Bellman, are analogous to the Euler-
Lagrange equations and the Hamilton-Jacobi equations of mechanics
respectively. A remarkably clear treatment of all these matters
may be found in
   Gelfand, I. A. and Fomin, S. V., *Calculus of Variations*.
   Wiley.
See also the chapter on optimal control in the volume by Kalman,
Arbib and Falb mentioned in Note 5 to 1.2 above. See also
   Hestenes, M. R., *Calculus of Variations and Optimal Control
   Theory*. Wiley (1966).

7.   The treatment of similarity given here was first developed in a
      paper of the author's (*Bull. Math. Biophys.* 40 (1978), 549-580).
      Further general references on the subject may be found in that
      paper. Particularly see the articles of Stahl referred to
      therein for incredibly complete bibliographies.

8.   The special theory of relativity asserted that the "laws of
      nature" were the same for all observers moving relative to each
      other with constant velocities. The general theory asserted
      the same for all observers, regardless of their relative states
      of motion. A good modern treatment of these matters may be
      found in
         Adler, R., Bazin, M. and Schiffer, M., *Introduction to General
         Relativity*. McGraw-Hill (1975).
      Some of the older books on relativity are full of interesting
      insights and suggestions. We may recommend particularly the
      book of H. Weyl (*Space, Time and Matter*, Dover 1948).

9.   At issue here are the groups of "symmetries" under which the
      Schrödinger equations of quantum mechanics are invariant. The
      classic references in this area are
         Weyl, H., *Group Theory and Quantum Mechanics*. Methuen (1923).
         Wigner, E., *Group Theory and its Application to the Quantum
         Mechanics of Atomic Spectra*. Academic Press (1959).
      The theory of group representations, which was mentioned in
      Note 10, 3.1 above, plays a crucial role in these developments.
      The review of Mackey, to which we have referred several times,
      provides a panoramic overview of these developments, as well as
      references to more detailed treatments.

10.   In a certain sense, renormalization is an admission that we
      measure the wrong things. As we have already noted, the passage
      from the ideal gas law to the van der Waals equation is a kind
      of renormalization. Ideas of this kind became decisive in
      physics with the study of the interaction of particles and
      fields in quantum physics; the results were plagued by diver-
      gences and other conceptual difficulties. A similar state of
      affairs emerged more recently in the study of phase transitions
      and other critical phenomena. For a treatment of these matters
      the reader may consult
         Amit, P. J., *Field Theory, the Renormalization Group and
         Critical Phenomena*. McGraw-Hill (1978).
      See also the relevant articles in the series *Phase Transitions
      and Critical Phenomena* (C. Domb and M. S. Greene, eds., Academic
      Press), especially volumes 1 and 6.

3.4 Encodings of Biological Systems: Preliminary Remarks

In the preceding chapter, we explored some of the ways in which physical systems could be encoded into formal ones. The present chapter is concerned with encodings of biological systems. The point of departure for all physical encodings was seen to reside in the fundamental concept of an *observable*. In phenomenological terms, an observable represented a capacity for interaction (manifested by the ability to move a meter) and in formal terms it could be regarded as a mapping from abstract states to real numbers. Correspondingly, we must begin our treatment of biological encodings with a discussion of observables of biological systems, and the nature of biological observations generally, before turning to specific examples.

Let us consider initially the most primitive of biological concepts; the recognition that a particular system is in fact an *organism*. The very word connotes that it is possible for us to discriminate in some fashion between systems which are organisms and systems which are not. The basis for such a discrimination must lie in some quality, or qualities, which are possessed by organisms but not by other systems, and in the fact that we can directly recognize these qualities.

Now we have seen that qualities in general, as percepts pertaining to the external world, are to be identified with definite observables of the systems which manifest them. As we have repeatedly noted, the diagnostic of a quality is precisely its ability to be recognized under appropriate circumstances; that is, its ability to move another system in a definite way. Insofar as the quality of being an organism is directly perceptible to us, we are ourselves playing the role of a measuring system for that quality; our very perception of an organism means that the quality in question is capable of moving us, or imposing dynamics on us, in a unique way. We cannot say precisely that we ourselves constitute *meters* for the numerical expression of this quality; nevertheless, the process whereby we recognize that a particular system is an organism is exactly analogous to the kinds of things we call measurement in dealing with physical systems.

This quality through which we can directly discriminate between organisms and non-organisms, which embodies the basic perception

171

underlying the very existence of biology as an autonomous natural
science, is in fact typical of the class of qualities with which
biology must deal. There are many ways in which such qualities
behave like the observables of the physicist, but there are clearly
many fundamental differences as well. The similarities allow us to
bring to bear on biological problems most of the machinery we have
developed above for dealing with observables of natural systems; in
particular, the basic concepts of abstract states and of linkage.
On the other hand, the differences between them endow biology with
its unique properties, and make the encoding of biological systems
much different from that encountered in our previous examples. Of
particular interest and importance are the cases in which we wish
to simultaneously encode biological qualities and physical observables,
and to establish linkages between them; as we shall see, the whole
question of reductionism in biology devolves onto the existence of
such encodings. Indeed, the basic (and as yet unanswered) question
as to whether or not we can define the quality of being an organism
in purely physical terms amounts precisely to *linking* the quality
to an appropriate family of physical observables through the analog
of an equation of state; i.e. of finding a family of physical observables which will serve as a complete set of invariants for the
quality of being an organism.

Just as we directly perceive the quality of being an organism, so
too do we directly perceive other similar qualities which in organisms
are linked to it. Such terms as irritability, adaptation, growth,
development, metabolism, reproduction, evolution, and indeed most
of the basic vocabulary of biology, refer precisely to such qualities.
Once again, we can say that our direct perception of such qualities
means that they share the basic attributes of numerical observables;
but the differences between them require a substantial modification
of the encoding procedure we have used heretofore. Likewise, our
encoding of the linkage relation itself must also be extended, in
such a manner as to encompass not only such qualities, but those
represented by the numerical observables with which we have so far
been exclusively concerned.

Let us try to characterize further these basic biological qualities,
and how they can be related to qualities which can be encoded as
real-valued functions. Indeed, any organism with which we are confronted must manifest qualities of *both* types; it must manifest
biological qualities precisely because we can recognize it as an
organism, and it must manifest numerical qualities because it is
above all a natural system. We must use these latter qualities to
discriminate between organisms, just as we use them to discriminate
between other kinds of natural systems. We note that this is the
basis of *taxonomy*, which rests on the fact that the quality of being
an organism can be manifested by an unlimited number of different
kinds of natural systems, whose numerical observables (and their
linkages) can be vastly different from system to system. Thus,
taxonomic concepts provide a good starting-point for our characterization of biological qualities, and the manner in which they are
linked to each other and to the more familiar numerical qualities.
There is indeed a sense in which it is correct to say that *the
quality of being an organism is represented by an observable which
takes its values in the taxa of the taxonomist*. We shall enlarge
on this point as we proceed.

Traditionally, a taxonomic unit, or taxon, is defined entirely through
the numerical-valued observables which any organism must manifest as
a natural system. Hence a specific organism is *assigned* to a taxon
if it manifests the defining observables, and if their values are

linked to each other in the appropriate way. Thus, to the extent that belonging to a particular taxon is a biological quality, we see that this quality is, by definition, itself linked to the numerical observables through which the taxon itself is specified.

We might use this fact to try to relate *any* biological quality of an organism to the real-valued observables which it manifests, in the following way. We could formally identify a taxon with the class of all organisms which belong to it, in much the same way as a cardinal number is defined in mathematics as the class of all sets of that cardinality. However, such a procedure is not generally valid here, for the following reason. Insofar as a taxon is defined *entirely* through linkages between numerical observables, it pertains to all natural systems, and not just to those we recognize as organisms. For instance, if we define the taxon "leopard" by *any* set of observables and linkages, however extensive, we can imagine constructing a completely artificial system which exhibits precisely those observables and linkages. Such an artificial system is clearly not an organism, but it must belong to the taxon because it satisfies the defining criteria. This indeed is precisely the difficulty faced in trying to *identify* the quality of being an organism with a set of numerical observables and linkages, which is basically the attempt to "define life". We could stipulate at the outset that our definition of a taxon is to be restricted to the class of organisms, but this simply begs the crucial question.

The basic problem exemplified in our discussion so far is in fact one which we have seen before. It involves the fundamental distinction made earlier between *recognition* and *generation* which we considered in Chapters 2.2 and 3.1. We saw, for instance, that for any system of axioms rich enough to be mathematically interesting, there must always exist propositions we can *recognize as true*, but which we cannot effectively *generate* from the axioms by means of the available production rules; this is the content of Gödel's theorem. Translating this situation to the terminology we have been using, Gödel's theorem asserts that the *quality* of being a theorem is one which can be recognized directly, but for which no specific linkage can be effectively constructed between this quality and our axioms.

We find similar situations in physics. The *quality* we call temperature, for instance, is directly perceptible by us, but cannot be directly linked to microscopic qualities measured in the conventional units of mass, length and time alone. To measure it, we need to construct a new kind of meter, and a special set of units (degrees); what we showed in Example 4 of the preceding chapter was that the quality of temperature was *consistent* with mechanical observables, but not directly derivable from those observables through specific linkage relations. Indeed, we saw that temperature is a property of an *ensemble* of mechanical system, and not of an individual one. Thus, temperature provides a specific, physical example of a quality which can be directly recognized, but not generated in a purely mechanical context. In a different physical realm, the basic qualities through which the electromagnetic field is defined can likewise be directly recognized, but not measured in terms of the same meters appropriate to mechanical systems; we must again invent new meters, and new units, to characterize these qualities. Thus it would not be an unprecedented circumstance for the qualities we recognize as pertaining to organisms to be of this character as well. Above all, it implies nothing mystical, vitalistic or unphysical about these qualities, just as there is nothing mystical or unphysical about such qualities as temperature and charge. At root, as we have emphasized, such a situation is merely an expression of the fact that we can recognize more qualities than we can generate.

In sum, there are three viewpoints which may be adopted regarding the relation of biological qualities of an organism to those which we can represent by numerical-valued observables. These are:

1. All biological observables are directly linked to an *appropriate* set of underlying purely physical observables. This is the reductionist position, and typically it is sought to link biological qualities directly to the character of specific particles (molecules) of which an organism is composed. In the words of one of the devoted postulants of this point of view: "The point of faith is this: make the polypeptide sequences at the right time and in the right amounts, and the organization will take care of itself". Although superficially plausible, and apparently directly related to observation, this position is in fact the least tenable alternative, for reasons which we have discussed in detail elsewhere.

2. Let us consider some specific biological quality, such as motility. This is a quality manifested by organisms, but it is not itself co-extensive with the quality of being an organism; in particular, there are many non-organic systems which are motile. Any non-organic motile system can be entirely represented by encodings of numerical observables, in the fashion we have already considered in detail. In such a system, we may expect that the quality of motility will be directly linked to an appropriate family of such observables. The class of such motile systems, then, can be regarded as consisting of *metaphors* for organic motility, in the sense we used that term in Chapter 2.3. In particular, we may hope to understand the specific quality of motility *in organisms* by considering them as elements of the larger class of motile systems, and thereby formally relating their motility to appropriate numerical observables in the fashion characteristic of that class. It is this procedure which underlies most of the approaches taken to a theoretical understanding of individual organic qualities; most of the examples we shall consider below are precisely of this character.

   The essence of this approach is to obtain insight into a *particular* quality, like motility, by embedding a given system manifesting the quality into a *class* of systems bearing a metaphorical relation to it, and for which linkages can effectively be established between this quality and others. In physics, for example, once we recognize some particular system as a gas, we can apply it to the full machinery of thermodynamics, simply because we know how this machinery can be applied to other gases. As we shall see, this exploitation of metaphoric relations provides us with a great deal of "free information" (to use a term of Eddington's) which we can bring to bear on *any* particular system simply from a knowledge that the system belongs to a certain class. In slightly different language: by embedding a given system into a class in this fashion, we create a *context*, which in itself is often sufficient to specify the form of the basic linkage relations pertaining to our system. It is by exploitation of such context, for example, that a paleontologist is able to reconstruct an entire anatomy from a single bone; utilizing the context created by the comparative anatomy of extant organisms as a source of information. Such considerations of metaphor, or context, also underlie many emprical studies of biological behaviors, such as the employment of inorganic films to elucidate properties of biological membranes, or the use of catalytic surfaces to help understand enzymes, or the employment of rats and other organisms to help understand disease processes and therapies in humans. In

the limit, metaphor converges to *analogy*, and the usages we have
described become identical with the employment of a scale model
to determine the exact behavior of all systems similar to it.

We have seen how we can employ the relation of metaphor to throw
light on how some specific biological quality, like motility, is
linked to other observables. We can in principle do the same for
any particular biological quality, we determine a class of systems
manifesting it, in which this quality is specifically linked to
others. Now let us imagine that we form the *intersection* of all
these classes. A system in this intersection will by definition
exhibit *all* of the basic biological qualities, and we will know
in principle how to link each such quality, considered individually,
to other observables. This intersection is not empty, because the
organisms themselves must lie in it. The question is whether this
intersection contains *only* the organisms. The conviction that this
is the case underlies what used to be called *biomimesis*; the
attempt to construct natural systems exhibiting the basic biological qualities. The idea was that a natural system manifesting
enough of the basic biological qualities would itself be an organism. It is important to recognize, though, that this approach to
biomimesis through an exploitation of relations of metaphors does
not itself imply reductionism; the biomimetic hypothesis can be
true without reductionism being true.

3.   The third approach strives to deal with biological qualities and
     their linkages directly, without relating them initially to
     numerical observables of any specific kind of natural system.
     This is the approach characterisitc of *relational biology*. We
     can then recapture individual systems, and the observables and
     linkages which characterize them, through a process of *realization*.
     The relational approach is thus analogous to the study, say, of
     transformation groups by regarding them initially as abstract
     groups. Ant particular transformation group can then be recaptured
     through a process of representation; i.e. by a "structure-preser-
     ving mapping" which maintains the abstract linkages while endowing
     the abstract elements with specific properties consistent with
     these linkages. We shall consider this relational approach, which
     is the most radical of those we have described, in more detail
     below.

3.5 Specific Encodings of Biological Systems

In the present chapter, we turn to some specific examples of encoding of biological systems, with special reference to the way in which characteristically biological qualities are related to the numerical observables manifested by all natural systems. For this reason, we shall not consider reductionistic approaches in detail, nor any of the encodings belonging entirely to *biophysics*. The essence of such encodings is precisely that they treat biological systems exclusively in terms of their numerical observables. Thus, for example, we shall ignore the large literature on the flow of blood as a hydrodynamic problem, pertaining to the flow of viscous fluid in a family of elastic vessels. For our purposes, this literature is part of hydrodynamics, and not of biology. It is of course true that such studies are often of vital practical importance, but they raise no question of principle beyond what we have already considered in Chapter 3.2 above; the biological origins of such studies and their application to cardiovascular problems are essentially irrelevant to the encodings themselves, and the manner in which inferences are drawn from them. We shall concentrate instead on examples of encodings which exhibit a basic metaphorical aspect, and on relational encodings. It is only in these cases that particular biological qualities play a dominant role.

EXAMPLE 1: THE MASS-ACTION METAPHOR[1]

We have seen, in Example 1 of Chapter 3.3 above, that one way in which to encode dynamical processes is to specify the manner in which the rates of change of observable quantities depends on their instantaneous values. Indeed, we stressed earlier (cf. Chapter 1.2) that such a specification is fundamental to the reactive paradigm itself. In mechanics, it is Newton's Second Law which allows us to do this, by linking the concept of force explicitly to the rate of change of velocity or momentum. Thus, if we are going to encode any kind of dynamical process in a natural system, or class of such systems, we need to find the appropriate analog of Newton's Second Law; i.e. we need to postulate the linkage relations which express instantaneous rates of change of observables as a function of their instantaneous values on states.

Let us suppose that the system under consideration consists of a
family of interacting units of various types. A natural set of
observables to employ for encoding such a system comprises the
instantaneous sizes of the populations of the "species" of units
involved in our system. More generally, if our units are arranged
in space in some fashion, we may regard these observables as *concentrations* or *densities*. Following the usual procedure, we shall
suppose that these observables have spectra which are *continua* of
real numbers. That is, if f is such an observable, and if there is
an abstract state s such that f(s) = r, then there is another abstract
state s' for which f(s') = r + ε, where ε is arbitrarily small. It
will be noted that this presupposition involves the compromise described in Example 2 of Chapter 3.3 above; our population of units
is in fact discrete and finite, while the representation of a concentration or density in the above fashion presupposes the properties of
the continuum. Thus, we must regard our observables f as *average*
quantities, to which the discrete and continuous pictures can only
be approximations.

Let us suppose that the units of our system may be inter-converted
as a result of their interactions, according to definite rules.
How are we to link the rates of change of our observables to their
instantaneous values in such a situation? The general postulation
whereby we may accomplish this is the *Law of Mass Action*, which
thereby plays exactly the same role here as Newton's Second Law did
for mechanical systems. This law states that the instantaneous rate
of change of any concentration or density is proportional to the
product of the concentrations of the interacting units involved. If
more than one type of interaction among the units can contribute to
the rate of change of concentration, then this rate of change is a
sum of such products.

The Law of Mass Action was originally proposed to account for the
rates at which chemical reactions proceed. A chemical system can be
regarded as a family of interacting populations of chemical species
(molecules); a particular reaction in the system is a mechanism
whereby specific kinds of units are converted into others. Thus,
for example, suppose that a particular reaction can be expressed in
the familiar chemical shorthand as

$$A + B \rightleftharpoons C + D.$$

Suppose we are interested in the rate at which the concentration [A]
of the chemical species A is changing. According to the Mass Action
Law, we note that there are two independent mechanisms contributing
to this rate of change: (a) the "forward reaction", through which
A is consumed, and (b) the "backward reaction", through which it is
produced. We can then write our linkage explicitly as

$$d[A]/dt = -k_1[A][B] + k_2[C][D],$$

where k_1, k_2 are constants (rate constants), and the choice of sign
of the summands is determined by whether the particular interaction
is producing reactant or consuming it. We can write down similar
rate equations for the other reactants; we obtain thereby a dynamical
system, which can be treated as a formal encoding, or *model*, of the
dynamical process in which we are interested. Thus, the Law of Mass
Action is the linchpin in the study of chemical kinetics, just as
Newton's Second Law is in mechanics.

It should be carefully noted that there is nothing in the discussion

so far which specifically singles out chemical systems; everything
we have said so far pertains equally well to *any* natural system of
interacting populations of units, in which units may be interconverted
as a result of their interactions. Chemical systems indeed represent
one large subclass of such systems, in which we also know that the
Mass Action Law generates faithful dynamical models. We can then
think of using the subclass of chemical systems as *metaphors* for
other systems of interacting populations, even though on physical
grounds these other systems may be far removed from chemistry. If
this is done, we may extend the Mass Action Law from its initial
restricted domain in chemistry, and postulate it as a universal
mechanism for linking rates of change to population size, valid
throughout the entire class.

It was the fundamental insight of Lotka and Volterra to carry out
this procedure in detail in an ecological context. Here the interacting units are not chemical reactants but biological individuals.
As a result of such interactions, the population sizes comprising
such an ecological system will change, just as the concentrations
of the reactants will change in a chemical system. The nature of
this change in ecological population sizes is particularly transparent
in the special case of predator-prey interactions. Thus, with Lotka
and Volterra, let us consider the simplest possible such system,
consisting of a single species x (the prey species) and a single
species y (the predator species). We suppose that three "reactions"
occur in such a system:

   (a) $x \rightarrow x$;   i.e. there is an autocatalytic first-order increase
         in the prey species;

   (b) $x + y \rightarrow y$;   i.e. there is a conversion of prey to predator
         as a result of their interaction;

   (c) $y \rightarrow 0$;   i.e. there is a first-order loss of predator, which
         can be regarded as a decay to an inactive or non-reactive
         form.

Applying the Law of Mass Action under these circumstances, we find
the following rate equations:

$$dx/dt = k_1 x - k_2 xy$$
$$dy/dt = k_2 xy - k_3 y$$

(3.5.1)

where k_1, k_2, k_3 are appropriate rate constants. These are the
prototypes of the general Lotka-Volterra rate equations for describing
the dynamics of interacting populations in an ecosystem.

The procedures we have just sketched shows in detail how the "chemical
metaphor" leads directly to a system of rate equations in a non-
chemical system, but which nevertheless shares certain *basic features*
with chemical systems. It should be noticed that the specific features on which the metaphor is based (namely, that both chemical
systems and ecological systems involve the interactions of different
kinds of populations, through which interconversions of these populations occur) are *themselves observable properties* and as such must
represent *qualities* manifested in common by both classes of systems.
The metaphor can then be regarded in the following way: it is a
linkage between this shared quality and the formal property of encodings embodied in the Mass Action Law. The Mass Action Law itself

expresses a specific linkage between rates of change of certain observables and their instantaneous values; thus *the metaphor serves
to identify this kind of linkage universally with the quality which
assigns a particular natural system to our class.* This is the
essential conceptual step involved in the employment of a metaphor;
we shall see it again and again as we proceed.

It should also be noted that, as with all relations of metaphor and
analogy between natural systems, there is no question of a *reduction*
of ecology to chemistry, or vice versa. The relation of metaphor
between natural systems involves a mathematical relation *between
encodings*, which is then regarded as embodying a quality manifested
by the systems themselves. In the present case, the mathematical
relation between encodings involves the presence of a certain kind
of linkage between rates of change of observables and their instantaneous values; we identify this with a *quality* manifested by the
systems themselves, but *which is not itself directly encoded* (or
indeed encodable) in terms of numerical observables evaluated on
abstract states of an individual system.

Once we have obtained the rate equations (3.5.1), the investigation
of their formal properties leads us to a number of other relations
between the ecosystems they describe and other classes of natural
systems which we have already considered. We shall here note only
one. It can readily be shown that the rate equations (3.5.1) can be
converted, through a simple mathematical change of variables, into a
form in which *all the conditions are satisfied which allow the
formalism of statistical mechanics (cf. Example 3 of Chapter 3.3
above) to be applied to them.* This was already noted by Volterra,
but has been most systematically exploited by E. H. Kerner.[2] By
exploiting this formal property of the encoding, we can construct an
exact analog for ecosystems of the procedure by which we can pass
from the microscopic Newtonian dynamics to a macroscopic thermodynamics. We can thus establish a relation of *analogy* between ecosystems
and thermodynamics systems, which is formally of the same character
as the mechano-optical analogy relating optics and mechanics in
physics (cf. Example 4 of Chapter 3.3 above). This "ecosystem-
thermodynamics analogy" is extremely suggestive in many ways. Unfortunately, its specific usefulness as an empirical tool has been
thusfar limited by the fact that we have, as yet, no empirical
analogs of the *meters* (such as thermometers and manometers) which
play the crucial role in physical thermodynamics. Stated another
way: our present perception of ecosystems is currently restricted to
the microscopic level specified by the dynamical equations (3.5.1).
We cannot, as yet, perceive them directly in macroscopic or thermodynamic ways. Therefore, we have no direct insight into the *significance* of the thermodynamic analogy for the behavior of ecosystems.
But exactly the same would be true if, in physics, we could not
perceive a gas except through the mechanical state variables describing
its individual particles. The thermodynamic analogy makes it clear
that there must be a "macroscopic" level in terms of which ecosystems
can interact; we must await the development of specific empirical
instruments to make their qualities directly perceptible to us.

EXAMPLE 2: MORPHOGENETIC METAPHORS

The phenomena of morphogenesis and pattern generation in development
are among the most picturesque and striking in all of biology. Until
recently, at any rate, there appeared to be nothing within the compass
of our experience with inorganic systems which was remotely like them.
Experience with the phenomena of embryology led experimentalists like

Driesch to despair *in principle* of finding physical explanations
(i.e. linkages between physical quantities and those characteristic
of developmental phenomena) and thus to a mystical vitalism. In a
similar vein, but from the opposite direction, the physicist Maxwell
proposed that living units were "demons" who could violate the Second
Law of Thermodynamics.[3]

What are the basic characteristics of morphogenetic phenomena, which
has so bemused successive generations of scientists up to the present
time? Let us list a few of them, initially in informal language;
we shall then see to what extent each of them can be captured through
metaphorical means.

The first, and most obvious, characteristic of morphogenesis is the
apparently magical emergence of successive novelties of structure
and function, which in simplest terms can be regarded as the growth
of heterogeneity.   Quite apart from the simple growth in size (which
is in itself remarkable), development proceeds from a relatively
structureless and homogeneous zygote to a complete functional organism
of almost unfathomable complexity in a very short time.   The pro-
gression from relative homogeneity to limitless heterogeneity, which
is contrary to all physical intuition, proceeds in an irreversible
fashion.   Furthermore, the gross features of the developmental process
itself are startlingly similar even in organisms of the utmost
diversity.

The second basic feature of morphogenesis which we shall note here
is its stubborn stability against external interference. It is in
fact very difficult to experimentally interfere with the process,
in any but trivial ways, without killing the organism. Let us give
a few examples of this stability: (a) It was shown by Driesch that
if the two blastomeres arising from the first division of a fertilized
frog egg, each of which normally gives rise to half the cells of
an adult frog, are separated from each other, then each blastomere
will develop into a complete frog (it was these experiments, more
than any other, which convinced Driesch that no mechanistic explanation
for developmental phenomena was possible in principle). (b) It was
shown by E. Newton Harvey that a fertilized sea urchin egg could be
centrifuged for hours at several thousand g, completely disrupting
all spatial relations between cellular structures; nevertheless,
such a cell would still give rise to a normal developmental sequence.
(c) It was shown by Holtfreter, Moscona and many others that if the
cells from an embryonic organ were randomized, they would spontaneously
"sort out" to restore at least an approximation to the original
histology of the organ. (d) If a limb bud or other rudiment from
one embryo is grafted onto a second, it will continue its development
as if it were still in its original site.

These stability phenomena, and many others which could be mentioned,
collectively came to be called *equifinality*;[4]   the tendency of a
developing organism to attain the same final configuration, despite
external interference of the type we have mentioned.

Finally, developmental phenomena are under exceedingly strict control
both in space and in time. Part of this control is exerted through
direct genetic mechanisms;   other parts are epigenetic. Examples of
this kind of control are shown by the experiments of Spemann on
organizer regions;   these produce specific signals (evocators) which
evoke specific developmental responses in competent populations of
target cells.   Both the capacity to organize, and the competence to
be organized, are sharply limited in time;   hence developmental events
of this character must be kept synchronous, and this synchrony, of

course, is evidence of the rigor of developmental control.

Let us now turn to the question of how such phenomena may be understood. As we said before, our approach will be of a metaphorical
character; we shall attempt to embed each of the behaviors we have
described in a wider context, in which it may be linked to more
conventional numerical-valued observables.

2A. Metaphors for the emergence of heterogeneity

Let us consider how we may approach the first of the phenomena we
described: the emergence of heterogeneity from an initially homogeneous state. We shall restrict our attention here to the simplest
form of this problem; the spontaneous generation of a polarity or
axis of symmetry in a system which originally does not possess one.

The crucial insight underlying the approach we shall develop was
first articulated by N. Rashevsky.[5] He recognized that a *spontaneous*
passage from a homogeneous to an inhomogeneous situation, in any
context, could only occur under circumstances which rendered the
homogeneous state *unstable*, in a mathematical sense. He proceeded
to show how such a situation could arise, within a plausible physical
context.

Heuristically, Rashevsky's argument was as follows: Let us imagine
a membrane-bounded chemical system, which to a first approximation
may itself be regarded as a metaphor for a biological cell. Suppose
that some reactant is produced at various sites distributed in this
system, and which then proceeds to diffuse away from the sites.
Suppose further that the system contains particles which inhibit the
activity of these sites. Rashevsky had shown earlier (in the course
of his investigation of a metaphor for cytokinesis, or cell division)
that flows of reactants down diffusion gradients could exert mechanical
forces on suspended particles. In the present situation, these forces
would drag the inhibitory particles to regions of low reactant concentrations. Since the particles by hypothesis inhibit particle sources,
the effect of the flow is to magnify any gradients which exist; this
much is clear intuitively.

Rashevsky then showed that if the initial distribution of particles
and sources were spherically symmetric, the spherical symmetry would
be preserved by such a flow. However, this condition of spherical
symmetry is *unstable*; if any hemisphere of the system should, by
chance, come to have a higher concentration of sources or inhibitory
particles than the other hemisphere, the effect of the flow would be
to *amplify*, or magnify, this initial asymmetry. Eventually, all the
inhibitory particles would come to lie in the hemisphere which
initially contained more of them, and all the sites at which reactant
is produced would come to lie in the opposite hemisphere. Moreover,
this new situation is stable; as Rashevsky pointed out, no matter
how the contents of the system are stirred or divided, the same kind
of final configuration would be produced (cf. the experiments of
Driesch and Harvey referred to above). Intuitively, a system of
this kind spontaneously establishes a polarity, in which two opposite
hemispheres come to possess completely different properties.

The elementary discussion we have given above exemplifies the basic
features of the metaphors we shall consider. These features are:
(1) a coupling of chemical reactions and diffusion in a spatially
extended system; (2) the rendering of the homogeneous state *unstable*

through such a coupling. (3) In such circumstances, the apparently
spontaneous transition of the system from homogeneity to inhomogeneity.

*Thus, the setting for our metaphors will comprise the class of en-
codings of diffusion-reaction systems.* (We shall, as usual, call
the *encodings* of a diffusion-reaction system also by that name.) It
should be observed that (a) we have seen informally that this class
of systems can indeed exhibit behaviors characteristic of those seen
in developing systems; (b) the operant dynamic features of the class,
namely chemical reactions and diffusion, are universally manifested
in developing systems.

The basic points which Rashevsky enunciated were independently re-
discovered a decade later by the English mathematician Turing,[6] who
proposed them in a far simpler context. To fix ideas, let us consider
the simplest possible Turing system, which is shown in Fig. 3.5.1
below:

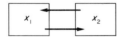

Fig. 3.5.1.

We envision here two identical "cells", each of which is completely
specified by the concentration of a single reactant (Turing used the
term "morphogen"); the amount of morphogen in the first cell at an
instant t will be denoted by $x_1(t)$; the amount of morphogen in the
second cell at the instant t will be denoted by $x_2(t)$. We suppose
that morphogen can flow between the cells by ordinary Fickian diffusion;
and that morphogen is produced at some constant rate S, and is lost
by a first-order process, which is the same for both cells. Thus,
according to Mass Action, we can encode these postulations into a
dynamical system of the form

$$
\begin{cases}
dx_1/dt = -ax_1 + D(x_1 - x_2) + S. \\
dx_2/dt = -ax_2 + D(x_2 - x_1) + S.
\end{cases}
\tag{3.5.2}
$$

where a is a rate constant for first-order decay or morphogen, and
D is a diffusion constant. This appears to be a completely linear
system; it is not in fact a linear system, because the morphogen
concentrations x_1, x_2 must remain non-negative. However, in the
interior of the first quadrant of the "state space" of the system,
it does behave linearly. Let us look at this behavior.

First, we observe that the system has a steady state given by

$$
x_1{}^* = x_2{}^* = S/a.
\tag{3.5.3}
$$

At this steady state, the concentration of morphogen is equal in the
two cells; i.e. the steady state is homogeneous.

Next, we inquire into the stability of this steady state. We know
that the stability is determined by the eigenvalues of the system
(3.5.2);   i.e. by the eigenvalues of the system matrix

$$\begin{pmatrix} D-a & -D \\ -D & D-a \end{pmatrix}$$

It is easy to verify that the two eigenvalues of this matrix are
given by

$$\lambda_1 = -a; \qquad \lambda_2 = 2D-a.$$

The first of these eigenvalues is always negative. The second is
negative as long as the diffusion constant D between the two cells
is not too large;   in more precise terms, it is negative as long as
D < a/2. In such a case, the steady state (3.5.3) is stable. However
if D > a/2. the eigenvalues λ_2 becomes positive;   the steady state
(3.5.3) becomes a *saddle point*, and the trajectories of (3.5.2) are
as indicated in Figure 3.5.2 below:

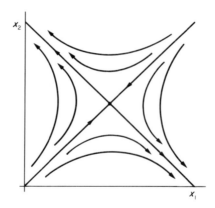

Fig. 3.5.2.

In this case, as in the Rashevshy systems mentioned earlier, any
deviation from homogeneity becomes successively amplified because of
the manner in which reaction and diffusion are coupled in (3.5.2).
Since by hypothesis morphogen concentrations cannot go negative, the
dynamics drives us to a situation in which all the morphogen is
either in the first cell or in the second cell, depending on the
character of the initial deviation from homogeneity. Thus, here
again a polarity is spontaneously established.

The situation we have just described can clearly be enormously
generalized. For instance, we can consider any finite number N of
cells, arranged in an arbitrary way in space.[7] We can suppose that
instead of a single morphogen we may have any finite number of n of
morphogens, interacting with each other according to any arbitrary
reaction scheme. Thus, if u_{ij} represents the amount of the ith

morphogen in the jth cell, we obtain analogous to (3.5.2) a system of Nn rate equations of the form

$$du_{ij}/dt = f_i(u_{1j}, \ldots, u_{nj}) + \Sigma\, D_{ijk}(x_{ij} - x_{ik}) \qquad (3.5.4)$$

where the summation is taken over all cells k adjacent to the jth.

In this scheme, the second index j plays the role of a position co-ordinate. We can pass to a continuum by allowing this index to range over a continuum in an appropriate fashion; we then find that the equations (3.5.4) become partial differential equations of the form

$$\frac{\partial u_i}{\partial t} = f_i(u_1, \ldots, u_n) + D_i \nabla^2 u_i,$$

$$i = 1, \ldots, n. \qquad (3.5.5)$$

which we have seen before (cf. (3.3.12) above).

It may be noted that the rate equations (3.5.2) or (3.5.4) or (3.5.5) always come equipped with the fluctuations required to manifest any instability of the homogeneous states. This is because, as we have repeatedly pointed out, the quantities whose rates of change are described thereby are *average* quantities, and thus they necessarily deviate in a random way from the observables they encode. These random deviations are precisely the fluctuations needed initially to move the system away from a steady state; thus, in this picture, the generation of inhomogeneity is indeed totally intrinsic.

Rate equations of this character have been intensively studied over the past decade or so, under the rubric of "symmetry-breaking" or "dissipative structures", especially by I. Prigogine[8] and his associates. A primary motivation for this study has been the recognition, motivated in large part by the phenomena of biological development which we have been describing, that classical thermodynamics is not adequate to deal with essential physical situations. We have already noted (cf. Example 3 of Chapter 3.3 above) that thermodynamics is essentially restricted to considerations of equilibrium in closed, isolated systems. In other words, we cannot hope to effectively encode into a thermodynamic context any kind of physical phenomenon which involves far-from-equilibrium behavior in an open system. Thus, from this point of view, *a main purpose of the reaction-diffusion metaphor is to suggest general procedures for encoding physical situations falling outside the scope of thermodynamics*. In fact, it is correct to say that biology is here providing a metaphor for physics. We shall return to this view in subsequent chapters, when we discuss the general properties of open systems and their relation to modelling.

Let us note one further feature of the simple formal system (3.5.2), which has provided the point of departure for another related field of active research. As we saw, the constitutive parameter D occurring in (3.5.2) plays a crucial role in determining the dynamical behavior of that system. When D is small, there is only one steady state for the system, corresponding to a homogeneous situation, and it is stable. As D is increased through the critical value D = a/2, this single steady state *splits*, or *bifurcates*, into (in effect) a pair of new stable steady states, while the original homogeneous state becomes unstable. Such bifurcation phenomena had long been known in purely physical contexts; an essentially similar behavior is shown by a vertical column on which a compressive axial force is imposed. For small values of the force, the vertical position is stable; past

a critical value, the vertical position becomes unstable, and new
steady states (corresponding to the buckled column) appear. A parameter like D in the system (3.5.2), or like the axial force imposed
on a vertical column, is generally called a *bifurcation parameter*.

We have already discussed the general notion of bifurcation in 2.3
above, and in Example 5 in 3.1. We here see the bifurcation phenomenon
appearing in yet another context, which it is instructive to relate
to our earlier discussions. As we noted above, a bifurcation is
generally to be regarded as manifesting a logical independence, of
loss of linkage, between two distinct modes of system encoding. In
the case of the systems (3.5.2), we can encode these systems either
in terms of the bifurcation parameter D, or in terms of the stability
of the homogeneous state. For small D, these two encodings are
equivalent; two systems characterized by similar values of D will
also exhibit similar stability properties. But in *any* neighborhood
of the bifurcation point D = a/2, we can find systems which are
arbitrarily close in terms of their D-values, and at the same time
qualitatively different in their stability properties. Thus, in
any neighborhood of the bifurcation point, we cannot generally
annihilate an arbitrary small change of D by means of a structure-
preserving co-ordinate transformation on the state space; the two
encodings have become completely independent of one another.

The upshot of these observations is the following. We have been
considering reaction-diffusion systems as metaphors for developmental
processes characterized by a spontaneous transition from homogeneity
to heterogeneity. We have seen that, in some sense, the *reason* that
reaction-diffusion systems exhibit such behavior resides in their
capability to exhibit bifurcations. Thus the reaction-diffusion
systems themselves can be regarded as metaphors for a wider class of
bifurcating systems; or stated otherwise, *any system which exhibits
a bifurcation can be a metaphor for these developmental processes*.
This approach to morphogenesis has been intensively exploited in
recent years, especially by Rene Thom, under the rubric of the *Theory
of Catastrophes*[9] The interested reader should consult the literature
for further insight into this kind of approach.

Let us conclude our discussion of reaction-diffusion metaphors by
observing that their power lies precisely in the fact that *any formal
reaction-diffusion system, like (3.5.5), is to be regarded as a
possible encoding of some natural system*. Any natural system, of
which a system like (3.5.5) is an encoding, must then exhibit the
characteristic spontaneous transition from homogeneity to heterogeneity. The class of systems (3.5.5) is thus identified as the
class of *potential models* for such behavior, because any system in
the class can, in principle, stand in the modelling relation to some
natural system. Conversely, insofar as developing biological systems
are encodable as diffusion-reaction systems, we tacitly expect that
such a system, when encoded, will yield a formal system in the class
(3.5.5), and thus, that any behavior exhibited by virtue of belonging
to that class will *a fortiori* pertain to natural systems encodable
into the class. This is the basic characteristic feature of a metaphorical approach to biological behavior in general.

2B. Phase transitions and phase separations as morphogenetic meta-phors

We saw, in our consideration of reaction-diffusion systems, that the
basic property through which they generate inhomogeneity is the
presence of a bifurcation parameter. Below some critical value of

this parameter, a homogeneous situation is stable; above the critical value, the homogeneous state becomes unstable; new (necessarily inhomogeneous) stable states appear, and the system will spontaneously tend to one of them. Consequently, we argued that any system with a bifurcation parameter of this type could be regarded metaphorically as an encoding of a morphogenetic process.

Many such situations are known to the physicist. A large class of them fall under the general heading of *phase transitions*. We have already considered certain phenomenological aspects of phase transitions, from a thermodynamic point of view, in our discussion of Example 5 of Chapter 3.3 above. In that discussion, we tacitly treated temperature as a bifurcation parameter, in the context of the van der Waals equation as an encoding of equilibrium states of non-ideal gases. If we look at Figure 3.3.3, we can actually see the bifurcation. Specifically, above the critical temperature $T = T_c$ all isotherms are monotonically decreasing. At the critical temperature T_c, a point of inflection (the critical point itself) appears on the corresponding isotherm. Below the critical temperature, this point of inflection splits, or bifurcates, into a minimum and a maximum. As we noted, it is this bifurcation which corresponds to the phase transition.

We can, of course, treat the same phenomenon from the point of view of statistical mechanics. A favorite device employed by physicists for this purpose, is a metaphor generally called the *Ising Model*.[10] In fact, the Ising model is a class of formal systems which can exhibit phase transitions, just as the diffusion-reaction systems are a class of formal systems which can pass from homogeneity to inhomogeneity. As we shall see in a moment, the two classes are in fact closely related.

It is worth while to spend a moment in briefly describing the Ising model. In its simplest form, we imagine a family of units arrayed in space in some regular fashion; e.g. on the vertices of a square lattice. At any instant of time, we suppose that a particular element can be in one of two possible states. We suppose further (a) that the elements can interact, in such a way that at any instant an element tends to be in a state favored by its nearest neighbors in the lattice; (b) the elements may be perturbed by an external influence (such as temperature, or an imposed field). Thus, interactions favor homogeneity of state throughout the lattice; the external perturbation favors inhomogeneity.

Under these circumstances, we can expect that there will be a critical value of the external perturbing influence, below which homogeneity is favored in the system as a whole, and above which heterogeneity is favored. Treating the external perturbation as a bifurcation parameter, we thus expect that at this critical value there will be an abrupt transition between the disordered situation (in which the states of adjacent elements are uncorrelated) to the ordered situation (in which adjacent elements will be in the same state). This is the Ising model version of the phase transition; this intuitive behavior is borne out by detailed statistical-mechanical considerations.

It is clear that the "Ising model" is not one system, but rather a large class of systems manifesting similar features. We can generalize it in many ways; we can consider more general spatial distributions of our elements, or we can consider that our elements have any number of possible states; we can postualte any type of non-nearest-neighbor interaction between the elements. Thus the Ising model is a *metaphor* for phase transitions, and not a "model" in our sense.

The main point at which we are driving can now be stated. We have interpreted the two states of our lattice elements as alternate states in which a definite element can be found at an instant of time. Thus, the transition of an element from one state to another can be looked upon as a *differentiation* of the element. But there are at least two other interpretations which can be made of the same situation:

a. Let us suppose that instead of a population of identical elements, each of which may be in one of two alternate states, we envision a population of two distinct kinds of elements, each of which possesses only a single state. In that case, a change of state must be interpreted as a *replacement* of an element of one type by an element of the other type. That is, we view a change of state in these circumstances as a *movement* of one type of element away from a particular lattice position, and a corresponding *movement* of the other type of element into that lattice position.

What is a phase transition under these circumstances? The "ordered" phase, in which elements tend to be in the same state as their nearest neighbors, will represent a situation in which all elements of one type are clustered together in one part of the lattice, and all elements of the other type are clustered together elsewhere in the lattice. The "disordered" phase will represent a situation in which the elements of both types are maximally intermingled. Thus, a "phase transition" in this situation will actually be a *phase separation*, like the breaking of an oil-water emulsion. We notice that the *formalism* describing this situation is exactly as it was before; only the *interpretation* has changed.

b. Let us suppose that our population consists only of one kind of element. The two states which can be assigned to a particular lattice position will now be interpreted as the *presence* of an element at that position, or the *absence* of an element. Thus, a change of state in these circumstances can be regarded either as the *birth* of an element, or the *death* of one. This situation is called the "lattice gas" by the physicist; the "disordered" situation corresponds to a uniform distribution of elements and "holes"; the "ordered" situation to a precipitation or accumu- lation of elements, with simultaneous generation of a "vacuum". Here again, the basic situation is exactly as it was before; only the *interpretation* has changed.

Let us now return to the problem of morphogenesis, after this brief detour into the Ising model. The biologist knows that there are three basic kinds of processes underlying all specific morphogenetic or developmental phenomena.[11] These are:

1. *Differentiation*; the cells of a developing system become pro- gressively different from one another, in their chemical consti- tution and their physiological properties.

2. *Morphogenetic movement*; the cells of a developing system sys- tematically change their relative positions, as for instance in the phenomena of "sorting out" to which we briefly alluded above.

3. *Differential birth and death*; the various cell populations of a developing system change their relative sizes through modulations

of their rates of multiplication and death.

It will be observed that these are exactly the three processes manifested metaphorically in the Ising model, arising from the different
interpretations of state transitions of individual lattice elements.
Thus, the Ising model provides us with metaphors for all of these
basic morphogenetic mechanisms.

Moreover, the reaction-diffusion systems we considered above are
themselves special cases of suitable Ising models. For at the molecular level, a chemical reaction is simply the disappearance ("death")
of elements of reactant, with the concomitant appearance ("birth")
of elements of reaction product. Likewise, diffusion is simply the
movement of a diffusing element from one lattice position to another.
Thus, the reaction-diffusion systems can be obtained from the Ising
models by a suitable superposition of movement with birth-and-death.
The phase transition in such a system is simply the bifurcation we
saw before.

Thus, we now have at our disposal a new and larger class of metaphors
for developmental processes. This is, as always, a class of *formal*
systems, each member of which is a presumptive encoding of some
specific physical or biological situation. Moreover, it is a class
of metaphors which serves to relate the morphogenetic processes
characteristic of developing biological systems to homologous phenomena
characterisitc of inorganic systems. It thus serves to exhibit a
continuity between the behaviors of the organic and inorganic realm,
which seemed initially so disparate. It should be carefully noted,
as always, that this conceptual continuity has nothing to do with a
reduction of developmental phenomena to physics; it rather asserts
that developmental phenomena may admit encodings falling into the
same class of formal systems as do certain phenomena of inorganic
nature.

2C. Metaphoric aspects of genetic control

We noted at the outset of this discussion that developmental phenomena
are under careful control, and that at least some portion of this
control must be of a *genetic* character. We wish now to consider the
meaning of this kind of assertion, within the context of the metaphors
for morphogenesis presented so far.

At the simplest level, the genome of an organism is to be regarded
as determining the *species* of biological system with which we are
dealing. Thus, almost by definition, any physiological, morphological
or developmental characteristic of an organism which is *species-
specific* must ultimately be referred to the genome. In particular,
if a developmental metaphor of the type we have been discussing is
to be fully meaningful biologically, we must be able to identify the
sense in which its specific properties are genome-determined. At
the same time, we note that the very concept of a genome seems
utterly alien to inorganic phenomena, which are also represented by
this same class of metaphors. We shall thus begin our considerations
of genetic control in morphogenesis by showing that this is not so;
incipient in even the simplest example of a morphogenetic metaphor
there is already present a genetic component which we can extract.

Let us take as an example a simple inorganic natural system; e.g.
a gas. There is clearly a sense in which such a gas possesses a
"species"; thus we can tell, for example, that chlorine and nitrogen
are *different* gases, or that two samples of nitrogen belong to the

same "species". A moment's reflection will reveal that the qualities
on which our perception of "species" depends reside in the *constitutive*
parameters which enter into the equation of state describing *all*
species of gas. To say that we have replaced one species of gas by
another means that we have, at bottom, made a change in one or more
of these constitutive parameters.

If we take, say, the van der Waals equation (3.3.25) as the equation
of state governing the various species of gas under consideration,
we see that there are three such constitutive parameters, which we
denoted by (a, b, r). Thus, within the confines of the encoding of
our gas into this formalism, it is reasonable to refer to the specific
values of these parameters as determining the *genome* of the gas. It
must, of course, be carefully noted that the property of being a
constitutive parameter belongs to a *formal* system; but we will as
usual *impute* this property to the natural system encoded into it.

In the example we are considering, the three constitutive parameters
(a, b, r) are related to the equilibrium values of the state variables
(P, V, T) by an equation of state of the form

$$\Phi(P, V, T, a, b, r) = 0.$$

Here two of the state variables (say P and T) can be fixed externally;
they can thus be regarded as properties pertaining to the *environment*
with which the gas is equilibrating. The equilibrium volume V is
then determined by the equation of state. Moreover, when P and T
are fixed, the specific *value* of the equilibrium volume under these
conditions is determined entirely by the genome (a, b, r). It is
not too great an abuse of language to refer to the volume so determined as the *phenotype* of the gas, determined by the genome (a, b, r)
and the environment (P, T).

In general, if the genome (a, b, r) is fixed, then the equation of
state defines a specific mapping Φ_{abr} from the space X of all environments (i.e. all (P, V) pairs) to the space Y of all phenotypes
(all values of V). That is, the equation of state can be expressed
as a relation of the form

$$\Phi_{abr} : X \rightarrow Y$$

which precisely determines what the corresponding phenotype will be
under a given set of environmental conditions.

Exactly the same kind of considerations can be applied to any linkage
between observables which involves constitutive parameters. The
equation of state which expresses this linkage can thus always be
interpreted as specifying phenotype as a function of genome and
environment. Thus, insofar as "genome" can be identified with
"species-determining", we can always specify a genome, for *any*
encodings of linkages, in *any* natural system. Moreover, we can do
so in a way which allows us to bring to bear the entire formal
apparatus of *similarity*. As we have seen, similarity governs the
relations which exist between systems with different genomes which
obey the same equation of state. This observation in itself dis-
closes an exceedingly rich and fertile area of study, but one which
we shall not pursue in detail here; our present point is simply to
show that the concept of a genome, in the limited sense of "species-
determining", is already present in any encoding; and in particular,
is available in the morphogenetic metaphors we have already discussed.

However, the term "genome" means much more to a biologist than simply "species-determining". Several decades of intensive research into the molecular basis of cellular activities have led to the conclusion that the ultimate role of the genome (in a cell) is to modulate the rates of the reactions which take place in the cell, by determining the kinds and amounts of the specific catalysts (enzymes) which catalyze these reactions. Furthermore, we can see from the facts of differentiation of cells in development that, even at this elementary level, the relation between the genome of a cell and the reactions which occur in the cell is not a simple one. For we must suppose that all cells in a developing organism possess the same genome; yet cell differentiation means precisely that *cells can possess the same genome and nevertheless be completely different from one another in chemical, morphological and physiological properties*. The question then becomes: how can this be?

Briefly, the answer to this question lies in the concept of *gene expression*. According to this viewpoint, we must imagine that any individual gene may at any instant of time be found in one of a number of *alternate states*. For simplicity, we may suppose that there are two states available to any gene, which we may designate simply as "on" and "off". Thus it is not merely a question of which genes are present in the genome; it is a question of which genes are *expressed* ("on") and which are not at specific instants; it is a question of the *time course* of gene expression. To a biologist, then, the term "species" means not simply genome, but refers to a temporal pattern of genome expression.

Now insofar as a temporal pattern of genome expression is a "species" characteristic, *it must itself be determined by the genome*. We are thus immediately led to the idea that the change of state of any individual gene at an instant must be determined by antecedent patterns of expression of the genome as a whole, and of course by whatever environmental influences may contribute directly to such a change of state. We are thus led to a situation not very different from that of the Ising model discussed above; a family of interacting elements, in which the change of state of any individual element depends on the states of its "neighbors", and on the character of the environment. In the present circumstances, the term "neighbor" is not necessarily to be understood in terms of geographic proximity, but in terms of a capability for direct interaction between elements; the two ideas are identified in the Ising model, but are in fact distinct. The picture of the genome itself which is thus emerging can be called a *genetic network*. Thus, a genetic network is a formal system representing an interacting population of two-state elements, and as such comprises a metaphor for the genome itself.

We thus see emerging two distinct metaphors for genetic control. The first one, which is shared by all natural systems, identifies the genome with appropriate constitutive parameters appearing in an equation of state. In biology this viewpoint is adequate for many purposes, especially those involving anatomical or taxonomic considerations; indeed, it was in this kind of context that the very concept of the gene was originally proposed. On the other hand, at a more microscopic level, we find a different picture: the idea of a genome as a network of interacting multistate elements, whose characteristic features involve temporal patterns of expression. This second kind of metaphor is apparently unique to biological systems; it is hard to imagine an analog of this kind of encoding for, say, a gas obeying the van der Waals equation. Thus, we may say that biological systems appear to admit a wide variety of different encodings of their genomes, while non-biological systems do not.

How are we to relate the encoding of a biological genome in terms of
constitutive parameters at a morphological level, and in terms of a
genetic network at a microscopic level? We are now in the situation
diagrammed by 2.3.4 above, in which the *same* system admits these two
distinct encodings. The question is: does there exist a mapping
between the encodings, which allows us to *reduce* one of them to the
other? Or is there a more general mathematical relation between
them? Or perhaps there may be no relation of a formal character
between them at all.

At the present time, these questions simply cannot be answered. All
that can be said is that, *as yet*, no such relation between these
pictures of the genome can be exhibited. It is, of course, an article
of faith of molecular biology that the picture of the genetic network
is in essence the fundamental one, to which every other encoding of
genetic activity can be effectively reduced. For the moment, however,
faith is the only vehicle for asserting such a conclusion; all the
other possibilities we have mentioned remain unexcluded.

EXAMPLE 3:   METAPHORS FOR THE CENTRAL NERVOUS SYSTEM

Of all the organs of man, the brain is perhaps the one which is the
subject of greatest interest. It is the seat of all the qualities
we perceive as peculiarly human, as well as perhaps the major biological organ of control. As such, it has been the subject of
modelling and metaphor from very early times. Of greatest interest
to the investigator is the manner in which the brain generates and
propagates the electrochemical signals which have come to be regarded
as the essential features of its activity. In the present section,
we will devote ourselves to two distinct modes of formally encoding
the phenomena of propagation. We shall then explore some of the
ramifications of these encodings, both for an understanding of the
brain itself, and to illuminate some of the general principles we
have been developing.

We must preface our description of the encodings themselves with a
brief description of the biological presuppositions on which they
are based. Each of these presuppositions is ultimately founded on
experimental observation, but the general form in which we shall
present them involves a substantial amount of theory as well. That
is, they already involve a considerable amount of tacit metaphorical
encoding. For our purposes, it is sufficient to treat them as we
would treat geometric postulates; the same metaphorical machinery
can be brought to bear on any similar system of presuppositions.
Since our major interest at this point is in the metaphors, it thus
suffices to regard these particular presuppositions merely as a
convenient point of departure.

The presuppositions we shall employ are then the following:

1.   The functional unit of conduction and propagation may be identified
     with an individual nerve cell or neuron. A neuron is initially
     an *anatomical* unit, which we now endow with specific functional
     capability.

2.   Neurons are anatomically interconnected in a definite spatial
     pattern. Hence, propagation and conduction phenomena can be
     thought of as restricted to this pattern of interconnected
     neurons, which we shall call a *neural network*.

3.   Individual neurons are *all-or-none* elements. That is, we may

think of them as being in one of two possible states at an instant
of time, which we may call "on" or "off".

4. The state of a neuron at an instant depends on its own state,
    and on the states of the neurons afferent to it in the network.

5. Neurons are *threshold elements*. In order to make a state tran-
    sition from "off" to "on", the magnitude of excitation reaching
    a given neuron from those afferent to it in the network must
    exceed some critical value, or threshold.

6. The excitation reaching a neuron from another neuron afferent to
    it may facilitate the transition from "off" to "on", or it may
    inhibit this transition. In the former case, we speak of an
    excitatory interaction; in the latter case, of an *inhibitory*
    interaction.

7. Neurons are *refractory*; when they have made the transition from
    "off" to "on" at some instant, they cannot make this transition
    again for a characteristic time (*refractory period*). During this
    period, we may regard the threshold of the neuron as infinite.

This is clearly a substantial set of properties, which we assume at
the outset. Most of them are subject to extensive qualification,
but we repeat that we are using them primarily for illustrative
purposes. We also repeat that most of them already involve a substantial amount of tacit encoding of experimental observation into a
quasi-formal system. The metaphors we now proceed to describe
complete this process of encoding in different ways.

3A. Two-factor metaphors[12]

The properties itemized above all us to regard a neuron as a kind
of *meter* for the excitation impinging upon it. That is, each excitation is capable of inducing a dynamics in the neuron, in a
manner linked to the magnitude of the excitation. The case of the
neuron is a particularly simple one, since we allow the neuron only
two states; thus, the spectrum of the neuron (considered as a meter)
consists only of two possible values, which we may take as 0 and 1.

The neuron can thus be considered as a "black box" (cf. 1.2 above),
which relates input signals (magnitudes of excitation) to its
responses or outputs. Indeed, observation of an individual biological
neuron typically takes the form of cataloguing its responses to
different magnitudes of input or excitation.

The two-factor theories of excitation now to be described represent
metaphors for what is inside such a "black box". They are thus
analogous to the treatment we have given of linear boxes in 1.2;
they are an attempt to carry out the equivalent of a state-variable
analysis for individual neurons. The treatment we describe was
pioneered by N. Rashevsky; several other equivalent formulations
are possible.

We shall suppose that the internal state of a neuron can be characterized by a pair of observables, or state variables, which we shall
call x and y. We shall suppose that the response of the neuron is
a function of these two state variables; $Y = Y(x, y)$. We shall
further suppose that these state variables possess the character of
chemical concentrations, as we have described extensively above.

We shall now impose a linkage between the rates of change of these
state variables, and an afferent excitation $I = I(t)$, considered as
a function of time. We shall suppose that both of these quantities
increase at a rate proportional to the instantaneous magnitude of
the excitation, and at the same time are subject to first-order
decay. Thus, by Mass Action, we can write these linkages as

$$\begin{cases} dx/dt = -ax + bI \\ dy/dt = -cy + dI \end{cases} \qquad (3.5.6)$$

Now we shall *define* an observable $Y = Y(x, y)$ by the relation

$$\begin{aligned} Y(x, y) &= 1 \quad \text{iff } x \geq \theta y, \\ &= 0 \quad \text{otherwise.} \end{aligned} \qquad (3.5.7)$$

The parameter θ appearing in this definition is to be identified
with the *threshold* of the neuron. Intuitively, if $Y(x, y) = 0$, we
shall say that the neuron is in the "off" state; if $Y(x, y) = 1$, we
shall say that the neuron is "on". Thus, we see that a state transition from "off" to "on" in the neuron requires that the state
variable x exceeds the value of y by an amount exceeding threshold.
Thus, it is natural to regard x as an *excitatory factor*, and y as an
inhibitory factor. This is the origin of the terminology, "two-
factor" for the metaphor we are describing.

Now let us take the next indicated step. Let us suppose that we have
some finite number N of two-factor elements, arranged in space in
some fashion. We shall imagine that these elements are organized
into a network, by specifying for each individual element which
others are afferent to it. We shall regard the output $Y_i(x_i, y_i)$
of the ith element as playing the role of an input to each element
efferent to it. Thus, the entire network can be described by a system of 2N rate equations of the form

$$\begin{cases} \dfrac{dx_i}{dt} = -a_i x_i + \sum_j \lambda_j Y_j(x_j, y_j) + b_i I_i(t) \\[2mm] \dfrac{dy_i}{dt} = -c_i y_i + \sum_j \mu_j Y_j(x_j, y_j) + d_i I_i(t) \end{cases} \qquad (3.5.8)$$

where the summations are taken over all elements afferent to the ith,
and the coefficients λ_i, μ_i can for simplicity be taken to be ± 1,

depending on whether the interaction is excitory or inhibitory. A
formal system of the form (3.5.8) will be called a *two-factor network*;
these rate equations then describe the manner in which excitation
flows in such a network.

The two-factor networks thus comprise a class of metaphors for the
behavior of real networks of neurons, considered as encoded into a
certain family of highly nonlinear dynamical systems. We shall have
more to say about this two-factor metaphor presently.

3B. McCulloch-Pitts networks[13]

We shall now consider a completely different kind of encoding of the
same basic biological situation. The basic element in this encoding
is a formal object, which we shall call the *McCulloch-Pitts formal
neuron*.

The crucial distinction between the McCulloch-Pitts metaphor and the two-factor systems just described involves the manner in which time is encoded in the two approaches. In the latter systems, time is encoded as a one-dimensional continuum, which we conventionally take as the real numbers $\mathbb{R}$. In the former, on the other hand, time is assumed quantized into a set of discrete instants, which we may take as the set of integers $\mathbb{Z}$. The rationale behind this drastic step lies in the refractory property of neurons (cf. property (3.5.7) above). The idea is that we need only consider the state of a neuron when it is *capable* of being excited, and that if we use the length of the refractory period as a time unit, we thus need only consider the neuron's state at integral multiples of the refractory period. The seems like a considerable idealization, but in fact it can be formally shown that the class of McCulloch-Pitts systems, which by definition satisfy this property, is essentially identical with the apparently far broader class of discrete-time systems which are not synchronous in this sense. We shall have more to say about this situation in a moment, as it reflects a most important property of the McCulloch-Pitts metaphors; namely their *universality*.

Let us now proceed to define the McCulloch-Pitts neuron, which we emphasize again is a *formal* object. This neuron will consist of the following data:

1. A number $e_1, \ldots, e_m$ of afferent *input lines*, which will be called *excitatory*. At any instant of time, each of these lines may be in one of two *states*, which we will designate as +1 ("active") or 0 ("inactive").

2. A number $i_1, \ldots, i_n$ of afferent input lines, which will be called *inhibitory*. At any instant of time, each of these lines may be in one of two states, which we will designate -1 ("active") and 0 ("inactive").

3. A non-negative number θ ("threshold").

4. A pair of states for the neuron itself, which will again be taken as +1 ("active") and 0 ("inactive").

5. If $s(t)$ denotes the state of our neuron at the instant t, then this state is linked to the above data at the *preceding* instant by the following rule:

$$s(t) = +1 \quad \text{iff} \left[\sum_{k=1}^{m} e_k(t-1) + \sum_{k=1}^{n} i_k(t-1) \right] \geq \theta;$$

$$= 0 \quad \text{otherwise.} \qquad (3.5.9)$$

That is, the formal neuron is active at time t if and only if the number of active excitatory lines at (t-1) exceeds the number of active inhibitory lines at (t-1) by at least the threshold θ.

We can now organize such formal neurons into networks in the obvious fashion; we regard the state of an individual neuron as its output, and we allow this output to flow to all other neurons efferent to it along appropriate input lines.

It is clear that if we know the connectivity of such a network, and any initial pattern of activity, we can determine the subsequent patterns of activity for every subsequent instant.

At this point, we may pause to notice the vast difference wrought by
the apparently purely technical passage from continuous time to
discrete time. If we compare the linkage (3.5.9), determining the
state-transition rule of a McCulloch-Pitts neuron with its two-factor
analog (3.5.6) and (3.5.7), we can see immediately that the former
is entirely an algebraic object, while the latter is an analytic
object. Thus, the inferential machinery which can be brought to bear
on these encodings of neural phenomena is vastly different. This
difference is reflected in the kinds of conclusions which can be
drawn within these metaphorical situations, which we shall notice as
we proceed.

It was already stressed by McCulloch and Pitts that the class of
networks of formal neurons is closely related to the kind of mathematical universe which we called $\mathfrak{p}$ in Chapter 2.1. It will be
recalled that $\mathfrak{p}$ was a universe of *names* of objects, relations and
operations arising in another mathematical universe $\mathfrak{u}$. We saw that
as we proceeded to define various structures in $\mathfrak{u}$, we simultaneously
created a calculus of *propositions* in $\mathfrak{p}$. The relation between $\mathfrak{u}$ and
$\mathfrak{p}$ revolved around the fundamental fact that it was essentially through
interpreting propositions in $\mathfrak{p}$ as assertions about $\mathfrak{u}$ that we could
assign definite *truth values* to these propositions. We saw that it
was essential to have a means of assigning truth values in order to
be able to develop any kind of mathematical theory in $\mathfrak{p}$ at all.

Now let us suppose that p is any proposition in $\mathfrak{p}$; any proposition
whatsoever. Let us *force* p to be synonymous with the following:
the neuron N_i in a particular neural net is active at the instant t_0;
i.e. p now *means* that $N_i(t_0) = 1$. Then the activity of this neuron
automatically *assigns* a truth value (1 or 0) to the proposition p.

If we make this kind of forcing in a judicious fashion, we find that
we can construct neural networks which will represent any proposition
in $\mathfrak{p}$. For instance, suppose that p, q are arbitrary propositions in
$\mathfrak{p}$. How would we represent the proposition p ∧ q?

We can do this with a network of three formal neurons; one (call it
N_p) to represent p, one (N_q) to represent q, and one ($N_{p \wedge q}$) to represent
p ∧ q. We need only arrange matters so that

$$N_{p \wedge q}(t) = 1 \qquad \text{iff } N_p(t-1) = 1 \quad \text{and} \quad N_q(t-1) = 1$$

$$= 0 \qquad \text{otherwise.}$$

Clearly, the neuron $N_{p \wedge q}$ must have two (excitatory) input lines, and
a threshold of exactly 2. The neurons N_p and N_q must be afferent to
$N_{p \wedge q}$, each connected along one of the input lines to $N_{p \wedge q}$. We see
that *we have thus represented the proposition p ∧ q by forcing its
truth or falsity to be determined by the activity of* $N_{p \wedge q}$.

By extending this idea in the obvious way, we can in fact represent
any proposition which can be constructed from a finite number of
others through application of the basic logical operations. Thus,
in a sense, the class of networks of formal neurons is *co-extensive*
with the calculus of propositions in $\mathfrak{p}$. It is this enormously

suggestive fact, arising as it does in a class of metaphors for the
brain, which has made the neural network idea so powerful an influence
in the theory of the central nervous system. For it asserts that,
if any behavior whatsoever can be described in propositional terms,
there is a neural net which will exhibit precisely this behavior.
In other words, the neural networks form a universal class for realizing all propositions of this type.

This universality result, which was already enunciated by McCulloch
and Pitts, was exceedingly influential in its day. For it showed
that the complexities of the brain could be approached in a constru-
tive fashion through the metaphor of the neural network. Thus, it
was a kind of existence proof arguing the possibility, and even the
feasibility of understanding brain function in neural terms. Only
later did it come to be recognized that the very universality of the
class of McCulloch-Pitts networks raised difficulties of its own.
We have already touched on this kind of difficulty when we considered
the universality of the reactive paradigm (to which the neural nets
in fact belong), at the very outset, in 1.1. Namely, the fact that
any behavior can be *represented* in terms of a universal class of
this type does not at all imply that the behavior is in fact *generated*
within the class. Thus, the class of neural nets may *simulate* any
behavior which the brain can exhibit, but we cannot conclude anything
from the fact of such a simulation about how the behavior was generated.

Despite this, we cannot overemphasize the historical importance of
the McCulloch-Pitts metaphor, and its intimate relation with the
logical machinery, on which all of mathematical theory is based.
Indeed, this circle of ideas closes upon itself; if mathematics is
a creation of the human brain, and if the human brain is representable
by the machinery of mathematics, then the intrinsic limitations of
mathematics (e.g. as exemplified by Gödel's theorem) are *a fortiori*
limitations of the brain. Such ideas have been the source of some
profound developments in both brain theory and the foundations of
mathematics, as well as of some lively controversy. We may refer
the reader to the literature for fuller discussions of these developments.

Let us note here, for further reference, that the logical correlates
of the McCulloch-Pitts metaphor seem unreachable from the continuous-
time universe of the two-factor metaphor. We content ourselves here
with the remark that this unreachability can in fact be fruitfully
circumvented.

EXAMPLE 4 :   RELATIONS BETWEEN THE MORPHOGENETIC AND BRAIN-
              THEORETIC METAPHORS

We shall now pause to point out some extremely interesting and
important formal relations which exist between the various metaphors
we have described, for morphogenesis on the one hand, and for the
central nervous system on the other. Since these relations pertain
to formal encodings of different classes of natural systems, they
involve corresponding relations of *analogy* between the natural systems themselves; cf. the diagram 2.3.3 above, and our discussion
of the mechano-optical analogy in Chapter 3.3.

Let us first direct our attention to the relation between the two-
factor metaphor for the central nervous system, and the reaction-
diffusion metaphor for morphogenesis. In particular, let us compare
the basic dynamical representation (3.5.6) - (3.5.7) of the former

with the simple diffusion-reaction system (3.5.2). On inspection, we see that these dynamical equations (which we recall can be regarded as equations of state; i.e. as linkage relations between states and their rates of change) are essentially identical; *the only difference between them is in the form of interaction assumed between the respective units*. Specifically, in the diffusion-reaction systems, the interaction was simple Fickian diffusion; in the two-factor systems, the interaction is through the observable Y. Thus, we can in effect transform a diffusion-reaction picture to a two-factor picture by modifying the postulated form of the interactions allowed between our units.

On the basis of this simple observation, we can see that the biologically quite disparate problems of chemical differentiation in population of cells, and the propagation of excitation in a network of neurons, are in fact *similar*. Indeed, we may regard the temporal properties of excitations in neural nets as a form of morphogenesis; or better, we can say that both morphogenesis in cell populations and excitation in neural networks are alternate concrete realizations of a class of abstract processes for *pattern generation*.[14]

A similar relationship exists between the McCulloch-Pitts networks and the genetic networks which were discussed in connection with gene expression. Indeed, the "genes" in such a network were considered exactly as two-state elements. A very influential treatment of genetic networks from this point of view is tacit in the familiar *operon hypothesis*, which was put forth in 1960 by the French microbiologists Jacob and Monod,[15] on the basis of their experimental work on adaptation in bacteria. It is instructive to spend a moment reviewing this work.

Jacob and Monod postulated a separation of the genome of a cell into two parts: (a) the "structural genes", which are identified with segments of DNA actually coding for a specific catalytic protein or enzyme, and (b) DNA regions called "operators", which contain specific binding sites for particular ambient metabolites. The complex consisting of one or more structural genes with the operator which controls them is called an *operon*. In the simplest version, the binding of a metabolite to an operator may render its associated structural genes unavailable for transcription, and thus *repress* these structural genes; in the terminology we used above, such repressed genes are simply not expressed, or are in the "off" state. Other metabolites, which may combine with the repressors or otherwise render them inactive, will clearly release the repression, or *induce* the expression of the structural genes; these will then be in the "on" state. If we regard the small repressor and inducer metabolites as themselves arising from reactions catalyzed by enzymes coded by other structural genes, we see that a population of such operons becomes a network; the "wiring" of the network in this case is determined entirely by the specificities of the operator binding sites. Moreover, the interaction between inducer and repressor is clearly identical with what we called "excitatory and inhibitory input lines" in our discussion of the McCulloch-Pitts neurons. We can thus take over our discussion of the McCulloch-Pitts networks word for word to the case of the operons; thus *the metaphor we developed for neural nets becomes simultaneously a metaphor for operon networks*. Stated otherwise, neural nets and operon nets are analogs of each other; they are alternate realizations of the same formal class of abstract mathematical objects.[16]

This striking fact was not noticed by Jacob and Monod; however, some of the examples they proposed of simple operon networks, which

illustrated how such networks exhibit differentiation in terms of
gene expression, are absolutely identical with neural networks
proposed 30 years earlier by N. Rashevsky and H. D. Landahl, to
illustrate how phenomena like learning and discrimination could
arise from differential neural excitation. This neural-genetic
analogy, which has so far been surprisingly unexploited, possesses
many remarkable properties, which the reader is invited to explore;
our purpose here is merely to point it out as a specific illustration
of our general treatment of modelling relations, analogies and metaphors. It should be regarded as a biological analog (this word is
chosen purposely) of the mechano-optical analogy in physics, which
was discussed previously.

One further ramification of this circle of ideas may be mentioned.
Precisely the same class of systems into which we may encode neural
and genetic networks also serves to encode an important class of non-
biological systems; namely, the class of *digital computers*. This
fact was noted almost from the outset, by McCulloch and Pitts themselves, and by many others; probably the most extensive early
exploitation of this fact was by the mathematician von Neumann. As
always, the fact that two distinct kinds of natural systems possess
a common encoding means that the systems themselves are *analogs* of
each other; thus from the beginning, it was recognized that we could
in principle construct artificial systems which would carry out brain-
like activities. Indeed, an entire field ("artificial intelligence")[17]
has grown up to exploit this analogy, and thereby simultaneously
obtain insight into the design of "intelligent" machines, and into
the activity of the brain. The close relation between such devices
and numerical computation, coupled with the universality to which we
have already alluded, are also responsible for the efficacy of digital
machines in solving dynamical problems. Indeed, there is a precise
sense in which a digital computer, programmed to solve a specific
dynamical problem, is analogous to any natural system described by
those dynamics. This is a very rich and fruitful circle of ideas,
which we can unfortunately only hint at here.[18] However, it should
be kept in mind as we proceed with our discussion.

So far, we have considered relations between encodings of distinct
classes of biological phenomena; namely those arising from development, and those arising from neural activity. Let us now turn briefly
to the relations which exist between *different* encodings of the *same*
class of phenomena. As an illustration, let us consider what, if
any, relation exists between the continuous encoding of neural phenomena as two-factor networks, and the discrete encodings of the same
phenomena as McCulloch-Pitts networks of formal neurons.

We have already pointed out the radical mathematical differences
which exist between the two kinds of encoding. Any kind of relation
we could establish between these kinds of encodings would be tantamount to constructing a continuous version of a logical system, or
of a formal theory (in the sense of Example 3 of Chapter 3.1), or
alternatively, a discrete version of an arbitrary dynamical system.
This has long been a tantalizing dream within mathematics itself;
the realms of the continuum and of the discrete have always resisted
all attempts at unification. However, in the present circumstances,
we have a new idea to bring to bear: namely, that specific discrete
and continuous systems can serve as encodings for the *same* natural
system. If the qualities encoded separately into the two realms are
at all linked in the natural system itself, then this linkage will
precisely specify a formal relation (like an equation of state) between the two encodings. This is an idea which we shall pursue
extensively in subsequent chapters.

EXAMPLE 5:   A RELATIONAL METAPHOR: THE RASHEVSKY PRINCIPLE
            OF BIOTOPOLOGICAL MAPPING

In this section we shall consider the first of two metaphors of a
quite different character from those which we have already seen. We
have so far considered certain qualitites associated with biological
activities, as for example those manifested by developing systems,
or the organized activity of the brain.   The thrust of the metaphors
we developed for these qualities was to establish how they might be
linked to the kinds of numerical valued observables which comprise
the basis of models of inorganic systems. We have not, as yet,
attempted to link such biological qualities to each other. The
exploration of such linkages of biological qualities, without the
necessary intervention of numerical-valued observables at all, is
the province of relational biology; a term coined by N. Rashevsky
in 1954. Our first illustration of a relational metaphor will be
that initially developed by Rashevsky, and which he termed the
"principle of biotopological mapping";[19] for reasons soon to become
apparent.

Before turning to the metaphor itself, let us begin with a few words
regarding the basic motivation for Rashevsky's approach. From what
has already been said in this chapter, the reader will recognize that
Rashevsky had been the outstanding pioneer in seeking to understand
the properties of biological systems by relating them to physics.
Thus, for example, he was the first to propose that cellular properties
could be understood by linking them directly to the ubiquitous phenomena of chemical reactions and diffusion; he was among the few who
understood that the brain could be productively approached as a network of excitable elements; he also carried out early and outstanding
work in a multitude of other biological areas from this point of view.
However, despite the fertility and success of the viewpoint which he
was the first to consistently espouse, and to which he contributed
so much, he came to feel a growing dissatisfaction with the entire
approach, primarily because of what seemed to elude capture in this
way. It is instructive to consider his own words in this connection:

> ...There is no successful mathematical theory which would treat the *integrated*
> activities of the organism as a whole. It is important to know how pressure
> waves are reflected in blood vessels. It is important to know that diffusion
> drag may produce cell division. It is important to have a mathematical theory
> of complicated neural networks. But nothing so far in those theories indicates
> that the proper functioning of arteries and veins is essential for the normal
> course of intercellular processes...And yet this integrated activity of the
> organism is probably the most essential manifestation of life. So far as the
> theories mentioned above are concerned, we may just as well treat, in fact *do*
> treat, the effects of diffusion drag forces as a peculiar diffusion problem
> in a rather specialized physical system, and we do treat the problems of
> circulation as special hydrodynamic problems. The fundamental manifestation
> of life mentioned above drop out from all our theories....[20]

Thus, Rashevsky's development of relational biology was an attempt
to circumvent this decisive shortcoming by introducing the essential
integrative aspects characteristic of biology from the very outset,
and by postulating that, whatever else may occur at the physical
level, these aspects must remain invariant.

Thus, Rashevsky was forced to deal from the outset with characteristic
biological qualitites, and with the manner in which they are linked.
The qualitites with which he chose to deal could initially only be
characterized crudely and verbally, through such terms as ingestion,
digestion, absorption, assimilation, respiration, locomotion,

reproduction, and the like. He hoped, and expected, that more precise
characterizations would become possible through the mathematical
form of the formalism into which they were encoded. This formalism
was to stress the manner in which these biological qualities are
linked; linkages which must be preserved invariant throughout the
entire class of biological organisms. To a large extent, this is
indeed true, as we shall see.

Now these biological qualities are directly recognizable by us, as
we noted earlier. Thus, they must formally correspond to the kinds
of observables with which we have been dealing all along, except
that they need not take their values in numbers. The whole essence
of the relational approach is to treat these qualitites exactly like
the observables which characterize all other qualitites of natural
systems. Let us see what this means in detail.

Suppose that v denotes a biological quality, which we can recognize
directly. Like any observable, then, v must be encoded into a mapping
of some kind. Our numerical-valued observables, we recall, were
encoded as mappings $f : S \rightarrow \mathbb{R}$ from a set S of *abstract states* to a
spectrum of numerical meter readings. Likewise, v must be encoded
as a mapping $v : \Omega \rightarrow M$, where Ω plays the role of the abstract states
on which the observable is defined, and M is a convenient set of
values. What intuitively are the abstract states on which a biological
quality is defined? It is clearly something like the "class of all
organisms"; an element $\omega \in \Omega$ must be regarded as an "abstract organism", on which the quality v assumes a certain value $v(\omega)$.

Let us suppose that we are given some arbitrary natural system N,
and a family of numerical observable qualitites $\} = \{f_1, \ldots, f_n\}$
defined on the abstract states S of N. The main task of science,
as we have abundantly seen above, is to establish the linkage relations which exist between the observables f_i on the states of N.

In general, as we have seen, we cannot expect there to be a single
linkage relation involving all these observables; rather, we can
find a variety of subsidiary relations linking various *subsets* of
these observables. Thus, if $\{f_{i_1}, \ldots, f_{i_r}\}$ is a subset of these

observables, we may be able to find an equation of state of the form

$$\Phi_i(f_{i_1}, \ldots, f_{i_r}) = 0. \qquad (3.5.10)$$

Let us suppose that $\Phi_1, \ldots, \Phi_k$ are such equations of state linking
the observables in $\}$. More precisely, each such equation of state
asserts that, for any abstract state $s \in S$, we have

$$\Phi_i(f_{i_1}(s), \ldots, f_{i_r}(s)) = 0 \qquad i = 1, \ldots, k \qquad (3.5.11)$$

for an appropriate subset $\{f_{i_1}, \ldots, f_{i_r}\}$ of $\}$. This is the essential
content of the discussion provided in Chapter 3.2 above, which the
reader should now consult once more.

The equations of state (3.5.10) or (3.5.11) which hold among the
family of observables $\} = \{f_1, \ldots, f_n\}$ introduce relations on $\}$
itself. For instance, if a subset of these observables is linked
through an equation of state, we must say that this subset constitutes

a *linkage group*. Let us say that two observables f_i, f_j are *related*
if there is some such linkage group to which they both belong. This
introduces a *binary relation* into $\mathfrak{F}$, which in fact turns $\mathfrak{F}$ into a
graph. Indeed, *this graph is characteristic of the natural system*
N *on which the observables are defined, and may in fact be regarded
as a new encoding of* N *itself*.

Suppose that we replace N by a new natural system N', on whose
abstract states precisely the same set of observables $\mathfrak{F}$ is defined.
We can repeat exactly the same procedure on N'. There is no reason
to expect in general that the new linkage groups into which $\mathfrak{F}$ is now
decomposed will be the same as before; hence the graph G(N') we
obtain in this way will be different from G(N).

Now let us see what these ideas amount to when translated into the
terminology of biological qualities. Let V = $\{v_1, \ldots, v_n\}$ by a set
of such qualities, defined on the abstract set Ω. Just as before,
we will expect these qualities to be linked on Ω in definite ways,
through the analogs of equations of state of the form (3.5.10) or
(3.5.11), and hence that V itself will fall into a family of linkage
groups. Thus, once again, we can define a binary relation, or graph,
$G(\Omega)$, characteristic of Ω. Moreover, given any particular $\omega \in \Omega$,
we can consider the corresponding graph of *values*, which we can
denote by $G(\omega)$.

Considerations of this type are the essential feature of Rashevsky's
construction. However, there is one further idea which must be
introduced before we can actually articulate that construction, and
which we can motivate in the following way. Consider once again
the class Ω of all "abstract organisms"; i.e. the class on which
the biological qualities v_i are defined. *Each* $\omega \in \Omega$ *can itself be
regarded as being a natural system*, and hence can be identified with
a set S of abstract states on which ordinary numerical observables
are defined. These are precisely the observables to which Rashevsky
referred in the quotation above, on which specific theories of
biological activity had heretofore been based. We can see now that
any such specific theory *must necessarily* miss the integrative
characteristics residing in the biological qualities, *because these
latter are defined on* Ω, *and not on any individual* S. Indeed, it
was Rashevsky's essential insight to recognize that, if we would
capture the missing integrative aspects, it is necessary to move the
discussion from an individual S to a *class* like Ω.

Rashevsky recognized that the *differences* we perceive between organisms reside in observables defined on individual abstract state sets
S, but that the *commonalities* shared by all organisms reside in the
qualitites defined on Ω (and in the manner in which they are linked).
Thus in his initial treatment, he allowed room for both kinds of
qualities. Specifically, he supposed given a set V = $\{v_1, \ldots, v_n\}$
of qualities defined on Ω, and another set $\mathfrak{F} = \{f_1, \ldots, f_m\}$ of
ordinary observables, defined on each individual $\omega \in \Omega$. He then
proceeded to form the graphs $G(\omega)$ appropriate to both sets of qualities. His *Principle of Biotopological Mapping* was an assertion
about how any two such graphs $G(\omega_1)$, $G(\omega_2)$ must be related. The
essence of the principle was, of course, that the portion of these
graphs coming from the biological qualities V must be maintained
invariant; i.e. any two such graphs could be homomorphically related

in such a way that there was always a certain invariant subgraph. This invariant subgraph is substantially what Rashevsky called the *primordial graph*, and on which he based his entire approach to relational biology.

Let us now observe that *any family of homomorphic graphs of this type could represent an encoding of biological qualities*. Thus, any such family of graphs could comprise what Rashevsky called an *abstract biology*. It follows that any proposition true for every abstract biology must *a fortiori* apply to biology itself. He established a number of such propositions, which are of the greatest interest. For example, he could show that under rather general conditions, the invariant primordial graph could be effectively determined from *any representative* of the class of graphs homomorphic to it. In effect, he showed that any biology is in principle completely determined by any organism in it. This is a startling kind of result, but one which has been entirely neglected by biologists. Indeed, it has ironically enough been dismissed as entirely alien to the spirit of biology, whereas the entire purpose of the relational approach was to capture in definite terms that which is intrinsically biological. We have seen that the relational approach, initially perceived as utterly abstract and remote from "experiment", is in fact based on exactly the same considerations which underlie any other kind of observation. It is thus no more remote, and no more abstract, than any other empirically-based theoretical development. In this regard, its only distinguishing characteristics are its universal significance, and the unusual insight required to perceive it initially.

It should be remarked that Rashevsky's initial treatment was superficially rather different from that presented above. However, we would as usual urge the reader to consult the original work for fuller details.

EXAMPLE 6:   ANOTHER RELATIONAL METAPHOR: THE (M, R)-SYSTEMS[21]

The (M, R)-systems represent another class of relational metaphors, this time developed within the more restricted confines of the biology of cells.

The point of departure for these ideas lies once again in this fact; that although the biologists can recognize many different kinds of cells, which may differ from one another more or less radically in physical terms, there are certain invariant commonalities which allow them all to be recognized as cells. As before, we can discern that these commonalities must be expressed in terms of biological qualities, and that these in turn must be defined on a class of systems, rather than on single ones. Once these are characterized and the linkages between them determined, we will have at our disposal a relational characterization of all cells. From such a characterization, we will be able to understand what cellular properties follow from cellularity *per se*, and which devolve upon the specific physical features of particular realizations.

Two basic biological qualities play the fundamental role in characterizing our class of systems. The first of these may be crudely summed up in the single word *metabolism*. However much individual specific cells differ from one another in chemical constitution, they are alike in that they are open systems, capable of ingesting and processing environmental materials, and converting them into new forms. The second of these qualities may roughly be called *repair*. It has to do with the utilization of processed materials to reconstitute the specific machinery by which metabolic processing occurs. Speaking very crudely, metabolism corresponds to cellular activities which are collectively called *cytoplasmic*, while repair corresponds to cellular activities generally called *nuclear* or genetic. We shall call a system capable of manifesting both these activities, linked to one another in a specific way, an (M, R)-system.

To proceed further, we must have some way of formally encoding the crude ideas of metabolism and repair just ennunciated into a more formal language. We shall regard a unit of metabolic activity, termed a *metabolic component*, essentially as a black box which transduces inputs into outputs. The inputs are drawn from the environment of the component, and the outputs also become part of the environment. Now we have seen before (cf. 1.2, for instance) that any such transducer can be regarded as a mapping $f : A \to B$ from an appropriate space A of inputs into a space of outputs. Thus our first step is to suppose that every metabolic component can be encoded into such a mapping.

As usual, whenever we are confronted with a family of transducers of this kind, we can arrange them into *networks*, through identifying the ranges (outputs) of certain of them with the domains (inputs) of others. In the present case, we can see that a network of metabolic components will comprise a finite family of mappings, related by the fact that the ranges of some of them are the domains of others, or are embedded in these domains as factors of larger cartesian products. Thus, for our purposes, a *metabolic system* M will comprise such a family of mappings. Conversely, any such family, as a possible encoding of a metabolic system, will be thought of as a metaphor for the metabolic activity of cells.

Let us now turn to the repair aspect. We wish to encode a repair element as a mapping, just as a metabolic element was so encoded. Let us see what such a mapping will have to be like. If $f : A \to B$ is a metabolic element in a metabolic system M, then f belongs to a *family* of mappings which we earlier (cf. Example 6, Chapter 3.1) denoted by H(A, B). Any process which generates copies of f must, if represented by a mapping Φ_f, have its range in H(A, B). Thus, it is suggested that we do the following: with *every* mapping f of a metabolic system M, we associate a corresponding repair element Φ_f. This element Φ_f will be a mapping into the set H(A, B) to which f belongs.

What, now, is the domain of such a repair element Φ_f? This domain must be related to the metabolic activity of the entire system M. We will thus suppose that the domain of each Φ_f must be a cartesian product of the ranges of mappings in M itself; the inputs to Φ_f represent outputs of M as a whole. A system composed of mappings f, and mappings Φ_f related to them in this fashion, is an (M, R)-system.

These (M, R)-systems possess many remarkable properties. Let us consider a few of them. One of the most obvious is intimately connected with the repair aspect of such systems. Let us suppose that by some means we remove a metabolic component f from the system. The associated repair component Φ_f, however, remains present and, if it receives its inputs, can continue to produce copies of f. Thus, the damage initially done to the system is in fact reparable. How-· ever, in order for this to be possible, it must be the case that the inputs to Φ_f do not depend on f; i.e. that the removal of f from the system should not affect the inputs to Φ_f or any of their necessary antecedents. If this is the case, then as we have seen, Φ_f will repair the damage. Let us call a component f with this property *re-establishable*; a component without this property will be *non-re-establishable*. Re-establishability of a component f thus depends entirely on (a) the manner in which the metabolic components are inter-connected, and (b) on the domains of the repair components Φ_f.

It can easily be shown that *every (M, R)-system must contain at least one non-re-establishable component*. That is, there must be at least one way of damaging such a system which cannot be repaired by the system. Moreover, we can show that there is an inverse relation be- tween the number of such non-re-establishable components and their importance for the functioning of the system as a whole. For instance, if there should be exactly one non-re-establishable component, then the removal of that component will cause the entire system to fail. In other words, although such a system can repair almost all such injuries, the single one which it cannot repair is lethal to every component.

Let us consider another kind of result which is unique to the theory of (M, R)-systems. We have argued that the repair components perform functions usually regarded as nuclear, or genetic, in cells. One of the decisive features of genetic activity in real cells pertains to the *replication* of the genetic material. Thus it would be most important to show that, already within the (M, R)-system formalism as we have defined it, and without the need for making any further *ad hoc* assumptions, a mechanism for such replication was already present. This is what we shall now proceed to show; namely, that already within our formalism, there exists machinery which can *replicate the repair components*. Let us see how this comes about.

Quite generally, if X and Y are arbitrary sets, we can define for each element x in X a mapping

$$\hat{x} : H(X, Y) \to Y$$

by writing

$$\hat{x}(f) = f(x).$$

This mapping is often called the *evaluation map* of x. We thus obtain an embedding $x \to \hat{x}$ of X into the set of mappings

$$H(H(X, Y), Y).$$

Let us suppose that this evaluation mapping x is *invertible*. Then clearly

$$\hat{x}^{-1} \varepsilon H(Y, H(X, Y)).$$

When will $\hat{x}$ be invertible? It is clearly sufficient that

$$\hat{x}(f_1) = \hat{x}(f_2) \qquad \text{implies} \qquad f_1 = f_2.$$

But by definition of the evaluation map, this means that

$$f_1(x) = f_2(x) \qquad \text{implies} \qquad f_1 = f_2.$$

That is, *the invertibility of $\hat{x}$ is a condition on* H(A, B); this latter set must be such that any two maps f_1 and f_2 which agree on x agree everywhere. (We may observe that this condition is reminiscent of the unique trajectory property in dynamical systems.)

Now in particular, let us put

$$X = A; \qquad Y = H(A, B).$$

We thus obtain, for any b in B for which $\hat{b}^{-1}$ exists, a mapping

$$\beta_b : H(A, B) \to H(B, H(A, B)).$$

where we have put $\beta_b = \hat{b}^{-1}$. It is now easy to see that this β_b plays the role of a replication for the simplest (M, R)-system

$$A \xrightarrow{f} B \xrightarrow{\Phi_f} H(A, B). \qquad (3.5.12)$$

By pursuing this kind of argument in more general settings, we obtain conditions under which replication maps exist for the repair components of any arbitrary (M, R)-system. To our knowledge, this kind of result is unique; there is no other situation in which replicative capacity can be made to *follow* from repair activity without the intervention of *ad hoc* assumptions. Thus it appears that this replicability is a *relational result*; i.e. independent of any particular physical mechanism or realization.

There are two other noteworthy features of the above construction. The first is that replication is not an *obligatory* feature of repair, but depends on the invertibility of a certain mapping. This in turn depends on the character of the entire set H(A, B) with which we are dealing. It may be expected that this condition will not usually be satisfied, and hence that most (M, R)-systems cannot replicate. Thus, as we would expect, replication is a relatively rare and unusual situation.

The second noteworthy aspect of our construction arises from the relation of the replication map (when it exists) to the other mappings in an (M, R)-system. This can be seen by extending the diagram of the simplest (M, R)-system, shown in (3.5.12), in the following way:

$$A \xrightarrow{f} B \xrightarrow{\Phi_f} H(A, B) \xrightarrow{\beta_b} H(B, H(A, B)). \qquad (3.5.13)$$

Let us now notice that the first three maps in (3.5.13) constitute our original (M, R)-system, in which f represents the metabolic component, and Φ_f represents the repair component. But let us now consider the last three maps in the diagram (3.5.13). It is easy to see that *these three maps themselves constitute an* (M, R)-*system*; but now one in which the original repair component Φ_f plays the role of metabolic component, and the original replication map β_b plays the role of the repair component. From this we see the curious fact that *there is nothing intrinsic about the biological qualities of metabolism, repair and replication*; out perception of them depends on the total system in which they are embedded. In fact, we can imagine the diagram (3.5.12) extended indefinitely on both sides, with any successive triplet of mappings being an (M, R)-system, and in which any map could be either a metabolic component, a repair component or a replication map, depending on which triplet was selected as primary. This too is a most remarkable result, of an entirely relational character.

These few results should suffice to give the flavor of the (M, R)-systems as cellular metaphors. It should be noted that, in formal terms, we may form (M, R)-systems in any category of sets and mappings (cf. Example 6, Chapter 3.1 above). Indeed, it can be shown that the totality of (M, R)-systems which can be formed in any category is itself a category in a natural way, and can serve as an index of the structure of the original category. Moreover, the property of being an (M, R)-system is preserved invariant by functors between categories. This fact has some interesting consequences which we cannot go into here; we refer the reader to the original paper for fuller details.

One final feature of the (M, R)-systems may be mentioned. As we have seen, such systems may be formed from any category of sets and mappings. In particular, we may think of the mappings appearing in an (M, R)-system as representing equations of state, or linkage relations, of some natural system. Now we saw in Example 2 above that one natural encoding of a biological genome is in terms of a set of structural or constitutive parameters appearing in such an equation of state. If we do this, then the output of the associated repair mapping can be thought of as precisely such a set of constitutive parameters; we obtain thereby a way of interpreting these repair components, which in fact represent nuclear activity in cells, in terms of the more familiar genetic concepts arising from morphological and biochemical considerations. Once again, we cannot pursue this interesting circle of ideas here, but perhaps the reader can observe from the outline presented above how rich such relational considerations can be.

REFERENCES AND NOTES

1.   The Law of Mass Action is at the heart of chemical kinetics. Roughly speaking, it allows us to convert a hypothesized chemical reaction mechanism into a system of rate equations, describing the rate of change of reactant concentrations in time. Although mass action had been known for a long time, the modern form of the law was derived from statistical mechanical considerations by Guldberg & Waage in 1867; their argument was based on the calculation of collision frequencies of the reactant molecules. It seems to have first been noticed by Alfred Lotka (*Principles of Physical Biology*, Williams and Wilkins 1925) that mass action was in principle applicable to any system of populations of interacting units. He applied this idea widely to problems in population biology. Similar ideas were developed at about the same time by the Italian mathematician Vito Volterra (*Lecons sur la Theorie Mathematique de la Lutte pour la Vie*, Gauthier-Villars, 1931.) Between them, Lotka and Volterra laid the foundation for all theoretical studies of the dynamics of populations e.g. mathematical ecology.

2.   For the original papers, see Kerner, E. H., *Bull. Math. Biophys.* 19, 121-146 (1957); ibid. 21, 217-255 (1959); ibid 23, 141-158 (1961). For a discussion of this and other attempts to exploit statistical-mechanical ideas in biology, see Rosen, R., *Dynamical System Theory in Biology*. Wiley (1970).

3. For an interesting discussion of the Maxwell Demon and its history,
    see Brillouin, L., *Science and Information Theory*, Academic Press
    (1963). Brillouin, as had others (notably Szilard) before him,
    attempted to circumvent the possibility of such demons by showing
    that in a closed system, a demon would have to pay for the infor-
    mation it extracted by becoming increasingly disordered. This
    kind of argument was one of the main justifications of identifying
    the formal notion of "information" with the negative of physical
    entropy.

4. Equifinality in developing systems was advanced by Driesch (cf.
    Note 2 to Chapter 1.1 above) as his "first proof of vitalism".
    In particular, Driesch pointed out that the characteristic feature
    of equifinality, the independence of the end state from initial
    conditions, was totally at variance with the equilibria studied
    at that time in physics and chemistry. It seems to have first
    been noticed by von Bertalanffy that such independence is in fact
    characteristic of stable steady states of open systems. This
    observation constituted major conceptual advance; it not only
    posed a counter-example to the arguments of Driesch, but also
    (a) revealed the inadequacy of contemporary physics (based on
    closed systems) for biological problems, and (b) opened a rich
    new field of investigation. A good discussion may be found in
    von Bertalanffy, L., *Problems of Life*, Harper (1960).

5. Rashevsky, N., *Bull. Math. Biophys.* 1, 15-25 (1940).

6. Turing, A. M., *Philos. Trans. R. Soc. B.* 237, 5-72 (1952).

7. See e.g. Othmer, H. G. and Scriven, L. E., *J. Theoret. Biol.*
    32, 507-537 (1971).

8. Prigogine was an early pioneer in the study of what may be called
    the thermodynamics of open systems. He and his collaborators
    have been remarkably prolific over the years, especially since
    belatedly recognizing the conceptual significance of the Rashevsky-
    Turing metaphor (cf. notes 5 and 6 above). The most recent ex-
    tended development of these ideas may be found in two books:
    Glansdorff, P. and Prigogine, I., *Thermodynamic Theory of Structure
    Stability and Fluctuations*, Wiley (1971), and Nicolis, G. and
    Prigogine, I., *Self-Organization in Nonequilibrium Systems*, Wiley
    (1977). For a further discussion of these ideas, see 4.3 below.
    See also the author's review of the book by Nicolis and Prigogine,
    Int. J. Gen. Syst. 4, 266-269 (1978).

9. The original book of Thom (*Stabilitie Structurelle et Morphogenese*,
    Benjamin 1972) still makes the most provocative reading. A recent
    book by Poston, T. and Stewart, I., *(Catastrophe Theory and its
    Applications*, Pitman 1978) provides a remarkably clear survey of
    the mathematical ideas and many of its areas of application.
    See also Zeeman, E. C., *Catastrophe Theory: Selected Papers*.
    Addison-Wesley (1977).

10. For a description of the Ising models in their traditional setting,
    see McCoy, B. M. and Wu, T. T., *The Two-Dimensional Ising Model*.
    Harvard University Press (1973). See also the relevant articles
    in the series *Phase Transitions and Critical Phenomena* edited
    by Domb and Green cited in Note 10 to Chapter 3.3 above.

11. The analysis of morphogenetic phenomena in biology into these
    three basic mechanisms was apparently first suggested by J. T.
    Bonner (*Morphogenesis: An Essay on Development*. Atheneum 1963).

12. For a good discussion of the various forms of the two-factor theories of excitation and conduction, their history and their biological implications, see Rashevsky, N., *Mathematical Biophysics*. Dover (1960).

13. The original paper on neural networks is McCulloch, W. S. and Pitts, W., *Bull. Math. Biophys.* 5, 115-134 (1943). For a survey of applications to the theory of the brain, see Rashevsky's book (cf. Note 12 above). A lively introduction to the relation of neural net theory to automata theory and logic as well as to biology is Arbib, M., *Brains, Machines and Mathematics*. McGraw-Hill (1964).

14. See Rosen, R., *Bull. Math. Biophys.* 30, 493-499 (1968).

15. Monod, J. and Jacob, F., *Cold Spring Harbor Symp. Quant. Biol.* XXVI, 389-401 (1961).

16. This fact appears to have been first pointed out by M. Sugita, (*J. Theoret. Biol.* 1, 413-430 1961).

17. The term "artificial intelligence" means different things to different individuals. The basic disagreement is over the interpretation of "intelligence". For instance, an early and acrimonious dispute in the field concerned whether chess-playing programs were or were not paradigmatic for intelligence. Several representative surveys of the field are:
     Bannerji, R. B., *Theory of Problem Solving*. Elsevier (1969).
     Nillson, N. J., *Problem-Solving Methods in Artificial Intelligence*. McGraw-Hill (1971).
     Slagle, J., *Artificial Intelligence*. McGraw-Hill (1971).
     Schank, R. and Colby, K. M., (eds.) *Computer Models of Thought and Language*. Freeman (1973).
     Simon, H. A. abd Siklossy, L., (eds.) *Representation and Meaning*. Prentice-Hall (1972).

18. The question here is the relation between discrete-time and continuous-time encodings of the same class of phenomena. The problem is not so much the establishment of a single over-arching mathematical formalism which encompasses both; this is relatively easy (cf. for instance Arbib, M. A., *Automatica* 3, 161-189 1963). The problem is rather whether a relation of correspondence is established between the encodings themselves, along the lines of Figure 2.3.4 above. It the answer is affirmative, it would provide a relation between the mathematical concept of a "machine" and the physical concept of a mechanical device; it would provide a physical analog to the mathematical concept of unsolvability (cf. Note 6 to Chapter 2.2 above); and among other things would reveal whether unsolvability in the mathematical sense places a constraint on *physical* laws. If the answer is negative, it would then be interesting to discover exactly why; i.e. why two encodings which seem so similar in spirit should be so unlinked.

19. Rashevsky, N., *Bull. Math. Biophys.* 16, 317-348 (1954). This work was pursued through a long series of papers, published mainly in the Bulletin of Mathematical Biophysics between 1955 and 1965. See also the posthumously published monograph *Organismic Sets*, published in 1972 by J. M. Richards Laboratory.

20. Rashevsky, N., *Mathematical Biophysics*. Dover (1960).

21. For a succinct review of the basic ideas, see Chapter 4: *Some Relational Cell Models: The* (M, R)-*Systems*, in Volume 2 of *Foundations of Mathematical Biology* (R. Rosen, ed.) Academic Press 1973).

3.6 Models, Metaphors and Abstractions

In the present chapter, we are going to draw some general conclusions about modelling relations from the specific examples we have developed. We shall begin with a discussion about the concept of a metaphor as an embodiment of some general quality, and the relation which exists between such qualities and those embodied by numerical observables.

Let us begin by recalling that a metaphor was defined (cf. 2.3 above) as a class of encodings (or possible encodings) which share some property. Since encodings are *formal* systems, the properties which they can share are mathematical properties. As always, the mathematical relation manifested by the encodings is then *imputed* to the natural systems so encoded. Let us then consider a few typical mathematical properties which may be so shared, and see how the properties themselves may be expressed in terms of the formal systems which exhibit them. We may for example consider the following:

1. An integer is *prime* if it has no divisors other than itself and unity.

2. A set X is *finite* if there is no 1-1 mapping of X onto a proper subset of itself.

3. A group is *simple* if it contains no non-trivial proper subgroup.

4. A topological space is *connected* if it cannot be expressed as a union of two subsets whose closures are disjoint.

5. A dynamical system

$$dx_i/dt = f_i(x_1, \ldots, x_n)$$

   is *closed* if $\sum_{i=1}^{n} f_i = 0$.

6. A mapping $f : X \to Y$ between two topological spaces is *stable* if every nearby map is conjugate to f.

7. A mathematical theory J is *consistent* if no proposition and its
    negation are both theorems.

Here the terms *prime*, *finite*, *simple*, *connected*, etc. name mathematical qualitites, which may or may not be shared by mathematical objects to which they are applicable.

Given any such mathematical property or quality, we can imagine the
totality of all mathematical structures which share or exhibit the
property. Thus, we can consider the set of all prime numbers; the
class of all finite sets; the class of all simple groups; etc.
Along with these mathematical structures typically come appropriate
families of structure-preserving mappings. Thus, each mathematical
property defines a *category* containing all the structures which
mainfest the property.

Let us consider such a category $\mathscr{C}$. Using the appropriate concept of
isomorphism between objects in $\mathscr{C}$, we can partition $\mathscr{C}$ into equivalence
classes; two objects X, Y in $\mathscr{C}$ fall into the same equivalence class
if and only if there is an isomorphism between them. Intuitively,
these equivalence classes represent the number of different *ways* in
which the mathematical property defining the category can be manifested.
In other words, the equivalence classes arising in this fashion can
be regarded as defining the *spectrum of values* of the quality in
question. Further, the class to which a particular object X belongs
can be regarded as a *label* or *name* for X; it precisely specifies
the value our quality assumes on the object X.

It will be noted that the situation we are describing is exactly
analogous to the manner in which we treated numerical-valued observables, as devices for naming or labelling the abstract states on
which they were defined. Indeed, suppose that f : S $\rightarrow$ $\mathrm{I\!R}$ is such an
observable. We saw in 3.1 above that the effect of such an observable
is to partition S into equivalence classes; two elements s, s' in S
fall into the same class if and only if f(s) = f(s'); i.e. if and
only if the observable f assigns to s and s' the same label in $\mathrm{I\!R}$.
We also saw that the set f(S) of such labels was in 1-1 correspondence
with the set S/R_f of equivalence classes. Thus, if we look upon f
as embodying some property or quality of the elements of S, the *values*
which this property can assume are identical with the classes of elements which assume these values.

Thus we can see, what we have repeatedly emphasized, that general
qualities can be regarded exactly like observables; in each case
there is an equivalence relation imposed on a class of objects bearing
the quality, and the set of equivalence classes is the spectrum or
set of values of the quality. The only difference lies in the interpretation given to the domains and ranges of the qualities.

In general, given an object X in such a category $\mathscr{C}$, how can we tell
what value of the defining quality is assumed on X? It is evident
that this is a general form of the *classification problem*, which we
saw repeatedly in Chapter 3.1. As noted at that time, one general
way of solving the classification problem arises from the concept of
a *canonical form*. Namely, suppose that we possess a means for extracting out of each equivalence class some specific representative.
We can solve the classification problem for X by determining to
which of these representatives X is isomorphic. In a certain sense,
this approach to the classification problem involves a kind of
"template matching", in which we use the canonical forms as a set of
"templates" to which any particular object X is to be compared. We

again note that this procedure is exactly analogous to the situation
for numerical-valued observables; we classify an unknown state s in
S by matching its "meter reading" f(s) to some set of standard readings, and assign s to the same class as the state which gave the
standard matched by f(s).

Thus, in most general terms, what we have called a *metaphor* is simply
a category with an equivalence relation on its class of objects.
The only restriction placed on this equivalence relation is that it
be preserved by the isomorphism of the category, and thus may be
thought of as arising from the isomorphisms. Any two objects in the
category are thus *metaphorically related*; they both manifest the
quality through which the category is defined. They assume the same
value of the quality if and only if they fall into the same equivalence
class; i.e. they are isomorphic as objects of $\mathscr{C}$. We stress again
that these notions are exactly the same as those arising in the case
of qualities encoded into numerical-valued observables; indeed, the
latter can be regarded simply as a special case of the former, if we
consider categories whose only mappings are the identity maps as sets
of abstract states.

Let us now extend these ideas, by imputation, to natural systems.
Suppose that a natural system N can be encoded in principle into
one of the objects in a category $\mathscr{C}$ of the type we have been describing.
There is thus a precise sense in which any object in that category
is a metaphor for N, since it shares the quality which assigns the
encoding of N to the category. It is in this sense that an arbitrary
diffusion-reaction system was regarded above as a metaphor for
morphogenetic processes; or that an arbitrary neural network could
be regarded as a metaphor for the brain. Thus, we can learn something
about N even without knowing how to encode it explicitly; in particular, anything true for the objects in the category in general will
a fortiori be true for the encoding of N, and hence, by imputation,
for N itself.

We will now turn to the more specialized circle of ideas involving
modelling relations. From the outset, these should be regarded as
special cases of the metaphors we have just described. We recall
that two formal systems are metaphorically related if they share
some general mathematical property, as we have described. In the
case of a model, this relation can be more precisely specified: it
involves the existence of a *homomorphism* of one of them into the
other; i.e. a dictionary through which the properties of one of
them can be translated into corresponding properties of the other.
We are now going to discuss the ramifications of this most important
situation by introducing some new terminology, which will be most
useful to us later. In the process, we shall see some important new
relations emerging between natural and formal systems, which belong
to the general area of *system analysis*. This new terminology will
center around the concept of abstraction; a term which we have not
used heretofore. It will also involve the concomitant concept of a
subsystem[1] of a natural system.

Let us return for a moment to the fundamental concept of an individual
observable. We recall that observables represent potential interactive
capacities, made manifest through the moving of corresponding meters.
The meter readings are labels for the values assumed by the observable on particular abstract states, and we have seen how these sets
of labels are the point of departure for all formal encodings.

Let us suppose we are given only a single meter, which may interact
with the states of some natural system N. As far as the meter is

concerned, the *only* quality of N visible to it is the one embodied
in the observable it measures. As far as that meter is concerned,
no other qualities of N exist; and indeed N behaves for that meter
as if it possessed no other qualities. Instead of seeing the full
range of interactive capabilities which N can manifest, then, the
meter sees only one.

It is in this sense that we shall say that *any observation procedure,
applied to a natural system* N, *generates an abstraction*. For instead
of telling us about N, the observation procedure can by definition
tell us only about a single quality of N; it must necessarily *forget*,
or neglect, all the other qualities which N may manifest. It allows
us to see only a *projection* of N along a single interactive dimension.
This kind of forgetting, or neglect, of existent qualities is the
essence of abstraction.

In popular parlance, "abstraction" has a pejorative connotation. The
antonym of "abstract" is "concrete"; thus in the popular view (which
is shared by many empirical scientists) abstraction is a property of
theory, and one engaged in the direct observation of nature cannot be
accused of performing abstractions. Above all, one who observes
nature directly must always be solidly anchored in concrete reality.

We see, however, that the facts are quite otherwise. The observing
procedure is the very essence of abstraction. Indeed, no theory, and
no understanding, is possible when only a single mode of observation
(i.e. a single meter) is available. With only a single meter, there
cannot be any science at all; science can only begin when there are
at least two meters available, which give rise to two descriptions
which may be compared with one another.

If an abstraction involves a loss or neglect of properties present
in the external world, then clearly the qualities which are in fact
captured in the abstraction can only refer to some restricted part
of the available qualities of any natural system N. We are going to
call this part a *subsystem* of N. Thus, for us, the concepts of
abstraction and of subsystem go hand in hand; a subsystem is that
part of N which a restricted family of observation procedures allow
us to see, and conversely, an abstraction can never capture more than
a subsystem.

It follows therefore that all the modes of system representation which
we have been considering can at best describe *subsystems* of a given
natural system N. Thus, any modelling relation which we establish
between N and any formal system, insofar as it proceeds from an encoding of a limited family of observables, really pertains only to
such a subsystem. Different encodings of the same system N must
then generally pertain to different subsystems. Conversely, it is
reasonable to say that if two *different* natural systems N_1, N_2 admit
an encoding into the same formal system, that N_1 and N_2 admit a *common*
subsystem (of which N_1, N_2 constitute *alternate realizations*).

It will be recalled that these were the two prototypic situations
discussed in a preliminary way in Chapter 2.3 above. They are the
basic situations of science, which as we have noted, can only begin
when we have two representations or encodings to compare. If the
two encodings we are comparing both pertain to the same natural system
N, then our science is directed towards ascertaining under what
circumstances these encodings are related, and under what circumstances they are not. As we have seen, the capacity to establish a

homomorphism between such distinct encodings of the same system
underlies the idea of *reduction* of one encoding to the other; in
that case, our two subsystems effectively collapse to a single one.
If the two encodings bifurcate from one another, then they each
capture separate aspects of the reality of N; neither of them can
be reduced to the other. Conversely, if our two encodings refer to
different systems, then the extent to which we can establish homomorphisms between them is the extent to which our two natural systems
share a common subsystem captured by the encodings; this determines
the extent to which our natural systems can be regarded as *analogs*
of each other.

Now the whole point of making models; i.e. of encoding natural systems into formal ones, is to enable us to make specific *predictions*
(particularly temporal or dynamical predictions) about natural systems, utilizing the inferential structure of the model as an image
of the processes occurring in the natural system itself. To what
extent can we hope to do this, if the best a model can capture is a
subsystem?

In general, if two natural systems N_1, N_2 interact, they must do so
because observables in each of them evoke dynamical changes in the
other. Indeed, the prototype of a general interaction between two
natural systems is the image of two meters looking at each other.
In general, such an interaction will not involve *all* the observables
of either system; rather, there will generally be two *subsystems*
$M_1 \subset N_1$, $M_2 \subset N_2$ which already contain all the *relevant* qualities.
To this extent, we could in fact replace N_1 by its subsystem M_1, and
N_2 by its subsystem M_2; the interaction between these subsystems
would be exactly the same as the interaction between the original
systems. In other words, the replacement of our original systems
by *these* subsystems would have no observable effect on the interaction; it would be *invisible* to that interaction.

Thus, if we had an encoding of each of these systems into formal
systems, or models, we would have captured all of the relevant interactive capabilities of both systems. Even though we are as always
dealing with abstractions, the abstractions in this case have only
neglected interactive capabilities irrelevant for the interaction in
which we are interested. Consequently, any predictions we make
regarding this interaction will be verified (at least to the extent
that our encodings are faithful). The conclusion to be drawn from
this argument is simply this: to say that any encoding is necessarily
an abstraction is not in itself a reproach; indeed, we have seen
that we can deal with nothing but abstractions. What we must do is
see to it that the qualities retained in our abstraction are precisely
the relevant qualities actually manifested in an interaction in which
we are interested. The diagnostic for this is, as mentioned above,
that we could replace each of the interacting systems by the subsystems we actually encode, with no effect on the interaction itself.

In such a case, it is correct to say that the subsystems M_i are themselves models of the larger systems N_i to which they belong. Thus,
any formal system into which the M_i are encoded will also be encodings
of N_i.

In the preceding discussion, we have considered subsystems as units of interaction between natural systems. We seek to understand such an interaction by identifying the relevant observables of the inter-acting system, where an observable is specified by a special kind of interaction between the system and a meter. The extraction and char-acterization of subsystems in terms of individual observables, and the employment of such characterizations to encode particular inter-actions, is the essence of *system analysis*.

Now we must note that there is another, quite different way in which the term "subsystem" has been employed in science. All of our dis-cussion so far has been framed in terms of observables which are measured by the dynamics they *impose* on the other natural systems (i.e., on meters). On the other hand, *we can ourselves impose dynamics on natural systems*. We could think of developing a parallel discussion of system analysis by considering the dynamics which can be *imposed upon* a natural system, and using these as a point of departure. Let us briefly see where such a discussion leads.

We have argued at great length elsewhere[1] that the general result of imposing dynamics upon a natural system N is a modification of the linkage relations which originally related the observables of N. In particular, linkage relations can be abolished by means of imposed dynamics; i.e. two observables initially related through an equation of state on N may become unlinked. The abolition of a linkage rela-tion of this type may be interpreted as a "partition" of our original system N into independent parts. For instance, if our original system N is a mixture of alcohol and water, we can by raising the temperature cause the alcohol to distill off, resulting in a spatial separation of the original mixture. This spatial separation uncorrelates the observables characteristic of the water from those of the alcohol, whereas in the mixture definite linkages existed between them.

Families of observables which have been unlinked by an imposed dynam-ics will be called *fractions* of the original system; the dynamics itself will be called a *fractionation*.[2] It is very common in science to identify such fractions, produced by a dynamics imposed on a system, with what we have earlier called subsystems. It is this identification of "fraction" with "subsystem" which we wish now to briefly discuss. We shall argue that, *although any fraction may (with some qualifi-cation) be regarded as a subsystem, not every subsystem is a fraction*. Thus, the concepts of fraction and subsystem are not co-extensive. It follows further that the capacity of a natural system N to induce dynamics on other systems need not be, and indeed is generally not, identifiable with the capacity of N to be resolved into fractions by dynamics imposed on it. As we shall see, the mistaken notion that (subsystem = fraction) is the main conceptual underpinning for *reductionism* as a general philosophy of systems analysis. The other, equally important, side of the coin, is: the existence of subsystems which are not fractions vastly enlarges the scope of system analysis in non-reductionistic directions. In these directions it is the concepts of modelling and metaphor which necessarily play the dominant role.

To show that the concepts of subsystem and fraction are not co-exten-sive, it suffices to exhibit a single natural system N for which we can characterize a subsystem which is not a fraction. Of the many examples which could be given, let us consider a simple biological one: namely, an enzyme molecule. The *subsystem* will be taken to be the *active site*. This subsystem can be characterized directly in terms of its interactive capabilities, and indeed encoded thereby into formal systems in a variety of ways. It is thus a well-defined

subsystem of the enzyme molecule. But we can conceive no fractionation which will unlink precisely those observables defining the
active site from all the other observables. That is, we can imagine
no dynamics, imposed on the molecule in which the site is embedded,
which will separate the molecule into a fraction which is site, and
a fraction which is "everything else". Moreover, it should be observed that the *same* site may be embedded in distinct enzyme molecules,
thus providing a concrete example of how different systems (i.e.
different molecules) can share a common subsystem (or alternatively,
how the same subsystem can be alternately realized in different ways).

Precisely this point was piquantly (if tacitly) argued long ago by
the organic chemist R. Willstäter, who would never accept the identification of enzyme with protein. He admitted, of course, that enzymic
activity was *associated* with protein, but he felt that the protein
constituted an unavoidable contaminant of the enzyme. Insofar as we
may identify enzymic activity with an active site, Willstäter was
entirely correct; the active site is *not* the molecule manifesting
the site, but the site cannot be separated from the molecule by any
imaginable dynamics. This is not a quibble over semantics; it is
a point of the deepest significance for the understanding of natural
systems.

In a completely different context, the same point was made by the
physicist Eddington, in considering the interactions of elementary
particles. He was forced to identify the units of interaction (what
we have termed subsystems) as possessing exactly the same physical
reality as "real" particles, even though they could not be fraction-
ated out of such particles. It is instructive to cite his words on
the subject:

> The word "particle" survives in modern physics, but very little of its classi-
> cal meaning remains. A particle can now best be defined as *the conceptual
> carrier of a set of variates*...
>
> We shall freely invent particles to carry the sets of variates which our
> form of analysis groups together. The provision of a carrier is not so much
> a necessity of thought as a necessity of language. It might seem desirable
> to distinguish the "mathematical fictions" from the "actual particles", but
> it is difficult to find any logical basis for doing so. "Discovering" a
> particle means observing certain effects which are accepted as proof of its
> existence, but it seems to be a matter of fashion or convention that one
> sort of effect rather than another is accepted as critical for this purpose..."[3]

Having seen that the concepts of fraction and subsystem are not co-
extensive, we may further observe that it requires quite a non-trivial
argument to accept that fractions are in fact subsystems. Indeed,
we may recall that linkage relations between observables are defined
in terms of the intersections of the equivalence classes which the
observables define on a common set of abstract states. To say that
a linkage is changed or broken means, in effect, that we must change
the set of abstract states on which the system is defined. In order
to fractionate a system, then, we must make radical changes in its
very definition, in such a way as to include new observables, belonging to the system imposing the fractionating dynamics; for fuller
details, we refer the reader to an extensive discussion of this
point in our earlier monograph on measurement. Thus, the most we
can actually conclude about a specific fraction is that it *contains*
a subsystem of the original system, but it is generally not identical
with such a subsystem.

Now let us briefly discuss the relation between fractionation and

reductionism. As we have defined the term, reduction refers to a
specific relation between encodings F_1, F_2 of the same natural system
N. More precisely, we say that we can reduce F_2 to F_1 if we can
construct a monomorphism $\Theta : F_2 \rightarrow F_1$, which allows us to express
every property of F_2 in terms of properties of F_1. A specific
example of reduction was given in Example 3 of Chapter 3.3 above,
where we utilized the machinery of statistical mechanics to reduce
a thermodynamic encoding to a dynamical one.

We now observe that the atomic theory itself (at least in its simplest
form) tacitly involves fractionations in an essential way. In asserting the particulate nature of every material system, we are inherently
granted the capability of (at least in principle) fractionating any
specific constituent particle from the system without changing its
nature. Indeed, the totality of fractions of such a material system
consists precisely of all subsets of its particles. In this sense,
the *analysis* of a material system *means* the characterization of the
particles of which it is composed. Once this is properly done, the
forces which these particles impose on each other can be determined,
and the equations of motion of the system follow from Newton's
Second Law. In such a way, as we have seen, we indeed obtain an
encoding of our original material system.

The basic hypothesis of reductionism is, of course, that *every other*
encoding of our system may be reduced to this one. In sum, then,
reductionism as a philosophy of system analysis posits the following:
(a)   There is a "universal" way of encoding any material system, so
that every other encoding is reducible to the universal one. (b)
This universal encoding can be canonically determined from an
appropriate series of *fractions*, which can be obtained from any
material system. (c)   These fractions constitute the individual
particles of which the system is composed, or sets of such particles.
These fractions may in turn be isolated by imposing well-defined
dynamics on the system.

Thus, reductionism is an *algorithm*, or recipe, for the analysis of
any material system. We merely apply a known spectrum of fractionating dynamics to any material system, appropriately characterize
the resulting fractions, and from these, a universal encoding is
obtained, to which any other encoding can be reduced.

Many forms of reductionism have been proposed, especially in biology.
Indeed, the well-known *cell theory*, originally propounded in the
nineteenth century, is a reductionistic theory; it asserts that
every quality of an organism can effectively be reduced to the
properties of individual cells, or groups of cells. Here the individual cells are the basic fractions. Molecular biology is at root
a refinement of this theory, insofar as it asserts that every property
of a cell can be effectively reduced to the properties of its constituent particles (molecules); here the molecules constitute the
fractions.

Unfortunately, the lack of correspondence between fractions and subsystems destroys the universality of the reductionist algorithm; an
encoding of a subsystem which is not itself a fraction cannot be
reduced to an encoding of fractions alone. This is a mathematical
or formal fact, which no ingenuity of argument can change. Moreover,
as we have seen, fractions need not in general even be subsystems;
they need only contain subsystems. Thus, the extent to which a

description of a fraction isolated from a natural system is even a description of the system itself is a question which cannot be settled in the abstract; it will depend on the details of the fractionating dynamics in each particular case.

On the other hand, we have argued above that the subsystems of a natural system, as interactive units, possess exactly the same physical reality as the system itself, or as any fraction extracted from the system. The characterization of such subsystems, and their expression as linked sets of observables, allows us many modes of system analysis which are intrinsically non-reductionistic. Such characterizations are always encoded in terms of models (or more generally, in terms of metaphors), from which specific predictions about interactions can be made. Thus the concept of a model, as a mathematical representation of a subsystem, comes to play a central conceptual role in system analysis. In this approach, there is no longer any over-arching universal encoding, to which all others can be reduced. Rather, we have a family of potential interactive or analytic units, whose encodings may be compared and related in the manner we have been describing.

To sum up: the reductionistic algorithm may tell us many things about a natural system, but it cannot tell us all about the system. To find out more about the system than the reductionistic recipe can tell us, the concepts of models and metaphors are our only recourse. As noted above, they vastly extend the arsenal of analytic weapons we may bring to bear on the study of natural systems. Indeed, the thrust of everything we have done in the present section, sketchy as it may have been, exhibits the power and fertility of this approach. Specifically, for most of the basic biological qualities we have discussed in the preceding chapter, there is in fact no other way.

REFERENCES AND NOTES

1. For fuller details regarding these ideas, consult Rosen, R., *Fundamentals of Measurement and the Representation of Natural Systems*. Elsevier (1978).

2. The idea that system analysis is synonymous with fractionation (i.e. dissection) finds its ultimate roots in Newtonian mechanics; we have seen that the Newtonian paradigm allows us to make complete predictions about any system of particles if we know (a) what the particles are like individually and (b) the forces they exert on each other. Somewhat independently came the rise of Baconian empiricism, which asserted essentially that the way to understand complex things is to take them apart into simple things. Such ideas are invariably found at the basis of most empirical sciences; the resolution of "mixtures" (complex things) into "pure substances" or "pure phases" (simple things). The postulation that the only acceptable mode of system analysis is to be found in a resolution of the system into such fractions is the essence of reductionism.

It may be noted that fractionation is entirely an operation on state or configuration. It is an operation which is intended to simplify state description. In the case of a dynamical system, however, each state has associated with it a tangent vector. An operation (fractionation) geared to simplify state description may, and generally will, do terrible things to the tangent vectors. This, in a nutshell, is the main reason why reductionism fails as a universal analytical scheme for natural systems.

3. See Eddington, A., *Fundamental Theory*. Cambridge University
    Press (1949). This is a remarkable book, which bases all of
    physical theory on principles of observation. Among other things,
    it argues that the basic physical constants (e.g. electron mass
    and charge) arise as consequences of the geometry of observation,
    and thus have the same status as do numbers like π and e. They
    are thus not arbitrary parameters in physical relations, to be
    determined empirically; rather they are to be *computed*, according
    to the calculus which Eddington describes. These ideas, however,
    have never made much impact on "main-stream" physics.

CHAPTER 4

The Encodings of Time

4.1 Time and Dynamics: Introductory Remarks

In the preceding sections, we have seen many examples of modelling relations, which have spanned a wide range of physical and biological contexts. Most of the models and metaphors we have introduced have involved dynamical processes, and the manner in which the inferential structure of a formal encoding represents the dynamical properties of the natural system so encoded. This is indeed the main thrust of the entire book; to determine how we may employ formal models of natural systems to make temporal predictions about the systems themselves, and ultimately to utilize such predictions to modify the systems' present behavior. In order to accomplish this, we must investigate modelling relations involving dynamical systems in more detail than we have heretofore done.

The crucial concept in dynamics, of course, is time. In all of the dynamical models we have considered, the essential step involves the establishment of linkages between instantaneous states and their rates of change. We have pointed out in 2.1 above that the concept of time involves two distinct aspects: an aspect of *simultaneity* and an aspect of *temporal succession*. Both of these are intimately involved in the encoding of dynamics. The very definition of an instantaneous state depends on simultaneity, while the definition of rate involves temporal succession. Thus, if we are to have a thorough understanding of the nature of dynamical encoding in general, and the nature of temporal predictions about a natural system based on a dynamical model, we must explicitly consider the encoding of time into our models. Specifically, we must clarify the relations which exist between time, instantaneous state, and instantaneous rate of change, and the properties of the linkage relations which can exist between them. This will be the main task of the present section.

If we look back over the examples we have developed above, it will become apparent that we have tacitly treated the concepts of time and rate in several quite different ways. At the very simplest level, we have employed two distinct encodings for the basic set of instants. In most of our physical and biological examples, we encoded the set of instants as the continuum $\mathbb{R}$ of real numbers. Indeed, in these examples, we made extensive and fundamental use of the mathematical properties of $\mathbb{R}$, especially the topological (metric) properties. The algebraic properties of $\mathbb{R}$ also enter in a fundamental

way, at several levels; the fact that $\mathbb{R}$ is an additive group is
basic to our treatment of dynamical systems as flows (cf. for instance Example 3 of Chapter 3.3 above). At an even deeper level,
the mathematical concept of a derivative makes essential use of all
the algebraic properties of $\mathbb{R}$; the encoding of rates of change of
observables as derivatives thus ultimately devolves directly upon
the algebraic properties of the set of instants. Nevertheless, we
also saw (cf. Example 3 of Chapter 3.5) that important kinds of
dynamical encodings could be obtained when the set of instants was
encoded as the discrete set $\mathbb{Z}$ of integers. Since $\mathbb{Z}$ is an additive
group, we can retain the idea of a (discrete) flow, but we lose all
of the metric and topological properties; this was seen to have
profound effects on every aspect of encoding.

Even in the continuous-time encodings, the role of time differs
greatly in the various examples we discussed. In the encoding of
particulate systems (cf. Example 1 of Chapter 3.1) time simply plays
the role of a parameter which indexes states along trajectories. On
the other hand, in thermodynamics, the restriction of our encodings
to equilibrium or near equilibrium situations implies an entirely
different treatment of time, arising from the fact that thermodynamic
systems can only approach equilibrium and not depart from it. This
fact, as we shall see below, imposes an "arrow" on temporal aspects
of thermodynamic phenomena which is absent from mechanics. This
"arrow" is formally manifested by the Second Law of Thermodynamics,
which basically asserts that certain kinds of linkages cannot arise
in thermodynamic encodings, and is intimately related to probablilistic
considerations which have no counterpart in mechanics.

The discrete-time encodings force on us a fundamental dissociation
between the concepts of *time* and *rate*, which are of course basic to
continuous-time encodings. Thus, discrete time stresses the *sequential* aspects of the set of instants. The idea of time as sequence
introduces yet another important aspect into our thoughts about time,
which we must develop carefully. We have already seen, (cf. Example
3B, Chapter 3.5) that discrete-time systems are closely related to
logic and to mathematical inference; indeed, there is a profound
sense in which the successive states of a discrete-time system can
be regarded as *theorems*, each arising from the preceding state as
axiom, and the dynamics itself as production rule or rule of inference
This idea of the temporal evolution of a state as a *logical* process,
independent of any notion of rate, represents still another aspect of
time; one which will have many important ramifications for us as we
proceed. Moreover, as we shall see, it has many important connections
with probabilistic ideas, which are also rate-independent.

All of these different aspects of time capture different essential
qualities of our time-sense, just as different observables capture
different qualities of natural systems. Each of them allows a
different kind of dynamical encoding to be built upon it. As always,
it then becomes important to *compare* these kinds of dynamical encodings; i.e. to establish relations between them. The establishment
of such relations tells us, in turn, how the different qualities of
our time-sense are themselves related, and perhaps more important,
the senses in which they are distinct and irreducible one to another.
From such an understanding, we will arrive at a clearer idea of what
a temporal prediction about a natural system actually entails.

Thus, in Chapter 4.2 below, we shall take up the question of "Newtonian
time"; i.e. the role of time in the encoding of particulate systems.
In Chapter 4.3, we shall consider thermodynamic or statistical time,
with its fundamental relation to irreversibility. In Chapter 4.4, we

shall extend these considerations to probabilistic time in general, and see how the laws of irreversible thermodynamics can be regarded as embodiments of such results as the Law of Large Numbers. In Chapter 4.5, we return to the notion of continuous dynamics; we shall see that despite the formal similarities which exist between Newtonian encodings and those arising in more general dynamical contexts, the notions of time in the two classes of systems are completely different from one another. In Chapter 4.6, we shall turn to another and quite distinct aspect of time; namely discrete or logical time, and the relation between time and sequence. In Chapters 4.7 and 4.8, we shall discuss the related notions of simi-larity in dynamical systems, and the inter-relationships between time and age.

4.2 Time in Newtonian Dynamics

Let us suppose that we are given a system of particles in space, whose displacements from some origin of co-ordinates at any instant can be represented as an n-tuple of numbers $x_1, \ldots, x_n$. In the terminology of Example 1 of Chapter 3.3 above, this n-tuple of numbers encodes a *configuration* of the system, and the totality X of all such n-tuples is the *configuration space*.

Let us further suppose that the forces imposed on the system depend only on the configurations, and moreover in such a way that the force F_i imposed on the ith configuration variable x_i can be encoded as

$$F_i = -\frac{\partial U(x_1, \ldots, x_n)}{\partial x_i} \tag{4.2.1}$$

for some definite function U defined on the configuration space X. The function $U(x_1, \ldots, x_n)$ is called the *potential*; forces F_i satisfying (4.2.1) for some potential are called *conservative*.

The theory of systems of particles under the action of conservative forces is the cornerstone of Newtonian mechanics. For such a system, it is shown in any textbook on classical mechanics that there is a function $H = H(x_1, \ldots, x_n, p_1, \ldots, p_n)$ defined on the *phase space* of the system, which has the following properties:

(a) $H = T(p_1, \ldots, p_n) + U(x_1, \ldots, x_n).$ (4.2.2)

That is, H is the sum of two terms, the first of which depends only on the momenta of the particles, and the second of which is our potential, which depends only on the displacements.

(b)   The equations of motion of our system can be expressed entirely in terms of H; explicitly, they can be put into the form

$$dx_i/dt = \frac{\partial H}{\partial p_i} \qquad\qquad dp_i/dt = -\frac{\partial H}{\partial x_i} \tag{4.2.3}$$

The function H is called the *Hamiltonian function*. It can be interpreted as the total energy of our system. The summand T(p) in (4.2.2),
which depends only on momentum, is accordingly called the *kinetic
energy*, while U is the *potential energy*. The equations of motion in
the form (4.2.3) represent the *Hamiltonian form* of these equations;
they are entirely equivalent to Newton's Second Law. Thus from (4.2.3)
we can see that the Hamiltonian function determines the entire dynamics

The Hamiltonian function, and the Hamiltonian form of the equations
of motion, are remarkable in many ways. For our present purposes, we
wish to stress the following: that the equations (4.2.3) serve to
relate the *temporal* rates of change of the state variables to the
gradient of a certain function H *in phase space*. These latter partial
derivatives themselves *contain no explicit mention of time*. In fact,
we shall take the viewpoint that the Hamiltonian equations (4.2.3)
implicitly *define* the time differential dt, and hence all temporal
rates of change, in terms of the quantity H and the differentials
dx_i, dp_i, all of which pertain entirely to the phase space. That is,
instead of taking the customary viewpoint (in which time is primary,
rates are specified as time derivatives, and Newton's Second Law
relates rates of change to forces), we shall *begin* with a Hamiltonian
on a phase space, and work backwards towards the equations (4.2.3) as
a *definition* of time.

Let us then completely forget about Newtonian dynamics, and about
Newton's Second Law. Let us retain only the following: (a) a family
of state variables $(x_1, \ldots, x_n, p_1, \ldots, p_n)$, where we may think of
the x_i as variables of configuration, but the p_i are simply other
observables; in particular, we do not think of them as velocities or
momenta; (b) there is a function $H = H(x_1. \ldots, x_n, p_1, \ldots, p_n)$
defined on the space XxP of all h-tuples $(x_1, \ldots, x_n, p_1, \ldots, p_n)$.

We will interpret the function H as imposing a *linkage relation*, or
equation of state, on the states of our system, in the following way:
the only states we shall consider are those satisfying the relation

$$H(x_1, \ldots, x_n, p_1, \ldots, p_n) = C \qquad\qquad (4.2.4)$$

where C is a fixed constant. There is in this picture no dynamics
visible; no forces, and no explicit mention of time.

Let us suppose that our system is initially in some state $(x_1^0, \ldots,$
$p_n^0)$, and that through some external intervention each of the values
of the state variables is changed slightly. Using the familiar abuse
of language, we shall say that the new state arising from the intervention is $(x_1^0 + dx_1, \ldots, p_n^0 + dp_n)$. If this new "perturbed" state
is again to be a state of our system, it must satisfy (4.2.4). On the
other hand, H itself can be expanded in a Taylor series about $(x_1^0,$
$\ldots, p_n^0)$, to give

$$H(x_1^0 + dx_1, \ldots, p_n^0 + dp_n) = H(x_1^0, \ldots, p_n^0)$$

$$+ \sum_{i=1}^{n} \left(\frac{\partial H}{\partial x_i} dx_i + \frac{\partial H}{\partial p_i} dp_i \right)$$

+ higher order terms   (4.2.5)

If we now invoke (4.2.4), and neglect the higher-order terms, we see that the following relation must be satisfied by the perturbations dx_i, dp_i:

$$\sum_{i=1}^{n} \left[\frac{\partial H}{\partial x_i} dx_i + \frac{\partial H}{\partial p_i} dp_i \right] = 0 \qquad\qquad (4.2.6)$$

Here the partial derivatives are, of course, evaluated at the initial unperturbed state $(x_1^0, \ldots, p_n^0)$, and are thus simply numbers. We can thus think of (4.2.6) as a *linkage relation* which must be satisfied by the perturbations, imposed on them by the linkage relation (4.2.4) governing the state variables.

We stress again that these perturbations dx_i, dp_i make no reference to any notion of time or rate. The relation (4.2.6) merely expresses a condition which must be satisfied by these perturbations (i.e. a linkage imposed on them) arising from the hypothesis that the perturbation of a state satisfying (4.2.4) once again gives rise to such a state. We have as yet no notion of "how long it takes" to go from the initial state to the perturbed one; such a question is as yet not even meaningful.

Now the relation (4.2.6) obtains between perturbations, or differentials of the state variables themselves. Let us suppose that we can find an analogous relation which involves only observables. That is, suppose the observables

$$M_i = M_i(x_1, \ldots, p_n)$$

$$N_i = N_i(x_1, \ldots, p_n)$$

are such that the relation

$$\sum_{i=1}^{n} \left[M_i \frac{\partial H}{\partial x_i} + N_i \frac{\partial H}{\partial p_i} \right] = 0 \qquad\qquad (4.2.7)$$

is identically satisfied. What relation can be established between the observables M_i, N_i and the corresponding perturbations dx_i, dp_i?

To put the matter simply, let us now *define* a differential quantity dt, as that quantity that simultaneously satisfies all of the relations

$$dx_i = M_i dt,$$

$$\qquad\qquad\qquad i = 1, \ldots, n \qquad\qquad (4.2.8)$$

$$dp_i = N_i dt.$$

In such a quantity dt can be defined, it will be called the *time differential* arising from the linkages (4.2.4) and (4.2.7).

Now we observe that we have natural candidates for the observables M_i, N_i. In particular, let us write

$$M_i = \frac{\partial H}{\partial p_i}$$

$$i = 1, \ldots, n \qquad (4.2.9)$$

$$N_i = - \frac{\partial H}{\partial x_i}$$

With this choice, (4.2.7) is always identically satisfied. Thus these observables define a time differential, according to (4.2.8). On the other hand, we can rewrite (4.2.8) as

$$dx_i/dt = M_i$$

$$i = 1, \ldots, n, \qquad (4.2.10)$$

$$dp_i/dt = N_i$$

thus explicitly defining the *rates of change* of the state variables themselves, with respect to the appropriate time differential. With the specific choice (4.2.9), these rates of change are precisely Hamilton's equations.

It is important to observe explicitly that *there is a different time differential* dt *arising from each choice of observables* M_i, N_i *satisfying* (4.2.7). Each such choice gives rise to a system of dynamical equations satisfying the equation of state (4.2.4). The specific choice of the time differential for which the dynamical equations (4.2.10) become Hamilton's equations is, in a sense, arbitrary; once made, however, it serves to *define time* consistently. Indeed, arguing backward from (4.2.9) to Newton's Second Law, we see that the forces imposed on our system are precisely those for which the time differential dt gives precisely the rates at which the states change as a function of force.

It is also important to observe that, if we carry out the same construction as above for a *different* conservative system, we will obtain a new time differential dt, defining time consistently *for that new system*. *There is a priori no guarantee that the time differentials so defined for different conservative systems are in fact the same.* Indeed, the entire problem of calibration arising from the use of particular conservative systems as clocks (e.g. harmonic oscillators) indicates that the time differentials arising from different systems are actually different, and a relatively elaborate system of mappings is required to transform consistently from the time variable of one system to the time variable of any other. We shall return to this question in Chapter 4.7 below; we merely call attention to the problem here, because it arises from the very outset, and it is especially transparent in this general context.

Let us note that we have so far only formally encoded the time differential dt into the formalism. We have yet to relate this differential, defined by (4.2.8) above, with the usual encoding of specific instants of time into real numbers. To do this requires a mathematical process of *integration*. If this is done, the usual properties of the definite integral translate the time differential into a set of instants identical with $\mathbb{R}$, and which is an additive group into the bargain. This, it must be stressed, is a purely mathematical (i.e. formal) procedure relating the differential of time (which is all that can be defined from a Hamiltonian) to a global set of instants.

The procedure we have used above is, of course, closely related to the traditional procedure of *virtual displacements*. Essentially, what we have done in passing from (4.2.6) to (4.2.9) is to introduce a time differential in such a way that a particular set of these virtual displacements becomes identical with the actual infinitesimal displacements along a trajectory in the state space. This trajectory is simply that (unique) trajectory of (4.2.10) on which our initial state lies. The global equation of state (4.2.4) is satisfied by every such trajectory. By repeating the procedure for every value of the constant C in (4.2.4), the equations (4.2.10) become the equations of motion describing every such system, and the corresponding trajectories fill out the whole of the state space in the usual fashion.

The procedure we have used is somewhat reminiscent of the concept of *ergodicity*, as it was defined in Example 3 of Chapter 3.3 above. This, it will be recalled, was one of the cornerstones of statistical mechanics, and it required that we be able to replace a notion of time (i.e. a sampling of states along a single trajectory) by a "phase average" (i.e. a sampling of points satisfying the equation of state (4.2.4)). Our procedure for defining a time differential dt is, in a sense, an inverse of ergodicity; it involves the replacement of operations in the phase space (namely, a perturbation of a point of the space in such a way that the equation of state continues to hold) by a new operation which involves time. We shall return to this important relation to ergodicity in the next chapter.

We already noted in Example 1 of Chapter 3.1 that the quantity t, whose differential we have defined by (4.2.8), can itself be treated as a variable of configuration. In general, each variable of configuration in a mechanical system is accompanied by a corresponding variable of momentum. Thus we can ask what would be the observable playing this role, as the "momentum" associated with t. The particular choice of M_i, N_i embodied in (4.2.9) allow us to answer this question in a simple way; the momentum associated with the time t defined by (4.2.8) and (4.2.9) is simply -H. Indeed, we can treat the mechanics of a conservative system with n co-ordinates of configuration as a problem in a phase space of 2n+2 dimensions, by considering time as a new configuration variable and -H as its associated "momentum" in a completely symmetrical way. Once again, we omit the details; they can be found in any standard text on Newtonian mechanics!

It is interesting to consider the relation between the procedure we have outlined for consistently defining a time differential dt, and the principle of causality. As we have already seen, one expression of causality appears in the "unique trajectory property", which says that any state of a system can give rise to only one future behavior, and can arise from only one past, as long as the forces on the system remain the same. In a certain sense, this causality principle is already implicit in the equation of state (4.2.6) relating the perturbations which may be imposed on a state satisfying (4.2.4). Indeed, a relation like (4.2.6) may be looked upon as itself expressing a kind of conservation law among the perturbations. Causality itself may be regarded as expressing such conservation conditions; indeed, the dynamical equations (4.2.10) say precisely that, it any state, *only one* infinitesimal perturbation is allowed; namely the one whose magnitude and direction are given by (4.2.8). These ideas relating causality and time will also be important to us later, especially in Chapter 4.4 below.

We turn now to one of the most important properties of the time differential dt which we have introduced. Namely, the dynamical equations (4.2.10) satisfy the property that they remain invariant to the replacement of dt by -dt; i.e. *these dynamical equations are symmetrical in the time we have defined*. Thus, for a conservative mechanical system, the distinction between future and past is entirely conventional; there is no way within such a system to attach an objective meaning to the "direction" in which time is flowing. In addition, the principle of causality holds equally well, whichever direction is (arbitrarily) chosen to represent the positive flow of time.

It has long been felt that this aspect of *time reversibility* in conservative mechanical systems is at variance with our own intuitive perception of the flow of time. Indeed, very few dynamical phenomena in our experience are actually symmetric to the flow of time; we perceive the sharpest possible assymetry between past and future. And yet, to the extent that the mechanics of conservative systems is itself a formalization of physical experience, and to the extent that any system can be regarded as composed of particles moving in potential fields, time reversibility appears as an inherent feature of the world. This situation has been correctly perceived as paradoxical. One immediate conclusion we can draw, which is nonetheless important, is the following: *the encoding of time in conservative mechanics is not the only encoding possible*. In particular, it fails to capture the basic quality we perceive in the distinction between past and future. Just from these simple remarks, we see that time is *complex*, in the sense that it allows (and indeed, requires) more than one encoding. Different encodings of time may then be compared with each other, just as different encodings of a natural system may be. Indeed, the characterization of such different encodings, and the relations which exist between them, is the main purpose of the present section. We may go so far as to say that many (though not all) of the problems traditionally associated with time arise from a failure to recognize that time is in fact complex, and that its different qualities *require* more than one kind of encoding.

Traditionally, there are two main kinds of suggestion available for resolving the paradox of time reversibility in a perceptibly irreversible world. These are:

(a) The dynamics of conservative systems is indeed fundamental, in some ultimate microscopic sense. Hence the irreversibilities we perceive in ordinary experience arise at another (macroscopic) level. Just as the quality of temperature appears to emerge when we pass from microscopic mechanics to macroscopic thermodynamics, so too does the apparent irreversibility of macroscopic experience. Like temperature, irreversibility depends on the fact that macroscopic experience involves statistical averages over large number of microscopic events. That is, irreversibility at the macroscopic level is connected with ensembles on which we can only deal with probabilities.

(b) The reversibility of time inherent in the mechanics of conservative systems shows that this formalism is not sufficiently general to encode all natural phenomena. That is, even at the most microscopic level, we must generalize the formalism of conservative Newtonian dynamics to include a broader class of systems for which time reversibility does not hold. The apparent time reversibility of Newtonian dynamics is thus essentially an artifact arising from the adoption of too narrow a formal framework for physical encodings. In a properly general framework,

.irreversibility will be manifested at the most fundamental
microscopic levels, independent of considerations of probabilistic averaging at a macroscopic level.

It should be noted that these two alternatives are *not mutually
exclusive.*

We shall consider the first of these possibilities in detail in the
next chapter. For the moment, we merely note that in developing it,
we are basically confronted with the necessity for developing a new
encoding of time *de novo*, this time on the basis of statistical
arguments. Such an encoding will necessarily be vastly different
from the one we have developed above.

The possibility (b) can itself be studied within the confines of
Newtonian dynamics. We can successively weaken the assumptions on
which the encoding developed above is based. For instance, we can
allow the potential U to depend not only on configurations but also
on momentum, and even on time itself; in the most general case, it
can readily be shown that the appropriate expression of (4.2.1) becomes

$$F_i = - \frac{\partial U}{\partial x_i} + \frac{d}{dt} \left(\frac{\partial U}{\partial p_i} \right) \qquad\qquad (4.2.11)$$

Such systems are in general no longer conservative. But the question
immediately arises; what is the time differential dt appearing in
this expression? It no longer has the meaning attributed to it by
the argument we have given above; that argument is in fact *equivalent
to* the conservation of total energy (this is a corollary to a famous
theorem due originally to E. Noether)? Thus, if we are to widen the
scope of our encodings in this fashion, *the time differential, and
time itself, must be redefined.*

Exactly the same is true if we give up the idea of a potential entirely, and allow forces which do not satisfy (4.2.1) or (4.2.11) for
any function U. This is the case with so-called *dissipative systems,*
of which the simplest example is the damped harmonic oscillator

$$\begin{cases} \frac{dx}{dt} = \frac{p}{m} \\[2mm] \frac{dp}{dt} = - kx - \beta p \end{cases} \qquad\qquad (4.2.12)$$

We can ask again: what is the meaning of the time differential dt,
in terms of which the defining rates are written? Is it the same as
the time differential which can be defined as above in the case $\beta = 0$?
Or must it be given a different interpretation? We shall consider
such questions more deeply in Chapter 4.4 below.

Considerations of this kind are essential if we are to attach any
definite meaning to temporal predictions arising from dynamical encodings of natural systems. It is well to stress again that such
considerations are not concerned with the question of what time
"really" is, but the manner in which its several perceptible qualities are captured within different kinds of encodings. Thus in a
real sense our considerations are entirely *formal*; they take place
entirely within mathematics. However, we shall impute these properties
to time itself, just as we impute topological qualities to sets of
abstract states through the observables defined on them. In particular,
of course, we wish to impute a definite meaning to such assertions as:

"if a system is in state $s(t_0)$ at an instant t_0, it is in some definite state $s(t_1)$ at another instant t_1". The fact that time itself is *complex* is what makes its difficult to do this in a universal fashion, valid for all encodings. But unless it is done, we have no way of converting an assertion of the kind given above into an actual temporal prediction about a specific natural system.

REFERENCES AND NOTES

1. See for example any of the references cited in Note 1 to Chapter 1.2 above. The assertion here is that energy and time are conjugate variables; this fact takes on profound formal significance (though in different ways) in both relativity and in quantum theory.

2. This theorem establishes a remarkable connection between one-parameter groups of transformations ("symmetries") in phase space under which Lagrange's equations (3.3.21) are invariant, and corresponding conserved quantities; i.e. observables which are constant on the trajectories. Indeed, the theorem shows that there is a reciprocal relation between such conserved quantities (like total energy in conservative systems) and corresponding *symmetries* of the equations of motion. It is very easy to show that the conserved quantity arising from symmetry to time reversal $t \to -t$ is the total energy H; in general, if some dynamical variable is subject to symmetry in the above sense, the conjugate variable is conserved. For a comprehensive treatment of these matters and their physical implications, see e.g.
    Lopes, J. L., *Lectures on Symmetries*. Gordon & Breach (1969).

4.3 Time in Thermodynamics and Statistical Analysis

We briefly discussed the character of thermodynamics and statistical mechanics in Example 3 of 3.3 above. In the present chapter, we will consider these matters in more detail, with special reference to the role of time.[1]

We have already noted that classical thermodynamics is restricted to essentially the situations of *equilibrium*. There are several reasons why this is so, which it is worth while explaining in some detail. In the first place, we have already seen that a thermodynamic description of e.g. a mole of gas requires only three state variables (namely pressure, volume and temperature), while a mechanical description of that same system requires on the order of 10^{25} state variables. This tremendous compression comes at a cost, and that cost is the restriction to equilibrium. When a macroscopic system is in equilibrium with its surroundings, there is a precise sense in which its state variables become functions of the environment with which the system has equilibrated. If this environment can be characterized in terms of a small number of quantities of state, then so can the system itself, no matter how many state variables might be necessary to describe the system in other circumstances. Thus, if pressure and temperature are regarded as parameters imposed by the environment, at equilibrium there will be an equation of state describing how every observable of the system is linked to them. Experience indicates that the only such observable we need to consider is volume, and the resultant linkage takes the form of the ideal gas law, or the van der Waals equation, or some corresponding state equation. In non-equilibrium situations, it is clear that not every state variable of the thermodynamic system under consideration will be uniquely determined by the properties of the environment, and hence any encoding of the system will necessarily be much larger; indeed, we will be essentially in the circumstances described in Example 2 of Chapter 3.3.

There is another, even more serious reason for the restriction of classical thermodynamics to equilibrium situations. This resides in the fact that *the fundamental thermodynamic observables of pressure and temperature are only meaningful at equilibrium*. Like all other observables, their values on (thermodynamic) abstract states are determined by the interaction of these states with meters. In the case of temperature, for example, the appropriate meter is a thermometer. However, the essence of a thermometer requires that we must allow our system to *equilibrate* with the thermometer before we can say that the temperature of the system is encoded into the reading of the thermometer. Hence in particular, it is very difficult to attach a meaning to a temperature measurement performed on a system which is not itself in equilibrium. Thus, the other crucial factor, restricting classical thermodynamics to equilibrium is simply that the observables with which it deals may simply not be defined in other circumstances.

Clearly, if thermodynamics were entirely restricted to states of equilibrium, there would be no need for a concept of time, and no thermodynamic sense in which such a concept could be introduced. However, even within the classical formulations of thermodynamics, there is some degree of flexibility, and with this flexibility the first tacit temporal notions come creeping in. If we imagine a thermodynamic system in equilibrium with some environment, we have seen that the thermodynamic quantities of state associated with the system are all functions of the environment. Let us now imagine the environment changes "slowly"; i.e. slowly enough so that we may imagine *the system is always in equilibrium with it*. In this way we can discuss the incremental changes (usually written as *differentials*) arising in our system as a result of such environmental changes, and introduce the concepts of work, energy, etc. which are the main subject-matter of classical thermodynamics. However, the restriction that the system be always in equilibrium with its environment (or in other words, that these changes are, in a certain sense, "infinitely slow") restricts us entirely to *reversible* changes in our system; i.e. to the cycles characterizing classical thermodynamic analysis. Such situations are called "quasi-static", and clearly there is no way to talk about temporal rates of change under these circumstances.

On the other hand, to the extent that thermodynamics is concerned with phenomena of heat, there must be some way within it to capture the basic fact of experience, that heat *flows* from warm bodies to colder bodies, and not the other way around. In other words, the flow of heat represents an *irreversible* situation, and any manner of encoding this aspect of the flow of heat must necessarily carry with it, at least tacitly, another notion of *time*. For the kind of irreversibility manifested by the flow of heat is intimately related with our intuitive ideas of temporal succession; a state of a two-body system in which there is a temperature difference between the bodies must *antedate*, or temporally *precede*, a state of the same system in which the temperatures of the two bodies are equal. Thus, any formulation of the notion of irreversibility tacitly partitions the class of thermodynamic states in to *earlier* and *later*, in which later states can be "reached" from earlier ones, but not vice versa. Hence we see that irreversibility carries with it an essential temporal component, but that this temporal component must be of a totally different character from the time of classical mechanics.

In fact, the fundamental thermodynamic concept of *entropy* can be regarded precisely as a partitioning of a set of states into *earlier* and *later* in this sense. Entropy can roughly be regarded as a real-valued function of thermodynamic state (at least, of thermodynamic state near enough to equilibrium so that we may imagine the thermodynamic variables to be well defined, and still be expressible as definite functions of the environment), defined in such a way that "later" states are characterized by higher entropy values than "earlier" ones. The thermodynamic state of maximal entropy is thus the state of thermodynamic equilibrium itself.

Thus it can be seen that the concept of entropy takes us out of the framework of classical thermodynamics, insofar as it characterizes situations which depart from thermodynamic equilibrium. On the other hand, the Second Law of Thermodynamics (which essentially was stated in the preceding paragraph) is traditionally considered an integral part of thermodynamics itself. It essentially involves the characterization of systems *approaching* thermodynamic equilibrium, but not at equilibrium. The *temporal* sense in which such a system is "approaching" equilibrium is characterized only insofar as the Second Law embodies the distinction between "earlier" and "later".

The detailed study of states of thermodynamic systems near enough to equilibrium to allow thermodynamic characterization, but not at equilibrium, is the province of "the thermodynamics of irreversible processes" or "nonequilibrium thermodynamics".[2] Let us briefly sketch how this kind of approach works. Let us suppose that we can characterize a system near equilibrium by a family $u_1, \ldots, u_n$ of thermodynamic variables of state. In more detail, if s is an *abstract state* of thermodynamic equilibrium, then $u_1(s) = u_i^*$ are well defined numbers associated with s by unambiguous measuring processes. If we apply these measuring processes to another state and obtain readings $u_i(s')$ which are close to u_i^*, then we say that s' is a state *near equilibrium*, and we characterize s' by the numbers $u_i(s')$. We do this *even though*, as we have seen, the meters applicable to equilibrium states are strictly not applicable to any other states. By ignoring this last fact, we obtain an encoding of abstract states s' which by imputation are "near" the equilibrium state s. Nonequilibrium thermodynamics works entirely with such neighborhoods, encoded into Euclidean n-dimensional space in the usual way.

On such a neighborhood of the equilibrium state, which of course is itself encoded into the n-tuple $(u_1^*, \ldots, u_n^*)$, we further suppose that entropy has been defined, i.e. as a real-valued function S defined on a neighborhood U of $(u_1^*, \ldots, u_n^*)$. By hypothesis, it assumes a maximum at equilibrium. Thus, by the mathematical theorem known as the Morse Lemma, there is a neighborhood $V \subseteq U$ of $(u_1^*, \ldots, u_n^*)$ in which S can be written as

$$S(u_1, \ldots, u_n) = \sum_{i,k=1}^{n} a_{ik} u_i u_k \qquad (4.3.1)$$

where we now interpret the quantities u_i in (4.3.1) as the *deviations* from their equilibrium values u_i^*. That is, in the neighborhood V of equilibrium, the entropy is essentially a quadratic function of the deviations from equilibrium. The coefficients a_{ik} appearing in (4.3.1) are the second derivatives

$$a_{ik} = \frac{\partial^2 S}{\partial u_i \partial u_k}$$

evaluated at the equilibrium $(u_1^*, \ldots, u_n^*)$.

Intuitively, our system is *approaching* equilibrium; thus we must express the manner in which the quantities u_i are changing in the neighborhood V. This is the essential dynamical step characteristic of irreversible thermodynamics. We shall relate an incremental change du_i of the ith thermodynamic state variable to the *Hamiltonian time differential* defined in the preceding chapter by writing

$$du_i = J_i dt \qquad\qquad (4.3.2)$$

where $J_i = J_i(u_1, \ldots, u_n)$ is called the *flow*, or *flux*, of u_i.

Let us pause to comment on this definition. It will be seen that the Hamiltonian time differential is rather dragged in by the heels; it does not arise intrinsically, as it did before. If we use it as indicated in (4.3.2), we have a way of talking about the incremental changes du_i of deviations from equilibrium in a common temporal framework. We recall that in the preceding chapter we *defined* the time differential dt in terms of increments in (mechanical) state variables, relating increments to states by virtue of an equation of state. Here we have no such equation of state, and we must use an extrinsic time differential dt to relate the increments du_i. This is a vast difference from the preceding situation, and it has some profound practical and conceptual consequences, as we shall see. For the moment, we simply point out that (a) the choice of time differential dt determines the nature of the flows J_i; changing this differential changes the form of the flows; (b) the choice of the Hamiltonian time differential is not conceptually compatible with the irreversibility expressed by the flow itself.

To construct the analogs of the equations of motion of a mechanical system from (4.3.2), we need, as usual, an analog of Newton's Second Law. This is obtained by *postulating* that the "forces" X_i responsible for the flows can be expressed in terms of the entropy (4.3.1) through the relations

$$X_i = \frac{\partial S}{\partial u_i} = -\sum_{k=1}^{n} a_{ik} u_k \qquad\qquad (4.3.3)$$

and that the resulting equations of motion are of the form

$$J_i = \sum_{k=1}^{n} L_{ik} X_k \qquad\qquad (4.3.4)$$

Thus, these equations are guaranteed to move the system encoded by (4.3.4) in the direction of increasing entropy; this is built in by the manner in which the "thermodynamic forces" X_i are defined.

In mathematical terms, the rate equations (4.3.4) are so constructed that the function S is a Lyapunov function for the system in the neighborhood V. The equations of motion (4.3.4) are, in a sense, the simplest of this kind which can be postulated; they assert that the flows J_i are linearly related to the forces X_i. The coefficients L_{ik} which serve to "couple" the flows to the forces are phenomenological coefficients, which obey the celebrated *Onsager reciprocal relations* $L_{ik} = L_{ki}$.

The Onsager relations are in a sense the backbone of irreversible thermodynamics. Onsager's own proof of these relations shows that they arise as a *consequence* of the introduction of the reversible Hamiltonian time differential dt. Indeed, if we were to choose any other time differential in defining the flows J_i, the reciprocal relations would not hold in general.

We may note that one of the basic quantities in irreversible thermodynamics is the "rate of entropy production"

$$dS/dt = \sum_{i=1}^{n} J_i X_i = -\sum_{i,k=1}^{n} a_{ik} u_k du_i/dt$$

which again depends crucially on the adoption of the Hamiltonian time differential.

It will be seen from this brief outline how restricted the domain of applicability of irreversible thermodynamics really is, and how contradictory are the assumptions on which it is based. On the other hand, the kinds of predictions which are obtained from the equations of motion (4.3.4) in specific situations are verified to perhaps a surprising extent. These equations (4.3.4) express how the thermodynamic (entropic) concepts of "earlier" and "later" are to be explicitly translated into a *reversible* Hamiltonian time frame.

Let us now see how the above thermodynamic considerations look when considered from the viewpoint of statistical mechanics, based on a Hamiltonian picture at the microscopic or molecular level.[3] We recall that the statistical-mechanical approach is based on the concept of an *ensemble*. The kinds of ensembles which are important for thermodynamics are, of course, the stationary ensembles (cf. Example 3 of Chapter 3.3 above). Among these, we single out for special consideration the *canonical ensembles*, which characterize a system in equilibrium with a "temperature bath" at a fixed temperature T. These represent systems at thermodynamic equilibrium. More explicitly, it is shown in any standard textbook on statistical mechanics that the canonical ensemble for a system of energy E and at a given temperature T is given by the Maxwell-Boltzmann distribution:

$$\rho = \frac{e^{-E/kT}}{\int_{-\infty}^{\infty} e^{-E/kT} u'(E) dE}$$

and thus, the probability of finding our system with an energy less than some fixed value E_0 is given by

$$\frac{\int_{-\infty}^{E_0} \mu'(E) e^{-E/kT} dE}{\int_{-\infty}^{\infty} \mu'(E) e^{-E/kT} dE}$$

(where the terminology is the same as that used in the discussion of Example 3 of Chapter 3.3 above).

Thus, in the statistical mechanical treatment, the situation of thermodynamic equilibrium is represented by a canonical ensemble. Likewise, measurements of thermodynamic variables are associated with averages over such canonical ensembles. We note that these averages can be regarded, by quasi-ergodicity, either as phase averages or as time averages.

A canonical ensemble is uniquely determined by the underlying

Hamiltonian function, and by the temperature T. In turn, at equilibrium, the Hamiltonian can be regarded as depending only on the
volume available to the system. Any change in such a system can
thus only arise from a change in temperature T, or from a change in
Hamiltonian (i.e. in the volume available to the system), or both.
This argument shows in another way why a thermodynamic system at
equilibrium can be characterized by such an exceedingly small number
of state variables.

Now let us turn to the statistical-mechanical view of entropy. Since
the Second Law of Thermodynamics is essentially concerned with non-
equilibrium situations, it deals essentially with non-canonical ensembles. It should be noted that if an ensemble is initially non-
canonical, it must remain non-canonical forever (this is a consequence
of Liouville's Theorem). The concept of entropy in statistical-
mechanical terms is basically a means of characterizing the deviation
between a given ensemble and a canonical one. As with entropy, this
deviation from canonicity is defined through a function of distributions $F(\rho)$ which assumes a maximum when ρ is the canonical distribution. Standard statistical-mechanical arguments again show that
such a function $F(\rho)$ can be written as

$$F(\rho) = - \int \rho \ln \rho \, dx_1 \ldots dp_n \qquad (4.3.5)$$

where the integral is extended over the entire phase space.

To see how this function F can be related to the entropy, let us
consider two initially separate (i.e. non-interacting) systems, with
phase spaces P_1, P_2 respectively. Initially, each system is represented by a canonical distribution in its respective phase space.
When the two systems are brought into interaction, the phase space
P of the composite system is simply the cartesian product $P_1 \times P_2$ of
the phase spaces of the original systems. The resulting distribution
in P is not canonical, and by Liouville's Theorem will never become
so (as along as P is isolated). However, we may compare it to the
canonical distribution in P, using the function F. In fact, it is
easy to show that

$$F(\rho) = F_1(\rho_1) + F_2(\rho_2)$$

where ρ_1, ρ_2 are the original canonical distributions in P_1, P_2
respectively, and ρ is the resulting distribution in P. But by
definition of F, we must have

$$F(\rho) \leq F(\rho_c)$$

where ρ_c is the canonical distribution in P uniquely determined by
the average energy and temperature of ρ. This is essentially the
Second Law, in statistical mechanical terms.

Finally, if we put this composite system, characterized by a distribution ρ with a definite average energy and temperature, in contact
with an external "temperature bath" at the same temperature, the
distribution will by definition ultimately become canonical. In
the process, the entropy will necessarily increase. The detailed
arguments regarding how the distribution changes from its initial
noncanonical character to the final canonical distribution are the
analog of (4.3.4) above.

It should be noted that the quantity $F(\rho)$ defined by (4.3.5) above becomes identical with thermodynamic entropy when ρ is the canonical distribution. For this distribution is determined entirely by the Hamiltonian (i.e. by the volume) and by the temperature, and thus $F(\rho_c)$ can be looked upon as a thermodynamic variable of state. If ρ is not canonical, the measure of its deviation from canonicity may be regarded as the statistical mechanical analog of S as defined by (4.3.1) above; but all of the difficulties associated with interpreting S as a thermodynamic quantity away from equilibrium remain in this situation as well.

Now let us return to the role of time in this statistical-mechanical treatment. As we saw in the preceding chapter, the Hamiltonian time differential dt is well defined in the phase spaces underlying the statistical-mechanical arguments. With respect to this time differential, the times required for time averages over ensembles to be meaningful (i.e. to have small variance) are exceedingly long. To interpret such averages as thermodynamic quantities thus requires, from the Hamiltonian point of view, correspondingly long times. Likewise, the time required for a non-canonical ensemble placed in contact with a temperature bath to become canonical is in general also exceedingly long compared to dt. On the other hand, it is precisely this same time differential which is employed in establishing the fundamental equations of motion of irreversible thermodynamics; we cannot in fact dispense with this time differential without also time giving up the reciprocal relations, and with them, the entire apparatus we developed earlier. Thus, the encoding of time into irreversible thermodynamic processes seems to possess fundamentally paradoxical properties. These paradoxical properties are enhanced rather than diminished by the arguments of statistical mechanics, because in these arguments the same time differential dt must necessarily play two distinct and incompatible roles, at the microscopic and macroscopic levels. In this peculiar situation, perhaps the most paradoxical result of all is that the dynamical encodings of statistical mechanics lead to predictions which are experimentally verified.

It may perhaps be pertinent to point out in this connection that the definition of a time differential by a Hamiltonian bears on the *total system* P which the Hamiltonian describes. If we consider the case of a system composed of weakly coupled subsystems, which is the standard situation in statistical mechanics, we could not establish a consistent time frame by considering any of the subsystems in isolation, for these subsystems are not energetically closed in P; i.e. not conservative, while to separate them from P changes their Hamiltonian. Thus, the establishment of a consistent time frame is a kind of *holistic property* of a conservative system. This remark should be considered in the light of our discussion of fractionation and reductionism given in Chapter 3.6 above.

Now let us briefly turn to a consideration of the probabilistic aspects of time in thermodynamics and statistical mechanics. The best way to do this is through the formulation of the Maxwell-Boltzmann distribution, and to the explication of the concept of entropy, which was originally given by Boltzmann himself (the procedure we have used previously was due to Gibbs). The Boltzmann argument depends essintially on probabilistic considerations, and in its simplest form arises from a combinatoric problem: in how many ways can N identical particles be distributed among M < N boxes? Each such distribution is characterized by M numbers $N_1, \ldots, N_M,$

where N_i is the number of particles in the ith box;   hence $N_1 + N_2 + \ldots$ $+N_M = N$.   It will be noted that these numbers N_i are discrete analogs of the continuous density ρ which we used before to characterize distributions in phase space.   Thus we will denote a distribution $(N_1, \ldots, N_M)$ of particles in our boxes by a similar symbol ρ.

It is easy to show that, given a particular distribution $\rho = (N_1, \ldots N_M)$, we can realize this distribution in

$$P(\rho) = \frac{N!}{N_1! \, N_2! \, \ldots \, N_M!} \qquad (4.3.6)$$

different ways;   that is, we can assign N particles to M boxes in such a way that the ith box receives N_i particles in $P(\rho)$ different ways.   We shall call $P(\rho)$ the *probability* of the distribution ρ. (Strictly speaking, $P(\rho)$ is only proportional to the actual probability, but following customary terminology we shall omit the normalizing factor of proportionality).

We can now ask: what is the distribution ρ_m of greatest probability; i.e. for which $P(\rho)$ is maximal?   If N and the numbers N_i are large enough, we can approximate to the factorials in (4.3.6) by using Stirling's relations

$$N! \cong N^N; \qquad N_i! \cong N_i^{N_i}.$$

Taking logarithms, we find that

$$\ln P(\rho) = N \ln N - \sum_{i=1}^{M} N_i \ln N_i \qquad (4.3.7)$$

which will clearly be maximal when $\sum_{i=1}^{M} N_i \ln N_i$ is minimal.   It is easy to see that this last sum is minimal when all the N_i are equal; i.e. when the density of particles in each box is uniform.   The quantity $\ln P(\rho)$ is essentially what Boltzmann identified with the entropy $S(\rho)$.   Indeed, the resemblance of (4.3.7) to (4.3.5) is already manifest.

Boltzmann's actual derivation of the Maxwell-Boltzmann distribution consists of adapting the above arguments to an appropriate phase space.   Phase space is partitioned into a family of small regions, which are analogs of the boxes considered above.   In phase space, each fixed region is associated with a certain average energy;   thus the distribution of states among such regions is associated with a conservation of average energy instead of conservation of number of particles.   The details of the argument, which leads to a discrete approximation to the Maxwell-Boltzmann distribution, can be found in the standard textbooks of statistical mechanics, and will be omitted here.

We see that Boltzmann's ideas identify the state of thermodynamic equilibrium (i.e. the state of maximal entropy) with the state which is "most probable". More precisely, a thermodynamic state corresponds to a distribution in some appropriate phase space; the thermodynamic state of maximal entropy is thus identified with the distribution of highest probability. In this sense, the transition of a system to thermodynamic equilibrium, which as we have seen automatically classifies such states as "earlier" and "later", can be expressed entirely in probabilistic terms; the *earlier* states are those corresponding to distributions which are less probable that the *later* states.

Another commonly employed terminology for these circumstances is the following: if we identify the distributions of high probability as *disordered*, and those of low probability as *ordered*, then the transition to thermodynamic equilibrium involves a passage from order to disorder. Thus, the Second Law itself is often formulated in the following way: that thermodynamic systems pass from ordered states to disordered states, and never the other way. In this language, the distinction between earlier and later becomes identical with the distinction between order and disorder. It is for this reason that, for instance, the phenomena of biological development (cf. Example 2 of Chapter 3.5) seemed so puzzling to physicists; they seem to involve a spontaneous transition from disorder to order, with a consequent reversal of the apparent sense of the arrow of time. To this point of view we must make the following remarks: (a) the systems encountered in developmental biology are *open systems*, to which the Second Law of Thermodynamics is not directly applicable; (b) the identification of "disorder" with distributions of high probability depends entirely on how probabilities are defined.

This last point is of fundamental importance. It deserves an independent discussion, which will be the substance of the next chapter.

REFERENCES AND NOTES

1. Some interesting discussions of the matters to be considered
    here, as well as the relation of the properties of "thermodynamic"
    time to problems of causality and determinism, may be found in
        Stuart, E. B., Bramard, A. J., and Gal-Or, B. (eds.), *A Critical
        Review of Thermodynamics*. Mono, Baltimore (1970).

2. Some classic standard references to the field of "irreversible
    thermodynamics" are
        Prigogine, I., *Introduction to the Thermodynamics of Irreversible
        Processes*. Wiley (1967).
        de Groot, S. R. and Mazur, P., *Non-Equilibrium Thermodynamics*.
        North-Holland (1963).
        Gyarmati, I., *Non-Equilibrium Thermodynamics*. Springer-Verlag
        (1969).

3. See the references in Note 5 to Chapter 3.3 above.

4.4 Probabilistic Time

The present chapter represents somewhat of a digression from the main line of argument, in that it concerns some purely formal considerations regarding probability. However, it is so closely related to the notions of thermodynamics and statistical mechanics described in the preceding chapter that it is natural to place it here. Moreover, it represents an interesting exercise in the general notions of encoding of observables which were developed in Section 2 above, and has had far-reaching implications for the general study of natural systems.

Let us return to the prototypic Boltzmann problem of throwing particles into M boxes. If M = 2, the problem is essentially one of coin-tossing, with the first box marked "heads" and the second box marked "tails"; if M = 6, it is that of rolling a die, etc. The first assumption we shall make about the problem is one of *ergodicity*. Namely, we shall assume that it is immaterial whether we throw N particles into our boxes at the same instant, or throw a single particle N times. For simplicity, we shall suppose that we are doing the latter; i.e. that our elementary operation is to throw a single particle into one of a family of M boxes.

In such a situation, each toss can result in one of M possible outcomes, which we shall designate as $u_1, \ldots, u_M$. The symbol u_i thus represents the outcome that our particle has landed in the ith box. Let the set of possible outcomes be U. Thus, $U = \{u_1, \ldots, u_m\}$.

Let us now suppose that we cast our particle N times. Each time we cast our particle, we obtain one of our M possible outcomes. Hence in this way we generate a *sequence*, or word, formed from the elements of U. The totality of all such sequences will be denoted by S_N.

In more formal terms, any element σ in S_N can be regarded as a mapping

$$\sigma : I_N \to U$$

where $I_N = \{1, 2, \ldots, N\}$ is the set of the first N integers. In what follows, we are going to regard these sets I_N as sets of "instants", and interpret $\sigma(k)$ as the outcome of the kth toss of our particle. In this way, we identify S_N with $H(I_N, U)$.

Now we are going to construct an encoding of the sequences $\sigma \in S_N$, with the aid of some new observables defined on S_N. Specifically, for each $i = 1, 2, \ldots, M$, define

$$\lambda_i(\sigma) = \text{the number of times the event } u_i \text{ occurs in } \sigma.$$

That is, $\lambda_i(\sigma)$ is the number of times our particle has landed in the ith box after our N tosses are completed. Since clearly we must always have

$$\sum_{i=1}^{M} \lambda_i(\sigma) = N,$$

it is convenient to normalize these observables, by writing

$$\mu_i(\sigma) = \frac{\lambda_i(\sigma)}{N}, \qquad i = 1, \ldots, M.$$

Thus, to each sequence $\sigma \in S_N$, we can associate an M-tuple of numbers

$$(\mu_1(\sigma), \ldots, \mu_M(\sigma)),$$

such that

$$0 \leq \mu_i(\sigma) \leq 1 \qquad \text{and} \qquad \sum_{i=1}^{M} \mu_i(\sigma) = 1.$$

In this way, we can encode *any* S_N into a common M-dimensional Euclidean space E_M.

Now we know (cf. Chapter 3.2 above) that any such encoding partitions S_N into a family of equivalence classes; specifically, two sequences σ, σ' fall into the same equivalence class if they both give rise to the same M-tuple; i.e. if

$$\mu_i(\sigma) = \mu_i(\sigma'),$$

for every $i = 1, \ldots, M$. Denote the resulting set of equivalence classes by S_N/R.

We shall now finally define a mapping $F : S_N/R \rightarrow \mathbb{R}$ by writing

$$F[\sigma] = \sum_{i=1}^{M} \mu_i(\sigma) \ln u_i(\sigma) \qquad\qquad (4.4.1)$$

It is easy to see that this function F takes its maximum value on that class in S_N/R containing the *most elements*;   indeed, F is a kind of measure of the *sizes* of the equivalence classes. We may call F[σ] the *entropy* of the sequence σ, by analogy with what we have done before.

Now let us consider this entire situation as a function of N, the number of throws or trials. In particular, we want to know what happens to the numbers $\mu_i(\sigma)$ as N grows very large. The answer to this question is essentially the Law of Large Numbers;[1] this asserts fisrt of all that the $\mu_i(\sigma)$ converge to definite numbers;   i.e.

$$\lim_{N\to\infty} \mu_i(\sigma) = p_i.$$

Furthermore, the numbers p_i possess the property that they maximize F;   i.e.

$$p_i = 1/M. \tag{4.4.2}$$

Let us see what this assertion means, especially in terms of the way in which sequences σ are encoded into E_M.

Intuitively, as we successively cast our particle at the boxes, the corresponding sequence σ of outcomes will grow in length. Regardless of the length of such a sequence, it will always be encodable as an M-tuple of numbers;   i.e. as a point in E_M. Each new cast of the particle will change the numbers μ_i slightly, so that the represen- tative point in E_M will appear to move in E_M as a function of "time" N. Consequently, a growing sequence σ will appear to trace out a trajectory in E_M (although since "time" is here discrete, the resulting trajectory will consist of discrete points of E_M). Thus the growth of a sequence σ by successive casts of our particle will be represented in E_M by something very much like a dynamics on E_M. The Law of Large Numbers, in the form we have sketched it here, asserts that this dynamics possesses a unique, asymptotically stable steady state; namely

$$(1/M,\ 1/M,\ \ldots,\ 1/M) \tag{4.4.3}$$

to which all (or more precisely, "almost all") of these trajectories converge as "time" (i.e. the number of successive casts of the par- ticle) becomes infinite.

Stated otherwise, the entropy of every growing sequence tends to increase as a function of N, so that these sequences become progress- ively more alike in terms of the observables M_i, the longer they grow. We can see also that the character of this dynamics on E_M is *irreversible*;   the trend of any sequence is *towards* the condition of maximal entropy, and never away from it.

The numbers $p_i = 1/M$ may be heuristically identified with the *sizes*

of the boxes at which we cast our particles. We have tacitly constructed the situation so that these boxes are of equal size; it is
easy to see how to modify the construction when the boxes are of
unequal size (so that the particle cast at the boxes is more likely
to land in a larger box than in a smaller one). In that case, the
Law of Large Numbers asserts that the $\mu_i(\sigma)$ will converge to numbers
p_i proportional to the sizes of the boxes. Thus, these numbers p_i
can be identified with the *a priori probabilities* of the outcomes
u_i of U.

Now let us look more closely at the "probabilistic time" which is
inherent in the above construction. We have already noted that (a)
this probabilistic time is discrete, and (b) that it is irreversible.
We may further observe that this kind of time carries with it no
notion of *rate*, at least at the level of the growing sequences σ.
However, for large N (i.e. close to the steady state (4.4.3)), we
may attach an approximate sense to the expressions

$$d\ \mu_i(\sigma)/dN \qquad\qquad\qquad (4.4.4)$$

in E_M. Indeed, if we now re-interpret the quantities $\mu_i(\sigma)$ as deviations from their steady-state values (4.4.3), we will obtain precisely the same equations (4.3.4) as we found earlier as the basic
equations of irreversible thermodynamics, with the function F defined
above playing the role of the entropy S.

From considerations of this kind, we see that there is a sense in
which the fundamental equations of motion of irreversible thermodynamics are simply re-interpretations of purely probabilistic
assertions, and in particular are reformulations of the Law of Large
Numbers. If this is so, we see that the probabilistic "time differential" dN is not related to Hamiltonian time directly at all, but
rather refers to the improvement of our averages by increasing the
length of σ through the addition of another sample. In statistical
mechanical terms, the addition of more samples means taking (Hamiltonian) time averages over longer pieces of trajectory; hence the
probabilistic time considered above is monotonically related to
Hamiltonian time, but this is as far as the relation between them
extends. For in our probabilistic considerations, the "time differential" dN is entirely *rate independent*, as we have seen.

Let us now briefly consider how the concepts of order and disorder
appear from a purely probabilistic point of view. If we make the
identification of disorder with high entropy, we see that the characterization of disorder depends entirely on the dynamics we impose on
E_M; i.e. on the specific relation we establish between the derivatives (4.4.4) and the points of E_M at which they are evaluated. That
is, *disorder depends on dynamics*. A disordered state is one to which
a dynamical system autonomously tends; or alternatively, a state
which requires work to keep the system out of. *There is no way to
characterize order or disorder in terms of states alone*; thus, to
the extent that entropy is *simply* a state function on E_M, unrelated
to any dynamics on E_M, an assertion that the state of maximal entropy
is the state of maximal disorder is entirely meaningless. It is
only when entropy possesses a very special relation to an imposed
dynamics (e.g., when it is a Lyapunov function for the dynamics)

that such an identification of entropy with disorder is meaningful.
In all the examples we have considered in the past two chapters,
what we have done is to define entropy *first*, and then *impose* dynamics *for which* entropy is a Lyapunov function. But if a dynamics
is given *first*, there is no reason to expect any *a priori* notion of
entropy, such as that embodied in (4.4.1) above, to have any meaningful relation to notions of order and disorder arising from that dynamics. What we are asserting, then, is the following: that order
and disorder are *dynamical* qualities, and not *thermodynamic* qualities.
One cannot define disorder in a dynamical vacuum, and this is what
classical thermodynamics essentially is. Consequently, except in
very special situations, the notions of entropy and disorder are
not co-extensive; entropy is always defined purely as a state function, independent of any imposed dynamics, while disorder can only
be meaningful in a specific dynamical context.

Precisely the same arguments hold for cognate fields, such as Information Theory. Information Theory is basically an attempt to associate numbers with words in a language, in such a way as to equate
"information" with improbability of a word (considered as a sequence
of letters from an alphabet analogous to the set U above). The limitations of this approach, which is often described as equating
"information" with "negative entropy" are well known; they revolve
around the fact that "information" is identified with purely syntactical aspects, totally divorced from semantics. This is simply
another way of saying that entropy, whether negative or positive,
is independent of dynamics. However, these fascinating matters are
tangential to our main considerations, and we cannot explore them
further here; we refer the reader to the literature for further
details. We shall, however, return to the general probabilistic
ideas developed above when we discuss *complexity* and *error* in
Sections 5.6 and 5.7 below.

The difficulties associated with attempting to define order and
disorder in purely probabilistic terms, which have been described
above, turn out to be closely related to the problem of reductionism
(cf. Chapter 3.6 above). This was first clearly pointed out by the
physicist Walter Elsasser. To Elsasser, reductionism is embodied
by the expression of all macroscopic quantities (as for instance
those encoded into biological descriptions or organisms) as averages
over some appropriate phase space, in the manner we have described.
By ergodicity, these averages may be regarded as time averages along
individual trajectories; this means that "almost all" trajectories
become statistically identical *if* we wait long enough. It is this
mysterious phrase "almost all" which Elsasser stresses. In mathematical terms, this phrase refers essentially to what happens in regions
of zero volume; such regions are always *necessarily* neglected in
any formal probabilistic argument. Nevertheless, sets of "zero
volume" can be appreciable in other mathematical senses. For instance,
the set of rational numbers is of "zero volume" in the set of all
real numbers, and hence "almost all" real numbers are irrational.
On the other hand, the rational numbers are actually topologically
dense in the real numbers; between any two rational numbers, however
close together they may be, there is another one. Nevertheless, in
any probabilistic argument, or more generally, in any averaging or
integration process over the real numbers, what happens on the
rational numbers is necessarily irrelevant.

Elsasser pointed out that the phase space of any organism, considered
as a purely physical system, is in general of very high dimension.
He argued further that the states in this phase space which are compatible with life will generally tend to be *sparesely distributed*

in such a phase space; specifically, they will form a set of zero volume. Hence "almost all" states, and thus "almost all" trajectories in this phase space, will be incompatible with life. Furthermore, any attempt to form averages over the entire phase space will necessarily discard the biologically relevant states. Consequently, Elsasser argued that insofar as physics must deal entirely with such averages at the macroscopic level, biology is *in principle* irreducible to physics. It further follows that the laws governing the behavior of biological systems are not inferable from physical laws although they are compatible with them. This is a very powerful argument. In general, insofar as we must identify "order" with the properties of sets of small volume, and insofar as averaging processes neglect what happens on such sets, general statistical laws of physics cannot in principle be applied to ordered situations. In slightly different language, the assertion is that encodings of ordered situations cannot be reduced to encodings pertaining to disordered ones.

We can see this very strongly if we return to our earlier example of the relation between the rational numbers and the reals. The fact that the rationals are a set of zero volume may be interpreted, in gross probabilistic terms, as asserting that it is "infinitely improbable" for a number taken at random from the real numbers to be a rational number. On the other hand, if we ask someone to "pick a number", the number picked will almost certainly be rational. The reason for this is that human beings are stongly biased towards the rational numbers, and we cannot explain this bias, nor understand our own relationship to the real number system, by means of *a priori* probabilistic or measure-theoretic considerations.

REFERENCES AND NOTES

1. The "Law of Large Numbers" is the name given to a class of related results, originating in probability theory, and asserting essentially that as the number of trials increases, the corresponding sequences of "average results" (i.e. outcomes averaged over all the trials that have already taken place) converges. This result and its ramifications are discussed in almost all standard texts on probability theory. A concise but comprehensive treatment may be found in
    Revesz, P., *The Law of Large Numbers*. Academic Press (1968).
    It is not surprising that there is a close relationship between the Law of Large Numbers and the notion of ergodicity as it was originally formulated in statistical mechanics. The relation is described e.g. in the review of Mackey to which we have had occasion to refer several times before (cf. Note 4 to Chapter 1.2).

2. On its mathematical side, Information Theory is closely related to the matters we have been discussing. A good treatment, which makes all sides of these relations visible, is
    Billingsley, P., *Ergodic Theory and Information*. Wiley (1965).

3. Elsasser's original arguments may be found in
    Elsasser, W., *The Physical Foundations of Biology*. Pergamon Press (1958).
    See also
    Elsasser, W., *The Chief Abstractions of Biology*. Elsevier (1975).

4.5 Time in General Dynamical Systems

In the present chapter, we shall be concerned with the role of time
as it appears in the general dynamical encodings of natural systems
into models and metaphors. We have seen many examples of such dynamical encodings in the preceding chapters. What we wish to do
here is to point out that the encodings of time into these systems
are as different from Hamiltonian and thermodynamic time as these
two are from each other.

Let us in general suppose that $x_1, \ldots, x_n$ represent the (actual or
metaphorical) encoding of observable quantities, in such a way that
every abstract state of the system is encoded into a point of a
manifold M in Euclidean n-dimensional space. We recall that such
an encoding already tacitly involves a definite temporal aspect;
namely, that of simultaneity. Indeed, the numbers $(x_1, \ldots, x_n)$
which identify a point of M are to be interpreted as the values of
the observables x_i, evaluated simultaneously on some abstract state
s, and thus serve to characterize s at some *particular instant* of
time.

We have also already seen that a set of rate equations on M, of the
form

$$dx_i/dt = f_i(x_1, \ldots, x_n), \qquad i = 1, \ldots, n \qquad (4.5.1)$$

embody several further hypotheses about our system. For one thing,
they assert that the rate of change dx_i/dt of each state variable x_i
is itself an observable, and in fact is precisely the observable f_i.
Thus each of the rate equations in (4.5.1) express a linkage between
the rates of change of an observable at an instant of time and the
values at that instant of the state variables themselves. Further,
in mathematical terms, the rate equations (4.5.1) serve to attach a
definite velocity vector to each point of the manifold M into which
the abstract states of our system are encoded; that is, they define
a vector field on M. Thus, these equations specify on each point of
M a unique *direction* in M associated with that point. Finally, we
observe that the mathematical operation of *integrating* the equations

(4.5.1) results in principle in the explicit expression of each state variable as a definite function of the time parameter t, and thus links a definite state of our system to each time instant t and every initial state $(x_1(t_0), \ldots, x_n(t_0))$.

We have also seen that, under very general conditions, the rate equations (4.5.1) manifest the basic properties of *causality*. These are expressed in the unique trajectory property, which says that any point of our manifold M uniquely determines the entire trajectory passing through it; hence only one future arises from each state, and only one past can give rise to each state, as long as the equations of motion (4.5.1) remain valid.

It will be observed that, in this general setting, there is no concept of force or potential visible, of the kind which was dominant in our consideration of the encodings of particle mechanics; in their place we have simply a postulated linkage between instantaneous rate of change of state variables and the instantaneous values of the state variables themselves.

Now in the employment of rate equations of the form (4.5.1) as encodings of dynamical processes in natural systems, the usual point of view is that, roughly speaking, the differential increments dx_i of the state variables are known, and the time differential dt is known, and the observable $f_i(x_1, \ldots, x_n)$ is their ratio. In what follows, we are going to take a different point of view, which is roughly this: the principles of causality, together with the differential increments dx_i of the state variables, essentially serve to specify the observables f_i; these together with the dx_i in fact *define* the time differential dt. The time differential dt which arises from such an argument in general is quite different from the Hamiltonian time differentials which were defined in Chapter 4.2, and in fact are generally different for different dynamical systems of the form (4.5.1). Thus, each dynamic encoding requires an encoding of time into a time differential unique to it. We shall consider some of the consequences of this curious fact at the conclusion of the present chapter.

Let us then proceed to the details. We shall initially suppose only that we are given a manifold M, whose points may be expressed as n-tuples of the form $(x_1, \ldots, x_n)$ as before. Since M is a manifold, we can give a definite and unambiguous meaning to the differentials $dx_1, \ldots, dx_n$ at each point of M. This much is available to us simply from the fact that M is a manifold.

We are now going to impose on this situation a notion of causality. Intuitively, if the manifold M encodes the abstract states of some natural system, the simplest form of causality we can impose is to require that *the differentials* dx_i *are not all independent, but satisfy some linkage relations*, depending on the particular point of M to which they refer. Moreover, we should require that *the totality of linkage relations satisfied by these differentials should suffice to determine them uniquely*. That is, to each point $(x_1, \ldots, x_n)$ of M, there will be attached a *unique* set $(dx_1, \ldots, dx_n)$ of differential increments, defined by these linkage relations.

Clearly, to define these differential increments dx_1, ..., dx_n
uniquely will require n independent linkage relations. We shall now
suppose that these linkage relations are of the simplest possible
form; namely, that they are *linear* in the dx_i. Let us then write
these relations as

$$\sum_{j=1}^{n} a_{ij} dx_j = \omega_i \qquad i = 1, \ldots, n \qquad (4.5.2)$$

where the numbers a_{ij} depend on the state $(x_1, \ldots, x_n)$ to which the
differentials dx_i are attached. The existence of such relations
(4.5.2), then, arise entirely from the weakest possible notions of
causality in the system whose states are encoded by the points of M,
as stated above. It is a consequence of the stronger causality
assertion that we may assume the determinant $|a_{ij}| \neq 0$.

Now we shall make our first real hypothesis. We shall suppose that
each of the ω_i in (4.5.2) can be written in the form

$$\omega_i = df_i \qquad (4.5.3)$$

where $f_i = f_i(x_1, \ldots, x_n)$ is an observable; i.e. a real-valued
function on the manifold M.

If (4.5.3) holds, then we can interpret the linkage relations (4.5.2)
as each specifying an *accounting*, or a *conservation condition*, relating
to the differential increments dx_i attached to a state. Each equation
of (4.5.2) says that these dx_i are not entirely arbitrary; some
linear combination of them is the differential increment of a particular observable f_i. The totality of these relations (4.5.2) then
define the dx_i uniquely.

Another consequence of (4.5.3) which may be noted is that the numbers
a_{ij} in (4.5.2) are immediately interpretable, as

$$a_{ij} = \frac{\partial f_i}{\partial x_j}$$

where the partial derivatives are evaluated at the point $(x_1, \ldots,$
$x_n)$ to which the differential increments dx_i are attached.

The final step in defining our differential time increment is now
clear. We shall suppose that we can write

$$dx_i = f_i dt \qquad (4.5.4)$$

for each i = 1, ..., n. These relations serve simultaneously to
define the time differentials dt, and to allow us to encode the
dynamical behavior of our system into the form (4.5.1). We stress
again the order of ideas here: (a) the differential increments dx_i
are related by causality by conservation conditions of the form

(4.5.2), which suffice to determine them uniquely;   (b) we *posit*
that these conservation conditions define, in mathematical terms,
exact differentials;   (c) these in turn define global observables
f_i, i = 1, ..., n; and finally (d) we define the time differential
by requiring it to satisfy the relations (4.5.4) for each i.   The
procedure we have used is strongly reminiscent of that employed in
Chapter 4.2 for defining the Hamiltonian time differential;   however
in that case we *started* from a global linkage (the Hamiltonian of the
system) and used it to derive conservation conditions on the differentials of the state variables analogous to (4.5.2) above.   In the
present case, we obtain these relations directly from a hypothesis
of causality, without postulating any global linkage (equation of
state) at all.

Now let us consider some of the consequences of the encoding of time
we have developed.   The first observation to make is that in general
the dynamical time differential dt defined by (4.5.4) is *not reversible*.   That is, the equations of motion (4.5.1) to which it gives
rise is not invariant to a replacement of dt by -dt.   Irreversibility
is thus built into such a system from the outset, without any notion
of equilibrium or any kind of probabilistic or entropic consideration.
In this context, irreversibility is exhibited entirely as a *dynamical*
phenomenon, and not as a thermodynamic one.

The next important observation to make is that every dynamical system
of the form (4.5.1) in general defines its own time differential dt,
and that *the differentials arising from different dynamical systems
are in general different from one another*.   This can be seen immediately from the defining relations (4.5.4).   Indeed, if we take two
different dynamical systems (4.5.1) defined on the same manifold M,
the differential increments dx_i are here the same for both systems,
but the conservation relations (4.5.2) (i.e. the numbers a_{ij}), and
hence the functions f_i, will in general be quite different from one
another.   Since we are *defining* the time differential dt for the two
systems in terms of a common set of differentials dx_i and different
sets of functions f_i, there is no reason to expect that the resulting
time differential dt will be the same for the two systems.   Furthermore, there is no reason to expect that any such time differential
will be related to a Hamiltonian time differential of the kind defined
in Chapter 4.2 above.   This fact raises some exceedingly deep questions
pertaining to the temporal relations which exist between different
dynamical systems, and in particular to the employment of a common
set of clocks (which invariably involve a Hamiltonian time differential) to "keep time" for all dynamical processes.   In effect, we
have shown that each dynamical process (4.5.1) defines its own
intrinsic time differential;   the question we are posing is this:
how are different intrinsic times, arising from different dynamical
processes, to be related to each other?   More specifically: how are
these different intrinsic times to be related to a common "clock
time", which in general is different from all of them?   Clearly, it
is hard to make meaningful dynamical predictions from an encoding
of the form (4.5.1) unless this question is answered.

To approach this kind of question, let us consider again the basic
rate equations (4.5.1), this time taking the point of view that the
parameter t (and its differential dt) appearing therein is simply
an arbitrary parameter;   e.g. we could take it to be arc length along

trajectories. In that case, we can multiply each of these rate
equations by the same non-vanishing function $a(x_1, \ldots, x_n)$ without
changing the trajectories or the stability properties of the system;
all we do is change the rates at which the trajectories are traversed, *relative to some fixed time scale*. In fact, this procedure
may be interpreted as replacing the intrinsic time differential dt
defined by (4) by a new time differential of the form $a(x_1, \ldots, x_n)$dt.

Indeed, when we write down a set of rate equations encoding some
natural dynamical system on the basis of a general law, like the Law
of Mass Action (cf. Chapter 3.5 above), the time differential arising
in these equations is only defined up to such an arbitrary function
$a(x_1, \ldots, x_n)$. There is no way within such a system to characterize
this function, and hence no way of predicting from knowledge of trajectories the state in which we will find the system at a particular
instant. The intrinsic time scale defined by (4.5.4) for these rate
equations will clearly be the one for which the scale factor $a(x_1,$
$\ldots, x_n)$ becomes identically unity in M, but we have no guarantee
(and indeed it will be false in general) that the time tacitly encoded into the Law of Mass Action is the intrinsic time to be associated with the natural system itself. Thus, we must regard all of
our dynamical models as containing an arbitrary scale factor, which
cannot be determined by employing any kind of intrinsic argument
pertaining to the model itself.

We attempt to take account of this arbitrary scale factor by choosing
the scale so that the intrinsic time differential dt defined by
(4.5.4) is related to a Hamiltonian time differential dt_H by a
relation of the form

$$dt = a(x_1, \ldots, x_n)dt_H. \qquad (4.5.5)$$

If this is done, the scale factor becomes absorbed into the constitutive parameters (rate constants) appearing in the equations of
motion, and the time differential appearing in the resulting rate
equations becomes interpretable directly in terms of "clock time".
But it must be recognized that this procedure involves a profound
distinction between the constitutive rate constants which are
measured, and the intrinsic rates at which our natural system is
changing. This distinction is far from trivial; for instance,
only for a particular choice of scale factor can the Lotka-Volterra
equations of population dynamics be converted into a Hamiltonian
form, for which Liouville's Theorem holds. In other words, our
ability to apply the machinery of statistical mechanics to the
Lotka-Volterra equations (which are, it will be recalled, based
precisely on Mass Action) depends entirely on making a proper
choice of scale factor relating intrinsic time to Hamiltonian time.

We can conclude then that *the encoding of time as a general dynamical
parameter cannot be effectively made within a limited dynamical
context*. Rather, we must in each case arbitrarily select a scale
factor $a(x_1, \ldots, x_n)$ which will convert intrinsic time to Hamiltonian
time via (4.5.5); only in this way can we use clocks to define a
"common time" in terms of which dynamical predictions can be made.
Even this is not the end of the matter, for we have already point
out that Hamiltonian time differentials can be different from one

another. Thus, if we change from one Hamiltonian time differential
to another, the resulting relations (4.5.5) force these Hamiltonian
differentials to be related in a particular way if (4.5.5) is to
remain invariant to this change. A change of this kind can be looked
upon as a change of *observer*, and thus we impinge on the kinds of
relativistic considerations which are intrinsic to any discussion of
synchronization. However, we shall not pursue this matter further
here; our main purpose is merely to show what is involved in attemt-
ing to consistently define temporal encodings and rates in such a
way that meaningful temporal predictions can be obtained. As we have
seen, any such dynamical encoding can only define what we have called
an intrinsic time, related to a common "clock time" through an
arbitrary scale factor, which cannot be specified by dynamical considerations entirely within the system.

We shall now briefly discuss the interpretation of the linkage relations (4.5.2), which as we have seen embody simply a hypothesis of
causality. We have seen that, if a relation (4.5.3) also holds, we
can interpret the numerical coefficients a_{ij} in (4.5.2) as

$$a_{ij} = \frac{\partial f_i}{\partial x_j} = \frac{\partial}{\partial x_j} \frac{dx_i}{dt} \qquad\qquad (4.5.6)$$

Let us now introduce the following terminology: we shall say that
the state variable x_j *activates* the state variable x_i in the state
$(x_1, \ldots, x_n)$ if the quantity a_{ij} in (4.5.6) is positive, and that
it *inhibits* x_i if this quantity is negative. Intuitively, if x_j
activates x_i, then an increase in x_j increases the *rate* at which x_i
changes (or alternatively, a decrease in x_j decreases the rate at
which x_i changes). Likewise, if x_j inhibits x_i, then an increase
in x_j decreases the rate at which x_i changes (and a decrease in x_j
increases the rate at which x_i changes). This terminology of activation and inhibition is in fact meaningful for any dynamical system
of the form (4.5.1); it is interesting to see how far we may characterize a system of rate equations on the manifold M through a
specification of functions $a_{ij} = a_{ij}(x_1, \ldots, x_n)$ which determine an
activation-inhibition pattern among the state variables $x_1, \ldots, x_n$.
As we see, such a pattern arises automatically from the expression
of conservation conditions (4.5.2) among the differential increments
dx_i at a state, as a direct consequence of causality.[1]

In this terminology, we may now re-interpret the conservation relations

$$df_i = \sum_{j=1}^{n} a_{ij} dx_j \qquad\qquad (4.5.7)$$

in the following way: *the differential change* df_i (i.e. the differential change in the rate of change of the ith state variable x_i)
is the sum of the activations and inhibitions imposed on x_i *by the
other state variables, each of which is weighted by the differential
change of the corresponding state variable*. Thus we can interpret
the sum $\sum_{j=1}^{n} a_{ij} dx_j$ as the *net excitation* received by the state

variable x_i in the given state. Likewise, we may interpret the resulting increment df_i as the *response* to this net excitation.

Using this language, we in effect construct a *network* of excitable
elements, very much like a neutral net (cf. Example 3B of Chapter
3.5 above).

In order for such an interpretation to be valid for an arbitrary
family of functions $a_{ij}(x_1, \ldots, x_n)$ *it is necessary and sufficient
that the net activations* $\sum_{j=1}^{n} a_{ij}dx_j$ *which we have defined should be
exact differentials*. This is, of course, exactly the requirement
we earlier stipulated in (4.5.3) above, and explicitly embodied in
(4.5.7). Furthermore it is only in this case that we are able to
define an intrinsic time differential dt, through which the concept
of rate itself becomes meaningful.

If the manifold M is simply connected, it is easy to write down
necessary and sufficient conditions on the functions $a_{ij}(x_1, \ldots, x_n)$
which turn the net activations into exact differentials. These
conditions involve only the partial derivatives of the functions
a_{ij} with respect to the state variables x_i in the manifold M. For
instance, if n=3, these conditions become

$$\frac{\partial a_{i1}}{\partial x_3} = \frac{\partial a_{i3}}{\partial x_1}; \qquad \frac{\partial a_{i1}}{\partial x_2} = \frac{\partial a_{i2}}{\partial x_1}; \qquad \frac{\partial a_{i2}}{\partial x_3} = \frac{\partial a_{i3}}{\partial x_2},$$

for each i = 1, 2, 3. Thus we can see that the kinds of functions a_{ij}
which can appear in the relations (4.5.2) above, which we noted are
merely an embodiment of causality on M, must be severely restricted
if a consistent notion of intrinsic time (and hence a corresponding
set of rate equations of the form (4.5.1)) is to be defined at all.
Thus we see emerging a close relation between time and causality,
which is of course at the heart of using dynamical models for predictive purposes. We also draw attention, for subsequent reference,
to the close formal relationship between general rate equations of
the form (4.5.1) and the excitable networks which we considered
earlier.

REFERENCES AND NOTES

1. The ideas embodied in this discussion go back to Lotka, but the
    first explicit connection between the coefficients a_{ij} and bio-
    logical function seems to have been made by Higgins (*Ind. Eng.
    Chem.* 59, 18-62 1977) in the context of developing a model for
    oscillations in sequences of enzyme-catalyzed reactions. A more
    detailed discussion of activation-inhibition patterns, and their
    relation to dynamical systems, may be found in Rosen, R., *Bull.
    Math. Biol.* 41, 427-446 (1979). Somewhat similar ideas can
    also be found in the dynamical analysis of ecosystems (e.g.
    Levins, R., *Lecture Notes in Biomathematics* 18, 152-199 1977).

4.6 Time and Sequence: Logical Aspects of Time

In the present chapter, we wish to explore yet another aspect of temporal encoding, different in character from those we have considered so far. This will concern the *logical* character of time. More specifically, we wish to develop the sense in which a dynamical prediction of the form "if a system is initially in state $x(0)$, then at time t it will be in state $x(t)$" can be regarded as a *theorem*, derived from $x(0)$ as axiom, with the aid of production rules (rules of inference) arising from the equations of motion. We thus wish to treat a dynamical system as a kind of *formal theory* in the sense of Example 3 of Chapter 3.1 above.

Let us begin by returning to the situation described in that earlier example, in which a formal theory was regarded as a family of axioms and production rules. The axioms themselves could be regarded as words $w_1, \ldots, w_n$ written in some alphabet, and the production rules were a set of operations $J = \{T_1, \ldots, T_m\}$. An operation T_i in J can be regarded as a mapping defined on r-tuples of words, and associating with each r-tuple in its domain a definite word in its range. Thus, in algebraic terms, each T_i is an r-ary operation on the set of all words, where of course r depends on the operation.

Let A_0 denote the set of axioms; $A_0 = \{w_1, \ldots, w_n\}$. We are now going to define a set of words A_1, which are the *immediate consequents* of the axioms in A_0 under the production rules in J. Briefly, A_1 consists of all the words that can be produced by applying the production rules in J to all possible r-tuples of axioms for which they are defined. That is, given any word w in A_1, we can find a production rule T_k in J, and axioms $w_{i_1}, \ldots, w_{i_r}$ in A_0, such that

$$w = T_k(w_{i_1}, \ldots, w_{i_r}). \qquad (4.6.1)$$

Thus, A_1 is a well-defined set of words; clearly, every $w \in A_1$ is
a *theorem* of our system, and the *proof* w consists precisely in exhibiting the appropriate production rule T_k and r-tuple of axioms which
yield w as a consequent.

Now let us go one step further. We shall define a set of words A_2,
which consist of all words produced by applying an operation in J to
an r-tuple consisting of axioms in A_0, or theorems in A_1. Once again,
A_2 is a well-defined set of words, and any word $w \in A_2$ is a *theorem*.
The *proof* of such a theorem now consists of several stages. We must
exhibit: (a) a production rule T_k such that (4.6.1) is satisfied,
and the operands w_{i_j} belong either to A_0 or A_1; (b) for each operand
w_{i_j} in A_1, we must exhibit an explicit proof; an expression of the
form (4.6.1) all of whose operands lie in A_0.

Thus, to prove that a word w is a theorem in A_2 requires a *sequence*
of elementary steps. These steps produce words in A_1 from the axioms;
the final step produces a word in A_2. Each step requires the specification of a production rule, and also of the r-tuple on which that
rule is to act. The sequence itself constitutes the proof.

We can obviously iterate this procedure. For instance, we can define
the set A_3 of words satisfying (4.6.1), such that each operand w_{i_j}
belongs either to A_0, A_1 or A_2. Once again, each such word is a
theorem, whose proof consists of exhibiting a sequence of elementary
steps of the kind we have described. We stress again that each of
these elementary steps requires us to specify a particular production
rule in J, and also to specify the particular r-tuple of words on
which this rule is to act. Likewise, we can generate the sets of
words A_4, A_5, ..., A_N, ... for every integer N.

We are now going to argue that *the set of indices for the A_i comprise
a temporal encoding*. That is, these indices may be regarded as a
(discrete) set of *instants* for a kind of logical time scale. To
say that a word w belongs to A_N says that it requires N "instants"
in this time scale for the word to be produced from the axioms.
Hence the axioms themselves play the role of "initial conditions";
they specify the situation at the initial instant N=0. Let us see
how this can be done.

Suppose w is a word in A_N. Then by definition, there is a production
rule T_k in J, and words w_{i_1}, ..., w_{i_r} belonging to the sets A_0, A_1,
..., A_{N-1} such that (4.6.1) is satisfied. We shall think of w as
being produced at the instant N. Now some of the operands of T_k will

lie in A_{N-1}. We will think of these as being produced *simultaneously* at the instant N-1, by means of expressions like (4.6.1), in which the operands now lie in A_0, ..., A_{N-2}. Thus, at each instant of our time scale, we will produce all of the words which will be required at the next instant. Carrying this procedure back to the axioms themselves, we can regard them as words produced at the 0th instant.

In this way, a proof can be regarded as a sequence of successive steps, indexed by the logical time we have defined. At each such step, a set of words is produced from the words generated at *earlier* steps, and which themselves will be utilized to produce new words at *later* steps. Thus, the procedure we are envisioning is a *recursive* one, in which each new step depends on the results of the preceding ones. We could write down explicitly how such a recursive procedure works, but the preceding discussion should be sufficient to illustrate how it works; we shall leave more precise formal statements to an exercise for the reader.

It may help fix ideas to pause at this point and give some concrete realizations. A simple and familiar one comprises a game[1] like chess. In chess, the axioms are embodied in the initial position; the production rules are the legal moves of the game. The logical time which we have introduced indexes the successive moves played by the players; the position which is arrived at following any particular move is the analog of the theorem, inferred from the starting position (the axioms) by means of successive applications of production rules. Of course, we can take any legal initial con-figuration of pieces on the chessboard as axioms; this is the format for the familiar chess problems, which require the establishment of theorems of the form "white to play and mate in two moves".

Another most important embodiment of the considerations developed above may be found in the McCulloch-Pitts neural networks, described in Example 3 of Chapter 3.5 above. Instead of a chessboard, we now have a definite array of interconnected neurons. The production rules specify which neurons shall be excited at a particular instant, as a function of those neurons excited at a preceding instant. The instants themselves are, of course, arbitrary. The pattern of excitation of the network at an instant N can thus be regarded as a theorem, derived from an initial pattern of excitation (the pattern at N = 0) through the successive application of the production rules. Thus we see, in another way, how the neural nets can be regarded as realizations of logical systems; this time as realizations of formal theories, in which the temporal structure of the network is directly interpretable into the logical or sequential time we have introduced above.

Before going further, let us itemize the main properties of the logical time frame we have constructed. First, we see that this time is *discrete*. Second, it is entirely independent of any physical notion of *rate*. Thus, the logical structure of a game of chess is entirely independent of the rates at which the individual moves are made, considered in any physical sense. The only thing which matters is the *order* in which the moves are made. Third, this logical time is *irreversible*. It will be noted that these properties were also manifested by the probabilistic time introduced in Chapter 4.4 above, and are at this point quite different from the properties of Hamiltonian or dynamical time.

Now the relation between logical time and neural networks on the one
hand, and between neural networks and dynamical systems on the other,
provides a motivation for supposing that dynamical time and logical
time may be related to one another. If such a relation could be
established, we could simultaneously view dynamical systems as very
special kinds of formal theories, and formal theories themselves as
generalizations of dynamics. The remainder of the present chapter
will be devoted to exploring how this can be done.[2]

Let M be any set, and let $T : M \to M$ be any automorphism of M; i.e.
a 1-1 mapping of M onto itself. Since any automorphism may be composed with itself, we can form the automorphisms T^2, T^3, ..., T^n, ...
If we define the identity automorphism I to be T^0, the set of all
these automorphisms is a group G_T, where we have $T^m T^n = T^{m+n}$ for
any integers m, n. This is the cyclic subgroup of all automorphisms
$\mathfrak{A}(M)$ of M, generated by T. We are going to think of T as a *production
rule* on M; if x ε M is regarded as an axiom, then T(x) is the
theorem obtained by applying T to the axiom.

With this terminology, the exponents of the powers of T in G_T become
interpretable as *instants of logical time*. Thus, if $x(m) = T^m x(0)$,
we can regard x(m) as the theorem (in this case, the unique theorem)
inferable from the axiom x(0) in m steps of logical time. In this
situation, we can characterize the theorems inferable from the axiom
x(0) very simply; they are the *orbit* of G_T on which x(0) lies.

More precisely, x is a theorem inferable from x(0) if there is an
instant m of logical time such that $x = T^m x(0)$.

In particular, if we take M to be a *manifold*, the specification of
a group G_T converts the manifold into a *discrete dynamical system*.

In this case, we have a manifold full of choices for our initial
axiom, but once having chosen an axiom, the set of theorems is
completely determined. Moreover, each theorem is indexed by an
instant of logical time, which recursively relates the theorem to
the axiom.

This situation is, of course, closely related to the specification
of a continuous dynamical system, as a one-parameter group $\{T_t\}$ of
automorphisms on a manifold M. Here the index t refers to a corresponding *dynamical time*, such as is embodied in the dynamical time
differential dt defined in the preceding chapter. Indeed, if we are
given a continuous dynamical system $\{T_t\}$ in this form, we can define
many discrete dynamical systems from it; for any real number r, we
can consider the cyclic subgroup generated by T_r (i.e. the subgroup
whose elements are $T_r^n = T_{nr}$ for each integer n), and this will define
a discrete dynamical system on M. In this case, we would have an
explicit interpretation (i.e. a *realization*) of the *logical* time in
the discrete system, in terms of the *dynamical* time t of the continuous system. Precisely this method is used in obtaining numerical
solutions of systems of differential equations by means of digital
computers.

Unfortunately, this procedure of relating logical time in a discrete
system to dynamical time in a continuous one only can work if the
dynamical time is defined *first*, and a logical time is specified by
choosing some arbitrary unit time step t = r. We cannot go backwards,

starting from a given logical time (i.e. a discrete group G_T) and embed it into a continuous one-parameter group. Moreover, there are many other possible relationships which can exist between discrete-time and continuous-time dynamical systems. For instance, suppose that M is embedded as a submanifold in a larger manifold N, and suppose that a one-parameter family $\{T_t\}$ of transformations is defined on the larger manifold N. Given a particular trajectory in N, we may define a mapping of M onto itself as indicated in Figure 4.6.1 below:

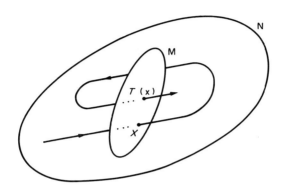

Fig. 4.6.1.

Here the image T(x) of a point x in M is defined as the point at which the trajectory through x next intersects M. Under appropriate circumstances, this mapping T : M → M defines a discrete dynamical system on M, but there is no continuous dynamical system on M of which G_T is a cyclic subgroup. It will be noted that the instants of logical time for the discrete system G_T in this case are not even a subgroup of the set of instants of dynamical time on N in general. The idea we have just sketched is often called the *suspension* of such a discrete system on M into a continuous one on a bigger manifold N, an idea originally due to Poincaré.[3]

Nevertheless, there is a sense in which we can interpret the dynamical time parameter t as a logical index for the theorems x(t) implied by an axiom x(0). It will be noted that in the case of a discrete dynamical system, the entire dynamics is determined by a generator T; an automorphism of M which can be applied to any point of M chosen as initial axiom. The logical time index m then refers to the number of times this generator must be applied to an axiom to yield a particular theorem. Thus there is an identification of this generator with the production rule of a formal system. If such ideas could be applied to the continuous case, we would need some concept of *infinitesimal generator*, from which any automorphism T_t could be obtained by an integration process.

In the continuous case, the role of such an infinitesimal production rule is played by the tangent vector. More precisely, if M is a manifold, we can turn M into a dynamical system precisely by specifying a tangent vector $\tau(x)$ for every point x in M; i.e., we define a vector field on M. As we saw in the preceding chapter, this is sufficient to impose conservation conditions on the differential increments attached to x, and hence to define the concept of dynamical time on M. From the present point of view, however, the tangent vector $\tau(x)$ can also be regarded locally as an infinitesimal production rule, specifying an infinitesimal change of state x → x+dx associated with the differential dt of dynamical time. Of course this production rule is in general different from point to point in M; indeed, the dynamical context is such that to each point x of M, a unique infinitesimal production rule $\tau(x)$ is also specified.[4] By means of an integration process, a trajectory on M can be looked upon as a *continuum* of theorems, indexed by the instants of dynamical time; thus we can force dynamical time and logical time to coincide.

In this way, a dynamics can be viewed as a very special kind of formal theory. It is special in that, given any initial point as M as axiom, there is exactly one production rule which can be applied to it (namely, the rule specified by the tangent vector to that point). On the other hand, this viewpoint leads to a significant generalization of formal theories; namely, that the theorems no longer form a discrete set, but are indexed by continua. The advantage of such a generalization is that discrete, rate-independent logical time coincides in this situation with rate-dependent dynamical time. Indeed, it is only under these circumstances that a relation between the two kinds of time can be established at all.

REFERENCES AND NOTES

1.   Indeed, any kind of game thus constitutes a formal system. However, games manifest additional structure, because the point of playing a game is to win. This means that there are certain distinguished propositions ("wins") in the system which a player attempts to establish, and others ("losses") which he wishes to avoid establishing. The theory of games is thus dominated by the idea of a *strategy*, the establishement of chains of propositions which culminate in "wins". Ordinarily, such strategies are generated through considerations of utility. The mathematical theory of games was originally developed in a classic book:
         von Neumann, J. and Morgenstern, O., *Theory of Games and
            Economic Behavior*. Princeton University Press (1944).
     It is interesting to observe that, just as the rules of the game comprise a formal system, the concept of utility which generates strategies relates game theory to control and optimal control theory; this point is taken up further in Note 4 below. Further, since the generation of "good" strategies ordinarily requires skill (i.e. intelligence) on the part of the players, it is not surprising to find a good part of the literature in Artificial Intelligence (cf. Note 17 to Chapter 3.5 above) to be concerned with game-playing. Thus, game theory is an exceedingly lively area. It also impinges directly on our present subject of anticipatory behavior, since a strategy may obviously be regarded as a model of the environment with which a player interacts.

2.   See Note 18 to Chapter 3.5 above.

3.   A good recent reference to Poincaré mappings, and to an approach to discrete dynamical systems based on them, is
         Gumowski, I. and Mira, C., *Recurrence and Discrete Dynamical
            Systems*. Springer-Verlag (1980).

4. If we regard the tangent vector to a state, not as fixed by the
    equations of motion, but as freely selectable from some submani-
    fold of the tangent space to each state, we find ourselves in the
    framework of *control theory*, rather than dynamical system theory.
    At the same time, such a *control system* becomes nearly analogous
    to the discrete logical systems which we considered initially.
    A choice of tangent vector (control) at each point then produces
    a trajectory; different choices will produce correspondingly
    different trajectories. If we then superimpose on this picture
    a notion of utility (or, in this context, of *cost*) the result
    is the theory of optimal control. The notion of utility can also
    be regarded as turning a control system into a *game*, and indeed
    one in which logical time and continuous time coincide. Such
    games are commonly called *differential games*, and the theory of
    differential games may be regarded as a generalization of ordinary
    optimal control theory. A good general reference to differential
    games is
        Friedman, A., *Differential Games*. Wiley (1971).
    The flavor of the relation between game theory and optimal control
    theory may be indicated by a sampling of the papers in the fol-
    lowing:
        Roxin, E. O., Liu, P. T. and Steinberg, R. L., *Differential
        Games and Control Theory*. Dekker (1974).

4.7 Similarity and Time

In the present chapter, we shall be concerned with exploring how the concepts of similarity and invariance, as we developed them in Examples 5 and 6 of Chapter 3.3, can be extended to dynamic and temporal situations.

The province of similarity studies, it will be recalled, is the study of those transformations of the arguments in an equation of state which leave that equation invariant. Thus, for example, in our study of the van der Waals equation (3.3.25), we found that this equation was invariant to: (a) an arbitrary replacement of the constitutive parameters (a, b, r) by any other values (a', b', r'). (b) a simultaneous replacement of each state (P, V, T) by the *corresponding* state (P', V', T'), where the values (P', V', T') are given by (3.3.27).

This invariance of the van der Waals equation was expressed precisely by the commutativity of the diagram of mappings displayed in (3.3.30). Conversely, all invariance properties of an equation of state can be expressed by such a conjugacy diagram; this fact was summed up in the relations (3.3.30).

Now in general, the introduction of dynamical considerations into our encodings of natural systems serves to introduce new equations of state into these encodings. Initially, of course, we have the equations of motion themselves, which as we have seen, express linkages between instantaneous rates of change of observables and the instantaneous values of the observables. The integrated form of these equations of motion are likewise linkages, between the values of observables evaluated at some initial instant, and the values of these observables at a later instant. Thus we may expect that considerations of similarity will be applicable to dynamics also. The question now is: *what transformations of the arguments appearing in dynamical equations of state leave those equations invariant?*

We have already seen a very special case of this kind of question in Chapter 4.2 above. Our assertion regarding the reversibility of Hamiltonian time is precisely an assertion of similarity; the Newtonian equations of motion remain invariant when an instant t is

replaced by its negative -t, and all other arguments remain fixed.
Conversely, the non-reversibility of the other kinds of time we have
discussed means that the equations of motion which define them do
not remain invariant under such a replacement. The remarks to follow
should be looked upon as generalizations of these simple results,
and those which we have developed previously.

To fix ideas, we will begin with a study of a particular example,
which we have seen before; namely, the undamped harmonic oscillator.
The equations of motion of this system were presented in (1.2.1)
above. These equations of motion are, as usual, to be regarded as
linkage relations, or equations of state, relating rates of change
of the state variables to the instantaneous values of these variables.
The integrated form of these equations of motion can, of course,
easily be written down:

$$x(t) = x(0) \cos \sqrt{\frac{k}{m}} \, t + \frac{p(0)}{m} \sqrt{\frac{m}{k}} \sin \sqrt{\frac{k}{m}} \, t \qquad (4.7.1)$$

There is a similar equation for $p(t)$, but it can be obtained from
(4.7.1) by differentiation. The equation of state (4.7.1) should
be considered as a linkage between an initial state $(x(0), p(0))$,
an instant t, and the corresponding value $x(t)$ of the displacement
at that instant.

The equation (4.7.1) can be regarded as a function of five arguments:

$$\Phi(x, t, m, k, x(0), p(0)) = 0. \qquad (4.7.2)$$

To study the similarity properties of the oscillator, we must as
always find those transformations

$$\begin{cases} x & \to & x' \\ t & \to & t' \\ m & \to & m' \\ x(0) & \to & x'(0) \\ p(0) & \to & p'(0) \end{cases} \qquad (4.7.3)$$

which leave (4.7.2) or (4.7.1) invariant. We shall proceed in general
just as we did with the van der Waals equation. It will be recalled
from Example 3 of Chapter 3.3 that we extracted a triple (a, b, r)
of arguments of the equation of state; this triple consists of the
constitutive parameters whose values determine the *species* of gas
with which we are dealing. These parameters we regarded as capable
of arbitrary variation; i.e. we placed no restriction on a transformation

$$(a, b, r) \to (a', b', r') \qquad (4.7.4)$$

of these arguments. We then found that the only transformations of
the remaining arguments of the van der Waals equation

$$(P, V, T) \to (P', V', T') \qquad (4.7.5)$$

which left the equation itself invariant were those given by the
Law of Corresponding States. We recall that this law is expressed
as follows: a state (P, V, T) of a gas with structural parameters
(a, b, r) is *similar*, or *corresponding*, to a state (P', V', T') of a
gas with structural parameters (a', b', r') of and only if

$$P/P_c = P'/P'_c; \qquad V/V_c = V'/V'_c; \qquad T/T_c = T'/T'_c \qquad (4.7.6)$$

(where the subscripts c refer to the critical point, determined by the values of the appropriate structural parameters alone).

We shall now do exactly the same with the equation of state (4.7.1) or (4.7.2), which now involves time instants t as values of one of the arguments. If we agree to allow *arbitrary* transformations of the form

$$(m, k, x(0)) \rightarrow (m', k', x'(0)), \tag{4.7.7}$$

we ask what are the transformations of the remaining two arguments

$$x \rightarrow x',$$
$$t \rightarrow t' \tag{4.7.8}$$

which leave the equation of state (4.7.1) or (4.7.2) invariant. It is easy to show that these transformations are given by

$$x' = \frac{x'(0)}{x(0)}x$$

$$t' = \sqrt{\frac{km'}{k'm}}t \tag{4.7.9}$$

From the first of the equations in (4.7.9), it is immediate upon differentiation that we must also have

$$p' = \frac{x(0)}{x'(0)}p. \tag{4.7.10}$$

The relations (4.7.9) and (4.7.10) are the exact analogs of the Law of Corresponding States for the van der Waals equation; just as in that case, we can use these relations to write the equations of state (4.7.1) or (4.7.2) in a *dimensionless* form, in which no constitutive parameters appear.

The equations (4.7.7), (4.7.9) and (4.7.10) express the full similarity properties of the class of one-dimensional frictionless harmonic oscillators. These relations may be summarized in the following general form: *two oscillators satisfying (4.7.7), (4.7.9) and (4.7.10) are in corresponding states at corresponding instants.*

Let us look more closely at the second relation in (4.7.9) above, which tells us which instants are corresponding instants. We notice that the time scales appropriate to the two oscillators are related by a factor depending on the masses and stiffness coefficients of the oscillators; hence any transformation (4.7.7) for which $m \neq m'$ or $k \neq k'$ *necessitates* a change of time scale. Conversely, any transformation (4.7.7) which leaves these constitutive parameters fixed, and only changes the initial displacement $x(0)$, does not affect the time scale. We also note that the scale factor connecting the two time scales involves a *radical*, with its attendant ambiguity of sign; this is simply a manifestation of the fact that a simple replacement of t by -t in (4.7.1) or (4.7.2) already leaves these relations invariant. The results just obtained thus reassert in another way our conclusions about the Hamiltonian time; that it is reversible, and that different Hamiltonian systems (such as two oscillators differing by a transformation of the form (4.7.7)) generate different intrinsic times.

In fact, the arguments we have given above are perfectly general, and can be applied to any dynamical equations of state. Indeed,

it will be recognized that the argument we have given is nothing
other than the establishment of the structural stability of the
class of systems satisfying the equations of state to arbitrary
perturbations of the form (4.7.7); the transformations (4.7.8) and
(4.7.9) of the remaining arguments are those which annihilate the
imposed perturbation (4.7.7). In general, we simply find an arbitrary
maximal set of arguments of an equation of state which serve to
parameterize such a structurally stable family; in both of the
cases we considered (namely the van der Waals equation and the
harmonic oscillator) it turned out that three such quantities sufficed.

We repeat the essential temporal feature of such arguments: *if time
is not used as one of the parameters subject to arbitrary perturbation,
then the effect of such a perturbation is to necessitate a change in
time scale if the equation of state is to be preserved invariant.*
Under such a change in time scale, *similar systems will be in corresponding states at corresponding instants.*

We will conclude this discussion of similarity in dynamical systems
by considering the sense in which the two dynamical systems

$$dx_i/dt = f_i(x_1, \ldots, x_n), \qquad i = 1, \ldots, n \qquad (4.7.11)$$

and

$$dx_i/dt = a(x_1, \ldots, x_n) f_i(x_1, \ldots, x_n),$$
$$i = 1, \ldots, n \qquad (4.7.12)$$

where $a(x_1, \ldots, x_n)$ is any arbitrary non-vanishing function of the
state variables, are similar to each other. It is clear that these
two systems possess the same trajectories and the same stability
properties; thus the only possible difference between them can
reside in the rates at which their trajectories are traversed, relative to some fixed external time scale.

Once again, it is simplest to proceed by examining first a special
case. Since we have already considered the harmonic oscillator at
some length, let us return to it once more for this purpose. Let
us simplify still further, and consider the case in which the arbitrary function $a(x, p)$ is put equal to some constant C. Thus our
question is: in what sense is the new system

$$\begin{cases} \dfrac{dx}{dt} = \dfrac{Cp}{m} \\[2mm] \dfrac{dp}{dt} = -Ckx \end{cases} \qquad (4.7.13)$$

similar to the original oscillator (for which C = 1)?

We observe that the transition from the original oscillator to
(4.7.13) is obtained by making the transformation

$$(m, k) \rightarrow (m/C, kC). \qquad (4.7.14)$$

We now look at our general similarity rules (4.7.7), (4.7.9), (4.7.10)
for the harmonic oscillator; we find that the state variables (x, p)
are unaffected by this transformation, but we must make a *time*
transformation $t \rightarrow t'$; specifically, we must have

$$t' = Ct. \qquad (4.7.15)$$

Now we observe that exactly the same argument holds if C is not constant, but is any non-vanishing function of state, C = a(x, p).
Thus, even in this general case, we find that

$$t' = a(x, p)t$$

which is indeed just what we would expect from our general considerations regarding dynamical time. We see then that the relation between a general dynamical system (4.7.11) and its derived systems
(4.7.12) is precisely one of similarity, and in particular, is entirely concerned with establishing a correspondence between their
intrinsic time scales which leaves the equation of state of (4.7.11)
invariant.

4.8 Time and Age

In the preceding chapters, we have abuntantly seen that the quality
we perceive as time is complex. It admits a multitude of different
kinds of encoding, which differ vastly from one another. Thus, we
have considered reversible Hamiltonian time; irreversible dynamical
time; thermodynamic time; probabilistic time; and sequential or
logical time. Each of these capture some particular aspects of our
time sense, at least as these aspects are manifested in particular
kinds of situations. While we saw that certain formal relations
could be established between these various kinds of time, none of
them could be reduced to any of the others; nor does there appear
to exist any more conprehensive encoding of time to which all of the
kinds we have discussed can be reduced. This, as we shall see later,
is indeed the essence of complexity.

Moreover, we saw that within each class of temporal encoding, many
distinct kinds of time were possible. Thus, there are many kinds of
Hamiltonian time; many kinds of dynamical time, etc. Each such time
was intrinsically generated by the particular kind of dynamics in
which it arose. As we indicated, these times cannot strictly be
reduced one to the other, but they can be *compared*, by means of more
or less complicated *scale factors*. As we saw in the preceding chapter,
this is most readily accomplished within a class of similar systems,
all of which obey a common equation of state in which the appropriate
intrinsic time enters as one of the arguments.

In the present chapter, we wish to illustrate further the complexity
of temporal encodings by considering the distinction between *time*
(or duration) and *age*. We shall show that these two concepts are
not co-extensive; in the process of establishing the differences
between them, we shall be able to gain additional insights into the
nature of temporal encodings of dynamical processes.

Let us begin with consideration of a simple example. Consider a
first-order decay process, such as the decay of a radioactive material.
Under conventional hypotheses, a natural system of this kind can be
encoded formally as a single first-order differential equation of
the form

$$dx/dt = -\lambda x. \tag{4.8.1}$$

Here the variable x denotes the amount of radioactive material present
at some instant t of clock time; the coefficient λ is a constitutive
parameter, representing the (constant) fraction of material which
decays in a single unit of clock time.

As usual, the equation (4.8.1) may be interpreted as a linkage relation
or equation of state, relating the rate of decay at an instant to the
amount of radioactive material present at that instant. By an integration process, we can convert this linkage to another one, of the
form

$$x(t) = x(0)e^{-\lambda t} \qquad\qquad (4.8.2)$$

which is of the general form

$$\Phi(x, x(0), \lambda, t) = 0 \qquad\qquad (4.8.3)$$

analogous to (4.7.2) above. We stress explicitly that the linkage
(4.8.2) or (4.8.3) relates the amount x(0) of material initially
present to that present at any *subsequent* instant of clock time.

We shall now treat (4.8.2) or (4.8.3) according to the general considerations of similarity developed in the preceding chapter. In
particular, we shall ask the following question: if we make an
arbitrary transformation

$$\begin{cases} \lambda \to \lambda, ' \\ x(0) \to x'(0), \end{cases} \qquad\qquad (4.8.4)$$

what transformations must we make of the remaining arguments in order
to keep the equation of state (4.8.2) invariant?

It is easy to see that the required transformations are:

$$\begin{cases} x \to x' = \dfrac{x'(0)}{x(0)}\, x, \\[2mm] t \to t' = \dfrac{\lambda'}{\lambda}\, t. \end{cases} \qquad\qquad (4.8.5)$$

If as before we say that two states x, x' are *corresponding* if they
satisfy the first relation in (4.8.5) above, and two instants t, t'
are *corresponding* is they satisfy the second relation, we once again
see that the equation of state (4.8.3) defines a two-parameter similarity class (parameterized by the pair $(\lambda, x(0))$, and the transformation rules (4.8.4), (4.8.5) express the Law of Corresponding States
for this class; any two systems in the class are in corresponding
states at corresponding instants if these rules are satisfied.

Indeed, if we introduce new (dimensionless) variables by writing

$$\xi = \frac{x}{x(0)}, \qquad \tau = \lambda t \qquad\qquad (4.8.6)$$

then the *entire class* can be represented by a single dimensionless
equation of state of the form

$$\frac{d\xi}{d\tau} = \xi \qquad\qquad (4.8.7)$$

in which no arbitrary parameters are visible; as usual, these parameters have been absorbed into the scales into which the remaining
quantities are measured.

This last assertion means the following with respect to the time
variable. If we measure time in units proportional to the rate of
decay (e.g., in *half-lives*), then all systems obeying (4.8.2) *decay
at the same rate*. On the other hand, if we persist in using a common
clock time, simultaneously imposed on all the systems obeying (4.8.2),
then different systems will necessarily appear to decay at different
rates. If the constitutive parameters λ, λ' are quite different for
two such systems, one of them will thus appear to *"survive" for a
greater duration*; but the systems will both survive for exactly the
same number of half-lives. What we now wish to assert is the following: *duration as measured in clock time is not an appropriate measure
of age*; the appropriate measure for age in this case is the dimensionless quantity τ defined in (4.8.6). The Law of Corresponding
States in this case thus asserts that *two systems satisfying (4.8.2)
are of the same age if and only if they are in corresponding states
at any instant* in the dimensionless quantities.

We are now going to assert that the distinction between elapsed time
(or duration) according to some fixed scale, and any natural concept
of *age*, possesses the qualities illustrated by the above simple
example. That is, age is a property shared by certain states belonging
to a *class* of similar dynamical systems. Two different systems in
such a class (i.e. characterized by different values of constitutive
parameters and/or initial conditions) are of the same age if and
only if they are related by a similarity transformation; i.e. they
are in corresponding states at corresponding instants of clock time.

The relation between elapsed time, age and similarity is a crucial
one for many purposes in biology. Thus, there is an obvious sense
in which a two-year-old human is "younger" than a two-year-old rat,
even though the absolute durations (measured in clock time) through
which their respective lives have extended are the same. However,
to explicitly write down the sense in which such an interspecific
comparison is meaningful is a far from trivial matter. What we
propose here is the following: that to the extent that two natural
systems can be compared in terms of age, they must be encoded into
a common similarity class of dynamical systems. The difference
between systems within the class is represented by a difference in
the specific values attached to particular constitutive parameters
and/or initial conditions. The ages of the two systems, at any instant
of clock time, are then expressed in terms of those transformations
of state and time which preserve the equation of state governing the
class invariant. Thus, to the extent that it is meaningful at all
to compare the ages of a rat and a human, we might say that a two-
year-old human is the same *age* as a two-week-old rat, expressed in
terms of duration. Age, in other words, is seen to be a reflection
of a more comprehensive similarity relation obtaining within a class
of similar dynamical systems; this similarity relation involves not
only elapsed time (duration), but also the instantaneous states of
the systems involved.

Thus we can see that, insofar as *age* represents a quality pertaining
to the states of a natural system, it is related only in a complex
way to the encoding of other qualities, and to the encoding of time.

The above considerations reflect only one of the various ways in
which the concepts of time and age can be juxtaposed. Other such
juxtapositions arise, for example, from attempts to relate the kind
of discrete, logical time described in Chapter 4.6 above to a continuous dynamical time. For instance, in discussions of "clonal aging"
in cell cultures, the "age" of a culture is expressed in discrete

time, as the number of *doublings* undergone by the culture[1] Normal
cells under these conditions exhibit a definite limit (the Hayflick
Limit) to the number of doublings they can exhibit, which is then
identified with their *life span*. This *logical* measure of age is
unrelated to any concept of *duration*, as measured in some external
continuous clock time. Thus, for example, a culture may be indefinitely arrested at any level of doubling (e.g. by immersing it in
liquid nitrogen); when restored to normal temperature conditions,
the cells proceed to complete precisely the expected number of
doublings required to reach the Hayflick Limit, as determined by
their logical age when arrested. Thus, the measure of age in terms
of discrete doublings is *rate independent*, in the same sense as a
sequence of moves in (say) a game of chess is rate-independent.
This situation represents another sense, distinct from those subsumed
under similarity, in which the concepts of duration and age are seen
to be independent.

Aside from the examples described above, many other situations in
which the notions of elapsed time and the quality of age are not co-
extensive can be imagined. For instance, we may express the age of
a system in terms of a probabilistic time (cf. Chapter 4.4 above),
which is again distinct from a continuous Hamiltonian or dynamical
time. All of these considerations point once again to the complexity
associated with temporal qualities and their various encodings, and
to the fact that there is no apparent way to describe temporal qualities in a single comprehensive fashion.

We shall conclude this section with some further remarks on similarity
time and age. Namely, we shall use the illustrations developed in
the last several chapters as examples of *modelling relations* between
natural systems, as these were defined in Chapters 2 and 3 above.
To do this, it is most convenient to refer to a refined version of
Fig. 2.3.2 above; namely, to the diagram

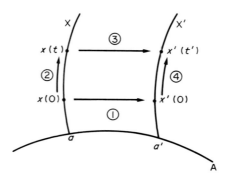

Fig. 4.8.1.

Here, as before, we let A represent an appropriate space of constitutive parameters, which identify individual systems within a similarity class. To each point a in A, we associate a copy of a common
state space X. In each of these state spaces, a specific dynamics
is imposed, such that any initial state x(0) is carried to a uniquely
determined state x(t) after some time interval t has elapsed. In the
Figure, two such points a, a' are indicated.

As we have seen, the linkages imposed on each state space X by the dynamics determines how the state x(0) at some initial instant is linked to the state x(t) at a future instant. Thus, *the dynamics determines how a present state can be regarded as a model of a future state of the same system*. This relation between present state and future state is represented in the Figure by the arrows labelled (2) and (4).

On the other hand, the similarity relation imposed on the entire class indicates how each specific system in the class can be regarded as a model of any other. In particular, we have seen that the dynamical form of the similarity relations determine correspondences between (a) the states of systems belonging to different parameter values a, a';   (b) the time scales used to parameterize the dynamics in these different systems. Thus, given any state of a given system in the class, there is a *corresponding* state in every other system;   moreover, the time scales between the systems are so related that *any pair of systems are found in corresponding states at corresponding instants*.

These relations are represented in the Figure by the arrows labelled (1) and (3). According to these relations, each state of a particular system in the class is also a model of all of its corresponding states;   i.e. is a model of state belonging to different systems.

By putting these two different kinds of modelling relations together, we can employ dynamical properties of *any* system in our class to obtain information about *every other system*. For instance, by symbolically composing the arrows (2) and (3) in Figure 4.8.1, we can see explicitly how the initial state x(0) of one system can be regarded as a model of the state x'(t') of a different system in the class, at a different instant. Hence, it follows that the combination of dynamics with similarity provides an exceedingly powerful inferential tool for the study of such classes of systems.

REFERENCES AND NOTES

1. The term "doubling" is used here as a kind of average replicative potential for a species of differential cell type in culture. More technically, a few cells are initially plated on a culture dish;   they will multiply until they cover the surface of the available medium in a monolayer ("normal" cells will only grow in a single layer on the medium, and they will stop multiplying when no more free surface is available to them, through a poorly understood mechanism called contact inhibition). At this point, some of the cells are replated on a fresh surface, and are once again grown to confluency. The major discovery of Leonard Hayflick is that this process cannot be continued indefinitely; normal cells can only be propagated for a relatively small number of such "doublings", depending on the species from which the cells are taken, the particular cell type involved, and the nature of the donor. This Hayflick Limit varies (roughly) directly with the longevity of the donor species, and inversely with the age of the individual donor; thus the Hayflick phenomenon is often called "clonal aging", and plays a major role in the search for relatively simple models for whole-organism senescence. For a more detailed review, and further references, see for instance Rosen, R., *Int. Rev. Cyt.* **54**, 161-191 (1978).

CHAPTER 5

Open Systems and the Modelling Relation

5.1 General Introduction

In the previous sections of this volume, we have developed in great detail the properties of the modelling relation, illustrated with a profusion of examples drawn from many scientific disciplines. The preceding section was specifically devoted to a consideration of dynamical modelling. Dynamical models are henceforward going to be our central concern, because they are the vehicles through which temporal predictions are made. Our most immediate item of business, to be taken up in the present section, is to combine our general insights regarding modelling relations with the specific properties of dynamical systems. The aim will be to obtain an integrated theory of dynamical models, which will play the central role in our treatment of anticipatory systems.

Let us begin by reviewing some of the salient features of the modelling relation, as we have previously developed them. We have seen that a model is essentially an encoding of qualities, or observables, of a natural system into formal mathematical objects. Just as the system qualities are interrelated in the original system, so these mathematical objects are related through corresponding linkage relations, or equations of state. It is then precisely the correspondence between the inferential structure of the model and the interrelation of qualities in the original natural system which allows us to utilize models for predictive purposes.

We have also seen that a model is by its very nature an abstraction, in the sense that any encoding must necessarily ignore or neglect qualities which are present in the original natural system. To that extent, a model represents a *subsystem* of the original system, rather than the system itself; much of our previous work was concerned with determining how, and whether, relationships between such subsystems could be established. In any case, the fact that a model is an abstraction means that the predictive capabilities of the model are limited to circumstances in which those interactive qualities of the system not present in the model are not significant. Stated another way: the model behaves as the real system would behave if it possessed *only* those interactive capabilities which are explicitly encoded into the model.

Thus the construction of a model intrinsically presumes an absence

of linkage between the behaviors we wish to study and those qualities
not encoded into the model itself. Our main present concern will be
to study the effects of such a presumption, in the special case of
dynamical models. We shall approach this study by bringing it within
the purview of the general theory we have already developed. Specifically, we have already seen how the properties of distinct encodings
of the same system may be compared. This comparison tells us, of
course, how the subsystems represented by the models are related to
each other in the natural system itself. We shall choose the two
encodings to be compared as follows: one of them will be a dynamical
model we wish to study, and the other will comprise that model together
with some further encoded interactive capabilities. The comparison
between the two will tell us the extent to which predictions made
from the original model can remain valid in the presence of uncoded
qualities.

This kind of question is of great importance within the sciences
themselves. Let us take a specific example; that of particle mechanics, which we have considered at great length above. The most
important systems of classical mechanics are frank idealizations, in
that they deliberately neglect or ignore qualities known to be present
in the world. Thus, the most important and deeply studied mechanical
systems are the conservative ones, in which the forces acting on the
system are derived from time-independent potentials, and in which
total energy is conserved. Such an idealization necessarily neglects
all dissipative or frictional aspects, which we know to be essential
and irreducible features of real natural systems. And yet, the
dynamical predictions of conservative particle mechanics have played
perhaps the central ròle in our attempts to understand the properties
of real systems.

Thus, the kind of question with which we shall be involved concerns,
as a special case, the relation between dissipative and non-dissipative
(conservative) systems. Indeed, this fact will dictate the nature
of the general approach we shall take to the relation between a model
(or abstraction) and the system being modelled. For a conservative
system is one in which we have neglected all dissipative or frictional
interactions between the system and its environment. It is a system
which is, in an important sense, *closed* to such interactions. The
distinction between a conservative system, such as an undamped oscillator, and its dissipative counterparts is thus essentially a distinction between a closed system and an open one; between a system uncoupled to its environment, and the same system in direct interaction
with a definite modality of that environment.

Thus, speaking very roughly, we are going to develop a kind of proportionality relation, of the form:

$$\frac{\text{model}}{\text{system}} = \frac{\text{closed system}}{\text{open system}}.$$

We shall begin by studying the right-hand side of this proportionality
in a dynamical context, by comparing the dynamical properties of a
system closed to environmental interactions with the corresponding
properties of the *same* system when open to such interactions. The
principal result in this connection, to be established in Chapter
5.4 below, is the following: *the discrepancy between a dynamical
behavior in a closed system and the corresponding behavior in an
open system is an increasing function of time.* The sense in which
"time" is to be understood in the above assertion will be made clear
in the course of the argument itself.

We shall then see how this result can be interpreted as embodying a proposition relating the predictions of a dynamical model to the actual behavior of the system being modelled.   In this context, the result will become: *the discrepancy between the dynamical behavior predicted from a model, and the actual behavior of the system being modelled, is an increasing function of time.*   This is in fact the main conclusion of the present section.   Because of its profound significance for many parts of system theory, and the crucial role it plays in understanding the properties of anticipatory systems, we shall examine it from a number of different points of view.   For instance, we shall argue that the concept of *error*, as a presumed quality of system behavior , arises precisely from the discrepancy between the actual behavior of a natural system and the behavior *predicted* on the basis of some dynamical model of the system.   This in turn will provide us a basis on which to rigorously discuss the relation between error and system complexity.   In subsequent sections we shall draw important corollaries pertaining to the reliability of anticipatory systems, and their physiological, behavioral and evolutionary implications.

We shall also stress the profound distinction between this result and the Second Law of Thermodynamics.   It will be shown that the increasing discrepancy between corresponding behaviors in closed and open systems has nothing whatever to do with entropy and disorder, or with approach to equilibrium in isolated systems, or with any considerations of probability or stochastics.   Yet it embodies in a rigorous form the same kind of result for which the Second Law is often (wrongly) invoked, and hence it is essential to be clear about the distinction between them.

5.2 Open, Closed and Compensated Systems

In many branches of science, such as thermodynamics, we can classify
the systems studied therein into a number of distinct classes,
depending upon the way they interact with the environment. Thus,
in thermodynamics, we can recognize a class of systems we call
isolated, which exchange neither heat nor matter nor any other form
of energy with their environment; much of the classical theory of
thermodynamics is restricted to this class of isolated systems.
Likewise, a system is called *closed* if it can exchange heat, but not
matter, with its environment. A system which can exchange both
energy and matter with its environment is generally called an *open
system*.

Let us note the two crucial features of such a classification. In
the first place, *we require above all an absolute distinction between
system and environment;* between what is "inside" and what is "outside". Indeed, without such a distinction, the categories of closed,
isolated, open, etc., are meaningless. Secondly, having made such a
distinction, *we need to stipulate the kinds of linkage relations we
allow between qualities which are internal to the system, and qualities which are assigned to the environment*. Thus, in an isolated
thermodynamic system, the system qualities are presumed *unlinked* to
any environmental quality; in a closed thermodynamic system, thermodynamic qualities of the system are linked to environmental temperature,
but to no other environmental qualities.

Thus, the first essential order of business is to examine the following
question: to what extent can we obtain an *intrinsic* characterization
of what is system and what is environment? Very roughly, we seek a
way of determining, from a consideration of the system qualities
themselves, whether there is anything outside the system. For, if
we cannot infer by intrinsic means that any environmental qualities
actually exist, this is equivalent to saying that the system is in
fact isolated (in the thermodynamic sense). It is clear that if
such a distinction between system and environment can be meaningfully
made at all, it must be represented in terms of the linkage relations
which characterize the system.

In most branches of system theory, the distinction between system
and environment is simply presumed to be given *a priori*, and not

further discussed. However, there is one field in which there is
indeed an absolute distinction between what is system and what is
environment; that field, not surprisingly, is classical Newtonian
mechanics. Accordingly, let us consider how an intrinsic system-
environment distinction arises in mechanics, and then proceed to
see how we may formulate this distinction in more general situations.

The simplest possible mechanical system consists of a single particle.
As usual, we suppose that this particle can be characterized at any
instant by its displacement x from some reference position, and by
its velocity v. We shall also suppose the particle endowed with a
single constitutive parameter; its (inertial) mass m. Hence at any
instant the particle possesses a momentum p = mv.

The situation in which such a system is totally uncoupled or unlinked
to any environmental quality is explicitly expressed in Newton's
First Law: such a particle is either at rest, or in uniform motion
in a straight line with constant velocity.[1]

Thus, if a particle is *not* moving in a straight line, and/or if its
velocity is not constant, then it is *by definition* experiencing some
interaction with its environment. This is expressed by saying that
there is a *force* (or more precisely, an external force) acting on it.
The extent of the deviation of the particle from uniform motion can
in fact be taken as a *measure* of the external force. This deviation
is characterized by the instantaneous value of the particle's *acceleration* a; thus the substance of Newton's *Second* Law is to identify
the environmentally imposed force with the acceleration, weighted
by the particle's inertial mass: F = ma.

Particle mechanics thus begins by explicitly characterizing what a
non-interacting system is; namely, it is a system in which acceleration is absent. This characterization is intrinsic, and in Newtonian
mechanics it has an absolute character.

Let us now consider a slightly more complex mechanical system; one
consisting of several particles. We suppose that these particles
can exert forces on each other, but such forces are entirely *internal*
to the system itself. How can we determine whether such a system is
also interacting with its environment; i.e. whether there are
external forces imposed upon it?

Here again, classical mechanics provides an absolute, intrinsic
prescription. We simply write down all the forces acting on each
particle of the system, including both those arising from the other
particles, and those arising externally. We now invoke Newton's
Third Law, which states that if any particle of the system exerts a
force on a second particle of the system, then the second exerts an
equal and opposite force on the first. Thus, when we add up all the
forces imposed on all the particles, *the internal forces will sum to
zero*. Consequently, if the sum of all the forces on all the particles
of the system is identically zero, there are by definition no external
forces acting on the system; the system is isolated. Conversely,
if the system is isolated, the sum of all the forces will vanish
identically. It is easy to show that the diagnostic that our system
be isolated from external forces is that its center of mass should
not accelerate.

Thus, the Three Laws of Newton can be precisely regarded as specifying
when a mechanical system is isolated. As we noted earlier, an isolated system is one for which we cannot infer the existence of anything outside the system by looking at the system itself. These

isolated systems thus provide the fundamental standards by which environmental interactions (i.e. impressed external forces) are recognized. It is precisely the deviation of a system from the behavior of an isolated system which allows us to infer that something exists outside the system, and which we can in fact take as the *measure* of that external quality. This situation is indeed analogous to that of a *meter*, which cannot provide meaningful measurements until a zero-point is established through isolating it initially from the quality it is intended to measure. Here, the behavior of a mechanical system unacted upon by external forces is the zero-point; that behavior is precisely what is characterized by Newton's Laws. This is in fact an important general point, which should be kept in mind as we proceed: a system which is open can be regarded as a meter for those environmental qualities with which it is in interaction, when its behavior is referred to that manifested in the *absence* of such an interaction.

Let us now recast these remarks in terms of explicit linkage relations. Suppose we have a system of N particles, with displacements x_1, ..., x_N, and velocities v_1, ..., v_N. Let us suppose further that the only forces acting on any particle are those arising from other particles, and that Newton's Third Law is satisfied. We shall now write down the equations of motion of the system.

According to the Second Law, the equation of motion of the kth particle in the system is

$$m_k \frac{d^2 x_k}{dt^2} = \sum_{i=1}^{N} F_{ik} \qquad (5.2.1)$$

where m_k is the inertial mass of the kth particle, and F_{ik} is the force imposed on that particle by the ith particle of the system. We suppose that the value of this force F_{ik} depends only on the distance between the ith and k^{th} particles at an instant. We allow the differential of time in this case to be arbitrary; it will "cancel out" in the considerations to follow. Indeed, if we multiply both sides of the equation (5.2.1) by the velocity dx_k/dt, we may rewrite the equation as

$$m_k v_k \, dv_k = \left(\sum_{i=1}^{n} F_{ik} \right) dx_k . \qquad (5.2.2)$$

There is a kind of linkage which we have seen extensively in the preceding section; specifically, it links a differential velocity increment dv_k with a differential displacement increment dx_k, when the system is in some state $(x_1, ..., x_N, v_1, ..., v_n)$. We have such a linkage relation (5.2.2) for each particle of the system; i.e. for each $k = 1, ..., N$.

The family of linkage relations (5.2.2) provide a local *accounting*, which tells us how an increment of displacement is to be converted into an increment of velocity at any state of our system. We have seen earlier that such linkages arise as simple expressions of causality; they must exist if a given initial state is to uniquely determine the state after a differential time increment has elapsed.

The specific *form* of the linkages is equivalent to the equations of
motion (for a suitable definition of time increment, as we saw
abundantly in Chapter 4.3 above), and in the present case is determined entirely by the forces imposed on the system.

Thus, if our mechanical system is isolated from external forces, the
local accounting by which differential displacement increments are
converted to differential velocity increments at any state must be
given by the linkages (5.2.2), in which $F_{ik} = - F_{ki}$ by Newton's
Third Law. If we think of these differential increments dv_k, dx_k as
representing *flows* of the state variables, then this accounting tells
us how any flow dx_k is compensated by a corresponding flow dv_k in any
state, and conversely. Thus, *according to these linkages (5.2.2),
every flow in the system is compensated; there are no uncompensated
flows.*

What happens if we now impose some external force on our system?
Obviously, the original equations of motion (5.2.1) must now be replaced by new equations of the form

$$m_k \frac{d^2 x_k}{dt^2} = F_k + \sum_{i=1}^{N} F_{ik} \qquad (5.2.3)$$

(where F_k denotes the external force acting on the kth particle, and
is assumed to be a function of displacements alone). Likewise, the
original accounting rules (5.2.2) are no longer valid; they must be
replaced by rules of the form

$$m_k v_k dv_k = \left(F_k + \sum_{i=1}^{N} F_{ik} \right) dx_k \qquad (5.2.4)$$

If we now compare (5.2.4) with (5.2.2), we see the effect of imposing
the external force F_k: *when such a force is present, the original
accounting rules (5.2.2) give rise to an uncompensated flow.* In
particular, we find discrepancies between the actual increments
dx_k arising from a given increment dv_k in a state, and those which
our accounting (5.2.2) tells us compensate for that increment. It
is in this sense that the imposition of an external force appears
to generate uncompensated flows.

Thus it is that the imposition of a new interaction between the
system and its environment (i.e. the imposition of an external force)
causes our initial accounting rules to break down. As we see, the
diagnostic of this breakdown is the appearance of uncompensated
flows; differential increments of state variables which cannot be
"paid for" by decrements elsewhere internal to the system. On this
basis, *the appearance of such an uncompensated flow implies the
existence of something outside the system,* which acts as a source
or sink for the uncompensated flows. The effect of passing from
(5.2.2) to (5.2.4) is to "internalize" such sources and sinks, by
establishing a *new accounting* in which all the flows are again
compensated.

Let us note two features of this situation, before we reformulate
its basic features in general dynamical terms. The first point is
the following: when we impose an external force on a system of

particles, the expression of that force as a conversion factor between
a differential increment of displacement and a differential increment
of velocity typically requires us to introduce new quantities into
the equations of motion, which play the role of new constitutive
parameters. Thus for instance, if we convert a single free particle
into a harmonic oscillator by introducing an external force of the
form $F = -kx$, the parameter k expresses precisely how a unit increment
dx of displacement in a state (x, v) is to be converted to an increment of velocity; the analog of (5.2.4) for this system is

$$kx \, dx + mv \, dv = 0. \tag{5.2.5}$$

This quantity k pertains to the *external* force imposed on a free
particle. But when the quantity is "internalized" to give the new
accounting relation (5.2.5), in which all flows are now compensated,
we can regard k as an *internal* constitutive parameter of our new
system, playing the same kind of role as does the inertial mass m.
Thus, in a sense, the number of constitutive parameters appearing
in accounting relations like (5.2.5) (and hence in the equations of
motion to which these relations give rise) indicate how many external
forces have been internalized in passing from an absolutely free
(i.e. non-interacting or isolated) system to the one under consideration. We shall return to this point in a moment.

The second feature we wish to discuss is the relation between a
particular kind of accounting, like (5.2.2) or (5.2.4), in which every
flow is compensated, and the formulation of global conservation laws.
Intuitively speaking, if there is no interaction between a system
and its environment, then there can in particular be no flow or exchange of qualities between them. Specifically, there can be no
sources or sinks for system variables in the external environment.
Thus, we would expect some kind of conservation law to be applicable
to the system, which would take the form of a global linkage relation
involving those system qualities which are sources or sinks for each
other. The differential accounting relation (5.2.2) or (5.2.4),
in which all flows are compensated, provide in fact a local expression
of this kind of expectation.

The passage from local accounting relations to a global conserved
quantity is formally equivalent to the integration of a differential
form. In general, a local accounting like (5.2.2) or (5.2.4) can be
expressed as

$$\sum_{i=1}^{N} M_i dx_i + \sum_{i=1}^{N} N_i dv_i = 0 \tag{5.2.6}$$

where the M_i, N_i are functions of the state to which the differential
increments dx_i, dv_i are referred. If this differential form (5.2.6)
is exact, then there is a single function $K = K(x_1, \ldots, v_n)$ such
that

$$dK = \sum_{i=1}^{N} M_i dx_i + \sum_{i=1}^{N} N_i dv_i; \tag{5.2.7}$$

i.e. such that

$$M_i = \frac{\partial K}{\partial x_i}; \qquad N_i = \frac{\partial K}{\partial v_i}$$

In that case, it follows that this observable K is a conserved quantity in a global sense, and we may say that there is no "flow" of
this observable between the system and its environment. In mechanics,
of course, such an observable is generally available; it is the
Hamiltonian or total energy of the system. To say that energy is
conserved in a system like (5.2.3) means precisely that the effects
of all forces have been internalized into the accounting relations
(5.2.4); i.e. that there are no uncompensated flows in the local
accounting. However, not every local accounting can give rise to a
global conserved quantity; even if all flows are locally compensated,
there need be no observable of the system which is conserved. This
is the case when the system is "dissipative"; we shall return to this
situation in more detail subsequently.

Let us now return to the main line of our argument, and consider the
extent to which the concepts we have introduced can be formulated in
general terms. The heart of the argument was to compare the properties
of a completely isolated system with its properties when allowed to
interact with its environment; i.e. when an externally arising force
is imposed on it. The non-interacting situation is characterized by
the presence of local accounting relations, in which every flow is
compensated. Relative to this accounting relation, the imposition
of an external force creates non-compensated flows. The nature of
these non-compensated flows then leads to a characterization of the
external force responsible for them, and thereby to a new accounting
relation, describing the properties of the interaction, with respect
to which all flows are again compensated.

The crux of this situation will be seen to rest upon the following
data:

1. a system in which all flows are compensated, to serve as a
    reference;

2. the same system, which is now placed in interaction with its
    environment in a particular way;

3. the generation of uncompensated flows, as measured against the
    reference system.

In our previous discussion, we have taken as reference system one
which is initially totally isolated. But we can now see that this
restriction is quite unnecessary; we may take as our initial reference *any system in which all flows are compensated*. In some absolute
sense, a system of this kind may generally be regarded to be interacting with its environment, but the assumption of compensation means
that these interactions have all been internalized. Hence, such a
system can be regarded as isolated from any other environmental interaction, aside from the internalized ones. It can thus be utilized
as a reference system, against which we may characterize the effects
of new environmental interactions. We need to have a name for such
a reference system, which need not be isolated in an absolute sense,
but can be regarded as isolated from the standpoint of a particular
modality of environmental interaction. In line with the above
arguments, we propose to call such a system a *compensated system*.
A compensated system is thus one for which local accounting rules
are given; these rules embody the internalization of all sources
and sinks for flows of the state variables. In thermodynamic terms,
a compensated system could only be described as "partially open".
The environment of such a system comprises every quality which has
not been internalized, and by definition, the system is totally isolated from that environment.

The study of such compensated systems, and the relations which can exist between them, will be the main object of the remainder of the present section.

REFERENCES AND NOTES

1. This kind of discussion always presupposes a single (fixed) observer. Otherwise, relativistic considerations immediately come into play; e.g. an accelerated observer will immediately impute a force (i.e. a particle-environment interaction) to account for the motion he observes.

5.3 Compensation and Decompensation

In accord with the ideas developed in the preceding chapter, let us
suppose we are given a compensated system $S°$, which will play the
role of a reference system. As we saw, $S°$ need not be isolated from
its environment in any absolute sense; but the hypothesis that it is
compensated means precisely that those interactions which it under-
goes with its environment have already been internalized into its
local accounting relations.

Let us express these ideas formally. Suppose that the states of $S°$
can be represented by means of the values assumed by a set $\{x_1,
..., x_n\}$ of state variables, and that the states so represented form
a manifold in Euclidean n-dimensional space. Then the hypothesis
that $S°$ is compensated means that there is a linkage relation of the
form

$$\sum_{i=1}^{n} M_i dx_i = 0 \qquad (5.3.1)$$

which relates the increments dx_i attached to a state to the state
itself. The coefficients M_i are, of course, functions of state
$(x_1, ..., x_n)$. However, they will in general also contain constitutive parameters $\alpha_1, ..., \alpha_r$ which arise from the internalization
of whatever environmental interactions to which $S°$ is exposed. Thus,
we may write $M_i = M_i(x_1, ..., x_n, \alpha_1, ..., \alpha_r)$.

Now let us suppose that an additional external force is imposed on
$S°$; i.e. a new interaction modality is established between $S°$ and
its environment. As we have seen in the preceding chapter, the
effect of this force will be to produce flows in the increments dx_i
which are uncompensated from the standpoint of the accounting (5.3.1).
Let us suppose that the uncompensated portion of the ith flow can be
expressed in the form

$$N_i dx_i \qquad (5.3.2)$$

where each N_i is a function of state, and in general also involves
some new constitutive parameters $\alpha_{r+1}, \ldots, \alpha_{r+s}$. The existence of
these functions N_i, in terms of which the uncompensated portion of
the flows can be expressed, is a consequence of the general hypothesis
of causality which we have employed repeatedly before.

We can now *internalize* these uncompensated flows (5.3.2), by combining
them with (5.3.1). Namely, each total flow in the new situation can
be regarded as a sum of two terms: (a) a term arising from the original accounting (5.3.1), and (b) a term comprising exactly that part
of the flow which is uncompensated according to that accounting.
Thus, the linkage relation appropriate to describe the effect of the
new force imposed on S° is no longer given by (5.3.1), but must be
written as

$$\sum_{i=1}^{n} (M_i + N_i)dx_i = 0. \tag{5.3.3}$$

The coefficients of the differential form (5.3.3) are functions of
the state variables, the original set of constitutive parameters
$\alpha_1, \ldots, \alpha_r$ describing the system when isolated from the new external
force, and the additional constitutive parameters $\alpha_{r+1}, \ldots, \alpha_{r+s}$
which enter into the expression (5.3.2) of the uncompensated flows
arising from that new force. The new accounting relations (5.3.3)
thus describe a new system S; S is itself a compensated system, but
it clearly has quite different properties from the isolated system
S° from which it arose. However, let us note explicitly that *(5.3.3)
is a generalization of (5.3.1); it reduces exactly to (5.3.1) when
$N_i = 0$ for each i;* i.e. when S is again isolated from the new
external force.

It is of great importance that this entire argument can be run backwards. Namely, suppose that S is now a compensated system, whose
local accounting is expressed by the linkage relation

$$\sum_{i=1}^{n} M_i dx_i = 0 \tag{5.3.4}$$

where $M_i = M_i(x_1, \ldots, x_n, \alpha_1, \ldots, \alpha_r)$. Let us now suppose that
we isolate this system from one of the environmental forces imposed
upon it, and suppose that this isolation is equivalent to placing
some subset of the constitutive parameters equal to zero. In this
way, we obtain a new compensated system S°, describable by a linkage
of the form

$$\sum_{i=1}^{n} M_i^{\circ} dx_i = 0. \tag{5.3.5}$$

where the M_i° are obtained from the corresponding functions M_i by
setting the appropriate constitutive parameters equal to zero. Then
S and S° are related as in the previous discussion; from the standpoint of S°, S appears to exhibit uncompensated flows given precisely
by

$$(M_i - M_i^{\circ})dx_i, \qquad i = 1, \ldots, n.$$

These relations will be of great importance to us when we come to compare the dynamical behaviors arising in two such systems S and S°.

Finally, let us see explicitly what happens to conserved quantities when we pass between systems related like S and S°. Thus, let us return to the expression (5.3.1) above, which we will suppose is a perfect differential; i.e.

$$\sum_{i=1}^{n} M_i dx_i = dH° = 0$$

where H° is some observable of the form $H°(x_1, \ldots, x_n, \alpha_1, \ldots, \alpha_r)$. Then we know that H° is conserved; there is no flow of H° between the system S° and its environment.

If S° is now exposed to a new external force, so that the new linkage between states and their differential increments is given by (5.3.3) rather than (5.3.1), we can still write (5.3.3) in the form

$$dH° + \sum_{i=1}^{n} N_i dx_i = 0. \qquad (5.3.6)$$

By definition, the differential form appearing in (5.3.6) cannot vanish; i.e.

$$\sum_{i=1}^{n} N_i dx_i \neq 0.$$

Thus, H° cannot remain conserved in the larger system S. However, it can happen that we can write

$$\sum_{i=1}^{n} N_i dx_i = dH$$

for some observable $H = H(x_1, \ldots, x_n, \alpha_{r+1}, \ldots, \alpha_{r+s})$, which depends on the original state variables and some new constitutive parameters. In that case, it is clear that the function $K = H° + H$ is conserved on S, although neither H° nor H is separately conserved. In the special case in which H° is a Hamiltonian for S°, and the N_i are mechanical forces arising from a potential, so that

$$N_i = - \frac{\partial U}{\partial x_i}$$

for some potential function U, then H is the additional energy arising from the applied force, and $K = H° + H$ is the Hamiltonian for the larger system S.

Just as before, this argument can be run backwards. Thus, if K is conserved on the larger system S, and we obtain S° from S by setting the new constitutive parameters equal to zero, there will be a conserved quantity H° on S° if and only if the resulting differential form (5.3.1) is exact.

5.4 The Main Theorem

We are now ready to develop some crucial results which relate the temporal behavior of a system which is closed to some modality of environmental interaction to that of the same system when open to that interaction.

Let us begin by restating our terminology. We shall start with a given system $S°$; this will be our closed system, or reference. We assume that it is encoded into a family $x_1, \ldots, x_n$ of state variables, and that the totality of states thus encoded fill a state space which is a manifold $X \subseteq E_n$. We suppose also that the system is further determined by a family $\alpha_1, \ldots, \alpha_r$ of constitutive parameters, which remain unaffected by any change of state which occurs in the system. Finally, we suppose that the temporal behavior of $S°$ is governed by a family of equations of motion, of the form

$$dx_i/dt = f_i(x_1, \ldots, x_n, \alpha_1, \ldots, \alpha_r) \qquad (5.4.1)$$

for $i = 1, \ldots, n$. These equations of motion are to be interpreted according to the discussion given in Chapter 5.2 and 5.3 above.

We shall be comparing the behaviors of $S°$ with those of a new system S, which intuitively is obtained by allowing $S°$ to be open to a new modality of environmental interaction. More specifically, we shall assume: (a) that the states of S are encoded into exactly the same state space X into which the states of $S°$ were encoded; (b) that in addition to the original structural parameters $\alpha_1, \ldots, \alpha_r$ of $S°$, we must adjoin an additional number $\alpha_{r+1}, \ldots, \alpha_{r+s}$ of new parameters; (c) that the equations of motion of S can be represented in the form

$$dx_i/dt = g_i(x_1, \ldots, x_n, \alpha_1, \ldots, \alpha_{r+s}) \qquad (5.4.2)$$

for $i = 1, \ldots, n$. Finally, we shall express the idea that $S°$ and S are the *same* system, albeit exposed to different environmental circumstances, by requiring that

$$g_i(x_1, \ldots, x_n, \alpha_1, \ldots, \alpha_r, 0, \ldots, 0)$$

$$= f_i(x_1, \ldots, x_n, \alpha_1, \ldots, \alpha_r).$$

That is, by putting new constitutive parameters $\alpha_{r+1}, \ldots, \alpha_{r+s}$ equal to zero in S, we obtain precisely the system S°.

Now let us suppose that at some initial instant of time t   0, both of our systems S° and S are in the same state, namely $(x_1(0) \ldots, x_n(0))$. Assuming that the unique trajectory property holds for both systems, this common initial state will determine a single trajectory in X representing the temporal behavior of S°, and another single trajectory in X representing the temporal behavior of S. This situation is diagrammed in Figure 5.4.1 below:

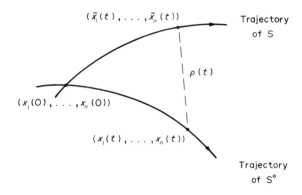

Fig. 5.4.1.

After some time interval t has elapsed, the system S° will be in a state $(x_1(t), \ldots, x_n(t))$ on its trajectory, while the system S will be in another state $(\bar{x}_1(t), \ldots, \bar{x}_n(t))$, as indicated in the Figure.

The time scale t is taken to be a common time valid for both systems, as can be chosen by selecting appropriate scale factors according to the discussion in Chapter 4.3 above; we henceforth assume that the dynamical equations (5.4.1) and (5.4.2) already incorporate these scale factors.

It is clear, from the way in which the systems (5.4.1) and (5.4.2) were defined, that the respective tangent vectors to the initial common state $(x_1(0), \ldots, x_n(0))$ *cannot be the same*. Hence the two trajectories determined in S° and S respectively by this common initial state must diverge from each other, at least initially. This divergence is represented explicitly in Figure 5.4.1 by the Euclidean distance $\rho(t) = [\Sigma(x_i(t) - \bar{x}_i(t))^2]^{\frac{1}{2}}$. *Our main interest will be to study the behavior of this divergence as a function of time.* Intuitively, this divergence can be regarded as the "dissipation" introduced into S° by opening it to a new modality of environmental interaction, this dissipation is a direct consequence of the creation of uncompensated flows.

We have already seen that the dissipation, or divergence, between
trajectories of $S°$ and S determined by a common initial state is
initially positive. We shall now argue that it is also terminally
positive; i.e. that

$$\lim_{t \to \infty} \rho(t) > 0.$$

We shall do this by showing that the transition from $S°$ to S can be
regarded as inducing a transformation $\alpha : X \to X$ of the common state
space of $S°$ and S. The effect of this transformation is to move the
states in X, and in particular, to move the limiting states (or more
generally, the limiting sets) to which trajectories of $S°$ and S tend
as $t \to \infty$. This kind of result is, of course, expected on intuitive
grounds; if we recall our analogy between an open system S and a
meter, we will observe that the essence of a meter is to manifest a
different limiting behavior when a measurement is being performed
than when the meter is isolated.

Let us then suppose that our system $S°$ satisfies the general accounting
relation

$$\sum_{i=1}^{n} M_i(x_1, \ldots, x_n) dx_i = 0 \qquad (5.4.3)$$

in accord with (5.3.1) above. We shall further suppose that the open
system S satisfies the accounting relation

$$\sum_{i=1}^{n} (M_i + N_i) d\overline{x}_i = 0, \qquad (5.4.4)$$

where we will denote the state variables for S by dashed quantities
$\overline{x}_i$ to distinguish them from those pertaining to $S°$. Thus, in particular, when discussing S, we shall write $M_i = M_i(\overline{x}_1, \ldots, \overline{x}_n)$,
$N_i = N_i(\overline{x}_1, \ldots, \overline{x}_n)$.

We next observe that, according to the discussion of Chapter 4.5
above, the equations of motion (5.4.1) and (5.4.2), describing $S°$
and S respectively, express the relations between differential increments of the state variables at a state and a differential increment of time. Thus, for $S°$, we have

$$dx_i = f_i dt, \qquad i = 1, \ldots, n; \qquad (5.4.5)$$

and for S we have

$$d\overline{x}_i = g_i dt, \qquad i = 1, \ldots, n. \qquad (5.4.6)$$

According to Chapter 4.5, we can take these differential time increments to be the same by incorporating an appropriate scale factor
$a(\overline{x}_1, \ldots, \overline{x}_n)$ into the functions g_i; for simplicity, we shall
assume this done, so that the trajectories of $S°$ and S are traversed
in a common time.

Combining (5.4.5) and (5.4.6) with (5.4.3) and (5.4.4), we obtain
global linkage relations for $S°$ and S: explicitly, we have

$$\sum_{i=1}^{n} M_i f_i = 0 \qquad (5.4.7)$$

for S°, and the corresponding relation

$$\sum_{i=1}^{n} (M_i + N_i) g_i = 0 \qquad (5.4.8)$$

for S. These relations are the basic ones we shall need to complete our argument.

Let us look initially at the relation (5.4.7). We observe that this relation has the form of an orthogonality condition; it basically asserts that two n-vectors, namely

$$\vec{f} = (f_1, \ldots, f_n)$$

and

$$\vec{M} = (M_1, \ldots, M_n)$$

are orthoginal to each other in some suitable vector space of functions. Likewise, the relation (5.4.8) asserts that the two vectors

$$\vec{g} = (g_1, \ldots, g_n)$$

and

$$\vec{M} + \vec{N} = (M_1 + N_1, \ldots, M_n + N_n)$$

are orthogonal in this *same* space.

Now the replacement of $\vec{M}$ by $\vec{M} + \vec{N}$ in this vector space must involve a *rotation* of the space. If we think of this replacement as a *perturbation* of $\vec{M}$, the result of the perturbation cannot simply be to multiply the components of $\vec{M}$ by a constant factor. For, by our preceding arguments, the effect of multiplying the M_i by such a constant factor would be simply to change the time scale according to which the trajectories of S° are traversed, while leaving the trajectories of S° invariant. On the other hand, we know that the trajectories of S° and S are different, as was indicated in Figure 5.4.1 above. From this it follows that the transition from $\vec{M}$ to $\vec{M} + \vec{N}$ must involve a rotation, as asserted.

One consequence of this rotation of $\vec{M}$ is that $\vec{M} + \vec{N}$ will no longer be orthogonal to $\vec{f}$. To restore orthogonality, we must correspondingly rotate $\vec{f}$; in effect, the vector $\vec{g}$ can be regarded as arising by *applying the same rotation to $\vec{f}$ as was applied to $\vec{M}$.* Indeed, the relation (5.4.8) embodies simply the statement that such a rotation of both $\vec{M}$ and $\vec{f}$ preserves orthogonality.

Now it is a general theorem that a rotation in a space of functions defined on a space X arises from a suitable transformation $\alpha : X \to X$ of that underlying space. More specifically, if U denotes such a rotation, and if $\vec{h}$ is a function of X, we can write

$$(U\vec{h})(x) = \vec{h}(\alpha x) \qquad (5.4.9)$$

for any x in X. Intuitively, this transformation α is the one which relates the points on the trajectories of S° to those of S, as for instance illustrated in Figure 5.4.1 above. In particular, it readily follows that the limiting behaviors of these trajectories will also be moved in general by α. Stated another way, the *attractors* to which trajectories of S° and S, initially determined by a common state, will move in X are different, and hence the distance between them must be positive.

Now let us obtain an estimate for the discrepancy between the state $(x_1(t), \ldots, x_n(t))$ of S° and the corresponding state $(\bar{x}_1(t), \ldots, \bar{x}_n(t))$ of S at a given instant t, given that the two systems were initially in the same state. As we noted above, this discrepancy is measured by the Euclidean distance

$$\rho(t) = \sum_{i=1}^{n} \left[(x_i(t) - \bar{x}_i(t))^2 \right]^{\frac{1}{2}} \qquad (5.4.10)$$

between these states in X. Using this relation, we can also obtain an expression for the rate at which this discrepancy is increasing at any time. In fact, by differentiating (5.4.10), and considering the quantities $x_i(t)$, $\bar{x}_i(t)$ as independent variables, we find

$$\rho\frac{d\rho}{dt} = \sum_{i=1}^{n} (x_i - \bar{x}_i)(\frac{dx_i}{dt} - \frac{d\bar{x}_i}{dt}) \qquad (5.4.11)$$

In fact, however, these quantities are not independent; they are connected by the transformation α defined above. That is, given that the two trajectories of S° and S respectively are determined by a common initial state in X, we can generally express the dashed quantities, pertaining to S, as explicit functions of the undashed quantities, pertaining to S°, evaluated at the same instant. Thus we can write

$$\bar{x}_i(t) = \bar{x}_i(x_1(t), \ldots, x_n(t)). \qquad (5.4.12)$$

Using these relations, the expression (5.4.11) can be considered as a function of the n variables $x_1(t), \ldots, x_n(t)$ alone, instead of as a function of 2n variables. Thus, from a knowledge of the state of S° at a given instant, and the transformation rules (5.4.12), we can compute the discrepancy between this state and the corresponding state of S determined by the same initial state as S° at t = 0.

As we noted earlier, the discrepancy $\rho(t)$ between states of S° and S which we have defined is a measure of the *dissipation* introduced by opening S° to a new modality of environmental interaction. It is thus of interest to express this dissipation explicitly in terms of the differential flows of the state variables at a state. From (5.4.11) and (5.4.12) this can be readily done. In fact, we can write

$$\rho d\rho = \sum_{i=1}^{n} (x_i - \bar{x}_i(x_1, \ldots, x_n)) (dx_i - \sum_{j=1}^{n} \frac{\partial \bar{x}_i}{\partial x_j} dx_j) \quad (5.4.13)$$

$$= \sum_{i=1}^{n} K_i(x_1, \ldots, x_n) dx_i \qquad (5.4.14)$$

where the functions $K_i(x_1, \ldots, x_n)$ can be written explicitly from

(5.4.13). These functions K_i depend both on the instantaneous
values of the state variables o S° and S, and of their instantaneous
rates of change. On the other hand, the expression (5.4.14) also
clearly represents the uncompensated flows arising at a state of S°
when S° is opened to the new modality of environmental interaction.
From this, we can see that these functions K_i are essentially the
same as the functions N_i introduced in Chapter 5.3 above, and allow
an alternative expression of them, measured now in terms of dissipation
arising from the interaction.

Finally, let us note that in order to compute $\rho(t)$ explicitly, it is
necessary and sufficient that both S° and S be known; i.e. that the
functions f_i in (5.4.1) and the functions g_i in (5.4.2) be given.
From this data, we can in particular compute the instant at which the
deviation between S° and S becomes greater than some pre-assigned
threshold quantity θ. As we shall see in subsequent chapters, this
kind of "critical instant" has a profound significance for the relation
between a system S and a dynamical encoding of it.

The results of the present chapter can be summed up succinctly in
the following way: *no system S can be indistinguishable from a subsystem S° of itself*. There must always exist a set of environmental
circumstances in which a discrepancy between the behavior of S, and
the corresponding behavior of the subsystem S° in those circumstances,
will appear.

5.5 Models as Closed Systems

We are now in a position to reconsider the modelling relation, in the light of the results just obtained. In particular, we are going to explore the proposition that the relation between a natural system and a dynamical model of it is the same as that existing between a system closed to some modality of environmental interaction and the same system which is open to such an interaction. In each case, there will be a discrepancy between the behavior of the system involved; between corresponding trajectories of the closed and open system, and between the predictions of the model and the behavior being modelled. And in each case, this discrepancy arises because of a tacit process of *abstraction*; the neglect or omission of interactions present in one of the systems (the open one) and necessarily absent in the other.

Let us begin by re-stating the modelling relation between a natural system and a formal one. We recall that a model is generated by an encoding of observables. It is necessarily an abstraction, because any observation or evaluation of observables on states is already an abstraction (cf. Chapter 3.2 above). Indeed, we may recognize that there are two distinct kinds of abstractions involved in such an encoding: (a) a neglect of observable quantities pertaining to the system itself, and (b) a neglect of environmental quantities, which are capable of causing change of state even in that subsystem retained in the encoding. Thus, as we have stated above, any such encoding serves tacitly to *unlink* the encoded observables from those other qualities of both system and environment which are not encoded.

Using the language introduced in the preceding chapters of the present section, let us designate that subsystem of a natural system S which has been encoded into a formal model by S°. We shall assume that the inferential structure present in the formal model is in fact a faithful representation of the behavior of S°, when S is in fact closed to all interactions not explicitly incorporated into the model. These interactions include both those arising from the remainder of the system S, and those which come from outside of S. We repeat that this formally assumes that the behavior of S° is *unlinked* to any quantity not explicitly encoded; i.e. an arbitrary change can be made in any such quality without affecting any behavior of S°.

It will now be seen that the relation we have posited between $S°$ and
S is precisely the one which has been discussed at length above. It
is this fact which makes it possible for us to discuss the relation
between a system and a model in the same terms that we used to discuss
the relation between a closed system and an open one. In particular,
we want to translate the growth of discrepancies between behavior of
$S°$ and S into the deviation between the predictions of a dynamical
model and the actual behavior of the system being modelled.

Let us restate these hypotheses, using the formal language developed
in Chapter 3.3 above. We assume that we have a natural system, whose
set of abstract states we will designate by S. We have also a family
of observables $x_1, \ldots, x_n$, which may be evaluated on these abstract
states. In particular, if $s_0 \in S$ is the abstract state of our system
at some particular instant of time, we encode this state into a corresponding n-tuple of numbers:

$$s_0 \rightarrow (x_1(s_0), \ldots, x_n(s_0)).$$

The totality of n-tuples arising in this way we suppose to fill out
a manifold X in Euclidean n-dimensional space; this is the state
space of the system arising from the particular encoding we have
chosen. The entire situation can be represented by a diagram of the
form

$$S \xrightarrow{\delta} S^n \xrightarrow{(x_1, \ldots, x_n)} X$$

which we have seen before.

We now suppose that the state of our natural system S is changing
in time. We further suppose, for the moment, that this change of
state in S can be faithfully represented in formal terms by a dynamics
imposed on the state space X. At this level of formalization, it
is sufficient to represent the dynamics by a one-parameter family of
transformations on X:

$$T_t : X \rightarrow X.$$

Explicitly, when we say that the change of state in S is *faithfully*
represented by the dynamics $\{T_t\}$, we mean the following: given any
initial state s_0 in S, we evaluate the observables $x_1, \ldots, x_n$ on s_0
to obtain a definite encoding $(x_1(s_0), \ldots, x_n(s_0))$ of s_0 in X. We
then apply any transformation T_t in our dynamics to this encoded
state. We obtain thereby a uniquely determined point of X, of the
form

$$T_t(x_1(s_0), \ldots, x_n(s_0))$$

which we may denote by $(x_1(t), \ldots, x_n(t))$. On the other hand, the
state of our natural system is also changing in S. Suppose that at
the particular instant t considered above, the system is in a definite
state s(t). Let us now evaluate our observables $x_1, \ldots, x_n$ on this
state s(t). This clearly gives us another n-tuple $(x_1(s(t)), \ldots,$
$x_n(s(t)))$ in X. We assert that the two n-tuples obtained in this

fashion *are the same* for each instant t;   i.e. that

$$x_i(t) = x_i(s(t))$$

for each i = 1, ..., n. In other words, the *prediction* about the state of our natural system at time t, given an initial encoded state in X, is always exactly verified. Thus, the inferential structure of our encoding (i.e the dynamics $\{T_t\}$) is a precise expression of the dynamical processes occurring in S; every *theorem* in our formal system (cf. Chapter 4.6 above) is verified by direct observation in S.

As usual, we can represent this kind of situation by means of a commutative diagram:

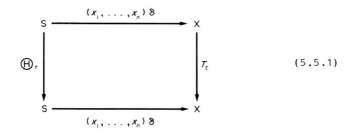

$$(5.5.1)$$

Here we have denoted by $\textcircled{H}_t$ the actual dynamical changes occurring in the abstract set of states S. The commutativity of the diagram means precisely that for each instant t, the mappings $\textcircled{H}_t$ and T_t are *models* of each other; we can translate between them precisely by means of the encoding mapping $(x_1, ..., x_n)\delta$. In more precise mathematical language, $\textcircled{H}_t$ and T_t are *conjugate*. We note explicitly that we will have a separate diagram of the form (5.5.1) for each instant of time t; i.e. (5.5.1) represents a one-parameter family of diagrams.

Now we observe that what we have in fact captured through the above encoding is a specific subsystem S° of S. The hypothesis that the dynamics $\{T_t\}$ on X precisely captures the change of state in S means that this subsystem S° is unlinked to the remainder of the system, or to any mode of environmental interaction besides those responsible for the changes of state $\textcircled{H}_t$ in S°. Under these circumstances, our model for S° is also a model for all of S.

Now let us assume that at some initial instant (which we may take as t = 0) these hypotheses fail to be satisfied. That is, at t = 0 some linkage relation is established between S° and uncoded observables in S, and/or between S° and a new environmental modality. As we have seen, this means that the system S° is no longer closed; it also means that the diagrams (5.5.1) will no longer be exactly commutative.

However, there is a sense in which the diagrams will remain *approxi-mately* commutative, in the following sense. Let $\varepsilon > 0$ be some small positive quantity. Then for any time t, we may compute for any initial state $s_0 \in S$ the discrepancy in X arising from the two paths in the diagram (5.5.1); i.e. the distance between

$$T_t(x_1, \ldots, x_n)\delta (s_0)$$

and

$$((x_1, \ldots, x_n)\delta) \circledH_t (s_0).$$

We may say that the diagram *approximately commutes* for this time instant t if this discrepancy is smaller than ε.

The results of the preceding chapter can now be invoked. In general, there will be some finite *critical instant* $t = t_c$ for which *the diagram no longer approximately commutes*. At this critical instant, the prediction obtained by applying our computative model T_{t_c} to the encoding of our initial state s_0 differs from the encoding of the actual state $\circledH_{t_c}(s_0)$ by more than the allowed amount ε. Thus, at the critical instant, we lose even the approximate conjugacy of the mappings $\circledH_t$ and T_t. In other words: for all times t such that $0 < t < t_c$, we retain an approximate conjugacy between our original model T_t on X and the actual dynamics $\circledH_t$ on S. For times greater then the critical time, this approximate conjugacy fails.

The actual value of the critical instant t_c obviously depends on (a) the specific character of the dynamics $\{T_t\}$ on X, and (b) the manner in which the subsystem S° has become linked to other non-en-coded quantities. It is clear that this latter is in principle *not predictable* solely from a knowledge of S° as a closed system. It can only be predicted if we know the new linkages established between S° and its environment. In the discussion of the preceding chapter, this knowledge was assumed; hence in that case it was possible to explicitly predict the value of t_c for any given initial state s_0 and any particular value of the measure of closeness ε. Thus, from the standpoint of S° alone, we cannot in principle predict that the modelling relation will fail, nor is it possible to predict when such a failure will take place.

It is important to cast these considerations into the language of *bifurcations*. As we saw in Example 5 of Chapter 3.1 above, bifurcation and the failure of a conjugacy relation are essentially synonymous; hence it should not be surprising to find that the opening of a system like S° should involve a bifurcation in an essential way. We stressed earlier that a bifurcation always involves the appearance of a logical independence between two descriptions; or what is the same thing, the failure of a specific linkage relation between the descriptions to be maintained. Of course, that is exactly what is happening in the present case; a description based on a closed system S° is becoming unlinked to the behavior of the same system when opened to further

interactions. In this case, it is the *time* which is acting as the
bifurcation parameter; at a definite critical instant $t = t_c$, the
discrepancy between the behavior of the two systems exceeds a pre-
assigned threshold.

In greater detail: let I denote the set of instants in which time
is measured in the original system S_0. Then in particular, the elements of I constitute the set of parameters for both of the one-
parameter families of transformations $\{T_t\}$, $\{H_t\}$ which represent
dynamical changes of state in X and S respectively. In what follows,
we are going to treat the mappings $t \rightarrow T_t$, $t \rightarrow H_t$, which associate
instants with transformations, as *observables of I*. That is, we
shall regard each transformation $T_t : X \rightarrow X$ *as a description of t*,
and each transformation $H_t : S \rightarrow S$ as another description of the same
time instant t. These observables thus defined on I are not numerical-
valued; rather, their values are themselves mappings of definite
types.

If we regard T_t and H_t as separate descriptions of the particular
instant $t \in I$ with which they are associated, the question arises
(as always) as to how these descriptions may be compared. We always
compare mappings or transformations by seeing if we can construct a
commutative diagram which allows us to translate between their actions;
if such a diagram can be constructed, the mappings are equivalent
(conjugate). In the present case, the diagram we need to construct
is already embodied in (5.5.1) above. It must be explicitly noted
that we cannot translate between the action of T_t on X and H_t on S
in an arbitrary way; rather, we are restricted to the encoding maps
$(x_1, \ldots, x_n)\delta$, by virtue of the way in which X and S are related.

Let us denote the situation we are describing diagramatically:

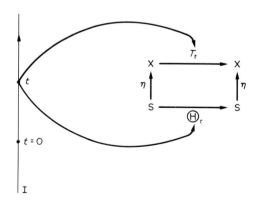

Fig. 5.5.1.

In this diagram, we have written $\eta = (x_1, \ldots, x_n)\delta$ as the encoding map relating X and S. If we think of t as moving in I, the maps T_t and $\textcircled{H}_t$ are correspondingly changing, but the encoding map η must remain fixed.

Let us now agree that the two descriptions T_t, $\textcircled{H}_t$ of an instant t in I are *equivalent* if the diagram (5.5.1) approximately commutes, in the sense defined above. In particular, the descriptions will surely approximately commute when t = 0; intuitively, this means that S and S° are in the same state. As we now let t increase in I, we have seen that there will be a growing discrepancy between the two arms of the diagram (5.5.1), but the diagram will still approximately commute. As t continues to increase, we will ultimately come to the critical value $t = t_c$, at which the property of approximate commutativity is lost. At this point, the two descriptions T_{t_c}, $\textcircled{H}_{t_c}$ of the time instant t_c are no longer equivalent; we can no longer translate between these descriptions. This, of course, is the essence of a bifurcation.

It is most interesting to note that the bifurcation parameter in this situation is most conveniently taken to be the set I of time instants. This fact points out in yet another way the crucial role which time plays in dynamical encodings. Indeed, throughout the above discussion, we treated I precisely in the same terms as we treated S; namely, as a set of "abstract time states", labelled or encoded by different families of dynamical processes. The fact that these labellings can bifurcate with respect to one another is simply a way of stating that time is complex; a conclusion we reached on other grounds in Section 4 above.

Another crucial aspect of the above discussion may now be noted. When the critical time t_c is exceeded, we have seen that we can no longer directly translate between the description T_t of S° and the actual dynamics in S. We can hope to restore the commutativity (or approximate commutativity) of the diagram (5.5.1) in a variety of different ways. The simplest is to "recalibrate"; namely, to restore the coincidence between the state of X at a time t and the actual state of S encoded into X at that time. Such a recalibration essentially puts the clock back to zero, and gives us a further time interval of approximate commutativity before a new critical time is reached. By repeating this process often enough, even a faulty model can retain approximate commutativity indefinitely.

Often, however, the continual recalibration of a model is impracticable, especially since the critical time cannot be predicted within the context of the model itself. The next simplest procedure for retaining approximate commutativity of the diagram (5.5.1) is to replace the dynamics $\{T_t\}$ on X by a new dynamics, while retaining all other features of the encoding (in particular, retaining the original encoding map η). Essentially, this can be done by recompensating the flows in X; i.e. introducing new accounting relations between the differential increments of the state variables at each point of X. This is the most obvious alternative, and is of course the one most generally adopted.

However, there are other alternatives. For instance, we may note that the loss of translation between the original dynamics $\{T_t\}$ on X and the actual dynamics $\{\textcircled{H}_t\}$ on S when the critical time t_c is exceeded arises *relative to the retention of the particular encoding map η which we are using*. It will be recalled that we have kept this encoding map fixed throughout the preceding discussion, as indeed we must if we are to preserve the given relation between S and X. How-ever, our discussion does not preclude the possibility of restoring the approximate commutativity of the diagram (5.5.1) when t_c is ex-ceeded, *providing we are willing to change the encoding map*. To make a change in the encoding map means, of course, that we are changing our description of the abstract states in S more or less radically. In the simplest case, we may retain the manifold X, but modify the manner in which the n-tuples in X are attached to abstract states. This confronts us with an abstract version of what the phy-sicist generally calls *renormalization*; a situation we have encoun-tered before (cf. Chapter 3.3) in what the reader will recognize to be an essentially similar context. A more radical change of encoding is to give up the manifold X entirely, and recode the abstract states of S into a new manifold Y, using different observables of S. These new observables may be more or less distinct from those originally used to define X, and their introduction is a manifestation of the phenomenon of *emergence*, or *emergent novelty*. It will be noted that what is "emerging" here is not an intrinsic property of S, but rather the failure of an encoding to model S over time. This is an essential point, which we will consider in detail in the following chapter.

In any case, we see that the existence of a critical time makes it necessary to replace a given description or encoding of S by another, which may differ more or less radically from the original one. At root, this necessity arises entirely because a model is an abstraction, tacitly supposing the system being modelled is closed to non-encoded interactions. From the failure of this tacit supposition, all of our conclusions immediately follow.

5.6 The Concept of Error

In the present chapter, we are going to recast the results we have obtained into another form, which will make manifest its intimate connection with the important concepts of *error* and system *complexity*. In the process, we shall see that the results obtained for continuous-time dynamics also hold for the other kinds of time-encoding discussed in Section 4. The procedure we shall develop also illuminates many of the general results on encoding obtained in that section, on which the entire concept of the modelling relation is based.

Let us fix ideas, as usual, with a few purely formal or mathematical considerations, which are of a particularly simple and transparent character. Let $\mathbb{R}$ be the set of real numbers. We are going to treat $\mathbb{R}$ like a set of abstract states, and put ourselves in the position of an observer who has access to the elements of $\mathbb{R}$ only through a limited family of "measuring instruments" at his disposal. At the same time, we shall retain the godlike perspective arising from our knowledge of $\mathbb{R}$ and its elements as mathematical objects, so that at every step we will be able to evaluate the limited results of our observations from a more comprehensive view of what is actually happening.

We know, as mathematicians, that every real number $r \, \varepsilon \, \mathbb{R}$ can be uniquely represented by a decimal expansion, which is generally infinite and non-repeating. On the other hand, as empirical observers of the elements of $\mathbb{R}$, we can only characterize these elements through some finite family of "observables" $f_1, \ldots, f_n$. We shall suppose that these observables have the following interpretation: $f_1(r)$ is the first (non-zero) coefficient in the decimal expansion of r; $f_2(r)$ is the second coefficient in the decimal expansion of r, and so on; thus in general, $f_i(r)$ is the ith coefficient in the decimal expansion of r. We suppose also that the observer can discriminate the decimal point; i.e. the numbers 213 and 2.13 are not counted as alike by the observer.

To see how $\mathbb{R}$ looks to such an observer, we may immediately invoke the general discussion of Chapter 3.2 above. Specifically, the observables

$f_1, \ldots, f_n$ which we have defined collectively impose an equivalence relation on $\mathbb{R}$; two real numbers r_1, r_2 fall into the same equivalence class under this relation if and only if we have

$$f_i(r_1) = f_i(r_2)$$

for $i = 1, \ldots, n$. Thus, our observer does not see all of $\mathbb{R}$; to him, two real numbers are indistinguishable if and only if their first n decimal coefficients coincide. From a mathematical point of view, our observer must replace any given real number r by a (generally different) number $r^{(n)}$; the first n decimal coefficients of $r^{(n)}$ coincide with those of r, but all the remaining decimal coefficients of $r^{(n)}$ are equal to zero. In other words, the decimal expansion of $r^{(n)}$ is a truncated initial segment of the expansion of r, and any two real numbers with the same truncated initial segment are counted as identical by our observer.

There are an infinitude of such truncated initial segments $r^{(n)}$, but from a mathematical point of view they comprise a *discrete subset* of $\mathbb{R}$. Moreover, each equivalence class defined by the observables f_i contains an uncountable set of real numbers, all of which are indistinguishable to our observer, both from each other, and from the single $r^{(n)}$ which represents the entire equivalence class. However, the mathematician can see that there is a *discrepancy* between any number r in such a class and the truncated initial segment $r^{(n)}$ which represents the class; a discrepancy which is of course invisible to our observer.

This invisible discrepancy can, however, be made visible to our observer under appropriate circumstances. In particular, we can allow two arbitrary real numbers r_1, r_2 to *interact*; say by forming their product $r_1 r_2$ in $\mathbb{R}$. Now our observer will see this interaction as occurring between the two corresponding truncated initial segments $r_1^{(n)}$ and $r_2^{(n)}$. Moreover, he can only see the first n coefficients of the product $r_1 r_2$; i.e. he can only see

$$f_1(r_1 r_2), \; f_2(r_1 r_2), \; \ldots, \; f_n(r_1 r_2),$$

which for him will specify the *result* of the interaction. Thus, for him, the multiplication operation will be represented in the form

$$r_1^{(n)} \times r_2^{(n)} = (r_1 r_2)^{(n)}.$$

From the more general mathematical perspective, we can recognize that *the operation of multiplication in $\mathbb{R}$ is not compatible with the observer's equivalence relation*. That is, if r_1 and r_1' are equivalent to our observer (i.e. have the same truncated initial segment), and r_2 and r_2' are equivalent, it need not be true that

$$(r_1 r_2)^{(n)} = (r_1' r_2')^{(n)}.$$

That is, multiplication in ℝ can *split* the observer's equivalence
classes. This splitting arises, of course, because the decimal
expansion of a product may involve decimal coefficients of the
factors beyond the ones visible to our observer; such coefficients
may vary widely within each of the observer's equivalence classes,
and are precisely the source of (invisible) variability within those
classes.

Let us now place ourselves in the position of our observer. Suppose
he repeats the "experiment" of multiplying two numbers r_1, r_2 a large
number of times. Since he can discriminate numbers only up to a
truncated initial segment, his repetition of the experiment will in
fact involve a sampling of the equivalence classes of the numbers
being multiplied. Thus, what appear to him to be the *same* numbers
are actually distributed over classes of numbers. In general, he
will conclude that "most of the time" the multiplication determines
a unique product; i.e. the equivalence class to which he assigns
the products he sees will be the same. Occasionally, however, he
will have to assign the resulting product to a different equivalence
class.

The visible splitting of the observer's equivalence classes by multiplication represents precisely what we called a *bifurcation*. In this
case, the bifurcation is between the observables f_1, ..., f_n and those
invisible decimal coefficients actually involved in the multiplication.

How will our observer describe such a bifurcation when it occurs?
To him, it will appear that a fixed interaction between two definite
numbers does not always give rise to the same result. In general,
he will be led to suppose that there is *some source of variability,
or noise, or error in the interaction*.[1] From our more general mathematical perspective, we can see that there is indeed a source of
variability, but it lies in the incompleteness of the observer's
description of his numbers, and not at all in their interaction.
On the other hand, since our observer is unaware that his description
is incomplete, he will conclude that his inability to uniquely
classify a product indicates a (stochastic) source of error *in the
interaction itself*.

Let us formulate the situation even more sharply. Suppose that our
observer possesses a calculating machine, which can multiply real
numbers exactly. To our observer, who can see only the truncated
initial segments of the numbers he supplies to the machine as input,
and who likewise classifies the output in terms of such a segment,
it will appear in the above circumstances as if the *machine* is making
errors. It must be stressed that the *error* involved here appears to
the observer as the assignment of a particular product to the "wrong"
equivalence class; it is a failure of classification. This error
arises from an invisible discrepancy between the numbers actually
being multiplied and those the observer believes are being multiplied,
but *this discrepancy is not itself the error* as seen by the observer.

From our more general mathematical perspective, it is clear that the
errors of classification seen by the observer are a form of round-
off error, or overflow, arising from a replacement of the actual
numbers being multiplied by abstract approximations to them. Since
actual multiplication splits the equivalence classes defined by these
approximations, the errors of classification are simply bifurcations
between the qualities retained in the approximation, and those

actually involved in forming a product. Such a bifurcation makes
the initially invisible variability appear in the form of errors of
classification, which are now patent to the observer. As we have
noted, the observer will tend to regard these errors of classification
as stochastic in nature; he can actually develop a detailed statistical theory of such errors. However, we can see that such a theory
will merely represent the manner in which he is sampling his equivalence classes as he repeats what (to him) is the experiment of
multiplying a pair of fixed numbers.

In a sense, the above discussion shows how errors of classification
arise when there are *hidden variables*;[2] i.e. degrees of freedom
invisible to an external observer, but manifesting themselves in a
particular interaction. The errors arise because the hidden variables
can bifurcate from the ones available to the observer. All of this
is clearly seen in the example we have presented.

In yet another picturesque mathematical terminology, the replacement
of a real number r by an initial segment $r^{(n)}$ is a passage from
actual numbers to *germs* of numbers. This terminology is drawn from
an exactly analogous situation, in which the local behavior of a
function at a point is referred to the equivalence class of functions
whose Taylor expansions at the point coincide up to the first n
terms. Here again, these equivalence classes (called *germs* of
functions) can be split by mathematical operations involving higher
terms; indeed, it is of the greatest interest to note that the
classical theory of bifurcations can be developed entirely from
this point of view (although to do so here would take us much too
far afield).[3]

For the most direct comparison of the situation we are presently
envisioning with what we have done in previous chapters, let us
suppose that a (discrete) dynamics is now imposed on $\mathbb{R}$, say by
defining $T^n(r) = r^n$. Here, the index n plays the role of a discrete
encoding of time; cf. Chapter 4.6 above. It is clear that such a
dynamics on $\mathbb{R}$ will in general also split our observer's equivalence
classes; by a repetition of the above argument, he will one again be
led to conclude that there is a source of error *in the dynamics*.

We shall now relate the situation we have just described to the
developments of the preceding chapters. As we have seen, our
observer is necessarily placed in the position of replacing a
general real number r, with its infinitude of decimal coefficients,
by an abstraction generated by his limited set of measuring instruments (i.e. by a truncated initial segment of these coefficients).
These decimal coefficients correspond to the degrees of freedom, or
interactive capabilities, of the abstract states of a natural system.
The abstraction retains only a small fraction of these. The abstractions thus correspond to what we earlier called a *closed* system S°.
In any interaction in which the neglected coefficients do not enter
significantly, the abstraction approximates sufficiently closely to
what it represents so that the behaviors in S° and in the full system
S remain indistinguishable to our observer. But in any interaction
for which the neglected coefficients become significant, there will
be an observable discrepancy, or bifurcation, between the behavior
of the abstractions in S° and the actual behavior observed in S.
This bifurcation is ultimately quite visible to our observer, but
as we have seen, it will tend to be ascribed to *error in the system*,[4]
and not to his description.

Indeed, it is curious and poignant, and not without deep epistemological significance, that our observer of the real number system,
armed as he is with only a limited capacity for discerning the
qualities of numbers, would regard the *mathematical* view of that
system as the abstraction, and his own description at the reality.
If our mathematician tried to convince the observer that the real
numbers involved unobserved qualities which, when properly formulated,
made numerical operations always associative, commutative, distri-
butive, etc., he would be dismissed by the observer as a metaphysician;
an inventor of abstractions totally divorced from observable reality.
The relation between the mathematician and the observer which we have
just sketched is in fact itself a model for the unfortunate chasm
which often separates theoretical from empirical sciences. For the
moment, we shall merely note that this chasm exists, and that its
roots are visible even in this purely formal discussion; its properties will become a major preoccupation in the sections to follow.

Let us return to the notion of error which we have introduced above.
We see that it arises because of a discrepancy between the behaviors
exhibited by actual real numbers, and the behaviors of corresponding
truncated initial segments, or number germs. It thus represents a
discrepancy between objects which are closed to certain interactive
qualities, and objects which are not closed to those qualities. We
see also that the character of this discrepancy is in principle
unpredictable from the standpoint of the number germs themselves.

We shall now argue that *the empirical concept of error always involves
such a discrepancy between objects open to certain interaction and
abstract representations which are closed to those interactions*.
In other words, error represents a deviation between how a given
system actually behaves, and the manner in which it *would* behave if
it were not open. This concept of error thus provides another
language in which to discuss the relation between natural systems
and their models, which is of the greatest importance.

In empirical terms, the concept of error arises already at the most
basic level; namely, in the operation of those meters or measuring
instruments through which we formalize the notion of an observable.
It is universally recognized that any measuring instrument is subject
to "noise" or variability; or, stated another way, that every
measuring instrument has a finite *resolving power*, below which it
cannot effectively discriminate.

To inquire further into the nature of this finite resolving power,
let us return to our consideration of the real numbers $\mathbb{R}$, as seen
from the standpoint of a mathematician, and from that of an empirical
observer who can only see number germs. Suppose that our observer
constructs a new measuring instrument, of the type sketched in Figure
1 below:

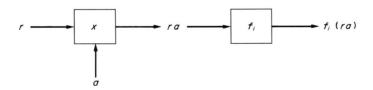

Figure 5.6.1.

From the mathematical standpoint, this instrument multiplies any number r to be observed with a fixed number a, and then specifies the ith decimal coefficient of this product. It thus defines an *observable* g_a of $\mathbb{R}$, defined by

$$g_a(r) = f_i(ra)$$

as seen in abstract mathematical terms. The structure diagrammed in Figure 5.6.1 above is thus a *meter* for g_a, which can be applied to any real number r. It thus *classifies* real numbers r in the usual way: r_1 and r_2 are alike if $g_a(r_1) = g_a(r_2)$.

Let us inquire into the resolving power of this meter, as it will appear to our empirical observer. Of course, he can only specify the number r to be observed to a limited number of decimal coefficients; i.e. he cannot discriminate real numbers which differ beyond the nth coefficient. It is easy to see that if r is large compared to a, our observer's inability to discriminate numbers belonging to the same germ will have no effect on $f_i(ra)$. In mathematical terms, the (invisible) variability in r will in these circumstances not affect the observed value of $g_a(r)$, and the operation of the meter for g_a will appear absolutely precise. However, as the input r becomes sufficiently small with respect to a, a *dispersion* will appear in the output of the meter, which will become more and more pronounced as r becomes smaller with respect to a. At some point, depending on the magnitude of a, the discriminating capability of the meter will be completely lost, and we would have to say that the *resolving power* of the meter has been exceeded.

What is happening here? To see this, let us actually perform a simple multiplication; say 534 x 27 = 14418. In terms of decimal expansions, we have

$$534 = 5 \times 10^2 + 3 \times 10^1 + 4 \times 10^0$$

and

$$27 = \qquad\qquad 2 \times 10^1 + 7 \times 10^0.$$

We obtain the decimal expansion of the product by multiplying these two decimal expansions. Let us look at this in some detail.

There will be a term in the product expansion of the form

$$(4 \times 10^0) \times (7 \times 10^0) = 28 \times 10^0$$

$$= 2 \times 10^1 + 8 \times 10^0.$$

Clearly there will be no other contributions to the coefficient of 10^0 coming from other terms of the product expansion. Thus the last term 8×10^0 has a coefficient which depends only on the last coefficients (4 and 7) of the factors. However, these last coefficients also produce a contribution (namely 2×10^1) to the coefficient of 10^1 in the product.

The other contributions to the coefficient of 10^1 in the product come from the terms

$$(3 \times 10^1) \times (7 \times 10^0) = 2 \times 10^2 + 1 \times 10^1$$

and

$$(4 \times 10^0) \times (2 \times 10^1) = 8 \times 10^1.$$

These two terms combine to produce a net contribution to the product of

$$2 \times 10^2 + 9 \times 10^1$$

and hence the total coefficient of 10^1 in the product is obtained by combining the results of the three terms we have considered; it is

$$9 \times 10^1 + 2 \times 10^1 = 11 \times 10^1$$

$$= 1 \times 10^2 + 1 \times 10^1.$$

No other terms can contribute anything further to the coefficient of 10^1 in the product. However, the terms we have already considered do make a contribution (3×10^2) to the next higher coefficient (that of 10^2) in the product.

Thus we see: (a) the coefficient of 10^0 in the product depends *only* on the coefficients of 10^0 in the factors; (b) the coefficient of 10^1 in the product depends *only* on the coefficients of 10^1 and those of 10^0 in the factors, but on all of these coefficients in general.

Pursuing this kind of argument, it follows that the coefficient of 10^p in a product depends only on the coefficients of 10^q in the factors, for $q < p$, but it generally depends on *all* of these coefficients. We also see that for large numbers, the *significance* of the lowest-power coefficients tends to diminish.

Let us now return to our observable $g_a(r)$. This involves forming a product rxa, and extracting the ith decimal coefficient of the product. From the above argument, we can see that if r is large compared to a, the ith coefficient of rxa will in general depend on the coefficients of 10^j in both r and a, where $j < i$. But the *effects* of coefficients of *both* numbers for which $j \ll i$ on this coefficient will generally be negligible; this negligibility will be sufficient to abolish the variability arising from working with number germs rather than with the numbers themselves. On the other hand, if r is small compared to a, the effect of multiplying r by a will be to *magnify* the contributions of lower-power coefficients of both r and a to the ith coefficient. At some definite point, this magnification will make the variability visible, and beyond this, we will ultimately come to see *only* the variability.

If we thus think of the infinitude of decimal coefficients of a real number $r \in \mathbb{R}$ as *degrees of freedom* of r, we see that the observable $g_a(r)$ ultimately depends on all these degrees of freedom. Replacing r by its "germ", which is what our observer is forced to do, makes most of these degrees of freedom invisible to the observer; in fact it tacitly puts them equal to zero. They become visible only when a number enters into an interaction in which they are important; e.g. in the formation of the product ra, where r is small compared to a.

The variability, or noise, or error we have noted in the meter displayed in Figure 5.6.1 above thus arises because these degrees of freedom are present in the numbers actually involved, but absent in the number germs by which the observer replaces them. The meter is thus telling us the net effect of *all* the interacting degrees of freedom present in both the number being observed and in the meter itself (i.e. in the number a), and *not simply those present in the germs of those numbers*. That is, the variables which are "hidden" in this case belong as much to a as they do to r.

To see that these apparently formal considerations actually do pertain to our intuitive concept of error in natural systems, let us consider a few specific contexts in which error plays an essential role.

1. Information theory

The basic problem with which Information Theory is concerned is the transmission of "messages" through a noisy channel. Let us recognize that such a "message" must always be carried by some physical vehicle. Such a vehicle may be regarded as an equivalence class of abstract states of some natural system S, corresponding to our number germs, and like them, defined through the values assumed on the states of S by some finite family F of observables. On the other hand, there are many other observables defined on the states of S, totally unrelated to those through which these states are classified as message vehicles. Likewise, the channel through which the message vehicles must pass are states of some natural system S'. Some of the observables of S' pertain to the channel's capability to transmit these message vehicles, but there are in general many other observables of S', unrelated to this capability.

To say that such a channel is noisy means precisely that discrepancies can arise between message vehicles observed to enter the channel and those observed to leave it; here observation means the evaluation of observables in F. Such a discrepancy, as usual, is referred to as an *error*, and it is localized *in the channel*; in such circumstances we say that the channel is noisy. However, through a line of reasoning exactly analogous to that carried out above, we can equally well suppose that the characterization of a message vehicle by *only* those observables in F, pertaining to message recognition, is equivalent to replacing a real number by a number germ, or to replacing a state open to certain interactions by another state closed to those interactions. Thus, the *physical* channel can interact with the *physical* message vehicles through observables entirely distinct from those in F on which the transmission of a message through the channel depends, and which are of course the only ones retained when the channel is regarded purely as a message transmission system. As we have seen, such an interaction can introduce a discrepancy between what the channel *actually* does to a message vehicle and what we *expect* the channel to do on the basis of our abstractions. This is exactly the noise, which we interpret as *error*.

Indeed, in a precise sense, the effect of a communication channel on a message vehicle can be regarded as an *observation* of the channel by the message vehicle; the message vehicle itself becomes analogous to a meter. The observable measured by this meter is, of course, distinct from those relating to the transmission of messages, and hence in general bifurcates from them. As we have repeatedly pointed out, it is such bifurcations which are interpreted as noise or error; their presence indicates that the systems involved are not closed to interactions which we have tacitly postulated to be absent.

Since the character of the "errors" arising in a channel are contingent upon observables distinct from those which characterize the messages, there is as usual no way to predict anything about the character of these "errors" from our descriptions of the messages themselves. The only way to gain access to these "errors" is to pass to a new description, which explicitly involves the observables and interactions on which they depend. In Information Theory, and indeed, in most treatments of noise and error, this is done in a roundabout fashion; namely, by superimposing on our original family of observables some kind of *probability distribution*. In this way, we treat the channel as a *stochastic* entity. The function of such a probability distribution is, of course, to take account of the observables not retained in our initial abstraction. However, this is not in general a good way to proceed; from our more comprehensive point of view, we see that the appearance of error is not a stochastic phenomenon at all.[5] Nevertheless, under many circumstances, the imposition of a stochastic element upon a closed system description can provide a useful model of the corresponding open system, and it does represent a general strategy for dealing with such open systems. We shall have more to say about this in later chapters.

2. "Errors" in genetic coding

One of the high points of molecular biology has been the identification of the "symbol vehicles" for primary genetic material with strands of DNA, and the specific "information" carried by such a strand with the order of nucleotide bases linearly arranged along such a strand. The genetic material itself must already be involved in at least two distinct kinds of information-transmission processes: (a) a *replicative* process, whereby genetic information is transmitted to descendants, and (b) a *decoding* process, comprising a transcription step (into RNA) and a translation step (whereby an initial DNA sequence is converted into a corresponding linear sequence of amino acids along a corresponding polypeptide chain).

We can obviously think of replication and decoding as comprising *channels* through which message vehicles are passed. Just as in the situation considered above, discrepancies can arise between a message vehicle entering a channel, and the corresponding vehicle leaving the channel; as always, such discrepancies are regarded as *errors*. Thus, a discrepancy between a DNA sequence entering a replication and a daughter sequence emerging from the replication comprises the kind of error called a *mutation*; a discrepancy between a DNA strand entering a decoding and (say) the polypeptide it codes for represents a *mistranscription* or a *mistranslation*.

Clearly, the only observables of a polynucleotide strand, or of a polypeptide chain, which are involved in the transmission of genetic information are those which determine sequence. The only operations retained to describe the transmission of this information are those which preserve sequence. Thus as far as coding is concerned, genetic transmission is closed to all observables and interactions which do not characterize sequence. On the other hand, it is clear that the vehicles which carry information in this case are chemical substances; hence there are many modes of interaction between these substances and their environment which can modify the perceived sequence. The occurrence of such an interaction (e.g., between a DNA strand and a chemical mutagen, or between such a strand and ambient radiation) may thus result in an error; i.e. a deviation between the initial sequence and the subsequent sequence. Once again, the source of these "errors" resides precisely in those observables not involved

in determining sequence, and hence abstracted out in any description
of information transmission. Consequently, as before, we must either
pass to a more comprehensive description of the actual information
vehicles, or else attempt to supplement our description with a
stochastic element; a probability distribution geared to take
account of the missing observables.

3. Errors in the central nervous system

An exactly parallel discussion to those given above may be developed
for the central nervous system. This should be clear already, on the
basis of the many formal relations we have established in preceding
sections between the central nervous system and genetic systems,
computation, information transmission and logic. However, it is well
to sketch the basis for this discussion independently.

As we saw abundantly in Example 3 of Chapter 3.5 above, the basic
theoretical tool for investigating the central nervous system is the
neural network; and the basic analytical unit for describing the
properties of such networks is the individual neuron. Let us therefore begin by considering such an individual neuron, say for simplicity the formal neuron of McCulloch and Pitts; an analogous
discussion can be provided for any other kind of formal unit.

As we saw earlier, the basic descriptive elements in the formal neuron
are the states of excitation of the input lines to the neuron at
specific instants of discrete time. The neuron itself can be regarded
as a *meter*, defining an observable on the set of instantaneous states
of the input lines through the relation (3.5.9). This observable is
defined through the state of excitation of the neuron's output line
at the succeeding instant, and it also depends on the threshold of
the neuron.

Let us note the similarity between this situation and that diagrammed
in Figure 5.6.1 above. In these terms, the neuron (as indeed any
meter) can be regarded as a classifier of the set of states on which
it is defined. Thus, as before, an *error* in the behavior of such a
classifier can only be recognized in terms of a discrepancy between
the class assigned to a particular input by the neuron, and the
class to which that input "should" be assigned according to (3.5.9).
That is, the error manifests a bifurcation between the classification
actually made and that embodied in the abstract description (3.5.9).

As usual, we recognize that our description (3.5.9) is that of a
system *closed* to interactions to which the neuron being described
is in fact *open*. Thus, the ingredients of that description are like
the number germs we considered earlier. If this is the case, then
as before, the actual interactions on which the output of a neuron
depends may generally bifurcate from those retained in our description.
The result will be, from our point of view, a mis-classification of
particular inputs, which we will ascribe to an *error* of the neuron.
Of course, the character of such an error will be unpredictable from
our description, which by definition has abstracted away the basis
for it. We will thus conclude that it is the neuron which is
erroneous or noisy, and we will be led to superimpose a probability
distribution on our description (3.5.9) to take account of its errors.

Ideas of this character have some interesting consequences when
elevated to the level of neural networks. In particular, let us
suppose that we have a population of such apparently fallible neurons,
organized in some network. The behavior of the network as a whole

will then be described by utilizing the description (3.5.9) as applied to each individual neuron in the network. As we saw earlier, such a network can be regarded as realizing some *proposition* in a logical system. If a neuron in the network appears to make an error, then the network need no longer realize that proposition; i.e. the *entire network* can thus be said to be in error. In other words, an error *of the network* is defined in exactly the same terms as is an error in an individual neuron; and indeed, the latter is the diagnostic of the former. In an analogous situation, we would recognize an entire mathematical proof as erroneous if any step of the proof is erroneous.

Thus in a general sense, the *reliability* of a neural network by definition devolves upon the errors made by its constituent neurons. This has had profound implications for theories of the brain. For it is observed that the brain as a whole appears to function "reliably" over prolonged periods of time (e.g. of the order of a century), despite the fact that its neurons randomly die at a significant rate, and even under conditions which greatly modify the properties of its constituent neurons (e.g. intoxication, anesthesia, sleep). Thus the question can be posed: how can the reliability of a neural network be greater than the reliability of its constituent neurons?[6]

This kind of question has received much attention over the past years, not only in the context of neural networks, but also in cognate areas of communication and computation. The general answer is: through the artful employment of redundancy, any statistically rooted variability in the individual elements of a network can be effectively neutralized or eliminated. However, it should be noted that this answer involves a tacit equivocation involving the term "reliability"; in particular, our heuristic argument requires us to identify the overall *functional* reliability of the brain with *freedom from error* of its constituent units. As we shall see later, there are no grounds for making such identifications in general; they involve different descriptions of the systems involved and these descriptions need not themselves be linked.

In a similar fashion, we can elevate the concept of *genetic error*, as outlined in the previous example, to the level of networks of interacting gene products; i.e. to the physiological behavior of cells and organisms. One such approach is embodied in the "error catastrophe" hypothesis of L. Orgel.[7] Briefly, Orgel's argument is as follows: The translation step of protein synthesis itself requires protein (the "synthetase" enzymes). Any error arising in these synthetases will introduce errors of sequence into *all* proteins subsequently synthesized, including the synthetases themselves. Thus, the subsequent generation of synthetase molecules will tend to be more erroneous than the initial one. This subsequent generation of synthetases will thus introduce still further errors of sequence into *all* proteins they synthesize, including again the synthetases themselves. Thus in effect a positive feedback loop exists, which serves to magnify the initial errors through successive rounds of protein synthesis. As a result of this positive feedback loop, it is concluded that all cell proteins become increasingly dysfunctional, until the entire cell becomes inviable. Further, as cells become inviable, so too must any organism composed of these cells. Hence, the "error catastrophe" itself escalates into a theory of mortality and senescence.

Here again, there is a tacit identification between reliability at some functional level and the occurrence of "errors" at a different level. That such an identification is not justified in general is

shown in this case from a more detailed dynamical investigation of
the "error catastrophe" itself. Such investigations show that the
positive feedback loop envisioned by Orgel can only arise under
physiologically unreasonable circumstances; thus there is no
necessary relation here between errors in constituent units and
reliability of larger systems composed of these units.[8] The same
is doubtless true in the central nervous system. Indeed, we shall
take quite a different approach to reliability in the following
section.

Now let us draw together the main features illustrated by the
examples we have considered, and relate them to the results of the
preceding chapters. We can state these features succinctly as follows.

1. The basis for error lies in the fact that any description of a
   system is an abstraction. As such, it cannot characterize the
   states of a system beyond assigning them to equivalence classes,
   generated by a limited set of observing instruments or meters.
   Hence there is an uncontrollable variability present in states
   which the observer classifies as identical.

2. This variability is not yet error. It *becomes* error when the
   states of the system enter into interactions which split the
   observer's equivalence classes. This splitting comprises a
   bifurcation between the observables employed in the classification,
   and those actually involved in the interaction.

3. The bifurcation or splitting of the observer's equivalence classes
   appears to him as a *mis-classification*, and will be interpreted
   by the observer as an *error* in the system being described.

4. Thus, error in the system appears to the observer as a discrepancy
   between the actual behavior of a system, and the behavior expected
   of the system, each determined by the observer on the basis of the
   descriptions generated by his observing instruments.

5. Any bifurcation can be regarded as a logical independence of the
   descriptions which are being compared. Hence in particular, the
   nature and character of the errors detected by the observer are
   unpredictable in principle from his descriptions.

6. In order to deal with the errors he detects, the observer must
   supplement his description, in order to take account of the
   observables involved in the interaction, but absent from his
   description. One general way of attempting to do this is to
   superimpose an appropriate probability distribution on his
   description; i.e. to treat error as a stochastic process
   intrinsic to the system.

7. In an interaction, the observables of *both* of the systems involved in the interaction must be taken into account. Hence in
   particular, error is in fact not intrinsic to a system considered
   in isolation. In fact, it is better regarded as a meter for
   environmental observables.

On the basis of these conclusions, we can now better appreciate the
relation between the phenomenon of *error*, and the discussion of
previous chapters. In essence, the distinction between an abstract
description of a system and the system itself is analogous to that
between a system closed to environmental interactions and the same
system opened to those interactions. As we saw in Chapter 5.4 above,
there will always be a discrepancy between the behavior of a closed

system and the same system opened to a family of environmental interactions; in a dynamical context, this discrepancy will grow with time. Such a discrepancy, as we have observed, is the underlying source of variability on which the perception of errors depends, but by itself it does not constitute error. Error, properly so called, arises when this underlying variability is sufficient to cause a bifurcation to appear under appropriate conditions of interaction. More specifically, two states which appear to be equivalent (or approximately so) under the observer's description are in fact sufficiently different in their other degrees of freedom to give widely different results when exposed to an interaction involving those other degrees of freedom. Hence, in a sense, error and bifurcation are equivalent terms; they both indicate the inadequacy of a particular mode of system description, and imply the existence of others. When such a bifurcation occurs, the original modelling relation which existed between the system and its description now ceases to hold. As we have seen, such a failure of a modelling relation can also be interpreted in terms of *emergence*; here too, a given description or model of a system must be replaced by another.

A most important conclusion can be drawn from these considerations, which underlies much of the distinction between biology and physics. Perhaps the most unassailable principle of theoretical physics asserts that *the laws of nature must be the same for all observers* (cf. Example 6, Chapter 3.5 above). By this is meant that these laws must be invariant to the position or state of motion of any observer. But the principle requires that the observers in question should otherwise be identical; i.e. equipped with precisely the same meters. If the observers themselves are not identical; i.e. if they are inequivalent, or equipped with different sets of meters, there is no reason to expect that their descriptions of the universe will be the same, and hence that we can transform from any such description to any other. In such a case, the observers' descriptions of the universe will *bifurcate* from each other (which is only another way of saying that their descriptions will be logically independent; i.e. not related by any transformation rule or linkage). In an important sense, biology *depends* in an essential way on the proliferation of inequivalent observers; it can indeed be regarded as *nothing other than* the study of populations of inequivalent observers and their interactions. These remarks lend a profound significance to the view that biology is the science of mutability; i.e. the science of error.

REFERENCES AND NOTES

1. The "error" we are considering here is well known to computer scientists and numerical analysts as overflow, or round-off error. It is discussed at length (though not from our point of view) in every standard text on numerical analysis, as for example
    Phillips, G. M. and Taylor, P. J., *Theory and Applications of Numerical Analysis*. Academic Press (1973).
    There is also an interesting discussion of "computer arithmetic" in the article by A. S. Householder, included in the collection:
    Sarty, T. L. (ed.), *Lectures on Modern Mathematics*. Wiley (1963).

2. There is an extensive and contradictory literature on hidden variables in quantum theory. The essentially statistical features of quantum theory have bothered many physicists (notably Einstein) and from the beginning the question was raised as to whether the quantum-mechanical description of nature was incomplete. If so,

a situation obviously analogous to the one we are discussing arises. For a good general discussion see, e.g.

d'Espagnat, B., *Conceptual Foundations of Quantum Mechanics*. Benjamin (1976).

Belinfante, F. J., *A Survey of Hidden-Variable Theories*. Pergamon (1973).

3. See for example Bröcker, T., *Differentiable Germs and Catastrophes*. Cambridge University Press (1976).

4. As we are employing the term, "error" refers to the discrepancy in behavior between a system and a model of that system. In the traditional canonization of scientific method, we are supposed to choose the observed behavior of a system as the standard, and refer the predictions of a model to it. If a discrepancy is found, the resultant error is to be imputed to the model; i.e. we would say that we have an erroneous model, and seek a better encoding. In the present circumstances, however, it is the model which is chosen as the standard, and the actual system behavior is referred to it; any discrepancy is then imputed to the system, and we say that the system is erroneous.

5. The viewpoint we are propounding here has certain analogies to, for instance, the calculation of absolute rate constants for chemical reactions in terms of the frequencies of molecular collisions. In order for two molecules to interact chemically to produce a new molecule, it is not enough that they collide; they must collide in a way adequate to pass over a potential barrier separating reactant configurations from product configurations. Whether this occurs or not depends upon a variety of circumstances; among them temperature, (formally, all these factors enter into the concept of chemical potential). Likewise, when a symbol is passing through a communication channel, an interaction of the symbol vehicle with the channel depends on a variety of circumstances characteristic of the vehicle and the channel. The coding theorems of information theory, which state that by suitable encoding and decoding the probability of "error" (i.e. interaction of symbol vehicles with channel) may be made arbitrarily small are analogous to the assertion that by suitably lowering the temperature, a reaction rate can be made arbitrarily small. It would be interesting to develop the relation between coding and "channel temperature", but so far this has not been done.

6. See for instance, von Neumann, J., in *Automata Studies* (Shannon, C. E. and McCarthey, J., eds.) Princeton University Press, 43-98 (1952).

7. See e.g. Orgel, L., *PNAS* 49, 517-519 (1963); Orgel, L., *Nature* 243, 441-443 (1973).

8. Goel, N. and Ycas, M., *J. Theor. Biol.* 55, 245-282 (1975); Goel, N. and Ycas, M., *J. Math. Biol.* 3, 121-132 (1976).

5.7 Error and Complexity

There has always been a close relationship between the notion of
error and the important notion of complexity. The relation between
the two can be summed up in the proposition that "simple systems do
not make errors". Thus, it is meaningless to speak of a system of
mechanical particles making an "error".[1] The capacity to behave
erroneously thus seems to be a function of complexity; hence it is
natural to consider in greater detail the relation between the two
notions, in the light of the discussion of the preceding chapter.
In particular, we want to consider the following question: to what
extent is complexity a *quality* of a system? That is: to what extent
can complexity be regarded as an observable, characterizing an
intrinsic property of systems?

To the ancients, complexity was epitomized by the movements of
celestial bodies. The hold which Newtonian mechanics continues to
exert on the human mind rests in large part on its ability to cope
effectively with such complexity, on the basis of a small number of
indisputably simple and universal laws. If celestial mechanics
continues to pose formidable problems, those problems are no longer
of a conceptual, but rather of a computational character; these
are of a quite different order. The rationalist point of view
towards any problem, however complex it may initially appear, is
colored by the experience of mechanics; surely any natural phenomenon,
however complex, can be resolved by exploiting the same techniques
which resolved the mysteries of the skies.

On the other hand, our views regarding the nature of complexity have
tended to remain as richly varied as the concept itself. There have
always been scientists uneasy with the view that all complexity could
be reduced or explained by means of simple laws, and not all of them
can be dismissed as "vitalists" or "holists". For one thing, we have
all heard it said that complex systems are those which are "counter-
intuitive", meaning that their behaviors are different from what
"common-sense" (i.e. extrapolation from simple rules) suggests that
it ought to be. John von Neumann[2] argued that there was a kind of
"threshold" of complexity, below which systems behaved with their
traditional regularities, but above which entirely new kinds of
phenomena emerge, such as self-reproduction, evolution, and free
will, which are sui generis, and which can have no counterpart in
systems of lesser complexity.

321

A corollary of the idea that complexity possesses such a threshold
is that it is a quality of systems which can in fact be measured,
or at least computed on the basis of other measurements. Thus, a
great deal of literature on system complexity exists; this literature
stresses such things as the number of components or variables involved
in a particular description of the system, or the richness of the
inter-connection of these components, or the length of the shortest
algorithm required to construct the system.[3] In all of these approaches, complexity is not only viewed as intrinsic to a system,
but even is referred to a single particular mode of description of
that system.

In what follows, we are going to take a quite different approach.
Namely, *we are going to define a system to be complex to the extent
that we can observe it in non-equivalent ways*. As we have seen
extensively, each mode of observation of a system involves the
evaluation of certain of the observables of the system on its
abstract states. Each of these in turn gives rise to a particular
kind of representation, encoding or description of the system. Thus,
for us, a system will be complex to the extent that it admits non-
equivalent encodings; encodings which cannot be transformed or
reduced to one another. Stated yet another way: since each encoding
describes a subsystem of the given system, a system is complex to the
extent that we can discern many distinct subsystems of it.

This approach to complexity is novel in several ways. For one thing,
it requires that complexity is not an intrinsic property of a system
nor of a system description. Rather, it arises from the number of
ways in which we are able to interact with the system. Thus, complexity is a function not only of the system's interactive capabilities, but of our own. A moment's reflection will reveal, however,
that this situation is not as strange as it may appear at first sight;
and indeed, is in accord with our intuitive notions regarding complexity. For instance, most of us would regard a stone, say, as a
simple system; an organism, on the other hand, is clearly complex.
Why do we believe this? Clearly, this intuition rests on the fact
that we typically interact with a stone in only a few ways, while
we can interact with an organism in many ways. As we multiply the
number of ways with which we interact with a stone, its complexity
appears to grow; to a geologist, who interacts with a stone in many
distinct ways, it can appear infinitely complex. Conversely, as we
circumscribe the number of ways we interact with an organism, its
complexity accordingly appears to diminish. Thus in this intuitive
sense, our characterization of complexity is a reasonable one.

Such considerations lead naturally to the ideas involved in the
analysis of complex systems. One such strategy for system analysis
is that of reductionism, which we have discussed at some length above.
The idea here is to resolve a given system into a spectrum of subsystems, and to reconstruct the properties of the entire system from
those of the subsystems into which it has been resolved. We have
already discussed some of the ramifications of this approach in
Chapter 3.6, and we need not repeat it here. We merely point our
once again that the multiplicity of descriptions which provide the
very definition of complexity precludes any one class of subsystems,
or any one mode of system analysis, from being universally valid
over all system properties. Indeed, the lack of such a universally
valid strategy for system analysis is but an alternate definition
of complexity.

We have related complexity to the idea of many non-equivalent sub-

systems; i.e. modes of description or encoding which cannot be transformed or reduced to one another. However, we have also seen that
such non-reducible, non-conjugate encodings must therefore bifurcate
from one another. It is exactly the appearance of such bifurcations
which we showed in the preceding chapter to be the essence of error.
Therefore according to our definition of complexity, we recapture
the intuitive result that a complex system is one in which errors
can occur; furthermore, the more complex a system, the greater the
number and kinds of errors which will appear, and the greater the
deviation between the behavior of the system as a whole and any
abstract (i.e. closed) subsystem of itself. Indeed, it is precisely
this feature which is responsible for the "counter-intuitive" behavior
of complex systems which we noted earlier; we can see that such
"counter-intuitive" behavior is simply another way of talking about
the capacity for making errors. Once again, this feature can in fact
be employed to provide another alternate definition of complexity
itself.

REFERENCES AND NOTES

1. In the computation of planetary orbits on the basis of Newtonian
    mechanics, for example, two major discrepancies arose between
    prediction and observation. These involved the planet Uranus,
    and the advance of perihelion of the planet Mercury. In the
    former case, an assumption that there was an additional force
    arising from an as yet unobserved planet culminated in the
    discovery of a new planet (Neptune). In the latter case, it
    turned out that the entire apparatus of Newtonian physics had
    to be replaced by a new encoding (general relativity).

2. See Note 6, Chapter 5.6 See also the article by von Neumann in
    Cerebral Mechanisms in Behavior (L. A. Jeffress, ed.; Wiley
    (1951) pp. 1-41), and the volume *Theory of Self-Reproducing
    Automata*, completed from von Neumann's notes by Arthur Burks
    (University of Illinois Press, 1966).

3. Indeed, there is an entire new field devoted to questions of
    "computational complexity", which is, roughly speaking, a finite
    analog of the theory of degrees of unsolvability (cf. Note 5 to
    Chapter 3.1). The complexity of an algorithm is measured by the
    number of instants $f(n)$ of logical time which the algorithm
    requires to process an input string of length n. Alternately,
    instead of such a "temporal" measure of complexity, we could
    substitute a "spatial" one, by asking how the amount of energy
    storage increase with the length of the input. The basic question
    is: can we place upper and lower bounds on the complexities of
    algorithms required to solve particular problems, or classes of
    problems? The interested reader may consult:
    Karp, R. M., *Network* 5, 45-68 (1975).
    Traub, J. F. (ed.), *Algorithms and Complexity*. Academic Press
        (1976).
    Garey, M. R., *Computers and Intractability*. Freeman (1979).
    Ferranti, J. and Rackoff, C. W., *Complexity of Logical Theories*.
        Springer-Verlag (1979).
    It may be noted explicitly here that one can approach probabilistic
    notions in the same way; for instance, the question of how "random"
    a sequence is may be related to the complexity of the algorithm
    which generates its successive terms.

4. See Rosen, R., *J. Theor. Biol.* 63, 19-31 (1976); also *Int. J.
    Gen. Syst.* 3, 227-232 (1977).

5.8 Order and Disorder

In this chapter, we shall return to the basic arguments developed in Chapters 5.4 and 5.5 above. We saw there that if we take initially identical states of a closed system S° and the same system opened to a new modality of interaction with its environment, a growing discrepancy will appear between the behaviors in S° and S. We have already discussed this discrepancy from the standpoint of error and complexity. We now wish to consider this discrepancy from another standpoint, namely that of *order and disorder*. In the process, we shall find that an interesting new light is thrown on associated thermodynamic concepts, especially the concept of entropy.

We have already briefly discussed the concepts of order and disorder in Chapters 4.3 and 4.4 above. We saw there that thermodynamics in essence provides a standard of disorder for a system, and that standard is *absolute*. Namely, the state of absolute disorder for any thermodynamic system S is the state of thermodynamic equilibrium which the system approaches *when it is closed and isolated*. This state is by definition the standard of absolute disorder; it is absolute in the sense that no matter how the system S was open, and no matter what interactions in which it participated, it will always reach the same state of thermodynamic equilibrium when the system is closed and isolated from these interactions. The closed, isolated system thus plays the same role for thermodynamics as the system of particles with non-accelerating center of mass does for Newtonian mechanics; it establishes an intrinsic standard of non-interaction.

We also saw that this standard of absolute disorder for a system S admitted two quite independent characterizations: (a) The state of maximal disorder for a system S is the state on which *entropy is maximal*. Entropy in this case can be regarded as a pure state function; it can in principle be evaluated on any state of S, irrespective of any dynamics or any interactions in which S is involved. (b) The state of maximal disorder of a system S is also the state to which S will autonomously tend when S is closed and isolated.

The former characterization of disorder, in terms of the concept of entropy is thus a static concept, while the latter pertains to a particular dynamics on S. By evaluating entropy, we could in principle

find the maximally disordered state of S without any knowledge of its
dynamical behavior. On the other hand, from (b), we could also find
the state of maximal disorder by isolating the system S and watching
the autonomous dynamics, without any knowledge of entropy at all.
The relation between these two independent characterizations of
disorder is, of course, the following: *the entropy function is also
a Lyapunov function for the dynamics arising when S is isolated from
all interactions*. Thus, in the particular case under consideration,
these two independent ways of defining disorder coincide.

If the system S is not completely closed to environmental interactions,
the two notions no longer coincide. In particular, the dynmmics
imposed on S through such interactions will be different from that
arising when S is completely isolated, and thus whatever attractor
states exist for this dynamics will be different from the state of
thermodynamic equilibrium. Thus, referred to that state of thermodynamic equilibrium as an absolute standard of disorder, such attractor
states necessarily appear ordered. Indeed, this is the standard
tacitly applied (e.g. by Prigogine and his collaborators) by identifying the departure from thermodynamic equilibrium in an open system
with *morphogenesis* (cf. Chapter 3.5 above). They dignify this departure with such names as *symmetry-breaking* and *dissipative* structures.

On the other hand, according to the criterion (b), the attractors of
S as an open system are themselves states of maximal disorder, *relative
now to the dynamics imposed on S*. For when such a dynamics is given
the attractor   states are the ones to which the states of S autonomously tend, and those for which work must be done on the system to
keep it away from. Thus, according to (b), the state of thermodynamic
equilibrium is now itself to be considered as an *ordered* state,
relative to the new dynamics. In particular, the entropy considered
in (a) is no longer a Lyapunov function for the dynamics, and indeed
need have no special relation to the dynamics at all.

Thus, we see that in effect the two notions of disorder, which
coincide when S is closed and isolated, fail to coincide under other
circumstances. Indeed, we may correctly say that these two characterizations of disorder *bifurcate* from one another.

Clearly, each of these bifurcating definitions possesses some valuable
features, which we would like to retain. The characterization of
disorder in terms of a state function (e.g. entropy) has the advantage
of being absolute; disorder can be characterized by a pure observable
universally applicable independent of any imposed dynamics. This
absolute characterization has the important property that it allows
us to compare the states of *different* systems with respect to order
and disorder. On the other hand, we have attained this absolute
standard at the cost of singling out, in an arbitrary way, the
properties of a closed and isolated system; there is no good *a
priori* reason to do this. Moreover, it is often of little interest
what the behavior of an open system S *would* be if that system were
to be closed and isolated; it thus seems entirely reasonable to
expect that any concept of disorder in a system should take some
account of its actual dynamics, even if this should mean that we
must relativize the concept, and even if we must give up the idea
of comparing disorder in systems with different dynamics.

In what follows, we shall attempt to resolve this contradictory
state of affairs by entirely reformulating the concepts of order
and disorder. This will be done in such a way that the desirable
features of both of the characterizations described above are

$$
\begin{cases}
\Phi_1(f_{11}, \ldots, f_{1r_1}) = 0 \\[2ex]
\Phi_2(f_{21}, \ldots, f_{2r_2}) = 0 \\
\qquad \cdot \\
\qquad \cdot \\
\qquad \cdot \\
\Phi_k(f_{k1}, \ldots, f_{kr_k}) = 0
\end{cases}
\tag{5.8.2}
$$

Then in the particular encoding of S into E^n which we employed above, the set of linkages (5.8.2) will define a subset $\Omega_P \subset E^n$; this is the subset on which the property P is satisfied. Thus, Ω_P is precisely the set of *ordered states* relative to the property P (and of course relative to the encoding we are using). This set Ω_P is fixed once and for all by the linkages (5.8.2) independent of any dynamics imposed on S (and hence on E^n). Therefore, regardless of any imposed dynamics, we can say whether or not a given state is ordered with respect to P, and if not, we can in principle say how disordered it is.

It will be noted that we successively identify the idea of a property P with a family of linkages, and thence with a specific subset of S (or E^n) which satisfies these linkages. The subset Ω_P we have defined is thus completely determined by its characteristic function, which is an observable of S; specifically, it is the observable $\chi_P : E^n \to \mathbb{R}$ which takes the value unity for states in Ω_P and the value zero for all other states. Superimposed on this *absolute* characterization of the property, there is a *metric* aspect; we specify the *degree* to which a state fails to possess the property P by the distance of that state from Ω_P in E^n. The incorporation of this metric aspect brings us very close to the notion of a *fuzzy set*, as originally designed by Lotfi Zadeh.[1] The reader may find it of interest to develop in detail the relation between the abstract concept of a fuzzy set and the picture of disorder relative to a particular property P which we have developed; we shall not pursue the matter further here.

The circle of ideas we have developed above allows us now to make explicit contact between the developments of Chapters 5.4 and 5.5 above, and the concepts of order and disorder. In particular, we are going to view the deviation $\rho(t)$, which specifies the discrepancy between trajectories determined by the same initial state in an open system S and a closed system S°, in terms of the loss of a property P. In other words, *we are going to treat this deviation as a disordering of S°.*

In order to do this, we must specify that property P which is satisfied by the given trajectory in S°, but which fails to be satisfied by the corresponding trajectory in S. But this is very easy. We shall take the linkages which specify the property P to be merely those linkages in E^n which determine the trajectory of S° in question. If we do this,

retained (and indeed, so that the thermodynamic situation is recaptured
as a special case). Moreover, this reformulation will automatically
relate to the modelling considerations inherent in our results of
Chapter 5.4 and 5.5 above.

Intuitively, what we shall do is the following. We shall begin by
relativizing the concepts of order and disorder, by always referring
them to some property P. However, this property P will be an absolute
property, in the sense that whether it obtains or not does not pertain
to whether a particular system is open or closed. We will call a
state of any such system an *ordered state* relative to P if it exhibits
the property; disordered relative to P if it does not exhibit the
property. Thus, the set of states of a system which exhibit the
property is the set of ordered states; the complement of this set
is the set of disordered states. For each disordered state, we may
in fact measure the *extent* to which it is disordered in terms of
its distance from the set of ordered states in the state space.
Thus, our definition of order will be relative, in that it pertains
only to a specific property P, specified in advance; it will be
absolute, in that the state of any system can be characterized,
independent of any dynamics on the system, as ordered or disordered
relative to the property in question.

The first step in making these heuristic considerations precise is
specifying what we shall mean by a property P of a system. For us,
such a property shall always be characterized in terms of specific
linkage relations between observables of our systems. We recall
that a linkage relation is of the form

$$\Phi(f_1, \ldots, f_n) = 0 \tag{5.8.1}$$

where the $f_i : S \to \mathbb{R}$ are observables of our system. More exactly,
we can define the set of abstract states of S on which such a linkage
relation holds. i.e. for which

$$\Phi(f_1(s), \ldots, f_r(s)) = 0.$$

The totality of these abstract states define a definite subset of
any encoding of S; in particular, they will define such a subset
in the encoding $S \to E^n$ arising from the state variables $x_1, \ldots, x_n :$
$S \to \mathbb{R}$ which we employed in 5.4 and 5.5 above.

Thus, for us, a property P will be a set of linkage relations between
observables of a system S, of the form (5.8.1). For each system S
on which these observables are defined, there will be a subset of
states (perhaps empty) which satisfy the property, and as we have
seen, this subset will be imaged in any specific encoding of S.
These imaged points in an encoding will be called *the ordered states
of S* relative to the property P. Clearly, this definition of order
is independent of any dynamics, or indeed of any other property
which might be possessed by such a system S; it thus has the same
kind of absolute character as that manifested by the entropy in
thermodynamics. On the other hand, it is relative in that it is
defined only with respect to a definite property P; i.e. a definite
family of linkage relations between observables of S.

In particular, let us suppose that a property P is defined through
a *family* of linkage relations of the form

then the corresponding set Ω_p of ordered states with respect to the property becomes merely the trajectory itself. Alternatively: the trajectory in question is specified by the linkages which define the dynamics in $S°$ (i.e. the linkages between the values of the state variables evaluated at a state and the instantaneous rates of change of these state variables) supplemented by the linkages which specify the initial state. These uniquely determine the trajectory, and hence again the property P. Under these circumstances, it is now immediate that the discrepancy between trajectories of $S°$ and S, specified by the same initial state, represents a disordering of $S°$, and in fact a disordering which grows in time.

But now let us further observe that the set of formal linkages which defines a property P can also be regarded as a *model* of P. Indeed, the set of linkages between states and their instantaneous rates of change in E^n which characterize the system $S°$ are precisely what we have called a model of $S°$. Thus, the disordering of $S°$ which we have demonstrated above, and which represents the discrepancy between the behavior of $S°$ and a more open system S, can be interpreted precisely as the discrepancy between the actual behavior of the system S and that of a model of the subsystem $S°$. Since $S°$ is itself regarded as a model of S, we may conclude that *the concept of disorder always refers to a discrepancy between the behavior of a system and the behavior of a model of that system.* Stated another way: order represents a concordance of behavior between a system and a model, in that the linkages which characterize the model are also satisfied by the system; disorder represents the extent to which those linkages fail to be satisfied. Hence, disorder is always to be understood relative to some particular description, or model, or property; it is thus perfectly possible for a system to be disordering with respect to one property, but not with respect to another. It is precisely this fact, which has long been intuitively sensed but not clearly articulated, which is responsible for much of the controversy which has arisen from the concepts of order and disorder.[2]

Let us now make some concluding observations about the circle of ideas which we have developed above. The first is to observe that, in our treatment of the deviation $\rho(t)$ between corresponding trajectories of $S°$ and S, given in Chapters 5.4 and 5.5 above, there is apparently a certain symmetry between the roles played by $S°$ and S. Namely, this discrepancy is the same, whether we regard it as arising from opening the system $S°$ to environmental interaction at t = 0, or whether we regard it as arising from closing the system S to those interactions at that instant. In the former case, it appears that we obtain a disordering of the closed system $S°$ by opening it; in the latter case, we obtain a disordering of the open system S by closing it. This is indeed the case; but we must recognize carefully that *the properties P which define order and disorder in the two situations are different.* Thus, if we opened a closed system $S°$, the linkages defining the property P (and hence which constitute the *model* against which order and disorder are characterized) are those pertaining to $S°$. On the other hand, if we close an open system S, these linkages are those pertaining to S. The discrepancy between the behaviors of the two systems is the same in both cases, and represents a disordering in our sense; but the property P against which order and disorder are recognized is determined by which of the two systems we take as the reference.

Finally, let us return briefly to the situation in thermodynamics, and the absolute characterization of disorder as the state of thermo-dynamic equilibrium of a system completely closed and isolated. In an intuitive sense, the state of thermodynamic equilibrium (as seen from a microscopic perspective, such as the Maxwell-Boltzmann distribution) is a state with no properties; it is characterized by total homogeneity, isotropy and stationarity in the underlying phase space. Thus, any departure from thermodynamic equilibrium will appear as the establishment of linkages between the underlying state variables, through which the departure from homogeneity, isotropy and stationarity can be described. These linkages correspond to *properties*, which are by definition lost as the system approaches thermodynamic equilibrium. With respect to any such property, then, thermodynamic equilibrium is indeed a state of maximal disorder. This is indeed, we believe, the intuitive sense underlying the identification of equilibrium with disorder; the loss of all properties involving departures from absolute uniformity. On the other hand, if we consider instead those properties which characterize absolute uniformity, and express these in terms of linkages, then the state of thermodynamic equilibrium becomes a state of maximal *order*. Thus, we see how important it is to specify in advance the property P with respect to which order and disorder are to be referred.

We will finally note, for future reference, that the disordering which arises from opening a system is ultimately to be identified with such things as "wear-and-tear", and the other kinds of deleterious effects which appear in the operation of real systems; it is also closely related to the "side-effects" about which we spoke earlier (cf. Chapter 1.1 above). All these things, as well as the "errors" discussed in the preceding chapters, are simply ways of expressing the growth of discrepancies between a real system S, open to environmental interactions, and a model of S, which represents a subsystem closed to such interaction.

REFERENCES AND NOTES

1. A fuzzy set was originally defined by Zadeh (*Information and Control* 8 (1965), 338-353) as one whose characteristic function takes values in the whole unit interval, rather than the two-point set {0, 1}. Since then, Zadeh and others have extended the idea enormously, into the theory of mappings, relations, systems, languages, etc. It has been Zadeh's contention that the preponderance of circumstances with which men deal are inherently imprecise; hence models built out of ordinary precise (i.e. non-fuzzy) mathematical objects are inadequate to deal with them. There is now a burgeoning literature in this area; for an overview, see e.g.
    Zadeh L. et al., (eds.) *Fuzzy Sets and Their Applications to Cognitive and Decision Processes*. Academic Press (1975).

2. Relevant here is the overly facile identification of "order" with "information" which characterized so many early attempts to apply Shannon's results on coding (cf. 5.6 above; also Note 3 to Chapter 3.5). Perhaps the responsibility for this ultimately rests with E. Schrödinger, who in his little book *What is Life?* (Cambridge University Press 1944) suggested that organisms avoid disordering (i.e. increase in entropy) by feeding on order; i.e. on *negative* entropy. From this it was a simple step from negentropy to order to information. Many valiant attempts were made, e.g. to calculate the "information content" of a DNA sequence, or even an entire organism (cf. for instance the volume *Information Theory in Biology* (edited by H. P. Yockey, R. L. Platzman and H. Quastler, (Pergamon, 1958); these essentially have come to naught, for reasons we have considered at great length above.

5.9 The Stability of Modelling Relations

The first four sections of the present volume were devoted to establishing the nature of the modelling relation, and exhibiting this relation in a profusion of particular cases. As we saw abundantly, a modelling relation can be regarded as an encoding of a natural system into a formal one, in such a way that the inferential structure of the formal system allows us to mirror the actual behavior in the system being modelled. The modelling relation thus establishes a kind of conjugacy between the system and the model; this enables us to employ the inferential structure in the model to make specific predictions about the system being modelled.

However, the present section has been devoted to exploring what must in effect be regarded as the failure of modelling relations, particularly in the context of dynamical models. We have argued that, since any model can only encode a fraction of the degrees of freedom, or interactive capabilities, of the system being modelled, it can only represent a closed subsystem of that system. Thus, the relation between a system and a model is the same as the relation between an open system and the same system when closed to particular environmental interactions. The result is a discrepancy which grows with time; a discrepancy between the inferential structure (and hence the predictions) of the model, and the actual behavior of the system to which these predictions are to be compared.

We have seen at length above how this growing discrepancy can be interpreted in terms of error, dissipation, disordering, and other similar phenomena, all of which represent a growing failure of the modelling relation; i.e. a growing loss of conjugacy between the actual temporal behavior of the system itself, and the predictions of that behavior made on the basis of a model.

Thus, it becomes necessary to reconcile the two basic propositions with which we have been concerned; namely: (a) modelling relations based on abstract encodings, can be established between natural and formal systems, and indeed provide essential tools of science; and (b) the properties of the modelling relation, particularly of dynamical models, tend to be lost in the course of time; i.e. the modelling relation initially established ultimately fails. This forces us to formulate problems relating to *the stability of the*

modelling relation itself. In the process, we shall learn some
important new things about the modelling relation, which must ultimately reflect some very deep properties of our world, and our
perceptions of it.

Let us begin to formulate the notion of the stability of a modelling
relation, in the light of these remarks. For simplicity, we shall
stay within the context of dynamical models, and in particular, we
shall contunue to regard the relation between system and model as
the relation between an open system S and the same system S° closed
to some modality of interactions.

Thus, we shall suppose that S° and S are encoded into a common set
of states, which we shall assume to be a manifold X. Let us further
suppose that the dynamics on S° can be encoded into a one-parameter
family of automorphisms

$$T_t^{\,a} : X \to X,$$

where a denotes an appropriate set of constitutive parameters, and
that the dynamics on S can be encoded into another one-parameter
family of automorphisms

$$T_t^{\,a'} : X \to X$$

where a' is a different set of constitutive parameters. Then for
each instant t, we can construct a diagram of the form

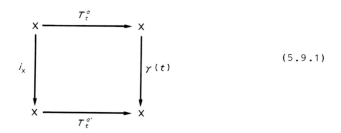

$$(5.9.1)$$

where i_X is the identity map on X, and $\gamma(t)$ is the map defined by

$$\gamma(t)(T_t^{\,a}(x_0)) = T_t^{\,a'}(x_0)$$

for each x_0 in X. Clearly, if the two dynamics were identical, then
$\gamma(t) = i_X$ for every t. However, as we have seen, the two dynamics
will generally not be identical; thus $\gamma(t)$ in effect measures the
discrepancy between the *predicted* state $T_t^{\,a}(x_0)$ and the *actual* state
$T_t^{\,a'}(x_0)$, when the system S and the model S° are started on the same
initial state x_0. It is clear that the map $\gamma(t) : X \to X$ is well
defined, because $T_t^{\,a}$ and $T_t^{\,a'}$ are automorphisms of X.

We can thus refer the discrepancy between the system S and the model
S° under these circumstances to the discrepancy between $\gamma(t)$ and the
identity map i_X. Namely, if $\gamma(t)$ is "close" to i_X in some appropriate
metric, then the discrepancy at time t between the predicted behavior
and the actual behavior will be small. Up to this measure of small-
ness, the predictions based on S° will approximate to the actual
behavior of S, and we can say that the modelling relation between S°
and S continues to hold. Of course, the *magnitude* of the map $\gamma(t)$
depends upon t; thus, as t varies, $\gamma(t)$ will trace out some trajectory in the space H(X, X) of mappings of X onto itself, and as we
have seen, will ultimately leave any small neighborhood of the
identity i_X in H(X, X). As long as this trajectory $\{\gamma(t)\}$ remains
in such a neighborhood, however, we may say that the modelling
relation between S° and S holds *to a particular level of approximation.*

Let us look at this situation in a another way. Let us suppose that
the set H(X, X) is given some appropriate metric. In this metric,
consider the sphere U of radius $\varepsilon > 0$ about the identity map i_X.
At time t = 0, we have by definition $\gamma(0) = i_X$. As t increases from
0, the map $\gamma(t)$ will trace out a trajectory or curve in H(X, X),
which we will suppose to be continuous in the metric on H(X, X).
As long as this trajectory stays within U, the discrepancy between
$T_t^a(x_0)$ and $T_t^{a'}(x_0)$ will also be small *in X*, for all x_0 in X; i.e.
the predictions about S based on the model S° will be approximately
verified. In other words, the diagram

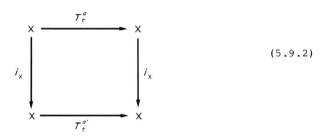

(5.9.2)

which embodies the hypothesized modelling relation between S and S°,
will *approximately* commute; i.e. will be insensitive to a replacement of i_X by $\gamma(t)$, for all values of t such that $\gamma(t)$ lies in U.
*We shall say that the modelling relation (5.9.2) is stable for all
such values of t.*

In a sense, the above ideas serve to define the stability of our
modelling relation between S° and S in terms of the stability of
the identity map i_X in H(X, X) with respect to the dynamics

$$i_X \longmapsto \gamma(t).$$

Diagrammatically, in H(X, X), we have the situation shown in Figure 5.9.1:

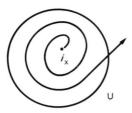

Fig. 5.9.1.

The situation we are describing must be carefully distinguished from that of the structural stability of the dynamics T_t^a. The above considerations are meaningful whether this dynamics is structurally stable or not; indeed, the question regarding the stability of the modelling relation (in which *time* plays the role of the "bifurcation parameter") has little to do with the structural stability of T_t^a (in which the constitutive parameters a are the bifurcation parameters). However, there is an important sense in which the two concepts are related. We recall that if the dynamics T_t^a is structurally stable to the replacement of a by new constitutive parameters a', then there are mappings α, β : X → X such that the diagram

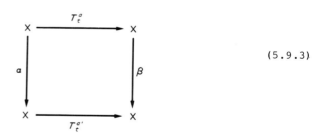

(5.9.3)

commutes for all times t; the mappings α and β depend only on the initial values and the perturbed values of the constitutive parameters (i.e. only on a and a'). This relation between the dynamics is one of *conjugacy*, and its interpretation is quite different from the situation diagrammed in (5.9.2) above. For in (5.9.2), we keep track of the states of S° and S through the *same* family of state variables for both systems; in (5.9.3) we must pass to *new* families of state variables for the system S, related to those describing the states of S° by the mappings α and β. However, let us observe that we can *reduce* (5.9.3) to the form (5.9.2) by rewriting it in the form

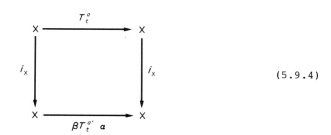

$$(5.9.4)$$

In this form (5.9.4), we retain the same state variable for describing
S° and S, but we must rewrite the dynamics on S; i.e. we replace
the original dynamics $T_t^{a'}$ by a new dynamics $\beta T_t^{a'} \alpha$, which directly
incorporates the passage to new state variables into the dynamics
itself.

The relation between the diagrams (5.9.3) and (5.9.4) allows us to
make two general comments, each of which is important:

(a) We have seen that the replacement of a closed system S° by an
     open system S (i.e. a perturbation of the constitutive parameters
     a to a different set a') changes the dynamics, when both of them
     are viewed with respect to the same set of state variables.
     However, if the respective dynamics T_t^a, $T_t^{a'}$ are conjugate
     (i.e. if S° is structurally stable to this perturbation) then
     the discrepancy between them can be annihilated if we are willing
     to pass to a new set of state variables to describe S. That is,
     we can *renormalize* either our state descriptions (as in the
     diagram (5.9.3)) or the dynamics itself (as in the diagram
     (5.9.4)). The effect of this renormalization, from the stand-
     point of the mapping $\gamma(t)$, is basically to keep forcing it to
     coincide with i_X in the renormalized coordinates. We thus
     force i_X to be stable in H(X, X), and hence we thereby stabilize
     the entire modelling relation (5.9.1) for all times t. We
     stress, however, that the price to be paid for this is the
     requirement to pass to a new encoding of S, different from that
     for S°. And obviously, if the dynamics T_t^a is not structurally
     stable to the perturbation a ⟼ a', then no renormalization
     of this kind can stabilize the modelling relation for all times.

(b) We recall that a conjugacy diagram of the form (5.9.3) already
     expresses a modelling relation between a pair of dynamics
     imposed on a manifold X. In this case, we can view both of
     these dynamics as pertaining to closed subsystems S°, S°' of
     different systems S, S' respectively. Invoking our previous
     results, the behaviors of S and S' will in fact be different
     from those encoded into S° and S°', and thus *the conjugacy
     relation between them will itself cease to hold under these
     circumstances*. However, by passing from the diagram (5.9.3)
     to the diagram (5.9.4), we can formulate the growing deviation

from conjugacy in terms of the stability of the diagram (5.9.4).
In this way, we can generalize our considerations of stability
from its initial setting, and make it apply to *any conjugacy
relation whatsoever*. We thus have an effective means of talking
about the stability of *any* modelling relation between systems,
and not merely of the stability of the dynamics of a single
system S° when the system is opened to environmental interactions.

The further development of these propositions raises numerous interesting technical problems, which are of great importance for the
epistemology of the modelling relation, but would here take us too
far afield to consider here. Their specific import for our main
argument is that they draw attention to the *domain of stability* of
a given modelling relation. More specifically, attention is drawn
to a definite span of time over which a modelling relation like
(5.9.1) or (5.9.3) remains stable. The very definition of stability
means that, within this time span, the predictions of the model (i.e.
the behavior of a closed system S°) gives us at least approximately
correct information about the corresponding behavior of the system
being modelled (i.e. the system S° opened to environmental interactions). When this time span is exceeded, we may say that the
behavior of the model, and of the system being modelled, have
become so different that a *bifurcation* has occurred between them;
in that case, the model becomes useless for predictive purposes, and
must be replaced by a different model in one way or another.

To talk in more detail about the span of time over which a modelling
relation remains stable, it is helpful to reformulate the problem
of stability in the other equivalent languages we have developed.
For the stability of a modelling relation means that, for practical
predictive purposes, *we may replace an open system S by a certain
closed subsystem S°; or that we may replace a complex system by a
simple one.* By definition, this replacement is *without significant
visible effect*, modulo the encoding we are employing, for as long
as the modelling relation remains stable. Our empirical experience
with modelling relations, as exemplified by the many specific illustrations we have given in the preceding sections, indicate that the
time interval over which stability persists can be substantial, even
if it cannot be indefinitely long in general. Thus, although the
behaviors of system and model will ultimately bifurcate, *they will
in fact remain similar until bifurcation occurs*.

This fact of experience can be stated in another way. Until bifurcation occurs, a *complex* system may be replaced by a simpler system
(the model) with no visible consequences, at least with respect to
a particular encoding. During this period, for as long as the
stability of the modelling relation persists, the complex system
is in fact behaving *as if it were* a simple system. This means that
as far as the modelled behavior is concerned, *only a few degrees of
freedom, or interactive capabilities, of the complex system are
actually involved in that behavior.* We may in fact elevate this
assertion to a general principle governing the interaction of complex
natural systems; namely, *given any specific interaction between
such systems, there is a definite time interval in which this interaction involves only a few degrees of freedom of the interacting
systems.* This means precisely that during such a time interval, the
complex systems may be replaced by simpler (abstract) subsystems,
or by models, without visible effect on that interaction.

The principle we have enunciated is perhaps the reason why science
is possible at all. Indeed, for periods of time which are substantial

to us, behaviors of complex systems do indeed appear as if they involved simple systems. These simple systems are themselves models for the complex systems they may replace, and further can be encoded into formal systems in a direct fashion. If it were not so, the world would appear as a total chaos, from which no laws, rules or principles could be extracted. For by definition, the formulation of scientific laws depends precisely on simple observable regularities which relate events, and such regularities are characteristic of simple systems. Indeed, if our measurement procedures could not isolate *single* degrees of freedom (i.e. single observables) the first step of the encodings on which science is based could never be made.

However, as we have seen, we cannot *indefinitely* expect a complex system to behave like a simple one, nor an open system to behave like a closed one. Ultimately, the two behaviors will bifurcate from one another. At such a time, we must replace our model by another; i.e. by another *simple* system, which encodes the degrees of freedom then dominating the interaction. From our point of view, as we have stated above, it will appear that *new properties of the system have emerged*; indeed, the phenomena of emergence so prominent in biology and elsewhere are nothing but the bifurcations between the behavior of a complex system and a simple model of it. In general, such a bifurcation represents the failure of linkage relations which previously existed, and the establishment of new ones; it is the encoding of these which lead us to the new model with which our original model must be replaced.

To these considerations, we must append a few general remarks. The first is this: all our considerations were based on the restricting of attention to a single behavior of our complex system. Any such behavior may be treated in the fashion we have indicated above, but different behaviors of the same system already require different encodings; i.e. different models. There need be no relation between the encodings appropriate to different behaviors of the same system, as we have abundantly seen. Thus, each modelling relation we establish, pertaining each to a distinct system behavior, will have its own domain of stability. We cannot therefore generalize about the stability of arbitrary system behaviors from the properties of a single one.

The second general remark is this: by definition, we cannot know the domain of stability of a particular modelling relation *from within the context if that modelling relation itself*. The bifurcation between system behavior and model behavior which we have described is itself an emergent novelty from the standpoint of the simple model; the basis for it has by definition been abstracted away in the very act of formulating the model. In order to *predict* this domain of stability, we need in fact another description; i.e. another model, with respect to which the original model will bifurcate. Indeed, this was the procedure we used when we initiated our discussion, and why we chose to do so in the context of closed and open systems. All we can say in general is that the domain of stability of a given modelling relation is *finite*; but we cannot in general predict the magnitude of this domain except through the agency of another model.

CHAPTER 6

Anticipatory Systems

6.1 General Introduction

At the very outset of this work, in Chapter 1.1 above, we tentatively
defined the concept of an anticipatory system; a system containing
a predictive model of itself and/or of its environment, which allows
it to change state at an instant in accord with the model's predictions pertaining to a later instant. Armed as we now are with a
clearer idea of what a model is, we may now return to this concept,
and attempt to obtain a deeper understanding of some of the principal
properties of such systems. It is well to open our discussion with
a recapitulation of the main features of the modelling relation
itself, which is by definition the heart of an anticipatory system.

We have seen that the essence of a model is a relation between a
natural system S and some suitable formal system M. The modelling
relation itself is essentially a linkage between behaviors in S and
inferences drawn in M become predictions about the behavior of S.
This linkage is itself expressed in terms of a commutative diagram
of mappings of the kind we have seen abundantly in the preceding
section, and which in mathematical terms expresses a *conjugacy* between the properties of S, and the properties of M which are linked
to it.

In the last analysis, a modelling relation of this kind is established
through an *encoding* of qualities or observables of S into formal or
mathematical objects in M. These mathematical objects serve as
labels or symbol vehicles which symbolically represent the qualities
of S with which they are associated. The very definition of a system
implies that such encoded qualities are *linked* to one another in
definite ways; such linkages are represented in M by relations
satisfied by the objects which represent the qualities. These
relations are called *equations of state* for the system. The rules
of inference in M allow us to draw conclusions from these relations,
which as we have seen then become predictions about behaviors of S.

We have also seen that a relation of analogy is established between
two natural systems S_1, S_2 which can be encoded into the same formal
system M. To the extent that an analogy exists between two such
systems, each of them can be regarded as a model for the other.
Analogous systems can thus also be regarded as *alternate realizations*
of a common formal system M.

We found that any encoding of a natural system S into a formal system M involved an act of abstraction, in which non-encoded qualities are necessarily ignored. Such an act of abstraction is not peculiar to theory; indeed, any act of observation (on which any kind of encoding must be based) is already an abstraction in this sense. What is captured by such an abstraction is thus not all of S, but rather a subsystem. In this sense, analogous systems are those which share a common subsystem. Almost by definition, however, any behavior of S which involves qualities not encoded into a particular model M is in principle unpredictable from M.

The relationship between M and S can thus be regarded as expressing what the behavior of S *would* be if S were closed to interactions involving non-encoded qualities. The actual relation of M to S is thus seen to be that between a system open to modalities of environmental interaction, and the same system isolated from those modalities. In the context of dynamical models, we saw that in general there will be a discrepancy between the behaviors of S and the corresponding behavior predicted by M, and that this discrepancy will generally grow in time. The character of this discrepancy is, of course, unpredictable from within M, since the basis for it has been abstracted away in the process of the encoding from which M was generated. It is the growth of such discrepancies which is responsible for phenomena associated with error and "disorder", and also with the emergence of novel behaviors (as judged from the standpoint of M) in complex systems. The root of these discrepancies lies in the appearance of bifurcations between corresponding behaviors of M and S over time, and was summed up in the principle: no natural system S is indistinguishable from a closed subsystem of itself.

Now let us see what is necessary in order to extend this discussion of the modelling relation, in such a way that it can be brought to bear on the characterization and study of anticipatory systems. Let us first observe that, according to our characterization of analogy between natural systems, two natural systems S_1, S_2 are analogous precisely when they may be encoded into a common formal system M; i.e. precisely when we can construct a diagram of the form for suitable encodings E_1, E_2.

$$(6.1.1)$$

As we have seen, this means precisely that the natural systems S_1, S_2 possess a common closed subsystem. Thus, it is certainly true that S_1 contains a model of S_2, and that S_2 contains a model of S_1; indeed, in formal terms, the relation $E_2^{-1}E_1$ can be regarded as an encoding of the states of S_1 into states of S_2; likewise, the relation $E_1^{-1}E_2$ represents an encoding of the states of S_2 into the states of S_1. Thus, the relation of analogy always gives rise to an essential feature of anticipatory systems; namely, that such a system possess a model of another system.

However, the mere fact that a model of S_1 can be found in S_2, while clearly necessary if S_2 is to be an anticipatory system, is far from sufficient to make it so. As we recall, the decisive feature of an anticipatory system is that, in effect, it employs its model to make predictions about S_1, and more important, change of state occurs in S_2 at an instant as a function of its predictions. Let us see, in a rough and heuristic way, how this decisive feature may be incorporated into our discussion; details and examples will be presented in subsequent chapters of this section.

First, it is trivially clear that those aspects of S_2 which comprise or embody the model of S_1 must not exhaust all of S_2. That is, there must be qualities of S_2 which are not related to the encoding E_2 displayed in (1) above. In terms of that diagram, we may say more formally that $E_2^{-1} E_1 (S_1) \neq S_2$.

The question then arises: how are the qualities of S_2 which are encoded into M related to those which are not so encoded? To answer this, let us suppose that $f : S_2 \to \mathbb{R}$ is an observable of S_2 not encoded into M, and let us consider what would happen if there were a linkage of M to f. Then by definition, given an arbitrary m in M, and an arbitrary number r in $f(S_2)$, there need be no state of $s \epsilon S_2$ such that $E_2 (s) = m$ and $f(s) = r$. Stated another way, fixing a value $r = f(s)$ will make some elements of M *inaccessible* if E_2 is linked to f. This follows immediately from the fact that in these circumstances the mapping

$$f \times E_2 : S_2 \to \mathbb{R} \times M$$

is into and not onto. Intuitively, this means that the *full model M of S_1 is not accessible from states of S_2 encoded in this fashion.* Thus, if every observable f of S_2 were linked to those comprising M, it would follow that M could not in fact be a model of S_1, which contradicts our initial hypothesis.

Thus, the set of all observables of S_2 unlinked to those in M is not empty. It follows from this that we can in fact construct an encoding of S_2 which is precisely of the form

$$S_2 \to M \times X \tag{6.1.2}$$

where X is a manifold, co-ordinatized by observables f such that M is unlinked to f. That is, the mapping 6.1.2 is *onto*. The existence of an encoding of the form 6.1.2, in which there is an orthogonality between the subsystem of S_2 comprising the model, and other observables of S_2 to which the model is unlinked, is the second necessary condition which must be satisfied if S_2 is to be an anticipatory system.

A third condition follows now from the fact that the model M serves to influence present change of state in S_2. This can be interpreted as follows: although the observables defining M are unlinked to those defining X in 6.1.2 above, a definite linkage exists between the observables of M and the *rates of change* of the observables of X. Thus, the behavior of S_2, as viewed through the encoding into X alone, will depend on M as well as on X. In a certain sense, the encoding of X alone defines thereby a closed subsystem of S_2, whose properties describe *how S_2 would behave if there were no model.*
Indeed, we may think of X as a closed system, and XxM as a corresponding open system; we may then apply the results of Chapters 5.4 and 5.5 directly to this situation. As we saw, there will be a growing discrepancy between the behaviors of X and XxM; in the present case, this discrepancy represents precisely *the effect of the model* M on the behavior of S_2.

This then represents the third necessary condition which is required if S_2 is to represent an anticipatory system: namely, the state of the model M must modify the properties of other observables of S_2 (namely, those involved in the encoding of S_2 into the manifold X). Indeed, we can regard the total encoding 6.1.2 of S_2 as follows: the elements of M represent particular values of constitutive parameters of S_2; to each $m \in M$ there is a copy of the manifold X, and the behavior in any such manifold depends on the value of M with which it is associated. The difference in behavior between two such copies of X is precisely the discrepancy we encountered before. We may ourselves anticipate future developments by calling the change in behavior as seen in X, arising from the particular element of the model M involved, an *adaptation* of X (or more accurately, in the case of a predictive model, a pre-adaptation).

Next, if we suppose that S_2 is modifying its present state (i.e. its behavior as seen through the encoding of S_2 into X) on the basis of a model, there would be no objective significance to this modification unless S_2 were interacting (or at least potentially interacting) with S_1 itself. For M is a model of S_1 by hypothesis; clearly, to attach significance to the conditions we have developed, it is necessary that the modification arising in S_2 have something to do with S_1. We will take the point of view that *the above described change in* S_2, *arising from the predictive model of* S_1, *must be manifested in a corresponding change in some actual or potential interaction between* S_1 *and* S_2. In other words, there must be some discrepancy between the interaction between S_1 and S_2 which actually occurs, and the interactio which would have occurred had the model not been present. This represents a fourth condition required to turn S_2 into an anticipatory system.

Finally, we must now introduce some dynamical considerations, to capture the idea that M is a *predictive* model. To do this, we must recall some properties of temporal encodings of dynamics, as they were described in Chapter 4.5 above. Let us suppose that $T_t : S_1 \rightarrow S_1$ is an abstract dynamics on S_1. If M is to be a dynamical model of this abstract dynamics, then there must exist a dynamics $\overline{T}_{x(t)} : M \rightarrow M$ such that the diagram

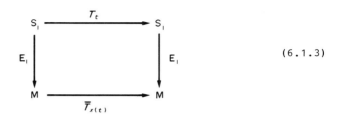

$$(6.1.3)$$

commutes. In this dynamics, the instant x(t) is that which *corresponds* to the instant t; it will be recalled that, in general, the time scales for the two dynamics will not be the same, and that a conversion factor (here denoted by x) is necessary between them.

If we ignore the conversion factor, and attempt to use the time scale of the dynamics T_t on S_1 as an *absolute* scale, then T_t and $\overline{T}_t$ are in general not conjugate. This is because with respect to any absolute time scale, the trajectories in S_1 and the corresponding trajectories in M are traversed at different rates. The temporal relations between such corresponding trajectories are illustrated diagrammatically in Figure 6.1.1.

In this Figure, we have supposed that $\alpha(t) < t$. Accordingly, suppose that the system S_1 is initially in state s(0), and the model M is in the corresponding state $E_1(s(0))$. Then after a time t has elapsed for S_1, this system will be in state $T_t(s(0))$. If we use the *same* scale for M, then M will at this instant be in state $\overline{T}_t(E_1(s(0)))$. As we can see from the figure, these two states *do not correspond*; in fact, M is now in a state *for which the corresponding state will not be reached in* S_1 *until further time has elapsed. In other words, if we look at the state* of the model M at time t, then this state of M actually encodes a state which S_1 will not reach until time t+h, where all times are referred to S_1. Intuitively, with respect to this time scale, the trajectories in M are traced out faster than are the corresponding trajectories in S_1; thus the state of M at an

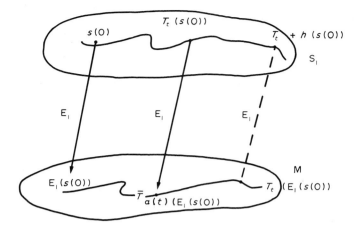

Fig. 6.1.1.

instant actually refers to the state of S_1 at a later instant. It is in this sense that we can regard M as a predictive model; the present state of M (i.e. its state at an instant t) is actually an encoding of a future state of S_1, when referred to the same time scale. In this scale, by looking at the *present* state of **M**, we obtain information pertaining to a *future* state of S_1.

Thus we arrive at our fifth and final condition for S_2 to be an anticipatory system: the model of S_1 which is encoded into S_2 must be a predictive model, in the sense we have just defined.

These conditions may be succinctly summed up as follows: An anticipatory system S_2 is one which contains a model of a system S_1 with which it interacts. This model is a predictive model; its *present* states provide information about *future* states of S_1. Further, the present state of the model causes a change of state in other subsystems of S_2; these subsystems are (a) involved in the interaction of S_2 with S_1, and (b) they do not affect (i.e. are unlinked to) the model of S_1. In general, we can regard the change of state in S_2 arising from the model as an *adaptation*, or pre-adaptation, of S_2 relative to its interaction with S_1. The conditions we have enunciated above establish precisely these properties.

Now let us focus our attention on the specific effect of a predictive model on an interaction. What we shall do is, as before, compare the actual interaction which occurs in an anticipatory system with the interaction which *would have occurred* if there were no predictive model; i.e. if the subsystem M of S_2 were absent. At the present level of generality, we can do this only in a correspondingly general way. Our approach will be to employ a modified version of the arguments used in a different connection in Chapters 5.4 and 5.5 above; namely, we shall argue that *there is some property P of* S_2 *which is satisfied when* S_2 *is anticipatory, and which is not satisfied when* S_2 *is non-anticipatory.*

Before taking up the specific argument required to establish this result, let us spend a moment assessing its significance. If such a property P can be identified, then we must say that the *role of the predictive model is to stabilize this property*; or, to put it another way, that the anticipatory behavior serves as a homeostat for the property P. To use another language: the predictive model *prevents a disordering* of S_2, with respect to the property P in question, which by virtue of its interaction with S_1 would otherwise occur. Indeed, it is *only* with respect to the stabilization of a property P that we can refer to the anticipatory change of state, occurring in S_2 in accordance with the state of its predictive model, as an adaptive change, or more precisely as a *pre-adaptation*. Seen in this light, the anticipatory change of state in S_2, determined by the state of the predictive model S_1 in S_2, serves precisely to modulate the interaction between these two systems in such a way that the property P is retained. We shall have a great deal more to say about these notions of adaptation and pre-adaptation as we proceed. We shall also have occasion to consider the following kind of converse question: *given* a property P which we wish to stabilize in S_2, can we convert S_2 into anticipatory system in such a way that the given property becomes precisely the one stabilized in the above sense? As will be seen, this is the central problem in what might be called the theory of predictive control.

With these words of motivation, let us return to the problem of finding a property P which is stabilized by the predictive model of S_1 in S_2. But this is now very easy; indeed, we shall simply exploit the character of the discussion already given in Chapter 5.8 above. Let us recall that the presence of the model M causes the interaction between S_1 and S_2 to be *different* from what it would have been, had the model not been present, and had it not been capable of pre-adapting the states of S_2. Moreover, we recall that the effect of any interaction between systems is to establish new linkages between particular observables of these systems. As we saw in Chapter 5.8, the specification of a linkage is equivalent to the characterization of an associated property P. Accordingly, we shall merely identify the property P in question with the linkages established through the interaction between S_1 and S_2 which actually occurs as a consequence of the predictive model M; by its very definition, this property is stabilized by the presence of the model, and will be lost if the model is not present. Hence there is always at least one property P which is stabilized by the presence of a predictive model in an anticipatory system. And if there is one such property, there will always be many others; namely, those which are in an obvious sense *linked* to P. These facts will be most important to us as we proceed.

It is now instructive to compare the conditions developed above to characterize a feedforward system with the heuristic discussion of Chapter 1.1 above, and in particular, with the diagram of such a system illustrated in Figure 1.1.1. It will be seen that all the features of this diagram are in fact embodied in the conditions we have posited. What we have called the anticipatory system S_2 in the above discussion comprises the three boxes labelled respectively M, E and S in Figure 1.1.1.; M represents that encoding of S_2 which comprises the model, S represents that encoding of S_2 which we called X, and E denotes the linkage between M and the dynamics in X through which a state of M establishes an adaptation, or pre-adaptation in X (and what we earlier called the *effectors* of the system). What we called the environment in Figure 1.1.1 is to be identified with the system S_1. Indeed, the only difference between the two discussions is the following: in Figure 1.1.1, we tacitly supposed that M, E and S were three *different* systems, with M controlling S through the effectors E; on the other hand, in the above discussion, M and S represented different encodings of the *same* system, and E corresponds to a linkage between the observables coded into M and the rates of change of those involved in the interaction with S_1. We thus see that our initial heuristic discussion of Chapter 1.1 was in fact well founded in terms of the more comprehensive conceptual treatment of modelling relations which we have developed.

The properties of anticipatory systems will be central to all of our subsequent discussion. Our aim is to develop at least the rudiments of a theory of anticipatory systems, whereby the behavior of such systems can be characterized. Most important, we wish to contrast the behavior of anticipatory systems with those of the reactive systems which have been our main preoccupation thus far, and thereby lay the foundations for what may be called an *anticipatory paradigm* for the treatment of such biological phenomena as adaptation, learning, evolution and other basic organic behaviors. Such a paradigm provides an important alternative to the pure *reactive paradigm*, on which all approaches to such behaviors have heretofore been based. Furthermore, we wish to develop as least some of the implications of such an anticipatory paradigm for human systems, through its bearing on questions of social organization, and its implications for social technologies involving planning and forecasting. These will be our major preoccupations for the remainder of the present volume.

Let us then outline the character of the discussion to follow. In Chapter 6.2, we shall consider in detail perhaps the simplest example of an anticipatory system. This is an example which was already briefly introduced in Chapter 1.1, and involves a forward activation step in a biosynthetic pathway. In particular, we shall see how the general considerations regarding anticipatory systems which were developed above appear in a concrete situation. In Chapter 6.3 we shall once again generalize from this example, with an emphasis on the property P which is stabilized in such a system, and the manner in which this property can be related to functional considerations bearing on fitness and survival. Chapter 6.4 will examine the implications of the stability of modelling relations which was developed in Chapter 5.9, for the long term behavior of anticipatory systems. In particular, we shall show that such systems can manifest novel modes of "system failure", characterized by the loss of properties (linkages) in the system as a whole, without anything which could be identified as a *local failure* occurring in any subsystem.

As an application of these ideas, we shall consider their bearing on
the senescence of organisms and human cultures. In Chapter 6.5, we
shall return to the general problem of adaptation, and develop the
ideas of selection and evolution in the context of anticipatory
systems. In Chapter 6.6, we shall turn to the general question of
the interaction between two systems which are both anticipatory; this
will lead us into problems bearing on *conflict* and *conflict resolution*
in the human realm. Finally, in Chapter 6.7, we shall consider what
may be called the *ontogenesis* of anticipatory systems, and the
general phenomenon of *learning*.

6.2 An Example: Forward Activation

In the present chapter, we shall be concerned with developing in some detail the properties of a particular example which we have seen before; namely, the biosynthetic pathway

$$
A_0 \xrightarrow{E_1} A_1 \xrightarrow{E_2} \cdots \rightarrow A_{n-1} \xrightarrow{E_n^+} A_n \qquad (6.2.1)
$$

with a forward activation step, as indicated. In such a pathway, the initial substrate A_0 also serves as an activator of the enzyme E_n; thus, the rate at which E_n catalyzes its reaction is a function of how much initial substrate A_0 is present. We have already indicated that such a pathway constitutes a simple example of an anticipatory system; we shall here consider its properties, not only as illustrations of the concepts developed above, but as motivation for subsequent theoretical developments.

Let us begin by reviewing the sense in which the pathway 6.2.1 actually constitutes an anticipatory system. We recall that, by virtue of the forward activation step, the concentration $A_0(t)$ of the initial substrate A_0, at any instant t, serves also as a *predictor* of the concentration $A_{n-1}(t+h)$ of the substrate of E_n at a later instant t+h. Therefore, by modulating the rate of the enzyme E_n, the initial substrate A_0 serves to adapt, or better, to pre-adapt, this enzyme so that it will be competent to process its own substrate A_{n-1} at that future time.

We may now formulate these heuristic remarks about the system 6.2.1 in precise mathematical terms. We begin by observing that the function of the pre-adaptation of enzyme E_n is obviously to prevent the accumulation of the intermediate A_{n-1} in the face of ambient fluctuations of the initial substrate A_0. We shall regard this feature of the forward activation step as precisely being the property

P of the system which is in fact stabilized by the pathway. This
represents a biologically plausible situation, and it illustrates
the manner in which such properties can be immediately related to
the biological concept of function.

As a first approximation, we can regard the pathway 6.2.1 as a simple
series of first-order chemical reactions; i.e. as a system of the
form

$$A_0 \xrightarrow{k_1} A_1 \xrightarrow{k_2} \cdots \to A_{n-1} \xrightarrow{k} A_n \qquad (6.2.2)$$

in which k_i denotes the apparent rate of the ith reaction in the
pathway. We shall treat all of these reaction rates k_i as constant,
except for the last one k_n; this last rate shall be taken as a
definite function $k_n(A_0)$ of the initial substrate concentration. The
explicit functional dependence of k_n on A_0 will thus embody the
forward activation step of the system 6.2.1 in the system 6.2.2.

With these hypotheses, the rate equations for the system 6.2.2 can be
immediately written down; they are:

$$dA_i/dt = k_i A_{i-1} - k_{i+1} A_i, \; i = 1, \ldots, n-1$$
$$\qquad (6.2.3)$$
$$dA_n/dt = k_n A_{n-1}$$

where we suppose that $A_0 = A_0(t)$ can be taken as an arbitrary function of time.

Let us consider first the specific rate equation governing the behavior of the intermediate A_{n-1}; namely

$$dA_{n-1}/dt = k_{n-1} A_{n-2} - k_n A_{n-1}. \qquad (6.2.4)$$

The hypothesis that A_{n-1} is not to accumulate can be embodied in the
requirement that dA_{n-1}/dt shall be non-positive; for simplicity, we
shall take the stronger condition that in fact dA_{n-1}/dt shall always
be zero, independent of the level of the initial substrate A_0. Thus,
from 6.2.4, we require that the condition

$$k_{n-1} A_{n-2} = k_n A_{n-1} \qquad (6.2.5)$$

shall hold. We attempt to achieve this condition by making k_n an
explicit funciton of A_0; the *form* of this function will embody the
model implicit in the forward activation loop.

Now we observe that the system of rate equations 6.2.3 is a linear
system, of the type we considered in Chapter 1.2 above; in fact,
these equations are precisely of the form (1.2.3). According to
(1.2.7), we can write the concentrations of the reactants A_{n-2}, A_{n-1}
appearing in 6.2.5 at any instant of time t, as explicit functions of
A_0:

$$A_{n-2}(t) = \int_0^t K_1(t-\tau)A_0(\tau)d\tau;$$

$$A_{n-1}(t) = \int_0^t K_2(t-\tau)A_0(\tau)d\tau. \tag{6.2.6}$$

Here K_1 and K_2 are determined entirely by the appropriate rate constants k_i appearing in the equations 6.2.3; their precise form is
not important for us here, but the reader may find it a useful
exercise to compute them according to the discussion given in Chapter
1.2. The main thing to note is that the values of these reactants
at any instant t is determined by the value of A_0 at earlier instants;
or, stated another way, that the value of A_0 at a given instant
determines the values of the reactants A_{n-2} and A_{n-1} at later instants
according to the reaction scheme 6.2.3.

We now express the control condition 6.2.5 in terms of the explicit
relations 6.2.6. We find that 6.2.5 will be satisfied if we put

$$k_n = k_{n-1} \frac{\int_0^t K_1(t-\tau)A_0(\tau)d\tau;}{\int_0^t K_2(t-\tau)A_0(\tau)d\tau.} \tag{6.2.7}$$

That is: the rate k_n of the final step of 6.2.2, at any instant of
time t, is determined by the value of the initial substrate A_0 at a
prior instant τ = t-h. Equivalently, the value of A_0 at a particular
instant τ determines k_n at a *subsequent* instant t = τ + h.

Thus, assuming that the behavior of the intermediates A_{n-2}, A_{n-1} is
in fact governed by the rate equations 6.2.3, a specification for the
forward activation step in accordance with 6.2.7 will guarantee that
the control condition 6.2.5 is satisfied; i.e. will assure that the
whole pathway satisfies the property P. Under these circumstances,
we can see the exact sense in which the concentration of the initial
substrate A_0 at an instant serves to *pre-adapt* the pathway, so as to
stabilize this property. The pre-adaptation itself is what we earlier
called the *competence* of E_n to maintain the property P; indeed, we
should stress that terms like adaptation and competence are only
meaningful relative to some property P which has been previously
specified.

Let us now reconsider this specific example in terms of the general
discussion of the preceding chapter. In particular, using the
terminology of Chapter 6.1, let us put

$$A_{n-1} = S_1,$$
$$A_0 = M,$$
$$E_n = X, \tag{6.2.8}$$
$$(A_0) \times (E_n) = M \times X = S_2.$$

That is: the anticipatory system, which is called S_2 in the preceding chapter, consists of two parts: (a) the part comprising the
model M, which in the present case is A_0, and (b) the part comprising
the interactive observables X, which is the present case is the enzyme
E_n. The system S_1, with which S_2 interacts, and which M models, is
in this case the substrate A_{n-1} of E_n. As before, the model M is not
linked to the observables in X (i.e. the value of A_0 is not dependent
upon the state of the enzyme E_n), but A_0 does determine the reaction
rate of the enzyme;   e.g. by inducing a conformational change in
enzyme molecules which modifies their rates in accordance with 6.2.7.
With respect to the property P, it is this conformational change, or
rather, its manifestation as a change in rate, which is precisely
the crucial pre-adaptation step. It is now immediate to verify that,
with these identifications, the pathway 6.2.1 does indeed satisfy all
the conditions of an anticipatory system which were developed in the
preceding chapter.

It is worthwhile to look more closely at the roles of the initial
substrate A_0 in this pathway. Clearly, A_0 plays a double role here:
it is on one hand a *substrate* for the entire pathway, and on the other
hand it is a *predictor* for subsequent values of the specific substrate
A_{n-1} of the enzyme E_n which it activates. As a predictor, *its role
is essentially a symbolic one*;   it represents, or encodes, or labels,
a *future* property of A_{n-1}. In this role, A_0 serves essentially as a
linguistic object;   it is a symbol, or more precisely, a symbol
vehicle, for the value of A_{n-1} to which it is linked by 6.2.6 above.
In a precise sense, A_0 in its capacity as activator of E_n is a *hormone*
("messenger"). This terminology is provocative in the present context,
but it is accurate, and is intended to be suggestive.

Let us also note that the homeostatis maintained in the pathway
6.2.1 is obtained entirely through the modelling relation between A_0
and A_{n-1} (i.e. entirely through symbolic processes) by virtue of the
relation 6.2.7 which links the prediction of the model to the actual
rate at which E_n operates. That is, the homeostatis is maintained
entirely through pre-adaptation generated entirely on the basis of
a *predicted* value for A_{n-1}. In particular, there is no *feedback*
in the pathway, and no mechanism available for the system to "see"
the value of the quantity which is in fact controlled, or indeed any
feature beyond that embodied in the predictive model relating A_0 to
A_{n-1}.

Let us make one further observation. The discussion so far has been
couched in terms of a property P, which can be defined entirely in
terms of the pathway 6.2.1 considered as an independent system. But
in fact, such a pathway can be regarded as a single component in a
larger biochemical network, which itself comprises a functional unit
of an intact cell. Thus, the property P of the pathway can be
directly related to properties P' of the successively larger systems
with which it interacts, and ultimately to properties pertaining to
the *viability* of the cell itself. Conversely, we may say that, at

the level of the intact cell, there will be properties pertaining to
its viability which are directly linked to the property P in the
pathway 6.2.1. This kind of "cascading" of properties, by means of
which properties of subsystems can be linked to properties of larger
systems not directly visible from within the subsystem, will become
most important to us shortly.

We shall now develop a further crucial property of the pathway 6.2.1
which is a direct consequence of its anticipatory character. To do
this, let us return to the relation 6.2.5 above which will be seen to
have two distinct but related meanings. On the one hand 6.2.5 expresses the actual behavior of the pathway, as seen from the standpoint of its chemical kinetics, *as a consequence of the hypotheses
we have made about the reactions in the pathway.* On the other hand,
this same linkage is built, via the relation 6.2.7, into the forward
activation step. *It is clear that the forward activation itself will
retain its adaptive character (with respect to the property P) only
as long as these two meanings coincide.* In other words: if the
actual chemical kinetic behavior of the pathway should cause the
linkage between the initial substrate A_0 and the product A_{n-1} to
depart from that expressed in 6.2.5, the forward activation step
governed by 6.2.7 will no longer be adaptive with respect to P, but
will rather have become *maladaptive.*

Stated another way: a particular linkage (namely (6.2.6)) between
the predictor A_0 and the substrate A_{n-1} is "wired in" to the forward
activation step of the pathway 6.2.1; this is expressed precisely
by the relation (6.2.7). On the other hand, these quantities are
actually linked by the detailed kinetic properties of the various
reaction steps in the pathway. As long as the actual linkage between
them is the same as that which is "wired in" to the forward activation
step, the property P will be maintained, and the rate changes in E_n
governed by 6.2.7 will be adaptive responses to fluctuations in A_0
with respect to the property P. However, if there should be a departure between the actual chemical kinetic linkage between A_0 and A_{n-1}
from that expressed in 6.2.7, those same rate changes in E_n will
represent maladaptive responses, to a degree measured by the departure
of the actual linkage from that "wired in" to the activation.

How could such a deviation come about? Ultimately, any such deviation
can be represented by changes in the apparent reaction rates k_i
governing the individual steps in the pathway 6.2.7 (which, we recall,
enter as constitutive parameters into the linkage (6.2.5)), or by the
presence of sources and sinks for the intermediate reactants A_i in
the pathway, beyond those which are explicitly represented in the rate
equations 6.2.3. The latter would correspond to *side reactions,*
competing with those occurring in the pathway; the former could arise
from such things as changes in ambient temperature, or from changes
in the rates of the intermediate enzymes E_i. Thus, the deviations
we are contemplating arise because the pathway 6.2.3 is in fact
immersed in a larger system, and is open to interactions with that
system in ways which are not explicitly represented, either in the
pathway 6.2.1, or in the kinetic equations 6.2.3 which describe that
pathway.

But now the reader may observe that our discussion is taking a

familiar form. In fact, it is nothing other than a reformulation of
the results of Section 5 above, in the context of the special case
we are now considering. In Section 5, we showed that there will
always arise discrepancies between the behavior of a system predicted
on the basis of a model, and the actual behavior of that system;
these discrepancies arise precisely because the actual system is
open to interactions to which the model is necessarily closed.
Relative to some appropriate property P, these discrepancies result
in errors or disordering; or in the present context, to a growing
maladaption of the pathway. And as usual, the character of the
discrepancies, and indeed, the maladaption itself, is unpredictable
and invisible from within the pathway itself.

Thus, we can conclude that a forward activation pathway like 6.2.1
can only retain its adaptive character, or its competence to maintain
the property P, for a characteristic time. The time interval during
which competence is retained does not depend on the pathway itself,
but on the nature of the larger system in which it is embedded, and
on the character of its interactions with that larger system. We may
sum this up by concluding that the property P, characterizing the
adaptive aspects of the pathway's behavior, is *temporally spanned*.
The time interval during which it persists may be quite long,
depending on the character of the ambient environment of the pathway,
but it is inevitably *finite*.

The same may of course be said for any properties linked to P,
including those pertaining to the larger system in which the pathway
is embedded.

It must be emphasized that the temporal spanning of the property P
which we have described does not arise from any localizable fault or
failure attributable to any step within the pathway 6.2.1 itself.
If we were to isolate each enzyme in the pathway, and each substrate,
it would be found individually to be identical in its properties to
the same enzyme or substrate at a time when the property P is maintained by the pathway. Likewise, the forward activation step, considered in isolation, is identical whether the property P is maintained
or not. Thus, if we identify the loss of the property P with a mode
of *system failure* in the pathway 6.2.1, that system failure cannot
be attributed to any localized failure in any one of the individual
steps in the pathway. Rather, it represents a kind of global failure,
which has its roots in the very nature of the modelling relation.
As we shall shortly see, this kind of temporal spanning, considered
as a form of system failure, is an intrinsic property of anticipatory
systems, which has no analog in non-anticipatory or reactive systems.
As we shall see in subsequent chapters, it is responsible for the
most far reaching characteristics of biological systems at all levels,
and allows us to understand in a unified way many puzzling features
of their behaviors.

6.3 General Characteristics of Temporal Spanning

We shall now proceed to recast the considerations of the preceding chapter into a more general form. This generalization will involve two rather distinct parts: (a) the replacement of the specific biosynthetic pathway (6.2.1) by a more general system, and concomitantly, the replacement of the forward activation of the pathway by a more general anticipatory signal, and (b) the replacement of the property P stabilized by the pathway by more general properties, pertaining not only to the system itself, but to larger systems in which the given one is embedded.

Let us begin by generalizing the relevant properties of the enzyme E_n in the pathway (6.2.1). In that pathway, E_n served as a transducer

$$A_{n-1} \xrightarrow{E_n} A_n \qquad (6.3.1)$$

which converted its substrate A_{n-1} to its product A_n at a definite rate. In its simplest terms, this transduction was described by the linkage relation

$$dA_{n-1}/dt = k_n A_n \qquad (6.3.2)$$

which expresses how the rate of change of A_n is linked to the instantaneous value of the substrate concentration.

We shall generalize the enzymic transducer of chemical qualities diagrammed in (1) by the more general transducer.

$$\vec{u} \rightarrow \boxed{\varphi} \rightarrow \vec{v} \qquad (6.3.3)$$

Here, we suppose that $\vec{u} = (u_1, \ldots, u_r)$ is an *input vector* to the transducer (and as such, generalizing the substrate A_{n-1} of 6.3.1, and $\vec{v} = (v_1, \ldots, v_s)$ is the corresponding *output vector* (hence generalizing the product A_n). As usual, the quantities u_i, v_j denote

specific observables of the natural system on which the transducer
acts, and we assume that their values are explicit functions of some
appropriately defined dynamical time t.

The transducer φ itself, which generalizes the enzyme E_n, must be
characterized by an appropriate *equation of state*, which links the
input and output vectors. We will take this equation of state to be
of the general form

$$\vec{v} = \varphi(\vec{u}) \tag{6.3.4}$$

which is an obvious generalization of (6.3.2). We leave open for the
moment the question of the time dependence in 6.3.4, in the sense that
we allow the possibility that 6.3.4 links the values of the input
vector $\vec{u}$ at an instant with those of the output vector $\vec{v}$ at some later
instant.

So far, we have not incorporated the forward activation step of our
pathway. As we recall, the activation step was represented by making
the rate constant k_n in 6.3.2 a specific function of a *predictor* A_0.
There were two aspects involved in doing this; first, there was the
positing of a linkage between the present value of the predictor A_0
and a later value of the actual input A_{n-1}; second, the *present*
value of the predictor A_0 was able to *pre-adapt* the transducer E_n
in a way which depended on the *predicted* value of the substrate A_{n-1}.
This last was accomplished by expressing the rate constant k_n in
6.3.2 as an explicit function of the predictor; i.e. by writing

$$k_n = k_n(A_0). \tag{6.3.5}$$

Let us now incorporate these features into the more general situation
we are constructing.

We accomplish the first of these steps by introducing a general
predictor $\vec{a} = (a_1, \ldots, a_m)$ to play the role of A_0 in our simple
pathway. We assume as before that the *present* value of this predictor
is linked with a future value of the input $\vec{v}$ to the transducer. The
second step is accomplished by supposing that *the equation of state
6.3.4 describing the transducer depends on the predictor $\vec{a}$.* This
will be denoted by rewriting 6.3.4 in the more general form

$$\vec{v} = \varphi_{\vec{a}}(\vec{u}). \tag{6.3.6}$$

For the sake of convenience, we have omitted from this equation of
state the crucial time dependences; however, 6.3.6 is meant to be
understood as follows: The value $\vec{a}(t)$ at some given instant predicts
the input $\vec{v}(t+h)$ at some subsequent instant. At that instant, the
transducer has been *pre-adapted* so that its activity on the *predicted*
input $\vec{v}(t+h)$ is described by 6.3.6.

With these modifications, which incorporate the essential features
of the forward activation of our biosynthetic pathway, we can enlarge
our diagram 6.3.3 accordingly; we may write

$$\vec{u} \;\to\; \boxed{\underset{\vec{a}}{\varphi}}^{\!\!\!\circ^{a}} \;\to\; \vec{v} \tag{6.3.7}$$

where the symbol ——o is meant to indicate that the vector a represents
a predictor, whose present value changes the *equation of state* describing the transducer.

As a final step, we shall now generalize the role of the intermediate
steps of the biosynthetic pathway. We do this by embedding the
diagram 6.3.7 into a *larger system* of unspecified structure. This
larger system serves to generate both the input $\vec{u}$ and the predictor
$\vec{a}$, and it also serves as a sink for the output $\vec{v}$. We need not, and
indeed we cannot, be more specific about this larger system; the
only assumption we can make about it is that its properties can be
encoded into appropriate equations of state which generalize the
relations (6.2.3) above. However, this unspecified larger system
will play several key roles in our subsequent development, both in
regard to the properties stabilized by the anticipatory step, and
the manner in which these properties are maintained over time.

We have thus accomplished the first step we mentioned at the outset;
we have seen how the essential features of our biosynthetic pathway
can be formulated in completely general terms. We now turn our
attention to the second step: namely, the formulation of the
properties stabilized by the presence of the anticipatory step.
We shall formulate these properties not only in terms of the diagram
6.3.7, but also in terms of the larger system in which the diagram is
embedded. That is, we shall investigate how the anticipatory step is
adaptive in terms of 6.3.7, and also in terms of the larger system
containing it.

We shall suppose as usual that the property P can initially be taken
as a linkage of the form

$$\Phi(\vec{u}, \vec{v}) = 0; \tag{6.3.8}$$

i.e. that it expresses the maintenance of a particular relation between the input vector $\vec{u}$ at some instant, and the output vector $\vec{v}$,
generally at some other instant. The anticipatory step, governed
by 6.3.6, is assumed to guarantee that 6.3.8 is satisfied, under the
assumption that the prediction of the model embodied in the anticipatory step agrees with the actual input vector seen by the transducer.

Let us formulate this last condition more precisely. We have seen
that the *present* value $\vec{a}(t)$ of the predictor a is linked to a future
value $\vec{u}(t+h)$ of the input u; this can be expressed by a linkage
relation of the form

$$\vec{u}_p(t+h) = \psi(\vec{a}(t)). \tag{6.3.9}$$

We use the subscript p here to denote the fact that the value $\vec{u}_p(t+h)$
is that predicted from the present value a(t) of the predictor a.
It is this predicted value to which the transducer is pre-adapted,
according to (6). On the other hand, the actual input value to the
transducer is $\vec{u}(t+h)$; therefore, since the property P embodied by
6.3.8 pertains to the actual inputs, the maintenance of this property
by the anticipatory step obviously requires that

$$\vec{u}_p(t+h) = \vec{u}(t+h).\tag{6.3.10}$$

That is, the maintenance of the property P invariant in time requires a concordance between the input value predicted from the model employed by the transducer, and the actual input presented to the transducer. In other words, the maintenance of the property P depends on the *fidelity* or stability of the model embodied in the anticipatory step.

Finally, we shall relate the property P embodied in 6.3.8, which pertains only to the system we have diagrammed in 6.3.7 above, to other properties of the larger system in which this diagram is embedded. We note in advance that if P' represents any property of this larger system, whose maintenance depends on the time-invariance of P, then P' also depends on the stability of the model which determines the anticipatory step.

To formulate such a property P' is very easy. In general, let y_1, y_2 be two observables of the larger system, which are linked to the predictor a and to the output v; i.e. such that we can write

$$y_1 = y_1(\vec{a}, \vec{v}, \ldots),$$

$$y_2 = y_2(\vec{a}, \vec{v}, \ldots).$$

Suppose that $\psi(y_1, y_2) = 0$ is a linkage in the larger system which holds if and only if 6.3.8 is satisfied; i.e. if and only if the linkage

$$\varphi_a(\vec{u}) = \vec{v}$$

satisfies the property P. Then clearly ψ defines a property P' of the larger system, and by definition, this property P' is contingent upon the presence of the property P in the system (7). In this fashion, we can construct many such properties P' which are *linked* to P, in the sense that they are maintained time-invariant only if P is likewise.

We have thus reformulated all of the basic features of the forward activation pathway described in the preceding chapter, but in a quite general setting. It only remains to consider what happens to the property P, and to the properties P' of the larger system which are linked to it, as the model embodied in the anticipatory step becomes unstable. Once again, we will find that the consequences will simply be a paraphrase of situations we have already described, adapted to the more general context developed above. In particular, we shall find that all these properties are *temporally spanned* by the growing instability of the model.

In the present case, the instability of the model is reflected precisely by the growing discrepancy between the two sides of equation 6.3.10 above. That is, the value $\vec{u}_p$ *predicted* on the basis of the model becomes increasingly different from the actual input u. Furthermore, the pre-adaptation step 6.3.6 is specifically geared to pertain to the predicted input u_p; thus if $\vec{u} \neq \vec{u}_p$, the pre-adaptation will to this extent be maladaptive with respect to the property P, and will become increasingly so as the discrepancy between the predicted behavior and the actual behavior grows. Accordingly, the linkage 6.3.8 which expresses the property P departs more and more from the relation between $\vec{u}$ and $\vec{v}$ actually manifested by the system, until at some characteristic time it is lost entirely. Likewise, any property P' of the entire system which is linked to P will also increasingly depart from the actual system behavior, until these properties are also lost. Hence all such properties, and the linkages which represent them, are temporally spanned.

The discussion of temporal spanning which has been presented above is, of course, closely related to the notions of *error* which were developed in Chapter 5.6 above. We may recall that error always refers to the deviation between the actual behavior of a system and the behavior of some abstract model or encoding of that system. We are going to invoke this discussion now, in the context of the property P which characterizes our anticipatory step in 6.3.7.

We have seen that the property P is preserved invariant only when 6.3.10 holds; i.e. only when the actual input to the transducer coincides with the input predicted on the basis of the anticipatory model. If we suppose that an external observer of the system 6.3.7 identifies its "correct function" with the maintenancy of the property P, he will in these circumstances conclude that the system is functioning correctly; i.e. without error. On the other hand, as the discrepancy between the predicted input $\vec{u}_p$ and the actual input $\vec{u}$ grows, the property P will eventually be lost, as we have seen. The external observer, who judges the "correct" functioning of the system by the persistence of the property, will under these circumstances conclude that the system is *malfunctioning*, or behaving *erroneously*. According to this criterion, we can see that the malfunction arises because of underlying errors in the predictive model employed in the anticipatory step. But it is clear that no *part* of the system 6.3.7 is itself malfunctioning in any sense; by any local criterion, each component of the system 6.3.7 is behaving "correctly" according to its equation of state. The ultimate source of the malfunction of 6.3.7 not lie in any local failure in any part of the system; rather, it resides ultimately in a *linguistic* or *symbolic* feature, which may be formulated as the loss of *synonymy* between the predictor a(t) and the transducer input which it is supposed to represent. Thus the malfunction of the system 6.3.7, as measured by the loss of the property P, will appear to the external observer to arise in spite of the fact that each constituent of the system is itself functioning correctly in any local sense. A malfunction of this type will be called a *global failure* of the system 6.3.7 it is to be distinguished from what we may call *local failures*, which would correspond to one or more of the constituents of the system itself departing from the behavior governed by its particular equation of state.

Since the property P is temporally spanned, we may identify the *lifetime* of the sytem 6.3.7 with the time at which the property P is lost. Thus, with respect to this property, the system 6.3.7 will have a definite lifetime. At the end of that time, the system will fail or malfunction in the global fashion we have described. It should be emphasized that the lifetime of the system 6.3.7, in this sense, is not determined by the system 6.3.7 itself; rather, it is a property of the larger system in which 6.3.7 is embedded. Thus, as we have seen, this lifetime is unpredictable from within the system itself. However, we can say, in a general way, that the longer the system 6.3.7 has functioned correctly, and hence the longer it has interacted with the larger system which contains it, the closer it must be to its spanned time at which the property P is lost.

6.4 An Application: Senescence

In the present chapter, we wish to develop the thesis that the
temporal spanning of properties in systems with anticipatory steps,
which we have demonstrated above, may be casually implicated in the
phenomena of *senescence* in complex systems. In order to do so, and
to place this thesis in a general perspective, we will preface our
discussion with a few general remarks concerning senescence, and
briefly describe some previous approaches and hypotheses which bear
upon it. [1]

In biology, senescence is an almost ubiquitous property of organisms,
but at present it remains one of the most poorly understood. The
concept of senescence, being intimately concerned with mortality,
has proved as difficult to define as life itself. Senescence is
also closely related to the concepts of time and age, which we saw
in Section 4 above to be exceedingly complex in themselves. Perhaps
the most satisfactory working definition, which has been adopted by
most of those concerned with senescence phenomena, is the following:
*senescence is an increase in the probability of death per unit time
with chronological age.* Put somewhat more picturesquely, senescence
is an increase in the force of mortality with time. Such a definition
is incomplete and unsatisfactory in many ways, as we shall see; but
it will serve as a point of departure. Moreover, it explicitly calls
attention to the basic conceptual notions involved: time, age,
mortality.

In order to relate our discussion of temporal spanning of properties
in anticipatory systems to this preliminary definition of senescence,
it will be necessary to analyze the components of that definition
further. The first step in this analysis will involve the "force of
mortality"; i.e. the probability of death per unit time. Let us
briefly consider what is meant by this notion.

Intuitively, we wish our definition of senescence to apply to *individual* organisms. On the other hand, the "force of mortality" is a
population concept. To see this, let us notice that in order to
determine empirically the probability of death of an individal organism
per unit time, we must imagine a large population of identical organisms, for which we can count the number of deaths per unit time as
a function of the ages of the organisms which have died. In this way,

we can form ratios which approximate to the probability that a representative individual in the population will in fact die at a
particular age. If this probability increase with age, then we may
say that the *individuals* in the population exhibit senescence. The
age at which this probability becomes unity can then be interpreted
as the *intrinsic life span* of the individuals comprising the population.

Thus, at the very outset, we can see that the very definition of
senescence, and of life span, is an *ensemble* concept, of the type
which we have met before; e.g. in statistical mechanics. On the
other hand, we desire to refer these properties, initially defined
in terms of ensemble or population, to the individual members of
such a population. We can only do this on the basis of some kind of
reductionistic approach, in which we suppose that the statistical
properties of the ensemble reflect some underlying properties of the
individuals which comprise the ensemble. But this raises difficulties
of its own, since we initially supposed that these individuals were
identical; it would clearly make no sense to attempt to define the
prbabilities of death per age in a heterogeneous population. On the
other hand, if there were no heterogeneity, the individuals in the
population would all behave identically, and there would be no
probabilistic sense to the "force of mortality".

Thus, we have to consider a population which is at least initially
identical with respect to some quality, but which we allow to be
heterogeneous with respect to another. We also need to visualize
the individuals in the population changing with respect to time in
some fashion, which is ultimately to be reflected in the mortality
of the individuals. Let us see if we can visualize this kind of
situation. To do so, we shall employ the same sort of picture which
we used earlier in our treatment of statistical mechanics, in a
fashion originally suggested by G. Sacher and E. Trucco.[2]

Let us suppose that we can encode the instantaneous states of the
individuals in our population into some suitable manifold X. Thus,
at any instant of time t (according to some suitable external clock)
the state of such an individual will be denoted by x(t), and is a
definite point of X.

Thus, we envisage a dynamics imposed on X, according to which any
point in X determines an entire trajectory in X.

We shall suppose further that initially (i.e. at t = 0) our population
is represented by a set of points $\Omega(0)$ in X. We shall suppose that
this set of points is such that the distance between any pair of
them in X is small; e.g. that they all lie within a sphere of small
radius in X. Thus, these initial states are essentially identical
in our encoding, but there is some small amount of initial heterogeneity.

We shall also suppose that the set $\Omega(0)$ of initial states of our
population is contained within some larger set $P \subset X$. We shall
identify this set P with the totality of *viable states* of our
individuals; a state outside this region is considered *dead*. In
this fashion, we replace the vague concept of viability with some
arbitrary property; which we further identify with the set of all
points which satisfy this property.

Now as time increases from zero, each point in $\Omega(0)$ will move along
its corresponding trajectory with X. Thus, the entire set $\Omega(0)$ will
move or flow in X, and will at each instant t<0 define a new set $\Omega(t)$.

The set us here is essentially that which we used in discussing Liouville's Theorem in Chapter 3.3 above.

At each instant t, we can consider the set $\Omega(t) \cap P$. This can be interpreted as specifying the totality of individuals in our population which are still viable at the instant t. Let us define the quantity

$$p(t) = \frac{\mu(\Omega(t) \cap P)}{\mu \Omega(t)}$$

Here μ denotes the measure or volume of subsets of X. For any instant t, we will have $0 \le p(t) \le 1$; i.e. $p(t)$ is essentially a probability. We may interpret $p(t)$ as the probability that a state initially in $\Omega(0)$ will still be viable at the instant t. The situation we are describing is shown diagrammatically in Figure 6.4.1 below.

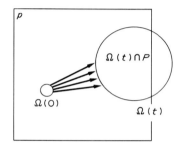

Fig. 6.4.1.

The intrinsic lifetime of a state in $\Omega(0)$ will thus be that time T for which its trajectory leaves P. It will be seen that these considerations depend on (a) the dynamics imposed on X, and (b) the nature of the property P.

It should be noted explicitly that although we have taken the source of variability to lie in the specification of initial state, we could just as easily incorporate the variability into the imposed dynamics. This would involve simply moving the appropriate constitutive parameters from the state description to the dynamics; it is entirely arbitrary where they are put. However, for pictorial purposes, it is more convenient to place them in the state space rather than the dynamics, and thus we shall continue to do so.

Let us also note that in this picture we have identified mortality or death with the loss of some property P by an individual in our population. In this sense, mortality is regarded as a kind of *system failure*, and the intrinsic lifetime of an individual is identified with the *maximum time to failure*, always determined with respect to the property P under consideration.

Now let us go a step further. Let us regard the individuals in our ensemble as complex systems, which can all be resolved into a common spectrum of subsystems. We shall take this to mean that our original state space X, into which the states of these individuals are encoded, are themselves cartesian products of the state spaces which characterize the subsystems. Thus, we can write

$$X = \prod_{i=1}^{n} X_i \qquad\qquad (6.4.1)$$

where the X_i are the manifolds into which particular sub-systems are encoded.

Just as we identified the viability of an individual in our population with a property P in X, so we can identify the "viability" of each subsystem X_i with a corresponding property P_i. This property P_i will as usual be identified with the set of points in X_i which satisfy the property. Thus, as long as a point in X_i lies in P_i, we shall say that the *subsystem* is viable; when the point leaves P_i, we shall say that the subsystem has become inviable, or has *failed*. Such a failure in a subsystem X_i will be called a local failure. Thus, the occurrence of a local failure in a subsystem X_i is a matter intrinsic to X_i alone; such a failure can be determined by looking at X_i, without reference to what is happening in the other subsystems.

We now inquire what is the relation between the *global* criterion of viability, namely the property P in X, and the *local* criteria of viability; i.e. the properties P_i in the individual X_i. Such a relation specifies, of course, the extent to which a *global* failure in an individual organism reflects a *local* failure in one or more of the subsystems into which the organism has been analyzed. Initially, there are three possibilities which can be entertained:

(a). $\prod_{i=1}^{n} P_i \subseteq P$;   (b). $\prod_{i=1}^{n} P_i \supset P$;   (c). Neither (a) nor (b) holds.

Let us consider the implications of these various possibilities.

The possibility (a) is indicated in diagrammatic form in Figure 6.4.2 below

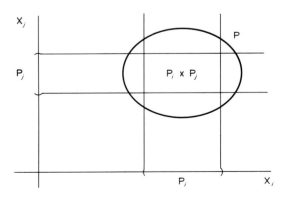

Fig. 6.4.2.

Comparing this situation to Figure 6.4.1 we see that it is impossible for any initial ensemble $\Omega(0)$ to leave P in X without simultaneously leaving at least one of the P_i in the corresponding X_i. In other words, in this situation *it is impossible for a global failure to occur without the associated appearance of at least one local failure in one of the constituent subsystems.* Thus, the two kinds of failure are in this case necessary concomitants of one another; if we wish, we can in fact *attribute* the global failure of the total system to the corresponding local failure which must occur in one or more of its subsystems in this case. That is, we can say that *global failures are in fact caused by local failures.*

The possibility (b) is sketched diagrammatically in Figure 6.4.3 below:

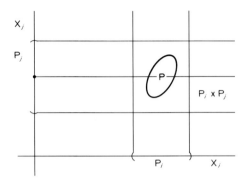

Fig. 6.4.3.

In this case, there is a complete separation between the notion of local failures in the subsystems and global failures in the total system. For, on comparing Figure 6.4.3 to Figure 6.4.1, we see that a global failure (i.e. inviability or death) of the organism is *never* associated with a local failure in any of the subsystems. Thus, in this case, if there is a local failure, we may perhaps say that such a local failure is *caused* by global failure, but never conversely.

The final possibility (c) is diagrammed in general form in Figure 6.4.4 below. In this case, on comparison with Figure 6.4.1, we see that there are two classes of ways in which an organism in our population can become inviable: (i) we can leave the region P as a result of local failures, as in the trajectory marked I in the figure; (ii) we can leave the region P without any local failures, as in the trajectory marked II. In this case, then, a global failure *may, but need not*, be associated with a local failure in a subsystem.

Now let us see what these general considerations mean in the context of senescence. Briefly, we shall show that all previous approaches to senescence have tacitly supposed that the hypothesis (a) is satisfied; i.e. that the senescence or loss of viability of an individual organism is causally related to local failures directly identifiable in particular subsystems of the organism. However much

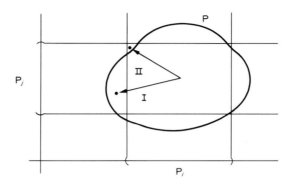

Fig. 6.4.4.

these approaches differ in detail, they are thus alike in supposing
that global failures all necessarily arise as a consequence of local
subsystem failures, which can be independently recognized.

The theories which have been heretofore proposed to account for
senescence in organisms fall logically into two distinct classes,
which we may call *error theories* and *program theories*. In intuitive
terms, the error theories all suppose that normal physiological
processes have superimposed upon them some source of randomness or
fluctuation, which causes them to behave *erroneously*. As we have
seen (cf. Chapter 5 above) the imposition of such fluctuations merely
reflects the fact that physiological subsystems are more open than
their physiologically significant interactions require; errors in
this sense are measured against our own models or ideas as to what
constitutes physiological interaction. To one degree or another,
the error theories regard such fluctuations, occurring in specific
subsystems, as antagonizing or opposing the maintenance of a local
property P_i in the subsystem; senescence and death occur through

the causal relation between such local properties P_i and the global

property P. Thus, an error theory of senescence typically involves
two aspects: (a) a specification of a source of fluctuation in a
particular physiological subsystem, and (b) a specification of the
effects of these fluctuations on the total viability of the organism.

As examples, let us consider a few of the well-known error theories.
Perhaps the simplest of these is the *somatic mutation theory*.[3] Here,
the essential locus of fluctuation is asserted to be the primary
genetic material itself; i.e. DNA in its role as template for
protein synthesis. According to this theory, the base sequence in
DNA is constantly subject to perturbation, through interaction with
ambient radiation or mutagenic substances, or through a variety of
other causes. Such perturbations constitute somatic mutation, and
result in a corresponding modification of amino acid sequences for
which these genes code. Since the primary sequence of amino acids
in a protein is the determinant of the protein's conformation, and
hence of its biological activity, such modifications in primary

structure will result in corresponding alterations of rate and specificity at the protein level; it is these alterations within cells, and their effects on intercellular interactions, which we collectively call senescence.

Another popular error theory is the "error catastrophe" of Orgel which was briefly mentioned in Chapter 5.6 above. Here, the source of the fluctuations is placed in the translation step of protein synthesis. Briefly, Orgel observed that the translation step itself involves protein in an essential way (e.g. the synthetase enzymes, which specifically attach individual amino acids to the correct species of transfer RNA). If the specificities of these enzymes is initially altered, through some random mechanism, then *all* proteins synthesized by the cell will be modified in primary sequence, including these synthetases themselves. Thus, the next "generation" of synthetase molecules will tend to be more erroneous than the first. By iterating the argument Orgel claimed that a positive feedback loop was effectively established, through which the initial synthetase errors are successively amplified until the cell becomes inviable; this is the "error catastrophe".

Other error theories involve different sources of fluctuation; e.g. the random extinction of crucial stem cell lines,[4] or the random cross-linking of collagenous supporting matrices. Still others implicate such systems as the immune system,[5] which may be the source of fluctuations (e.g. by the random appearance of cells in the system which attack "self proteins"), or the effector (e.g. by recognizing aberrant protein, generated through somatic mutation or other errors, as foreign). The catalog of such theories is virtually limitless, both as regards source of fluctuation and its physiological effects. However, we can see immediately that all the error theories are alike in proposing that the ultimate cause of senescence lies in localized (random) failures in specific physiological sub-systems.

At the other logical extreme appear the "program theories" of senescence. In these theories, it is asserted in general that the primary causes of senescence are not of a random character, but rather represent the accurate expression of genetic programs similar to those expressed during development. Essential ingredients in these theories are various types of clocks, counters and timers, which cause lethal events to occur when a particular time interval, or a particular sequence of preceding events, has elapsed. Here again, the locus of the initial lesion, and the propagation of its physiological effects, can be of the widest latitude.

Ironically, despite the apparent logical polarity between the error theories and the program theories of senescence, they are in fact indistinguishable from one another on any empirical ground. Worse that this: not only are these theories inseparable from one another in logical terms, but it is empirically impossible to distinguish between theories belonging to the same class. It is safe to say that at the present time, every observation can be made compatible with any theory; conversely, every theory is equally well supported by the available empirical data.

This fact means one of two things: either senescence simply comprises a catalog of the unlimited number of ways in which physiological sub-systems can locally fail, or else some radically different approach to senescent phenomena is indicated.

The former possibility has been advocated e.g. by Medawar;[6] according to such a view, senescence is simply the sum total of all physiological defects which appear after reproductive maturity, and hence cannot be selected against. There are strong reasons for believing that this is not so, but it would at least explain the featureless character of the empirical data concerning senescent organisms, and the multiplicity of plausible hypotheses regarding senescence which may be entertained on the basis of that data. However, it would also imply that there could be no *theory* of senescence; rather there would only be an encyclopedia of local failures.

The second possibility is far more interesting; namely, that a radically different approach to senescence, both conceptually and empirically, is called for. The essence of such an approach may be found in the recognition of the possibilities sketched in Figures 6.4.3 and 6.4.4 namely, it is possible for complex systems to exhibit global modes of failure which are not causally related to local sub-system failures. So far, these possibilities exist only formally; to make them significant for senescence, we would need to show by example that such possibilities can actually arise in complex systems.

To do this, however, we need only recall the preceding chapters in the present section. In those chapters, we showed precisely that *any system possessing an anticipatory step exhibits properties which are temporally spanned*; and moreover, that *such a temporal spanning represents a kind of global failure which is independent of any local subsystem failures*. But these are precisely the characteristics we have seen to be required, if there is to be any comprehensive theory of senescence phenomena.

We have thus seen that any anticipatory system can in effect exhibit senescence, in the sense that it will automatically possess temporally spanned properties; and this temporal spanning is independent of any local subsystem failure. The next important question then becomes: are anticipatory systems widespread in nature, or at least are they sufficiently so to make it reasonable to seek a comprehensive theory of senescence on this basis? To this question, we have already given an affirmative answer in Chapter 1.1; indeed, we have argued that anticipatory behavior is in fact *ubiquitous* at all levels of biological organization. If this is so, and if temporal spanning is a universal concomitant of anticipatory systems, then it becomes at least plausible to construct a general theory of senescence in terms of such spanning.

Once this much is admitted, a number of interesting and suggestive conclusions immediately follow. One of these is the following: if indeed senescence arises from the temporal spanning of an anticipatory system, it instantly becomes clear why it has been so difficult to learn about senescence through empirical studies of physiological subsystems. Indeed, we may say that every technique of empirical analysis pertains precisely to such a subsystem, and the essence of our argument is that no local property of such a system, considered as an isolated system in its own right, is pertinent to the global failure of the larger system in which it is embedded. On these grounds, then, we would *expect* that an exclusive pre-occupation with the local empirical study of subsystems must fail to clarify the "mechanism" of senescence, since that mechanism is independent of the subsystems, and will be called into play even though no local subsystem failure occurs. An immediate corollary of this point of view is the following: an effective empirical study of senescence must proceed from an entirely different basis than has heretofore been the case; present techniques which are based entirely on analysis into physiological subsystems, are simply not adequate to deal with temporal spanning based on anticipatory loops. It is not

possible to decide at the moment what the most effective approaches
will in fact be; only experience with the behaviors of anticipatory
systems in general, initially based on the careful study of model
systems, is likely to clarify this question.

One further tantalizing corollary to these considerations may be
mentioned. We have seen above that the temporal spanning of anticipatory systems arises from a growing discrepancy between the predictions of the internal model, and the actual inputs processed by the
anticipatory step. We have also seen that this discrepancy can be
eliminated by *recalibrating* the model; i.e. by applying an external
dynamics which will bring the predicted and actual inputs once again
into concordance as they are initially. In the present situation,
such a recalibration would amount to a *rejuvenation* of the entire
system. It is conceivable, for example, that the function of mitosis
is to effect precisely such a recalibration at the cellular level.
Here too, only the careful study of model systems will indicate how
these kinds of possibilities may be further explored in an effective
manner.

We conclude by observing once again that our arguments regarding the
temporal spanning of properties are perfectly general; they apply
to any complex system which contains anticipatory steps. Thus, they
may be also applied to social and cultural systems, in which antici-
pations are likewise ubiquitous. We may recall in particular that
it was the thesis of historians such as Spengler and Toynbee[7] that
human cultures and civilizations exhibit many of the properties of
biological organisms, including phases which may at least be analogized with senescence. Such considerations lead us back towards
the view of societies as superorganisms, which was briefly discussed
in Chapter 1.1 above. These analogies, taken together with the
ubiquitous properties of temporal spanning in anticipatory systems,
suggest that a comprehensive study of all these phenomena is possible;
from such a study, it is certain that much of great value will be
learned.

REFERENCES AND NOTES

1.   Some good general references on senescence are the following:
        Comfort, A., *The Biology of Senescence*. Rinehart (1956).
        Strehler, B., *Time, Cells and Aging*. Academic Press (1962).
        Burch, P. R. J., *An Inquiry Concerning Growth, Disease and
          Aging*. Oliver & Boyd (1962).
     For a critical review of the various theoretical and experimental
     approaches to senescence, see e.g. Rosen, R., *Int. Rev. Cyt.* 54,
     161-191 (1978). See also Nore 1, Chapter 4.8 and Note 8, Chapter
     5.6.

2.   See Sacher, G. and Trucco, E., *Ann. N.Y. Acad. Sci.* 96, 985-999
     (1962). See also Trucco, E., *Bull. Math. Biophys.* 25, 303-324;
     343-366 (1963).

3.   Although somatic mutation has long been considered as a mechanism
     for carcinogenesis, it does not seem to have been implicated in
     senescence before 1956 (cf. Danielli, J. F., *Experientia* Supp.
     #4, 55-81 (1956)). This is not surprising, since senescing cells
     and malignant cells seem to manifest opposing properties. A
     general theory of senescence based on somatic mutation was
     developed by Szilard in 1959 (*PNAS* 45, 30-45); similar ideas
     were later developed by many others.

4. The two most popular kinds of cells involved in these random
    extinction hypotheses are those of the hemopoietic system and
    the neurons in the brain; see the general references cited in
    Note 1 above.

5. The great advocate of this idea has been M. Burnet. See for
    instance *The Clonal Selection Theory of Acquired Immunity*,
    Cambridge University Press (1959); *Immunological Surveillance*,
    Pergamon (1970). See also Walford, R. L., *The Immunologic
    Theory of Aging*, Munskgarrd (1969).

6. See Medawar, P. B., *Modern Quart.* <u>2</u>, 30-38 (1945).

7. See Spengler, O., *Der Untergang des Abendlandes*. Beck (Munich)
    (1922); Toynbee, A., *A Study of History: Reconsiderations*.
    Oxford University Press (1961).

6.5 Adaptation, Natural Selection and Evolution

Throughout the foregoing sections, we have had ample occasion to
mention the concept of *adaptation*. This is an idea utterly basic to
the biological realm, and which is becoming increasingly important in
an understanding of the properties and control of social systems and
the human sciences. Indeed, the main point of our entire development
has been that systems which anticipate are thereby rendered adaptive,
and in fact are more adaptive, in some appropriate sense, than systems
which simply react.

It is now time to consider the concept of adaptation in more detail.
As we shall see, the circle of ideas on which this concept depends
are very rich indeed;[1] this very richness accounts in large measure
for the confusion, controversy and acrimony with which the concept
has been associated. During the course of this development, we shall
not only be able to obtain a better understanding of what adaptation
means, but we shall find that anticipatory behavior is in some sense
a corollary of the general mechanisms by which adaptations are generated. During the course of our previous development, we did not ask
why so much biological behavior should be of an anticipatory rather
than a reactive character; the simple fact that it was so provided
sufficient grounds for studying such systems in depth. It is thus of
great interest to find that a study of adaptation automatically bears
on the question of why anticipatory mechanisms are so prevalent in
biology.

In order to best motivate and focus our discussion of adaptation, it
is convenient to proceed *metaphorically*, as we did for example in our
treatment of morphogenesis in Chapter 3.3 above. To do this, we shall
initially elaborate on one of the first and simplest examples of
adaptation, which we introduced at the outset in Chapter 1.1; namely,
the example of a simple tropism, such as the negative phototropism
or photophobia which is so common in simple organisms. We shall
elaborate our metaphor by idealizing this kind of behavior.

To begin, let us imagine an organism which is free to move on a two-
dimensional surface. Thus, at any instant of time, the organism can
be located at a definite point of this surface, and thus its position
may be characterized by a pair of numbers (x,y) relative to some
convenient system of co-ordinates in the surface.

We shall also assume that the organism can perceive some environmental quality E (such as light intensity). This quality is assumed to have a definite value at every point (x,y) of the surface, and thus defines a *scalar field* thereon. We further suppose that this scalar field is such that a gradient ∇E may be defined at every point of the surface. Thus, the environmental quality E also defines for us a *vector field* on the surface in which our organism moves.

For our purposes, the *behavior* of our organism will be specified by determining the *direction* of its motion at any point on the surface. The components of the vector which specify the direction are just dx/dt and dy/dt, and we suppose that these components depend on *both* the gradient ∇E of the imposed vector field, and on the internal constitution of the organism itself. Thus, the behavior of the organism is determined by equations of state of the form

$$\begin{cases} dx/dt = \varphi(\alpha, \nabla E), \\ dy/dt = \psi(\alpha, \nabla E) \end{cases} \qquad (6.5.1)$$

where we have denoted by α a set of constitutive parameters, characteristic of the organism, which we shall call the *genome* for these equations. This is in accord with our earlier discussion (cf. Chapter 3.5, Ex. 2c), in which we saw that the quantities entering into any equation of state can generally be characterized as genome, environment and phenotype; here the variable α denotes genome, the gradient ∇E denotes environment, and the resulting direction of motion (i.e. the components of the tangent vector at a point of our surface) is the phenotype. From these equations of state, we can infer, as usual, the path of our organism on the surface as a function of the genome, and the scalar field E = E(x, y).

For our purposes, we shall assume that *different organisms are characterized by different values assigned to the genome* α. Thus, different organisms will generally follow different paths through our surface, even though they start initially at the same point, and are exposed to the same scalar field E(x, y). The question is: how can we say whether the path followed by a particular organism is adaptive or not? When is one such path more adaptive than another?

In point of fact, there is as yet no way of characterizing adaptation within the confines of the description introduced so far. Indeed, all we have done is to characterize the manner in which an organism's state (i.e. its position on the surface) changes as a function of genome and environment. In order to specify whether such a change of state is adaptive or not, an entirely different element of structure must be introduced. This is what we now proceed to do.

Let us then suppose that we are given another scalar field U = U(x, y) on our surface; one which is initially entirely independent of the environmental modality E to which our organism is responding. This scalar field likewise determines a vector field by forming its gradient ∇U. This vector field in general fibers out surface into a family of integral curves, which are trajectories of the associated dynamical system which can be written in the form

$$\begin{cases} dx/dt = \partial U/\partial x; \\ dy/dt = \partial U/\partial y. \end{cases} \qquad (6.5.2)$$

What we are now going to do is to compare the curves arising in this

way, as solutions of the system (6.5.2), with the paths followed by
our organisms *in the same surface*, which are the solutions of the
system (6.5.1).

In Figure 6.5.1 below, we indicate pictorially two such curves.   The
heavy curve is assumed to represent the path of an organism, as
determined by (6.5.1), the dashed curve is the corresponding path
through the same initial point of our surface which is determined
by (6.2.1).   There is of course no reason why there should be any
particular relation between these paths.

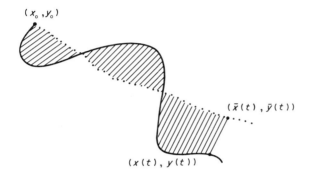

Fig. 6.5.1.

However, what we want to do now is to introduce a numerical measure
of the degree of discordancy between the two paths we have shown.
There are many ways in which this can be done.   Because of the
metaphorical character of our discussion, our subsequent conclusions
will be essentially independent of our specific choice of a measure
of discordancy between the paths;   accordingly, we are free to choose
the simplest.   This simplest measure, which is also indicated in
Figure 6.5.1 above, is the area of the region bounded by the two
curves, and (if necessary) by the geodesic of the surface connecting
the corresponding points on the curve at a common instant t.   For
a given initial point (x_0, y_0) in the surface, the resulting measure
A(t) is clearly a monotonically increasing function of t.   As noted,
this function A(t) is clearly a measure of how far the actual path
of an organism deviates from a corresponding integral curve of
(6.5.2); the greater the deviation, the bigger is A(t).

The measure A(t) just introduced, or rather its inverse F(t) = 1/A(t),
is what we shall call the *fitness* of a path.   Thus , given any solution
of (6.5.1), and any fixed time T, we can associate with the resulting
path a *number*.   Thus, *the fitness we have defined can be regarded as
an observable of paths*.   As usual, we can utilize such an observable
to impute properties to the paths on which the observable is defined.
In particular, we shall say that *one path is more adaptive than
another if its fitness is larger*.   In particular, we can see that
the most adaptive paths, in this sense, are the integral curves of
(6.5.2);   their fitness is infinite.

Let us pause here to stress that, in order to introduce a notion of

adaptation, we require: (a) a way of associating numbers with paths,
in such a way that two paths can be compared;   (b) this number must
be introduced in a manner initially independent of the specific mechanism (6.5.1) by which the compared paths are actually generated.
The condition in effect introduces a *common currency* in terms of which
any paths can be compared, regardless of how they are generated;   the
condition (b) means that the organism does not have any intrinsic mechanism for perceiving the fitness, and hence for determining whether
the path it is following is adaptive or not.   The point to stress is
that, at this stage, there is no linkage whatever between the mechanism for generating specific paths, and the mechanism whereby their
fitnesses, and hence their relative adaptive values, are assessed.

It must be emphasized that it is in fact meaningless to characterize
a phenotype, or behavior, as adaptive apart from a postulated measure
of fitness.   Therefore, for example, the autonomous behavior of non-
biological systems cannot be considered as adaptive in our sense.
A familiar example of such behavior which is often regarded as
intrinsically adaptive is expressed by the well-known Principle of
Le Chatelier;[2] if a system in equilibrium is disturbed by the variation of one of the environmental quantities which determine that
equilibrium, the system will move to a new equilibrium is such a way
as to oppose the initial variation.   In this example, there is no
postulated measure of fitness, and hence no adaptation.   The same is
true of the homeostasis exhibited by open systems in the vicinity of
a stable steady state, which we earlier (cf. Chapter 3.5) considered
as a metaphor for the biological phenomenon of equifinality;   and
indeed, of any kind of homeostasis whatsoever.   It must be stressed
that, until a measure of fitness is introduced, no simple
state can be meaningfully characterized as adaptive or maladaptive;
and this includes all the cybernetic mechanisms which have been
proposed as examples of adaptation.[3]   This is a subtle point, but it
cannot be emphasized too strongly.

At this stage, however, we can already frame such questions as: what
are the maximally adaptive paths in our surface?   In mathematical
terms, such questions are simply problems in *optimality*;   they can be
framed whenever a mechanism like 6.5.1 is proposed for generating a
space of possible paths, and a criterion like 6.5.2 is available to
associate numbers with these paths.   In the light of our discussion
so far, the solution of such an optimality problem can be regarded
as *the determination of those genomes α in* (6.5.1) *whose paths deviate
minimally from the integral curves of* (6.5.2).   However, we must note
that, so far, the solution of such an optimality problem possesses no
necessary relevance to our problem, because as we have stressed, there
is so far no relation between the procedure by which paths are generated and the procedure by which their adaptive character is determined.

The final step in our metaphorical discussion is then to introduce
precisely such a relation, which will be called *selection*.   As we
shall see, in its broadest terms, selection links the generation of
paths to their fitnesses by, in effect, *allowing phenotypes (i.e.,
paths) to act back on the genomes which generated them.*   This is the
fundamental property of selection, which we shall describe, and then
interpret in biological terms.

Our first observation is the following: *we can utilize the fitness
F defined above to define a scalar field on the space A of genomes.*
Namely, to each α in A, we can associate the number $F(α)$, the fitness
of the path generated according to 6.5.1 with the genome α, evaluated
as some definite fixed instant T of time.   Next: *from this scalar
field on A, we can construct the vector field ∇F on A.*   Finally:

we can construct a dynamics on A itself, of the general form

$$d\alpha/d\theta = K\nabla F(\alpha)$$ (6.5.3)

It is this dynamics (3) which embodies the essence of a selection
mechanism. As we shall see in a moment, it is crucial that the time
parameter θ entering into this dynamics be *different* from the time
parameter t entering into the dynamics 6.5.1, in terms of which
phenotypes (i.e. paths) are generated.

The essential feature of the selection dynamics 6.5.3 is that *it
moves the genome in the direction of increasing fitness*. The stable
steady states for this dynamics are thus those genomes for which
fitness is *maximal*, in the ordinary mathematical sense. Thus, not
only does fitness serve to link genomes to their adaptive consequences,
but through the action of selection, the genome itself is controlled
so as to generate phenotypes which are maximally adaptive. It is
for this reason that the abstract optimality problem which can already
be posed in terms of 6.5.1 and 6.5.2 can be claimed to have biological
significance; selection forces organisms towards genomes for which
fitness is maximal. This is the essential content *of the Principal
of Optimal Design*[4] as a tool for probing biological phenotypes, as
proposed by N. Rashevsky many years ago; and for the appearance
of optimality problems in any discussion of adaptation.

Now let us discuss briefly the biological basis for postulating a
dynamics of the form 6.5.3. To the biologist fitness is invariably
related to fecundity; and is measured by the size of the progeny
left by any particular organism in a given set of environmental
conditions.[5] Let us suppose then that the fixed time T which we used
in defining the scalar field F(α) is interpreted as the *generation
time*. Next, we shall suppose with the biologist that the progeny
left by an organism of a given genome are not genetically identical
but rather populate some neighborhood of α in A. The picture is
thus rather like treating A as an excitable medium, and α as a point
source of excitation. Intuitively, some of the progeny α' of this
genome α will be more fit than was α, according to how close they
are to the gradient vector ∇F evaluated at α. Translating fitness
into differential fecundity or reproductive rates means that the
propagation of "excitation" in A away from the source α will be
attenuated in all directions *except in the direction of ∇F*. This
is precisely what is asserted by the dynamics described in 6.5.3,
when all inessential transients and attenuations are neglected.

We now draw attention to the time scale for the dynamics 6.5.3,
which we emphasized *must* be different from that occurring in 6.5.1.
In some sense the "time unit" for the dynamics 6.5.3 can be regarded
as the generation time T. If fitness and selection are to be meaningful, this generation time must be very long with regard to the time
unit in the dynamics 6.5.1, through which the behavior evaluated with
the fitness function F is actually generated. On the other hand,
this unit of generation time for 6.5.3 must itself be treated as an
infinitesimal in describing a dynamics on the space A of genomes.
These requirements are incompatible, in much the same sense that the
time scales governing irreversible macroscopic processes and the
underlying micro-dynamics are incompatible (cf. Chapter 4.3 above);
they cannot be combined into a common temporal frame which encompasses
both the adaptive dynamics 6.5.1 and the selective dynamics 6.5.3.
The fundamental incompatibility of these two time scales has troubled
many authors, and has even led a number of them to claim that any
understanding of selection as a dynamical process is impossible.[6]
However, the basic difficulty here (as it was in the relation between

irreversible macro-dynamics and the underlying micro-dynamics) arises
from the complexities of temporal encodings in general, and from the
fact that not all such encodings can be reduced to one another.

The dynamics 6.5.3, which occurs in a space of *genomes* is thus of
quite a different character from the dynamics 6.5.1 which generates
phenotypes or behaviors. In any equation of state, an observable
appearing as genome may be regarded as pertaining to the essential
identity of the specific system with which we are dealing; a change
in the value of such a quality means precisely that a change of
identity, cr a *change in species*, has occurred. For instance, in
the case of an equation of state like the van der Waals equation
for non-ideal gases (cf. equation (3.3.25) above, and the related
discussion) a change in value assigned to one of the constitutive
parameters a, b, r amounts to changing the *species* of gas with
which we are dealing. On the other hand, a change in the value
assigned to an environmental or phenotypic quantity in such an
equation of state is not to be regarded as a change of identity;
it is simply a change of state in a system whose identity is remaining
fixed.

In order to emphasize the difference between dynamical processes in
which genome or identity is held fixed, and dynamical processes in
which genome is changing, it is well to refer to them by different
names. A dynamics like 6.5.1, in which genome is held fixed and
only environment and phenotype are changing will accordingly be
called *developmental dynamics*. All of the specific dynamical encodings with which we have heretofore been concerned have been of
this character; as we have noted, they involve simple changes of
state in a system whose identity is remaining constant. On the
other hand, a dynamics like 6.5.3, which encodes precisely a change
in system identity, will be called an *evolutionary dynamics*, or an
evolution. This terminology is in exact accord with biological intuition, since evolution is exactly concerned with the appearance
of new species. In these terms, it is not surprising to find that
developmental dynamics, dealing entirely with change of state within
a fixed species, and evolutionary dynamics, dealing with change of
species, require entirely different temporal encodings.

Let us rephrase the above comments in a slightly different language.
We have seen repeatedly above (cf. Chapter 3.3 Ex. 1) that the separation of variables occurring in an equation of state into the categories of genome, environment and phenotype amounts to the construction of a fiber space, in which the genomes constitute the base space,
and the remaining quantities constitute the fiber. In this picture,
developmental dynamics refers to dynamical processes in a particular
fiber; evolutionary dynamics refers to dynamical processes in the
base space itself. In these terms, the distinction between the two
kinds of dynamical processes emerges most clearly.

Let us pause here to recapitulate the essential features of the
metaphor we have drawn. We have seen that, in order to characterize
a particular phenotype or behavior (in our case, a path through a
surface) as adaptive requires a numerical measure through which
different behaviors (paths) can be compared with one another. We
called this measure fitness; the higher the fitness, the more
adaptive the behavior with which it is associated. The processes
by which behavior is generated and through which fitness is assessed
are independent of one another; they involve entirely different
observables of both the environment and the organism. However,
they are coupled through the imposition of a *selection mechanism*;
this, as we have seen, allows phenotypes to act as genomes through

the fitnesses with which they are associated. A selection mechanism thus generates an evolution in the space of genomes, which is of such a character that the adaptive value, or fitness, of the behaviors arising in the course of the evolution continually increases. Thus, in our terms, evolution is a mechanism for generating behaviors which are increasingly adaptive. Indeed, what we have shown is that, within the confines the validity of the metaphor we have been using, the concepts of adaptation, fitness, selection and evolution are themselves *linked*; none of them can be completely understood unless all of the others are taken into account. The specific expression of the linkage between these concepts is given by the relations 6.5.1, and 6.5.2 and 6.5.3 above.

Now let us proceed to a discussion of the proposition which we enunciated at the beginning of this chapter: namely, *that a behavior or phenotype which is adaptive necessarily is of an anticipatory character*. We shall now proceed to show how this comes about.

Let us recall two basic facts about the scheme which we have developed above:

1. Our organism is by hypothesis capable of perceiving only the environmental qualtiy we called E, the scalar field defined on the surface on which the organism moves. On the other hand, the adaptive character of the organism's behavior is determined not by E, but rather by a different environmental modality, which we called U.

2. What the organism does at a given instant (i.e. which direction it turns in the surface at a given point) contributes to the evaluation of the fitness of the behavior *at a later instant*. Thus, the organism's present change of state has an important effect on what *will* happen to the organism subsequently.

Let us now suppose that the environmental quality E, which the organism sees, and which generates its behavior according to 6.5.1, is *linked* in some fashion to the environmental quality U, which the organism does not see, but which determines the extent to which its behavior is adaptive. For sake of illustration, let us suppose that E represents light intensity, and U represents something like a predictor density, or a nutrient density. Thus, we are supposing that there is an equation of state of the form relating the two vector fields defined

$$\Phi(\nabla E, \ \nabla\sigma) = 0 \qquad\qquad\qquad (6.5.4)$$

on our surface by these qualities. If we knew this equation of state, we could predict the value of the field U at a point of our surface from a knowledge of the field E at the point; likewise, we could predict the gradient ∇U from a knowledge of the gradient ∇E at any point of the surface.

Now according to 6.5.2, the characterization of a behavior of our organism as adaptive is measured by the extent to which its path through the surface follows the gradient of U. The selection mechanism, embodied in 6.5.3, is defined in such a way that, by controlling the genome α, we generate organisms which will respond to E in such a way that they must closely follow the gradient of U. Thus, these adapted organisms treat E as an indicator or predictor for U; by orienting themselves properly with respect to the vector field ∇E, they *automatically* follow the integral curves of the vector field ∇U. Their instantaneous behaviors at any point of our surface thus

in effect embody the equation of state 6.5.4 through which these two
vector fields are related. This is one basic aspect of how selection
for increased adaptation generates a model.

A second, and perhaps more important aspect, arises through the tacit
prediction that, *by orienting themselves appropriately with respect
to ∇E, at any specific instant of time, they will thereby be maximizing
their fitness, when evaluated at some later time.* That is, the retrospective or reactive mode through selection generates adaptation,
becomes converted in the adapted organism to a *prediction* about how
present behavior will affect future behavior.

All of this is transparently visible in the case of our negatively
phototropic organism, which we may suppose to be fully adapted to an
environment in which light intensity E is correlated to, say, predator
density U. Thus, by following negative gradients of light intensity
(i.e. moving towards regions of darkness) the organism automatically
follows negative gradients of predator density, even though it cannot
directly perceive the predator gradient. It also simultaneously
maximizes its fitness; by moving to dark *now*, it guarantees maximal
fecundity *later*. Indeed, it is now trivial to show that our organism
now satisfies the five conditions given in Chapter 6.1 above, which
characterize an anticipatory system. We leave the explicit verification
as an exercise for the reader.

Moreover, we see from this kind of discussion the relatively minor
role played by the specific *mechanism* by which the fully adapted
behavior is actually generated; i.e. of the manner in which the
organism actually orients itself in a scalar field of light intensities.
In this regard let us recall the description of phototropism as given
by Wiener (cf. p.   above), which as we saw dealt *entirely* with
mechanism. In this case, the fully adapted behavior is simply *described* independent of the selection mechanism which generated it ,
and excised from the context of adaptation and selection from which
it arose. Such a discussion is carried out entirely within the confines of a specific equation of state of the form 6.5.1; as we have
seen, from 6.5.1 alone we can have no concept of adaptation at all,
let alone a concept of selection which produces an adaptive organism
from imperfectly adaptive precursors. Consequently, the anticipatory
features of the fully adaptive organism disappear, and with them, any
chance to understand the nature and character of adaptation itself.

The picture of adaptation, selection and evolution which we have
drawn, and which is embodied in the relations 6.5.1, 6.5.2, 6.5.3,
and 6.5.4 above, is an exceedingly rich one, even when expressed within
the confines of the particular metaphor we have been employing so far.
It is well to stress again that none of these concepts can be properly
understood unless all the others are taken into account. Failure to
recognize this fact clearly has contributed more than anything else
to the strife and controversy characterizing the literature pertaining
to adaptation and evolution, closely akin to the "nature-nurture"
controversies which clutter the literature on behavior.

Even from this limited discussion, we can draw quite a number of
general conclusions. One simple illustration will suffice for us here

Let us imagine a family of different kinds of organisms moving in
our surface, each kind responding to a different kind of sensory
modality E_i (for instance, to temperature, or to the concentration
of some chemical species) according to an equation of state

$$dx/dt = \varphi_i(\alpha_i, \nabla E_i)$$

$$(6.5.5)$$

$$dy/dt = \psi_i(\alpha_i, \nabla E_i)$$

analogous to 6.5.1 above. The forms of these equations (i.e. the functions φ_i, ψ_i) can be completely different from one kind of organism to another; i.e. the mechanisms by which the motions are generated can be entirely dissimilar. We suppose only that the same quantity U determines the fitnesses of the paths followed by each kind of organism (i.e. that the relation 6.5.2 is imposed on all organisms), and that there is for each E_i an equation of state of the form

$$\Phi_i(\nabla E_i, \nabla U) = 0$$

analogous to 5.5.4, where again the forms of these relations can be different for the different kinds of organisms. Then the imposition of the selection mechanism 6.5.3 will clearly generate, for each kind of organism, a genome α_i^* for which the equations 6.5.5 yield paths which follow the integral curves of 6.5.2. That is, selection will yield adapted organisms which behave similarly, even though each of them is responding to a different sensory modality, and even though the mechanism by which paths are generated are entirely dissimilar. This conclusion can be interpreted as what the biologist calls *convergence*, or *convergent evolution*.[7] In words: different kinds of organisms experiencing the same kind of selection mechanism will tend towards the same kind of behavior, independent of the specific mechanisms by which the behaviors themselves are generated.

Before proceeding further, let us pause to extract from the special metaphor developed above the essential aspects which serve to characterize any system in which adaptation, and consequently associated notions of fitness and selection, can be formulated. This will involve nothing more than a restatement of the basic relations 6.5.1, 6.5.2, 6.5.3 and 6.5.4 in a general context.

The first pre-requisite, of course, is a family of behaviors or phenotypes, which are generated according to some equation of state analogous to 6.5.1. Let us suppose then that S is any natural system, which can be described in such a way that an equation of state of the form

$$\Phi(E_i, \alpha_i, v_i) = 0 \qquad\qquad (6.5.6)$$

holds. Here the observables v_i correspond to phenotypic quantities, the E_i are environmental quantities, and the α_i constitute genome for the equation of state 6.5.6. It should be emphasized that this equation of state characterizes only one possible description of the natural system S; i.e. pertains to a particular encoding of that system. There will, of course, in general be many other equations of state characterizing S, depending on which observables of S (and the environment) are chosen to generate our encoding.

The next prerequisite, as we have seen, is the introduction of a measure of *fitness*, with respect to which phenotypes or behaviors generated by equations of state like 6.5.6 can be compared with one another. As we have noted, such a notion of fitness amounts to the introduction of a common currency, adequate for the comparison not

only of alternate phenotypes of a single system, but of phenotypes
arising from diverse systems governed by entirely different equations
of state. The stipulation of such a common currency for comparison
of utterly diverse systems is not by any means unique to biology.
For example, in physics, such a common currency is found in the
concept of *energy*. All motions, and all interactions occurring
between physical systems of any character, can be canonically formulated into propositions about the flow, exchange and conversion of
energy. Indeed, it is this fact above all which allows us to characterize physics as a discipline, and to recognize the diverse phenomena
of mechanics, electrodynamics, acoustics, optics, and a host of others
as amenable to physical description in a unified way. It is perhaps
the fact that the common universal currency of physics, which is
energy, is no longer adequate as a measure of biological activities
which distinguishes biological phenomena from the purely physical
ones which are associated with them. In another realm, the science
of economics, which is concerned with the diverse forms of wealth,
begins with the introduction of a common currency (value) which does
for economics what energy does for physics. The concept of fitness
plays an analogous role in biology, as we have seen, in establishing
the basis for discussing adaptation, selection and evolution.

Let us then suppose that there is a quantity F (the fitness) which
is determined by each particular phenotype (v_i) arising from 6.5.6,
and a family (U_i) of environmental qualities. This hypothesis may
be expressed as another equation of state relating the system S and
its environment, and will generally be of the form

$$\psi(F, U_i, v_i) = 0. \tag{6.5.7}$$

Thus, given any phenotype (v_i) generated according to 6.5.6, and any
environment characterized by particular values of the qualities U_i,
a definite value of fitness is associated.

It should be noted that the relation 6.5.7 defining the fitness is
itself contingent upon a particular encoding of the natural system
S. It states in effect that *if* the phenotype of our system is
encoded through the observables v_i, and *if* only the environmental
qualities U_i enter into the interaction between S and its environment
through which fitness is determined, then that fitness would be
expressed by 6.5.7.

In any case, once the common currency F is postulated, we may compare
the adaptedness of any phenotype to any environment by substituting
the (v_i) defined by 6.5.6 into the relation 6.5.7. In this way, the
concept of fitness may be extended from phenotypes to the genotypes
and environments which generated them.

We thus have formulated two of the basic pre-requisites, which allow
us to generate phenotypes, and to compare them with respect to a
common currency. This allows us to speak of phenotypes (or their
genotypes) as adaptive to a particular degree under a given set of
environmental conditions. The third pre-requisite is a notion of
selection, which as we have seen, allows us to act on genotypes
through their corresponding phenotypes. Such a selection mechanism
induces a dynamics in a space of genomes; it is thus a mechanism

for modifying the *identity* of the natural system with which we are
dealing, and hence generates an *evolution* of the system. Thus,
analogous to 6.5.3, we shall write

$$d(\alpha_i)/d\Theta = K \ \nabla F(\alpha_i).$$
(6.5.8)

In general, the trajectories of this dynamics will take us to
stationary values of the fitness in a fixed set of environmental
conditions. As before, we emphasize that the time scale (defined
by the differential $d\theta$) is *necessarily* different from the time scales
appearing in the relations governing the generation of phenotypes
through 6.5.6; it it were not so, we would not be dealing with
evolution.

Our final pre-requisite is the existence of a definite linkage between the qualities U_i which determines the fitness, and the qualities
E_i which generate the behaviors or phenotypes. For generality, we
shall write this linkage in the form

$$\Gamma(E_i, \ U_i, \ V_i) = 0$$
(6.5.9)

where E_i and U_i are as in (6) and (7) respectively, and the V_i represent other environmental qualities on which the relation beween
the E_i (which are the qualities our system perceives) and the U_i
(which are the qualities which define the fitness or adaptive character of system behaviors or phenotypes) may depend. Under the special
hypothesis of V_i = constant, we recover the situation described
explicitly in our previous metaphor. However, if the V_i are not
constant, then the linkage relation between the U_i and the E_i will
not be fixed; accordingly, the nature of the selection mechanism
6.5.8 will change, and with it the character of the evolutionary
dynamics 6.5.8.

It is now very easy to see, by means of essentially the same argument
as before, that the effect of the selection mechanism 6.5.8 is twofold:
(a) it serves to generate within the evolving systems an image of the
linkage between the perceived qualities E_i and those qualities U_i on
which fitness depends; i.e. it generates an image of the linkage
6.5.9 within the system; and (b) because of the fact that the time
scale for the selection dynamics is *slower* than that for the behavior
dynamics, a *predictive model* for the fitness F (i.e. an image of the
equation of state 6.5.7 is likewise generated within the system.
Indeed, if in 6.5.7 we replace the U_i by the E_i according to relation
6.5.9, and we replace the v_i by the specific function of E_i and α_i
obtained from 6.5.6, then the fitness F becomes a function of the α,
and the E_i alone; clearly, the selection dynamics 6.5.8 will drive
us towards that genome for which the resultant phenotype maximizes
fitness, and possesses all of the other properties we have described.

It would take us far beyond the scope of the present volume to consider the various implications of the selection picture we have

drawn.[8] We have merely attempted to indicate how it is that selection
and ·adaptation in fact generate specific predictive models, in such
a way that the behavior of an organism at an instant of time bears
a definite relation to an internal prediction about a *later* instant.
In fact, a general theory of macroevolution can readily be built on
the framework we have introduced, incorporating all of the traditional
biological features of the Darwinian picture; the reader should ex
plore for himself how such a general macroevolutionary theory would
look. In particular, the reader should consider how the properties
of the linkage 6.5.9 bear upon the *stability* of the models generated
by selection, and how this in turn manifests itself on the effect of
selection in changing environments. We shall consider some aspects
of this circle of ideas in more detail in Chapter 6.7 below.

REFERENCES AND NOTES

1. There are at least three distinct spheres in biology in which
    the term "adaptation" plays an essential role: evolution,
    physiology, and behavior. In evolution (and more generally,
    in population genetics) the whole thrust of natural selection
    is to generate what we may loosely call adaptation to definite
    environments on niches. Almost any book about evolution is a
    treatise about adaptation and how it is generated; for specific
    discussions and further references, see e.g.
       Leigh, E. G., *Adaptation and Diversity in Natural History and
       the Mathematics of Evolution*. Freeman (1971).
       Williams, G. G., *Adaptation and Natural Selection: A Critique*.
       Princeton University Press (1966).
    In physiology, a host of adaptive mechanisms are studied, such
    as the "pupillary servomechanism", which controls the amount of
    light admitted to the eye (cf. Chapter 1.1, and Note 6 to that
    chapter). At one time, there was intensive study of "adaptation"
    in bacteria, by which was meant their capacity to rapidly adjust
    their internal chemistry to utilize whatever carbon source was
    available; this ultimately led to the discovery of inducible
    and repressible enzyme synthesis, the control of gene expression,
    and the operon hypothesis of Jacob and Monod (cf. Chapter 3.5,
    Note 15), among other things. On the behavioral side, which
    overlaps with physiology to an indefinite extent, depending on
    the author, we have the entire spectrum of learning and condition-
    ing, which we shall discuss separately in Chapter 6.6 below.
    All of this sprawling biological literature is related in two
    ways: (a) one can argue that the capacity to manifest physio-
    logical and behavioral adaptations must itself evolve; and (b)
    the encodings appropriate for the study of *all* adaptive mechanisms
    are metaphorically related. Indeed, in all cases, the problem
    of adaptation involves a functional relation or linkage $\Phi(x_1, \ldots,$
    $x_n) = 0$ between systematic and environmental observables; the
    problem is to transform the systematic variables so as to maintain
    the linkage when the environmental variables are modified. This
    is the essence of our previous assertion that adaptation (i.e.
    something being modified) and homeostasis (something remaining
    invariant) are two sides of the same coin; adaptation is con-
    cerned with what is changing, and homeostasis with what is
    invariant.

    It might be remarked parenthetically that one aspect of adaptation
    studies which has become clinically popular is the study of
    "stress" (cf. Selye, H., *Stress*. McGraw-Hill 1950); here, the
    main interest lies in the untoward effects of physiological adapta

to "stressful" environmental modifications, and how they may be controlled. This has led to quite an extensive literature in which the term "adaptation" plays an important role; cf. Helson, H., *Adaptation-Level Theory*, Harper & Row (1964), or Coelho, G. V., *Coping and Adaptation*, Basic Books (1974).

Adaptation can also be studied in areas remote from biology, as in the context of human systems (cf. Day, R. H. and Groves, T., *Adaptive Economic Models*, Academic Press 1975), or in terms of mechanical artifacts and their control (cf. the extensive literature on adaptive control. In technical terms, an *adaptive* control system is one in which controller characteristics are modified according to the performance of the system being controlled. There is thus a close relation between adaptive control and the idea of a differential game; cf. Note 4 to Chapter 4.6 above). See for instance Yakowitz, S. J., *Mathematics of Adaptive Control Processes*, Elsevier (1969).

Finally, adaptation can be studied in quite abstract terms, yielding results which simultaneously illuminate all the various topics we have mentioned above. One example of this may be found in a long series of papers by Bremermann, in which a frank mutation-selection model is utilized to solve general optimization problems (cf. Bremermann, H., in *Biogenesis, Evolution, Homeostasis* (A. Locker, ed.), Springer-Verlag 1973, pp. 29-37). Abother extensive formalism of this character was developed by John Holland (*Adaptation in Natural and Artificial Systems*, University of Michigan Press 1975).

Thus, it is clear that the spectrum of studies of adaptation is broad indeed.

2. In particular, this Principle refers to the equilibria of closed systems, and the response of such an equilibrium to an externally imposed perturbation. Specifically, if such an equilibrium is disturbed through a change in *one* of its state variables, the system will move to a new equilibrium; in moving to that equilibrium, the state variable which was originally perturbed will move in the direction opposite to the one in which it was originally perturbed.

3. However, it may be argued that it a cybernetic homeostat, the controller imposes a measure of fitness on the states of the controlled system; this fitness is measured by the deviation of a state of the controlled system from the set-point in the controller.

4. For a fuller discussion of the Principle of Optimal Design and its correlates, see N. Rashevsky 1960. *Mathematical Biophysics*, Dover (1960).

5. The identification of fitness with fecundity is probably due to R. A. Fisher. Strictly speaking, it is most correctly used in population genetics as a measure of how the frequency of a particular gene is increasing or decreasing per generation in the gene pool under consideration. See e.g. Fisher, R. A., 1930. *Genetic Theory of Natural Selection*. Reprinted Dover 1958.

6. For an extreme statement along these lines, see e.g. Williams, M. B., *Lecture Notes in Biomathematics* #13, 226-240, Springer-Verlag (1977).

7. In evolutionary biology, convergence is usually restricted to
    morphological rather than behavioral characteristics; for a
    typical discussion, see e.g. Rensch, B., *Evolution Above the
    Specific Level*, Wiley (1959). However, it is clear that our
    discussion can be entirely recast into morphological terms.
    Similar ideas of convergence appear from time to time in the
    social and political sciences, with respect to bureaucracies,
    firms and even entire states.

6.6 Learning

In the present chapter, we wish to explore the following proposition: that the apparently disparate phenomena of evolution and of learning are in fact linked to each other, in the sense that a metaphor for the one is, at the same time, a metaphor for the other.[1] In fact, we can translate an evolutionary metaphor into a learning metaphor by means of a specific mapping process in which observables of the former are simply re-interpreted, or translated, into observables of the latter. From this it will immediately follow, from the arguments of the preceding chapter, that *learning processes generate predictive models*.

To see this, it is most transparent to proceed by developing a specific learning metaphor, and show how it comprises a realization of the evolutionary formalism developed in the preceding chapter. We will develop this metaphor within the context of the neural networks described in Example 4 of Chapter 3.5 above, which, it will be recalled, were themselves metaphors for the activity of the central nervous system in organisms.[2] What we will describe is a class of devices commonly called *perceptrons*, and which received a great deal of attention not so many years ago.

Let us then suppose that we are given an arbitrary neural network, as indicated schematically in Figure 6.6.1 below:

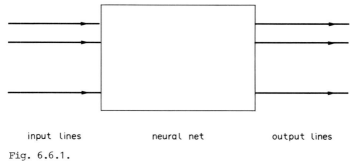

input lines   neural net   output lines

Fig. 6.6.1.

We will consider the inputs coming into the network from the left as
sensory inputs, whose states of excitation at any instant is determined completely by the environment of the network. These are the
afferent lines to the network. Likewise, the output lines, leaving
the network on the right, are the efferent lines, which may intuitively be regarded as driving specific responses to the sensory inputs.

Let us imagine that all of these efferent lines innervate a single
organ, which can be in one of two states ("on" or "off"). If this
is so, we may as well consider the innervated organ to itself be
represented by a formal neuron which we shall call the response
neuron. Thus, the network of Figure 1 can be enlarged to give the
network shown in Figure 6.6.2 below:

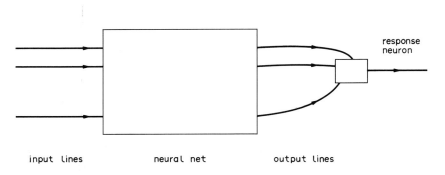

response
neuron

input lines   neural net   output lines

Fig. 6.6.2.

Let us suppose at some initial instant t_0 the neural network N is in
some definite state; e.g., the state in which no neuron in the network is on. At that instant, we impose a specific pattern of excitation on the afferent in input lines to the network. It is easy to
see that, if there are k such input lines, there are 2^k distinct
patterns of excitation which can be so imposed. According to the
theory of neural networks as we developed it previously, at some
subsequent instant, the response neuron will either fire or not.
Whether it fires depends on both the nature of the input pattern,
and on the constitutive parameters of the network (i.e. on its wiring
diagram, the neural thresholds, and the magnitudes of the weights
assigned to each of the internal axons of the network). If the
response neuron fires at a subsequent instant under these conditions,
we shall say that the network *recognizes* the initial input pattern;
otherwise, we shall say that the network does not recognize the
pattern.

Let us denote by ξ the set of possible input patterns to our network;
as noted above, ξ contains 2^k elements, where k is the number of input
or afferent lines to the net. It is clear that our network necessarily decomposes ξ into two disjoint subsets which together exhaust
ξ; namely, the class of patterns which are recognized by the network,
and the class of patterns which are not recognized. The specific set
of input patterns which are recognized is thus a function of the
constitutive parameters of the network we are using; if these are
changed, so is the partition of ξ defined by the network. Any such
network can thus be regarded as a meter, which defines a particularly
simple kind of observable on ξ.

Now let us suppose that we arbitrarily choose a subset $\xi_r \subset \xi$, which we wish the network to recognize. That is, we wish the response neuron to fire at some subsequent instant if and only if the input pattern imposed on it belongs to ξ_r. In general, of course, the class of patterns recognized by the network will not coincide with ξ_r. However, we can *modify* the class of patterns recognized by the network by *changing the constitutive* parameters which define the network; i.e. by changing the pattern of interconnection and/or the thresholds and/or the weights which characterize the network. Let us focus our attention on the weights. Imagine that at an initial instant t_0 we impose some input pattern E from ξ on the input lines to the network. We shall say that the network responds *correctly* to this pattern if either: (a) E ϵ ξ_r, and the output neuron of the network fires at a subsequent instant, or (b) E $\notin$ ξ_r, and the output neuron of the network does not fire at that instant. If the network has responded correctly, we make no change in it. If the network has not responded correctly, however, we shall modify the weights of its internal connections, according to some fixed algorithm, called a reinforcement algorithm, whose precise nature need not concern us here. We then repeat the process, by resetting the network to zero, picking another input pattern from ξ, and ascertaining whether the response of the network is correct or not. Then, it is a theorem that, under these conditions, there exists a reinforcement algorithm such that, if all the patterns in ξ are shown to the network as indicated a sufficient number of times, the reinforcement algorithm will force the network to "converge"; i.e. so that the correct response will thereafter be made to any pattern in ξ. That is, the network will "learn" to recognize precisely those patterns which belong to the pre-assigned set ξ_r. Moreover, the reinforcement algorithm in question does not depend on ξ_r; i.e. the *same* algorithm will force convergence to any ξ_r. This is the principal theorem on which the study of perceptrons as paradigms for learning is based.

A great many experiments were performed at one time in constructing perceptrons of the above type which could be "trained" to recognize visual patterns. This was done by connecting the afferent inputs to a network of threshold elements to an array of photocells, which could be differentially illuminated; such an array of photocells was termed the "retina" of the perceptron. Of particular interest was the training of perceptrons to recognize relatively abstract classes of patterns characterized by the presence of specific qualitative *features*; e.g. to train the device to recognize the letter "E" regardless of its size or orientation on the retina.

Obviously, by increasing the number of response neurons, we can partition the set ξ of input stimuli into any number of classes. An analogous result to that stated above holds in this more general case; the same network can be trained to *discriminate* between the patterns belonging to each of these classes. Thus, we could in principle train a network to recognize (i.e. to discriminate) between, say, the 26 characters comprising the English alphabet. However, we shall restrict attention to the case of a single response neuron, because of its simplicity, and because it already exhibits the essential features to which we wish to draw attention.

Let us now reformulate the situation we have described, which is clearly a metaphor for learning (in this case, learning to discriminate between afferent excitation patterns belonging to different classes) in the language developed in the preceding chapter.

First, let us note that for any neural network, there is a definite equation of state of the form

$$\Phi(E, \alpha, v) = 0 \qquad\qquad (6.6.1)$$

where $E \varepsilon \xi$ is a particular pattern of excitation imposed on the input lines to the network at an initial instant t_0, the quantity α denotes the totality of constitutive parameters characterizing the network (and in particular, the weights of the internal axons), and v is the state of the response neuron at some subsequent instant. Thus in this equation of state, E is environment, α is genome, and v is phenotype.

Next, we suppose that we have a distinguished observable $U : \xi \rightarrow \{0,1\}$, which has the property that $U^{-1}(1) = \xi_r$, the set of inputs we wish the network to recognize. We shall define the *fitness* $F(v)$ of a phenotype v, arising from a given environment $E \varepsilon \xi$, to be 1 if $v = U(E)$, and zero otherwise.

Third, we observe that the imposition of a reinforcement algorithm precisely embodies a *selection mechanism*, which allows phenotypes to act on the genomes which generated them, according to the fitness of the phenotype. In this discrete setting we cannot of course talk about gradients; however, if we denote by α' the genome arising from the genome α from the implementation of a reinforcement algorithm, it is clear that there is an equation of state relating α and α' which is of the form

$$\Psi(\alpha', \alpha, F(v)) = 0. \qquad\qquad (6.6.2)$$

It is clear that the time scale governing the transition $\alpha \rightarrow \alpha'$ has no relation to the time scale in which the phenotype v is actually generated by the network. In the present context, the "time scale" in which the genotype transitions take place is given simply by the *sequence* in which the rules of the reinforcement algorithm are applied. The only constraint on this time scale is clearly that the "time unit" for the application of the reinforcement algorithm must in some sense be *slower* than the time unit governing the dynamical processes by which the phenotype v is generated.

Finally, we note that there is a definite relation between the input E "seen" by the network and the quantity U which determines the fitness of the resulting phenotype. This relation can be expressed by another equation of state of the form

$$\Gamma(E, U(E)) = 0. \qquad\qquad (6.6.3)$$

It is now clear that there is an exact analogy between our discussion of selection in the preceding chapter, and our metaphor for the generation of a particular discriminatory capability (i.e. learning) in perceptrons. Accordingly, the selection mechanism which "trains" the perception thereby creates a predictive model of the selection mechanism itself. Insofar as defining a class ξ_r of inputs to be recognized can be thought of as specifying a "feature", which is common to all the elements of ξ_r but is missing from all other inputs, the selection mechanism embodied in the reinforcement algorithm converges to a genome which *extracts* this feature, and uses it as a predictor. It is indeed correct to say that the "training" of a perceptron is equivalent to the establishment of a *tropism* in the system.

The simple metaphor for learning embodied in the perceptron is of course capable of infinite variation and extension. This has been one of the major driving forces in the study of "self-organizing" systems, both in their own right, and as metaphors for biological activities characterized by learning, evolution, intelligence, etc. Indeed, the perceptrons themselves constituted one of the early pillars of the field of "artificial intelligence"; an attempt to construct alternate realizations (in the form of machines) of behaviors mani- fested in organisms through metabolic, genetic and neural mechanisms. There is an enormous and sprawling literature devoted to these prob- lems, but the field is still in a state of relative immaturity. Part of this stems from a failure to take account of the distinction be- tween a metaphor and a model; part of it involves the absence of a sufficiently comprehensive viewpoint (including a failure to clearly articulate the separate ingredients which must enter into a coherent theory of adaptation).

Perhaps the most general formulation of perceptron-type metaphors was suggested by Norbert Wiener in one of the appendices to the second edition of his book *Cybernetics*. This suggestion uses the fact, which we alluded to at the outset, that any behavior which can be described can be simulated. For definiteness, suppose that a particular behavior can be represented as a function $f(x_1, \ldots, x_n)$ of n variables. Under very general conditions, such a function can be represented in terms of a suitable basis set; say polynomials. Thus we can write

$$f(x_1, \ldots, x_n) = \Sigma \; a_i \; \varphi_i(x_1, \ldots, x_n).$$

The coefficients a_i appearing in such an expansion can be considered as analogous to constitutive parameters, or genome for the behavior in question; in a precise sense, these coefficients *code* for that behavior.

Let us now suppose that we possess devices which can generate the basis functions φ_i. If we think of the coefficients a_i as *weights* to be associated with the outputs of these devices, then we can imagine a selection mechanism which will "tune" these coefficients in such a way that our array of devices precisely simulates the original behavior. This is an obvious generalization of the ideas embodied in the percep- tron; it was used by Wiener to provide a metaphor for, among other things, "self-reproduction" through the employment of the original system as a kind of template to which the selection mechanism must converge. The reader may find it a useful exercise to express these ideas in terms of the formalism we have developed in the preceding chapters.

For our purposes, the essential point to emphasize is that any such selection mechanism can be regarded as creating a system which con- tains a predictive model of the selection which gave rise to it; i.e. to a system which changes state in the present in accord with some internal model of the subsequent effect of the change of state on

fitness. It is of great interest that the selection mechanism itself,
which as we have formulated it proceeds entirely within a reactive
paradigm, generates a system which thereby falls outside that paradigm.
Namely, if the adapted system is considered in isolation, its behavior
will generally be anticipatory rather than reactive. These facts
lend a most important perspective to any attempt to understand the
behaviors of any system whose behaviors have been shaped by selection.

REFERENCES AND NOTES

1. In fact, the sprawling literature on learning runs closely parallel
    to that on adaptation. Depending on one's viewpoint, it can be
    regarded either as a part of adaptation, or as a metaphor for it.
    For instance, the enormous body of work devoted to establishing
    the relation between neuro-physiology and learning relates to
    psychology in the same way that population genetics relates to
    descriptive evolutionary biology. In both cases, it seems hardly
    fortuitous that under very general conditions, inter-unit inter-
    actions automatically generate the right kind of gross behavior.
    Moreover, as we have seen, learning can be extrapolated from
    biology to mechanical artifacts (cf. our earlier discussion of
    "Artificial Intelligence"; e.g. Note 19 to Chapter 3.5 above);
    this is analogous to the study of adaptiveness in non-biological
    systems which was discussed in the preceding chapter. In any case,
    we can only hint here at the vast literature, which runs in an
    enormous stream, with many deep canyons, north from neurophysio-
    logy; the few samples we cite are hardly representative, but
    they perhaps connect most closely with the main thread of our
    discussion:
        Anokhin, P. K., *Biology and Neurophysiology of the Conditioned
            Reflex and its Role in Adaptive Behavior*. Pergamon (1974).
        Hebb, D. O., *The Organization of Behavior*. Wiley (1949).
        Pribram, K., *The Languages of the Brain*. Prentice-Hall (1971).
        Arbib, M. A., *The Metaphorical Brain*. Wiley (1972).
        Rosenzweig, M. R. and Bennett, E. L. (eds.) *Neural Mechanisms
            of Learning and Memory*. MIT Press (1976).

2. The original concept of the perceptron was developed in
        Rosenblatt, F., *Principles of Neurodynamics*. Spartan (1962).
    Perceptrons constituted an initial paradigm for the area of
    pattern recognition, which in many ways overlaps with Artificial
    Intelligence, as well as with learning theory, and with applied
    technology. A more recent and abstract treatment may be found
    in
        Minsky, M. and Papert, S., *Perceptrons*. MIT Press (1969).

6.7 Selection in Systems and Subsystems

In the present chapter, we shall consider some implications of the
phenomena of adaptation and selection, when these are viewed from
the standpoint of *subsystems* of a given system. Such subsystems
may be thought of as individual cells, or organs, of a multicellular
organism; or as individuals or institutions in a society. As we
shall see, a number of surprising implications emerge when the
machinery we have described, which pertains to whole systems, is
projected down onto constituent subsystems. Conversely, the same
circle of ideas bears on the inverse situation; namely, the possibility that selection mechanisms acting on a number of initially
independent systems may establish definite linkages between them,
leading to the emergence of a new system at a higher level.

It is convenient to begin our discussion with a particular example,
which we have already explored in some detail. Thus, let us consider the perceptrons described in the preceding chapter. As we
have seen, these are systems for which a measure of adaptation is
at hand, and for which a selection mechanism (the reinforcement
algorithm) for generating adaptive behavior can be defined.

Each neuron in the basic neuron net which constitutes the perceptron
may be regarded as a subsystem of the perceptron. As such, each
neuron has its own equation of state, whose variables can be cate-
gorized as environment, genome and phenotype for that particular
neuron. It may happen that the environmental quantities for such a
neuron are a subset of the input pattern imposed on the system as
a whole, in which case the neuron "sees" a portion of the overall
stimulus imposed on the entire network; or it may be that these
quantities are entirely internal to the network, and hence linked to
the input pattern only through relations involving other neurons;
in this case such a neuron "sees" only the properties of other
neurons afferent to it. Likewise, the genomic qualities of the
neuron may be regarded as contributing to the overall genome of the
entire perceptron, or as linked to that genome through relations
involving other neurons. Finally, the phenotype of a constituent
neuron is linked to the phenotype of the entire perceptron only
through an equation of state involving all the other neurons.

As we have seen, the entire perceptron allows a notion of fitness

to be defined on it, with respect to which changes in its structure
may be regarded as adaptive. In particular, the imposition of a
reinforcement algorithm causes precisely such changes in structure.
With respect to such a definition of fitness, which obviously pertains only to the system as a whole, we may characterize any change
occurring in an individual neuron of the system as adaptive or not,
depending on whether the fitness of the entire system is increased
or decreased by that change. Thus we may conclude that *a notion of
fitness defined for the system as a whole, with respect to which
behavior can be characterized as adaptive or not, induces a corresponding notion of adaptation on the behaviors of its subsystems*.

Now let us consider each of these subsystems as if it were an independent system subject to the selection mechanism induced on it, as
we described, by the selection mechanism imposed upon the entire
system. As the entire system converges to a maximally adaptive
structure, so will each subsystem converge to some structure which
will be maximally adaptive with respect to the *induced* selection
mechanism. Consequently, as we have seen, each of these subsystems
will automatically generate a predictive model of the selection
induced on it, and in terms of the environment imposed on it. However, from the standpoint of the individual subsystems, *these induced
selection mechanisms are all different from one another, as are the
imposed environments which they experience*. As a result, the predictive models which they generate are also all different from one
another, and from the total model generated in the total system.
Thus, if we consider these subsystems individually, their predictive
models will all be different; *i.e. they will bifurcate from one
another*. Indeed, not only will they bifurcate from each other, but
also from the model generated in the system as a whole.

From these simple observations, a number of conclusions can be drawn
which are of considerable interest and importance. For one thing:
it is immediately obvious that we cannot in general hope to reconstruct the properties of the predictive models embodied in a fully
adapted system by considering the corresponding models generated in
subsystems. In a sense, this conclusion is another form of the
failure of reductionism as a universal mode of system analysis, which
we have already considered at great length above. Our previous
discussions of reductionism were cast entirely within the context
of the reactive paradigm; what we can conclude now is that the same
kinds of difficulties arise (perhaps even more sharply) in the anticipatory paradigm as well.

This kind of situation is quite general; it pertains to any situation
in which a system, containing a family of subsystems, is exposed to
a selection mechanism. Since each of the subsystems sees only a
fragment of the total situation, it can only form a model of that
fragment through the selection imposed on the whole system. We can
see this most clearly from our own experience, considering ourselves
as subsystems of an evolving social structure. Each of us occupies
a different position within the structure; thus each of us generates
predictive models about the structure as a whole and utilizes them
for generating his behavior. These models are all different, and
depend at least in part upon the information we receive about the
overall behavior of the structure; since our positions in it are
generally different, so too will be our information, our models and
our behaviors.

So far, we have considered the situation in which the *only* selection
mechanism imposed on the subsystems is the one induced from that
acting on the whole system. Let us suppose, however, that each of

the subsystems has a separate selection mechanism imposed upon it, apart from that induced on it by the system to which it belongs. That is, for each subsystem, we suppose that we can separately define a local notion of *fitness*. Accordingly, the behaviors of each sub-system can be classified as adaptive or not *with respect to its own local measure of fitness*. Let us further suppose that this local measure of fitness or adaptation imposes a selection mechanism, whereby the phenotype of the subsystem can act upon its genome. We can then ask: what will happen to the system as a whole under these circumstances? Let us briefly discuss some ramifications of this kind of situation.

First, there is of course no reason to expect that the local selection mechanisms acting on the subsystems will be concordant with the mech-anism induced on the subsystems by the global selection acting on the entire system. Stated another way, the two selection dynamics imposed on the subsystem genomes, considered separately, will *bifurcate* from each other. This means that a behavior in a subsystem which is adaptive from the global standpoint will be maladaptive from the local one, and conversely. In such circumstances, it is clear that the evolutionary process will depend on the relation between the *time scales* characterizing the local and global selection dynamics. Specifically, the selection with the faster dynamics will dominate the behavior of the subsystems, at least over the short term. If the local selection mechanisms are faster, the subsystems will each evolve *independently*, to generate behavior which is adaptive with respect to the local fitness measure, but generally maladaptive with respect to global fitness. If the global selection is faster, the subsystems will evolve so as to generate behavior which is adaptive from the standpoint of the whole system, but maladaptive with respect to the local fitness measure. Likewise the predictive models gener-ated within the subsystems will correspondingly be determined by the faster selection dynamics.

There are any number of intermediate cases which can be envisioned, in which some subsystems are evolving according to a local selection mechanism, and others evolve according to the induced global mechanism, once again depending on which is the faster.

Attention is thus drawn inevitably to the *rates* at which these various selection mechanisms operate. These rates are themselves time-de-pendent in general, so we may expect that whether evolution is di-rected by local or global mechanisms in the subsystems is itself time-dependent. In particular, we may expect that there will be definite intervals in which the evolution of the system as a whole is dominated by the local mechanisms, and other intervals in which that evolution is dominated by the global mechanism. The situation emerging here is somewhat reminiscent of the kinds of phase transitions which characterized the Ising models (cf. Example 2B, Chapter 3.5 above), although strictly speaking these are not evolving systems in our sense. It will be recalled that, in the Ising models, under certain sets of environmental conditions, the interaction between neighboring elements (i.e. subsystems) was such that their states became corre-lated; under these circumstances the system as a whole could be thought of as "ordered". Conversely, under other circumstances, the environment favored uncorrelated states between neighboring elements, and hence a "disordered" character for the system as a whole. It is precisely the transition between the global character of "order" and "disorder" which is manifested as a phase transition. Similarly, in the evolutionary situation we have been considering, we may expect transitions between a situation in which the global selection mech-anism dominates (i.e. is faster) and those in which local selection

mechanisms dominate; these will appear very similar to phase transitions between an ordered or co-operative phase, and a disordered
or individualistic phase.

The kind of "phase transition" in evolving systems which we have just
described has been graphically described by the biologist Garrett
Hardin,[1] in a special case which is termed "the tragedy of the Common"
The situation he envisaged concerned a common pasture, on which any
member of a community could bring a flock to graze. When the number
of individuals using the Common, and the sizes of their flocks, are
small, the situation is stable, and can persist indefinitely. The
situation is individually beneficial to each member of the community,
and this is manifested by an increase in the size of each individual
flock, and by the number of flocks which utilize the Common; this
increase tacitly embodies the selection rule imposed on the community,
and the model of the situation which each individual forms to guide
his actions. However, at some point the utilization of the Common
exceeds its carrying capacity. At this point, a new local selection
mechanism comes into play, which acts faster than that imposed by the
limited carrying capacity of the Common. Specifically, over the short
term, each individual will find it advantageous to utilize the Common
as heavily as he can, and increase the size of his flock as fast as
he can, as Hardin has so vividly described. The result will be, of
course, as increasingly maladaptive behavior generated in each individual, as judged by the (unfortunately slow) selection mechanism
imposed by the limited carrying capacity of the Common on the community. Ultimately, of course, the community will crash completely;
the Common will be destroyed, and all the flocks will be completely
and uniformly wiped out.

Such a situation arises whenever the selection mechanism imposed on
a system depends on an environmental resource which is depleted by
increasing adaptation of the system as a whole. In another form,
it appears in the "technological catastrophe" which has been described
by numerous authors.[2] Consider, for instance, the evolution of a
fishing industry. Initially, the fish population is large; this
is the Common. As the number of fishermen, and the sizes of their
catch, increases, the resource supporting them becomes scarcer. At
this point, an apparent local advantage goes to those fishermen who
employ technological means to find fish and maintain their catch;
radar, mechanized trawling equipment, etc. As the resource becomes
even more scarce, the associated technology is driven to become ever
more refined by this local selection mechanism; in the limit, the
technology becomes maximally sophisticated just as the resource becomes completely extinct. Here again, the local selection, acting
rapidly, drives the population to behavior which is increasingly
maladaptive from the viewpoint of the slower global selection; but
it is the global mechanism which is ultimately decisive.

Speaking in purely biological terms, the generation of maladaptive
behavior in subsystems, created by a fast-acting local selection
mechanism of the kind we have described, results in the establishment
of a *parasitic* relation between the subsystems and the total system.
Such a relation is characterized precisely by the fact that what
appears to be an adaptive response by the subsystem, according to
its own local selection criterion, actually decreases the fitness
of the total system to which the subsystem belongs. Under appropriate
circumstances, as we have seen, the more adaptive the subsystem (i.e.
the more effectively parasitic it behavior) the greater is the decline
of fitness of the overall system, including the parasite. Because
of the disparity of time scales in the local and global selection
mechanisms, and precisely because the observables determining global

fitness are generally not directly perceptible by the subsystems, the catastrophic effects ultimately generated thereby are not manifested until it is too late for the subsystems to re-adapt.

Such situations, in which fast-acting local selection rules overshadow slower global selection mechanisms, are also unfortunately familiar in physiological contexts as well. For instance, the concepts of "health" and "pathology" largely pertain to such situations. A malignancy, for instance, is pathological precisely because it represents the manifestation of a local selection rule which becomes increasingly maladaptive from the standpoint of the total system to which it belongs; the malignancy is indeed a parasite, which ultimately causes the collapse of the entire system to which it belongs, and of itself as well. Conversely, the state of "health" is manifested when any local selection rules which may exist are too slow to affect behavior in a maladaptive fashion, or when they act in the same direction as global selection (i.e. so as to increase the fitness of the system as a whole).

The situation we have been describing can be expressed in another language. In effect, the generation of a parasitic relation between a system and its subsystems arises because local selection and global selection bifurcate from one another, so that a behavior adaptive from the local standpoint becomes maladaptive from the global one. We may express this by saying that such a bifurcation manifests a *conflict* between the local and global selection rules. It is a kind of conflict which arises entirely from the differential effects of selection mechanisms on systems and their subsystems. It can only be "resolved" in one of two ways: (a) by arranging matters so that the global selection mechanism always acts faster than local mechanisms, or (b) by eliminating local selection altogether. This last amounts to the imposition of specific constraints on the subsystems, which eliminates their capacity to respond to any local measures of fitness, apart from those induced on them by the system as a whole. The circumstances under which this can be done are, of course, not yet known; however, that it can be done is rendered plausible by the persistence of multicellular organisms, and indeed, the successive growth of their complexity, through biological evolution; and by the similar emergence and persistence of complex social structures, which have independently evolved many times in a number of different phyla. Such organisms and societies are characterized precisely by the fact that at least under most circumstances, selection does not act locally on the individual cells or members respectively, but globally on the system as a whole. On the other hand, the ecosystems to which such organisms and societies belong are characterized by the absence of global selection, and the predominance of local selection mechanisms on the individual constituents. Thus, for instance, it is hard to imagine a measure of fitness which would pertain to an ecosystem as a whole; and hence we cannot characterize a behavior of a constituent organism as "adaptive" from the standpoint of the ecosystem to which it belongs. On the contrary, the concept of adaptation prevalent in biology is defined completely in terms of the fitness of *individual* organisms.

It might be relevant to point out that elimination of local selection mechanisms according to (a) or (b) above, while eliminating the conflicts that lead to parasitism of subsystems on the total system, comes at a high cost. Namely, it leaves the total system vulnerable to the phenomena of *senescence* which were described in the preceding chapters. For once an internal model is generated, the absence of local selection mechanisms means that there is no way to change it. As we saw abundantly, there must be in general a growing discrepancy between the predictions of such a model and the actual properties of the organism; consequently, the behavior generated by the model must necessarily become increasingly maladaptive. For instance, the model incorporated in the forward activation step described in Chapter 6.2 above, once genetically encoded into a particular individual, cannot be changed by selection mechanisms imposed on that individual. The enzyme involved in this step cannot become parasitic on the cell which contains it, but on the other hand, we have seen that its behavior becomes increasingly maladaptive, ultimately leading to a generalized system failure which can be identified with senescence. In biology, of course, the kind of failure is at least partially circumvented by *proliferation*, which keeps resetting the model to zero in the progeny. But they too, in their time, must necessarily senesce in this fashion.

This kind of conflict we have been describing, which involves a bifurcation between local and global selection rules, is only one of the kinds of conflict which can emerge in evolving systems. A somewhat different kind of conflict can arise *between* the constituent subsystems of such a system, and is based on the fact alluded to above, that each such subsystem generates a *different model* of the global selection mechanism imposed on the system as a whole. Under appropriate circumstances, these models can themselves bifurcate from one another, and we can thus speak of "conflicts" between these models. Such a conflict between models becomes important when the subsystems involved are both required to generate some phenotypic behavior which pertains to the system as a whole. To put the matter somewhat anthropomorphically, when the models employed by the subsystems to generate behavior bifurcate, each subsystem will "decide" that a particular phenotypic behavior is adaptive, and the two decisions will be different. Indeed, this is the source of conflict which is most visible in human societies, either between individuals, or between institutions. Under such circumstances, the same objective situation will be perceived differently by the subsystems, and different courses of action will be advocated and pursued. In a complex society, for which by definition many models are possible, there are accordingly many such sources of conflict.

Such situations of conflict can, of course, also arise within a single organism possessing a number of sensory modalities. Thus, a stimulus imposed on such an organism, processed through several such modalities, may simultaneously activate contradictory impulses to effector or motor organs. For instance, an organism which is both chemotropic and phototropic may be placed in an environment in which the phototropic response requires movement in one direction, and the chemotropic response requires movement in the opposite direction. In such organisms, there generally exists specific mechanisms which serve to resolve these conflicts, and commit the organism to a single response in the presence of ambiguous environments; these are collectively called "integrating mechanisms".[3] The point to stress here is that such an integrating mechanism is required precisely because different subsystems of a complex system necessarily generate different models of that system, which will typically bifurcate from one another; when such models both effect a common response, conflict will arise which must be resolved before any response can be made. Most conflict in human societies appears to be of this form, and the integrating mechanisms available to resolve them are unfortunately not always adequate. For these purposes, an understanding of the nature of bifurcation between alternate models, which we have considered in great detail in the preceding sections, must play a crucial role.

So far, we have considered the relations which may exist between an evolving system and its subsystems. Let us now take up the converse question; namely, if we start with a number of initially independent (i.e. unlinked) systems, under what circumstances can they interact so as to form a composite system which itself can evolve?

Such a question is of considerable importance, not only for dealing with biological questions bearing on the evolution of multicellularity or social organization, but also for social technologies within our own society. For instance, it is a common belief that the institutions of our society are in some sense not sufficiently adaptive; that the various crises with which our society is increasingly faced arise from a state of non-adaptation or maladaptation. Implicit in this view is the idea that we must treat our institutions as if they were *individuals* in the biological sense; we must intrinsically define a measure of fitness for them, and a selective mechanism which would allow them to evolve in the direction of increasing fitness; as we have seen, that is what making them adaptive means. Cn the basis of the preceding discussion, however, two essential aspects of this situation must be considered: (a) as we have pointed cut above, fast local adaptive mechanisms (e.g. those which might be imposed on societal institutions, as opposed to society as a whole) will generally bifurcate from each other, as well as from any slower selective mechanism operating on the whole society. Under such circumstances, unless very special (and very imperfectly understood) conditions are satisfied, an integrated social structure may not be possible at all. (b) The perceived "malfunctioning" of social institutions, far from arising because they are insufficiently adaptive, may well cccur because they are *already too adaptive*. That is, they are already behaving as biological individuals, at the expense of the social structure to which they belong; i.e. they are already parasitic on that structure, in the sense we have described above. In such a case, a casual increase in their adaptive capabilities will only render them more parasitic, and again make any overarching social structure impossible.

In any case, we see that questions of adaptation and maladaptation must be approached with great care. Moreover, they cannot be meaningfully discussed apart from general notions of fitness, which give them meaning and from selection mechanisms, which serve to generate adaptive behavior. These in turn depend in the last analysis entirely upon modelling relations, and especially on the manner in which predictive models can bifurcate from one another. Thus, the questions in which an understanding of social organization must be based, as well as the basic questions of biology, all ultimately devolve on those with which we have been concerned at such great length above. It thus appears that the concept of a model, and the relationships which exist between models, lies at the root of everything which we need to know.

REFERENCES AND NOTES

1. Hardin, G., *Science* 131, 1292-1297 (1960).

2. See for example
    Ellul, J., *The Technological Society*. Knopf (1973).

3. The problem of establishing coherent behavior in a population of semi-autonomous units is one of the great problems facing any reductionistic analysis of complex systems, or any attempt to generate them from structural subunits. In principle, the easiest way to generate coherent behavior is to provide the population with some external cue (e.g. the conductor of an orchestra);

this is what generates coherent behavior in systems like the
Ising models. Somewhat more interesting are situations in which
the units generate the coherence internally, as in populations
of weakly coupled oscillators; these will generally entrain to
a common frequency (see e.g. Winfree, S., *The Geometry of Biological Time*, Springer-Verlag 1979). At a somewhat higher level,
coherence-generating mechanisms are often called integrating mechanisms, and are much studied from the standpoint of the control
of complex neuromotor activities (see for example Kilmer, W.,
McCulloch, W. and Blum, J., *Int. J. Man-Machine Studies*, 1, 279-
309 1979). At still higher levels, coherence is often called
consensus; its absence is called *conflict*. One of the great
mysteries is how to generate concensus; one approach, applicable
in very limited situations, has been called "Delphi"; see for
instance Linestone, H. A. and Turoff, J., *The Delphi Method:
Techniques and Applications*, Addison-Wesley (1975). In general,
however, the ontogenesis of coherent behavior is shrouded in
obscurity, though it is obviously a matter of some importance.

6.8 Perspectives for the Future

It is now time to pull together the various threads we have woven;
to see where they have taken us so far, and where they direct us for
the future. To that end, we will review the basic ideas which have
entered into our development, and specifically pose a few of the many
open questions which remain.

The point of departure for our entire development was the recognition
that most of the behavior we observe in the biological realm, if
indeed not all of the behavior which we consider as characteristically
biological, is of an anticipatory rather than a reactive character.
In fact, if it were necessary to try to characterize in a few words
the difference between living organisms and inorganic systems, such
a characterization would not involve the presence of DNA, or any other
purely structural attributes; but rather that organisms constitute
the class of systems which can behave in an anticipatory fashion.
That is to say, organisms comprise those systems which can make predictive models (of themselves, and of their environments) and use
these models to direct their present actions.

We saw very early that the behaviors of systems which employ predictive models are vastly different from those which do not. At the
most fundamental level, anticipatory systems appear to violate those
principles as causality which have dominated science for thousands
of years. It is for this reason that the study of anticipatory systems *per se* has been excluded routinely from science, and that therefore we have had to content ourselves with *simulations* of their behavior, constructed in purely reactive terms. Restriction to such
simulations has limited us to the study of the *mechanisms* whereby
biological actions are effected, thereby distorting our approach to
biological processes, and in fact precluding from the outset any basic
understanding of how these processes actually work.

Once we recognized that anticipatory behavior is the general rule in
biological systems, and that it depends essentially on the presence
of predictive models, our attention was inexorably drawn to the
nature of the modelling relation itself. What, indeed, is a model?
The better part of our development was concerned with attempting to
clarify this question. In its most general terms, we found that a
modelling relation between systems is established through an encoding

of qualities pertaining to one of them into corresponding qualities
of the other, in such a way that the linkages between these qualities
are preserved. In science, we generally attempt to encode qualities
of natural systems into purely formal (i.e. mathematical) ones, in
such a way that the rules of inference of the mathematical system
correspond to causal relations, and particularly dynamical relations.
in the natural system. We found that the same natural system generally admits many models, depending on which of its qualities are thus
encoded; indeed, the *complexity* of a natural system is perceived
through the number of distinct modelling relations into which it can
enter. Conversely, we found that many different natural systems can
admit the same model; this provided the basis for the fundamental
concept of *analogy* between systems, and the use of analogy as a powerful scientific tool. We sought to illustrate these ideas with many
examples, drawn from the widest possible variety of scientific disciplines; not only to show their universality, but also to demonstrate that the concept of a model is not something exotic or unusual,
but rather of the broadest currency imaginable.

The raw material for the construction of modelling relations is, and
must be, the result of observation. In the broadest sense, observation provides the means by which the qualities of natural systems
are defined and represented. As we developed it, observation involves
the dynamical *interaction* of natural systems, and the employment of
the change of state induced in one of the interacting systems as a
label for the value of some corresponding quality of the other system.
Thus, we stressed that the making of observations, which is generally
considered the hallmark of empirical or environmental science, already
involves the concept of a model in an essential way, and thus theoretical science (i.e. the study of models) is simply a kind of extension of the process of observation itself.

We also pointed out in this connection that an act of observation is
a quintessential act of abstraction; the observation of a single
quality of a natural system is indeed the greatest kind of abstraction
which can be made of that system. From this point of view, the
development of theoretical science is an attempt to combine observations in such a way that our view of systems becomes *less* abstract
than it could be if we were restricted to observation alone. Thus,
we stressed what should be a commonplace; that there is no antagonism
between "theory" and "experiment"; it is unfortunately not a commonplace, because it has been obscured by the antagonism between "theor-
ists" and "experimentalists".

Even though models are, in this sense, less abstract than observations,
they are nevertheless abstractions. Thus it becomes of great importance to understand how different models of the same system are inter-
related. The crucial concept here was that of bifurcation. Indeed,
a modelling relation can generally be formulated in mathematical
terms as a conjugacy; the failure of a modelling relation, which
is a logical independence between two modes of description, thus
becomes exactly a bifurcation in the mathematical sense. We saw how
this concept of bifurcation was related, on the one hand, to phenomena
of emergence, and on the other hand, to the concept of error. As we
formulated it, error is not a stochastic phenomenon, but rather
indicates a discrepancy between the behavior of a natural system and
the corresponding behavior of a particular model of that system.

Since the point of our development was the consideration of *predictive*
models, it was necessary to describe the concept of time in some
detail. We found that time itself is complex, in the sense that it
admits many different kinds of encodings, and these encodings can

themselves bifurcate from one another. Indeed, it is only within a
class of systems which are themselves already similar in some non-
temporal sense that a concept of time can be uniformly introduced
which is valid for all the systems in the class. It was in fact the
non-comparability of time scales generated by different kinds of
dynamical processes which was at the heart of our discussion of
selection and adaptation, which is the process by which predictive
models are actually generated in biological systems.

Armed with a deeper understanding of the modelling relation itself,
how then shall we approach the study of systems whose behavior is
controlled by models? As we saw, there are several different kinds
of questions we can ask about such systems, each with its own emphasis
and point of departure. Let us illustrate a few of them.

First, we may ask how best to study the "physiology" of an anticipatory
system. That is, we suppose given a system which contains some predictive model, and uses that model to determine its present behavior.
We do not ask how that model was generated, either ontogenetically
or phylogenetically, but rather seek to understand the behavior of
the system as a whole. Certain aspects of the behavior of such a
system can be understood without knowing the specific nature of the
model employed by the system, but follow from the general character
of modelling relations. For instance, we know that the model, as
an abstraction, must ultimately bifurcate from what it models; thus
any such system is in a sense *spanned*, and must undergo a characteristic form of senescence, as we have seen. We indicated how the
character of this senescence can tell us something about the nature
of the model, and how it is linked to the other qualities of the
system.

However, for detailed understanding of such a system, we need to know
specifically what the model is which the system is employing to
generate its behavior. Thus the basic question arises: *how can we
determine this model, from observations performed on the system
itself?* This is the basic question underlying the "physiology" of
anticipatory systems; it is one which has no counterpart in the
theory of purely reactive systems, and raises a host of entirely
new problems of both a theoretical and a practical character. Analogous problems which can be formulated in a formal context should be
of great help in telling us how to approach this basic question; for
instance, how do we need to observe a computer, or a Turing machine,
in order to determine its program? It should be noted that the
reactive paradigm itself, based on developments initiated in particle
mechanics, presume that there are in general effective procedures for
extracting system laws (i.e. linkages between observables, or equations
of state) from appropriate observations of the observables themselves;
we are now asking explicitly how (and indeed, whether) this can be
effectively done in the context of anticipatory systems. Such questions have received relatively scant attention in the past; they
now are seen to be of the essence.

Another kind of basic question we can ask about anticipatory systems
concerns their "ontogeny"; the manner in which they are generated.
We have suggested in the preceding chapters of the present section
that the ontogeny of the models, and their role in control of anticipatory behavior, is the natural consequence of selection mechanisms;
that these in turn involve the closely linked ideas of fitness, adaptation and a mechanism through which genome can act on phenotype.
Here, of course, the terms "genome" and "phenotype" are to be understood in very general terms, they are ways of classifying the qualities which appear in an equation of state. Thus, the operation of

a selection mechanism is a metaphor both for biological evolution and for the structurally quite different phenomena usually associated with the notion of learning. It is quite clear that a study of the onto-genesis of anticipatory systems, governed by the requirement that adaptation (as measured by fitness) increases, can throw some light on the physiological problems articulated above. Of particular interest in this regard, as we sketched in the preceding chapter, is the circle of ideas relating the several subsystems of an adaptive system, and the manner in which a study of subsystems might bear upon the determination of an anticipatory model in the system as a whole. However, here too, the necessary ideas have only just begun to be formulated, and are themselves still in an essentially embryonic state.

A third circle of questions concerns the basic question of how we can hope to apply an understanding of anticipatory systems to develop a technology of anticipatory control. Such a technology would be of vast importance, in many vital areas. For instance, in a medical context, it is clear that many of the so-called metabolic diseases, which are as yet so imperfectly understood, can be thought of as derangements of anticipatory mechanisms. For instance, as we have suggested, senescence can be regarded as a generalized maladaptation arising from a growing discrepancy between what the system's internal models are predicting, and what the system itself is actually doing. As we saw, the hallmark of this type of senescence is a kind of generalized maladaptation, without any localizable failure in specific subsystems. Likewise, hormonal control seems to be of an essentially anticipatory character; a hormone is thus to be regarded as a pre-dictor, representing some anticipated future state of the organism. To approach endocrine mechanisms in this way is to cast an entirely new light on endocrine disorders, and points up once again the need to extract from an anticipatory system some information about the character of the models employed by the system. Exactly the same may be said about other vital physiological subsystems, such as the central nervous system and the immune system, which in some sense seem to work entirely off models. Hence a theory of anticipatory systems seems bound to find crucial applications in medicine.

Finally, of course, we must return to the circle of applications which were the initial point of departure for our entire development; namely, the management of our own societies. Here, too, we feel that a deep understanding of anticipatory systems in general, and the character of the modelling relations which direct them, will be central. Furthermore, the ubiquitous character of anticipatory mech-anisms in biology, and their emergence through selection mechanisms, provides for us a vast encyclopedia for how to solve complex problems of the type with which we are presently confronted (and also, equally usefully, of how not to solve them). This encyclopedia represents a natural biological resource to be harvested; a resource perhaps ultimately more important to our survival than the more tangible resources of food and energy. To learn to exploit this resource to the full involves an understanding of the metaphoric relations be-tween biology and social systems, which we are only beginning to be able to grasp. Indeed, it was for this purpose that we went so deeply into the character of metaphorical relationships between systems in the above pages. The formal tools arising from these considerations represent a beginning, but still only a beginning, in these directions.

One other problem regarding anticipatory systems, unique to the human realm, may also be mentioned. The basic situation with which we have dealt so far involves the interaction of an anticipatory system with an environment that is non-anticipatory; i.e. is describable entirely

within a reactive paradigm. We may, however, ask what happens when
an anticipatory system must interact with an environment which is
itself anticipatory. This is the situation embodied most graphically
in the illustration below:

The behavior of such systems is characteristic of human interactions.
The closest approach to a theory of such interactions is found, of
course, in the Theory of Games. But this theory is in many ways
phenomenological and unsatisfactory; it is like a probabilistic
theory of error, and awaits a more basic theory arising from fundamental principles. The development of such a theory of interacting
anticipatory systems represents yet another direction for future
research.

Finally, we come full circle to the ideas of Robert Hutchins, with
which we started. His basic question, it will be recalled, was:
"What ought we to do now"? The crucial word here is "ought"; a
word which has traditionally been regarded as foreign to science.
Indeed, if we stay entirely within a reactive paradigm, this word
never arises. Perhaps this is the fundamental reason why Hutchins
was so suspicious of scientists, and hence of science; in his view,
there had to be something fundamentally missing in a field in wiich
the word "ought" was excluded as a matter of principle. However,
in the study of anticipatory systems, we find that "ought" is of the
essence; the character of a predictive model assumes almost an
ethical character, even in a purely abstract context. We might even
say that the models embodied in an anticipatory system are what comprise its individuality; what distinguish it uniquely from other
systems. As we have seen, a change in these models is a change of
identity; this is perhaps why, for human beings, the preservation
of models becomes identical with the preservation of self. The
identification of one's self with one's models explains, perhaps,
why human beings are so often willing to die; i.e. to suffer
biological extinction, rather than change their models, and why
suicide is so often, and so paradoxically, an ultimate act of self-
preservation.

The study of anticipatory systems thus involves in an essential way
the subjective notions of good and ill, as they manifest themselves
in the models which shape our behavior. For in a profound sense, the
study of models is the study of man; and if we can agree about our
models, we can agree about everything else.

CHAPTER 7

Appendix

7.1. Prefatory Remarks

In this final part of the book, we shall briefly sketch some of the
more recent developments which have grown out of the material presented in the preceding sections.

In their way, these newer developments are very revolutionary. Their
revolutionary character lies in the questions they raise about the
class of mathematical systems which can be the images of natural
systems. Throughout the present book, we have stressed that the
essence of science lies in the modelling relation; the establishment
of a correspondence between percepts and the relations which link
them, and the ingredients which make up a formal or mathematical
system. This correspondence must match what we call the causal
properties of the natural system with the inferential properties of
the formal one, as we have amply seen. Also, as we have seen, we
can and do use the characteristics of a formal model to *impute* corresponding properties back to the natural system being modelled.

One fundamental imputation, which has been preserved essentially intact since the time of Newton, is the idea that nature is to be represented in such a way that there is a partition into *states* and
dynamical laws, or into *propositions* and *production rules*. However
much our system descriptions may differ from each other technically,
they all, to this day, share or partake of this dual structure. Even
in quantum mechanics, which seems to be the most radical departure
from the Newtonian picture, the primary difference between the two
is the argument over what constitutes a state or state description;
thus, even here the duality between states and dynamical laws persists intact.

Thus, the class of mathematical images of natural systems, or the
class of mathematical structures which could be images of natural
systems, is tacitly assumed to be some kind of category of general
dynamical system. What I assert in the Appendix to follow, and what
is the main revolutionary content of that Appendix, is that this
class of mathematical images is too small; it is not enough to do
physics in, let alone biology.

I try to make it plausible that this category of general dynamical
systems, in which all science has hitherto been done, is only able
to represent what I call *simple systems* or *mechanisms*. Natural systems which have mathematical images lying outside of this category
and which accordingly do not admit a once-and-for-all partition into
states plus dynamical laws, are thus not simple systems; they are
complex. However, as we argue, complex systems can be approximated,
locally and temporarily, by appropriately chosen simple ones; indeed,
Parts 5 and 6 below were essentially concerned with the nature of such
approximations.

The reader will also find a number of unsuspected relationships between the notion of complexity and the old Aristotelian categories
of causation. In particular, we will argue that the category of
Final Cause, excluded from science for so long because of its incompatibility with the science of simple systems or mechanisms, is not
excluded from the science of complex systems. A corollary is: an
anticipatory system must be complex; a complex system may be anticipatory. I believe that the reader will find a number of other
such surprises. But then, this is the essence of complexity.

I hope that the reader will indulge my closing this Preface with a
few personal remarks about the material to follow. It was never my
hope or ambition or expectation to embark on the kind of epistemological investigations whose results are reported here. What I
wanted to do was to get a better insight into the material basis of
organic phenomena. I entered into this endeavor with a complete
faith in the generality of physical laws, and in the explanatory
powers of mathematics. This kind of faith is not abandoned lightly,
and in fact I have never abandoned it. What I have had to abandon,
indeed have been forced to abandon, is the conceptual framework in
which physics and biology have heretofore been done, and limitations
this framework imposes on the relation it admits between mathematics
and the material world. One does not lightly or gladly abandon the
traditions of centuries and millenia; it would be much nicer and
more convenient to be able to work within those traditions than to
have to move outside them. I have tried to indicate why and how
they must be departed from. I hope that the reader will agree that
these departures are indeed forced upon us; that there is nothing
whimsical, speculative, or fanciful about them; and that to at
least some extent they can reflect Newton's own words: Hypothesis
non fingo.

7.2. Introduction

We shall introduce the rather wide-ranging considerations which follow
with a discussion of the concept of *information* and its role in
scientific discourse. Ever since Shannon began to talk about
"Information Theory" (by which he meant a probabilistic analysis of
the deleterious effects of propagating signals through "channels";
cf. Shannon, 1949) this concept has been relentlessly analyzed and
re-analyzed. The time and effort expended on these analyses must
surely rank as one of the most unprofitable investments in modern
scientific history; not only has there been no profit, but the
currency itself has been debased to worthlessness. Yet, in biology,
for example, the terminology of information intrudes itself insist-
ently at every level; code, signal, computation, recognition. It
may be that these informational terms are simply not scientific at
all; that they are an anthropomorphic stopgap; a *facon de parler*
which merely reflects the immaturity of biology as a science, to be
replaced at the earliest opportunity by the more rigorous terminology

of force, energy, and potential which are the province of more mature
sciences (i.e. physics) in which "information" is never mentioned.
Or, it may be that the informational terminology which seems to force
itself upon us bespeaks something fundamental; something which is
missing from physics as we now understand it. We shall take this
latter viewpoint, and see where it leads us.

In human terms, information is easy to define; it is anything which
is or can be the answer to a question. Therefore we shall preface
our more formal considerations with a brief discussion of the status
of interrogatives, in logic and in science.

The amazing fact is that interrogation is not ever a part of formal
logic, including mathematics. The symbol "?" is not a logical
symbol, as for instance are "∨", "∧", "∃", or "∀"; nor is it a
mathematical symbol. It belongs entirely to informal discourse, and
as far as I know, the purely logical or formal character of interrogation has never been investigated. Thus, if "information" is indeed
connected in an intimate fashion with interrogation, it is not surprising that it has not been formally characterized in any real sense.
There is simply no existing basis on which to do so.

I do not intend to go deeply here into the problems of extending
formal logic (always including mathematics in this domain) so as to
include interrogatories. What I want to suggest here is a relation
between our informal notions of interrogation and the familiar logical
operation "⇒"; the conditional, or the implication operation. Collo-
quially, this operation can be rendered in the form "If A, then B".
My argument will involve two steps. First, I will argue that *every*
interrogative can be put into a kind of conditional form:

          If A, then B?

(where B can be an indefinite pronoun like "who", "what", etc., as
well as a definite proposition). Second, and most important, I will
argue that every interrogative can be expressed in a more special
conditional form, which can be described as follows. Suppose I know
that some proposition of the form

          If A, then B

is true. Suppose I now change or vary A; i.e. replace A by a new
expression which I will call δA. The result will be an interrogative,
which I can express as

          If δA, then δB?

Roughly, I am treating the true proposition "If A, then B" as a
reference, and I am asking what happens to this proposition if I
replace the reference expression A by the new expression δA. I
could of course do the same thing with B in the reference proposition;
replace it by a new proposition δB and ask what happens to A. I
assert that every interrogative can be expressed this way, in what
I shall call a *variational form*.

The importance of these notions for us will lie in their relation
to the external world; most particularly in their relation to the
concept of *measurement*, and to the notions of causality to which
they become connected when a formal or logical system is employed
to represent what is happening in the external world; i.e. to
describe some physical or biological system or situation.

AS-N

Before doing this, I want to motivate the two assertions made above
regarding the expression of arbitrary interrogatives in a kind of
conditional form. I will do this by considering a few typical
examples, and leaving the rest to the reader for the moment.

Suppose I consider the question

        "Did it rain yesterday?"

First, I will write it in the form

        "If (yesterday), then (rain)?"

which is the first kind of conditional form described above. To
find the variational form, I presume I know that some proposition
like

        "If (today), then (sunny)"

is true. The general variational form of this proposition is

        "If δ(today), then δ(sunny)?".

In particular, then, if I put

        δ(today) = (yesterday),

        δ(sunny) = (rain)

I have indeed expressed my original question in the variational form.
A little experimentation with interrogatives of various kinds taken
from informal discourse (of great interest are questions of classification, including existence and universality) should serve to make
manifest the generality of the relation between interrogation and
the implicative forms described above; of course this cannot be
proved in any logical sense, since as noted above, interrogation sits
outside logic.

It is clear that the notions of observation and experiment are closely
related to the concept of interrogation. That is why the results of
observation and experiment (i.e. data) are so generally regarded as
being information. In a formal sense, simple observation can be
regarded as a special case of experimentation; intuitively, an
observer simply determines what *is*, while an experimenter systematically perturbs what is, and then observes the effects of his pert-
bation. In the conditional form, then, an observer is asking a
question which can generally be expressed as:

        "If (initial conditions), then (meter reading)?"

In the variational form, this question may be formulated as follows:
assuming the proposition

        "If (initial conditions = 0), then (meter readings = 0)"

is true (this establishes the reference, and corresponds to cali-
brating the meters), our question becomes

        "If δ(initial conditions = 0), then δ(meter readings = 0)?"

where simply

$$\delta(\text{initial conditions} = 0) = (\text{initial conditions})$$

and

$$\delta(\text{meter readings} = 0) = (\text{meter readings}).$$

The experimentalist essentially takes the results of observation as his reference, and thus, basically asks the question which in variational form is just

"If δ(initial conditions), then δ(meter readings)?"

The theoretical scientist, on the other hand, deals with a different class of question; namely, with the questions which arise from assuming a δB (which may be B itself) and asking for the corresponding δA. This is a question which an experimentalist cannot approach directly, not even in principle. It is mainly the difference between the two kinds of questions which marks the difference between experiment and theory, as well as the difference between the explanatory and predictive roles of theory itself; clearly, if we give δA and ask for the consequent δB, we are predicting, whereas if we assume a δB and ask for the antecedent δA, we are explaining.

It should be noted that exactly the same duality arises in mathematics and logic themselves; i.e. in purely formal systems. Thus a mathematician can ask (*informally*): If (I make certain assumptions), then (what follows)? Or, he can start with a conjecture, and ask: If (Fermat's Last Theorem is true), then (what initial conditions must I assume to explicitly construct a proof)? The former is analogous to prediction, the latter to explanation.

When formal systems (i.e. logic and mathematics) are used to construct images of what is going on in the world, then interrogations and implications become associated with ideas of causality. Indeed, the whole concept of natural law depends precisely on the idea that causal processes in natural systems can be made to correspond with implication in some appropriate descriptive inferential system (e.g. Sec. 3 above, where this theme is developed at great length).

But the concept of causality is itself a complicated one; this fact has been largely overlooked in modern scientific discourse, to its cost. That causality is complicated was already pointed out by Aristotle. To Aristotle, all science was animated by a specific interrogative: why? He said explicitly that the business of science was to concern itself with "the why of things". In our language, these are just the questions of *theoretical* science: if (B), then (what A)? and hence we can say B *because* A. Or, in the variational form, δB *because* δA.

But Aristotle argued that there were four distinct categories of causation; four ways of answering the question *why*. These categories he called *material cause*, *formal cause*, *efficient cause*, and *final cause*. These categories of causation are not interchangeable. If this is so (and I will argue below that indeed it is) then there are correspondingly *different kinds of information*, associated with different causal categories. These different kinds of information have been confused, mainly because we are in the habit of using the same mathematical language to describe all of them; it is from these inherent confusions that much of the ambiguity and murkiness of the concept of information ultimately arises. Indeed, we can say more than this: the very fact that the same mathematical language

does not (in fact, cannot) distinguish between essentially distinct
categories of causation means that the mathematical language we have
been using is in itself somehow fundamentally deficient, and that it
must be extended by means of supplementary structures to eliminate
those deficiencies.

7.3. The Paradigm of Mechanics

The appearance of Newton's *Principia* towards the end of the 17th
century was surely an epochal event. Though nominally the theory of
physical systems of mass points, it was much more than this. In
practical terms, by showing how the mysteries of the heavens could
be understood on the basis of a few simple universal laws, it set
the standards for explanation and prediction which have been accepted
ever since. It unleashed a feeling of optimism almost unimaginable
today; it was the culmination of the entire Renaissance. More than
that; in addition to providing a universal explanation for specific
physical events, it also provided a language and a way of thinking
about systems which has persisted essentially unchanged to the present
time; what has changed has only been the technical manifestation of
the language and its interpretation. In this language, the word
"information" never appears in any formal technical sense; we have
only words like "energy", "force", "potential", "work", and the like.

It is important to recognize the twin roles played by Newtonian mechanics in science; as a reductionistic ultimate, and as a paradigm
for representation of systems not yet reduced to systems of interacting particles. The essential feature of this paradigm is the
employment of a mathematical language with a built-in duality, which
we may express as the distinction between *internal states* and *dynamica
laws*. In Newtonian mechanics, the internal states are represented
by points in some appropriate manifold of phases, and the dynamical
laws represent the internal or impressed forces. The resulting
mathematical image is thus nowadays what is called a *dynamical system*.
However, the dynamical systems arising in mechanics are mathematically
rather special ones, because of the way phases are defined (they
possess a symplectic structure). Through the work of people like
Poincaré, Birkhoff, Lotka, and many others over the years, however,
this dynamical system paradigm, or its numerous variants, has come
to be regarded as the universal vehicle for representation of systems
which could not be technically described mechanically; systems of
interacting chemicals, organisms, ecosystems, and many others. Even
the most radical changes occurring within physics itself, like
relativity and quantum theory, manifest this framework; in quantum
theory, for instance, there was the most radical modification of
what constitutes a *state*, and how it is connected to what we can observe and measure; but otherwise, the basic partition between states
and dynamical laws is relentlessly maintained. Roughly, this partitio
embodies a distinction between what is inside or intrinsic (the states
and what is outside (the dynamical laws, which are formal generalizations of the mechanical concept of impressed force).

This, then, is our inherited *mechanical paradigm*, which in its many
technical variants or interpretations has been regarded as a universal
language for describing systems and what they do. The variants take
many forms; automata theory, control theory, and the like, but they
all conform to the same basic framework first exhibited in the
Principia.

Among other things, this framework is regarded as epitomizing the concept of causality. We will look at this closely, because it will

become important to us momentarily, when we turn to the concept of information in this framework.

Mathematically, a dynamical system can be regarded simply as a vector field on a manifold of states; to each state, there is an assigned velocity vector (in mechanics it is in fact an acceleration vector). A given state (representing what the system is intrinsically like at an instant) together with its associated tangent vector (which represents what the effect of the external world on the system is like at an instant) uniquely determines how the system will change state, or move in time. This translation of environmental effects into a unique tangent vector is already a causal statement, in some sense; it translates into a more perspicuous form through a process of *integration*, which amounts to "solving" the equations of motion. More precisely, if a dynamical system is expressed in the familiar form

$$dx_i/dt = f_i(x_1, \ldots, x_n) \quad i = 1, \ldots, n \quad\quad (7.3.1)$$

in which time does not generally appear as an explicit variable (but only implicitly through its differential or derivation dt), the process of integration manifests the explicit dependence of the state variables $x_i = x_i(t)$ on time:

$$x_i(t) = \int_{t_0}^{t} f_i(x_1(\tau), \ldots, x_n(\tau))d\tau + x_i(t_0). \quad\quad (7.3.2)$$

This is a more traditional kind of causal statement, in which the "state at time t" is treated as an *effect*, and the right-hand sides of (7.3.2) above are the *causes* on which this effect depends.

Before going further, let us take a look at the integrands in (7.3.2), which are the velocities or rates of change of the state variables. The mathematical character of the entire system is determined entirely by the *form* of these functions. Hence, we can ask: what is it that expresses this form (i.e. which determines whether our functions are polynomials, or exponentials or of some other form? And given the general form (polynomial, say), what is it that picks out a specific function and distinguishes it from all others of that form?

The answer, in a nutshell, is: *parameters*. As I have written the system (7.3.1) above, no such parameters are explicitly visible, but they are at least tacit in the very writing of the symbol "f_i".

Mathematically, what these parameters do is to serve as coordinates for function spaces; just as any other kinds of coordinates do, they label or identify the individual members of such spaces. They thus play an entirely different role from the state variables which constitute the arguments or domains of the functions which they identify.

Here we see the first blurring. For the parameters which specify the form of the functions f_i can *mathematically* be thrown in as arguments of the functions f_i themselves; thus we could (and in fact always do) write

$$f_i = f_i(x_1, \ldots, x_n, a_1, \ldots, a_r) \quad\quad (7.3.3)$$

where the a_i are *parameters*. We could even extend the dynamical
equations (7.3.1) by writing

$$da_i/dt = 0$$

(if the a_i are indeed independent of time); thus mathematically we
can entirely eradicate any distinction between the parameters and
the state variables.

There is still one further distinction to be made. We pointed out
above that these parameters a_i represent the effects of the "outside
world" on the intrinsic system states. These effects involve *both*
the system *and* the outside world. Thus some of the parameters must
be interpreted as intrinsic too (the so-called *constitutive* parameters), while the others describe the "state of the outside world".
These latter obey their own laws, not incorporated in (7.3.1), so
they are, from that standpoint, simply regarded as *functions of time*
and must be posited independently. They constitute what are variously called *inputs* or *controls* or *forcings*. Indeed, if we regard
the states $(x_i(t))$, or any mathematical function of them, as corresponding *outputs* (that is, output as a function of input rather than
just of time) we pass directly to the world of control theory.

So let us see where we are. If we divide the world into state variables plus dynamical laws, this amounts to dividing the world into
state variables plus parameters, where the role of the parameters
is to determine the *form* of the functions which in fact define the
dynamical laws. The state variables are the arguments of these
functions, while the parameters are coordinates in function spaces.
Further, we must additionally partition the parameters themselves
into two classes; those which are *intrinsic* (the constitutive parameters) and those which are extrinsic, i.e. which reflect the nature
of the environment. The intrinsic parameters are intuitively closely
connected with what we might call *system identity*; i.e. with the
specific nature or character of the system itself. The values they
assume might, for example, tell us whether we are dealing with oxygen,
carbon dioxide, or any other chemical *species*. The values assumed
by these parameters, therefore, cannot change without our perceiving
that a *change of species* has occurred. The environmental parameters,
as well as the state variables, however, can change without affecting
the species of the system with which we are dealing.

These distinctions cannot be accommodated with the simple language
of vector fields on manifolds; that language is too abstract. We
can only recapture these distinctions by (a) superimposing an informal
layer of *interpretation* on the formal language, as we have essentially
done above, or (b) by changing the language itself, to make it less
abstract. Let us see how this can be done.

Just to have names for the various concepts involved, I will call
the constitutive parameters, which specify the *forms* of the dynamical
laws, and hence the species of system with which we are dealing, the
system *genome*; I will call the remaining parameters, which reflect
the nature of the external world, the system *environment*. The state
variables themselves I will call *phenotypes*. This rather provocative

terminology is chosen in deliberate reflection of corresponding
biological situations;   in particular, I have argued (cf. 3.3 above)
that, viewed in this light, the genotype-phenotype dualism which is
regarded as so characteristically biological has actually a far more
universal currency.

The mathematical structure appropriate to reflect the distinctions
we have made is that of genome-parameterized mappings from a space
of environments to a space of phenotypes;   i.e. mappings of the form

$$f_g : E \to P$$

specified in such a way that given any initial phenotype, environment
plus genome determines a corresponding trajectory. Thus we have no
longer a simple manifold of states, but rather a fiber-space structure
in which the basic distinctions between genome, environment, and
phenotype are embodied from the beginning. Some of the consequences
of this picture are examined in Rosen (1978, 1983);   we cannot pause
to explore them here.

Now we are in a position to discuss the actual relation between the
Newtonian paradigm and the categories of causation which were described earlier. In brief, if we regard "phenotype of the system
at time t" as *effect*, then

   a.   *Initial phenotype is material cause;*

   b.   *Genome* g *is formal cause;*

   c. $f_g(a)$, *as an operator on initial phenotype, is*
        efficient cause.

Thus, the distinctions we have made between genome, environment, and
phenotype turn out to be directly related to the old Aristotelian
categories of causation. As we shall soon see, that is why these
distinctions are so important.

We may note in passing that one of the Aristotelian categories is
missing from the above;   there is no *final cause* visible in the above
picture. Ultimately, this is the reason why final cause has been
banished from science;   the Newtonian paradigm simply has no room
for them. Indeed, it is evident that any attempt to superimpose
a category of final causation upon the Newtonian picture would
effectively destroy the other categories in this picture.

In a deep sense, the Newtonian paradigm has led us to the notion
that we may effectively *segregate the categories of causation* in
our system descriptions. Indeed, the very concept of system state
segregates the notion of material cause from the other categories
of causation, and tells us that it is all right to deal with all
aspects of material causation independent of the other categories.
Likewise with the concept of genome and environment. I would in
fact claim that *this very segregation into independent categories
of causation is the heart of the Newtonian paradigm*. When we put
it this way, however, the universality of the paradigm perhaps no
longer appears so self-evident. Indeed, that it is not universal
at all will be one of our main conclusions as we now turn back to
the concept of information with which we began.

7.4. Information

We said above that information is, or can be, the answer to a question,
and that a question can generally be put into what we called the variational form: If δA, then δB?. This is going to serve as the connecting bridge between "information" and the Newtonian paradigm we
have described. In fact, it has played an essential role in the
historical development of Newtonian mechanics and its variants, under
the rubric of *virtual displacements*.

In mechanics, a virtual displacement is a small, imaginary change
imposed on the *configuration* of a mechanical system, while the expressed forces are kept fixed. The animating question is: "If such
a virtual displacement is made under given circumstances, then what
happens?" The answer, in mechanics, is the well-known *Principle of
Virtual Work*: If a mechanical system is in equilibrium, then the
virtual work done by the impressed forces as a result of the virtual
displacement must vanish. This is a static (equilibrium) principle,
but it can readily be extended from statics to dynamics where it is
known as *D'Alembert's Principle*. In the dynamic case, it leads then
directly to the differential equations of motion of a mechanical
system when the impressed forces are known. Details can be found
in any text on classical mechanics.

In what follows, we are going to explore the effect of such virtual
displacements on the apparently more general class of dynamical systems of the form

$$dx_i/dt = f_i(x_1, \ldots, x_n), \quad i = 1, \ldots, n \qquad (7.4.1)$$

(In fact, however, there is a close relationship between the general
dynamical systems (7.4.1) and those of Newtonian mechanics; indeed,
the former systems can be regarded as arising out of the latter by
the imposition of a sufficient number of non-holonomic constraints.[1]

As we have already noted, the language of dynamical systems, like
that of Newtonian mechanics, does not include the word "information".
Rather, the study of such systems revolves around the various concepts
of *stability*. However, in one of his analyses of oscillations in
chemical systems, J. Higgins (1967) drew attention to the quantities

$$u_{ij}(x_1, \ldots, x_n) = \partial/\partial x_j (dx_i/dt).$$

These quantities, which he called "cross-couplings" if $i \neq j$ and
"self-couplings" if $i = j$, arise in an essential way in the conditions which govern the existence of oscillatory solutions of
(7.4.1). In fact, it turns out that it is not so much the magnitudes, as the signs, of these quantities which are important. In
order to have a handy way of talking about the signs of these quantities, he proposed that we call the jth state variable x_j an
activator of the ith, at a state $(x_1^0, \ldots, x_n^0)$, whenever the quantity

$$u_{ij}(x_1^0, \ldots, x_n^0) = \frac{\partial}{\partial x_j}\left(\frac{dx_i}{dt}\right)(x_1^0, \ldots, x_n^0) > 0$$

and an *inhibitor* whenever

$$u_{ij}(x_1^0, \ldots, x_n^0) < 0.$$

Now activation and inhibition are *informational* terms. Thus, Higgins'
terminology provides an initial hint about how dynamical language
might be related to informational language, through the Rosetta Stone
of stability.

Now let us see what Higgins' terminology amounts to. If x_j activates
x_i at a state, it means that a (virtual) increase in x_j increases the
rate of change of x_i, or alternatively, that a (virtual) decrease of
x_j decreases the rate of change of x_i. It is eminently reasonable
that this is what an activator should do intuitively. Conversely,
if x_j inhibits x_i at a state, it means that an increase in x_j decreases the rate of change of x_i, etc.

Thus the n^2 functions $u_{ij}(x_1, \ldots, x_n)$, i, j = 1, $\ldots$, n constitute
a kind of informational description of the dynamical system (7.4.1),
which I have elsewhere (Rosen, 1979) called an *activation-inhibition
pattern*. As we have noted, such a pattern concisely represents the
answers to the variational questions: "If we make a virtual change
in x_j, what happens to the rate of production of x_i?".

There is no reason to stop with the quantities u_{ij}. We can, for
instance, go one step further, and consider the quantities

$$u_{ijk}(x_1, \ldots, x_n) = \partial/\partial x_k (\partial/\partial x_j (dx_i/dt)).$$

Intuitively, these quantities measure the effect of a (virtual)
change in x_k on the *extent* to which x_j activates or inhibits x_i.
If such a quantity is positive at a state, it is reasonable to call
x_k an *agonist* of x_j with respect to x_i; if it is negative, an
antagonist. That is, if u_{ijk} is positive, a (virtual) increase
in x_k will increase or facilitate the activation of x_i by x_j, etc.
The quantities u_{ijk} thus define another layer of informational interaction, which we may call an *agonist-antagonist pattern*.

We can iterate this process, in fact to infinity, producing at each
state r a family of n^r functions $u_{ij\ldots r}(x_1, \ldots, x_n)$. Each layer
in this increasing sequence describes how a (virtual) change of a
variable at that level modulates the properties of the preceding
level.

In the above considerations, we have considered only the effects of
virtual changes in state variables x_j on the velocities dx_i/dt at
various informational levels. We could similarly consider the effects
of virtual displacements at these various levels on the second derivatives d^2x_i/dt^2 (i.e. on the *accelerations* of the x_i), on the third

derivatives d^3x_i/dt^3, and so on. Thus, we have a doubly infinite web
of informational interactions, defined by functions

$$u^m_{ijk...r}(x_1, ..., x_n) = \frac{\partial}{\partial x_r}\left(\cdots \frac{\partial}{\partial x_j}\left(\frac{dx^m_i}{dt^m}\right)\cdots\right)$$

If we start from the dynamical equations (7.4.1), then nothing new
is learned from these circumlocutions, beyond perhaps a deeper insight into the relations between dynamical and informational ideas.
Indeed, given any layer of informational structure, we can pass to
succeeding layers by mere differentiation, and to antecedent layers
by mere integration. Thus in particular, knowledge of any layer in
this infinite array of layers determines all of them, and in particular the dynamical equations themselves. For instance, if we know the
activation-inhibition pattern $u_{ij}(x_1, ..., x_n)$, we can reconstruct
the dynamical equations (7.4.1) through the relations

$$df_i = \sum_{j=1}^{n} u_{ij}dx_j \qquad\qquad (7.4.2)$$

(note in particular that the differential form on the right-hand
side is like a generalized *work*), and then putting the function
$f_i(x_1, ..., x_n)$ so determined equal to the rate of change dx_i/dt
of the ith state variable.

However, *our ability to do all this depends in an absolutely essential
way on the exactness of the differential forms which arise at every
level of our web of informational interaction*, and which relate each
level to its neighbors. For instance, if the forms in (7.4.2) are
not exact, there are no functions $f_i(x_1, ..., x_n)$ whose differentials
are given by (7.4.2), and hence *no rate equations of the form (7.4.1)*.
In fact, in such a situation, the simple relations between the levels
in our web (namely, that each level is the derivative of the preceding
level and the integral of the succeeding one) breaks down completely;
and levels become independent of each other, and must be posited
separately. Thus, for instance, two systems could have the same
activation-inhibition patterns, but vastly different agonist-antagonist
patterns, and hence manifest entirely different behaviors.

Just to fix ideas, let us see what is implied by the requirement
that the differential forms

$$\sum_{j=1}^{n} u_{ij}dx_j$$

defined by the activation-inhibition pattern be exact. The familiar
necessary conditions for exactness here take the form

$$\frac{\partial}{\partial x_k} u_{ij} = \frac{\partial}{\partial x_j} u_{ik}$$

for all i, j, k = 1, ..., n. Intuitively, these conditions mean
precisely that *the relations of agonism and activation are entirely
symmetrical* (commutative); that x_k as an anogist of the activator
x_j is exactly the same as x_j as an agonist of the activator x_k. And
likewise for all other levels.

Clearly, such situations are extremely degenerate in informational terms. They are so because the requirement of exactness is highly nongeneric for differential forms. Thus, these very simple considerations suggest a most radical conclusion: that *the Newtonian paradigm, with its emphasis on dynamical laws, restricts us from the outset to an extremely special class of systems, and that the most elementary informational considerations force us out of that class.* We shall explore some of the implications of this situation in the subsequent section.

Meanwhile, let us consider some of the ramifications of these informational ideas, which hold even within the confines of the Newtonian paradigm. These will concern the distinctions we made in the preceding section between environment, phenotype, and genome, the relations of these distinctions to different categories of causation, and the correspondingly different categories of information which these causal categories determine.

First, let us recall what we have already asserted above, namely, that according to the Newtonian paradigm, every relation between physical magnitudes (i.e. every equation of state) can be represented as a genome-parameterized family of mappings

$$f_g : E \to P$$

from environments to phenotypes. It is worth noting specifically that, in particular, every dynamical law or equations of motion are of this form, as can be seen by writing

$$d\vec{x}/dt = f_g(\vec{x}, \vec{a}). \tag{7.4.3}$$

Here in traditional language, $\vec{x}$ is a vector of states, $\vec{a}$ is a vector of "external controls" (which together with states constitutes

environment) and the phenotype here is precisely the tangent vector $d\vec{x}/dt$ attached to the state $\vec{x}$.[2] In this case, then, tangent vector or phenotype, constitutes *effect*; genome g is identified with formal cause, state x with material cause, and the operator $f_g(\ldots, \vec{a})$ with efficient cause.

By analogy with the activation-inhibition networks and their associated informational structures which were described above, we are going to consider formal quantities of the form

$$\frac{\partial}{\partial (\text{cause})} \left(\frac{d}{dt} (\text{effect}) \right) \tag{7.4.4}$$

As always, such a formal quantity represents an answer to a question: If (cause is varied), then (what happens to effect)? This is exactly the same question we asked in connection with the definition of activation-inhibition networks and their correlates, but now set into the wider context to which our analysis of the Newtonian paradigm has led us. That is, we may now virtually displace *any* magnitude which affects our relation (7.4.3), whether it be a genomic magnitude, an environmental magnitude, or a state variable. In a precise sense, the effect of such a virtual displacement is measured precisely by the quantity (7.4.4).

In particular, then, it follows that there are indeed different *kinds* of information. What kind of information we are dealing with depends

on whether we apply our virtual displacement to a genomic magnitude
(associated with formal cause), an environmental magnitude (efficient
cause), or state variable (material cause), Formally, then, we can
initially distinguish at least the following three cases:

1. Genomic information:

$$\frac{\partial}{\partial (genome)} \left(\frac{d}{dt} (effect) \right) ;$$ (7.4.5)

2. Phenotypic information:

$$\frac{\partial}{\partial (state)} \left(\frac{d}{dt} (effect) \right) ;$$

3. Environmental information:

$$\frac{\partial}{\partial (control)} \left(\frac{d}{dt} (effect) \right) .$$

We shall confine ourselves to these three for present purposes, which
generalize only the activation-inhibition patterns described above.

We now come to an important fact; namely, *the three categories
defined above are not equivalent*. Before justifying this assertion,
we must spend a moment discussing what is meant by "equivalent". In
general, the mathematical assessment of the effects of perturbations
(i.e. of real or virtual displacements) is the province of *stability*.
The effect on subsequent dynamical behavior of modifying or perturbing
a system state is the province of Lyapunov stability of dynamical
systems; the effect of perturbing a control is part of control
theory; the effect of perturbing a genome is the province of structural stability. To fix ideas, let us consider genomic perturbations,
or *mutations*. A virtual displacement applied to a genome g replaces
the initial mapping f_g determined by g with a new mapping $f_{g'}$. Mathematically, we say that the two mappings f_g, $f_{g'}$ are equivalent, or
similar, or conjugate, if there exist appropriate transformations

$$\alpha : E \rightarrow E,$$

$$\beta : P \rightarrow P$$

such that the diagram

$$
\begin{array}{ccc}
 & f_g & \\
E & \rightarrow & P \\
\alpha \downarrow & & \downarrow \beta \\
E & \rightarrow & P \\
 & f_{g'} &
\end{array}
$$

commutes; i.e. if

$$\beta (f_g (e)) = f_{g'} (\alpha (e))$$

For every e in E. Intuitively, this means that a mutation g → g'
can be offset, or annihilated, by imposing suitable *coordinate transformations* on the environments and phenotypes. Stated yet another
way, a virtual displacement of genome can always be counteracted by

corresponding displacements of environment and phenotype so that the
resultant variation on effect vanishes.

We have elsewhere (see e.g. 3.3 above) shown at great length that
this commutativity may not always obtain; i.e. that there may exist
genomes which are bifurcation points. In any neighborhood of a
bifurcating genome g, there exist genomes g' for which f_g and $f_{g'}$
fail to be conjugate.

With this background, we can return to the question of whether the
three kinds of information (genomic, phenotypic, and environmental)
which we have defined above are equivalent. Intuitively, equivalence
would mean that the effect of a virtual displacement δg of genome,
say with everything else held fixed, could equally well be produced
by a virtual displacement δa of environment, or by a virtual displacement δp of phenotype. Or stated another way, the effect of a virtual
displacement δg of genome can be annihilated by virtual displacements
$-\delta a$, $-\delta p$ of environment and phenotype respectively. This is simply
a restatement of the definition of conjugacy or similarity of mappings.

If all forms of information are equivalent, it would follow that there
could be no bifurcating genomes. We note in passing that the assumption of equivalence of the three kinds of information we have defined
above thus creates terrible ambiguities when it comes to *explanation*
of particular effects. We will not consider that aspect here, except
to note that it is perhaps very fortunate for us that, as we have seen,
they are not equivalent.

Let us look at one immediate consequence of the non-equivalence of
genomic, environmental, and phenotypic information, and of the considerations which culminate in that conclusion. Long ago (cf. von
Neumann, 1951; Burks, 1966) von Neumann proposed an influential
model for a "self-reproducing automaton", and subsequently, for automata which "grow" and "develop". This model was based on a famous
theorem of Turing (1936) establishing the existence of a universal
computer (universal Turing machine). From the existence of such a
universal computer, von Neumann argued that there must also exist a
universal constructor. Basically, he argued that computation (i.e.
following a program) and construction (following a blueprint) are
both algorithmic processes, and that anything holding for one class
of algorithmic processes necessarily holds for any other class. This
universal constructor formed the central ingredient of the "self-
reproducing automaton".

Now a computer acts, in the language we have developed above, through
the manipulation of efficient cause. A constructor, if the term is
to have any shred of its intuitive meaning, must essentially manipulate material cause. The inequivalence of the two categories of
causality, in particular manifested by the non-equivalence of environmental and phenotypic information, means that we cannot blithely
extrapolate from results pertaining to efficient causation into the
realm of material causation. Indeed, in addition to invalidating
von Neumann's specific argument, we learn that great care must be
exercised in general when arguing from purely logical models (i.e.
from models pertaining to efficient cause) to any kind of physical
realization, such as developmental or evolutionary biology (which,
as noted, pertain to material cause).

Thus, we see how significant are the impacts of informational ideas,
even within the confines of the Newtonian paradigm. In this paradigm,
as we have shown, the categories of causation are essentially segre-
gated into separate packages. We will now turn to the question of what
happens when we leave the comforting confines of that paradigm.

7.5. An Introduction to Complex Systems

I am going to call any natural system for which the Newtonian paradigm
is completely and eternally valid a *simple system*, or *mechanism*.
Accordingly, a *complex system* is one which, for one reason or another,
falls outside this paradigm. We have already seen a hint of such
systems in the preceding section; e.g. systems whose activation-
inhibition patterns u_{ij} do not give rise to exact differentials
$\Sigma u_{ij} dx_j$. However, some further words of motivation must precede an
immediate conclusion that such systems are truly complex (i.e. fall
fundamentally outside the Newtonian paradigm). We must also justify
our very usage of the term "complex" in this context.

What I have been calling the Newtonian paradigm ultimately devolves
upon *the class of distinct mathematical descriptions* which a system
can have, and the relations which exist between these descriptions.
As we have noted extensively above, the touchstone of system description arising in this paradigm is the fundamental dualism between
states and dynamical laws. Thus, in this paradigm, the mathematical
objects which can describe natural systems comprise a category, whose
objects may be called general dynamical systems. In a formal sense,
it looks as if any mathematical object falls into this category,
because the Newtonian partition between states and dynamical laws
exactly parallels the partition between propositions and production
rules (rules of inference) which presently characterize all logical
systems and logical theories. However, as we shall soon see, although
this category of general dynamical systems is indeed large, it is not
everything (and indeed, as we shall argue, it is far from large
enough).

As noted, the Newtonian paradigm asserts much more than simply that
every image of a natural system must belong to a given category. It
asserts certain relationships between such images. In particular,
(and this is the reductionistic content of the paradigm) it asserts
that among these images there is a biggest one, which effectively
maps on all the others. Intuitively, this is the master description
or ultimate description, in which every shred of physical reality
has an exact mathematical counterpart; in category-theoretic terms,
it is much like a free object (a generalization of the concept of
free semigroup, free group, etc.)[3]

There is still more. The ingredients of this ultimate description,
by their very nature, are themselves devoid of internal structure;
the only things about them which can change are their relative positions and velocities. Given the forces acting between them, as
Laplace noted long ago, everything that happens in the external
world is in principle predictable and understandable. From this
perspective, everything is determined; there are no mysteries, no
surprises, no errors, no questions, and no information. This is as
much true for quantum theory as for classical; only the nature of
state description has changed. And it applies to everything, from
atoms to organisms to galaxies.

Let us look now at how this universal picture manifests itself in
biology. First from the standpoint of the physicist, biology is
concerned with a rather small class of extremely special (indeed,
inordinately special) systems. The theoretical physicist, in his
quest for general and universal laws, has thus never had much to do
with organisms. As far as he is concerned, what makes organisms

special is not that they transcend his paradigms, but rather that their specification within the paradigm requires a plethora of special constraints and conditions, which must be superimposed on the universal canons of system description and reduction. The determination of these special conditions is an empirical task; essentially someone else's business. But it is not doubted that the relation between physics and biology is the relation between general and particular.

The modern biologist, in general, avidly embraces this perspective.[4] Historically, in fact, biology has only recently caught up with the Newtonian revolution which swept the rest of Natural Philosophy in the 17th century. The three-century lag arose because biology has no analog of the solar system; no way to make immediate and meaningful contact with the Newtonian paradigm. Not until physics and chemistry had elaborated the technical means to probe microscopic properties of matter (including organic matter) was the idea of a "molecular biology" even thinkable. And this did not happen until the 1930's.

At present, the fact is that there is still no single inferential chain which leads from anything important in physics to anything important in biology. This is in fact; a datum; a piece of information. How are we to understand it? There are various possibilities. Kant, long ago, argued that organisms could only be properly understood in terms of Final Causes or intentionality; hence from the outset he suggested that organisms fall completely outside the canons of Newtonian science which work for everything else. Indeed, the essential telic nature of organisms precluded even the possibility that a "Newton of the grassblade" would come along, and do for biology what Newton had done for physics. Another possibility is the one we have already mentioned; we have simply not yet characterized all those special conditions which are necessary to bring biology fully within the scope of universal physical principles. Still a third possibility has grown up within biology itself, as a consequence of evolutionary ideas; it is that much of biology is the result of *accidents* which are *in principle* unpredictable and hence governed by no laws at all.[5] In this view, biology is as much a branch of history as of science. At present, this last view sits in a kind of double-think relation with reductionism; the two are quite inconsistent, but do allow modern biologists to enjoy the benefits of vitalism and mechanism together,

Still a fourth view was expressed by Einstein, who said in a letter to Leo Szilard: "One can best appreciate, from a study of living things, how primitive physics still is".

As we have noted, the present prevailing view in biology is that the Newtonian canons are indeed universal, and we are lacking only knowledge of the special conditions and constraints which distinguish organisms from other natural systems within those canons. One way of saying this with a single word is to assert that organisms are *complex*. This word is not well defined, but it does connote several things. One of them is that complexity is a system property, no different from any other property. Another is that the *degree* to which a system is complex can be specified by a number, or set of numbers. These numbers may be interpreted variously as the dimensionality of a state space, or the length of an algorithm, or as a cost in time or energy incurred in solving system equations.

On a more empirical level, however, complexity is recognized differently. If a system surprises us, or does something we have not

predicted, or responds in a way we have not anticipated; if it makes
errors; if it exhibits emergence of unexpected novelties of behavior,
we also say that the system is complex. In short, complex systems
are those which behave "counter-intuitively".

Sometimes, of course, surprising behavior is simply the result of
incomplete characterization; we can then hunt for what is missing,
and incorporate it into our system description. In this way, the
planet Neptune was located from unexplained deviations of Uranus
from its expected trajectory. But sometimes, this is not the case;
in the apparently analogous case of the anomalies of the trajectory
of the planet Mercury, for instance, no amount of fiddling within
the classical picture would do, and only a massive readjustment of
the paradigm itself (General Relativity) could avail.

From these few words of introduction, we see that the identification
of "complexity" with situations where the Newtonian paradigm fails
is in accord with the intuitive connotation of the term, and is the
alternative to regarding as complex any situation which merely is
technically difficult within the paradigm.

Now let us see where "information" fits into these considerations.
We recall once more that "information" is the actual or potential
response to an interrogative, and that every interrogative can be
put into the variational form: "if δA, then δB?". The Newtonian
paradigm asserts, among other things, that the answers to such
interrogatives follow from dynamical laws superimposed on manifolds
of states. In their turn, these dynamical laws are special cases
of what we have elsewhere called *equations of state*, which link or
relate the values of system observables. Indeed, the concept of an
observable was the point of departure for our entire treatment of
system description and representation (cf. Rosen, 1978); it was
the connecting link between the world of natural phenomena and the
entirely different world of formal systems which we use to describe
and explain.

However, the kinds of considerations we have developed above suggests
that this world is not enough. We require also a world of variations,
increments, and differentials of observables. It is true that every
linkage between observables implies a corresponding linkage between
differentials, but as we have seen, the converse is not true. We are
thus led to the notion that a differential relation is a generalized
linkage, and that a differential form is a kind of generalized observable. A differential form which is not the differential of an
observable thus is an entity which assumes no definite numerical
value (as an observable does), but which can be incremented.

If we do think of differential forms as generalized observables,
then we must correspondingly generalize the notion of equation of
state. A generalized equation of state thus becomes a linkage or
relation between ordinary observables and differentials or generalized
observables. Such generalized equations of state are the vehicles
which answer questions of our variational form: If δA, then δB?

But as we have repeatedly noted, such generalized equations of state
do not generally follow from systems of dynamical equations, as they
do in the Newtonian paradigm. Thus we must find some alternative
way of characterizing a system of this kind. Here is where the
informational language which we have introduced above comes to the
fore. Let us recall, for instance, how we defined the activation-
inhibition network. We found a family of functions u_{ij} (i.e., of

observables) which could be thought of in the dynamical context as modulating the effect of an increment dx_j on that of another increment, df_i. That is, the values of each observable u_{ij} measure precisely the extent of activation or inhibition which x_j exerts on the rate at which x_i is changing.

In this language, a system falling outside the Newtonian paradigm (i.e. a complex system) can have an activation-inhibition pattern, just as a dynamical (i.e. simple) system does. Such patterns are still families of functions (observables) u_{ij}, and the pattern itself is manifested by the differential forms

$$\omega_i = u_{ij} dx_j$$

But in this case, there is no global velocity observable f_i which can be interpreted as the rate of change of x_i; there is only a velocity *increment*. It should be noted explicitly that the u_{ij} which define the activation-inhibition pattern need not be functions of the x_i alone, or even functions of them at all. Thus, the differential forms which arise in this context are different from those with which mathematicians generally deal, and which can always be regarded as cross-sections of the cotangent bundle of a definite manifold of states.

The next level of information is the agonist-antagonist pattern u_{ijk}. In the category of dynamical systems, this is completely determined by the activation-inhibition pattern, and can be obtained from the latter by differentiation:

$$u_{ijk} = \frac{\partial}{\partial x_k} u_{ij}.$$

In our world of generalized observables and linkages, the u_{ijk} are independent of the u_{ij}, and must be posited separately; in other words, complex (non-Newtonian) systems can have identical activation-inhibition patterns but quite different agonist-antagonist patterns.

Exactly the same considerations can now be applied to every subsequent layer of the informational hierarchy; each of them is now independent of the others, and must hence be posited separately. Hence a complex system requires an *infinite* mathematical object for its description.

We cannot go into the mathematical details of the considerations we have sketched so briefly above. Suffice it to say that a complex system, defined by a hierarchy of informational levels of the type we have described, is quite a different kind of object than is a dynamical system. For one thing, it is quite clear that there is no such thing as a set of *states*, assignable to such a system once and for all. From this alone, we might expect that the nature of causality in such systems is vastly different than it is in the Newtonian paradigm; we shall come to this in a moment.

The totality of mathematical structures of the type we have defined above forms a category. In this category the class of general dynamical systems constitutes a very small subcategory. We are suggesting that the former provides a suitable framework for the mathematical imaging of complex systems, while the latter, by definition, can only image simple systems or mechanisms. If these considerations are valid (and I believe they are), then the entire epistemology of our approach to natural systems is radically altered, and it is the basic notions of information which provide the natural ingredients for this.

There is, however, a profound relationship between the category of general dynamical (i.e. Newtonian) systems, and the larger category in which it is embedded. This can only be indicated here, but it is important indeed. Namely, there is a precise sense in which an informational hierarchy can be *approximated*, locally and temporarily, by a general dynamical system. With this notion of approximation there is an associated notion of *limit*, and hence of topology. Using these ideas, it can in fact be shown that what we can call the category of complex systems is the completion, or limiting set, of the category of simple (i.e. dynamical) systems.

The fact that complex systems can be approximated (albeit locally and temporarily) by simple ones is a crucial one. It explains precisely why the Newtonian paradigm has been so successful, and why, to this day, it represents the only effective procedure for dealing with system behavior. But in general, we can also see that it can supply *only* approximations in general, and in the universe of complex systems, it amounts to replacing a *complex* system with a *simple subsystem*. Some of the profound consequences of doing this are considered in detail in Section 5 above.

This relationship between complex systems and simple ones is, by its very nature, without a reductionistic counterpart. Indeed, what we presently understand as "physics" is seen in this light as *the science of simple systems*. The relation between physics and biology is thus not at all the relation of general to particular; in fact, quite the contrary. It is not biology, but physics, which is too special. We can see from this perspective that biology and physics (i.e. contemporary physics) grow as two divergent branches from a *theory of complex systems* which as yet can be glimpsed only very imperfectly.

The category of simple systems is, however, still the only thing we know how to work with. But to study complex systems by means of approximating simple systems puts us in the position of early cartographers, who were attempting to map a sphere while armed only with pieces of planes. Locally, and temporarily, they could do very well, but globally, the effects of the topology of the sphere become progressively important. So it is with complexity; over short times and only a few informational levels, we can always make do with a simple (i.e. dynamical) picture. Otherwise, we cannot; we must continually replace our approximating dynamics by others as the old ones fail. Hence another characteristic feature of complex systems; they appear to possess a multitude of partial dynamical descriptions, which cannot be combined into one single complete description. Indeed, in earlier work we took this as the defining feature of complexity (cf. Notes to Chapters 5.5, 5.6, 5.7).

We shall add one brief word about the status of causality in complex systems, and about the practical problem of determining the functions which specify their informational levels. As we have already noted, complex systems do not possess anything like a state set which is fixed once and for all. And in fact, in complex systems, the categories of causality become intertwined in a way which is not possible within the Newtonian paradigm. Intuitively, this follows from the independence of the infinite array of informational layers which constitutes the mathematical image of a complex system. The variation of any particular magnitude with such a system will typically manifest itself independently in many of these layers, and thus reflect itself partly as material cause, partly as efficient cause, and even partly as formal cause in the resultant variation of other magnitudes. We feel that it is, at least in large part, this involvement of magnitudes simultaneously in each of the causal categories which make biological systems so refractory to the Newtonian paradigm.

Also, this intertwining of the categories of causation in complex systems makes the interpretation of experimental results of the form "If δA, then δB" extremely difficult to interpret directly. If we are correct in what we have said so far, such an observational result is far too coarse as it stands to have any clear-cut meaning. In order to be meaningful, an experimental proposition of this form must isolate the effect of a variation δA on a single informational level, keeping the others clamped. As might be appreciated from what has been said so far, this will in general not be an easy thing to do. In other words, the experimental study of complex systems cannot be pursued with the same tools and ideas as are appropriate for simple systems.

Our final conceptual remark is also in order. As we pointed out above, the Newtonian paradigm has no room for the category of final causation. This category is closely tied up with the notion of anticipation, and in its turn, with the ability of systems to possess internal predictive models of themselves and their environments, which can be utilized for the control of present actions. We have argued at great length above that anticipatory control is indeed a distinguishing feature of the organic world, and developed some of the unique features of such anticipatory systems. In the present discussion, we have in effect shown that, in order for a system to be anticipatory, it must be complex. Thus, our entire treatment of anticipatory systems becomes a corollary of complexity. In other words, complex systems can admit the category of final causation in a perfectly rigorous, scientifically acceptable way. Perhaps this alone is sufficient recompense for abandoning the comforting confines of the Newtonian paradigm, which has served us so well over the centuries. It will continue to serve us well, provided that we recognize its restrictions and limitations as well as its strengths.

LITERATURE

1. Burks, A. 1966. *Theory of Self-Reproducing Automata*. University of Illinois Press, Urbana, Illinois.
2. Handler, P. (ed). 1970. *Biology and the Future of Man*. Oxford University Press, N.Y.
3. Higgins, J. 1967. "The Theory of Oscillating Reactions". *J. Ind. & Eng. Chem.* <u>59</u>, 18–62.
4. Monod, J. 1971. *Chance and Necessity*. Alfred A. Knopf, N.Y.
5. von Neumann, J. 1951. "The General and Logical Theory of Automata" in *Cerebral Mechanisms in Behavior* (L. A. Jeffress, ed.), 1–41. John Wiley, N.Y.
6. Rosen, R. 1978. *Principles of Measurement and Representation of Natural Systems*. Elsevier, N.Y.

7.   . 1979. "Some Comments of Activation and Inhibition".
    Bull. Math. Biol. <u>41</u>, 427-445.
8.   . 1983. "The Role of Similarity Principles in Data
    Extrapolation". *Am. J. Physiol.* <u>244</u>, R591-599.
9.   Shannon, C. 1949. *The Mathematical Theory of Communication.*
    University of Illinois Press, Urbana, Illinois.
10. Turing, A. 1936. "On Computable Numbers". *Proc. London Math.
    Soc.* Ser. 2, 42, 230-265.

APPENDIX: NOTES

Note 1, Section 7.4.

Newton's original *particle mechanics,* or *vectorial mechanics,* is hard
to apply to many practical problems, and was very early, through the
work of people like Euler and Lagrange, transmuted into another form,
generally called *analytical mechanics.* This latter form is what is
usually used to deal with extended matter; e.g. with rigid bodies.
From the standpoint of particle mechanics, the rigidity of a macroscopic body is a consequence of interparticle forces, which must be
explicitly taken into account in describing the system. Thus, if
there are N particles in the system (however large N may be) there
is a phase space of 6N dimensions, and a set of dynamical equations
which expresses for each particle the resultant of *all* forces seen
by that particle. In analytical mechanics, on the other hand, any
rigid body can be completely described by giving only five configurational coordinates (e.g. the coordinates of the center of mass, and
two angles of rotation about the center of mass), however many particles it contains. From the particulate point of view, the internal
forces which generate rigidity are replaced by *constraints;* supplementary conditions on the configuration space which must be identically satisfied. Thus, the passage from particle mechanics to analytical mechanics involves a partition of the forces in an extended
system into two classes: (a) the internal or *reactive* forces, which
hold the system together, and (b) the *impressed* forces, which push
the system around. The former are represented in analytical mechanics
by algebraic constraints, the latter by differential equations in the
configuration variables (five for a rigid body).

A system in analytical mechanics may have additional constraints
imposed upon it by specific circumstances; e.g. a ball may roll on
a table top. It was recognized long ago that these additional constraints (which, like all constraints, are regarded as expressing
the operation of reactive forces) can be of two types, which were
called by Hertz *holonomic* and *non-holonomic.* Both kinds of constraints can be expressed locally, in infinitesimal form, as

$$\sum_{i=1}^{n} u_i(x_1, \ldots, x_n) dx_i = 0$$

where $x_1, \ldots, x_n$ are the configuration coordinates of the system.

For a holonomic constraint, the above differential form is exact;
i.e. is the differential of some global function $\varphi(x_1, \ldots, x_n)$
defined on the whole configuration space. Thus the holonomic constraint translates into a global relation

$$\varphi(x_1, \ldots, x_n) = \text{constant.}$$

This in turn means that the configurational variables are no longer
independent, and that one of them can be expressed as a function of
the others. The constraint thus reduces the dimension of the configuration space by *one,* and therefore reduces the dimension of the
phase space by *two.*

A non-holonomic constraint, on the other hand, does not allow us to
eliminate a configurational variable in this fashion. However, since
it represents a relation between the configuration variables and
their differentials, it does allow us to eliminate a coordinate of

velocity, while leaving the dimension of the configuration space
unaltered. That is, a non-holonomic constraint serves to eliminate
one degree of freedom of the system. It thus also eliminates one
dimension from the space of impressed forces which can be imposed on
the system without violating the constraint.

Similarly, if we impose r independent non-holonomic constraints on
our system, we (a) keep the dimension of the configuration space what
is was originally; (b) eliminate r coordinates of velocity, and thus
reduce the dimensionality of the phase space by r; (c) likewise, we
reduce by r the dimensionality of the set of impressed forces which
can be imposed on the system.

Let us express these facts mathematically. A non-holonomic constraint
can be expressed locally in the general form

$$\left(x_1, \; \ldots, \; x_n, \; \frac{dx_1}{dt}, \; \ldots, \; \frac{dx_n}{dt} \right) = 0$$

which can (locally) be solved for one of the velocity coordinates
(dx_1/dt say). Thus, it can be written in the form

$$\frac{dx_1}{dt} = \left(\psi \; x_1, \; x_2, \; \ldots, \; x_n, \; \frac{dx_2}{dt}, \; \ldots, \; \frac{dx_n}{dt} \right)$$

$$= \psi(x_1, \; \vec{\alpha})$$

where we have written $\vec{\alpha} = (x_2, \; \ldots, \; dx_n/dt)$. (At this point the
reader is invited to compare this relation with (7.4.3) above.)

Likewise, if there are r non-holonomic constraints, these can be expressed locally by the r equations

$$dx_i/dt = \psi_i(x_1, \; \ldots, \; x_r, \; \vec{\alpha}) \qquad i = 1, \; \ldots, \; r$$

where now $\vec{\alpha}$ is the vector $(x_{r+1}, \; \ldots, \; x_n, \; dx_{r+1}/dt, \; \ldots, \; dx_n/dt)$.
These equations of constraint, which intuitively arise from the
reactive forces holding the system together, now become more and
more clearly the kind of equations we always use to describe general
dynamical or control systems.

Now what happens if r = n? In this case, the constraints leave us
only *one degree of freedom; they determine a vector field on the
configuration space*. There is in effect only one *impressed* force
that can be imposed on such a system, and its only effect is to get
the system moving; once moving, the motion is determined entirely
by the *reactive* forces, and not by the *impressed* force. Mathematically, the situation is that of an autonomous dynamical system, whose
manifold of states is the *configuration* space of the original mechanical system.

This relation between dynamics and mechanics is quite different from
the usual one, in which the manifold of states is thought of as generalizing the mechanical notion of *phase*, and the equations of motion
generalize *impressed* force. In the above interpretation, however,
it is quite otherwise; the manifold of states correspond now to
mechanical *configurations*, and the equations of motion come from the
reactive forces.

Note 2, Section 7.4

The reader should be most careful not to confuse two kinds of propositions, which are equivalent mathematically but completely different epistemologically and causally. On the one hand, we have a
statement like

$$d\vec{x}/dt = f_g(\vec{x}, \vec{\alpha}).$$

This is a local proposition, linking a tangent vector or velocity
$d\vec{x}/dt$ to a state $\vec{x}$, a genome g, and a control $\vec{\alpha}$. Each of these
quantities is built up out of observables assuming definite numerical
values at any instant of time, and it is *their values at a common
instant* which are related by this proposition.

On the other hand, the integrated form of these dynamical relations
looks like

$$\vec{x}(t) = \int_{t_0}^{t} f_g(x, a(\tau))d\tau.$$

This is a relation which involves time *explicitly*, and links the
values of observables *at one instant* with values (assumed by these
and other observables) *at other instants*.

Each of these epistemically different propositions has its own causal
structure. In the first of them, we can treat the tangent vector
$d\vec{x}/dt$ as effect, and define its causal antecedents as we have done.
In the integrated form, on the other hand, we take $\vec{x}(t)$ as effect,
and find a correspondingly different causal structure. In general,
the mathematical or logical equivalence of two expressions of linkage
or relationship in physical systems does not at all connote that their
causal structures are identical. This is merely a manifestation of
what we said earlier, that the mathematical language we use to
represent physical reality has abstracted away the very basis on
which such causal discriminations can be made.

Note 3, Section 7.5

It should be recognized that this reductionistic part of the Newtonian
paradigm can fail for purely mathematical reasons. If it should
happen that there is no way to effectively map the master description,
then this is enough to defeat a reductionistic approach to those system behaviors with which the partial description deals. This is
quite a different matter from the one we are considering here, in
which no Newtonian master description *exists*, and the program fails
for *epistemological* reasons, rather than mathematical ones.

Note 4, Section 7.5

This statement is not simply my subjective assessment. In 1970 there
appeared a volume entitled "Biology and the Future of Man", edited
by Philip Handler, then president of the National Academy of Sciences
of the U.S.A. The book went to great lengths to assure the reader
that it spoke for biology as a science; that in it biologists spoke
with essentially one voice. At the outset, it emphasized that the
volume was not prepared as a (mere) academic exercise, but for
serious pragmatic purposes:

Some years ago, the Committee on Science and Public Policy of the
National Academy of Sciences embarked on a series of 'surveys' of the
scientific disciplines. Each survey was to commence with an appraisal
of the 'state of the art'....In addition, the survey was to assess the
nature and strength of our national apparatus for continuing attack on
those major problems, e.g., the numbers and types of laboratories, the
number of scientists in the field, the number of students, the funds
available and their sources, and the major equipment being utilized.
Finally, each survey was to undertake a projection of future needs for
the national support of the discipline in question to assure that our
national effort in this regard is optimally productive....

To address these serious matters, the Academy proceeded as follows:

....Panels of distinguished scientists were assigned subjects....Each
panel was given a general charge....as follows:

The prime task of each Panel is to provide a pithy summary of the status
of the specific sub-field of science which has been assigned. This should
be a clear statement of the prime scientific problems and the major questions currently confronting investigators in the field. Included should
be an indication of the manner in which these problems are being attacked
and how these approaches may change within the foreseeable future. What
trends can be visualized for tomorrow? What lines of investigation are
likely to subside? Which may be expected to advance and assume greater
importance?....Are the questions themselves....likely to change significantly?....Having stated the major questions and problems, how close are
we to the answers? The sum of these discussions, panel by panel, should
constitute the equivalent of a complete overview of the highlights of
current understanding of the Life Sciences.

There were twenty-one such Panels established, spanning the complete
gamut of biological sciences and the biotechnologies. The recruitment
for these Panels consisted of well over 100 eminent and influential
biologists, mostly members of the Academy. How the panelists themselves were chosen is not indicated, but there is no doubt that they
constituted an authoritative group.

In due course, the Panels presented their reports. How they were
dealt with is described in colorful terms:

....In a gruelling one week session of the Survey Committee....each
report was *mercilessly* exposed to the criticism of all the other members.
....Each report was then rewritten and subjected to the *searching, sometimes scathing*, criticisms of the members of the parent Committee on
Science and Public Policy. The reports were again revised in the light
of this exercise. Finally, the Chairman of the Survey Committee....
devoted the summer of 1968 to the final editing and revising of the
final work.

Thus we have good grounds for regarding the contents of this volume
as constituting a true authoritative consensus, at least as of 1970.
There are no minority reports; no demurrals; biology does indeed
seem guaranteed here to speak with one voice.

What does that voice say? Here are a few characteristic excerpts:

The theme of this presentation is that life can be understood in terms
of the laws that govern and the phenomena that characterize the inanimate,

physical universe and, indeed, that at its essence life can be understood *only* (emphasis added) in the language of chemistry.

A little further along, we find this:

Until the laws of physics and chemistry had been elucidated, *it was not possible even to formulate* (emphasis added) the important, penetrating questions concerning the nature of life....The endeavors of thousands of life scientists....have gone far to document the thesis....(that) living phenomena are indeed intelligible in the physical terms. And although much remains to be learned and understood, and the details of many processes remain elusive, those engaged in such studies hold *no doubt* (emphasis added) that answers will be forthcoming in the reasonably near future. Indeed, *only two major questions* (emphasis added) remain enshrouded in a cloak of *not quite* (emphasis added) fathomable mystery: (1) the origin of life....and (2) the mind-body problem....yet (the extent to which biology is understood) even now constitutes a satisfying and exciting tale.

Still further along, we find things like this:

While *glorying* (emphasis added) in how far we have come, these chapters also reveal how large is the task that lies ahead....If (molecular biology) is exploited with vigor and understanding....a shining, hopeful future lies ahead.

And this:

Molecular biology provides the closest insight man has yet obtained of the nature of life - and therefore, of himself.

And this:

It will be evident that the huge intellectual triumph of the past decade will, in all liklihood, be surpassed tomorrow - and to the everlasting benefit of mankind.

It is clear from such rhapsodies that the consensus reported in this volume is not only or even mainly a scientific one; it is an emotional and aesthetic one. And indeed, anyone familiar with the writings of Newton's contemporaries and successors will recognize them.

The volume to which we have alluded was published in 1970. But it is most significant that nothing fundamental has changed since then.

Note 5, Section 7.5

In the inimitable words of Jacques Monod ("Chance and Necessity", pp. 42-43):

We can assert today that a universal theory, however completely successful in other domains, could never encompass the biosphere, its structure and its evolution as phenomena deducible from first principles....The thesis I shall present....is that the biosphere does not contain a predictable class of objects or events but constitutes a particular occurrence, compatible with first principles but not deducible from these principles, and therefore *essentially unpredictable* (emphasis added).

Index